GW00818624

Economics of Money and Income

Economics of
Money and Income

JOHN HACCHE

Senior Lecturer in Economics
at the Polytechnic, Manchester

 HEINEMANN · LONDON

Heinemann Educational Books Ltd
LONDON   EDINBURGH   MELBOURNE
TORONTO   JOHANNESBURG   AUCKLAND
SINGAPORE   IBADAN   HONG KONG
NAIROBI

Cased edition SBN 435 84395 8
Paperback edition SBN 435 84396 6

To D. J. E. and F. B. E.

Published by Heinemann Educational Books Ltd
48 Charles Street, London W1X 8AH
Printed in Great Britain by Butler and Tanner Ltd
Frome and London

Contents

v

Part II

Part III

Part IV

Part V

Appendices

Examination Questions

The following list provides a key to the sources of the examination questions to be found at the end of each chapter.

U.L.	University of London: G.C.E., Advanced Level.
J.M.B.	Joint Matriculation Board (Universities of Manchester, Liverpool, Leeds, Sheffield and Birmingham): G.C.E., Advanced Level.
A.E.B.	Associated Examining Board for the General Certificate of Education: Advanced Level.
W.J.E.C.	Welsh Joint Education Committee: G.C.E., Advanced Level.
S.U.J.B.	Southern Universities' Joint Board: G.C.E., Advanced Level.
I.B.	Institute of Bankers: Banking Diploma Examination Part II, Monetary Theory and Practice.
I.M.T.A.	Institute of Municipal Treasurers and Accountants: Final Examination (Part B), Economics or Banking and Public Finance.
C.I.S.	Chartered Institute of Secretaries: Final Examination, Economic Policies and Problems.
C.S.	Corporation of Secretaries: Final Examination, Economics.
B.A. Gen.	University of London: B.A. General Examination.
B.Sc.(Econ.)	University of London: B.Sc. (Economics) Part I (External Students).

Preface

This book attempts to present a large area of macro-economics and monetary economics at a beginner's level. It is intended especially for the more intelligent and ambitious 'A' level student who wishes to read further in this field but finds full-blown specialist works a little daunting; for the undergraduate in need of an introductory text; and for candidates preparing for the Monetary Theory and Practice Paper of the Institute of Bankers. It should also prove useful to students preparing for the various secretarial and accounting qualifications and higher national certificates and diplomas in business studies, as well as (I would like to think) to the ordinary citizen who wants to understand more about the complex monetary system in which we live.

I am profoundly indebted to the publisher's readers for innumerable helpful suggestions and for the great stimulus that their criticism provided. I acknowledge my debt also to a large number of colleagues at the (former) Manchester College of Commerce, for advice and discussion on a variety of topics. I am deeply indebted, again, to many people in the financial world for dealing with my queries so patiently and courteously. Any errors and distortions that remain are, of course, exclusively my own contribution. Michael and Valerie Standen encouraged me to start the book, and the publishers have been kind and tolerant during its long gestation. Mrs Joan Hinchey typed successive drafts with accuracy and good humour. I was fortunate in having access to the resources of the College of Commerce Library, the University of Manchester Library and the Manchester Central Library, and I appreciate the help I enjoyed there.

My gratitude is due to the examining bodies listed for allowing me to reproduce their questions, and to the bodies and institutions which permitted the reproduction of the various financial documents in Appendix A. I also thank my friends who lent their names for the narrative to be found there, under the heading 'A Specimen Cheque'.

J. M. Hacche
Manchester,
September, 1969

xi

Part one

Part one

1

Money: its Nature and Functions

1. *Functions of Money*

MONEY is anything which people are generally prepared to accept in return for the goods or services they want to trade. To understand more fully what this means, and what money does, it is useful (if paradoxical) to begin by considering a simple barter economy. Whether or not such a non-money economy has ever in fact existed is, in this context, of no importance. It is helpful to theorize about its workings in order to be able to highlight, as the next step, the part that money plays in our own sort of economic system.

Under a barter system, all sorts of goods and services would be swapped directly for one another. It follows that someone who finds he has too much of one good and too little of another would need to find someone else in precisely the reverse position before an exchange could take place. Thus a fisherman who had a lot of fish, but no bread, could trade only if he found someone who not only had bread available but also happened to want fish. Without this double coincidence of wants, exchange would not be possible.

A second drawback to this rudimentary system arises on any attempt to compare the terms on which various transactions are carried through. Thus in one case six fish might exchange for two loaves; in another, four loaves for two dozen eggs; in a third, a dozen eggs for two pounds of potatoes; and in a fourth, three pounds of potatoes for six fish. It is far from obvious that the fisherman would have done better, at these rates, to trade four of his fish for two pounds of potatoes, swap these for a dozen eggs, then swap the eggs for two loaves, finishing up two fish to the good!

A third difficulty would arise as people attempted to regulate their affairs over a period of time. A man who wanted to put something by for a future occasion would have two alternatives. He might lay in a stock of durable goods, or he might part with goods now, on the understanding that he would be repaid with material goods on a future date. In either case, the subsequent value of his 'savings' would depend upon

3

the exchange value, at any future date, of the particular goods he had
stored or to which he had a claim.

A rise in this value would, of itself, make him richer than previously,
and vice versa. When he came to trade the goods from his stock, or the
goods which had been repaid to him, he might get more (or less) in
return than would originally have been the case. The fortunes of a debtor
would lie in the opposite direction from those of his creditor. If, for
example, the exchange value of the commodity fell during the period
of the loan, the debtor would enjoy a gain. The goods he hands over in
repayment will now command a smaller quantity of other goods in an
exchange than when the loan was first made.

A barter system, it is seen, suffers from three major drawbacks. The
first is the need to achieve a double coincidence of wants before an
exchange can take place, and the second lies in the difficulty of comparing exchange values. Third, wealth may be held (directly, or indirectly as a claim) only in the form of particular goods, the exchange
value of which may fluctuate over time. All three problems are solved to
a greater or lesser extent by a monetary system, depending upon the
efficiency with which the system is performing.

Money was earlier defined as anything which people are generally
prepared to accept in return for the goods or services they trade. This
means that the fisherman, for example, is prepared to trade his fish for
a commodity which, unlike the bread, he does not want for its own
sake. Rather, he accepts it because he is confident that, in turn, the baker
will take it from him in return for loaves. The use of this commodity—
money—as a medium of exchange removes the need for a double
coincidence of wants: the fisherman who wants bread need not seek
out a baker eager for fish.

The willingness of a community to use one specific commodity (or
group of commodities) in this way greatly facilitates the process of
exchange. This in turn encourages the division of labour, since each man
and firm can easily exchange the product of their specialized activity.
This leads to much higher output per head, with its implication of higher
living standards. The economy becomes more complex, and its members
more interdependent on one another.

Trade is also encouraged by the extreme simplicity, in a monetary
system, of comparing the relative value of goods in the market. The price
at which, say, the fisherman sells his fish is the rate or ratio at which he
changes it 'into' money, e.g. one pound of fish for 5s. Since the 'exchange
rates' of all goods and services are expressed in this common denomi-
nator of money, it becomes possible to compare all values at a glance.

In a monetary system people will hold fairly small sums of money
from day to day or week to week. When, for example, they are paid
wages at the end of one week they will hold some money over the course

of the next week, to make purchases as they need day by day. Money balances are clearly a much more convenient way for 'storing value' than the various commodities a person would need to stock under a barter system.

For their savings, however, most people are not likely to hold money, because (in general)[1] it does not bring them any return. They are much more likely to put money they save at someone else's disposal, in return for a promise of interest or some other sort of payment. Where their claims are fixed in money terms, they appear to be free from the risk of exchange value fluctuations which characterize commodity claims in a barter system. For this reason, money is often said to act as a standard for payments which have been deferred to a future date. However, money itself is a sort of commodity, and the holder of the claim is now exposed to fluctuations in the value of money itself! This problem we shall take up in Section 2.

2. *Qualities of Money*

Money, we have seen, functions as a medium of exchange and a store of value, and acts as a measuring rod for present (and future) payments. However, it will discharge these functions efficiently only if the monetary system satisfies certain conditions or, to put it another way, if money 'possesses' appropriate qualities.

Money is anything which people are generally prepared to accept in settlement of debts. As, for example, we make purchases in the course of our daily lives we momentarily become the debtors of, e.g. shopkeepers, debts we redeem promptly by handing the purchase price over the counter. It follows that the prime 'quality' of money is its general acceptability. This is really another way of stating what money does because, of course, if it were not generally acceptable in transactions, it would not be money.

People are prepared to use a commodity as money if they expect that, by and large, they will be able to dispose of it on the same terms as they acquired it. This means that they must feel both that there will be things available for them to buy and that prices next week will be more or less what they are this week. If these two conditions cease to hold good, then what *was* money may quickly lose its general acceptability and therefore no longer *is* money!

In 1923, for example, there occurred in Germany a whirlwind rise in the prices of goods and services (known technically as a hyper-

[1] An exception are balances on deposit account with the commercial banks which, as explained in Chapter 2, yield interest and are usually included in the money supply.

inflation). Prices rose so rapidly that even to hold currency for a few days, to make purchases during the week after wages were paid, could lead to a dramatic loss in its purchasing power. Accordingly, people became more and more reluctant to accept currency in return for goods or services. For the time, therefore, currency ceased to be money, even though the German authorities may still have considered it to be money.[1] German experience provides a second example. The disruption of the Germany economy through invasion in 1945 meant that people could no longer rely on being able to obtain in the shops the goods they wanted. For a time, accordingly, sellers of goods, etc., were often reluctant to accept currency which they feared they might themselves have difficulty in spending.

It is possible, again, for the general level of prices to rise gradually, say a few per cent each year. This means that the purchasing power or value of money is falling at the same rate, since at the end of each year £1 (say) will, in general terms, buy rather less than at the start of the year. The gradual rise in the price level also leads to a gradual erosion of the value of claims—both capital and income—fixed in money terms. Money in this case does not function efficiently as a standard for deferred payments. Of course, the shorter the period for which the claim is outstanding, the smaller this erosion will be, and vice versa. These and other aspects of a rising price level are further considered in Chapter 14.

Apart from the major qualities of acceptability, and stability in value, there are minor features which, nonetheless, it is desirable money should possess. As an aid to memory, these qualities may all be expressed in words ending in -ity. First, divisibility; to facilitate its work as a unit of account especially, money must split into appropriately small units. Second, portability; crowns were too large, silver threepenny pieces too small for convenience. Third, durability; money with a physical existence is clearly less trouble to the issuing authority the longer its life. Fourth, cognizability; the various units of money should be clearly distinguishable one from another.[2]

---

[1] A contrary situation may be imagined in which a rapid fall in prices makes people reluctant to use money currently as money (i.e. to settle transactions), since they prefer to hoard it to spend later. This notion seems of little practical significance.

[2] The Bank of England consults the organizations for the blind before issuing notes of new design, since blind people are able to distinguish notes by their size.

3. Money in the United Kingdom

Let us now apply our definition to the U.K. economy, and see what the British people use as money.

First, notes and coins[1] are money when they can be used to settle debts. This is always the case, provided that the denominations tendered by the debtor fall within the normal range of everyday commercial practice. Thus the five sixpenny pieces paid for a half-crown bus ticket are undoubtedly serving as 'money', but one could not regard as money a bag of 4,000 sixpences offered in settlement of a debt of £100, as they would very likely be refused by the creditor.

To protect himself from an inconsiderate or malicious debtor, a creditor may rely on the rules of law governing 'legal tender'. He may, if he chooses, refuse to accept more than 1s. in bronze coins, more than 2s. in nickel brass coins (3d. pieces), or more than 40s. in 'silver' coins (actually made of cupro-nickel alloy). Bank of England notes in denominations of 10s., £1, £5 and £10 are legal tender up to any value, though the creditor is able to insist upon the tender of the exact amount, without a request for change. In practice, of course, creditors will usually choose not to bother with these rules, so it would be quite wrong to infer that a shilling, when used to buy a 6d. newspaper, is not 'money' because its use involves a request for change! Notes and coins, we conclude, serve as money when they are used within the conventional pattern of making payments.

Second, the liabilities of some banking institutions satisfy our definition of money as anything generally acceptable in settlement of debts. Let us see why. A man who, in the everyday expression, 'has got money in the bank' is in fact the holder of a bank account with a positive balance standing to his credit. Suppose he has £50 in his account with Lloyds bank. From his viewpoint he has an asset of £50, but from the bank's viewpoint the sum of £50 is owed by the bank to the customer and forms therefore a liability. Now, this gentleman is able to use his claim against the bank as a means for settling his own debts. If he owes a friend £20 he may pay him by writing an instruction[2] to his banker to transfer £20 worth of his claim against the banker (i.e. the bank's liabilities) to the credit of his friend. The friend will now have his account credited accordingly, and so the debt has been settled by transferring £20 worth of banker's liabilities from one person to another: therefore banker's liabilities have been used as money. If the friend had not had a bank account, of course, he would have insisted on the banker's meeting his liability straight away, by handing notes over the

[1] The proposed decimal system is outlined in Appendix A.
[2] Strictly, this is true only for the holder of a current account, not a deposit account (see text below).

counter. Practically all business firms, however, and many private people have bank accounts, and are quite prepared to leave their wealth in the form of balances in their banks, drawing out and paying in notes and coins as convenience requires.

In this example, the transfer of the banker's liabilities from one customer to another was carried out by giving him an instruction to this effect. Such an instruction is written on the cheque form supplied to its customers by the bank. An examination of the specimen in Appendix A will reveal its nature as an order to a banker to pay a given person a certain sum from the account of the writer of the cheque (who is said to be drawing a cheque on his bank—the drawee—in favour of the named payee). Every cheque must by law bear a twopenny stamp—a device first hit on by the Government for raising funds in 1694.

Superficially it might seem that cheques are money: but this is not the case. The cheque is the instrument for transferring bank deposits (current account) from one person to another, and it is the deposits which are transferred—not the device for transferring them—which constitute money as we have defined it.

A second apparent difficulty may have occurred to the reader, namely that there is no obligation on any creditor to accept a cheque; cheques are not legal tender, and the creditor may insist on payment in notes or coin. This does not mean, however, that bankers' liabilities are not generally used in making payments, but that the possession of a cheque book in itself is no guarantee of a credit balance in the bank account. Once the creditor is satisfied on this score he would almost invariably accept the cheque, thereby acquiring a claim against the bank to the sum stated.

A more serious problem is presented by the fact that deposit accounts held with the banks are not 'cheque-able', which throws some doubt on the role of deposit-account balances in the payments system. Difficulties also arise in deciding which institutions to include within the banking sector for the purpose of defining the money supply. Some of the difficulties under both heads will be considered in the course of Chapters 2–5. At this stage it is important to examine official usage in the definition of the money supply and its constituents. Details are set out in Table 1.1.

Notes and coin in general circulation (column 2) represent much the greater part (typically about 80 per cent) of all notes and coin outstanding. The remaining 20 per cent is regularly held within the banking sector (for reasons explained in Chapters 2 and 4), so it would be unrealistic to include this proportion in the money supply.

Column 3 shows net deposits held by U.K. residents with the banking sector. 'U.K. residents' are people, firms and other institutions (except banks) in the U.K. Balances that banks hold with one another are thus

TABLE 1.1
Money Supply in the U.K.
(£ million)

Year	(1) Total money supply [(2) + (3a)]	(2) Currency in circulation with the public	(3) Net deposits by U.K. residents with the banking sector			
			Total (a) [(b) + (c) + (d)]	Deposit banks (b)	Accepting houses, overseas and other banks (c)	Discount houses (d)
1964	11,426	2,341	9,085	8,180	811	94
1965	12,165	2,517	9,648	8,585	982	81
1966	12,974	2,702	10,272	9,017	1,174	81
1967	13,759	2,796	10,963	9,456	1,397	110
1968	15,091	2,887	12,204	10,078	2,029	97

Note: (i) Figures for each year are quarterly averages.
(ii) Changes in coverage, book-keeping procedure, etc., may affect the figures (notably under 3c) from time to time.

Source: Financial Statistics (H.M.S.O.)

excluded, as also are balances on account to customers resident overseas, and to the banks' own foreign-based offices. The figures are
designed, accordingly, to show the balances of the 'U.K. public' on the
one hand with the 'U.K. banks' on the other.

Net deposits are all deposits—on both current and deposit account—
held by this public with the banking sector, excluding cheques 'in course
of collection' and similar items in transit between the offices of the
same bank. To understand the significance of this deduction, consider
a simple example. X pays into his account with Bank A a cheque for
£100 drawn on Y's account with Bank B. Bank A will usually credit
X's account immediately, but Y's account with Bank B will not be
debited until Bank A has presented the cheque to Bank B for payment.
In the meantime, therefore, the total liabilities of the banking 'sector'
(Banks A and B) to their customers (X and Y) are overstated by £100.
To avoid overstatement of this sort, liabilities of the banking sector
to the public are accordingly stated *net* of cheques in course of collection. (Similar principles require the *inclusion* of 'credits in transmission'
under the credit transfer scheme, but this is held over for explanation in
Chapter 2.)

Finally, the 'banking sector' is defined in Table 1.1 to include the
thirty or so deposit banks in the U.K. (alternatively called joint-stock
or commercial banks); sixteen accepting houses and a number of 'other'
(merchant) banks; eleven discount houses; and a large number of
'overseas' banks. Though the recently-established national giro is not
a deposit bank, its liabilities are also conveniently included under
heading 3b (1968 only). The nature and activities of all these institutions
are considered in the following chapters.

Though not included in Table 1.1, deposits are also held by the
public with local authorities, building societies, finance companies and
savings banks. All except the first may provide some payment facilities comparable with those of the joint-stock banks. Though the line is
sometimes difficult to draw, a case may nonetheless be made for not
regarding the deposit liabilities of these institutions as part of the money
supply. These problems are taken up in Chapter 5, under the heading of
'quasi-money'.

The reader unacquainted with the monetary system may be surprised
to find that only about 20 per cent of our money supply (as defined)
consists of notes and coin, the remainder consisting of the liabilities
of bankers on current and deposit account. It is for this reason that
notes (and coin) may be considered the small change of the monetary
system. It will also be apparent that the liabilities of the banks considerably exceed their holdings of notes and coin. Let us see how these two
situations have arisen.

4. The Evolution of Money (I): Coins and Notes

We may imagine that the members of any community, however primitive, will at least have made a little progress towards a monetary system. This is true if its members are often prepared, in an exchange, to take a commodity not wanted for itself but easily disposed of subsequently. In various communities in the past farm livestock, ornaments and important foods, e.g. salt, have all served as 'exchange commodities'. Gold and silver have been outstandingly important as exchange commodities from which has evolved a coinage clearly recognizable as money. Their attractiveness may have lain in their ornamental (or religious) appeal, or may be considered part of the spell gold especially has always cast over men's minds.

A community in which gold, silver, animals, etc., are *regularly* used to facilitate trade has in fact developed its own forms of money. This conclusion follows since the commodities concerned are 'generally accepted in settlement of debts'. Of course livestock, for example, is not the most convenient form of money to have, and it is easy to imagine that communities growing less primitive would gradually confine general acceptability to gold, silver and other desirable metals. At some stage or other the government or rulers intervene and attempt to make the money supply a profitable business by minting gold and silver into regular coins. This in itself would encourage the use of the coins as money since they would carry the seal of the ruler, could be used for paying taxes and unless (or until!) debased would imply an official guarantee of quality or metal content. Indeed coins of a particular monarch (though of another country and long since dead) may acquire such a reputation among an unsophisticated people as to continue in use over many generations. This was the position in the Yemen until late 1962.

For over 150 years the normal currency in circulation had been the Maria Theresa thaler,[1] a large silver coin originally issued in Austria and brought to Arabia by European traders, its value being about 6s. 6d.; thalers bearing the effigy of the Empress Maria Theresa and the date 1780 (the year of her death) had continued to be minted in Vienna for use in the Persian Gulf area. It was originally intended to introduce paper currency, but the Government subsequently decided that it would be unwise to break with silver coinage at one step. The thaler was accordingly withdrawn from circulation on December 30th and replaced by another silver coin, the bakcha—Yemen's first domestic currency.[2]

Let us turn now from these rather general considerations to something more specific—the evolution of money in Britain since the Middle

[1] A German word from which is derived the English 'dollar'.
[2] Keesing's Contemporary Archives 1963.

Ages. Coins minted by the rulers of the period were in use before the Norman Conquest, and formed the money supply in the country. From the mid-seventeenth century onward, and especially during the Civil War and the Commonwealth period (1642–60), merchants with substantial sums of gold and silver (in bullion or in coin) developed the habit of leaving them with goldsmiths for safekeeping. The goldsmith would give the depositor a note acknowledging his receipt of the valuables, and this note might be used by the merchant as evidence of his wealth in a subsequent transaction. From this it was a short step for the merchant to hand over his note with a suitable endorsement to his creditor, and the note might change hands many times before being presented in the end to the goldsmith for redemption in gold.

By the eighteenth century goldsmiths (whom we may now more properly call bankers) were taking advantage of this development to make loans of notes to customers without receiving any deposit of gold, so that total liabilities in the form of notes exceeded assets in the form of gold, the balance of the assets comprising the borrowers' promises to repay the banker (with interest). As the century progressed so notes became more and more generally acceptable in settlement of debts, and from the mid-century onwards money may be regarded as comprising notes as well as coin. From this time on, moreover, the supply of notes from the London goldsmith-bankers was increasingly augmented by new formed banking businesses in the provinces (hence 'country' bankers).

The notes of both London and country banks were redeemable in gold or silver at the offices of the issuing banks concerned, and this undoubtedly gave the public the confidence to use 'pieces of paper' as money. Unfortunately, some of the banks abused their note-issuing powers by making issues far in excess of their gold reserves, so that a 'run' on them for redemption (the consequence perhaps of rumoured bad management) found them unable to redeem their 'promises to pay'. This meant of course the failure of the banks concerned, while their notes often became of little or no value, imposing losses upon their holders.

This problem was aggravated by the special position of the Bank of England. This bank had been founded in 1694 and, in return for a loan to the Government, had received a charter as a joint-stock company, enabling it to raise capital with a public issue of shares. From the first its notes had enjoyed public confidence by virtue of its privileged foundation. Acts of Parliament of 1697 and 1708 extended its privileges by providing that in England and Wales (the law in Scotland and Ireland was different) no other joint-stock banking company should issue notes. This meant accordingly that the London bankers and subsequently the country bankers were limited in size to partnerships of (by the Act of 1708) not more than six members, so that capital resources could not be greater than the wealth six men could get together. This weakness was highlighted by a banking crisis in 1825, when a run on many of the small country banks led to substantial failures. The remedy of Parliament in 1826 was twofold: first, joint-stock banking companies were given a right of note issue, provided they stayed 65 miles or more from London (to protect the Bank of England's privileges). Second, future issues of notes by any bank were to be in denominations of not less than £5.

A campaign for joint-stock company banking continued nonetheless after 1826, and in 1833 Parliament took the opportunity, when renewing the Bank of England's charter, to allow joint-stock banks to set up business in London and within the 65-mile radius, provided they did not issue notes. A further provision made the Bank of England £5 notes legal tender for amounts above £5 (except at the Bank of England, which still had to redeem them in gold). From this time on the emphasis in commercial banking moved away from note issue, and a scheme which led to the ultimate disappearance of their private note issue was introduced by the Bank Charter Act, 1844. This Act was intended, among other things, to regulate the supply of money in the country by restricting the note issue in England and Wales to the Bank of England (the arrangements made for Scotland and Ireland are briefly considered in Chapter 2). The Bank, in turn, was free to issue notes to any amount provided it held a corresponding value of gold. Beyond this, the Bank was allowed by the Act to issue notes only to the value of £14 million, and against this issue the Bank had to hold a corresponding amount of British Government securities. This part of the note issue was known as the fiduciary issue, presumably because it was backed only by faith or trust (Latin fides) in the notes or the securities. The greater part of the total issue, of course, was backed by gold, in that the Bank held an equivalent amount of gold, and until 1925 the Bank was under a legal obligation to meet any tender to it of a £5 note with gold on request.

The other banks which still had issues outstanding at the time of the 1844 Act were allowed to maintain but not increase them. Further, it was provided that their note issue would lapse in the event of an amalgamation, and the Bank of England would be able to increase its fiduciary issue by up to two-thirds the size of the lapsed issue. Amalgamations among the banks were very popular in the second part of the nineteenth century, and the operation of this rule led to the gradual extinction of the private note issue and a slow growth in the fiduciary issue. The last bank to lose its note issuing power in England and Wales was Fox, Fowler and Company, a Somerset bank which merged with Lloyds Bank in 1921. By this time the fiduciary issue had increased to just under £20 million.

By the mid-nineteenth century, therefore, we may safely say that notes were an established form of money in the United Kingdom,[1] virtually a monopoly of the Bank of England and convertible there into gold on demand. For smaller sums, however, gold and other coins were used as money, since (until 1928) only notes for at least £5 were issued by the Bank. Thus the position remained until 1914 when, at the start of the Great War, the Government took power to issue £1 and 10s. currency notes through its finance department, the Treasury. Soon after, the Bank began to withdraw gold coins from circulation, and convertibility was suspended in practice though not in law. It was not restored until 1925 when, however, the minimum sum the Bank would change into gold was put at about £1,700,[2] obtainable in gold bars and not coin. The significance of the restoration of this gold-bullion standard—as it was called—and its final disappearance in 1931 is considered in the context of international trade (Chapter 19). After 1915, then, we may say that our currency comprised Bank of England £5 notes, Treasury £1 and 10s. notes and a dwindling quantity of sovereigns and half-sovereigns. This arrangement was tidied up in 1928 when the Currency and Bank Notes Act authorized the Bank of England to issue £1 and 10s. notes, and absorb the outstanding Treasury issue.

By this date, of course, sovereigns had virtually disappeared from circulation. Nonetheless, silver coins with an appreciable (though reduced) bullion content continued to be struck until 1946, when they were replaced by a cupro-nickel coinage. Outstanding silver coins were called in (as far as possible) by the Government, to be used in the following ten years to finance the repayment of silver borrowed from the U.S.A. during the war. Coins with a very small worth as metal, such as our 'silver' coinage today, are known as token money. In our economy, of course, people have confidence in them and accept them despite their low bullion value. In fact, a token coinage has a distinct advantage in that, when bullion prices are high, there is no temptation for people to sell the coins as metal (which has happened in the past with coins of high bullion value).

Current practice in issuing notes and coin is considered in Chapter 4. At this point, however, it is useful to comment on the absence from the system of any significant gold 'backing' for the note issue. This lack of convertibility would probably have been impossible a hundred years ago, and certainly so two hundred years ago. Then paper money was still a novelty, and the issuing banks rather frail institutions. Many years of complete security in using bank notes since the mid-nineteenth century has given the public a deep confidence in paper money, and so convertibility into gold is no longer necessary to enhance paper

[1] And had been so since the second half of the eighteenth century.
[2] 400 troy ounces of fine gold at £3 17s. 10½d. a standard ounce.

money's acceptability: it is used as money in its own right. Were this confidence to be impaired, however, the nature of its backing might once again become relevant to its acceptability. For example, when after the inflationary difficulties of the early 1920s the German authorities sought to restore confidence in paper money, they introduced a rentenmark said to be backed by a charge on the land of Germany. In practice this meant nothing; but the almost mystical connection between the money and the land helped people regain their faith in paper currency.

The system of convertibility between notes and gold also served the Government as an instrument of economic policy, designed to promote stability in the general level of prices and equilibrium in economic relationships with other countries. These goals were prime objectives of the 1844 Bank Charter Act: the ways in which they were carried through are considered, in abstraction, in Chapter 19. Emphasis in economic policy has long since moved away from regulation of the note issue to other techniques for influencing the economy, based on modern developments in economic theory. These matters are considered from Part III onwards.

5. The Evolution of Money (II): Bank Liabilities

Cheques were in use as early as the seventeenth century, though understandably their use was confined to well-off people who might reasonably be expected to have the balances to meet them. Their use remained strictly limited until the 1820s, the commercial banks in general making loans by issuing notes. As we have seen, this activity simultaneously increased their liabilities (the notes) and their assets (the promises to repay, with interest). The Acts of 1826 and 1833 (discussed in the previous section) both encouraged the establishment of joint-stock banks and discouraged the private note issue, while the Bank Charter Act of 1844 restricted the latter to the average for the Spring of 1844. From the 1830s onwards, therefore, the banks were under strong pressure to develop an alternative technique of lending. Such an alternative lay to hand, in consequence of the increasing willingness of the general public to make payment by cheque, which in turn reflected growing public confidence in the banking system. The use of cheques was further encouraged after the 1844 Act by the inadequacy of the supply of Bank of England notes and coin to meet the monetary needs of an expanding economy.

The technique of lending developed by the joint-stock banks is explored in some detail in Chapter 2, but it may be helpful at this stage to outline the system in broad terms. In effect, the banks placed balances at the disposal of customers who wanted a loan, by making appropriate entries in the books. Holders of balances in account with the banks would make payment to one another by instructing the banks to transfer balances from one account to another. The instrument by which this instruction was given was, of course, the cheque. The banks would thus be carrying on their business with liabilities to customers (i.e. the balances on account) considerably in excess of their holdings of gold and silver coins and Bank of England notes. Their other assets would consist of promises to repay given them by their customers, and the interest on these promises would give the banks their profit.

The banks could function in this way because customers would make most payments by cheque, and so would not require notes or coin over the counter. Withdrawals would of course occur but, provided a bank was holding its own in competition with the others, these would normally be offset by customers paying in notes and coin for the credit of their accounts. Banks creating balances on these lines would be careful not to extend their liabilities too far on a narrow 'base' of notes and coins. They would also be concerned to ensure that some loans were of shorter duration than others. In modern times both these precepts of sound banking have hardened into conventional ratios of 'cash' and 'liquid assets' to total deposit liabilities, discussed in Chapter 2.

6. *Money as a Claim*

It is often said that money is a claim. Let us see in what senses this is true.

Money in the U.K. today consists of notes and coins together with the deposit liabilities of (principally) the joint-stock banks. Historically notes originated as claims against the issuing banks concerned, and were redeemable in gold. Indeed, the legal right to present notes for payment in gold at the Bank of England did not disappear until 1925. While today Bank of England notes may still, technically, be regarded as claims in practice this means nothing. The Bank could only honour its 'promise to pay the bearer on demand' (printed on the note) by offering him other notes or coins instead. From a legal view, of course, coins are not claims upon the Bank of England. Indeed, before 1925 gold coins were precisely the substance to which the notes gave a claim.

We shall see in Chapter 4 that, under the arrangements for issuing extra notes, a rise in the note circulation of itself gives the Government extra funds to spend. For this reason, notes today are sometimes described as a type of Government security carrying no interest and no date for redemption! Today's token coins are sometimes described as 'small notes printed on metal', and the Government will also derive a profit from their issue (Chapter 4).

Secondly, bank liabilities are money, and these are 'claims' against (in the main) the joint-stock banks, so that today most of our money consists of claims against a particular type of business—namely a bank. Some readers may still find it odd to reflect that money, which seems superficially to be the creation of the Government, is largely the product of private initiative. And this is true in two senses. First, the joint-stock banks take the initiative in regulating the size of their liabilities (though the Government through the Bank of England can influence their behaviour). Second, in a more fundamental sense, money is the creation of the public itself, since people are, or are not, prepared to use things as money, and if they are prepared to use them as money, then the things *are* money! Thus the liabilities of banks are money because the public use them as money. However, if a bank were thought to be insolvent then the depositors would immediately ask the banker to honour his liabilities with notes or coin: nobody during this crisis would regard or use this banker's liabilities as money. Similarly with notes: during the economic disruption of Germany in 1945 the official currency could not be regarded as generally acceptable in settlement of debts. For a time, indeed, people used commodities such as cigarettes as a medium of exchange: they could be regarded as money, though temporary and unofficial.

Finally, 'money as a claim' may be interpreted not in the narrower sense of a claim against a bank, but in the deeper sense of 'a claim against real wealth'. Money is wealth to the individual, but only because he is normally able to spend his money to buy the goods and services which alone are capable of satisfying his needs. The usual way of acquiring money is by making some contribution to the production of goods and services. This contribution may be made by working personally, or by lending savings from past money receipts. The contribution is rewarded by wages and salaries for those who work in or organize production; interest and rent for those who facilitate production by financing it; and profits for those who undertake production and bear its uncertainties. The wages, etc., are received as money; spending it enables the recipients to draw, upon the great flow of output, goods and services in proportion to the value of the contribution they themselves have made.

Questions

1. What are the functions of money? How are these affected by the existence of inflation? U.L.

2. 'The most important function of money is that it should be stable in value over time'. Discuss.	S.U.J.B.

3. Consider whether a fall in the value of money affects the ability of money to fulfil its various functions.	I.B.

4. It has been stated that 'in modern societies money consists predominantly of claims against certain institutions'. Explain what this statement means, and in the course of your answer show, for any particular country with which you are familiar, how its money supply is composed.	I.B.

5. Consider the special characteristics that distinguish 'money' from other economic goods.	I.B.

6. Critically assess the efficiency of gold as the basis of a country's currency.	A.E.B.

7. What is meant by the 'backing of the Note issue'? Is it a necessary condition of a sound monetary system?	U.L.

2

Deposit Banking in the
United Kingdom

1. *A Preview*

This chapter is principally concerned with the activities of the London clearing banks, which are the leading deposit banks (alternatively called, joint-stock or commercial banks) in England and Wales. The clearing and other deposit banks are to be sharply distinguished from the Bank of England which, as we shall see in Chapter 4, occupies a unique position as the United Kingdom's central bank. They are also to be distinguished from merchant banks and 'overseas' banks, whose activities are more briefly reviewed at the end of this chapter. Discussion of the clearing banks necessarily entails reference to the discount houses (also a part of the U.K. banking system), but the discount market receives separate and more detailed consideration in Chapter 3.

About 90 per cent of deposits with commercial banks in the United Kingdom are held with the London clearing banks. They take their name from membership of the London Bankers' Clearing House, which was set up around 1770 for sorting and clearing cheques. For many years the number of clearing banks stood at eleven, namely: Barclays Bank; Coutts and Co.; District Bank; Glyn, Mills and Co.; Lloyds Bank; Martins Bank; Midland Bank; National Bank; National Provincial Bank; Westminster Bank; and Williams Deacon's Bank.

However, in 1968 National Provincial and Westminster merged to form National Westminster which will, in due course, operate as one integrated concern. National Provincial had owned two of the smaller clearing banks, District and Coutts and Co., and the District is also to be incorporated into National Westminster. In the same year Barclays Bank acquired Martins, and plans for its integration are similarly under way. Williams Deacon's and Glyn, Mills were subsidiaries of the Royal Bank of Scotland, while the National Bank had been acquired by the National Commercial Bank of Scotland in 1966 (National's major interests—in Ireland—passing to the National Bank

19

of Ireland, a subsidiary of the Bank of Ireland). A merger of these two Scottish banks (below) was followed in 1969 by the integration of the new group's three clearing-bank subsidiaries into one concern, Williams and Glyn's Bank. In terms of total deposits (1968) the two biggest clearing banks are Barclays (with Martins) and National Westminster (with District and Coutts and Co.), followed by Midland with Lloyds in fourth place.

The Co-operative Bank (i.e. the banking division of the Co-operative Wholesale Society) is not a member of the Clearing House, although— if all the latter's members were ranked individually—it stood eighth in order of total deposits in 1968. It has access to the facilities of the Clearing House through National Westminster, which acts as its agent. Other English commercial banks which are not members of the Clearing House are C. Hoare and Co., the Isle of Man Bank, Lewis's Bank and the Yorkshire Bank. Of these the Isle of Man Bank is an affiliate of the National Provincial, Lewis's is a subsidiary of Lloyds, while the share capital of the Yorkshire Bank is held by four of the London clearing banks.

The four major Scottish banks maintain their own clearing system. These are the Bank of Scotland; the British Linen Bank; the Clydesdale Bank; and the Royal Bank of Scotland Limited (the name used since 1968 by the merged Royal Bank of Scotland and National Commercial Bank of Scotland Limited). A commercial banking business is also carried on by the Scottish C.W.S. Bank. Each of the major Scottish banks has English connections. The Clydesdale Bank is affiliated with the Midland, while the National and Commercial Banking Group (i.e. the group comprising the Royal Bank of Scotland Limited and Williams and Glyn's Bank) is associated with Lloyds. Barclays Bank acquired an interest in the Bank of Scotland in 1969, the latter taking over in return the British Linen Bank, until then a Barclays'.subsidiary. All the Scottish banks operate nonetheless as independent institutions in their day-to-day affairs. Some of their special features are briefly considered in Section 6.

The commercial banks operating in Northern Ireland are: the Bank of Ireland; the Belfast Banking Company, which is affiliated to the Midland Bank; the Hibernian Bank and the National Bank of Ireland, both subsidiaries of the Bank of Ireland; the Munster and Leinster Bank; the Northern Bank, affiliated to the Midland; the Provincial Bank of Ireland; and the Ulster Bank, which is a subsidiary of National Westminster. Since 1966 the Munster and Leinster Bank and the Provincial Bank of Ireland have been in an alliance—Allied Irish Banks —along with the Royal Bank of Ireland. The latter is active in the Republic of Ireland, though its U.K. branch (at Birkenhead) qualifies for inclusion in the U.K. commercial banking sector.

2. The Creation of Bank Credit

Before considering the major assets and liabilities of the clearing banks, it is useful to investigate more fully the 'bank credit' which, it was suggested in Chapter 1, the commercial banks are capable of creating. For this purpose we shall analyse the path by which bank assets and liabilities might grow in a very simple system, which has just one (commercial) bank. Subsequently, we shall consider the complications that may arise when there are two or more commercial banks. It is important to appreciate that bankers themselves would not necessarily view their activities in terms of the framework we shall construct. Further, it hardly needs saying that the monetary system in the real world is highly complex, so that only a partial understanding is obtained from the sort of analysis which follows.

The money supply in our imaginary economy consists, to start with, of £100 million worth of notes and coin. These are technically the liabilities of the government, by which they were originally issued (we do not need to consider how). A commercial bank—Bank A—now opens its doors for the first time, and invites deposits of notes and coin from the public. A number of firms and people decide to place cash deposits with the bank, and very soon the bank's balance sheet reads:

Liabilities	£m.	Assets	£m.
On account to customers	20	Notes and coin	20

For simplicity, we ignore any capital put up by the proprietors themselves.

The original motive of the depositors may have been safety for their notes, but they quickly find it convenient, we take it, to start making payments to one another by cheque. Instead of drawing out notes, a customer (X) simply instructs Bank A (by cheque) to transfer part of his claim on the bank to his creditor (Y). If Y has no account, he will ask Bank A for notes over the counter. In this case, the bank loses assets (notes) and liabilities (through its debit of X's account) by an equal amount. Alternatively, if Y has an account he will pay in X's cheque for its credit. Bank A simply credits Y's account and debits X's account correspondingly, and no movement of notes is involved.

As the practice of making payment by cheque grows, Bank A makes two very important discoveries. First, that its customers are making most of their major payments by cheque, so that they are not continuously asking for, or re-depositing, very large quantities of notes over the counter. Second, that while it needs each day to part with some notes, both to customers and to non-customers who present cheques drawn by customers, this outflow is (with some variation) offset by fresh deposits of notes, e.g. from customers who have been paid in this way by non-customers.

These two observations lead the bank to conclude that it could, quite safely, have more liabilities on account to customers than it has holdings of notes. Let us suppose it tries an experiment. It is approached by a customer (Z) with a request for a loan. At the moment, Z has no balance at all in his account, but the bank agrees to allow him to overdraw his account up to (say) £100,000. Z immediately draws a cheque on his account for this amount and pays W for goods supplied. W pays the cheque into the bank for the credit of his account. Bank A's balance sheet now reads:

Liabilities	£m.	Assets	£m.
On account to customers	20·1	Notes and coin	20
		Promise to repay by Z	0·1
Total	20·1	Total	20·1

In return for his loan, Z promises to pay Bank A interest, which will give it a profit. He may subsequently make repayment with a cheque paid him by a fellow customer of the bank. In this case, the bank debits the drawer's account by £0·1 million, while its assets also revert to £20 million, since Z has redeemed his promise to repay. Alternatively, Z may pay cash over the counter, in which case Bank A has a new asset (£0·1 million in notes) in place of the old asset (Z's promise to repay). However, we may ignore this second possibility, because it was earlier assumed that deposits of fresh cash are, by and large, offset from day to day by cash withdrawals. This is also the reason for not exploring the outcome if W (in the first instance) asked for cash over the counter when he arrived at Bank A with his cheque.

At the time when Z's loan was outstanding, Bank A's total liabilities were £20·1 million, and its holdings of notes and coin (which, for brevity, we shall now call its cash) were £20 million. Its ratio of cash holdings to total liabilities—its cash ratio—was therefore about 99·5 per cent. Its excess of liabilities over cash did not cause it any difficulties, and it decides accordingly to make a number of further loans in the same way, provided that suitable applicants present themselves. Ultimately, its balance sheet reads:

Liabilities	£m.	Assets	£m.
On account to customers	250	Cash	20
		Promises to repay	230
Total	250	Total	250

At this point it has a cash ratio of 8 per cent, and does not consider it expedient to expand its assets (and so its liabilities) any further. If all its customers asked for cash, at once, over the counter, the bank would fail, unless the government came to its rescue with more notes. In practice, however, the bank finds its small reserve of cash quite adequate because, as already mentioned, cash withdrawals are by and large offset by cash deposits, while customers make large payments by cheque anyway.

This sort of explanation of bank expansion is useful as far as it goes, but it takes no account of the complications which arise from the existence of more than one bank. Let us therefore introduce a second bank (Bank B) into the system, and see how its existence could affect Bank A's expansion of assets and liabilities. The argument could, clearly, be generalized for any number of banks.

At the moment, then, that Bank A decides to start giving its customers loans a second bank is established in competition. We shall ignore any fresh cash deposits it receives from the public, of the same sort originally made with Bank A. The establishment of Bank B makes Bank A very cautious, and it decides to back its loans fully with cash. Let us see what this means. It has, currently, £20 million liabilities on account to customers, and £20 million in notes. It decides that it needs only an 8 per cent cash ratio in respect of these existing liabilities, so that it has $92/100 \times £20$ million (i.e. £18·4 million) surplus to 'support requirements'. Accordingly, it allows some customers to overdraw their accounts by £18·4 million. The borrowers pay their cheques, totalling £18·4 million, to their creditors, who all use them to start accounts with Bank B! Bank A, however, is not embarrassed. It simply hands over notes to this value to Bank B, and is left with cash of £1·6 million and promises to repay of £18·4 million. It has therefore a cash ratio of 8 per cent, with which it is quite content.

Consider, now, Bank B's balance sheet.

Liabilities	£m.	Assets	£m.
On account to customers	18·4	Cash	18·4

Bank B decides to behave in exactly the same way as Bank A, and allows some new customers to overdraw accounts by $92/100 \times £18·4$ million, i.e. by £16·928 million. The borrowers proceed to draw cheques to this value and pay them to creditors who, in turn, pay them into accounts with Bank A. Bank B now has:

Liabilities	£m.	Assets	£m.
On account to customers	18·4	Cash	1·472
		Promises to repay	16·928

This, of course, is because Bank A has had £16·928 million in notes back off Bank B in settlement. Bank A's balance sheet now reads:

Liabilities	£m.	Assets	£m.
On account to customers	20	Cash	1·6
	+16·928		+16·928
		Promises to repay	18·4
Total	36·928	Total	36·928

Bank A therefore has cash equal to 92/100 × £16·928 million surplus to 'support requirements', and proceeds to lend £15·57376 million to customers, with the same consequences as before.

It is apparent that the two banks will go on giving loans as long as they have cash over and above their 8 per cent support requirements, since the process of giving loans is profitable; it yields the bank the interest the customer must pay for the privilege of overdrawing his account. The inter-play between the two banks will continue until the 'surplus' cash balance becomes so small that neither bank finds it worth bothering about. Between them, the banks will have total liabilities of (£ million):

$$20 + 18·4 + 16·928 + 15·57376 + \ldots$$

which may also be written

$$20 + (0·92)\,20 + (0·92)^2\,20 + (0·92)^3\,20 + \ldots.$$

This will be recognized as a convergent geometric series, of which the sum (S) is given by the formula.

$$S = a/(1 - r)$$

where $a = 20$ and $r = 0·92$. It follows that $S = 20 \div 0·08 = 250$ (£ million).

Between them the banks' total liabilities ultimately stand at £250 million, which was the level attained by Bank A in the original example, when it had no competitor. Bank A's balance sheet (it can be shown) will now read:

Liabilities	£m.	Assets	£m.
On account to customers	130	Cash	10·4
		Promises to repay	119·6
Total	130	Total	130

Bank B's balance sheet will read:

Liabilities	£m.	Assets	£m.
On account to customers	120	Cash	9·6
		Promises to repay	110·4
Total	120	Total	120

Although Bank A has expanded little over half as much as before, its expansion nonetheless was not completely frustrated by the loss of cash to the other bank which occurred during the process. This is because Bank B followed an identical expansionist policy.

It will be recalled that, before the establishment of Bank A (and subsequently Bank B), the economy's money supply consisted of £100 million in notes and coin. There are now only £80 million in circulation, as £20 million is regularly held by Banks A and B. This forms their cash 'float', regularly turning over, but remaining roughly stable at this level. In respect of this £20 million, of course, people and firms have claims on the banks, which *they* regard as money. In a sense, therefore, the community has changed £20 million of 'government money' for £20 million of 'bank money'. Additionally, people and firms now 'hold' a further £230 million on account with the banks, balances which they also regard as money. The total money supply in the economy now consists, accordingly, of £80 million in notes and coin plus £250 million bankers' liabilities (compare Table 1.1). The banks' activities have increased the money supply by £230 million, not £250 million.

In the example, the banks extended their liabilities in order to acquire their customers' (interest-bearing) promises to repay. Alternatively, the banks might have acquired other sorts of profitable asset, for instance certificates carrying the promise of the government to pay the holder a capital sum in final redemption at some future time, with annual interest in the meanwhile. Such a document is known as a (redeemable) government bond. The bank pays the seller with a cheque drawn on itself, which the seller in turn (we assume for simplicity) pays into an account with this same bank. The bank's liabilities increase by the value of its purchase, while at the same time its assets increase by its holdings of government debt.

This discussion serves to illustrate the two senses in which the expression 'bank credit' is used. In some contexts it means the total of bank liabilities as, for instance, in the sentence, 'Bank credit is the major part of the economy's money supply'. In others, it means the total of loans (say) to businessmen, as for example in the statement, 'Bank credit is important for the short-term finance of business'. It is apparent that a bank may increase credit in the first sense but not in the second. If a bank buys a government bond from a private person it increases its liabilities, but it is not giving anyone a loan. The seller, in turn, has exchanged his bond, which he cannot spend, for a bank deposit, which he can.

It is useful to sum up the argument so far.

(a) Commercial banks are able to extend their liabilities beyond their holdings of cash, because of the public's willingness to hold bank deposits and use them as money. We may conceive, accordingly, of a cash base supporting an inverted pyramid of deposit liabilities.

(b) The ratio of cash to total deposit liabilities appears a critical factor in determining how far the banks can extend liabilities on the basis of their cash holdings. With a cash ratio of 8 per cent, they can extend liabilities by 100 to 8, or $12\frac{1}{2}$ to 1, which is the inverse of the cash ratio. This ratio of $12\frac{1}{2}$ to 1 is known as the cash multiplier: its significance is further considered in Chapter 4.

These results provide some insight into the British banking system, but should not be applied too literally. They were obtained by analysing the workings of a very simple and artificial system, and are subject in practice to some important qualifications. First, the reader should not imagine that the banks devote their energies to trying to coax more deposits of cash from customers, to have a bigger cash base on which to extend their assets (and so their liabilities). As already suggested, the cash paid into the banks is in the short run fairly evenly offset by cash withdrawals. For the clearing banks, the truly important source of cash lies in their relationships with the Bank of England, which are explored in Chapter 4.

Second, commercial banks do not settle indebtedness to one another with actual note transfers, as did Banks A and B. They maintain accounts at a central bank (in the U.K. the Bank of England), and settle their debts by having balances switched from one account to another (Section 5). The working balances[1] they maintain in account with the central bank are regarded as cash by the commercial banks, since at any time the central bank will give them notes and coin and debit their accounts correspondingly. This possibility was not considered in the worked example but, of itself, does not alter the argument.

Third, while the clearing banks in fact work to an 8 per cent cash ratio, this is today required of them by the Bank of England as part of its apparatus of control over the banking system. In the absence of this control, 8 per cent is not necessarily the cash reserve the banks would consider expedient in modern conditions.

Finally, in their acquisition of assets the clearing banks pay more regard to the resultant 'liquidity' pattern than did Banks A and B in the example. To any commercial bank cash is a perfectly liquid asset, since it can always be used to meet customers' demands for 'payment' of their claims upon the bank. Other assets held by the clearing banks are classed as more or less 'liquid', according to the ease and certainty with which they can be turned into cash, as we shall see in the next section. Any bank would in practice consider it prudent to hold some assets in a fairly liquid form, since by definition these could be readily turned into

---

[1] They might also be obliged to keep 'special' balances, which they could not regard as cash (Chapter 4).

cash should (for whatever reason) its cash reserve appear insufficient. Business prudence apart, however, the clearing banks are required by the Bank of England to keep a part of their assets—equal to at least 28 per cent of total deposit liabilities—in the form of cash and certain other specified assets of high liquidity. This 28 per cent liquidity ratio must be sharply distinguished from the 8 per cent cash ratio, though both requirements constitute Bank of England control devices.

3. The Balance Sheet of the London Clearing Banks

The composite balance sheet in Table 2.1 sets out the main liabilities and assets of the London clearing banks. The figures are averages of the balances on the third Wednesday[1] in each month of 1968. We are not here concerned with the balance sheet as an accounting document: this is discussed in general terms at the start of Chapter 7. Rather, we need to analyse the items in the balance sheet, using the concepts developed in the previous section. The contribution of the banks to our economic life is examined in Section 4, largely in terms of these balance sheet items.

1a, b. These items represent the balances 'in' the accounts of the customers themselves. A customer may have a current account or deposit account (or both).

(a) A current account gives the holder the right to draw cheques on it without any notice, commanding the transfer of part or all of his balance to the person named as payee. If he wants cash out, he simply names himself as payee and presents the cheque at the counter[2] of the branch of the bank where he has his account. The clearing banks have agreed among themselves to pay no interest on balances in current account. Moreover, the customer is charged a (relatively) small sum each year, for the expense involved in running his account. The more cheques he writes, and the smaller his average balance, the bigger his bank charges will be.

(b) A deposit account does not give the holder the right to draw cheques on it. If the holder wants payment he will either have cash over the counter or his current account credited correspondingly. The bank reserves the right to receive seven days' notice of withdrawal, though this requirement may be waived subject to loss of interest. The rate of interest paid on deposit account balances is agreed among the clearing banks, and usually stands at 2 per cent under Bank Rate (Chapter 4),

[1] Except December, second Wednesday.
[2] An innovation likely to be widely introduced is the use of electronic devices to dispense cash at the counter and, for approved customers, to provide a cash-dispensing service when the banks are closed.

TABLE 2.1

Balance Sheet of the London Clearing Banks 1968

	£ million
Liabilities	
1. Total deposits:	
(a) Current Accounts	5,334
(b) Deposit Accounts	4,177
(c) Other Accounts	920
Assets	
2. Cash:	
(a) Notes and coin	542
(b) Balances with Bank of England	309
3. Money at call and short notice:	
(a) To Discount Houses	896
(b) Other	439
4. Treasury Bills discounted	468
5. Other bills discounted:	
(a) U.K. commercial bills	341
(b) Other	186
6. Special deposits with Bank of England	208
7. Investments	1,375
8. Advances	5,075
Note the omission of:	
9. Cheques in course of collection;	
10. Acceptances and endorsements;	
11. Paid up capital and reserves;	
12. Bank premises and investments in other banks and companies.	

Source: Financial Statistics (H.M.S.O.)

with a minimum of 2 per cent. On 'savings account' balances, however, interest is fixed at $4\frac{1}{2}$ per cent for the first £250, and at bank deposit rate thereafter. This type of deposit account is intended for the small saver, and sums up to £10 (sometimes £20) may be withdrawn on demand at any branch of the customer's bank.

1c. 'Other accounts' include internal funds of the banks themselves, and suspense accounts. The latter play an important part in the mechanics of the credit transfer system (Section 4).

2. Cash, the first item in the assets column, falls into two parts:

(a) 'Notes and coin' are the coins and notes the banks keep in their tills and safes.

(b) 'Balances with the Bank of England' are credit balances in the accounts all the clearing banks have at the Bank of England. They are considered as good as cash, since a bank that wanted more notes and coin would be given them by the Bank, which would correspondingly debit the account of the bank receiving them.

3. Loans are made at call and short notice to the eleven members (3a) of the London Discount Market Association, who borrow to finance their holdings of bills of exchange, Treasury bills, Government bonds and other assets (Chapter 3). A discount house will be allowed to draw cheques on the lending bank up to an agreed limit, but may be required to repay at least part of its debt 'at call' or on demand by the lender (see Chapter 3). Other borrowers (3b) are bill brokers (Chapter 3) and, for periods up to one month, members of the Stock Exchange (Chapter 7) and bullion brokers (i.e. dealers in gold bullion). Also included under this head are the balances which the various clearing banks may hold for convenience with other banks in the United Kingdom and overseas.

Loans at call and short notice are highly liquid assets to the clearing banks. If any one bank found itself short of cash, it could call in some of its loans from the discount houses, which would (in general) make repayment by borrowing off the other banks. The discount houses would hand over cheques drawn on these banks, and the first bank could secure payment on the cheques by having its account at the Bank of England credited correspondingly (Section 5). Of course, if for some reason all the clearing banks were calling in their loans, the discount houses could not finance repayment in this way. An alternative method of raising the necessary funds is, however, always open to them: this is discussed in Chapters 3 and 4.

4. We saw in Section 2 that the banker is not limited in his quest for profitable assets to the acquisition of customers' promises to repay. He may instead buy, for example, Government securities of various sorts—in this case not bonds but Treasury bills.

A Treasury bill is simply a written promise of the British Government to pay the bill's holder the face value of the bill (say £10,000) on a given date. Each Friday the Bank of England, acting on the Government's behalf, offers a quantity of bills for sale, in various denominations but all with a life of 91 days to maturity. Their sale provides short-term finance for the Government, since the initial purchase price paid to the Bank of England for a bill goes to the credit of the Government's account at the Bank. Suppose that a purchaser paid the Bank £9,900 for a bill with a face value of £10,000. If he kept it until its maturity date in three months' time the Bank would give him £10,000 for it, so he would have earned £100 for lending the Government £9,900 for three months.

The discount houses, as we shall see in Chapter 3, are major buyers of these bills from the Bank of England when each week's issue becomes available. They will, however, hold relatively few bills to maturity, but look for the opportunity to pass them on at a profit. Their leading customers are the clearing banks, though by convention the banks do not buy bills (for themselves) with more than 84 days to run. A bank buying bills from a discount house would credit the seller's account, thus increasing its own liabilities. At the same time its assets would increase by the amount of the bills thus purchased. The redemption of its bills in due course by the Government will, as we shall see in Chapter 4, lead to a corresponding increase (other things being equal) in the banks' balances at the Bank of England. They are therefore regarded as a highly liquid asset.

The price a bank pays for its bill purchases would be somewhere between the nominal value and the price originally paid by the discount house. Suppose that, on a given day, a bank's purchases included a £10,0C0 bill in the 46th day of its life, for which it paid the discount house £9,951; the discount house, we may assume, had originally paid £9,9C0 for it on issue. In this case the discount house earns £51 for providing the Government with £9,9C0 for just over 45 days, while the bank earns £49 for financing the loan for the remaining period.

5. The use of the commercial bill (i.e. the bill of exchange) is slightly more complex than the Treasury bill. At this point we need simply record that the 'acceptor' of a bill of exchange incurs a liability to pay the face value of the bill (say £10,000) to whoever may hold it on the maturity date (say three months after it was first 'drawn'). Banks buy these bills both from their own customers and from the discount houses, paying rather less than their face value. The seller's account is credited, thereby increasing the bank's liabilities, while the corresponding asset is the bill(s) purchased. Holdings of commercial bills are also regarded as highly liquid, because of their short lives to maturity (mainly up to 3 months) and because of the financial standing of the acceptors of certain sorts of bill.

'Other bills' (5b) include re-financeable export credits (Section 4), and Treasury bills of foreign governments and Commonwealth governments (other than the U.K.). Both Treasury bills and commercial bills are discussed in greater detail in Chapter 3.

6. These are special accounts which, as part of the Bank's system of control, the clearing banks have on occasions since 1960 been required to maintain at the Bank of England (Chapter 4). Balances in these accounts are not regarded as a liquid asset.

7. 'Investments' are mainly British Government bonds, though (other) Commonwealth government bonds and some local authority and public company securities are also held (about 10 per cent of the total). Shares held in other banks or in finance companies are not included under this head.

The issue through the Bank of England of interest-bearing bonds (alternatively known as Government stock or gilt-edged securities) represents a major source of Government borrowing, discussed more fully in Chapters 4 and 8. These bonds are attractive investments to many different sorts of financial institution, as well as to some private holders, and are daily traded in large quantities on the Stock Exchange (Chapter 7). It follows that a bank wanting to buy some bonds need not wait until a new issue is made, but will ordinarily instruct its broker to buy them on its behalf in the Stock Exchange.

The purchase of the bonds may be made, through the machinery of the Stock Exchange, from some other financial institution, or a member of the public (compare Section 2). However, the Bank of England may also make bonds available from day to day on the Stock Exchange through its own broker. Purchase of these, either by the banks or their customers, has important consequences for the clearing banks' cash reserves, discussed in Chapter 4.

The banks are almost exclusively interested in 'short' bonds (redeemable by the Government within five years) and 'medium' bonds (with a maturity date between five and ten years distant). 'Long' bonds (with a life to maturity beyond ten years) and irredeemable bonds (which have no fixed maturity date at all) occupy an insignificant place in most clearing bank bond portfolios. One reason for the banks' preference is that, the shorter the life of a bond to maturity, the closer will its market price (i.e. in Stock Exchange dealings) approach its redemption (i.e. its nominal) value. The risk of capital loss on sale is therefore smaller on a short bond than on a long bond, and much smaller than on an irredeemable bond.

The Government's redemption of its bonds will lead, other things being equal, to a corresponding increase in the banks' balances at the Bank of England (Chapter 4). Accordingly, by holding some bonds which mature this year, some which mature next year, and so on, the banks are assured of a given cash inflow each year from bond maturities.

8. Advances are loans to customers for a variety of purposes and on a range of terms reviewed at some length in the following section. We may note in passing, however, that advances are considered the least liquid of the banker's assets. While they are most often legally repayable on demand, in practice the banks would not expect repayment without reasonable notice.

The usual method of lending is to allow the customer to overdraw his account up to an agreed limit as and when he requires. This is the 'overdraft' system, already illustrated in Section 2. An alternative though less common technique is to open a separate 'loan account', to which the value of the loan is immediately credited in full.

9 to 12. These items are not included in official financial statistics,

because they do not possess any broad monetary significance. They will, however, be found in the annual balance sheet published by each bank.

9. At the date on which it draws up its balance sheet, a bank will be in the process of collecting some cheques just recently paid into their accounts by its customers. As normally the customers' accounts are credited straightaway, thereby increasing the bank's liabilities, it is necessary to enter 'cheques in course of collection' as a matching asset.

10. For a commission, a bank may 'accept' bills of exchange on behalf of its customers. The bank thus acquires an asset in the form of a claim against the customer, but incurs a corresponding liability to the holder of the bill in due course (Chapter 3). Item 10, accordingly, is usually entered in a bank's balance sheet as both an asset and a liability.

11. Each of the clearing banks is a company, with capital subscribed by its shareholders. The latter receive the profits of the business, after the bank has set aside an appropriate sum as a 'reserve'. The balance sheet treatment of share capital and reserves is explained in Chapter 7.

12. The balance sheet will also show, as assets, the value of bank premises and the shares a bank may itself hold (in other banks or in hire-purchase finance companies). It is instructive to recognize that, when a bank buys a new building, it is able to make payment in just the same way as when it buys Government bonds. It simply increases its liabilities by giving a cheque on itself.

We are now in a position to consider the overall liquidity pattern of the assets in the balance sheet. Cash, comprising notes, coin and working balances at the Bank of England, is by definition the perfectly liquid asset to a banker, since he can use it to meet claims presented to him for payment. Other assets are more or less liquid, according to the ease and certainty with which the banker may turn them into cash. The assets in Table 2.1 are in fact ranged in a descending order of average liquidity for each category. This is also the broad order followed in the balance sheet published by each individual bank.

Money at call and short notice represents, as we have already seen, a highly liquid asset, since a bank may require repayment on demand of part of its loans outstanding. Bills are only slightly less liquid, as a bank would arrange its portfolio so that some bills reached maturity each day, while none of its Treasury bills would have more than twelve weeks to run to maturity. On average, bonds are rather less liquid than bills. Their prices are liable to fluctuate in the day-to-day dealings on the Stock Exchange, and a quick sale may be made only at a loss in relation to what was paid for them. Advances are least liquid of all, as already noted.

Within each category of asset, however, items do not possess a uniform liquidity, and particular items positioned fairly 'low down' the balance sheet may in fact have a liquidity greater than other items placed nearer the top. Thus a bank may hold some Government bonds which, as it happens, are going to be redeemed next week: these particular bonds are accordingly more liquid than most of its bill portfolio. Again, a few borrowers on overdraft may be able and willing to repay virtually on demand, so that advances to them possess a greater liquidity than loans at one month's notice, to, say, members of the Stock Exchange (3b). It remains true, nonetheless, that the balance sheet position (in Table 2.1) reflects the average liquidity within each principal class of asset.

It is also true, in general terms, that less liquid assets earn the banker a higher rate of return than the more liquid assets. Thus cash, which is perfectly liquid, earns the banker no return at all. Loans at call and short notice bring in less than bills discounted, while investments are generally less lucrative than advances. The correspondence is not perfect, however, since (for example) advances for export finance (below) may be less profitable than investments, while 'trade' bills (Chapter 3) may top the yield on investments. With some reservations, accordingly, we may regard the banker's principal assets, as set out in Table 2.1, as ranged not only in order of descending average liquidity but also in order of ascending profitability.

If the less liquid assets are more profitable, it would seem superficially that the banker might increase his profits by reducing his relatively liquid assets (cash, money at call and bills) and increasing his relatively illiquid assets (bonds and, especially, advances). There are two reasons, however, why he will want to keep a proportion of assets in a relatively liquid form. First, he will be interested not only in his immediate returns but also his profitability in the years ahead. For long-run profitability, the banker must retain the public's confidence in his ability to meet his liabilities in cash whenever he is called upon to do so. To this end, it is expedient for the bank to maintain a part of its assets in relatively liquid form. In a sense, therefore, the balance sheet represents a compromise between, on the one hand, the goal of immediate profit and, on the other, the desire for 'safety' which is one necessary condition for long-run profitability.

Business prudence apart, the clearing banks today are required by the Bank of England to maintain in an appropriate liquid form assets corresponding to at least 28 per cent of total deposit liabilities. Cash (2), money at call and short notice (3) and bills (4 and 5) all satisfy the Bank's requirement, and are conventionally known as 'the liquid assets' of the clearing banks. As already noted in Section 2, the clearing banks are also expected by the Bank to work to an 8 per cent cash ratio. The operation of both ratios as central bank instruments of control is considered in Chapter 4.

4. *The Work of the Clearing Banks*

The analysis of the clearing banks' balance sheet will enable us to assess the contribution they make to our economic life. They have other important functions, however, which are not reflected in the balance sheet, though they find reflection in the profit and loss account! These will be considered subsequently.

First, in the liabilities column, stand the balances on current and deposit account. As we saw in Chapter 1, bank balances of this sort represent much the greater part of the total supply of money in the country. It is an especially convenient way to hold money, free from the risks of theft or physical destruction, while current account balances are easily transferable to a creditor by request to the bank, i.e. by drawing a cheque or using the credit transfer system (below). A bank customer who produces to his creditor a 'guarantee card', issued by nearly[1] all the clearing (and other) banks, should have no difficulty in making (small) payments by cheque, as in these cases the bank guarantees to honour cheques up to £30, whatever the balance in the drawer's account.

Even though it is not possible to draw cheques on them, balances on deposit account with the clearing (and other commercial) banks may reasonably be regarded as part of the money supply, for two reasons. First, most deposit account holders also have current accounts, and if a cheque on the latter is rather bigger than the balance, the banker will normally meet the difference by debiting the deposit account. Further, the banker tends to a uniform attitude towards current and deposit account liabilities, treating them as both repayable on demand.

The facilities the clearing banks provide for settling debts were extended in 1961 with the development of the 'credit transfer' scheme, which may be used by both customers and non-customers. A non-customer with, for instance, a gas bill to pay may pay cash over the counter at a branch of any bank, for the credit of the Gas Board's account at whatever bank it is held. A customer, for example, who owes various sums of money to creditors banking with different banks in various parts of the country is able to pay them all with one single instruction to his own branch. The branch debits his account by the total sum payable and, within (in general) two business days, the accounts of the beneficiaries are duly credited by their respective banks, through the machinery of the Clearing House (Section 5).

In the meantime, having debited the customer's account, the bank credits an internal account, known as a 'suspense account', to represent the 'credit in course of transmission'. When the settlement is finally

[1] One leading clearing bank operates instead its own 'credit card' system—see text.

made through the Clearing House, the suspense account is debited correspondingly. For the banking system as a whole, therefore, liabilities to the public will consist of (net) balances on current and deposit account plus credits in the course of transmission, which are reflected in the banks' internal suspense accounts. This explains why these 'credits' are included in estimates of the total money supply (Chapter 1).

In 1967 the banks further developed their money transfer facilities with the introduction of a 'direct debit' system, which enables the *payee* to initiate a payment from a customer's account. At the same time improvements were made in the details of the credit transfer system, and the two presented to the public as the 'bank giro' (see Chapter 5, Section 5).

Operation of the direct debit system is best explained by contrasting it with the use of the cheque. Thus a wholesaler might submit monthly accounts to a number of retailers, who pay with cheques they draw on their accounts, which the wholesaler in turns pays into his account. Should the retailers now agree to settle by direct debiting, they will authorize their respective bank branches to meet the request for payment that the wholesaler will, henceforward, present each month directly to the banks concerned. The retailers are thus relieved of the responsibility of arranging payments (i.e. sending off the cheques each month), while overall the wholesaler achieves a quicker settlement.

Turning now to the list of assets, we note a second function of the banks, in the (indirect) provision of short-term finance for the Government. The clearing banks are the principal lenders to the discount houses who, in turn, are always willing to meet the Government's short-term borrowing requirements at the weekly Treasury bill tender (Chapter 3). Further, the discount houses are subsequently able to pass bills on to the banks, as already noted.

Third, in their advances to customers the banks provide at least six different varieties of financial assistance.

(a) They are an important source of short-term finance for the businessman, enabling him to pay wage and raw material bills while his goods are in process of production, etc. Traditionally this sort of loan is particularly favoured by the banker as it finances a 'self-liquidating' transaction. This means that the loan enables the fairly quick production of goods which can be sold off (or liquidated) to repay the loan if the banker is not prepared to extend his credit.

The customer would be allowed to overdraw his account, as he required, up to an agreed limit, with interest payable only on the sum actually overdrawn. The loan would be legally repayable on demand, but in practice it would be usual to give a few months' notice before requiring a reduction in the overdraft level. Advances are often made against the security of property owned by the borrower, e.g. buildings, company shares or debentures, Government securities, life insurance policies with a surrender value, etc. If the customer failed to repay, the bank's *ultimate* remedy would be to dispose of the property, and recoup itself from the proceeds.

The rate of interest charged on overdrafts by the clearing banks is generally 2 per cent or so above Bank Rate (see footnote on page 73), with a minimum of 5–6 per cent. Borrowers who are exceptionally credit-worthy may pay only 1 per cent above Bank Rate, while the nationalized industries (whose overdrafts are guaranteed by the Government) borrow at Bank Rate itself (with a minimum of 4 per cent).

(b) The banks provide 'bridging finance', e.g. to enable a firm to go ahead with a capital scheme while devising other ways of raising funds on a long-term basis. Thus a company may plan a new share issue to finance the construction of a factory, but in the meantime can get on with the job with the aid of a bank advance.

(c) The banks recognize the special problems that small businesses (Chapter 7) and farmers have in securing medium-term and long-term finance. It appears, accordingly, that the banks will in general lend to these special classes of borrower to enable them buy equipment, or premises or land. With most banks such loans remain legally repayable on demand, though in practice there would probably be an informal understanding that the advance would remain outstanding over a number of years. However, at least one of the 'Big Four' has put such lending on a formal basis, both for farming and for small business borrowers. The latter, for instance, may in appropriate cases obtain a 'term loan', generally up to a ceiling of £10,000, with a rate of interest fixed at Bank Rate plus 2 per cent (minimum 6 per cent). Where these loans are used to buy property, repayment is made over ten years (possibly more) by half-yearly instalments.

Other developments in the provision of medium-term loans for capital finance have occurred in recent years. Thus since 1967 the clearing (and Scottish) banks have been willing to lend for up to five years, at usual overdraft rates, to finance the purchase of British-made machine tools. Since 1967, further, the same banks have been prepared to finance the purchase of British-built ships with loans up to eight years in duration,[1] at a fixed interest rate of $5\frac{1}{2}$ per cent per annum.

(d) Over the past decade several innovations have been made by the clearing banks in the provision of 'consumer finance'. Under the 'personal loan' scheme, customers of good standing are able to borrow,

[1] The whole of such an advance is re-financeable by the lending bank at the Bank of England, while 30 per cent of its value may be entered in the balance sheet as a liquid asset. The arrangements are thus comparable with those for medium- and long-term export finance, explained in the text.

without security, to buy durable consumer goods (e.g. cars) and for other personal uses (e.g. house decoration). Personal loans may also be used by small businesses to finance equipment purchases. The usual maximum is £500, generally repayable over two years, at interest rather higher than on normal overdraft terms. Banks which do not offer 'personal loans' as such may nonetheless lend for identical purposes by way of the normal overdraft arrangements.

In 1965 a leading clearing bank acquired virtually a 50 per cent interest in a credit card scheme operated by a dining club, and shortly afterwards a second major bank introduced its own credit card scheme, which is not restricted to its account holders. The holder of a credit card is able to obtain goods or services (as appropriate) from approved suppliers, and periodically receives a bill for his total purchases. In the meantime the suppliers are paid by the bank (or club), which takes a discount on the supplier's sales under the scheme. Under these arrangements, the card holder has a short period of credit interest-free. A subsequent development of the clearing bank's scheme, however, allows the card holder to enjoy an extension of credit from month to month, subject to a fixed interest charge.

Under the 'budget account' scheme introduced in 1967 by several clearing banks, the account holder pays a specified sum into his account by twelve monthly instalments. He is then able to make recurring payments (e.g. school fees) over the year up to the value, in total, of this sum, the bank automatically extending credit for any month(s) the account is in deficit.

(e) All the clearing banks (except one of the smaller banks) own shares in hire-purchase finance companies, and further assist in their finance by making advances to them. These funds in turn are used by the finance companies to give hire-purchase credit (Chapter 5). It is not unfair to say, therefore, that the banks engage indirectly in hire-purchase finance.

(f) Finally, the banks make a substantial contribution by way of advances to the finance of exports. The pattern of arrangements in this field is complex, and has changed considerably in the last few years. The most useful approach is to consider them under the heading of short, medium and long term requirements. The British exporter, whose foreign customer wants credit (for, typically, consumer goods) up to six months will often carry this within his normal overdraft arrangements. Alternatively, he may be able to discount a bill of exchange with his bank (Chapter 3). Further, under a scheme introduced in March, 1966, the London clearing banks, the Scottish and the Northern Ireland banks are prepared on certain conditions to put exporters in funds immediately after shipment of goods, for a period up to two years, at a rate of interest equal to the current Bank Rate (subject to a minimum of 4½ per cent). The exporter is required to give the bank a bill of exchange drawn on the importer, or comparable document, and must also satisfy certain requirements of the Export Credits Guarantee Department of the Board of Trade. The E.C.G.D. will, in turn, guarantee repayment to the exporter's bank should the importer default on the bill. The scheme was extended in 1967 to enable (E.C.G.D. approved) exporters to borrow from the banks for up to six months on the security of their own promise to repay, with recourse for the bank to E.C.G.D. in the event of their default.

The overseas importer may, however, require credit for a medium period of two to five years, say on a £1 million order on which he is prepared to pay the first 20 per cent immediately and the balance by eight six-monthly instalments of £100,000 over four years. Provided the exporter secures appropriate credit insurance from E.C.G.D.—to guard the bank against the risk of the importer's default—the bank will put him in funds straight away, and collect the balance over the four years. Since 1962, this finance has been provided by the banks at a fixed rate of 5½ per cent per annum.

The reader will appreciate that the bank has acquired a highly illiquid asset. The illiquidity of this sort of asset has in the past caused the banks some concern, and in February, 1961, the Bank of England introduced a scheme to improve liquidity in these cases. In the example, the bank would be allowed to re-finance at the Bank of England instalments due over the next eighteen months (which for the first two and a half years would be £300,000). Initially, therefore, of the £800,000 outstanding, £300,000 would be re-financeable and so highly liquid. It would offset the remaining £500,000 illiquid part of the advance. By lending for the finance of exports on these terms the banks actually increase their liquid assets, by a proportion of the total advance made. 'Re-financeable export credits', as they are known, appear in the balance sheet (Table 2.1) in item 5b.

Finally, in January, 1965, the London clearing and Scottish banks announced their willingness to lend beyond the five-year period at a fixed rate of interest of 5½ per cent. Thus the importer of electrical generating plant for a major project may want fifteen years to pay off his debt. Provided E.C.G.D. is willing to give insurance cover (i.e. against default in payment), the financing bank (or consortium of banks) will lend directly to him enabling him to pay cash to his British supplier. To relieve the banks of the burden of illiquidity which such facilities represent, the Bank of England announced an extension of the original re-finance scheme. Under these 1965 arrangements, the clearing banks and Scottish banks will be able to re-finance (at the original loan rate of interest) the outstanding balance of an eligible export credit which has been on the banks' books for five years or more. The banks will not be allowed to count as liquid assets sums which are re-financeable under this particular arrangement, though the facility explained in the preceding paragraph still, of course, applies.

Apart from acceptances (Chapter 3), this completes the list of functions derivable from the banks' balance sheet. But it does not finish the account of the functions the banks perform.

First, they are active dealers in foreign exchange, buying and selling the currencies their customers need for buying (and get from selling) goods overseas.

Second, they offer a variety of financial services, advising on tax problems, advising on and making share purchases, collecting dividends, etc. The banks also play a part in the 'new issue market' and in unit trust arrangements (Chapter 5).

Third, they offer two very important legal services. As executors for wills, they carry out the wishes of the testator in disposing of his property after his death. As trustees of estates, they administer the trust property in the interests of the beneficiaries as required by the settlor in the deed of settlement.

Fourth, they provide facilities for the safe keeping of customers' valuables (e.g. jewellery), either in the general strong room or in private safes.

By following a common formula related to Bank Rate, the clearing banks avoid interest competition for balances on deposit account, though their subsidiaries (Section 7) may offer competitive rates for large deposits made for a fixed term. In their overdraft business, on the other hand, there is not a rigid margin between Bank Rate and lending rates, and a bank may reduce its rate to retain a valuable customer. Competition among the banks is, however, more apparent in their attempts to improve the quality and extend the variety of the services they offer. Thus each bank is keen to put up new branches, in order to reach new customers and to serve existing ones better. New loan techniques of especial interest to the private customer have, again, been introduced by various banks in the last ten years.

The recent improvements in their payments facilities have been standardized by the clearing (and Scottish) banks, and represent an instrument not of inter-bank competition but of competition by the banks with other financial institutions (Chapter 5). The new payments facilities are associated with the increasing use of computers by the banks, and this is likely to bring further progress and development in the next few years. Thus direct linkage between a bank's computer system and those of its large business customers may be anticipated, while co-operation between the banks and their customers in various matters of computer-system operation is already well established. Plans are also under way for setting-up computer centres which will take over from a bank's branches the book-keeping involved in handling customers' accounts. These arrangements for centralization can be expected to become operative with the change to decimal currency in 1971 and should enable virtually instantaneous transfer of balances from one account to another.

5. *Settling Inter-Bank Indebtedness*

On any given day, a number of, say, Lloyds Bank customers will draw cheques on their accounts and hand them over in settlement of debts to Midland Bank customers, who will pay them into their accounts. The Midland Bank will then have £x worth of claim against Lloyds Bank on behalf of its customers. On the other hand by the same process Lloyds may have acquired £y worth of claim against Midland on behalf of its customers. If we ignore for the moment any transactions involving the other clearing banks, the simplest way of settling is for the one bank to pay the other the balance between the two claims. If £y is the smaller, then Lloyds would arrange for Midland to receive £(x — y) from its account at the Bank of England. The Midland and Lloyds branches, meanwhile, proceed to debit and credit the accounts of, respectively, the customers who drew cheques and the customers who received them.

Settling inter-bank indebtedness in this way has involved crediting Midland's and debiting Lloyds' account at the Bank of England. Lloyds has accordingly lost a part of its cash reserve. In practice, of course, on another day it would probably be a net creditor on balance for its customers, so that its account would increase a little. The net loss of customers, on the other hand, is a serious matter for any bank, as the transfer of each customer's account means that much more taken from the credit of its account at the Bank of England for the credit of other banks. Part of the cash reserve, accordingly, is lost, and (as we have seen) the size of the cash reserve is one of the factors determining how many other (profitable) assets it can acquire.

The machinery for sorting and clearing cheques is provided by the London Clearing House and various local arrangements in the provinces. The Clearing House is organized by its joint-stock members (Section 1). The Bank of England is also a member, and has a representative at the House, since it is ultimately involved in the settlements. However, it takes no part in the administration of the Clearing House, and is not in any sense a clearing bank.

The work of the Clearing House is divided into three main sections, Town, General and Credit. 'Town Clearing' deals with cheques (in general, for £2,000 or over) paid into, and drawn on, the hundred or so offices and branches in the City of London only. As many financial institutions have accounts at banks in the City, the total value of the Town Clearing is much higher than the General Clearing, though the number of cheques handled is much smaller (see Table 2.2). In operating the Town Clearing, the emphasis is on speed. Eligible cheques paid into a branch within the City will be taken the same day to the Clearing House, and handed over to the representatives of the other clearing banks on which they were drawn. Each bank's representative straightway sends round its cheques by messenger to the branches involved, where the drawers' accounts are debited. Meanwhile each bank's representative in the House is busy compiling a balance sheet of total debits and credits. This will form the basis for the subsequent transfers of funds between the clearing banks' accounts at the Bank of England.

TABLE 2.2

Bank Clearings 1968
(average for each month)

	£ million
Debit clearing:	
Town	42,977
General	6,985
Provincial	59
Credit clearing	970

Source: Financial Statistics (H.M.S.O.)

Cheques which are ineligible for the 'Town Clearing' or any local arrangements (below) are dealt with through the 'General Clearing'. Thus a branch of Lloyds Bank in Swansea may have paid into it a cheque drawn on a Midland branch in Manchester. It sends the cheque to Lloyds clearing department in London, from which it goes via Midland clearing department to the Manchester branch where the drawer's account is debited. The debits and credits involved in all these transactions are noted, and the totals finally incorporated with the Town Clearing balances for settlement.

A customer using the credit transfer scheme to make a payment (Section 4) has his account immediately debited, so the subsequent clearance is concerned only with crediting the account(s) of the beneficiary (or beneficiaries). This apart, the Credit Clearing is run in very much the same way as the General Clearing, and net balances are counted in with Town and General balances for settlement.

The settlement is made daily on a multilateral basis, not a bilateral basis (as the earlier example assumed for simplicity). Thus Lloyds, for instance, may on a given day be (say) a net debtor of Coutts and Co., a net creditor of Midland, a net creditor of Barclays, and so on. Overall, it may be a net creditor of all the other banks, and three other banks may be in the same position. The remainder, it is apparent, must be net debtors, and each will authorize the transfer of the appropriate amount from its account at the Bank of England to a special intermediary account held at the Bank by the Clearing House. This sum, in turn, will be transferred in the appropriate amounts from the intermediary account to the accounts at the Bank of the four net creditor banks. Thus each bank meets all its obligations and receives all its dues through just one transfer to or from its account at the Bank.

Until 1968 twelve leading provincial towns and cities had their own Clearing Associations for handling locally drawn cheques, but early in that year the work of all except one was transferred to the General Clearing. Transactions at the surviving Liverpool clearing figure in Table 2.2, as 'Provincial debit clearing'. Banks in the same town or district may have their own informal arrangements for clearing locally drawn cheques, but progressive centralization through absorption in the General Clearing can be expected.

Cheques drawn on some of the non-clearing-banks (including the Trustee Savings Banks) may be handled in the General Clearing, through the agency of one of the members.

6. *The Scottish Banks*

A well-known distinction of the four Scottish banks is their power to issue their own notes. The Bank Notes (Scotland) Act of 1845 gave each of the Scottish banks a fixed fiduciary issue, but authorized the issue of notes beyond this limit, provided the excess was backed by equivalent holdings of gold. Similar arrangements were made for Ireland and, in further contrast to the position in England and Wales (Chapter 1), there was no provision that issue powers should lapse if banks amalgamated. In 1914 the banks were authorized to hold Treasury notes as a backing in place of gold, and Bank of England notes after 1928. Each Scottish bank holds some of its Bank of England 'cover' notes in two of its offices authorized for this purpose, and a part (probably the greater) with the Bank itself. These latter holdings should not be confused with the balances which the Scottish banks keep (though at a very low level) in account with the Bank of England.

In their services to depositors, the Scottish banks exhibit two features of especial interest. The first is the relatively high number of branches per head of population. Thus despite a considerable increase in the English ratio since the early 1950s, Scotland in 1965 still had a substantial lead[1] with one bank office per 3,000 people, compared with one per 4,000 in England and Wales. One possible reason for this abundance is the ease with which the Scottish banks can equip their branches with a cash float of (largely) their own notes, which do not need backing till they are actually put into circulation. The second feature is the emphasis which the Scottish banks place on the encouragement of savings (especially small savings). This is reflected in the lower proportion of deposit liabilities on current account—about 40 per cent in 1968 compared with the clearing banks' ratio of 51 per cent.

The banks offer the public two alternatives to the current account. The 'deposit receipt' is a document issued to the customer in return for a given deposit: it is repayable on demand at the office of any bank in Scotland. The deposit account was introduced as recently as 1928, especially to encourage the deposit of small savings, though it now has a broader character. The depositor has a pass book, may operate the account in terms of shillings, and may withdraw his total balance on demand at the branch keeping his account. Interest rates are agreed among the banks at—normally—$2\frac{1}{2}$ per cent below Bank Rate on both types of deposit, though sometimes a little more favourable on deposit accounts.

On a monthly average for 1968, the Scottish banks had total deposit liabilities of some £1,106 million; notes outstanding were £139·2 million, of which only £2·7 million formed their fiduciary issue. (Corresponding figures for the Northern Ireland banks for 1968 are £252 million, £10·6 million and £2 million respectively.) Their cash reserves are today conventionally regarded as their balances at the Bank of England, their holdings of coin and all Bank of England notes (including those held at the Bank of England) and their holdings of each other's (but not their own) notes. The inclusion of the latter may be considered a little artificial, as they are largely self-cancelling at the regular note exchanges that take place between the banks. On the other hand, the definition excludes the balances held in account with the clearing banks, yet these possess a liquidity hardly inferior to their balances at the Bank of England.

The assessment of the Scottish banks' cash position is further complicated by their holdings of Bank of England notes as cover for the issue of their own notes beyond the tiny fiduciary limit. It is apparent that, in principle, these 'cover holdings' (averaging £136·5 million in 1968) could be regarded as supporting both the 'excess' note issue and a

---

[1] Scotland also possesses apparently the only boat bank in the U.K., owned by the National and Commercial Banking Group and serving the North Islands of Orkney.

part of their liabilities on account to customers (on the pattern outlined in Section 2). Scottish bankers themselves will not necessarily hold the view that their cover holdings discharge this second function. If, nonetheless, the Scottish banks had no notes outstanding, it is probable that their cash reserves would be higher than the current difference between total cash (as conventionally defined) and their cover holdings of Bank of England notes.

An important supplement to the Scottish banks' cash reserves is provided by their loans at call and short notice, mainly to the discount houses. In recent years these have been about two or three times greater than their bill holdings, and of course possess rather higher liquidity than the bill portfolio. For the clearing banks, in contrast, total money at call has until recent years been well below the bill portfolio in size.

Unlike the clearing banks, the Scottish banks have received no intimation from the Bank of England about the size of an appropriate liquidity ratio. However, in published statistics this ratio is calculated by expressing liquid assets as a percentage of total deposit liabilities plus notes outstanding. Liquid assets for this purpose are defined as cash (i.e. holdings of notes and coin, and balances at the Bank of England), balances at other banks, call money, bills, and cheques in course of collection. Calculated on this basis, the liquidity ratio has in recent years regularly been just over 30 per cent. However, a substantially lower value is obtained if cover holdings of notes are omitted from liquid assets and the banks' own note issue from liabilities.

Holdings of Government bonds are significantly higher for the Scottish banks than the clearing banks, and until fairly recently the average life to maturity of their bond portfolio was notably greater. Traditionally, too, the Scottish banks were more willing to recognize explicitly the long-term nature of some of their advances. Possibly, with a lower proportion of liabilities on current account, they felt less need to stress liquidity as an attribute for investments and advances. Today, however, it is probable that in their investment policy the Scottish and clearing banks are very close to each other; in the light of the discussion in Section 4, this also appears true of their advances policy.

A further traditional feature of Scottish banking practice disappeared in 1964. Until that date, the banks regularly published a jointly agreed list of the minimum interest rates at which they were prepared to lend, graded according to the security offered. Today the banks quote their rates as a percentage on Bank Rate, and work to the same pattern as the clearing banks.

7. The Merchant Banks

There are in the City of London forty or fifty financial institutions which may be described as 'merchant banks'. Some of them are old established firms, in business since the last century or before, which at one time combined overseas merchandise and banking interests. Others—perhaps subsidiaries of British or foreign-based joint-stock banks—are more recent in origin. Today all are best regarded as specialist banking institutions, each with its particular interests (which may still include trading), but mainly engaged in international finance and the higher reaches of company finance.

Sixteen leading merchant banks are members of the Accepting Houses' Committee, and are alternatively known as accepting houses. They include such distinguished financial names as Baring, Guiness Mahon, Morgan Grenfell, Rothschild and Warburg. Statistics of their principal assets and liabilities are regularly published by the Bank of England, and appear in Financial Statistics (H.M.S.O.). The same information is also published for twenty or so other merchant banks (the 'other banks' of Table 1.1).

The traditional functions of the accepting houses are the acceptance of bills of exchange (Chapter 3) and the issue of bonds on behalf of foreign governments and companies. This second activity was largely in eclipse in the post-war years, but has revived since 1963. Both sorts of business may, of course, be undertaken by other merchant banks. Bond issue by a foreign company or government puts funds at its disposal to finance overseas purchases. An alternative may sometimes be a very large long-term loan from a consortium of clearing and 'overseas' banks (Section 8), organization of which will often be undertaken by a merchant bank. A merchant bank may also act as agent for an overseas company in placing its funds on temporary loan with, say, a finance company or local authority in this country. This is to be distinguished from the deposit business in which these banks engage (below).

Domestically, the accepting houses and some other merchant banks are active in the new issue market (Chapter 5), a business which grew out of their traditional work in arranging foreign bond issues. Apart from handling the issue of shares and other company securities, they advise on, and carry through, company reconstructions and mergers. They may also look after the investment of e.g. pension funds, or advise the funds' managers on their investment. Interesting developments in recent years have been their participation in the growth of unit and investment trusts (Chapter 5), and the attempt by some banks to cater for the financial needs of industrial and trading firms in the provinces.

In their deposit-taking and loan-making activities the merchant banks seem more nearly comparable with the clearing and other joint-stock banks, though many substantial differences in fact exist (below). Business in deposits and loans has grown with exceptional rapidity in the last decade. Thus in the five years between late 1963 and December 1968 deposits with the accepting houses more than doubled to reach a level of £1,877 million. Deposits with the twenty-two 'other banks' which figure in official statistics seem to have grown even more steeply, though comparison is difficult because of changes in the number of banks covered. In December, 1968 their deposit liabilities totalled £1,544 million. For the accepting houses in 1968, about 20 per cent of deposits came from U.K. banks, 40 per cent from other residents in the U.K., and the remainder from overseas residents. Comparable figures for the 'other banks' are, roughly, 35 per cent, 40 per cent and 25 per cent.

The deposit and loan business of the merchant banks has grown in line with the expansion in the 1960s of the 'new' or 'secondary' money markets, in which they play an important part. Thus deposits which the merchant banks hold on account to other U.K. banks and to one another reflect their participation in the 'inter-bank' market, briefly described in Chapter 3. They are broadly matched by loans to (described as 'balances with') other banks and to one another. Deposits held on account to overseas residents are mainly denominated in foreign currencies, and these would in general be used by the merchant banks for loans to other overseas residents. The workings of this 'Euro-currency' market are considered in Chapter 17. The great bulk of deposits from (non-bank) U.K. residents is in sterling and these (together with the sterling deposits of overseas residents) enable the banks to support, among other assets, sizeable short-term loans to U.K. local authorities (Chapter 8) and hire-purchase finance companies (Chapter 5). The corresponding 'deposit' market is briefly considered in Chapter 3.

A further important outlet for the sterling funds of the merchant banks are advances to U.K. industrial and commercial companies. Unlike the predominantly overdraft system of the clearing banks, advances are usually for a fixed term, though not necessarily at a fixed interest rate. The term of the loan might sometimes be five years or more, and the loan itself made specifically to finance a 'capital' project like machinery purchase. Loans to the discount market by the accepting houses are (today) small in relation to their other assets, as are their holdings of bills discounted and Government bonds. These three classes of asset have even less significance for the twenty-two 'other banks'.

The merchant banks take balances both on current account and on deposit for a fixed term. Current account facilities are used almost entirely by their non-bank customers (notably industrial and commercial companies) in the U.K., though even among this group most balances are held on deposit. Sums may be placed overnight, for a few days, a month or so, or even a year, and come in large units from, say, £50,000 upwards. The merchant banks do not follow the clearing bank practice of paying Bank Rate less 2 per cent on deposit account balances, and need to keep rates internationally competitive if they are to retain overseas residents' funds.

Sums placed on deposit with the merchant banks may be evidenced by a certificate of deposit, which is interest-bearing and transferable. The depositor is thus enabled to sell his certificate (typically to a discount house—Chapter 3) should he want cash before the maturity date, and for conferring this advantage the issuing bank would pay a somewhat lower rate than otherwise on a deposit for that term. Dollar certificates of deposit have been available for a few years, and were originally pioneered in 1966 by the American banks in London (Section 8). Dollar C.D.s are issued only in respect of deposits of U.S. dollars made by foreign residents. Sterling C.D.s—issued in respect of sterling deposits to U.K. or overseas residents alike—have been available only since late-1968 (Appendix A).

The fixed-term nature of so large a part of total deposits gives the merchant banks a somewhat different liquidity requirement from the clearing banks, for whom slightly more than half of all deposits are on current account. This requirement they may meet by aiming, more or less closely, at a 'match' between deposit liabilities and assets of comparable duration in the same currency. Thus a given value of dollars deposited for one month might be 'matched' by (roughly) equivalent dollar loans for one month, and so on.

With so much of their deposits at fixed term the merchant banks, in contrast to the clearing banks, play a relatively small part in the economy's payments system. This explains their minimal holdings of notes and coin and balances in account with the Bank of England. Deposits of non-bank U.K. residents with the accepting houses and 'other banks' are included in the official definition of the money supply (Table 1.1). However, only the smaller part (perhaps 25 per cent) of these balances are on current account and hence unambiguously 'money' by the definition of Chapter 1. The remainder is on deposit, and the fixed-term nature of these deposits precludes their use as a 'supplement' to current account balances after the fashion of deposit accounts held with the clearing banks. Inclusion of these fixed-term deposits in the money supply thus seems difficult to justify.

The merchant banks are not subject to cash and liquidity requirements in the same way as the clearing banks, though the accepting houses come under some supervision by the Bank of England as a consequence of their acceptance business (Chapter 3). Since 1968, however, the Bank of England has reserved the right to call for 'cash deposits' from the accepting houses and twenty-two other merchant banks, should it wish to restrain their lending in the interests of official monetary policy (Chapter 4).

8. *Overseas Banks*

The London offices of about a hundred and fifty banks with interests mainly overseas are conveniently described as 'overseas' banks. Four groups are distinguished in the published statistics (to which most of the banks contribute). The thirty or so members of the British Overseas and Commonwealth Banks Association are either the head offices of British banks with most of their other offices overseas, or the London offices of banks with head offices elsewhere in the Commonwealth. The remainder (sometimes distinguished as 'foreign banks') are the London branches of banks whose head offices are outside the Commonwealth. About twenty are members of the Foreign Banks and Affiliates Association, a similar number are definable as American banks in London, while thirty-five to forty may be designated simply as 'other overseas banks'.

Like the merchant banks, the overseas banks have enjoyed an exceptionally rapid growth in their loan and deposit business in the last decade, largely reflecting their participation in the fast-expanding secondary money markets. Both in deposits and in numbers, expansion has been especially marked for the American banks and for the group of 'other overseas banks'. By end-December, 1968, liabilities on current and deposit account for all the overseas banks were a little under £10,200 million, compared with a mid-December gross deposit level of just over £10,700 million for the clearing banks. One difficulty in such a comparison, however, is that the deposit level of the overseas banks (and, indeed, the merchant banks) will to some extent reflect the level of turnover in the inter-bank market (Chapter 3), while this is not the case for the clearing banks.

As their leading role in the secondary money markets might suggest, statistics of the overseas banks' principal assets and liabilities reveal a pattern broadly comparable with the merchant banks. Section 7's account of the merchant banks' loan and deposit business provides a reasonable general guide to the activities of the overseas banks, though the extent of their participation in the Euro-currency market should be emphasized. Thus at end-December, 1968, rather more than half their total assets took the form of foreign currency advances to overseas residents. Asset proportions do, however, vary widely among the banks, and in the case of the American banks, for instance, the corresponding figure was about 75 per cent.

Like the merchant banks, the overseas banks are not subject to cash or liquidity ratio requirements, but are included in the Bank of England's 'cash deposit' scheme. Their liabilities on account to non-bank customers in the U.K. are counted in official statistics as part of the money supply, and this is open to the criticism made in Section 7.

Credit for Exports and Domestic Shipbuildings: New Re-Finance Facilities

In September, 1969, the Bank of England published details of new arrangements made the previous May with the London clearing and Scottish banks. Part I of the revised scheme relates to fixed-rate loans for domestic shipbuilding (p. 36), and E.C.G.D.-guaranteed export credits made for a minimum period of two years (p. 38). A bank whose operations are hindered by a liquidity shortage, or which needs cash to meet deposit withdrawals, will be able to re-finance at the Bank (on the original terms) up to 30 per cent of the sum outstanding on each eligible transaction, or, in the case of export credits, the balance payable in the next eighteen months if this is greater than 30 per cent. Amounts thus re-financeable may be treated in the bank's balance sheet as a liquid asset.

Under Part II of the new scheme, a bank may re-finance that part of its fixed-interest export and shipbuilding loans total which—excluding the proportion definable as liquid assets—exceeds 5 per cent of its total gross deposits. The banks thus enjoy an assurance that the expansion of their fixed-rate advances will not, after a certain point, restrict their other forms of lending. The facility for re-financing export credits of more than five years' duration (introduced in 1965) and for re-financing fixed-rate shipbuilding loans (1967) is discontinued.

Questions

See end of Chapter 4.

3

The London Discount Market

1. *The Market Defined*

The London discount market centres around the activities of the eleven discount houses which are members of the London Discount Market Association. Their work principally involves dealing in bills of exchange, Treasury bills and short-dated Government bonds (Table 3.1). To finance their activities, they borrow at call and short notice, mainly from the London clearing banks, but also from the accepting houses and overseas banks (as defined in Section 8, Chapter 2), the Scottish banks and other U.K. commercial banks. The eleven houses also hold Loan Accounts at the Bank of England's Discount Office, which carry the unfailing right to borrow from the Bank, though on terms of the Bank's own choosing. Such borrowing has special significance for the whole banking system, considered in some detail in Chapter 4.

A similar sort of business may be included in the activities of a few foreign exchange and bullion brokers, for example, and is also undertaken by a few smaller discount houses and running bill-brokers (who earn commission by acting as intermediaries). These firms—numbering a dozen or so in total—may be regarded as part of the 'discount market', though in practice the term is often restricted (as in Table 3.1) to the twelve members of the Association. These other institutions have no *right* of access to the Bank of England for a loan.

The market for short-term loans thus created by the discount market is described as the London money market, and the two expressions are often used interchangeably. There are, however, other financial firms which may regularly borrow at call or short notice, for example, brokers in the market for local authority finance, who could be regarded as part of the money market. On the other hand, the term is sometimes restricted to just the eleven members of the London Discount Market Association.

Reference was made in Section 7, Chapter 2, to an 'inter-bank market', a 'market for short-term deposits', and a 'Euro-currency market'. These have all developed since the late 1950s, and are sometimes

TABLE 3.1

*Principal assets and liabilities of London Discount Market
Quarterly average, 1968*

	£ million
Assets	
1. British Government Treasury bills	364
2. Commercial and other sterling bills	484
3. British Government bonds	464
4. Other assets	250
Borrowed Funds	
5. Bank of England Banking Department	104
6. London clearing banks	966
7. Scottish banks	88
8. Other deposit banks	17
9. Accepting houses, overseas and other banks	179
10. Other sources	119

Source: Financial Statistics (H.M.S.O.)

described as the 'new', 'parallel' or 'secondary' money markets, in
contradistinction to the traditional or 'primary' money market revolv-
ing around the discount houses. This chapter is concerned with the
traditional market, though its relationships with the new are briefly
considered in Section 6.

2. The Bill of Exchange

The discount market has its origins in the early nineteenth century,
when the forerunners of today's discount houses developed a business in
the purchase and sale of bills of exchange. These bills were used in the
finance of inland or domestic trade, but it was in the sphere of international finance that the discount market and the bill of exchange grew
together in the fifty years or so preceding the First World War. Let
us therefore take an example of how a bill may be used to finance an
international trading transaction.

  Suppose that Smith of Birmingham is selling Gonzalez of Buenos
Aires £10,000 worth of goods. As part of the deal, perhaps, Smith is
giving Gonzalez three months' credit. We may consider, first, the
procedure which is simplest to understand but which would not actually
involve a discount house! Smith writes out an order to Gonzalez,

telling him to pay, in three months' time, £10,000 either to Smith or to whomever Smith orders should have the money, in return for the goods received. This document is a bill of exchange, and under English law it must carry a 2d. stamp. Brief details of the shipment would also be entered upon the bill (see specimen in Appendix A). The bill will be sent to Gonzalez, who accepts it by writing his name across the face of the bill, thereby becoming liable to pay £10,000 on presentation of the bill in three months' time.

Bills accepted by overseas traders in this way are not discounted by discount houses, as they cannot be used by the houses as security for the loans they get from the clearing banks. In this example, accordingly, Smith might choose to hold the bill for three months, then claim the £10,000 from Gonzalez. Alternatively, he might secure immediate funds from his bank against the bill, under the E.C.G.D. scheme (Chapter 2). Otherwise, he may (on the strength of his own good name) be able to discount the bill with his bank, selling it to them now for, say, £9,800. In this case, the bank will receive the £10,000 in three months' time, and is making a profit of £200 for putting Smith in funds three months before the bill matures.

If Smith had wanted to discount the bill with a discount house, he could do so with ease if he arranged with Gonzalez for it to be accepted by an accepting house, a London clearing bank, a Scottish bank or an overseas bank with a London office. Under this system, Gonzalez (say) is given an 'acceptance credit' with the bank up to e.g. £100,000 at any given time. Exporters to Gonzalez are then able to draw their bills, not on Gonzalez, but on the bank concerned which accepts the bill in its own name. The bank in turn becomes liable on the bill in three months' time, while it makes its own arrangements for collecting this sum from Gonzalez. For this service, it charges him an 'acceptance commission' of, typically, about $1\frac{1}{2}$ per cent per annum. With the name of the London bank on the bill as drawee and acceptor, Smith will have no difficulty in selling his bill to a discount house.

Bills accepted by a bank (or accepting house) are described as 'bank bills', and those drawn on and accepted by the accepting houses and by London banks of the very highest standing are known as 'fine bank bills'. They are particularly attractive to the discount houses not only because of the standing of the acceptors but also because they can be used by the houses as security for a loan from the Bank of England (Chapter 4). The 'fine' or 'prime' bill rate is the lowest rate at which bank bills may be discounted in the market, and is fixed weekly by the twelve discount houses. In the example, Smith might have sold the bill to a discount house for £9,850, which represents a discount rate of £150 in £10,000 or 1·5 per cent for three months. On an annual basis, therefore, the rate of discount here is $4 \times 1·5$, or 6 per cent. The total cost of bill finance would, of course, include the acceptance commission.

Bills accepted by the London branch of an overseas bank (known as Agency Bills) will very often command the prime rate, but may in some cases or on some occasions stand at $\frac{1}{16}$ per cent or so above fine bills. A drawback is that these bills are not eligible security for a loan to the discount houses from the Bank of England, while at times there may be some uncertainty about the financial situation in the country in which the parent bank is located.

A trade bill is a bill drawn by the seller of goods on his customer in the U.K. They may be bought in limited quantities by the discount houses, but are more often discounted with the drawer's bank, or used as security for an advance from the bank. Rates of discount will reflect the acceptor's (and drawer's) business standing, but will anyway stand above the prime rate. Thus in late December, 1968, 3-month bank bills were being bought in the discount market at rates between $7\frac{1}{4}$ and $7\frac{5}{16}$ per cent, but 3-month trade bills of good average quality at $8\frac{1}{4}$ to $8\frac{3}{4}$ per cent. It would appear, anyway, that most trade bills are held outside the banking system, representing a means of finance between firms comparable with trade credit (Chapter 7).

The example constructed to illustrate the use of the bill involved an actual shipment of goods, and it is to finance such movements that most bank bills are in fact drawn. A firm may, however, use a bill simply to raise funds, without any such movement, in which case it is described as a 'finance bill'. Thus after making rather heavy purchases of raw materials a firm may find itself short of ready funds. It may be able to secure an acceptance credit with a merchant bank, draw a bill on them, and discount it with a discount house. In principle, by the time the firm is called upon to put the accepting house in funds the raw materials have been worked up and sold, and the proceeds would be available to make repayment.

The maintenance of the high standards of the discount market is a concern of the Bank of England. Accordingly on most days the Bank will make 'sample purchases' of prime bank bills from the discount houses, to ascertain the type of business for which bill finance is being used. Further, the accepting houses must make their balance sheets open to the Bank, and be prepared to answer the Bank's inquiries about their acceptance business. It is on this condition that the Bank is prepared to recognize an accepting house's signature as making a bill a prime bank bill, and so eligible for use by a discount house as security for a loan from the Bank.

c

3. *Short-dated Bonds*

On several occasions in their history the discount houses have demonstrated their resilience in the face of adversity. Thus when the inland
bill of exchange yielded place to the bank overdraft in the second half
of the nineteenth century, the market was able to take up, and grow
with, the international bill. When the latter virtually disappeared in
the First World War, the discount houses were able to switch to the
Treasury bill, which for the first time became an important means of
Government finance. The 1930s, again, put the discount market to the
test. A severe contraction in international trade meant a sharp decline
in 'commercial paper'. Bill discounting became, anyway, a profitless
affair, as at home the Government pursued a policy of low interest
rates, in an attempt to encourage trade in a depressed economy. The
discount market nonetheless survived these lean years, largely through
applying some of their borrowed funds to the purchase of short-dated
Government bonds.

This development did not, at first, meet with the Bank of England's
approval: bonds are liable to fluctuate in value on the Stock Exchange,
so a discount house obliged to sell might suffer a capital loss. However,
the growth of Government borrowing in the later 1930s, and in particular during the war years, underlined the advantage of extending
the market for Government securities. The discount market's bond
activities accordingly received official recognition, the Bank at the same
time encouraging the formation (through amalgamation) of rather
fewer houses with bigger capital resources. 'Official recognition' meant
that the discount houses were given the same special facilities as jobbing
members of the Stock Exchange for effecting the transfer of short-dated
Government bonds at the Bank of England (which looks after such
matters for the Government). This in turn made it easier for the
houses to deal in short bonds, buying or selling as the opportunity
presented.

By thus extending the market in short bonds, the discount houses
may make some contribution to their price stability, e.g. selling by other
institutions need not depress prices on the Stock Exchange if the bonds
are readily purchased by the discount houses. Further, as we shall see
in Chapter 4, the Bank of England is regularly looking to buy in bonds
that are approaching maturity, and it is convenient to have a significant
proportion already to hand and available for purchase from the discount market. It would appear, nonetheless, that the Bank has made
known to the discount houses its wishes regarding the size and pattern
of their bond holdings. A house's bond portfolio should not, in general,
be more than eight or ten times greater than its own capital resources,
nor are the houses expected to carry, on borrowed funds, bonds with a

life longer than five years to maturity. In practice, the bulk of the portfolio would consist of bonds with two years or under to redemption.

4. *Treasury Bills*

The Bank of England's weekly sale of Treasury bills on behalf of the Government forms, it was noted in Chapter 2, the regular method of short-term Government finance. Each Friday the Bank announces the maximum number of bills to be allotted the following Friday, and on that subsequent Friday it is open to receive tenders from any London bank, discount house or bill-broker (see specimens in Appendix A). Tenders must be received by 1 p.m.; they are then checked, and sorted according to the price offered. Tenders offering the highest prices (i.e. asking the lowest discount rates) are met in full, and so on downwards until all the bills on offer have been allotted.

By an agreement dating from the mid-1930s, the clearing banks do not submit tenders on their own account, though they may do so on behalf of their customers. Any bills that they want are, in fact, purchased from the discount houses (Chapter 2), though not before they are seven days old. A bank may, however, buy bills from a discount house on their day of issue ('hot Treasury bills'), as an alternative to tendering for customers. The discount houses, also by informal arrangements dating from the 1930s, operate in effect as a syndicate in their submission of tenders. All the houses put in tenders at the same price (subject to some minor qualifications), the size of each house's bid reflecting (among other things) its own size and the amount of its working capital. Their tenders, taken together, exactly match the total of bills on offer.

While the discount houses do not face the competition of the clearing banks as such, applications for bills will be received by the Bank from other ('outside') sources. Apart from clearing bank bids for their own customers, tenders may be submitted by houses and brokers outside the Association, by the accepting houses and overseas banks, and perhaps by one or two of the Scottish banks. The Bank of England may itself submit tenders, on behalf of its own Banking Department, and as agent for overseas central banks.

These 'outside' tenders are met in full, in so far as they offer prices higher (i.e. ask for lower rates of discount) than the discount houses. What is left of the issue is allotted to the discount houses, who may expect on average to take up about 30 to 40 per cent. If the houses wish to increase their share of the tender it is open to them to quote higher prices, which means reducing profit margins (Section 5).

On Friday afternoon the Bank of England announces the average rate of discount (expressed on a yearly basis) at which bills were allotted in that day's tender. This may be termed the Treasury bill rate. Thus an average rate of £5 per cent (per annum) means a rate of £1 5s. per cent for 91 days (the life of a Treasury bill). In this case the average purchase price on allotment would be £98 15s. per cent, or £9,875 for a £10,000 bill.

5. *Borrowed Funds*

To finance their asset holdings the discount houses have, as their main source of funds, 'money at call and short notice' (Chapter 2) from the London clearing banks. A bank is always able to 'lend its surplus cash', at interest, to the discount market, and subsequently make good any cash shortage by calling in some of these loans. To understand what these propositions imply, it is useful to construct a very simple example, involving the discount market and just two clearing banks, A and B. All values are in units of, say, £10 million.

Suppose that, initially, each bank has deposit liabilities of 100 and assets consisting of cash 8, loans at call 10, bills 12, and bonds and advances together 70. Each bank has a cash ratio, accordingly, of 8 per cent, which it maintains by adjusting its loans to the money market.[1] Assume now that Bank A's customers pay Bank B's customers cheques of total value 5, and B's customers pay A's customers cheques of total value 3. On the subsequent clearing, Bank A will have an adverse balance of 2. The corresponding debit to its account at the Bank of England would reduce its cash to 6, while at the same time its liabilities to customers fall to 98 (i.e. it will credit some accounts by 3, but debit others by 5). With liabilities of 98, it will need a cash reserve of 7·84 (i.e. $8/100 \times 98$). It therefore calls in 1·84 loans from the discount market.

Bank B, on the other hand, will gain 2 on the clearing, which would give it a cash reserve of 10. Its liabilities on account to customers will rise to 102, as it credits some accounts by 5, and debits others by 3. Its necessary cash reserve is accordingly 8·16 (i.e. $8/100 \times 102$), which means it has 1·84 'surplus cash'. It is therefore prepared to increase loans at call by 1·84, which it backs fully with cash. The discount houses are, of course, looking for funds and take up the new loans from Bank B, immediately paying cheques drawn on Bank B to Bank A to meet the latter's request for repayment. Bank B accordingly loses 1·84 of its balance in account with the Bank of England, while Bank A gains 1·84. B's balance sheet will now read: liabilities 102; cash 8·16; loans at call 11·84; bills 12; bonds and advances 70. A's balance sheet will now

---

[1] The alternative—to buy or sell bonds—is considered in Chapter 4.

read: liabilities 98; cash 7·84; loans at call 8·16; bills 12; bonds and advances 70.

This simple example shows how, if we could treat the amount of cash in the clearing bank system as given, adjustments in the daily cash requirements of the banks could be made in effect by switching balances at the Bank of England from one bank to another through the machinery of the money market. In the real world, however, the amount of cash in the banking system is *not* a constant, for reasons considered in Chapter 4. It follows that, if most or all of the clearing banks find themselves short of cash, and obliged to call in some loans from the discount market, the latter would have to look for funds outside the clearing bank system. In fact, the discount houses may always turn to the Bank of England as a last resort, as we shall see in the next chapter.

It also follows that, in deciding its daily cash requirements, each bank has to consider all the influences upon its cash position (Chapter 4), not only the effects of the clearing. In practice, each bank makes an estimate early in the day of probable changes in its cash position during the day. On this basis it will decide whether to increase loans at call, buy bills or call in some loans. By convention, it will not call in loans after twelve noon, though it may make fresh loans available at any time.

Of its total borrowing from any given bank, a discount house would be able to regard some minimum sum as regularly available to it, and so 'regular' money. The remainder is liable to fluctuate from day to day, depending on the lending bank's cash position and might be appropriately termed 'night' money. Finally, by agreement with various banks, a discount house will have the privilege of borrowing relatively small sums towards the close of the day's business, should it need assistance in balancing its books: such loans are known as 'privilege' money.

Since 1958 the clearing banks have lent part of their regular money to the discount houses at their own deposit rate plus $\frac{3}{8}$ per cent (sometimes $\frac{1}{4}$ per cent when the deposit rate has reached 6 per cent). The remainder of their regular money, and their night money, will be made available at rates higher than this 'basic rate', depending upon the demand for and availability of funds in the market. Privilege money is lent at $\frac{1}{2}$ per cent on top of the basic rate. The Scottish banks, it appears, follow the clearing banks in their minimum rates. The rates of the accepting houses, other merchant banks and the overseas banks, on the other hand, are more flexible, and may be above or below the clearing banks' 'basic rate', reflecting the relative shortage or abundance of funds in the market.

A discount house needs to provide security for its loans from these institutions, and this will consist of the bills and bonds acquired, very largely, with the borrowed funds. However, the bills or bonds it places as security with the lending banks will be rather greater than the value of the loan, and this 'margin' of extra security is provided by the discount house out of its own resources. The need to provide such a margin from its own capital thus sets a limit to the range of its activities financed on borrowed funds.

The discount houses obtain a relatively small part of their funds from sources outside the U.K. banking system. Some of these balances come to the houses directly from foreign residents, while others are placed on deposit by (say) U.K. industrial or commercial companies with funds temporarily to spare. Deposits may be taken at seven days' notice, or on a day-to-day basis, and those from U.K. (non-bank) residents are included in the official definition of the money supply (Table 1.1). Their inclusion seems difficult to justify in so far as deposits placed on these terms are not readily usable as a means of payment and do not serve as a 'supplement' to current account balances (compare Chapter 2, Section 7).

We saw in Chapter 2 that the clearing banks buy all their Treasury bills and some of their commercial bills from the discount houses. In buying their bills the banks take a forward view, and generally try to match the maturities of the bills they purchase with any foreseeable commitments which are going to involve them in a loss of cash, i.e. a debiting of their accounts at the Bank of England. This cash outflow may then be more or less offset by the cash inflow from the maturing bills. The discount houses sell the banks parcels of bills of the desired maturities, with the further advantage, in the case of commercial bills, of the discount house's endorsement and its original scrutiny of the parties to the bill. For these services a bank is prepared—on the lines of the Treasury-bill example on page 30—to take the parcel at a slightly lower rate of discount than the current market rate.

Dealing in bills, accordingly, may yield the discount houses a profit from two sources. First, there is a 'running profit' derived from the difference between the rates at which a house discounts bills and the rates at which it borrows. Second there is a 'selling margin' representing the difference between the rate at which the discount house bought a bill and the rate at which it sells it. Similarly in bond dealing there may be a running profit and a 'jobbing profit', the latter deriving from the slightly higher price at which the discount house would aim to sell the bonds it had purchased. A rise in interest rates, of course, spells losses for the houses in so far as they dispose of bills (or bonds) on less favourable terms than they acquired them. Further, higher rates on sums borrowed from day to day could mean a running loss on bills previously discounted at a lower level of rates. However the market has a very high turnover, selling perhaps about £70/80 million of bills daily, and anything from nothing to £60 million in one day for bonds. It is this enormous volume of business which enables the discount houses to secure a reasonable return on their shareholders' capital.

6. Recent Developments

An outstanding feature of the 1960s has been the development of several 'new' money markets, in only one of which the discount houses play a leading role. Four such markets may be distinguished: the local authority (and finance company) temporary loan market; the Euro-currency market; the inter-bank market; and the market in sterling certificates of deposit.

The first of these emerged in the second half of the 1950s, when local authorities and (hire-purchase) finance companies developed the practice of accepting sums on deposit from large industrial and commercial companies with funds temporarily to spare; from merchant and overseas banks; and from banks and other institutions located overseas. These deposits come to the local authorities in large amounts (ranging, say, from £50,000 to £1 million), and the greater part is repayable with seven days; deposits with the finance companies seem usually to be for a fixed term of three or six months.

The Euro-currency market, which emerged at roughly the same time, is best held over for explanation in Chapter 17. At this stage, however, it is useful to recall from Chapter 2 that dollars deposited by foreign residents with overseas and merchant banks may sometimes be evidence by transferable certificates, known as dollar certificates of deposit.

Expansion of the temporary loan and Euro-currency markets in the 1960s stimulated the development of an inter-bank market, in which merchant and overseas banks could borrow short-term (very largely from one another) to meet liabilities presented for payment. For example, following the repayment of a loan (by, say, a local authority), merchant bank X will have enjoyed an increase in its balance in account with clearing bank A. This it may lend to overseas bank Y, which is in need of funds to meet a loan to one of its customers. Loans among the merchant and overseas banks are generally made through the agency of brokers, mostly for periods up to fourteen days.

Rates of interest offered by borrowers in all three markets are significantly higher than the average available on loans to the discount houses. This explains their relative attraction to the merchant and overseas banks, since they in turn are enabled to attract deposits by quoting rates higher than the clearing banks' deposit rate. The three markets have a large turnover in short-term funds in which, until quite recently, the discount houses had no share. Since 1965, however, several houses have acquired an interest in the local authority and inter-bank markets, in general by establishing connections with broking firms active in these fields. A number of discount houses, further, deal in the dollar certificates of deposit which first appeared in 1966.

The most recent of the 'new' money markets is the market in sterling certificates of deposit, which were introduced in late-1968 (Chapter 2). Here, by contrast, the discount houses have from the beginning played the leading part in providing a market for holders of certificates who wish to regain their cash before maturity. Some demand may develop, however, from merchant and overseas banks. The discount houses are not able to use sterling (or dollar) C.D.s as security for a loan from the Bank of England (Chapter 4).

Apart from temporary borrowing by taking deposits (above), larger local authorities may be able to raise funds with the issue of 'revenue' bills, i.e. bills issued in anticipation of revenue from the rates. These bills—which may be thought of as a local authority version of the Treasury bill—are attractive to the discount houses, since (on certain conditions) they can be used as security for a loan from the Bank of England. They are issued either by placing them directly with one or more discount houses or by open invitation to submit tenders. Their use is not widespread, but has increased in recent years.

More important, both for the local authorities and the discount houses, was the introduction in 1964 of the local authority 'yearling' bond (life span one year minimum to four years maximum). Initially these were regularly placed by issuing authorities with various discount houses, though in recent years most bonds have been placed 'through' the Stock Exchange, in which case they enjoy a Stock Exchange quotation (Chapter 7). A drawback for the discount houses is that the bonds cannot be used as security for a loan from the Bank of England, which might encourage the houses to pass them on to other institutions seeking such an investment.

Alongside these new financial developments it is interesting to record the revival, in the 1960s, of a traditional method of finance, viz., the bill of exchange. Thus the discount houses' holdings of commercial (and other) bills rose from just under 10 per cent of total assets at the end of 1960 to just under 34 per cent at end-December, 1968. 'Other bills' include local authority bills and Treasury bills of the Northern Ireland Government, and would make relatively little difference in the comparison of the two percentages. A number of factors underlie the increase. First, bill finance received some encouragement from the standardization of stamp duty, in 1961, at the flat rate of 2d. per bill. Second the growth of international trade may have found some reflection in increased bill finance. Third, the bill has been popular with finance companies as a method of raising funds (Chapter 5).

Fourth, there was in the late 1950s and early 1960s a notable swing to bill finance when bank advances were under official restraint. Since 1965, however, the discount houses have been explicitly asked by the Bank of England to limit commercial bill holdings during periods of general credit restraint (Chapter 4).

Membership of the London Discount Market Association

The membership which for some years stood at twelve is reduced to eleven by a merger between two of the houses initiated in the Summer of 1969.

Questions

See end of Chapter 4.

4

Central Banking in the United Kingdom

---

1. *The Bank of England a Central Bank*

A central bank is an institution at the very centre of the monetary system. It is often regarded as the pivot on which the system turns, or (to vary the metaphor) as the regulator necessary for the system's smooth operation. It invariably enjoys special relationships with the government, and an ascendancy over other financial institutions, especially other banks. Its activities are not carried on for its own maximum profit, and may be designed to influence the quantity of money in the economy, and the cost and availability of finance.

In the United Kingdom, the central bank is the Bank of England. The Bank received its charter in 1694 as a banking company, and from its foundation acted as banker to the Government, as well as engaging in a variety of commercial banking business. In the course of the nineteenth century, a growing awareness of its unique power led it to assume increasing responsibilities within the banking and monetary system. The Bank let its commercial business dwindle into insignificance, and its own profitability ceased to be its principal objective. By the end of that century, the regular exercise of its responsibilities had hardened into the art and practice of central banking. Let us see what this constitutes today.

As banker to the Government, the Bank holds the Government's two main accounts, respectively the Exchequer account and the National Loans Fund, as well as the subordinate accounts operated for convenience by various Government departments. In broad terms, all Government borrowing, and most of its lending within the U.K., pass through the National Loans Fund; tax revenue, and spending by the various Government departments (very largely on goods and services), pass through the Exchequer account. More details are given in Chapter 8. As the Government's financial agent, the Bank raises short-term loans through the Treasury bill issue, and longer term loans by issue of gilt-edged securities. It also acts as registrar for Government stock, recording transfers and arranging the interest payments to security holders.

Second, the Bank holds accounts for most of the other institutions in the domestic banking system, notably the clearing banks, the Scottish and Northern Ireland banks, the discount houses, the accepting houses, and some of the overseas banks in London. This arrangement greatly facilitates the settlement of indebtedness among the clearing banks (Chapter 2), and plays its part in the mechanics of the note and coin issue. It also enables the clearing banks—in principle, through the discount houses—to draw on the Bank of England for the support of their cash reserves. The Bank holds accounts, moreover, for a number of overseas central banks, as well as international organizations like the International Monetary Fund (Chapter 19).

Third, the Bank is the main agent of the Government's monetary policy. As the source of cash and as the prime operator in Government securities, the Bank is able to influence the total quantity of money, the working of the discount market, the pattern of interest rates in the financial system, and the lending policies of the clearing banks. The lending policies of other banks and financial institutions also come under the Bank's surveillance.

Fourth, the Bank attends to various international monetary duties on the Government's behalf. It manages the Exchange Equalization Account, maintains relationships with monetary authorities in other countries and—along with the Treasury—provides representatives for the Government in the work of the International Monetary Fund. It also operates whatever system of controls the Government may desire on the purchase and sale of foreign currencies by British residents. These international aspects of the Bank's work are postponed for consideration in Chapters 18 and 19.

Most of these activities are reflected in the Bank's balance sheet. This is published every Wednesday in a statutory form known as the Bank Return, as required under the Bank Charter Act, 1844. This Act was particularly concerned with the regulation of the note issue (Chapter 1). To this end the Bank was required to separate its business of note issue from its (other) banking business, and publish a return showing each separately. The old method of presentation for two 'Departments'— Banking and Issue—has been preserved, but the Bank is not (and never has been) organized on this basis.

Table 4.1 sets out the Bank Return for Wednesday, 5th February, 1969. It is convenient at this stage simply to define the items, returning to them in passing as we review the Bank's functions in later sections.

1. *Notes issued:* these are the £1, £5 and £10 notes with which we are all well acquainted. Most are in circulation; some are 'held in'

TABLE 4.1

Bank Return, Wednesday, 5th February, 1969

Issue Department

	£		£
1. Notes Issued		2. Government Debt	11,015,100
In Circulation	3,105,721,115	3. Other Govt.	
In Banking		Securities	3,137,940,396
Department	44,698,535	4. Other Securities	784,504
		5. Coin other than	
		Gold Coin	260,000
		6. Fiduciary Issue	3,150,000,000
		7. Gold Coin and	
		Bullion	419,650
	£3,150,419,650		£3,150,419,650

Banking Department

	£		£
8. Capital	14,553,000	13. Govt. Securities	549,045,735
9. Rest	3,805,476	14. Other Securities:	
10. Public Deposits	11,679,649	(a) Discounts and	
11. Special Deposits	230,990,000	Advances	
12. Other Deposits:		£80,911,226	
(a) Bankers'		(b) Securities	
£311,327,271		£39,333,824	120,245,050
(b) Other Accounts		15. Notes	44,698,535
£142,364,667	453,691,938	16. Coin	730,743
	£714,720,063		£714,720,063

the Banking Department preliminary to circulation. All these notes are technically a liability of the Bank of England (Issue Department).

2. *Government debt:* this entry represents loans from the Bank to the Government made before 1844. This Government debt to the Bank accordingly appears in the Bank's books as an asset.

3. *Other government securities:* are gilt-edged securities and Treasury bills.

4. *Other securities:* are securities of any other sort, e.g. the securities of other Commonwealth Governments.

5. *Coin other than gold coin:* the Issue Department may 'hold' up to £5·5 million of silver coinage, as a part of the 'backing' of the note issue.

6. *Fiduciary issue:* has already been discussed in Chapter 1, and is

further considered in Section 2. The fiduciary issue, of course, is the £3,150 million of notes backed by assets 2 to 5, not the assets themselves. In practice it is usual to say that the fiduciary issue is backed by Government securities (item 3 and—in effect—item 2). Strictly, however, a tiny part of the fiduciary issue is backed by other securities (4) and subsidiary U.K. coinage (5).

7. *Gold coin and bullion:* the bulk of the Bank's gold was transferred to the Exchange Equalization Account in 1939, and there forms part of our gold and foreign currency reserves (Chapter 17). This nominal sum was left with the Issue Department, so that the note issue is not completely a fiduciary issue.

8. *Capital:* comprises the original share capital of the Bank, now held by the Treasury since the Bank passed into public ownership in 1946 (Section 8).

9. *Rest:* these are undistributed profits of the Bank, regarded technically as a liability (Chapter 7).

10. *Public deposits:* these include the Exchequer account and National Loans Fund of the Government, and the subordinate accounts operated by various Government departments.

11. *Special deposits:* a particular variety of account the English clearing banks and the Scottish banks are sometimes obliged to hold with the Bank. They should be regarded entirely as a Bank of England control device.

12. *Other deposits:* (a) the Bankers' accounts are those of the clearing banks, discount houses, etc., mentioned above.

(b) 'Other accounts' comprise accounts of overseas central banks and international monetary institutions, and the (current) accounts of a small number of private customers. Most of the latter have had their accounts at the Bank since the nineteenth century, but recently the Bank has opened some new private accounts, notably for City firms. This may be interpreted as an attempt by the Bank to increase the range of commercial banking experience open to its staff: it does not in any sense represent 'competition' with the clearing banks. The Bank also holds accounts of those of its staff who wish to exercise this privilege. The Bank's liabilities on account to private customers are comparable with the current account liabilities of the clearing banks, and may for this reason be included in the estimates of the money supply (Chapter 1).

13. *Government securities:* comprise bonds, Treasury bills and temporary loans to the National Loans Fund known as 'Ways and Means advances'.

14. *Other securities:* (a) The eleven discount houses have a right of access to the Bank, either rediscounting eligible bills or taking advances on approved security (Section 4). The Bank may also discount bills for (or make advances to) customers holding accounts under 12b.

(b) 'Securities' comprise any other securities of whatever sort, including market purchases of commercial bills (Chapter 3).

15. *Notes and* 16. *Coin:* are entered here as assets of the Banking Department. Coins in circulation are not, at law, a liability of the Bank of England, though it may be useful, from a financial viewpoint, to regard them as a liability of the Government (Section 2). The notes may be imagined as temporarily resident in the Banking Department, en route from the Issue Department to general circulation via the commercial banks.

2. *The Issue of Notes and Coins*

The coins and notes in general circulation have all reached the public by way of the commercial banks, very largely the clearing banks. Table 2.1 shows that the latter hold about 5 per cent of their assets in the form of notes and coins in their tills, and about 3 per cent in account with the Bank of England (item 12a in the Bank return). An increased desire by the public to use notes and coins in transactions shows itself in withdrawals from the banks by the holders of bank accounts. To maintain their cash float, the banks will secure more notes and coins from the Bank of England, and have their accounts (12a) debited accordingly. The banks thus have more cash in their tills, but smaller balances in account with the Banking Department, while the Banking Department shows fewer assets (i.e. notes and coin) and fewer liabilities (bankers' balances).

The Bank is able to replenish its own reserve of notes by printing more at its printing works. What happens then, in effect, is that the Issue Department 'hands' the new notes to the Banking Department, thus increasing its own liabilities (1), while at the same time it takes up from the Government a corresponding value of Treasury bills (3), thereby increasing its assets. The Banking Department pays the Government for the bills by crediting Public Deposits (10), thus putting corresponding funds at the Government's disposal while simultaneously increasing its own liabilities. To match this increase in its liabilities, it has the notes (15) received from the Issue Department, ready for issue to the clearing banks as required. Indirectly, therefore, the public 'lends' to the Government by taking up additional notes, which may accordingly be regarded as a special sort of Government security, carrying no interest and with no redemption date! Of course, the securities held in the Issue Department yield a return, but this is kept within the system of Government finances, as explained in Chapter 8.

A legal limit is set to this process of note creation by the Currency and Bank Notes Act, 1954. This Act limited the size of the fiduciary issue to its actual value in 1954 (£1,575 million), but gave the Bank power to vary the amount subject to Treasury approval and a Parliamentary power to veto any increase. In fact the note issue has doubled since 1954, as Table 4.1 shows.

The clearing banks may obtain coins from the Banking Department in the same way as notes. The Bank in turn purchases coins from the Royal Mint, a Government department, making payment by crediting the Exchequer account (10) with the face value of the coinage acquired (16). It thus increases its liabilities (to the Government) by an amount equal to its newly acquired assets.

Since the issue of coins puts the Exchequer account in credit it is not unreasonable, by analogy with the consequences of the note issue, to regard coins likewise as a liability of the Government. On the other hand the costs of minting must be set against the gross revenue derived from their purchase by the Bank of England.

It was suggested in Chapter 2 that, in the short run, withdrawals of notes and coin from the banks are fairly evenly offset by deposits of cash. There are, nonetheless, changes in the public's requirements of notes and coin, which are reflected in net withdrawals from or net payments of cash into the commercial banking system. Three situations may be distinguished. First, the demand for cash from the banks varies from day to day. It is highest from Wednesday to Friday, when firms are drawing out notes and coins for wage payments, while on Monday and Tuesday a net cash inflow may occur, as firms (especially retailers) are paying in their takings from the weekend shopping. Second, the public's requirements vary seasonally, being particularly high in the weeks before the great public holidays, notably Christmas and the Late-Summer Holiday. Third, over the years the demand tends to reflect the general trend of income, employment and price levels. Full employment and rising incomes and prices can be expected to occasion a greater public demand for cash, as evidenced by the increase in the note issue between 1954 and 1969.

A net outflow of notes and coin from the clearing banks would lead (other factors remaining constant) to a corresponding fall in bank liabilities to customers, as the banks make the appropriate debits to customers' accounts. At the same time, however, the banks would lose an equal sum—in absolute terms—from their cash reserves, which would accordingly stand below the desired 8 per cent ratio. In anticipation of a net cash outflow, therefore, the banks might call in some loans from the discount houses, with consequences examined in Section 4.

3. *The Management of the Exchequer Account and National Loans Fund*

The scale of the Government's transactions involve the official accounts in a very considerable daily turnover, amounting perhaps to several hundred million pounds. The Exchequer account is put in credit as taxes are paid, and debited as Government departments pay their staffs and make all sorts of purchases. The National Loans Fund is credited as securities are sold to the public and past loans by the Government are repaid, and debited as fresh lending is undertaken. These various categories of Government payment and receipt are considered more fully in Chapter 8. At this stage, it is useful to see their effects both on Public and Bankers' Deposits by following through, first, a tax receipt and, second, a purchase by a Government department.

A taxpayer paying his taxes to the Commissioners of Inland Revenue[1] (or the Board of Customs and Excise) will normally draw a cheque on his clearing bank. The Inland Revenue (say) will pay the cheque into its account at the Bank of England, from which it will be transferred to the Exchequer account. Public Deposits (10) in the Banking Department have risen, while the Bank debits correspondingly the clearing bank's account, so that Bankers' Deposits (12a) will be reduced. The process of tax payments accordingly puts funds at the disposal of the Government, while at the same time reducing the balances of the clearing banks.

The system operates in reverse when a Government department makes a payment to a member of the public. The department gives him a cheque drawn (effectively) on the Exchequer account, which he pays into his account with a clearing bank. The bank credits his account, and presents the cheque for payment at the Bank of England. The Bank credits the clearing bank's account, and debits the Exchequer account: Bankers' Deposits (12a) are thereby increased and Public Deposits (10) reduced.

It follows that net Exchequer receipts from the public increase the balance in the Exchequer account and reduce the clearing banks' cash reserves, while net Exchequer payments to the public increase the clearing banks' cash reserves and—unless the appropriate steps are taken—may put the Exchequer account into deficit. Similarly, net receipts by the National Loans Fund from the public increase its balance and reduce the clearing banks' cash reserves, and vice versa. The variations in clearing bank and official balances thus present two major problems for the 'authorities', i.e. the Treasury and the Bank of England. First, an

[1] For wage and salary earners, of course, income tax is deducted from their remuneration and paid on their behalf by their employers.

anticipated deficit on official account must be financed, or any surplus put to profitable use for the Government. Second, some control must be achieved over the impact, upon the banking system, of clearing-bank cash gains or losses. This, in fact, gives the Bank of England an opportunity to influence interest rates in the money market, as we shall see in Section 4.

In its day-to-day management of the Exchequer account and National Loans Fund, the Bank will switch balances between the two as necessary to enable a surplus on the one to finance a deficit on the other. The Bank will also make use of any temporary surplus in the subsidiary accounts held at the Bank by various Government departments and statutory funds (e.g. the National Insurance Fund). Surplus funds may be lent to the National Loans Fund in return for Treasury bills, which will be held by the Government department making the loan. Such bills are said to be issued 'through the tap': the rate of discount they carry is fixed each Friday by the Treasury. As an alternative to taking up tap Treasury bills, the lending department may make a Ways and Means Advance, which means simply that the Bank debits the lending account and credits the National Loans Fund correspondingly.

The Bank cannot rely on transfers of this sort to keep the two main accounts in balance at the close of each day's business. To prevent a deficit it is always prepared to lend to the Government as a last resort, simply by crediting the National Loans Fund. Such loans might, however, damage the Government's creditworthiness if they were made frequently or on a large scale. The public might conclude that the Government was obliged to rely on the central bank, because other lenders were unwilling to meet all its requirements. In practice, therefore, Ways and Means Advances by the Bank are confined to overnight assistance, on the few occasions when the Bank has miscalculated the needs of the account at the end of the day.

It follows that the authorities will need to make regular—in fact, weekly—short-term forecasts of official receipts and payments, and arrange to finance any anticipated deficit by short-term borrowing. The method of borrowing used is the sale, by tender, of Treasury bills (Chapter 3). In simple outline, the system works as follows.

Suppose that, towards the end of Week 1, the Treasury has calculated that during Week 3 payments from the Exchequer account will exceed receipts by £50 million, and that payments from the National Loans Fund will exceed receipts by £250 million. On the Friday of Week 1, accordingly, the Bank of England will announce that £300 million[1] of bills will be available for tender on the Friday of Week 2. On that Friday, it will allot bills on the principles already explained in Chapter 3. The discount market, we have seen, submits in effect a joint tender for

[1] In practice, the figure would generally be a little higher (page 74).

the whole of the bills on offer. The Bank can, therefore, be certain that the tender will always be fully covered. Applicants for bills specify in their tenders on which day in the subsequent week (Week 3) they wish to take their bills up, and on the appropriate day pay for them with cheques drawn on Bankers' Deposits at the Bank of England. The latter are accordingly debited, while corresponding balances are placed in the National Loans Fund. These balances will, in turn, meet the N.L.F. net payments and enable a transfer of £50 million to the Exchequer account to meet its net payments.

We may now consider, in very broad terms, the outcome of these operations over Week 3 taken as a whole (a more detailed exposition is given in the course of Section 6). Let us assume that the anticipated excess of Government payments over receipts does, in fact, materialize. Of itself, this would raise the cash reserves of the clearing (and other) banks by £300 million, enabling some increase in loans at call to the discount houses. Concurrently, however, the discount houses and other successful applicants are taking up £300 million worth of Treasury bills. This both removes the extra balances from the bankers' accounts and finances the net expenditure from the official accounts. When the week finishes, the clearing banks have more loans at call, while the discount houses hold more new bills. The remainder of the £300 million worth of bills are held by the other successful tenderers. In this way, the £300 million net expenditure has been financed by Treasury bill issue.

It is apparent, nonetheless, that the needs of the National Loans Fund will now be greater by some £300[1] million in thirteen weeks time, when the bills reach maturity. Accordingly, even if tax and other receipts exceed current spending on goods etc., during Week 16 by (say) £100 million, it would still be necessary to borrow £200 million to finance the maturing debt. This explains why the size of the bill issue varies during the course of the year. It is generally at its lowest from January to March, when tax payments by the public are particularly heavy (Chapter 8).

In addition to using the Treasury bill to meet the immediate needs of the National Loans Fund and the Exchequer account, the Government might also finance part of its annual spending programme by allowing an increase, over the year, in the bills made available to the banking sector and the public in general. On the other hand, the Government might succeed in borrowing sufficient funds by other methods—notably bond issues (Section 5) and the sale of small savings securities (Chapter 8)—to enable a reduction, over the year, in the volume of bills outstanding. The Bank has, therefore, to weigh the advantages and disadvantages

[1] Less, in fact, if the Bank has bought some of these bills in the market during the interval (Section 4).

of extending the various forms of Government borrowing. In fact it has endeavoured since the war to reduce the Government's reliance on finance by bill issue, for reasons explained in Section 6.

4. *The Management of the Money Market*

In order to manage the official accounts effectively, and to deal with the problems mentioned in Section 3, the Bank of England needs to intervene or 'operate' almost daily in the London money market. This, in turn, gives it the opportunity to exercise a strong influence upon money market interest rates, particularly Treasury bill rate and the fine bill rate (Chapter 3).

Suppose that, on a given day, the clearing banks anticipate a fall in their cash reserves below the desired level of 8 per cent. This may be the consequence of an excess of Government receipts over disbursements. Thus customers' tax transfers to the Inland Revenue account may be particularly heavy, and the proceeds of maturing Treasury bills and Government payments to the banks' customers particularly light (Section 3). Alternatively, the cash shortage may reflect a net outflow of notes and coin from the clearing banks to the public (Section 2).

A bank might decide to deal with this problem by selling some of its holding of Government bonds on the Stock Exchange. If these happened to be bought by its own customers, this would reduce its liabilities and so the amount of cash needed to maintain the 8 per cent ratio. If they were bought by the customers of other banks, it would increase the selling bank's claim on the others at the clearing, so aggravating their cash shortage. If they happened to be bought by the Bank of England's broker on the Stock Exchange (Section 5), the Bank's payment would lead to a corresponding increase in the bank's cash reserves.

Let us assume, however, that all the banks decide to meet their anticipated cash shortage by calling in some of their loans from the discount houses. In contrast to the position examined on page 56, the latter will not be able to meet one bank's calls by increased borrowing from another, because there is a *general* cash shortage among all the clearing banks. The discount houses may be able to increase their borrowing from 'outside' sources, for example, the Scottish banks, accepting houses or overseas banks. But if this assistance is inadequate, the discount houses will still be in need of funds to meet the calls from the clearing banks. They will also need funds to take up any Treasury bills they have agreed (the previous Friday) to take up on that particular day.

In this situation, the Bank of England has two alternatives. In the first case it may take the initiative in helping the discount houses, by buying Treasury bills[1] from them at current market rates. Purchases are made by the Bank's agent in the discount market, the Special Buyer, who is in fact a member of one of the discount houses. The Bank pays for the bills by crediting the discount houses' accounts: the latter thus acquire the wherewithal to meet the calls of the clearing banks, and to finance any required take-up of Treasury bills. The banks, in turn, acquire balances at the Bank to offset (as appropriate) the drain occasioned by (say) the excess of Government receipts over payments.

The Bank's purchase of bills in the discount market thus limits the effects of a clearing bank cash shortage to a loss of Treasury bills by the discount houses: some of their bills are, in effect, turned into cash for the clearing banks. The Bank is also given the opportunity to utilize any temporary surplus on the official accounts, where an excess of Government receipts over disbursements is the cause of the prospective clearing bank cash shortage. Its purchase of bills on the market is made (in effect) on behalf of the Government, the National Loans Fund being debited correspondingly. In this way the Bank is helping reduce the cost of Government borrowing. The saving it effects is the difference between the price the N.L.F. pays for the bill on purchase, and the full nominal value which the N.L.F. would have had to meet on maturity.

Operations of this sort also give the Bank the opportunity to plan ahead to offset disturbances anticipated in the near future. To take this opportunity, however, it may be necessary for the Bank to deal, not with the discount houses, but with the clearing banks themselves. Suppose, for example, that in three weeks time there will be a particularly heavy call upon the National Loans Fund, as a bond issue comes to maturity. The Bank will want to buy bills maturing at this date, to minimize the additional burden bill maturities will create. It will be recalled, however, that the discount houses will almost certainly have sold such bills to the clearing banks (Chapters 2 and 3). The Special Buyer will therefore intimate to the leading clearing banks that the Bank is prepared to take from them a given quantity of Treasury bills of the appropriate dates. The subsequent crediting of their accounts at the Bank will not only relieve their own cash shortage, but enable them to pass funds on to the discount market, who are thus enabled to repay the other clearing banks. By giving direct assistance to the clearing banks, the Bank has given indirect assistance to the discount houses.

The purchase of bills at current market rates from the discount houses or the clearing banks is one way in which the Bank may help the money

[1] In February, 1969, the Bank for the first time bought fine bank bills instead of Treasury bills from the discount houses, as a means of making funds available to them. This purchase is to be distinguished from the small amounts the Bank frequently buys as 'samples' (Chapter 3, Section 2).

market over its shortage of funds. The alternative, when the discount houses are faced with demands they cannot meet, is for the Bank of England to wait for the discount houses to make an approach for assistance. The Bank is always prepared to help the eleven members of the London Discount Market Association on application at its Discount Office, but in this case it may inflict a substantial loss on the applicants as the price of its aid.

At the Discount Office the discount houses have a choice between selling the Bank eligible bills with at least twenty-one days to run to maturity, or (the usual practice) borrowing from the Bank against approved security.[1] In this second case it is customary for the Bank to lend either for a minimum of seven days or just until the next day. When it lends for seven days (or should it rediscount bills), the Bank nearly always charges Bank Rate (its official rate of rediscount) as a minimum, though since January 1963 it has reserved the right to charge up to 1 per cent more than Bank Rate (Chapter 20). When it lends overnight (a technique first used in mid-1966), the Bank may charge Bank Rate, or it may lend at any other rate down to the current market level for overnight loans.[2]

Bank Rate is always higher than Treasury bill rate, and has often been above prime bill rate[3] (the rate on trade bills, however, is typically higher than Bank Rate). Suppose for the illustration that, at a time

---

[1] Eligible bills are British Government Treasury bills, U.K. local authority bills (on certain conditions) and commercial bills bearing two reputable British signatures, of which one must be the acceptor's. A 'reputable signature' in the case of the acceptor is that of a British bank or accepting house, while the second signature could be that of the discount house, which would itself sign the bill on rediscounting it. 'Approved security' constitutes Government bonds with five years or less to maturity, and eligible bills, though in recent years the Bank has asked for trade bills occasionally to be included among the bills put up as security, as a means of sampling their quality—compare page 53.

[2] Since 1966 the Bank has introduced greater flexibility into its dealings with the market, which makes it difficult to summarize its activities in clear-cut 'rules'. Thus in early 1967 it lent not overnight but for two days at the current market rate, and this has been repeated on occasions since. In August, 1967, it lent for the first time for seven days at the current market rate, and in September, 1967, for the first time for five days, again at the market rate. The Bank may develop yet further variations on the 'basic pattern' set out in the text.

[3] The possibility of substituting bill finance for bank overdrafts suggests that (in such circumstances) the clearing banks would find it difficult to charge more than 1 or 2 per cent above Bank Rate on much of their advances (Chapter 2). The full cost of finance by bank bill, of course, also includes the acceptance commission (Chapter 3).

when Bank Rate is 7 per cent, a discount house borrows a sum from a clearing bank at 5⅝ per cent (¼ per cent above the 'basic' rate), and uses it to discount some bank bills at 6⅞ per cent. It is then obliged to borrow from the Bank at 7 per cent (Bank Rate) to repay the loan to the clearing bank. It is apparent that, while the loan from the Bank is outstanding, it suffers a running loss on these bills in its portfolio. Assistance at Bank Rate, therefore, enables the discount houses to meet the calls of the clearing banks only at some cost to their own profits. Their reaction, accordingly, will often be to raise their own discount rates for new business (Section 6).

It follows that in deciding their rates the discount houses take into account the current level of Bank Rate, in what direction it might be changed, and what level of interest rates the authorities would probably prefer. The higher Bank Rate is now (or likely to be soon), the greater the cost of official assistance, unless the Bank should decide to lend overnight at market rates. The higher, therefore, will the discount houses' own rates tend to be. This apart, any rise in Bank Rate will affect the discount houses through the corresponding increase in the 'basic' rate for clearing bank 'regular' money (Chapter 3).

Its ability to choose its terms for helping the discount market means that the Bank can exert a decisive influence upon interest rates in the money market. Since the pattern of official receipts and disbursements is uneven during the week, there will generally be some days on which the clearing banks are calling in loans, and the discount houses are looking to the Bank for assistance. Further, the Bank strengthens its hold by normally raising through the Treasury bill tender rather more than it estimates the Government will spend during a given week. At some time, accordingly, the discount market will find itself short of funds to take up its bills, a shortage the Bank can relieve on its own terms. In brief, if the Bank is content with current market rates, it buys bills; if it wants to see them rise, it lends at Bank Rate.

If the Bank raised Bank Rate (Section 8) and was eager to see the discount market follow suit, the authorities might engineer a situation in which the discount houses find themselves short of funds, and with no alternative but to seek official assistance—at the punitive Bank Rate. For example, net sales of bonds by the Bank to the public (Section 5) would lead (other things being equal) to a fall in Bankers' Deposits at the Bank, as the purchasers paid with cheques drawn on the clearing banks. The latter would call in some loans from the discount market, which would be obliged to seek official assistance. In this case the authorities will have 'put the market in the Bank', in order to 'make the new Bank Rate effective'.

So far the narrative has illustrated how the Bank, through its operations in the money market, can make cash available to the clearing banks, can utilize official surpluses to reduce the cost of Government borrowing, and can decisively influence discount rates. We may now consider briefly how the Bank may operate in the money market to offset the effects of a net excess of Government payments over receipts.

On a particular day, for instance, Exchequer and N.L.F. disbursements to the banks may exceed receipts by a considerable margin. At the same time, the number of new bills to be taken up by the discount houses and others may be rather low. The banks, accordingly, have 'surplus cash', and increase their loans at call to the discount market. If the Bank took no remedial action, the competition among the discount houses for appropriate assets would increase. This would tend to push up the prices of any bills being offered on the market, as well as the prices of short bonds.

However, by *selling* bills to the market through the Special Buyer, the Bank is able to match an increased demand with an increased supply. It thus prevents bills and bond prices rising i.e. interest rates falling. The discount houses pay for the bills with cheques drawn on the clearing banks, which removes the 'surplus cash' from the banking system. The National Loans Fund is credited with the proceeds of the bill sale, which thus finances the prospective deficit.

5. *Operations in the Bond Market*

The issue of bonds (variously called stock or gilt-edged securities) is handled for the Government by the Bank of England. The Bank also attends to the subsequent work of registering transfers and paying holders their interest. The Bank invites applications for a new issue with the publication of a prospectus, which sets out the terms, notably the rate of interest and date of redemption (though some bonds, issued in the past, have no redemption date). Applicants will include financial institutions—banks, discount houses, insurance companies, pension funds, etc.,—as well as large industrial and commercial companies and ordinary members of the public. They pay the Bank for their securities with cheques drawn on the clearing banks, and this leads by the familiar process to a crediting of Public Deposits and a debiting of Bankers' Deposits.

It does not happen today that an issue of gilt-edged securities is fully subscribed. The unsubscribed—usually the greater—portion is taken over by the Issue Department, which makes room in its portfolio by, in effect, substituting them for some of the Treasury bills it holds. The Bank thus has a ready supply of the new securities it can offer through its own broker on the Stock Exchange (Chapter 7), whenever the demand seems appropriately brisk. Very often the Bank will have a short-dated, a medium-dated and a long-dated security available 'on tap' in this way. Further, it will take the opportunity to sell other bonds (i.e. not issues on tap) from the Issue Department's portfolio should buyers develop an appetite for a particular maturity.

The Bank, through the 'Government Broker', will also buy gilt-edged securities in the Stock Exchange. It is generally prepared to buy short bonds and finance the purchase by the sale of long bonds, at current market prices. In this way it can effectively take a short bond out of the public's hands and replace it with a long bond, thereby pushing the need to redeem the debt further into the future. The Bank will also be eager to buy in bonds as they approach their maturity dates. When the maturity date arrives, the Bank will sometimes offer holders other bonds n place (a 'conversion issue'). Holders who decline the offer will receive ithe full nominal value of their bonds in cash, i.e. cheques drawn (in effect) on the National Loans Fund. These cheques will be paid into accounts with the clearing banks, thus increasing Bankers' Deposits at the Bank by the familiar process. It follows that the more of a given bond issue the Bank has bought in before its maturity date, the less the disturbance to the money market from the rise in clearing bank cash.

The frequency of the Bank's bond dealings and the size of its resources clearly give it an opportunity to influence the prices at which bonds change hands in the market. The Bank may pursue various objectives, but its main concern is to preserve the attractions of Government bonds for investors by maintaining their 'marketability'. This and other objectives of the Bank, along with its methods and underlying motives, are considered in Chapter 20.

6. *Influencing the Clearing Banks' Cash and Liquidity*

We saw in Section 4 that, if the clearing banks react to a cash shortage by calling in loans from the discount houses, the latter can always turn to the Bank of England for assistance in making repayments. The Bank, however, may choose the terms on which it helps the discount houses. If it decided to assist *only* at Bank Rate, then it appears possible for the Bank to force through a contraction of clearing bank assets and liabilities by a multiple of their original cash shortage. To illustrate how this process might work, it is useful to construct a simplified illustration. All values are expressed in units of, say, £100 million.

Suppose that, at the start of a given week, the clearing banks between them have total liabilities, on account, of 100. Assets consist of cash 8, money at call 10, Treasury bills 6·5, commercial bills 3·5, bonds 22 and advances 50.[1] During the week, Government disbursements to the banks' customers exceed receipts by 2, so that the banks' liabilities rise to 102, and their cash reserves rise to 10. During the week, also, Treasury bills—value 1—reach maturity, so that the net cash requirement of the official accounts is 3. Of the bills reaching maturity, 0·5 are held by the banks, and 0·5 by their customers. It follows that the banks' cash reserves rise to 11, their own Treasury bill holdings fall to 6, and their total liabilities on account to customers increase to 102·5.

At the bill tender on the previous Friday, the discount houses secured 2·5 of the bills on offer, and the general public 0·5. During the week, the latter take up their bills with cheques drawn on the clearing banks, reducing the banks' cash to 10·5 and their liabilities to 102. With liabilities of 102, they need a cash reserve of $8/100 \times 102$, or 8·16: it follows that they have 2·34 'surplus cash'. The banks accordingly buy 0·5 Treasury bills from the discount houses, thus restoring their Treasury bill portfolio to 6·5, and increase loans at call by 1·84. Their balance sheet now reads: cash 8·16, loans at call 11·84, Treasury bills 6·5, commercial bills 3·5, bonds 22, advances 50. It is apparent that their total liabilities, and hence the money supply, has increased by 2.

The discount houses have 2·34 funds available from the banks to take up 2·5 bills. On the assumption that no other sources are open to them, they are obliged to turn to the Bank of England which lends them 0·16 *at Bank Rate*. As long as this loan is outstanding, the discount houses suffer a running loss on a corresponding part of their bill portfolio (Section 4). It is reasonable to suppose, therefore, that they will make every effort to pay it off as quickly as possible. Several techniques may be available to them but all, as we shall see, will have the same consequences.

The first possibility is that the discount houses will try and sell the banks more Treasury bills than they take up in the new tender, and use the balance to pay off the debt (0·16) to the Bank of England. Thus suppose that on the Friday of the week under review new bills value 1 are on offer from the Bank, replacing 0·5 maturing bills held by the public and 0·5 maturing bills held by the banks (other Government disbursements and receipts in the following week are expected to balance exactly). On this Friday, accordingly, the discount houses may reduce their tender price (i.e. raise their rate of discount) and, in consequence, are allotted (say) only 0·34 bills. In the subsequent week the banks buy 0·5 bills from the houses to replace their maturities, thereby enabling the latter both to take up their new bills (0·34) and to make good their outstanding debt (0·16) to the Bank of England.

[1] Only assets of 'monetary' significance are included in this balance sheet. The ratios are, nonetheless, either fully or reasonably realistic, except for bond holdings, which currently stand around 12 per cent.

So far, so good. The banks, however, will not be in equilibrium. The total bill maturities of 1 increased their cash reserves from 8·16 to 9·16, and, since half these bills were their customers', their liabilities rose at the same time to 102·5. The purchase of 0·5 bills from the discount houses has maintained their Treasury bill holdings at 6·5, but has reduced their cash to 8·66. Since the discount houses took up only 0·34 of the bills available on the preceding Friday, the banks' customers (we take it) took up the other 0·66. When in the course of this second week they actually pay the Bank for their bills, the banks' cash reserves will further decline to 8. At the same time, the banks will debit their customers' accounts by 0·66, thereby reducing their liabilities to 101·84. At this level they need a cash reserve of 8/100 × 101·84, or 8·1472. They accordingly remedy their cash shortage by calling in 0·1472 from the discount houses, who are obliged to borrow this sum from the Bank, *at Bank Rate*.

To vary the illustration, assume that the discount houses' next move is to reduce the prices they offer for commercial bills. Their hope now is to discourage fresh business, and thereby achieve an excess of maturities over bills newly discounted of 0·1472. The acceptors of the maturing bills will pay with cheques drawn on the clearing banks, and the discount houses will use the balances thus acquired to pay off the Bank of England. Alternatively, the discount houses might consider raising the interest rates offered to non-bank customers, to attract new deposits worth 0·1472. Their new customers would open their accounts with cheques drawn on the clearing banks, enabling the discount houses to repay the Bank of England. The clearing banks debit their customers' accounts, as appropriate, thereby reducing their liabilities from 101·84 to 101·6928, at which level they need 8·135424 cash reserves. If they take no action their reserves will fall to 8, so they call in 0·135424 from the discount houses. The latter meet these calls by borrowing from the Bank of England *at Bank Rate*, and then attempt to attract this amount in the same ways as before. If they succeed, clearing bank liabilities fall by a further 0·135424.

So far the total fall in clearing bank liabilities has been

$$0·16 + 0·1472 + 0·135424,$$

which represents the first three terms of the convergent geometric series

$$0·16 + (0·92)\,0·16 + (0·92)^2\,0·16 + \ldots$$

It can be shown that, if the process is allowed to work itself out, bank liabilities (and therefore assets) will fall overall by $0·16/(1 - 0·92)$, or 2, from 102 to 100 (compare page 24).

This example suggests that, if the Bank occasions an initial cash shortage (here 0·16) in the banking system, it can force a reduction 12·5 times as great (here 2) in the level of clearing bank assets and liabilities.

This it is able to do despite its obligation as lender of last resort to the discount market provided it exercises this obligation only at the punitive Bank Rate. In more general terms, it appears that its role as lender of last resort does not (on this proviso) deprive the Bank of its power to influence clearing bank deposit levels through the cash ratio. Such a system of control, however, may have various drawbacks from the viewpoint of the monetary authorities.

First, short-term Government finance would become more expensive, in so far as the discount houses' reaction to their losses (as in the example) pushed up Treasury bill rate. Second, the monetary system would be under some stress, with consequences it would not be possible to predict. Thus with assistance available only at Bank Rate the discount houses might be reluctant to continue to cover the Treasury bill tender. This implies a greater reliance by the Government on borrowing from the public, which might be more expensive and anyway difficult to achieve. Third, interest rates in the money market might move erratically from day to day, as the Bank would lose the opportunity to smooth out shortages or surpluses of cash with bill purchases or sales. This instability might, in turn, affect bond prices, as short bonds—in which the discount houses are important dealers—are (more or less) close substitutes for Treasury bills. We shall see in Chapter 20, however, that the Bank tries to encourage an 'orderly' market in bonds, to maintain their attractiveness to investors.

These difficulties perhaps explain why, in recent years, the authorities have not attempted to influence the clearing banks by operating on their cash ratio. Thus from 1939 to 1951 the discount houses were invariably assisted by the Bank at ruling market rates. Since 1951 assistance at market rates has been the general rule, though occasionally the Bank assists at Bank Rate if it wants to see interest rates in the money market rise. This willingness of the Bank to do business 'at the back door' has produced a situation in which, from the viewpoint of the clearing banks, Treasury bills and cash are interchangeable. If the banks are short of cash, and unless the Bank wants to push interest rates up, they can always get their accounts at the Bank credited by selling bills to the Bank (or having the discount houses sell them following a call from the banks).

This in turn means that the cash ratio has lost much of its importance for the banks, as the reserve is readily adjustable to the 8 per cent the Bank requires them to maintain. More important, accordingly, is their minimum liquidity ratio of 28 per cent (30 per cent before September, 1963). To support each £72 worth of advances and bond holdings, the banks need £8 in cash and £20 in the form of loans at call and short notice, Treasury bills and commercial bills. Given £28 overall of these liquid assets, the adjustment to £8 cash and £20 other liquid assets is a mere technicality (in the light of the Bank's willingness to operate at the 'back door'). This position prompted the Radcliffe Committee (Appendix B) to comment that: 'the effective base of bank credit has become the liquid assets (based on the availability of Treasury bills) instead of the supply of cash' (para. 376).

The importance of Treasury bills as a liquid asset to the clearing banks gives the Bank an opportunity to influence their activities through its management of Government borrowing. In so far as the authorities can raise funds with bond rather than bill issues, they are able to deprive the banks of a major liquid asset. The banks may be able (more or less) to offset this reduced supply of Treasury bills by acquiring other liquid assets (below). Their liquidity ratio may, nonetheless, be kept under some pressure, with two important consequences. First, their ability to increase their holdings of less liquid assets—bonds and, notably, advances—will be restricted by the lack of the necessary liquid assets to serve as a 'base'. Second, a restraint on the level of assets represents a corresponding restraint on the level of liabilities, i.e. on the greater part of the U.K. money supply.

When the Bank borrows for the Government by issuing bonds rather than Treasury bills it is, of course, lengthening the average life of the Government's debt (or 'National Debt', Chapter 8). Such a policy is known as 'funding'. Events in the year 1951 provide an interesting example of a 'forced funding'. At that time the banks, as a residue of war-time finance, held a very large quantity of Treasury bills which put their liquidity ratio at 39 per cent. This tended to weaken the discipline which the liquidity ratio exercises upon the banks. Accordingly they agreed to take up £500 million of short-dated bonds in return for £500 million bills. This transferred £500 million from 'liquid assets' to 'investments', so reducing the liquidity ratio from 39 to 32 per cent (*Radcliffe Report*, para. 406).

A possible limitation on a funding policy might be imposed by the reactions of the discount houses. Faced with a reduction in the total Treasury bill issue, they could attempt to increase their share by raising their bid prices. In this way the consequences of the Treasury bill shortage would fall upon the 'outside' tender, while the supply of bills within the banking system remained unchanged.

The clearing banks might also counter a funding policy by increasing loans at call and commercial bill holdings, since both these are acceptable 'liquid assets'. In the mid-1950s, for instance, the banks sold short bonds to the discount houses which the latter were able to take up with increased loans at call from the banks (*Radcliffe Report*, para. 175). In this way the banks strengthened their liquidity by effectively turning an illiquid asset (bonds) into a liquid asset (money at call). In the 1960s, a revival in the use of the commercial bill has enabled the banks to overcome a shrinkage in the Treasury bill issue (partly a reflection of a successful funding policy). The banks have also increased loans at call, especially to borrowers other than the discount houses, while 're-financeable export credits' (page 38) have made a further addition to their liquid assets.

Even a successful restraint upon clearing bank liquid assets will not, of itself, place a decisive curb on bank advances. By selling bonds on the Stock Exchange, the banks may effectively substitute advances for investments: in this way they change the proportions of their less liquid assets, but not the total. The sale of bonds by the banks does however meet with two difficulties. A sale may involve a capital loss, if the prices of securities have fallen since the bank initially purchased them, or if heavy sales by the banks combine to depress prices significantly. Second, the Bank of England is alive to the possibility of security sales, and might by direct request give the banks no alternative but to limit advances (Section 8).

It is interesting in this context to note that, in post-war years, the banks have been eager to restore their advances/total deposits ratio to a figure closer to the 50 per cent (average) ratio of the 1920s. The depressed economic circumstances of the 1930s kept advances to an average 40 per cent level, while during the war they fell below 20 per cent. The effects of official restraint (Section 8) had limited their increase to only 29 per cent by 1958, while in the same year investments were 32 per cent. By the mid-1960s, however, advances had reached the 50 per cent level, while investments had fallen to around 12 per cent.

7. The Creation of Bank Deposits

The ability of the clearing (and other commercial) banks to support their deposits on a fractional cash reserve has already been considered in Chapter 2. However, the process of deposit expansion is much more complicated than this simple picture might suggest, and with the aid of the material in the preceding sections we may explore further some of its intricacies and limitations.

We have seen that the Bank of England operates almost daily in the money market, making extra cash available by bill purchase to avert a shortage, or selling bills to absorb a surplus. The consequence of these open-market operations in Treasury bills is that the cash reserves of the clearing banks are brought into adjustment at 8 per cent of their current deposit liabilities. Suppose, however, that the Bank took no steps to absorb a cash surplus with bill sales, and made cash available—through the discount houses—only at the punitive Bank Rate. In this event the critical ratio for clearing bank assets and liabilities would become the

cash ratio. A loss of cash would then force upon them a multiple contraction of deposits, while an increase in cash would enable a multiple
deposit expansion.

To illustrate this first proposition, it is convenient to use the example
already worked through at the start of Section 6. With liabilities of 102
(£00 million), the banks' cash reserves fell from 8·16 to 8, as the discount
houses succeeded in repaying a loan of 0·16 to the Bank of England.
At the same time the banks' liabilities fell to 101·84, a level at which
they needed a cash reserve of 8·1472. Their reaction was a fresh call
on the discount houses, and so on, until deposits and assets had shrunk
to a level which could be supported with the cash (8) available to the
banking system other than on penal terms. The ultimate contraction
(2) is a multiple of the initial cash loss (0·16), viz. 12·5 or 100/8. In
simple terms, the 0·16 cash was 'supporting' liabilities of 2, and the loss
of the cash meant the disappearance of these liabilities.

The ultimate size of this contraction, however, might be influenced
by forces which the process of contraction itself engenders. In this case
the 'cash multiplier' may have a lower value than 12·5. Suppose, for
example, that the general public holds the two main forms of money—
clearing bank liabilities and currency—in stable proportions. A fall in
the first thus implies a proportionate fall in the second. People can hold
less currency, however, only by paying it into bank accounts (thereby
increasing bank liabilities!) or into accounts with other financial institutions, e.g. building societies, which would in turn pay it into *their*
bank accounts. Holdings of notes by the banks would accordingly tend
to rise, thus providing a partial offset to the initial cash loss to the Bank
of England.

We turn next to consider the implications for multiple deposit
expansion of the Bank of England's money market policy. Since the
Bank's operations in the market enable the banks to adjust their cash
reserves to their total deposits, the cash ratio loses its significance as a
regulator of the total deposit level. Its place is taken by the liquidity
ratio, which the banks are required to keep at a minimum of 28 per cent.
The relevant banking multiplier becomes, accordingly, a liquid assets
multiplier of 100/28 or 3·57.

Suppose that, in the worked example of Section 6, the Bank of
England had bought 0·16 bills off the discount houses to enable them to
take up their Treasury bill allotment of 2·5 without any loss. Both the
discount houses and the banks would be in equilibrium, though an
inspection of the figures on page 77 will show that the banks' liquidity
ratio has increased to 29·4 per cent. If this process were repeated week
after week the liquid assets of the clearing banks would progressively
expand, and they would be able to carry additional bonds and advances
while maintaining a minimum liquidity ratio of 28 per cent. Should the

banks' liquid assets increase by £280 million then—subject to various qualifications—they could carry additional bonds and advances of £720 million.

The total expansion might be expected to fall short of ($100/28 \times$ £280 million), because of the leakages of liquid assets the process would engender. To take the example of a few paragraphs back, the public might draw out more notes as they found bank balances growing, to preserve a stable proportion in their holdings. This, in turn, would entail the loss of some Treasury bills by the clearing banks to the Bank of England, as they made their cash loss good.

Second, the increased appetite of the clearing banks for bonds would give the Bank an opportunity to increase its net bond sales in the market. A rise in finance by bond issue, however, means that the Treasury bill issue need not be maintained at its new level. In effect, the banks would use some of the proceeds from maturing bills to take up bonds, and liquid assets would contract until a new equilibrium was reached.

Finally, it may be the case that the public seeks to keep in stable proportions its holdings of currency, bank deposits and other forms of financial claim. The latter may include, for instance, deposits with building societies and finance houses, company securities, and Government debt of various sorts. If, however, the Government can finance a greater part of its borrowing by sales of (say) bonds to the public, then its reliance on bill issue will be reduced. This in turn implies some contraction—other things being equal—in the banks' liquid assets base. The implications for the banks of a rise in deposits with building societies and comparable institutions are considered in Chapter 5.

8. *The Organization and Role of the Bank of England*

From its foundation in 1694 to its nationalization in 1946 the Bank of England had its existence as a joint-stock company. On its nationalization by the Bank of England Act, it was given the legal status of a public corporation. The former shareholders were compensated with Government securities, and their shares taken over and held by the Treasury.

As regards the Bank's organization the main innovation of the Act was a provision for the appointment of four full-time 'executive' directors. These hold departmental responsibilities under the Governor and the Deputy Governor, who head the Bank's administration. The Governor and Deputy Governor hold office for five years, and the directors for four, though they are eligible for reappointment. There are, additionally, twelve part-time directors (on four-year appointments), who are at the same time engaged in other industrial, commercial or financial activities. The Governor, the Deputy and the sixteen directors are all appointed by the Crown (i.e. by the Queen on the advice of the Prime Minister). Together they form the Court of the Bank, which meets each week, normally on a Thursday morning, to give consideration to the Bank's affairs.

The day-to-day running of the Bank is in the hands of the Governor, the Deputy Governor and the executive directors. In addition, some responsibility is borne by various Standing Committees made up of executive and part-time directors. The latter may thus contribute their specialist knowledge and experience at the appropriate points in the Bank's administration. The most important of these committees is the Committee of Treasury, which formulates the Bank's policy and examines the reports of the other committees before they are submitted to the Court. The Committee of Treasury is made up of the Governor, the Deputy Governor and five directors (chosen by the others in a secret ballot) of whom not more than one is an executive director. The Governor, accordingly, always has the Committee of Treasury with whom he may consult. Additionally, he may at any time turn to a part-time director whose background would make his advice particularly valuable.

We shall see in Chapter 20 that the general objectives of Government economic policy comprise full employment, price stability, rising productivity and satisfactory international economic relationships. In the pursuit of these goals the Government will wish to influence the economy by, among other things, measures which affect the monetary system. Such measures make up the monetary policy of the Government, and in giving effect to this monetary policy the Bank of England is the Government's principal agent. Because of its unique position in the monetary system, the Bank is able to influence interest rates, the quantity of money and the availability of finance. If, however, the Bank is to interpret, execute and indeed help formulate official monetary policy, it must enjoy appropriate relationships with the Government and with the various financial institutions. Let us accordingly examine these relationships.

There exists in this country a long tradition of co-operation between the central bank and the Treasury, which is the main Government department responsible for financial affairs. This convention received a statutory basis only in 1946, when the Bank of England Act (Clause 4, Sections 1 and 2) provided that the Treasury might give directions to the Bank when it appeared in the public interest to do so. Such directions were, however, only to be given after consultation with the Governor. This provision has not in any sense reduced the Bank to the status of a Government department subordinate to the Treasury. Thus officials of Bank and Treasury co-operate daily in such matters as the management of the money market. The 'guide-lines' of monetary policy will, however, be decided by Bank and Government in consultation together, while the ultimate decision is the Government's.

This relationship is illustrated by the arrangements for deciding a change in Bank Rate. If either the Chancellor of the Exchequer or the Governor thinks there is a case for changing the Bank Rate, then the matter is discussed informally between them. In such a discussion, the Governor will be able to contribute his central banking and monetary experience. If they disagree, then the final authority rests with the Chancellor: it is not necessary to invoke the 1946 Act. If in fact Bank Rate is to be changed, then the Governor will formally propose this in writing to the Chancellor, who will give formal written approval. Bank Rate for the week ahead is announced after the meeting of the Court every Thursday morning, so it is on this occasion that changes are normally made. At this meeting the Governor will have reported the proposed change, but on this particular aspect of policy neither Court nor Committee of Treasury are consulted. The Governor may, however, have obtained the views of individual directors.

The Bank's advice is the more helpful because it understands how the various financial institutions react to, and are affected by, official monetary policy. This understanding springs from its daily contact with, in particular, the clearing banks and the discount houses. Additionally, the Governor has a weekly meeting with the Chairman and Deputy Chairman of the London Discount Market Association. There are also 'regular and frequent meetings with the Chairman and Deputy Chairman of the Committee of London Clearing Bankers, and there are frequent meetings on particular matters between the chief executives of the clearing banks and the executive directors and senior officials of the Bank' (*Radcliffe Report*, para. 354).

In their dealings with the Bank, the clearing banks, discount houses and accepting houses have long recognized its ultimate authority. Nonetheless, Clause 4 (Section 3) of the 1946 Act gave legal expression to the Bank's position: 'The bank, if they think it necessary in the public interest, may request information from and make recommendations to bankers and may, if so authorized by the Treasury, issue directions to any banker for the purpose of securing that effect is given to any such request or recommendation, provided that:

(a) such request or recommendation cannot refer to the affairs of a particular customer of a banker;
(b) the banker may make representation to the Treasury.'

In point of fact, this clause (with its reservation to protect the traditional secrecy of the banker–customer relationship) has never been invoked. To continue the quotation of the penultimate paragraph, the

D

Radcliffe Report (para. 354) observes that: 'It is on this relationship, and on the mutual trust and confidence that are the basis of the relationship, rather than on formal powers or the regular provision of statistical information that the Bank has relied in seeking to inform itself about and influence the policies of the clearing banks.' This technique of 'moral suasion' received, however, a sharper edge in June, 1969, when the Bank imposed a financial penalty upon the clearing banks for their failure—overall—to achieve the full reduction in their advances level earlier requested of them by the Bank (below). The sanction took the form of a cut by one half in the interest rate paid to the banks on their Special Deposits with the Bank (below). The reduced rate was to remain effective until the clearing banks had brought their advances down to the specified level.

The ways in which the Bank may seek to influence the activities of the clearing banks may now be specifically described. First, the Bank's management of the National Debt is of the greatest relevance to the clearing banks (and the discount houses). Its operations in bills in the money market enable the banks to adjust their cash to an appropriate level, while its pursuit of a funding policy brings the banks' liquid assets under some pressure. The Bank thereby exercises some influence both on the level of advances (see, however, page 81) and on the money supply (the greater part of which consists of clearing bank liabilities).

Second, the Bank's operations in the gilt-edged market has some influence upon bond prices, the level of which must be considered by the banks in deciding, for example, whether to sell bonds to make room for an expansion of advances. In the money market, the Bank exercises a decisive influence on interest rates by its bill dealings, by its adjustment of Bank Rate, and by its occasional assistance at Bank Rate (or above). The fact that interest rates on advances (and indeed on deposit account balances) follow Bank Rate suggests that the Bank has it in its power to influence the demand for advances via Bank Rate changes. In fact, however, the demand for advances seems insensitive to interest rate changes (Chapter 13).

Third, the Bank may make direct requests to the clearing (and Scottish) banks on the composition and the level of their advances (hence 'qualitative' and 'quantitative' credit restrictions). Such requests (normally expressed in a letter from the Governor to the chairmen of the respective bankers' associations) have been made periodically since 1945, in line with the requirements of the Government's monetary policy. In recent years, for example, the banks have variously been asked to restrain the growth of, not to increase, or even to reduce the general level of advances, bill finance and acceptance facilities. Such requests are always subject to a strong exception for export finance, which is expected to receive every encouragement; priority is also attached to loans for capital investment in manufacturing industry, and for shipbuilding. By contrast, restriction is expected to fall with especial weight on loans for personal consumption (e.g. buying a car), for imports, for building up stocks, for property speculation, and (by way of the finance companies) for hire-purchase finance. In this context it is useful to recall that, in recent years, the banks have developed special facilities both for export finance and for financing the purchase of two important 'import substitutes', British-made machine tools and ships (Chapter 2).

A fourth and more recent method of control is provided by the Special Deposit scheme. This was foreshadowed in 1958 when, in announcing the relaxation of its limitations on advances, the Bank reserved the right to call for Special Deposits should changed monetary circumstances require it. The first 'call' was actually made in March, 1960, for a Special Deposit to be paid in June equivalent to 1 per cent of their total liabilities in the case of the London clearing banks, and $\frac{1}{2}$ per cent for the Scottish banks.

Under this scheme, the Bank opens a special account for the clearing banks, and debits their normal accounts (under Bankers' Deposits) while crediting their special account with the appropriate sum. Similar arrangements are made for the Scottish banks. The effect, accordingly, is that the banks have lost a part of their cash reserve (equivalent in value to the percentage of liabilities specified), as the Special Deposits are not to be counted as part of their cash reserve. They do, however, carry interest at the current Treasury bill rate (halved for the clearing banks in June, 1969, as a sanction against them). Now, given the willingness of the Bank to buy Treasury bills at the back door, the banks will be able to restore their cash balances quite easily by selling Treasury bills. For the immediate future, however, they will be able to support rather less illiquid assets than they could have otherwise, as they have lost some of their liquid assets (i.e. bills), while still needing to observe a liquidity ratio of at least 28 per cent.

It was observed in Section 7 that the banks are able to reduce illiquid assets either by reducing advances or selling securities. In this light it is interesting to record that, when the first call was made in 1960, the banks maintained advances and sold bonds. Subsequent calls by the Bank have been accompanied by the intimation that advances, not bond holdings, should bear the consequences.

Whether or not the Bank calls for Special Deposits will depend, of course, on the overall economic policy of the Government. Thus the call for 1 per cent (clearing banks) of April 1960 was followed by four successive calls of $\frac{1}{2}$ per cent, which had increased the total to 3 per cent by September, 1961. These were released progressively from June, 1962,

88 ECONOMICS OF MONEY AND INCOME

and the last was repaid in December, 1962. A fresh call for Special Deposits was made in April, 1965 (clearing banks 1 per cent, Scottish banks ½ per cent). The amount required was raised to 2 per cent for clearing banks and 1 per cent for Scottish banks in July, 1966: the increases were payable in two equal instalments by July 20th and August 17th.

The requests made to the clearing and Scottish banks on their advances levels, etc., are matched by similar requests to the accepting houses, other merchant banks, overseas banks, discount houses and leading hire-purchase finance companies. Members of the British Insurance Association, the National Association of Pension Funds and the Building Societies Association have also been asked for their co-operation in the appropriate restriction of lending (excluding loans on mortage for owner occupiers—Chapter 5). In 1968, further, the Bank of England announced details of a 'Cash Deposit' scheme, designed as a means of restricting lending by the accepting houses, other merchant banks and overseas banks, at times which required rather less severity than that imposed through quantitative control by request. Under the scheme, the Bank would require the banks concerned to deposit with itself sums equal in value to a given percentage of specified (mainly sterling) liabilities. A new method of regulating lending by the finance companies is also under consideration by the Bank.

Questions

1. To what extent can bank deposits be regarded as money, and how are they created?   S.U.J.B.

2. In what sense can it be said that commercial banks 'create money'? What is the limit to this power?   W.J.E.C.

3. Analyse the factors that determine the supply of money in present-day Britain.   I.B.

4. Examine the connection in Britain today between changes in the supply of money and changes in the assets of the banking system.   I.B.

5. 'Advances create deposits.' Explain and discuss.   B.A.Gen.

6. Describe by means of a hypothetical example, the major items in the balance sheet of a joint stock bank, explaining briefly some of the principles that regulate the asset structure.   I.M.T.A.

7. Describe briefly any changes since the end of the war in the com-

position or relative proportions of the main assets and liabilities of the London clearing banks. I.B.

8. Consider to what extent the functions and services of a British commercial bank are reflected in its balance sheet. In the course of your answer draw up a present-day balance sheet, giving the relative proportions of the main items. I.B.

9. How does a well-developed banking system assist economic activity? C.I.S.

10. Discuss the main functions of the commercial banks in Britain, with special reference to their role in the economy as a whole. S.U.J.B.

11. 'The distribution of a bank's assets is determined by a balance between the needs of liquidity and of profitability'. Discuss this statement. I.B.

12. With reference to the London clearing banks:
(a) explain precisely what is meant by their 'liquidity ratios'; and
(b) show the significance of such ratios for the conduct of their business. I.B.

13. Discuss, with reference to the Bank of England, the role of the Central Bank. I.M.T.A.

14. Describe the controls which the Bank of England has today over Britain's commercial banks. I.B.

15. Describe and assess the various ways in which the Bank of England exercises control over the monetary and banking system of the country. W.J.E.C.

16. How can the Central Bank exercise control over the supply of money? B.A.Gen.

17. Describe the main functions of the Bank of England. To what extent have these changed since the thirties? U.L.

18. What comprises and what determines the money supply of a country? Give a brief account of the consequences of open market purchases by a central bank. S.U.J.B.

19. What will determine the relationship between a given increase in the cash reserves of a country's commercial banking system, and the total increase in deposits associated with it? B.A.Gen.

20. The following data represents the combined balance sheets of the commercial banks in the British economy.

Liabilities (£'000)		Assets (£'000)	
Deposits:		Notes	500
(i) Current accounts	5,000	Balance at the	
(ii) Deposit accounts	5,000	Central Bank	500
		Bills	2,000
		Securities	3,000
		Advances	4,000
Total	10,000	Total	10,000

(a) (i) What is the cash ratio of the Banks?

(ii) If the central bank purchases £500,000 of securities in the open market, what is likely to happen to the level of deposits, assuming that the commercial banks keep the proportions between assets unchanged? Explain how you arrive at your answer.

(b) What are the main factors which govern the asset structure of the commercial banks in Britain?　　　　　　　　　　　　　J.M.B.

21. Describe the Bank of England's role as 'lender of last resort'.
　　　　　　　　　　　　　　　　　　　　　　　　　　　S.U.J.B.

22. What is meant by 'funding' operations? Can 'funding' enable the monetary authorities to regulate the volume and the terms of credit?　　　　　　　　　　　　　　　　　　　　　I.M.T.A.

23. Why did the Radcliffe Committee conclude that the cash ratio is no longer the key to the regulation of British bank credit?
　　　　　　　　　　　　　　　　　　　　　　　　　　　W.J.E.C.

24. Explain the view of the Radcliffe Committee that the cash ratio has ceased to be the primary means of controlling commercial bank credit.　　　　　　　　　　　　　　　　　　　　B.Sc.(Econ.)

25. Why is it argued that the existence of large amounts of short-term government debt makes the working of traditional monetary policy ineffective?　　　　　　　　　　　　　　　　　　　　B.A.Gen.

26. What is meant by the term 'liquid assets' in the context of British banking? If the monetary authorities make available to the commercial banks an extra £100,000,000 of liquid assets, what would be the effect on the volume of deposits?　　　　　　　　B.Sc.(Econ.)

27. 'The liquid assets of the joint stock banks are, today, their effective credit base.' Discuss this statement.　　　　　　　　　　I.B.

28. Write a brief account of the role and operations of the London discount market.　　　　　　　　　　　　　　　　　　I.B.

29. Set out the pattern of short-term interest rates in the London money market and consider how far the level of such rates is within the control of the monetary authorities.   I.B.

30. 'The London money market is an obsolete relic.' Consider this view.   B.Sc.(Econ.)

31. Discuss the role of the Treasury bill in Britain's public and private financial systems.   I.B.

5

Other Financial Intermediaries in the United Kingdom

INSTITUTIONS which conduct a business in taking deposits (from those with funds to spare) and making loans (to those in need of funds) are appropriately described as 'financial intermediaries'. They include the commercial banks, merchant banks, overseas banks and discount houses, whose activities have already been considered. Other deposit-taking and loan-making bodies are the finance companies, building societies, savings banks and Post Office giro, whose activities are sketched in Sections 1–4. This will enable some consideration, in Section 5, of the extent of their competition with the banks in providing finance and accepting deposits; and, in Section 6, of the relationship between their deposits and the money supply, as defined in Chapter 1.

The term 'financial intermediary' may also be defined to include loan-making institutions like pension funds and life insurance companies, which take sums not on deposit but on a long-term basis. Their activities are outlined in Chapter 7.

1. *Finance Companies*

Finance companies are variously known as finance houses, hire-purchase finance companies and industrial bankers. The second title gives the best guide to their activities, since they are primarily concerned with the provision of hire-purchase finance and its main variant, the 'credit-sale'. Under a hire-purchase agreement, the customer undertakes to hire a commodity over a year or two, paying weekly or monthly hire instalments, with the right to buy the good for a nominal sum when all the hire instalments have been paid. While the customer enjoys the practical benefit of immediate possession, the legal ownership does not pass to him until he exercises his purchase option with the final payment. By contrast, a credit sale confers (in general) immediate ownership as well as possession upon the customer, who is allowed to pay his debt by

92

instalments over a comparable period. The rights of the parties to these and similar contracts are defined in the Hire Purchase Act, 1965.

While the total number of finance companies may approach fifteen hundred, about three-quarters of their business is in the hands of the forty or so members of the Finance Houses' Association. A profusion of small concerns was probably encouraged by restrictions[1] which, up to 1956 (with one short exception), prevented finance companies from raising more than £50,0C0 in any twelve months with an issue of shares or other securities. Between 1956 and 1958 this limit was set at £10,000. Until the late 1950s the clearing banks had, very largely, taken no part in the post-war growth of hire-purchase finance. However, within a short time of the complete relaxation of this 'capital issues' control in July, 1958, a minority or majority share interest had been acquired in one or more larger finance houses by all the clearing banks (except Coutts) and by the Scottish banks.

Many of the small companies are subsidiaries of firms such as garages and T.V. dealers, concerned with the finance of their parent companies' sales. The big finance companies (and 'independent' smaller concerns) obtain a lot of their business through the agency of retail dealers, to whom they pay the purchase price of articles sold and from whom in turn they receive the regular instalments paid by the customers. A less frequent alternative is for the dealer to sell a company his rights in a batch of hire-purchase contracts he himself has previously made with his customers ('block discounting'). Some companies describe themselves as 'industrial bankers', though the Radcliffe Report notes (para 217) that 'what this is meant to imply is not altogether clear'. While some of the larger houses clear cheques, for instance, this service seems limited to their business customers. It is open to any company to apply to the Board of Trade, under the Companies Act, 1967, for recognition as a banker for the purposes of the Moneylenders Acts. Recognition in this context may be important for a finance company, as it might otherwise encounter legal difficulties in recovering some of its loans.

In 1968 the amount of instalment credit outstanding in Great Britain was somewhat over £1,200 million. Roughly two-thirds of this was owed directly to the finance companies and the remainder to a variety of department stores, general stores, durable-goods shops, mail order houses, etc. Of the new instalment credit extended by the finance houses during 1968, about 58 per cent financed the purchase of private motor vehicles, and a further 6 per cent the purchase of household goods. The proportion devoted to commercial vehicles was 13 per cent, and to industrial and agricultural equipment 14 per cent. However, business

[1] Between 1939 and 1959 the Government operated (through the now-defunct Capital Issues Committee) a control on company finance by share (etc.) issue, as one technique for regulating the economy.

enterprise received further assistance by way of loans and advances which in recent years has formed about 12 per cent of the finance houses' main assets. Under a 'stocking plan', for example, a finance company will lend to a motor dealer to enable him to buy new cars for his showroom, taking from him a bill of exchange drawn on the dealer and payable to itself.

Of their principal liabilities of £1,116 million at end-December, 1968, the finance houses had £190 million in issued capital and reserves, £116 million bills discounted with U.K. banks and discount houses, £78 million bank advances (net of deposits with the banks) and £620 million deposits. Companies secure bill finance either by opening an acceptance credit with a bank and drawing bills on it for discount in the discount market or, especially for smaller companies, by accepting a bill which the bank supplying the credit draws upon the finance house. Of their total deposits of £620 million, 18 per cent came from U.K. banks (notably merchant and overseas banks), 15 per cent from other U.K. financial institutions, 44 per cent from industrial and commercial companies and 16 per cent from (mainly) private persons. A further 7 per cent came from companies, banks and private persons resident overseas. It is the large finance houses which attract the deposits of the big industrial and commercial companies, taking any sum up to £100,000 in the normal range of business, and bigger amounts by individual negotiation. The smaller companies rely more heavily on small deposits, in which the funds of private individuals would figure significantly. Deposits may be for a fixed term (up to 12 months) or on terms ranging from call to 3 or 6 months' notice.

As a liquidity reserve against their deposit liability, the smaller houses generally hold a lot more cash than the larger houses, which place greater reliance on unused overdraft and acceptance facilities. Further, the instalment payments on outstanding agreements provide a regular cash flow, which could be used to repay depositors if houses were prepared to let their volume of business contract. Members of the former Industrial Bankers' Association—most of whom joined F.H.A. in April, 1966—were required to hold cash or Treasury Bills to the value of 10 per cent of all deposits or 30 per cent of deposits repayable within fourteen days, whichever amount was greater.

The 'interest' rate which the houses charge their customers includes as well a service charge for operating the customer's account. These rates normally follow movements in Bank Rate, because in their deposits at short notice the houses compete directly with other short-term investment outlets, especially (for larger sums) with local authorities (Chapter 3). Further, the larger houses may take deposits at a rate specifically quoted as a premium on Bank Rate.

Business prudence suggests that the size of the initial deposit should reflect the difference between the new and second-hand value of commodity, and that the instalment period should be related to the r at which it loses value. In fact, the Board of Trade will often decide the minimum deposit and maximum repayment period by statutory order, as one weapon of the Government's monetary policy (Chapter 20). While the stricter terms required by a contractionary monetary policy may reduce the houses' turnover, they may nonetheless derive some benefit in that only relatively risk-free customers will be able to afford the higher deposit and bigger instalments. Some heavy losses, for example, were suffered between 1958 and 1960, when controls were completely relaxed and the more intense competition led some houses to offer over-generous terms (e.g. a five-year repayment period).

Since 1961, members of the F.H.A. (and, during its existence, the I.B.A.) have been asked by the Bank of England to observe a comparable restraint at times when the clearing and other banks have been under restriction. In 1965 this informal control was extended to include a number of leading houses outside the F.H.A. Other methods of regulation are being officially considered, for use when circumstances require a less rigorous control than that imposed by a 'ceiling' on the level of financing. A possibility is that the finance houses could be required to work to a minimum liquidity ratio, along the lines (for example) of that imposed by the former I.B.A. upon its members.

2. *Building Societies*

The earliest recorded building societies were established towards the end of the eighteenth century as self-help 'mutual' societies. Their object was to build houses for their members, the construction of which would be financed from the members' regular savings. Once the members were all housed the society was dissolved. By contrast, the 'permanent' building society of today provides an investment outlet for predominantly small savers, many of whom will never borrow from the society. The great bulk of their funds are lent at interest to finance house purchase by owner occupiers, and as the loans are repaid so the capital is lent again to further applicants. However, societies have retained the important characteristic of being 'mutual' rather than 'commercial' in nature. They seek to hold a balance between the respective interests of investors and borrowers, while earning sufficient to pay competitive interest rates, meet expenses and taxes, and build up appropriate reserves. In their policy, the societies are guided by the 'social' objectives of encouraging thrift and promoting home ownership.

Societies secure their funds by the sale of shares and the acceptance of deposits. Share purchase confers membership of the society, but in other respects building society shares are quite different from company shares (Chapter 7). They are purchased with a minimum of formality at the society's office, the investor receiving in fact simply a book of account with the share value standing to his credit; they are not transferable; and they are repayable by the society. From the investor's viewpoint, accordingly, the share may be regarded as a category of deposit under another name. The rules of the societies prescribe a longer notice of withdrawal for shares than for deposits, but in practice small sums in both categories may be withdrawn on demand. Further, shareholders would be repaid after depositors should the society be wound up. These are in practice very small disadvantages and, since shares carry interest on average $\frac{1}{2}$ per cent higher than deposits, it is not surprising to find them more popular. In 1968, the total liabilities (plus reserves) of building societies in the U.K. exceeded £8,000 million: of this total, about 90 per cent was due to shareholders, and only about 4 per cent to depositors.

The great bulk of the societies' funds comes from small savers: in 1968, over eight million individual shareholdings had an average value of about £910, while roughly 600,000 deposits averaged about £540 in value. Investors are limited to a maximum holding of £10,000 in any one society, though they may hold this maximum in each of many societies. The societies provide a useful outlet for temporarily surplus funds of the smaller business, but are not a suitable investment for the temporary funds of the big concerns.

The principal outlet for the societies' funds is the finance of house purchase for owner occupation. The society advances the borrower an agreed proportion of the purchase price (possibly though not usually 100 per cent), to enable him to buy the property. The borrower becomes the legal owner of the house, but the society takes a mortgage as a security for the loan. Should the mortgagor fail to maintain his monthly payments (usually a mixture of interest and capital), the society may foreclose on the mortgage, i.e. sell the property and recoup itself from the proceeds. When the debt and the interest it bears are finally paid, the society's legal rights as mortgagee come to an end: the pledge (Norman French 'gage') of the property as security becomes dead ('mort'). Of the funds lent for house purchase by building societies, local authorities and insurance companies, the societies provide about 80 per cent: roughly one-third of their loans relate to new houses.

The unwise use of funds for property speculation by a few societies in the 1950s led to the imposition of certain restraints in the Building Societies Acts, 1960 and 1962. In brief, societies are not allowed to lend more than 10 per cent of total advances in any one year as 'special advances', save with the permission of the Registrar of Friendly Societies. 'Special advances' are defined as loans of any amount to a company or loans in excess of £10,000 to any one private person.

While the societies may lend for a 30-year period, the bulk of their loans are made for 20 or 25 years. At any given time, of course, all their outstanding loans will be at various stages of repayment. Since, further, some loans will be repaid before the agreed date, it follows that the loan assets of the societies (i.e. their claims against the borrowers) are not quite so long term as might superficially appear. It remains true, nonetheless, that the societies are accepting funds at short term from shareholders and depositors, and lending them for substantially longer periods. As a precaution against an abnormal volume of withdrawals, therefore, they need to hold some of their assets in a liquid form, even though a cash inflow is provided by loan repayments. Although in recent years share withdrawals have averaged about 17 per cent of year-end balances, and deposit withdrawals 30 per cent, in fact these outflows have been more than covered by the inflow of new money. Investment in building societies has, indeed, shown a strong upward trend since the 1930s.

In practice, societies tend to hold about 15 per cent of their total assets in the form of cash and investments. The latter consist of gilt-edged and local authority securities, the maturity pattern of which is prescribed by the Registrar under powers conferred by the Building Societies Act, 1962. The societies are obliged to hold a reasonable proportion of securities with a fairly short life to redemption, since their prices in Stock Exchange dealings would normally be close to their maturity values. Thus they could readily be sold to finance abnormal withdrawals, with little risk of capital loss.

Societies with assets of at least £1 million (£500,000 up to 1968) are able, on certain further conditions, to secure 'trustee status' for their shares, i.e. they become an eligible investment for trust funds. The other principal requirements are, first, a minimum liquid assets ratio of $7\frac{1}{2}$ per cent and, second, a minimum reserve ratio of $2\frac{1}{2}$ per cent.[1] 'Liquid assets' are defined as cash and investments less current liabilities such as bank overdrafts and interest due to shareholders. 'Reserves' represent the accumulation of profits retained by the societies after paying shareholders and depositors their interest and meeting administrative expenses and tax liabilities. The reserves could accordingly be used to offset capital losses on investments, or on the sale of the property of defaulting mortgagors, without prejudice to the sums subscribed by shareholders or depositors. In practice, reserves as a percentage of total assets vary from about 4 per cent on average for the largest societies to about 6 per cent on average for the smallest.

[1] A sliding scale is operated for societies with assets over £100 million, which serves to make their reserve-ratio requirement somewhat lower.

In their competition with other institutions for the funds of the small saver, the societies enjoy the advantage of being able to quote 'tax free' interest rates. By a special arrangement with the Inland Revenue, the societies pay the income tax in respect of their investors' liability on the interest received. This is to the advantage of the investor who is paying the standard rate of tax (Chapter 8), though it does mean that the investor with no tax liability receives less interest than he otherwise would if all investors made their own tax arrangements.

Traditionally, the societies have seen their main competitor as the National Savings Movement, which has relatively stable interest rates. However, it is probable that a significant number of investors are alive to other outlets, for example deposit accounts with the clearing banks, since a rise in bank deposit rate is in general associated with a decline in the net inflow of funds. Despite a shrinkage in their new money, the societies are slow to follow other interest rates upwards. Instead, they may 'ration' available funds by, for instance, advancing a lower proportion of the house purchase price, or favouring loan applications from their own shareholders.

Their marked preference for stability of interest rates may be explained on several grounds. To finance the payment of higher rates to investors, rates have to be raised for existing as well as new borrowers (though an increase for the former may be delayed for a short period). Although all this constitutes a major administrative task, it does not necessarily maintain the societies' lending powers to the extent that might at first be thought. While the societies will encourage existing borrowers to increase their monthly payments, some will wish to exercise their option of extending, instead, the total loan period. The capital element in the payments of such borrowers will accordingly decline, reducing in turn the ability of the societies to make fresh loans from the repayments of principal. Further, societies tend to the view that the supply of investment funds is insensitive to interest rate changes, and they are reluctant to set in motion a competitive bidding-up of rates. Accordingly, when other interest rates rise, the societies wait until a new interest level seems reasonably well established before following suit.

Amalgamation (especially among the smaller societies) has brought the number of societies down from 819 in 1950 to 744 in 1958 and 525 in 1968. The range of size among the societies is notably wide. Thus about a dozen societies have assets over £100 million and between them hold roughly two-thirds of all building society assets; at the other extreme more than 300 societies have assets of less than £1 million each. In 1968, 301 societies were members of the Building Societies Association, and between them they accounted for 98 per cent of all building society assets. Two leading membership requirements of the B.S.A.

are the liquidity and reserve minima prescribed for trustee status. The Council of the B.S.A. makes recommendations on interest rates to its members, which in practice are followed by the majority. The Council also serves as a channel for any requests the Bank of England may make to member societies for restraint in their lending (Chapter 4).

3. *Savings Banks*

The Trustee Savings Banks and the Post Office Savings Bank[1] both owe their origins, in the nineteenth century, to the desire to bring savings facilities within easier reach of the poor. An important goal continues to be the provision of completely secure deposit facilities for relatively small sums, at modest interest, with (limited) withdrawal rights on demand. In more recent years, however, the savings banks have developed a significance beyond that of simple 'thrift institutions'.

The 'ordinary departments' of the 77 Trustee Savings Banks in Great Britain offer their customers facilities very similar to those provided by the P.O.S.B. in its 'ordinary account'. Both place an upper limit of £10,000 on deposits, allow very small sums to be withdrawn on demand, and pay interest at 2½ per cent. In both cases, too, the funds of the depositors are automatically[2] invested by the National Debt Commissioners in loans to the Government (Chapter 8). The interest the banks receive[2] enables them to pay depositors their 2½ per cent, but is less than the rate the Government would (in recent years) have to offer in a public issue of gilt-edged securities. Apart from their role as a source of Government finance the savings banks, as a part today of the National Savings Movement, have a relevance in the broader field of Government economic policy (Chapter 20).

Nearly all the Trustee Savings Banks operate 'special investment departments', which have shown especially rapid growth since the early 1950s. Accounts are available only to customers with a minimum £50 balance in the ordinary department, and there is a limit to the maximum deposit of £10,000. At least 20 per cent of depositors' funds in the special investment department must be held in liquid form (notably cash, temporary loans to local authorities and marketable securities with less than five years to maturity). The remainder is invested pre-

---

[1] When the Post Office achieves full 'public corporation' status in 1969 (Chapter 8), the P.O.S.B. will be re-named the National Savings Bank and come under the control of a new Department of National Savings, responsible to the Treasury.

[2] However, the Trustee Savings Bank Act, 1968, provides for the grant to the T.S.B.s of some powers to invest these funds directly; it also enables the interest rate they receive to be increased.

dominantly in gilt-edged stocks and (especially) the securities of local authorities, to whom they have thereby become an important source of long term finance. Special investment departments are not allowed to hold company securities,[1] but their freedom of choice among the various classes of central and local government debt enables them to offer a return averaging between 6 and 7 per cent (before tax). They thus compete significantly with the building societies, especially for the funds of those savers who do not pay income tax at standard rate (Chapter 8). In June, 1966, the P.O.S.B. introduced a comparable 'investment account', which is able to offer better returns than its ordinary account through investment in higher yielding Government securities and in loans to local authorities.

Both categories of savings bank offer facilities for settling debts. Thus the P.O.S.B. and many T.S.B.s are prepared to undertake certain regular payments to creditors on their depositors' behalf. Further, most T.S.B.s now provide non-interest-bearing current accounts, first introduced in 1965. Cheques drawn on these accounts are subject to a fixed charge of 6d. per cheque, and are cleared through the London clearing banks' facilities. Holders are not allowed to overdraw their accounts, though a limited personal loan scheme for customers is being considered by the banks. A banker's (guarantee) card scheme—comparable to that of the clearing banks (page 34)—was introduced in 1968.

4. *The Post Office Giro*

A payments system rivalling that of the clearing banks was introduced by the Post Office in 1968. The essential principle of the Post Office (or national) giro is the centralization of all accounts at one headquarters, to which transfer, payment and deposit instructions are sent by account holders and non-account holders (as appropriate) from all parts of the country. These giro accounts, of course, are quite separate from the P.O.S.B. accounts previously described. Suppose that the holder of a giro account (minimum initial deposit, £5) who lives in Nottingham wishes to make a payment to an account holder in Truro. He will fill in the appropriate instruction form and post it to giro headquarters at Bootle (Lancs) on day 1. On day 2, his giro account will be debited and the Truro man's credited, by modern methods of automatic data processing. On day 3, he can receive and his creditor will receive a statement of account, posted from Bootle. Had the Truro man not had a giro account, the giro headquarters would instead have sent him a 'cheque' which he could cash at a Truro post office. Had the Nottingham

[1] The T.S.B. unit trust (Chapter 7) is a quite separate activity.

man not had an account, he would have paid cash over the counter of a Nottingham post office, for the credit of the Truro man's giro account. Transfers between account holders, and deposits by an account holder to his own account, carry no service charge, but in consideration no interest is paid on balances. The assets corresponding to these balances are principally short-dated Government bonds and local authority loans and securities of comparable duration, with—as a liquidity reserve—loans to the discount market (included in entry 8 in Table 3.1) and in the local authority 'temporary loan' market, as well as some Treasury bills and balances at the clearing banks.

Various refinements on this basic system are provided by the giro service. Thus a company receiving periodic payments from a large number of customers might arrange (with their approval) for the 'automatic' debit of their giro accounts at the appropriate intervals. The company itself would then initiate the debiting of its customers' accounts, and have the balances transferred to its own account. Alternatively, the customers might place a standing order with the giro to make the payments on their behalf. Employers might also arrange with employees for wages (and for retired employees, pensions) to be paid through the giro. The giro service, however, is essentially a payments service, and customers are not allowed to overdraw their accounts.

5. Competition with the Clearing Banks

There are two areas in which these institutions might compete with the clearing banks. The first—relevant only to the building societies and finance companies—is in the provision of finance for firms and private borrowers. The second, relevant also to the savings banks and national giro, is in the acceptance of deposits.

We have already seen that the building societies are, predominantly, long-term lenders of funds on mortgage to finance house purchase. During 1968, for example, some 98 per cent of new mortgage advances were given for this purpose. On the other hand, the banks do not as a rule engage in this sort of business, though they assist their own staff in house purchase. Indeed, the banks complement the work of the building societies, by providing 'bridging' loans to enable the borrower, for example, to buy his new house before he has succeeded in selling the old. They might also advance a part of the purchase price of a house if the borrower were able to repay within a few years. These activities, taken together, probably explain the 6 per cent of total advances outstanding to the clearing banks for house purchase during 1968.

The clearing banks do not themselves engage in hire-purchase finance, though all (with one unimportant exception) have an interest in one or more finance companies, and make advances to the finance companies for their business (Chapter 2). This apart, bank overdraft facilities and loan schemes for personal uses do represent an alternative to hire-purchase finance for more expensive consumer goods (e.g. cars). The credit card has also been developed to provide consumer credit for periods comparable with hire-purchase arrangements. On the other hand, business borrowers might find the facilities of finance companies an alternative to finance by bank overdraft, for the purposes shown in Section 2.

Commercial, merchant and overseas banks, the national giro, savings banks, building societies and finance companies all accept sums on deposit from private persons and business firms. Deposits with the clearing banks are in turn held by all other forms of financial intermediary, while the clearing banks themselves hold balances with other deposit banks. The interaction of their deposit business is a highly complex affair. Thus if people use some of their deposits with the clearing banks to open accounts with building societies, there may be effects on the community's income and savings, which could in turn react back upon the total and proportionate distribution of deposits. The discussion in this section, however, is limited to the implications of such deposit movements for the finance of Government, and so for the availability of Treasury bills to the clearing banks.

Suppose that, to take the example considered in Chapter 4, Section 7, an increase in liquid assets enabled the clearing banks to expand advances and bond holdings. Their liabilities on account to customers would necessarily rise in correspondence with the net increase in assets, so that the total supply of bank-deposit money in the economy will have increased. Firms and private persons with bank balances may decide to hold some of their new wealth in the form of deposits with building societies, finance companies or savings banks.

If clearing bank customers move some of their deposits into account with the building societies, this has no immediate effect on the banks. The societies are now the holders of the balances with the clearing banks, in place of the other customers: the ownership of some bank deposits has changed, but the total is (as yet) unaffected. The societies will use most of their new balances to finance loans for property purchase, which means a further change in the ownership of the balances, as they pass to the sellers of the property. Some of their new balances, however, will be used by the societies to increase their reserve holdings of Government bonds (Section 3). In so far as the Bank of England sells the extra bonds, the Government's reliance on bill finance will be reduced. This in turn implies (*other things being equal*)[1] a

[1] As Chapter 4 explained, the clearing banks countered a shrinkage in the Treasury bill issue in the 1960s by holding more 'private sector' liquid assets.

contraction in the clearing banks' liquid assets, a decline in their less liquid assets, and so a fall in the total of bank deposits. The profitability of the banks, of course, is reduced by the contraction of assets, not of deposits.

This sort of leakage could hardly result from an initial switching of deposits from the clearing banks to the finance companies, since the latter are not significant holders of Government debt. It seems particularly important, however, where deposits are switched into account with the savings banks, since almost all the P.O.S.B.s' funds, and much of the T.S.B.'s funds, find their way into the National Loans Fund. The T.S.B.s are, further, an important source of long-term funds for the local authorities, which (of itself) serves to reduce the amounts that the latter need to borrow from the Government (Chapter 8), and that the Government in turn needs to raise from the public. An expansion in balances at the savings banks, therefore, implies a reduction in Government reliance on 'market borrowing', including bill issue.

The same sort of reasoning is useful in assessing the 'competition' which the giro system is likely to afford the clearing banks. As Section 4 noted, the major outlet for the funds of the national giro are short-term Government bonds and local authority loans. This implies some reduction in other Government borrowing, with possible consequences for the clearing banks' liquid assets base. The giro system gives the public the opportunity to use a special type of Government debt— balances with the giro—as a means of making certain payments in a convenient way. The Government may thus increase the total demand for its debt among the public by attaching to part of it not interest but special payment facilities.

The clearing banks have co-operated in establish ng arrangements for payments between giro and bank accounts. At the same time, they have increased the attractiveness of balances held on current account with themselves, by refining the payments facilities they offer. Further progress and development in this field is expected in the next few years (Chapter 2). The banks have also developed their loan facilities for the private customer, an attraction which, of course, the national giro is unable to rival.

6. Quasi-Money

'Money' was defined in Chapter 1 as anything generally acceptable in settlement of debts. On this definition, coin, notes and the public's current account balances with the commercial, merchant and overseas banks emerge unambiguously as 'money' in the U.K. today. Balances on deposit account with the commercial banks are not, as such, transferable in settlement of a debt. In practice, however, they may be so closely involved in the operation of current accounts that their exclusion from the coverage of the money supply would seem artificial.

In official usage, term deposits with the merchant banks, overseas banks and discount houses are also regarded as 'money' (Chapter 1). As earlier chapters noted, a difficulty with this view is that deposits for a fixed term cannot be drawn down, if necessary, to supplement a current account balance, and so cannot be involved in the payments system in the same way as deposit account balances with the commercial banks. When, further, a term deposit reaches maturity, it would be customary to transfer it to a current account as a preliminary to drawing on it to make a payment. It seems appropriate therefore to regard term deposits with these institutions not as money but, by virtue (nonetheless) of their closeness to other bank deposits, as 'near' money or 'quasi' money (Latin 'qua si' means 'as if').

This reasoning suggests a broad basis on which to classify the liabilities to the public of the various financial institutions considered in this chapter. In their everyday affairs, people or firms would probably regard their balances with finance companies, building societies or the savings banks as part of their 'money'. Like coin, notes and bank balances, they all function as a store of value, with a worth fixed in money terms. However, with some exceptions (below), the holder of any of these assets would need first to turn them into notes, or into a current account balance, in order to make a payment to his creditor. It seems best, accordingly, to regard them as quasi-money, not money, since (for the most part) they are not transferable in settlement of debts.

On this criterion, further, it is quite appropriate to broaden the coverage of the money supply to include balances with the newly-established national giro. Giro balances can be used interchangeably with notes and coin as a means of payment between account holders and non-account holders. Many people and firms may choose to hold some balances with the giro as an alternative to notes, coin and bank balances, in order to make some of their everyday payments. Like notes and coin, also, balances with the giro are a form of non-interest-bearing Government debt. Giro balances, therefore, seem best regarded as money, not quasi-money.

Those balances held with the trustee savings banks on current account might also, at least in principle, be singled out as 'money', by virtue of the part they play in the payments system. Thus the holder of such a balance will draw cheques on it to pay his creditors, and the T.S.B. in turn will meet the resultant claims through the debiting of its account with a clearing bank, in the same way as various other non-clearing banks in similar circumstances. This seems a different situation from one in which, say, a depositor or shareholder with a building society arranges for it to make a payment to a third party on his behalf. In this case, the society is simply acting as a paying agent: it debits the account of (say) its depositor, but the latter's creditor gets a cheque not on the society but on the society's (clearing) bank. It is the clearing bank balance, accordingly, which serves as the means of payment. On the other hand, *if* many people and firms held accounts with building societies, and often made payments to each other by the movement

TABLE 5.1

Some items of Quasi-Money in the United Kingdom end-1968

	£ million
1. Building Societies: Shares and Deposits	7,764
2. Finance Companies: Deposits	509
3. Local Authority Debt repayable within a year	1,390
4. Post Office Savings Bank Balances:	
(a) Ordinary accounts	1,589
(b) Investment accounts	190
5. Trustee Savings Bank Balances:	
(a) Ordinary departments	1,054
(b) Special investment departments	1,311
6. National Savings Certificates	2,602
7. Premium Savings Bonds	690
8. British Savings, Defence and National Development Bonds	917

Note: (i) Entries 2 and 3 do not include deposits (2) or debt (3) held by banks.
 (ii) Entries 4, 5 and 6 include interest accrued to date.

Source: Financial Statistics (H.M.S.O.)

of these balances from one account to the other, then it would be difficult not to regard them as the equivalent of clearing bank liabilities as a means of payment, i.e. as money.

It is clear that, in some cases, the line between money and non-money is difficult to draw. It would be even more difficult to attempt a sharp distinction between quasi-money and other (non-money) financial claims, and the list given in Table 5.1 is admittedly arbitrary. Thus temporary borrowing by local authorities (3) is included because of its closeness to 2, and small savings securities (6 to 8—explained in Chapter 8) because of their nearness to 4b and 5b. All represent claims which can be turned into money at a pre-defined value after a given (minimum) period of time, which varies in length from one year down to zero. These are also features, however, of Treasury bills and bills of exchange, as well as all Government bonds and company debentures (Chapter 7) with one year or less to maturity. The latter, in turn, are very close to bonds with a little over a year to run, and so on.

The importance of the distinction between money and other forms of financial claim will depend upon the problem or piece of analysis under attention. Thus in considering the determinants of how much people spend on consumer goods and services (Chapter 10), it is probably not important to distinguish people's money balances from their other financial assets which are readily convertible into cash. On the other hand, a distinction between money and other forms of (interest-bearing) financial claim is at the root of the theory of interest explained in Chapter 13.

Questions

1. Examine the probable effects on the volume of commercial bank deposits in Britain of a significant difference between the rates of interest paid on commercial bank deposit (time) accounts and on:
   (a) Treasury bills;
   (b) deposits with hire purchase finance houses.   I.B.

2. Trace the effects on the total volume of bank deposits in Britain if certain customers of the banks buy:
   (a) Treasury bills;
   (b) shares in a building society.   I.B.

3. What is the economic importance of Building Societies?   A.E.B.

4. Write a short essay on *either* building societies *or* finance houses.
                                                                  I.M.T.A.

5. The Government has announced plans for the establishment of a post office giro system for the convenient settlement of monetary transactions. What effects do you believe it will have on the activities of the commercial banks?   J.M.B.

6

Other Banking Systems

(I) United States of America

1. *The Structure of Banking in the U.S.A.*

The Bank of England, we saw in Chapter 4, was not founded expressly as a 'central bank', but came gradually to assume its special responsibilities in the developing monetary system of the nineteenth century. By contrast, the Federal Reserve System of the United States came into operation in 1914 specifically as the American central banking organization, though the contemporary conception of its appropriate duties was understandably narrower than that of today.

The System operates in two tiers. Situated in Washington, D.C., is the Board of Governors of the Federal Reserve System. It has seven members who are appointed on fourteen-year engagements by the President of the United States. Their task essentially is the supervision and co-ordination of the twelve Reserve Banks, and the definition of the guide lines of central banking policy. The twelve Federal Reserve Banks form the second tier of the System. The country has been divided into twelve regions or districts, with a Reserve Bank in a leading city in each district. Thus the Federal Reserve Bank of Boston serves District No. 1, on the eastern seaboard, while Reserve Banks for the other districts are located at New York, Philadelphia, Cleveland, Richmond, Atlanta, Chicago, St. Louis, Minneapolis, Kansas City, Dallas and San Francisco. Between them, the Reserve Banks have twenty-four branches.

The structure established by the Federal Reserve Act of 1913 was the resultant of a variety of influences active at the time. In particular, it represented a compromise between a desire for centralized and a desire for regional control (though the subsequent trend has in fact been towards increased central power). This compromise is also apparent, for example, in the administration of each Reserve Bank. Thus of its nine directors, six are chosen by its 'member banks' (below) which own the Bank's share capital. Only three of these six may have banking affiliations, while the others should be representative of industry, etc., in the District. The remaining three are appointed by the Board of Governors of the Federal Reserve System. One of these acts as Chairman of the Reserve Bank's board, and also as Federal Reserve Agent in the District, while another serves as Deputy Chairman.

A banking institution which has no parallel in the U.K. is the Federal Deposit Insurance Corporation. This was established in 1934 to provide 'deposit insurance' for commercial banks, the bank paying a small annual premium proportionate to its deposits. The principle here is that, should the bank fail, F.D.I.C. will refund depositors' balances up to a maximum of $10,000 on each account. F.D.I.C. is not part of the Federal Reserve System, though its activities may be included loosely in American central banking.

Commercial banks in the U.S.A. are incorporated by charter, received either from the state or from the federal authorities. Each bank, accordingly, is classified as a state bank or as a federal bank (alternatively called, national bank), subject principally to state or federal laws. An investment bank, it may be noted, is not a variety of commercial bank but the American counterpart of the British issuing house (Chapter 7). Membership of the appropriate Federal Reserve Bank is compulsory for national banks, but optional for state banks. Deposit insurance with F.D.I.C. is compulsory for all 'member banks', but also available to those state banks outside the Federal Reserve. At end-1968, national banks in the U.S.A. numbered 4,716 and state banks 8,963. Of the state banks 1,262 were members of the Federal Reserve System. Between them, the 5,978 members of the Federal Reserve held about 80 per cent of total commercial bank assets. Of the non-members of the Federal reserve, only 197 were not insured with F.D.I.C.

The total of 13,679 American commercial banks stands in contrast to the United Kingdom, where about 90 per cent of joint-stock bank deposits are held with the London clearing banks, which in turn are dominated by the Big Four. The British system is, outstandingly, a system of branch banking: each of the Big Four has over 2,000 branches (or agencies) in towns and villages throughout England and Wales. The American system, however, is less easy to characterize. The decision whether or not to permit the development of branch banking rests with each state authority so that, where branch banking is permitted, it cannot extend beyond state boundaries. *Nation-wide* branch banking is not therefore possible in the U.S.A. under these arrangements.

Attitudes towards *state-wide* branch banking vary from state to state. Roughly one-third of the 50 states permit state-wide branch banking and in California, for instance, the Bank of America (the largest bank in the world with assets exceeding $17,000 million) has nearly 900 branches. In a second group of states branch banking is restricted to, for example, the county in which the head office is located. Finally, in a dozen or so states branch banking is prohibited, either absolutely or with insignificant exceptions. Thus the greater Chicago area is served by nearly 300 banks, each of which (under Illinois State law) operates from a single building and has no branches. This illustrates in extreme form the pattern of 'unit banking', which is sometimes thought (incorrectly) to be typical of the whole of the United States.

An arrangement similar in some ways to branch banking may, however, be achieved by the 'bank chain' and the 'bank group'. In the first case, a family (say) may hold a controlling share interest (Chapter 7) in two or more commercial banks. In the second, the formation of a holding company (Chapter 7) enables a number of banks to achieve a high measure of common ownership and control, though they remain independent in title. Bank holding companies, which are not permitted in all states, are in general subject to regulation by the Federal Reserve. Banks may also effectively acquire 'branches' by a direct merger with other banks, though this process again is controlled by state and federal law.

To the British student, a notable absentee from the American banking system is any direct transatlantic counterpart to the London discount house. The London money market is largely a market in very short-term loans by the joint-stock banks to the discount houses, and in bill sales by the discount houses to the banks. It thus forms an adjunct to the liquidity position of the banks, enabling them to achieve an appropriate liquidity pattern. By contrast, the emphasis in the New York money market lies on dealings with all comers: commercial banks, other financial institutions (e.g. insurance companies), and industrial and commercial enterprises seeking to acquire, or liquidate, short-term investments. The items traded comprise U.S. Treasury bills, promissory notes, bankers' acceptances, federal funds and time certificates of deposit—all of which are explained in subsequent pages. The dealers who make a regular market in these financial assets comprise about 20 bank and non-bank security dealers, centred on New York but trading (often through representatives) throughout the United States. Unlike the London discount houses, they do not rely heavily on bank finance, nor do they have the same interest in maintaining large holdings of Treasury bills.

The staple short term security of the New York money market is the Treasury bill. This is an instrument of federal, not of state finance, as most state borrowing is on a long-term basis. The American Treasury bill is essentially the same as the British version, and fulfils the same role in federal short-term finance. The U.S. bill, however, is available for 6 and 12 months, as well as the 91 days of the British bill. The tender is held weekly on a Monday (except for 365 day bills, which are auctioned monthly) for payment on a Thursday. In contrast to the British system, anyone can tender directly, though in practice most tenders are submitted through banks. Bills are widely held by companies and even private individuals as short-term investments, in contrast to the U.K. where bills are held predominantly in the narrow circle of joint stock banks, discount houses and overseas central banks. Perhaps the appeal of U.S. bills to small investors is that the smallest U.S. denomination is $1,000 (£416) in contrast to the smallest British unit of £5,000.

Corresponding rather to the bill of exchange in the London discount market are, in the New York money market, the promissory note and the banker's acceptance. The former, as its name suggests, is simply a written promise to pay the holder a given sum (say) three or six months hence. This 'commercial paper' is put out by large business firms and, especially, in a continuous flow by finance companies as a method of raising funds. Bankers' acceptances are bills of exchange accepted by bankers, similar to the 'bank bill' in the London discount market.

2. *Commercial Banking in the U.S.A.*

Table 6.1 sets out the principal items in a composite balance sheet for all U.S. commercial banks at end-1968.

1 and 2. Demand deposits correspond to 'balances on current account' in the composite balance sheet of the London clearing banks (Table 2.1). They likewise carry no interest, while most banks levy a service charge for operating the account. However, a number of smaller banks (not members of the Federal Reserve System) follow an alternative practice of deducting a small sum (typically $\frac{1}{10}$ of 1 per cent) from the face value when meeting a cheque. This practice explains their title of 'nonpar' banks.

The significance of the separate entry for the U.S. Government is discussed in Section 3.

3. Under the general heading of 'time deposits', the American banks offer four major alternatives to the demand deposit. The closest parallel to the English deposit account is the American savings deposit account, operated for private persons and non-profit-making organizations. The account holder has a passbook, and while 30 days' written notice of withdrawal is formally required, in practice balances may be withdrawn on demand. In early 1969, these accounts formed about 51 per cent of all time deposits held with insured commercial banks by individuals, partnerships and corporations (I.P.C.).

Since 1961, the larger business corporation has had available the negotiable (time) certificate of deposit, offered by the large banks active in the money market—typically in $1 million units—as a counter-attraction to the U.S. Treasury bill. The depositor receives an interest-bearing certificate with a maturity between (in general) three and twelve months, but easily sold beforehand in the New York money market. These certificates are also issued by the smaller banks, and

TABLE 6.1

All U.S. commercial banks
31st December, 1968

	$000 million
Selected Liabilities	
1. Demand Deposits (*less* cheques etc., in collection)	167
2. Demand Deposits (U.S. Government)	5
3. Time Deposits	204
4. Balances with domestic banks	19
5. Borrowings	9
Selected Assets	
6. Currency and coin	7
7. Deposits at Federal Reserve Banks	21
8. Balances with domestic banks	19
9. Investments:	
(a) U.S. Government Securities	64
(b) Other	72
10. Loans	260

Note: Entries 1 and 3 are exclusive of deposits amont U.S. commercial banks.

Source: Federal Reserve Bulletin, May, 1969.

latterly have become popular with the general public in units as low as $25. In early 1969, negotiable certificates of deposit issued in larger denominations mainly to businesses represented about 8 per cent of insured commercial banks' time deposits (I.P.C.).

Third, the banks issue interest bearing non-negotiable savings certificates, savings bonds and time certificates. Typically, these entitle the holder to principal and accrued interest on a specific maturity date, and cannot normally be redeemed without appropriate notice.

A fourth category of account is the time deposit (open account). In general, this is individually designed for the client's needs, the terms being set out in a written contract.

In the light of the discussion of earlier chapters, it is interesting to record that time deposits with the commercial banks are excluded from official U.S. calculations of the money supply. Not all American economists follow this practice.

4 and 8. The size of these balances serves to illustrate the importance of 'correspondent relationships' in U.S. banking. Thus to facilitate access to the foreign exchange market, the securities market and the money market in New York, most major banks outside that city maintain an account with a New York bank. Banks in other important financial centres (e.g. Chicago) will also have correspondent relationships throughout the country. Further, small banks which are not members of the Federal Reserve System will often hold an account with a larger bank to facilitate cheque clearing. Under state laws, these balances would generally count as part of the cash reserves required by the supervising state authorities.

5, 6 and 7. Borrowing from the Federal Reserve Banks (included in 5) and required federal cash reserves for member banks (included in 6 and 7) are both considered in Section 3.

9. Investments: (a) U.S. Government securities are holdings of federal bonds, notes and bills. Treasury 'notes' are issued with a life from one to five years, and 'bonds' with an initial maturity over five years. For our purposes, both may be described as 'bonds'. The maturity pattern of the bond portfolio is reasonably close to that of the London clearing banks, the great majority being for ten years or under.

After the emphasis on Treasury bills in the British system, it may come as a surprise to the reader to find them included with bonds in Table 6.1. In a similar fashion, loans at call (to banks, bond brokers, etc.) are included with the less liquid loan in item 10. However, unlike the London clearing banks, American member banks are not expected to follow a minimum liquid assets ratio—though cash ratio requirements are outstandingly important (Section 3). In general, they hold fewer bills relative to deposits than do the clearing banks, though the liquidity pattern varies considerably from bank to bank.

(b) 'Other securities' mainly comprise holdings of state and local government securities.

10. 'Loans' are (largely) the counterpart of the British 'advances', though the usual technique of lending is against the borrower's signature on a promissory note. Most often the note provides for repayment of the whole sum at a specified future date, but payment on demand may be undertaken (e.g.) by security dealers, or payment by regular instalments may be required (e.g.) for consumer or home mortgage loans (below).

While the traditional American preference, as in England, is for the short-term business loan, the American banks show a notably greater willingness to lend explicitly on a long-term basis. An outstanding feature is the use of the 'term loan'. Here a number of banks will group together (except for small sums) to provide a loan up to ten years or so in duration, repayable in regular instalments. Typically, these loans are used to finance building construction or machinery purchase by corporations too small for a share issue, or by enterprises which wish to anticipate the proportion of future profits earmarked for capital finance (Chapter 7). In this country, comparable facilities seem limited to farmers and small businesses, though the clearing banks are important lenders at medium- and long-term for export finance, and offer term loans for the purchase of U.K. ships and machine tools (Chapter 2). American banks are also significant lenders on a long-term basis for house purchase, a category of business in which the clearing banks seem more or less reluctant to engage (page 101).

In contrast to the U.K., commercial banks in the U.S.A. play an important part in the direct provision of instalment credit for consumer durables. In late 1968, loans for this purpose represented about 11 per cent of total loan assets for the 350 or so largest banks (which hold about three-fifths of all U.S. commercial bank deposits). It must be remembered, however, that the London clearing banks have made important innovations in the provision of consumer credit in recent years (Chapter 2), though they do not engage in hire-purchase finance as such.

Like their English counterparts, American banks provide a variety of services not reflected in these balance sheet entries. Of interest are their assistance in debt collection, their provision of information about credit-worthiness, and their management of pension funds for business corporations.

The composite balance sheet of Table 2.1 serves as an accurate guide to the activities of all the London clearing banks, since the proportions in which they hold their various assets do not differ widely from bank to bank. For the United States, by contrast, the composite balance sheet of Table 6.1 is far less useful, because the great variation in the banks' size and location entails a wide variation in their asset structure. While the correspondent system encourages quite small banks to buy money market assets or participate in a pool for a term loan, balance sheets nonetheless tend to reflect the predominant activities of the area in which the bank is located. Thus a small bank in a Mid-West town would be substantially involved in farm loans and mortgages, while a New York bank could be heavily committed in money market assets and industrial loans.

The 'local colouring' thus imparted to the asset structure has in times of economic depression (Chapter 12) been a source of weakness in the American banking system. A recession in the leading industry of the area could spell heavy losses for local banks. The smallness of many

American banks has served, more especially in the past, to increase their vulnerability. Their resources would be inadequate to enable them to take losses in their stride, or to withstand a panic 'run' by (small) depositors eager to get their deposits back in currency.

Both factors contributed to the failure, during the depression years 1930–3, of nearly 9,000 banks (out of about 25,000) in the U.S.A. The establishment of F.D.I.C. in the mid-1930s followed as a direct consequence. Its duties are supervisory (Section 3) as well as the provision of deposit insurance, though the limit of $10,000 (Section 1) means that the insurance scheme has little *direct* value to the big corporation account holder. Its existence, however, is reassuring to the small private depositor, and so makes a 'bank run' less likely.

It is interesting to record that, during the same period 1930–3, not a single U.K. bank was obliged to suspend payments. This may in part be attributable to the branch banking system operating in this country. The number of branches might of itself serve to reassure a bank's depositors, while losses in depressed regions might be balanced by profits in more prosperous areas.

3. *Central Banking in the U.S.A.*

Like the Bank of England in this country, the Federal Reserve System in the U.S.A. exercises the primary central bank responsibilities of seeking to regulate the money supply and the cost and availability of finance. In detail and techniques, however, and in relationships with their respective Treasuries, there are some substantial differences between the British and American central banks. The Federal Reserve System also undertakes some routine banking 'chores' which, while of great administrative convenience, are really incidental to its central banking.

The Federal Reserve Banks play a more active part in cheque clearing than does the Bank of England in this country. Suppose Smith draws a cheque on his bank in Oklahoma (Ok.) and sends it to Brown in Portland (Oregon); we assume that both Smith and Brown have accounts with member banks. Brown's bank in Portland will credit his account, then send the cheque to its Reserve Bank, the Federal Reserve Bank of San Francisco, where its account is credited. The latter airmails the cheque to the Federal Reserve Bank of Kansas City, which debits the account which the Oklahoma bank maintains with it; the latter, in turn, debits Smith's account. Finally the F.R.B. of Kansas City settles with the F.R.B. of San Francisco through an adjustment in the accounts all the Reserve Banks keep for this purpose in the Interdistrict Settlement Fund, operated by the Board of Governors in Washington.

The balances which member banks hold in account with their respective Reserve Banks thus serve as a basis for settlement on cheque clearing, as well as forming part of their required cash reserve (below). Some non-member banks maintain accounts at a Federal Reserve Bank for clearing purposes, but most of them effect settlements through their 'correspondent' relationships. Nonetheless, the facilities the System offers for cheque clearing are available to member and non-member banks alike, with the exception of the nonpar banks.

A routine but very convenient service operated by the Federal Reserve system is the telegraphic transfer of funds: this has no counterpart at the Bank of England. Thus a Birmingham (Alabama) man wishing to pay a Detroit (Michigan) man, say $1,000, may effect the payment in minutes through a series of telegraphic instructions from his bank to the Federal Reserve Bank of Atlanta to the Federal Reserve Bank of Chicago and thence to the creditor's bank in Detroit. The appropriate settlements are made as with a cheque clearing, with a final Reserve Bank adjustment in the books of the Interdistrict Settlement Fund.

For denominations of $5 and above, the currency of the U.S.A. is made up of the notes of the Federal Reserve Banks. Notes below this value, and the coinage, are the responsibility of the U.S. Treasury, though since 1963 the Reserve Banks have also been authorized to issue $1 and $2 notes. Today, almost 90 per cent of U.S. currency in circulation consists of Federal Reserve notes. Until recently, the Reserve Banks' note issue was still linked with gold, in that by Act of Congress their issue of notes could not exceed 4 times their holding of gold certificates. This rule—a survival from days when Reserve Bank notes were freely convertible—was considered by the Board of Governors to serve no useful purpose, while its existence perhaps tended to throw a little doubt on the ability of the U.S. authorities to use their gold freely for its primary purpose, as an international monetary asset (Chapter 19). The gold-reserve requirement was, accordingly, eliminated in early 1968.

The bulk of their gold certificates was acquired by the Reserve Banks in 1934, in return for their holdings of gold which they surrendered to the U.S. Treasury. Gold certificates, however, are still actively added to or 'retired', in consequence of U.S. Treasury gold dealings. Under United States law, the Treasury stands ready to buy or sell gold at a fixed price of $35 per ounce. In practice, purchases by U.S. residents are restricted to industrial and comparable users, while the Treasury does not normally deal with individuals or non-official bodies overseas. Its principal dealings, accordingly, take place with the central banks of other countries and international monetary institutions. While this has significance mainly in international finance (Chapter 19), it also has implications for the domestic U.S. money supply. Suppose the Federal Reserve, acting as the agent of the Treasury, buys gold from an overseas central bank. The Treasury puts the gold in Fort Knox, and hands over a corresponding value of gold certificates to the Federal Reserve. The latter increases its assets with these certificates, but at the same time increases its liabilities correspondingly by crediting the account of the overseas central bank with the value of the gold it has bought from it. When, accordingly, the overseas bank draws on its new balance, the cheques will come into the hands of the American commercial banks, thus increasing their cash reserves at the Reserve Banks.

Like the Bank of England, the Federal Reserve System exercises controls over the volume and cost of bank credit, though there may be significant differences in technique. Additionally, the Federal Reserve Banks examine and supervise the banking practices of the member banks, to ensure conformity with federal requirements. This has no parallel in English central banking. Thus a Federal Reserve Bank has it within its power to remove a member bank director for 'unsound banking practices'. The Reserve Banks are not alone in their supervisory powers. Jurisdiction is exercised over all national banks by the U.S. Comptroller of Currency, over all insured banks by F.D.I.C., and over state banks by state banking commissioners. To prevent supervision turning into inquisition, banks are normally inspected each year by only one agency, which circulates its report to the others.

An instrument of monetary control without parallel in the English system is the power of the Board of Governors to establish the maximum interest rates which member banks may pay on time and savings deposits. 'Regulation Q' was first introduced in 1933; by curbing the interest costs of the banks, it was hoped to limit any pressure upon them to acquire assets which were risky but carried possibilities of big returns. On their last review in April, 1968, maximum rates of 4 per cent were established on savings deposits, and from 4 to 6¼ per cent for the various other categories of time deposits. These are also the maxima applied by F.D.I.C. to non-member insured banks. They do not currently apply to accounts held by foreign governments and central banks.

Second, under Regulation U, the Board of Governors fixes the 'margin requirements' on loans made to finance security purchases or holdings. Under the minimum margin requirement (fixed in June, 1968) of 80 per cent, a borrower may obtain no more than $200 from a bank to finance the purchase of $1,000 worth of stocks (i.e. company shares): he has to find the margin of $800 himself. By varying margin requirements, the Board of Governors can influence the demand for securities through the availability of bank finance, and so help moderate price fluctuations in security dealings (Chapter 7). This rule was introduced in 1934, in consequence of the notorious rise and collapse of share prices in the late 1920s.

Other forms of 'selective' credit control have been operated in the past, for example, over finance for house construction and hire-purchase during the Korean War, 1950–3. These controls were likewise embodied in Regulations, and it is often considered that the number of banks would make 'informal control by request' less practicable than in the U.K. Nonetheless, the banks co-operated fully in the Voluntary Foreign Credit Restraint programme inaugurated by the U.S. President in 1965. Under this programme, the banks were requested to limit their expansion of foreign lending and investment within 'guidelines' periodically defined by the Board of Governors. Subsequently, in 1968, the Board was given standby authority to make its requirements compulsory, though this measure was introduced in the context of generally increased restraint on U.S. investment overseas.

The third control device constitutes a weapon of great power. Under Regulation D, the Board of Governors determines the minimum ratio of cash to total deposits which member banks are required to observe. A higher cash ratio is imposed in respect of demand deposits than for time deposits, while the reserve requirement on demand deposits is higher for banks in leading cities ('reserve city banks') than for others ('country banks'). 'Cash' is defined, for these purposes, as balances in account with Federal Reserve Banks plus cash in vaults: balances with other banks are excluded. The ratios (as at 30th April, 1969) are: demand deposits under $5 million—reserve city banks 17 per cent, country banks 12½ per cent; demand deposits over $5 million, respectively 17½ and 13 per cent; savings deposits—both categories, 3 per cent; time deposits up to $5 million—both categories, 3 per cent; time deposits over $5 million—both categories, 6 per cent.

Suppose that, at a given time, the cash holdings of the member banks (considered as a whole) were exactly in line with these requirements. In this case, a reduction in the minimum ratios would encourage credit expansion, and an increase would entail some contraction. Further, if cash reserves were above the stipulated minimum, a rise in requirements would inhibit potential expansion, and vice versa. Requirements are not, however, varied to achieve week to week adjustments, for which the System relies on open market operations (below). Variations are used, rather, to impart a distinct change of emphasis to monetary policy.

The counterparts of Bank Rate in this country are the discount rates charged by the various Reserve Banks on their loans to member banks. These rates are 'established' from time to time[1] by each Reserve Bank,

[1] Under proposals published in 1968, access to the Reserve Banks would be broadened by giving each member bank a basic borrowing facility in-

E

but 'reviewed and determined' by the Board of Governors. The Reserve Banks are normally prepared to lend to member banks to help them meet their reserve requirements, but only on a temporary basis.[1] To avoid borrowing from its Reserve Bank, a commercial bank may, of course, always sell off some of its assets, for example Treasury bills. It follows that a rise in discount rates, which makes loans from Reserve Banks less attractive, will encourage Treasury bill sales and, by depressing their prices, raise market interest rates.

Day-to-day variations in deposit levels and so reserve requirements are often met by dealings in the 'federal funds' market. Thus a bank with a surplus balance in account with its Reserve Bank will frequently lend it, mostly on a one-day basis, to another bank with a prospective deficit. Balances can be switched immediately by telephone or cable, and interest rates vary hourly with the supply of and demand for 'funds'. Small banks make up local markets, while the bigger banks participate in a national market centring especially on New York. The London inter-bank market (Chapter 3) functions in a basically similar fashion, though here of course it is the merchant and overseas banks which deal among themselves in surplus balances with the clearing banks.

Finally, control over the member banks is exercised through open market operations, conducted in the U.S.A. by the Federal Open Market Committee. This consists of the seven members of the Board of Governors, the President of the Reserve Bank of New York and four other representatives from the other eleven Reserve Banks. Dealing decisions are made by F.O.M.C., and carried out on its behalf by the Reserve Bank of New York, all the Reserve Banks participating according to their relative financial strength.

We have seen that, in dealing in Treasury bills, the Bank of England is typically concerned with stabilizing their prices (i.e. Treasury bill discount rates) at a level it considers appropriate in the context of Government monetary policy (Chapter 20). In consequence, cash and bills are virtually interchangeable in the U.K. banking system. The Federal Reserve followed a broadly comparable policy in the U.S.A. between 1942 and 1951, though here their objective was to prevent both bill and bond prices falling below (for most of the period) the pre-war level, by buying without limit in the market as the pressure of private sales might require. Since 1951, however, the prime objective of the Federal Reserve authorities' open market operations has been to

---

versely proportionate to its share capital (hence beneficial especially to small banks), as well as more explicit seasonal borrowing privileges. These plans are thought (1969) almost certain to be adopted. Greater frequency in discount rate changes was also suggested.

[1] Ibid.

influence the cash reserves of the member banks, which is achieved mainly (and, between 1953 and 1961, almost exclusively) by dealing in Treasury bills. Thus a sale of Treasury bills will lead to a corresponding reduction in member bank balances at Reserve Banks, as the purchasers hand over cheques drawn on their commercial banks (compare Chapter 4). This loss of cash reserves must, in turn, exercise a strong contractive influence upon bank credit.

In its exercise of these various regulatory powers, the Federal Reserve System is not responsible to the U.S. Treasury or Administration, though it is of course subject to Congressional constraint. By contrast, the Bank of England is essentially the agent of the Government's monetary policy; though the Bank's advice and opinions carry a unique weight, the formulation of this policy is the ultimate responsibility of the Government. The Federal Reserve's relationships with the administration are complex and controversial. While in general their policies are in harmony, conflict may sometimes arise, more particularly in periods of inflation. Thus it was contrary to the wishes of the Administration that the Federal Reserve abandoned, in 1951, its policy of supporting Government security prices by open market dealings (above). Subsequently, however, both 'sides' jointly published a statement of accord, announcing their agreement in policy matters arising from Federal debt management.

On an administrative level, the Federal Reserve Banks discharge a variety of routine financial services for the U.S. Treasury. Thus they attend to the issue and redemption of bills and bonds on its behalf, pay bond holders their interest, and act as Treasury agent in gold and foreign exchange dealings. The U.S. Treasury also holds accounts with the Reserve Banks, though in other respects its arrangements for payments and receipts are in sharp contrast with the British system.

It was explained in Chapter 4 that the British Government keeps its two principal accounts (the Exchequer account and National Loans Fund) with the Bank of England: all tax and loan proceeds are promptly paid into these accounts, and from them in turn all payments are financed. Tax payments, etc., thus reduce the balances of the clearing banks in account with the Bank of England, while Government spending increases them. However, by dealing in Treasury bills in the money market, the Bank is able to offset these disturbances as it wishes.

While F.O.M.C. may engage in similar smoothing operations, the banking arrangements of the U.S. Treasury serve in themselves to minimize disturbance to member banks' balances with the Reserve Banks. The Federal Government holds 'tax and loan accounts' with some 10,000 commercial banks (item 2 in Table 6.1), and receipts from taxes and security issues are left in these accounts until required for the finance of expenditure, when they are transferred to accounts at the

Reserve Banks. In this way, payments to the U.S. Government cannot lead to a reduction in member banks' balances at the Reserve Banks until the sum is actually needed to finance Government spending. Further, the cash loss occasioned by such payments can be more or less offset by concurrent Government expenditure. Thus, by synchronizing as far as possible its expenditure with its receipts from the commercial banks, the Treasury will in general attempt to limit disturbances to the banks' cash reserves. On the other hand, were F.O.M.C. seeking to increase or diminish these reserves by open market operations, then the Treasury would provide support by the appropriate re-timing of its receipts and (where possible) payments.

(II) Nigeria

This short account of the Nigerian banking system is intended to illustrate some of the monetary problems of a developing country. The Nigerian system has made rapid if uneven progress since the country gained independence in 1960, and presents some interesting comparisons and contrasts with banking in Britain and the U.S.A.

Fourteen commercial banks are currently active in Nigeria, of which five are 'expatriate' banks, with their head offices overseas. A further four, while possessing head offices in Nigeria, are owned at least in part by foreign banks, so that of the total only five may be classified as purely 'indigenous' banks, i.e. exclusively Nigerian in operation and control. Two expatriate banks, one of the banks under foreign control and one indigenous bank between them conduct about 90 per cent of commercial banking business in Nigeria. Offering a rather more specialized financial service is the Nigerian Industrial Development Bank, formed in 1964 particularly to provide development finance for industrial and mining enterprises. Two finance houses also undertake bill business and accept money at call (below).

The deposit facilities offered their customers by the Nigerian banks are reminiscent more of American than English banking practice. Three types of account are available—demand, savings and time. Demand deposits, of course, are 'cheque-able', carry no interest, and entail bank charges for their operation. Savings deposits are designed particularly for the small savings of private people: withdrawals are technically liable to three days' notice, though this may in practice be waived. Time deposits are intended for the larger sums deposited by firms and government institutions. Withdrawal terms are stricter, while a slightly higher rate may be paid for sums deposited beyond a twelve-month period.

Total bank deposits have grown very considerably over the past decade, from about £N40 million in 1954 to a high of £N164 million in early 1967. While balances on demand have increased in absolute terms, the ratio of demand deposits to savings and time deposits has declined from about 4/3 in 1960 to roughly 5/6 in early 1968. The most popular account with the general public is the savings account. Demand accounts are operated mainly by firms, governmental institutions, the state governments and the Federal Government itself in areas lacking a Central Bank branch. Private persons, other than the rich, use cheques for making payments far less than in Britain or the United States. Their reluctance may be partly explained by the greater formality involved in opening a demand account, by the attraction of interest on savings accounts, and by the inadequate number of bank branches. While the number of branches increased from 86 in 1954 to 298 in operation at the end of 1968, banking facilities are not yet available in a large part of the country.

Official statistics of the money supply show that, in early 1968, cheque-able balances represented rather more than 40 per cent of the total, the remainder comprising currency and coin. This ratio, of course, contrasts with the corresponding proportions in the U.K. and U.S.A. An increased willingness among the general public to use cheque-able balances as money would represent an increase in the credit-creating powers of the commercial banks. We saw in Chapter 4 that a rise in the liquid assets base of a commercial banking system enables an expansion of credit, the size of which is limited by (among other things) the leakage of cash the process of expansion engenders. This suggests that the value of the banking multiplier would be raised if the public developed a taste for bank liabilities rather than currency to use as money.

The Central Bank of Nigeria came into operation in 1959 under legislation passed in 1958 (subsequently amended in 1962 and 1967). As in the U.K. and (largely) the U.S.A., the Central Bank is responsible for the currency issue. The 1958 Banking Act required the Bank, during the first five years of its operations, to keep 'external reserves' equal to (at least) 60 per cent of its currency in circulation plus 35 per cent of its other demand liabilities. These reserves were held initially entirely in the form of gold and sterling assets though, since 1962, other foreign currencies have also been permitted.

Historically, this requirement reflects the practice of the West African Currency Board, which before the formation of the Central Bank was responsible for the issue of currency in Nigeria and other West African countries. The W.A.C.B. issued its notes in direct correspondence to its holding of sterling assets. Currently, the prime function of these reserves is to enable the Nigerian authorities finance any deficit in the balance of payments, while maintaining the Nigerian rate of exchange at the parity agreed with the International Monetary Fund. In this respect, they have a role comparable with the British Exchange Equalization Account (Chapter 17). However, the statutory limitation these external reserves place on the size of the note issue (and of Central Bank lending) has no parallel in the English system, where the note issue is overwhelmingly fiduciary.

In the 1960s, an increasing fiduciary element (i.e. Government securities) has in fact been introduced into the 'backing', and the required foreign-assets reserve ratio successively reduced in 1962 and 1967. The requirement of the 1958 Banking Act that the Central Bank should buy or sell, on demand, Nigerian pounds for sterling (and, since 1962, gold and other currencies at its discretion) is of practical significance only in international finance. However, the 'backing element' of a currency may at times enhance its domestic acceptability (Chapter 1). It is accordingly interesting to read the following passage in the Central Bank's Annual Report for 1960, a time when the Bank had just substituted Nigerian currency for W.A.C.B. currency: 'The introduction of a fiduciary element into the currency backing, under which the Bank would hold domestic securities in place of overseas assets, must be gradual and conducted in such a way as not to *cast any doubt on the strength of the currency*' (Author's italics).

The growth of the British financial system during the eighteenth and nineteenth centuries occurred spontaneously in a context of general economic expansion, i.e. it was not purposefully engineered as an act of official policy. The development of each of the institutions—the Bank of England, the commercial banks, the merchant banks, the discount houses, the London Stock Exchange—reacted upon and helped form the growth of the others slowly, and sometimes with difficulty, over a period of many years. By contrast, the Central Bank of Nigeria came to its tasks in 1959 with a clear conception of its role as a central bank but only a rudimentary financial system in which to exercise it. There was no Stock Exchange, no bankers' clearing house, no money market, and no (significant) instruments of government finance, such as bonds or Treasury bills. It is understandable, accordingly, that the early energies of the authorities were devoted to encouraging the growth of financial institutions which, it was hoped, would in turn contribute to the country's general economic development.

The first Nigerian clearing house was established in the Central Bank's premises in Lagos in 1961, with a set of rules drafted by a committee of bankers who form the Lagos Clearing House Company. It is the Central Bank's policy to promote further clearing arrangements when branches are opened, as for instance, at Kano in 1963, at Port Harcourt in 1964, at Ibadan in 1965, at Enugu in 1966 and at Benin in 1967.

The Central Bank acts as agent for the Federal Government in its long-term borrowing, issuing stocks on its behalf, acting as registrar, and underwriting the issue. This latter duty means that, when an issue is not fully subscribed by the public, the Central Bank takes up the balance and gradually disposes of it as opportunity presents. The Bank has, in fact, taken the initiative in encouraging security dealings. When, in May 1959, it undertook the issue of Federation of Nigeria First Development Loan Stock, the Bank at the same time made arrangements which would serve to foster the growth of a securities market. The banks agreed to record the names of potential buyers and sellers, and pass them on to a central register established at the Bank. The Bank was then able to effect suitable introductions, and contribute its own suggestions on appropriate prices.

The Bank's efforts were rewarded in June, 1961, with the opening of the Lagos Stock Exchange: security dealings have since taken place through the Exchange, not through the Bank. Further development of a market in securities has encountered some difficulty, partly because the Nigerian public has not yet grown accustomed to investment in stocks and shares. The requirements of the Nigerian National Development Plan, 1962–8, on the other hand, have necessitated large bond issues, averaging about £N16 million per year up to 1968. Correspondingly, the Central Bank has been obliged to take up a growing proportion— in the last few years about 90 per cent—of new stock on the occasion of issue. It appears that much (in value terms) of Stock Exchange transactions represent the subsequent sale of stock by the Central Bank to local governments and (especially) savings institutions.

Starting in April, 1960, the Central Bank (as the Federal Government's agent) has made a regular (since 1963, weekly) issue of 91 day Treasury bills. The bills are issued at a fixed rate of interest determined by the Central Bank, the latter taking up those—between 1963 and 1967 roughly one half—not elsewhere subscribed. The principal demand (excluding the proportion absorbed by the Central Bank) comes from commercial banks, statutory boards, and savings institutions (including pension funds and insurance companies). The growth of the latter's subscriptions may partly reflect official encouragement to 'repatriate' overseas assets. The main volume of subsequent dealing in Treasury bills appears to be between the banks and the Central Bank, though the latter would like to see inter-bank dealing develop.

The facilities open to the banks for lending money at call are also partly the creation of the Central Bank. Under arrangements made in July, 1962, any funds above a certain minimum balance kept by the banks at the Central Bank may be lent to a 'call money fund' in multiples of £N5,000. These loans are invested in Treasury bills which the Central Bank provides from its own portfolio, and carry interest at rates fixed variously between 1 and 2 per cent below the Treasury bill rate. In the London money market, by contrast, interest rates on call loans more directly reflect the availability of funds. Call facilities are also provided by two finance houses and ten commercial banks, on a scale which has expanded considerably since their inception in the early 1960s.

The appearance of Nigerian Government bonds and Treasury bills has given the banks an opportunity of acquiring investments within Nigeria which they had not enjoyed in the past. Interestingly, the bulk of their investments is in Treasury bills: indeed, their holdings of Government Development Stocks have seldom risen above virtually nominal levels. However, the principal outlet for bank credit continues to be the private sector, with a marked emphasis on the finance of commerce, particularly the export of agricultural produce. Agricultural credit requirements are heaviest from about November to February, when two leading export crops of cocoa and groundnuts are harvested, slackening off somewhat during the rest of the year. The banks meet this seasonal pressure by running down their Treasury bill holdings (so that the Central Bank takes up more of the bill issue) and using their facilities for rediscounting Treasury and commercial bills at the Bank (below).

The bill of exchange plays an important role in Nigerian banking and, since 1962, the inland bill has been the instrument of finance for a number of the Marketing Boards. Under arrangements made between the Boards, the Central Bank and a consortium of commercial banks and finance houses, a Board will draw a 90-day bill on the Nigerian Produce Marketing Company, Ltd, and discount it with one of the consortium. This enables the Board to pay the small farmers who have produced the crops, pending their sale in the world markets through the central agency of the Produce Marketing Company. This 'produce paper' is eligible for rediscount with the Central Bank, and to this extent the Central Bank may provide indirect finance for the Boards. The Marketing Boards have thus been freed from their former dependence for seasonal finance on London banks, a development in line with official emphasis on harnessing domestic as opposed to overseas financial resources.

In the practice of banking, some indigenous banks have at times been criticized for their failure to achieve the high standards set by their expatriate rivals. Thus some may make inadequate provision for bad debts, or may readjust their asset structure specifically for the occasions when the balance sheet is made up ('window dressing'), in order to show greater liquidity than is normally the case. The Government has made several legislative attempts to raise standards, with Acts in 1952, 1958 and 1962. Under the 1958 Banking Act (as amended in 1962) all commercial banks in Nigeria must be licensed and must have a minimum capital of £N250,000. All banks, further, are open to inspection, and must submit regular statements of their financial position to the Central Bank. Additionally, the Central Bank maintains close contact with the banks through the meetings of the Bankers' Committee, held regularly to consider matters of general banking interest.

The authorities are, understandably, eager to foster the growth of the indigenous banks. Nigerian businessmen, also, claim that they are able to get loans more easily from the indigenous than the foreign banks, though this may be because the former do not insist as rigorously as the foreign banks on both good security and good prospects of repayment. There has, however, been a high rate of failure among the indigenous banks and, in the early 1960s, the two largest indigenous banks were taken over by, respectively, the (then) Eastern and Western Nigerian Regional Governments.

The 1958 Banking Act also required the commercial banks to keep a minimum proportion of their assets in a liquid form. This provision was designed both to serve as a protection for depositors and to give the Central Bank an instrument of control over the banks. Under the amending Act of 1962, assets to be regarded as 'liquid' for this purpose are: cash in hand, balances at the Central Bank, net balances at other Nigerian banks, money lent at call to other Nigerian banks and Federal Government Treasury bills. Certain other assets might also be eligible to satisfy the liquidity requirement, at the discretion of the Central Bank. They are inland bills of exchange and promissory notes, net balances with banks in other approved countries, and money at call and bills payable in other approved countries.

The 1958 Act did not specify what proportion of their assets the banks were to keep in liquid form, but left the size of the liquidity ratio to the discretion of the Central Bank. It has in fact stood at 25 per cent, and might be difficult to increase in so far as some of the indigenous banks have had difficulty anyway in maintaining this level. A third instrument of control conferred by the 1962 Act was a requirement that the interest rate on bank advances should be linked to the minimum Central Bank Rediscount Rate. The Central Bank, further, had to 'approve' the interest rate structure of each licensed bank.

The relatively underdeveloped condition of the securities and money markets offers little scope for open market operations on the American pattern. Further, market dealings in Treasury bills by the Central Bank which involved only the banks would (other things being equal) leave their liquidity ratio unchanged, since both cash and Treasury bills are eligible liquid assets. On the other hand, bill sales to non-banks would reduce the banks' cash without, of course, occasioning a compensating increase in their own bill holdings.

The first positive monetary measures—to restrict credit—were in fact introduced towards the end of 1964, and restrictions were first tightened then slackened during 1966, with changing economic circumstances. In October, 1964, the Governor of the Central Bank wrote to the commercial banks asking them to restrict the rate of growth of advances in general, and in particular to curb finance for less essential imports, hire-purchase companies and personal borrowers. Second, the minimum Rediscount Rate was raised from 4 to 5 per cent, the commercial banks following with a half per cent rise in deposit and lending rates. Third, the proportion of 'overseas liquid assets' eligible for inclusion in the specified liquidity requirement was reduced from $7\frac{1}{2}$ to 3 per cent of total deposits. This eligibility was abolished altogether in April, 1966, which in turn prompted the banks to increase their investment in Nigerian Treasury bills.

Recent Changes in Nigerian Central Bank Powers, Marketing Board Finance Arrangements and Government Borrowing Instruments

1. In late 1968 the Central Bank added to its powers of credit control by acquiring authority to: (a) establish a cash ratio for the commercial banks; (b) vary the composition of the specified liquid asset holdings; (c) call for special deposits; (d) impose a ceiling on credit; (e) establish minimum ratios for each bank's loans to indigenous borrowers (compare p. 125).

2. Difficulties in the consortium arrangements for the finance of the Marketing Boards (p. 124) led the Central Bank in 1968 to assume direct and exclusive responsibility for the provision of funds to the boards. To make up for the consequent shortage of commercial paper (aggravated by a sluggish private-sector demand for credit in a war-controlled economy) the banks have greatly increased their holdings of Treasury bills. This in turn has reduced very sharply the proportion of Treasury bills held by the Central Bank (p. 123).

3. From end-1968 a greater variety of Government debt has become available with the introduction of the treasury certificate. The certificate—which possesses a life of one to two years and offers a yield higher than treasury bills—proved popular with the commercial banks.

Questions

1. Outline the differences between the banking system in the United Kingdom and that of any other country you know about.   A.E.B.
2. Compare and contrast the commercial banking system of the United Kingdom with that of any other country.   I.B.
3. Compare and contrast the banking system of the United Kingdom with that of the U.S.A.   I.B.
4. Compare and contrast the development, structure and operations of the Bank of England and the Federal Reserve System of the U.S.A.   I.B.
5. Write a brief account of the Federal Reserve System of the U.S.A.   I.B.
6. Write a brief account of the banking system of the U.S.A.   I.B.

Part two

PART TWO

7

The Finance of Business and the Securities Market

---

1. *The Capital Requirements of Business*

To carry on production of goods or services, a firm will need to use human resources (labour) and material resources. For some firms, material resources may include natural resources in their original condition as 'gifts of Nature', e.g. coal deposits or uncultivated forests, conveniently designated in economics by the omnibus term 'land'. However, except for extractive industries like mining and forestry, the material resources required will normally comprise stocks of raw materials and more durable items such as plant and machinery, the latter usefully distinguished as capital (producer, investment) goods. Both raw material stocks and capital goods represent 'goods which have been produced and are then employed to make more goods', which is the definition of capital used in economics.

This definition may, however, be taken more widely to include the money balances which, in an exchange economy, firms are obliged to hold in order to finance the process of production (Chapter 13). On this approach, money may be considered a capital good, 'produced' by the banking system and helping increase the yield from material resources through the greater division of labour its use makes possible (Chapter 1).

The firm itself would probably regard as its 'business capital' all the assets of which it was legally the owner (or would eventually be through hire-purchase!). This definition would exclude any equipment on short-term hire to the firm (e.g. bulldozers), but include the firm's property rights over e.g. natural resources under a lease for a term of years. Apart from the firm's physical capital and financial assets, 'business capital' would also include intangible assets such as 'goodwill'—the value of the firm's trading connections.

The accounting document of first importance in analysing business capital is the balance sheet. In its traditional form, the right-hand

129

side of the balance sheet sets out the categories of asset which the firm owns, while on the left hand side appear the sources of finance which, in total, enabled their acquisition. There is not, however, any simple link between the individual assets on the right-hand side and the individual 'sources of finance' on the left-hand side. These sides are reversed in the conventional United States presentation. Further, a vertical lay-out is today frequently adopted in both countries, as certain information of interest to company shareholders may be displayed more explicitly in this form.

The owner(s) of a business will themselves have put up some funds, a contribution described in the balance sheet as their 'capital'. In the

TABLE 7.1

Balance Sheet of Davies Electricals
31st December, 1968

Capital and Liabilities	£	Assets	£
1. Richard Davies, capital	10,000	FIXED ASSETS	
CURRENT LIABILITIES		4. Premises	5,000
2. A.B.C. Bank, Ltd	2,000	5. Plant	3,000
3. Account payable	500	6. Van	500
		CURRENT ASSETS	
		7. Work in Progress	1,000
		8. Raw Materials	500
		9. Debtors	1,500
		10. Cash	1,000
	12,500		12,500

conventional lay-out, the owners' capital appears above a list of liabilities in the left-hand column, and indeed the business could be regarded as 'indebted' to them for their contribution. On the other hand, it may be more illuminating to reserve the term 'liabilities' for the other sources which have helped finance the acquisition of the assets. This enables us to define the owners' capital as equal to 'assets minus liabilities', which is often referred to as the owners' 'equity' or 'net worth'.

The simplest sort of balance sheet is normally that of a business owned by just one man. Suppose that Richard Davies has set up in business producing small electrical gadgets, trading under the name of Davies Electricals. His firm's balance sheet for a given date might read, in essentials, as Table 7.1.

On the right-hand side of Table 7.1 are the assets which constitute the firm's business capital. Items 4, 5 and 6 are classified as fixed assets, items 7 to 10 as current assets. Fixed assets are defined as items which do not change hands in the course of the business, for instance, the machinery and equipment (item 5) which make the firm's product, or the premises (4) where the business is conducted. Current assets are turned over regularly in the course of business: cash, raw materials, work in progress and debts owed to the firm are in a constant process of circulation. What is a fixed asset in one business may, of course, be a current asset in another. Thus the van is a fixed asset in Davies' business, but a current asset in a motor dealer's.

The left-hand side of the balance sheet indicates the sources which financed the acquisition of the assets, items 4 to 10. First, Davies put up £10,000 himself, specified in the balance sheet as 'Richard Davies, capital'. Second, the A.B.C. Bank, Ltd, has lent Davies £2,000 by way of overdraft for the use of his firm. The business is, accordingly liable to A.B.C. Bank, Ltd. Third, the business has obtained £500 worth of raw materials on credit from a supplier, and has received but not yet paid their account (or bill). Here, then, is the third source of finance or capital. Liabilities such as these last two which fall due within a year are known as 'current liabilities'.

The finance which a firm obtains is often classified as short term, medium term or long term. Short-term finance denotes funds legally if not actually repayable in a matter of months, for example, a bill of exchange, a bank loan or credit provided by trade suppliers. In the second case, repayment of the overdraft is legally on demand, though in practice some months' notice would be given if the overdraft level had to be reduced. In the third case, payment of the account is required in a matter of weeks. The sources of short-term finance are to be found, with certain other items, under 'current liabilities' in the firm's balance sheet. Short-term finance is traditionally associated with the provision of current assets.

Long-term finance denotes, typically, funds put up by the owner(s), or borrowed on a long-term basis (say 20 years). These funds are traditionally associated with the acquisition of fixed assets which have a long life (items 4 and 5 in Table 5.1). They may, of course, also be used to finance the other items. Medium-term finance denotes, typically, funds obtained for a few years only, such as a hire-purchase finance loan. It may be used to finance a fixed asset with a relatively short life. A motor van would be an example, though from Table 7.1 it is seen that Davies has not in fact financed the purchase of his van in this way.

The balance sheet shows, for any given point of time, the value of the firm's assets and the sources which, in total, financed their acquisition. However, the proprietor will also be interested in the size of the profit (or loss) made by the business over a given period of time. This information is obtained from the trading account, the manufacturing account (where relevant) and the profit and loss account. These are, basically, records of the incomings and outgoings of the business over the period in question. The principal incoming is the revenue from the sale of the final product (or service). Against this are set the various out-goings, i.e. the expenses or costs of production, and any surplus is the profit of the business over the period for which the accounts are drawn up, say a year.

Some obvious costs of production are expenditure on the raw materials used up, on labour and on fuel and power consumed. The corresponding current assets go through a regular cycle of transformation, which explains the name often given them of 'circulating capital'. Thus cash is 'turned into' raw materials; the raw materials are worked up by labour in return for further cash (wages and salaries) with the aid of fuel and power (more cash for fuel bills). The finished commodity is then sold for a return that covers these and other expenditures, thus yielding a profit for the proprietor and financing the continuation of the production cycle.

A less obvious cost of production is the depreciation allowance made in respect of fixed assets. Thus when new machinery is purchased, it is necessary to make an estimate of its useful life. After so many years, either rising maintenance costs will make it more profitable to replace it with new plant, or the machinery will be markedly inefficient relative to the more up-to-date equipment subsequently installed by business rivals. In the first case, the machinery will have to be scrapped because of its deterioration; in the second, because of its obsolescence.

Suppose machinery costs £10,000 new, and is estimated to have a useful life of 10 years, at the end of which its scrap value is assessed at £1,000. Each year one of the costs to be set against revenue will be a depreciation allowance or charge. By the straight line method, the same annual charge will be made each year, of £(10,000 − 1,000) ÷ 10, or £900. By the reducing balance method, a constant percentage (calculable at 20 per cent) is deducted each year, so that the first year's depreciation would be $\frac{1}{5}$ × £10,000, or £2,000, the second year's would be $\frac{1}{5}$ × £(10,000 − 2,000), or £1,600, and so on. Of course, other fixed assets, as well as machinery, undergo depreciation. Thus a firm with a 40-year lease of its premises will make an appropriate annual depreciation charge to show that, each year, the lease is one year nearer expiry.

By making a charge for depreciation in the profit calculation, the firm takes account of the fact that, over the year, the fixed assets have lost a part of their reasonable expectation of life. To put it another way, the fixed assets have over the year yielded up a part of their value, which has become incorporated in the value of the products made during that year. The depreciation allowances also figure in the balance sheet, where fixed assets stand at cost *less* depreciation to date (this was not shown in Table 7.1 to avoid complication).

In making its depreciation allowances the firm is, in effect, choosing to regard a certain part of its revenue, which would otherwise be considered profit, as necessary instead to maintain its capital stock to offset the depreciation of its fixed assets. It follows that the writing down of the value of existing fixed assets in the balance sheet is exactly offset by an increase in the value of other assets. This increase may take any form the firm wishes, for example, an increase in cash, in raw material stocks, in new fixed assets or a reduction in creditors. It is, accordingly, wrong to imagine the firm setting aside sums of cash each year, to have enough funds to buy replacement machinery. While the firm will ultimately have to replace most fixed assets, this is a part of the general problem of 'capital budgeting', i.e. planning the finance of fixed asset acquisition, whether for replacement or expansion. In fact, funds corresponding to current depreciation allowances on existing plant may be used to finance the purchase of additional plant. The prime significance of the depreciation allowance is that, by representing an appropriate charge against revenue, the profits are not overstated by ignoring the deterioration or obsolescence of the firm's fixed assets.

2. *The Legal Framework of Business*

Whether or not a business has corporate status at law is critically important in its financial affairs, affecting, for example, its techniques of raising capital, the way in which it is taxed, and the liability of its proprietor(s) for the firm's debts. It is necessary, therefore, to see what corporate status means, and how it is acquired.

Consider the case of a man who establishes and runs his own business, like Davies in the previous section. He and his accountant will make a sharp distinction between his personal assets and liabilities and those of his business. Thus one might interpret the balance sheet (Table 7.1) as showing the business as 'liable' to its owner in respect of the capital he has put into it. This liability of his business Davies would consider his personal asset. However, at law the business has no identity of its own separate from that of Davies. When a sales contract is made, property bought or money borrowed in connection with the business, the transaction is made by Davies and the legal responsibility is his personally.

This legal identification of Davis with his business is well illustrated by the consequences of the firm's insolvency. Suppose that the greater part of the capital is lost through unwise trading, and the business becomes insolvent, i.e. unable to meet the creditors in full. Their remedy is to present a petition at the County Court for Davies' bankruptcy. The Court will investigate the affairs of the business, and may

order the sale not only of the business assets but of such of Davies'
personal effects as the law permits, e.g. his house and his car. The proceeds are used to pay off the creditors, in full or in part, in final settlement of their claims.

Suppose that (instead of this unhappy outcome!) Davies' business
prospers, and he takes on a partner. They will almost certainly have a
written partnership agreement, defining their respective capital contributions, profit shares, etc. The only legal limitation is that the number
of partners must not exceed twenty, though this limit does not apply to
partnerships of solicitors, accountants or Stock Exchange members.
Again no distinction is made at law between the partners and the
business they conduct, from which it follows that, should the business
become insolvent, all or both partners may be made bankrupt. However, it is possible, under the Limited Partnerships Act, 1907, to register
(with the Registrar of Companies) one or more partners with limited
liability: in the event of the partnership's insolvency, a limited partner
loses his capital in the business, but no more. At least one partner in
such an arrangement must be a general partner, i.e. has unlimited
liability and can be made bankrupt. Moreover, the running of the business is restricted to the general partner(s).

The proprietor or proprietors of a business may, if they so wish,
establish their business as a separate legal entity, with a 'personality' at
law quite distinct from themselves. This is done by incorporating the
business, i.e. making it a business corporation. Business corporations
are generally known as companies, though this latter term may also be
applied to unincorporated associations. If Davies and his partner formed
their business into an (incorporated) company, then the company would
exist as a legal person in its own right. It could enter contracts, own
property, be fined for not paying its taxes, etc. Davies and his former
partner would now be the members of the company, and (of course) the
company would have to act through human agency. However, though
both sold their interest, and ceased to be members, the existence of the
company would be unaffected.

Companies are today usually formed by registration under the
Companies Act, 1948, though incorporation may also be obtained by
Royal Charter or by Private Act of Parliament. Registration may be
made either as a limited or unlimited company, but the former is
almost universally the case, because of the benefits of limited liability
explained below. Under the Companies Act, 1948, the promoters
of a limited company (normally the proprietors of the business for
which incorporation is desired) submit to the Registrar of Companies,
among other documents, a Memorandum of Association and an
Articles of Association, along with a fee proportionate to the size of the
company's nominal capital. If these are in order and satisfy the require-

ments of the Act, the Registrar issues a Certificate of Incorporation, and the company thereupon comes into existence.

The Memorandum will state the name of the Company; its objects, to which the conduct of its business must subsequently be confined; and the national location of its registered office, thus determining its liability to English or Scottish law. The capital of the company is normally divided into shares, ownership of which denotes membership of the company. Shares have a nominal value (e.g. £1 shares, 10s. shares, and so on) determined by the company on issue. Once this full nominal value has been paid to the company by the shareholder, he cannot be called upon to make a further contribution, however large the company's debts may be. Should the company become insolvent, the shareholders cannot be made bankrupt, since they enjoy limited liability. As a warning to suppliers, therefore, companies must register, and use, the word 'limited' as the last word of their names.

The amount of the nominal or authorized capital will also be stated in the Memorandum, along with the number of shares into which it is divided, e.g. £10,000 capital divided into 10,000 £1 shares. This figure merely sets a ceiling to the company's share issue (though it can easily be increased subsequently). It does not mean that the company will ever necessarily issue shares to this extent. The promoters of the company may plan to issue shares with varying rights (as to dividends, voting powers, etc.) attached to them. These matters are defined in the Articles of Association, along with other details of the internal organization of the company as a company, e.g. the calling of meetings, and the powers and share qualifications of the directors. The directors run the business on behalf of their fellow shareholders. In a small company, of course, the few shareholders may all be directors.

A company need not require the full nominal value of the share to be paid when it is first issued. It follows that a company with a nominal or authorized share capital of, say, £10,000 may have an issued share capital of £5,000 and a paid-up share capital of £1,000. This means that the directors are able at any time to call up the balance of 16s. in the £ from the shareholders. When shares are fully paid up the company may convert them into stock, which to the holder has the advantage of being transferable in any units he pleases (e.g. £49 6s. 3d. worth), irrespective of the original share denomination.

The company may attach whatever names and rights it wishes to its shares, but in practice ordinary and preference shares generally have the following characteristics. A (e.g.) 5 per cent preference share entitles its holder to a dividend equal to 5 per cent of its paid-up value, before any dividends are paid to the ordinary shareholders. Should this dividend be passed one year, because the company made no profit, the holder of a *cumulative* preference share is entitled in later, more profitable years to all arrears before the ordinary shareholders receive a dividend. A preference share may also be preferential as to capital, in which case the preference shareholder ranks before the ordinary shareholder (but after the creditors) in the distribution of capital should the company be wound up or liquidated.

The ordinary share entitles the holder to whatever size dividend the directors choose to declare from the profits after paying the preference shareholders. This, of course, will depend both upon the size of the profits and upon the outlook of the directors, who will often want to retain part to finance future activities. Frequently only the ordinary shares carry voting rights, though the Articles may give the preference shareholders voting powers if their dividend remains unpaid for, e.g., more than six months. Ordinary and preference shares may be divided into classes with different rights, the Articles giving voting rights for example to Class A but not Class B ordinary shares, or entitling Class A preference shareholders to dividend preference over Class B preference shareholders.

A company may raise funds by borrowing, giving its creditors in return securities known as debentures. These acknowledge the debt of the company, and undertake, first, to pay interest at the agreed rate before any classes of shareholder receive a dividend; and second, to repay the capital on a given date (if the debenture is redeemable, as most are). In practice, most debentures are mortgage debentures, conferring a charge upon certain of the company's assets as security for the loan to the company. These assets may be more easily disposed of and replaced by the company if the charge is a floating charge (e.g. on the company's buildings), which crystallizes on the property currently owned when interest or capital payment is not met. Such default gives the debenture holders various rights, including the sale (in this case) of the company's buildings by a receiver they appoint for the purpose. It will be apparent that shareholders and debenture holders are quite different in legal status, the former being members of the company and the latter creditors. From the viewpoint of the investor, however, the debenture has some resemblance to the preference share. Further, a company may issue 'convertible debentures', constituting loans to the company for a few years with the option subsequently to take up shares on favourable terms.

A company may be formed either as a public or as a private company. A private company does not permit, in its Articles, the free transfer of its shares by members to non-members, nor does its Articles allow it to raise funds by inviting subscriptions from the public for its shares or debentures (Section 3). A public company is simply one which does not impose these restraints upon itself. Private companies are obliged to have no less than two and no more than fifty members; public companies have a minimum of seven, with no maximum. Every limited company, whether private or public, must submit to the Registrar of Companies an annual return and a copy of its annual accounts[1] showing information specified by the Companies Acts, 1948 and 1967. Banking companies are exempt from the need to disclose their full annual profits, and are thereby enabled to accumulate 'secret' reserves (section 3) which could be used to mask fluctuations in the market value of investments or occasional losses on loans. Full profit disclosure has, nonetheless, been promised by the London clearing and Scottish banks from 1970 onwards.

Corporate status may make it easier in various ways for a business to obtain fresh capital, as explained in Section 3. These financial reasons alone make it inevitable that the large concern which raises funds from the general public be organized as a company; the same reasons also make incorporation essential for the smaller but expanding business. Many companies, however, especially private companies, are simply small family businesses, and while financial considerations may be relevant, other reasons for incorporation probably predominate.

A prime benefit is that, as shareholders, the proprietors of a business incorporated with limited liability cannot be made bankrupt should it become insolvent. This limitation of their liability to their fully paid up share capital contrasts with the partnership, where the incompetence of one partner may lead to the bankruptcy of all. A sole trader may also enjoy the benefit of incorporation, getting (say) his wife to take up at least one share to satisfy the minimum membership requirement of a private company. Private companies cannot, of course, invite the general public to take up its shares or debentures, but the fact that liability is limited may encourage friends to put up capital. A company may also issue a floating debenture (above) as a security for a bank loan, which an unincorporated business cannot do.

Corporate status may also bring tax advantages. Thus in a small company most of the revenue which remains after meeting expenses may be taken by the proprietors not as dividends in their role of shareholders but as fees in their role of directors. In one year, the company may pay its directors bigger fees than its actual profits, carrying the deficit forward to set against the bigger (anticipated) revenue of a subsequent year. In this way, the directors in the first year get the full benefit of their personal, etc., tax allowances (Chapter 8), and they may, accordingly pay less income tax over all than if they had been members of a partnership.

Finally, the splitting of company membership into transferable

[1] Anyone may inspect these and other company documents filed with the Registrar at his office in Bush House, London, on payment of a search fee of one shilling.

shares carrying rights defined in the Articles has provided a very flexible instrument of business ownership useful to small and large company alike. Thus if a small business is organized as a partnership, the death of one partner leaves the surviving partners with the choice of paying back the deceased's capital in cash to his heir, or accepting the latter into the business. If the same business is organized as a company, the heir gets the deceased's shares carrying pre-defined rights and involving no capital withdrawal. At the other end of the scale, if the shareholders of two companies (X and Y) wish their companies to merge, they may set up a holding company (A), and sell (most of) their shares in X and Y to A in return for shares in A. The former X and Y shareholders thus all become shareholders in A, which in turn controls its subsidiaries, X and Y.

3. *Sources of Business Finance*

Consider a firm set up by one man, who is going into business on his own. He may conduct his affairs as an unincorporated 'sole trader', or he may secure incorporation for his business from the very start, his wife taking up a few shares to become the second shareholder necessary as a minimum for a private company. In either case, his initial capital will come from his (or his wife's) personal resources, typically his savings, or perhaps a legacy. His capital will be needed to provide the fixed assets, though some capital savings may be effected by leasing instead of buying property or equipment. Hire-purchase finance would also be suitable for short-lived fixed assets—for example, earth-moving equipment or motor vehicles.

A part of the proprietor's capital will also be needed to finance the current assets. The remainder of this (very) small firm's circulating capital may come from the bank overdraft (discussed in Chapter 2) and trade credit. By trade credit is meant simply the period of grace offered by many suppliers to their customers, in which to settle the account for goods delivered. A firm may, for instance, send a bill at the beginning of each month for goods supplied in the previous month, offering a discount of, say, $\frac{1}{2}$ per cent for payment within fourteen days, or adding a surcharge of, say, $1\frac{1}{2}$ per cent if the account has not been settled within four weeks. These terms give the customer a period in which to work up (or sell) his purchases before actually paying for them. His benefit will be more pronounced if he himself is paid more promptly than he pays his supplier. The 'cash discount' for prompt payment and the surcharge for tardy settlement are, however, strong inducements to settle reasonably promptly, as while the figures seem small they represent on an *annual* basis a substantial interest benefit (or cost).

The growth of trade credit in post-war years may perhaps be explained by the economy's freedom from major depressions (Chapter 20), which has tended on average to increase the reliability of debtors through reducing the number of business failures. The extension may also have encouraged (and been encouraged by) the practice of 'factoring'. Factors or dealers in trade debts are specialist firms which buy the claim that the firm giving credit has against its customer, paying in cash a purchase price rather less than the full nominal value of the debt, in order to cover its own expenses, risk and profit. This arrangement provides immediate finance for the supplying firm although at a cost, while enabling it to attract custom by offering credit terms. The factor makes further arrangements for collecting from the debtor firms.

To expand his business in its very early stages, the sole proprietor may be able to secure more capital from his personal circle, or take on a partner. In either case, the balance of advantage is now strongly in favour of incorporating the enterprise as a private company, if this has not already been done. As explained in Section 2, incorporation will give the proprietors or participants the well defined rights and the limited liability which attach to shares in a limited company. While these external sources of long-term capital may sometimes be important, the major source of funds for expansion generally comes from the firm's own profits. By limiting the amount of the profits taken out of the business as income, the proprietor(s) will have a balance to finance the extension of the firm's activities. Fixed or current assets may also be financed, at all stages of the firm's growth, from the depreciation allowances the firm makes on its fixed assets, as explained in Section 1. Since 1945, these allowances have often been made more valuable by attracting tax relief under the initial and investment allowance scheme, now largely replaced by the investment grant scheme (Chapter 20).

The great increase in direct taxation in the twentieth century has made inroads, among other places, in the profits which firms are able to 'plough back' to finance their expansion. Accordingly, while internal funds may enable the firm to achieve considerable growth, it will, if it is to maintain progress, usually need long-term capital from external sources in greater quantities than the proprietors' personal circle could provide. In its report on finance and industry, published in 1931, the Macmillan Committee noted the existence of a gap in this section of the 'capital market', i.e. the network of arrangements by which smaller firms secure funds. While large companies may raise long-term capital with security issues to the public (see below), there was no such clear-cut source of long-term capital available for the medium and small business. By 1959, however, the Radcliffe Committee (*op. cit.*) was able to write (para 938): 'The facilities for financing investment which are available to the small industrialist have grown substantially since the time of the Macmillan Committee.'

Thus for specifically long-term funds, an insurance company may make a loan to finance the purchase of industrial property, taking a mortgage of the property as security. Alternatively, property bought in the past may be sold to the insurance company, the firm staying on as its new landlord's tenant. A company may also be able to arrange to have its debentures or some of its shares 'placed' privately with a financial institution, such as a life insurance company or an investment trust. Business suppliers or customers, again, may put up funds in order to cement a trading connection. The smaller concern may also be helped by one of a number of institutions that have come specifically into the field to cater for their long-term capital needs. Thus the Charterhouse Industrial Development Company, Ltd, was set up to this end in 1936, and the Industrial and Commercial Finance Corporation, Ltd, in 1945. The shareholders in the latter are the London clearing and Scottish banks and the Bank of England, with debenture finance subscribed by the public. The I.C.F.C. provides capital in amounts from £5,000 to £300,000 to small- and medium-sized businesses, and for existing borrowers may extend this upper limit to £500,000. More specialized institutions are the Agricultural Mortgage Corporation, Ltd, which gives long term loans to farmers on a mortgage of their lands, and the Ship Mortgage Finance Company, Ltd, which assists in the finance of shipbuilding.

Companies too small to make a securities issue carrying a Stock Exchange quotation (see below) may choose to merge one with the other to achieve an appropriate size. One technique of amalgamation is to form a holding company, as explained in Section 2, in which the voting ordinary shares are taken up by the shareholders of the trading companies and non-voting preference shares are offered to the public. The encouragement of industrial concentration, rationalization and merger is the objective of the Industrial Reorganization Corporation, established by the Government in 1966. To this end the Corporation is intended to provide ideas and encouragement in some cases, financial assistance of various kinds in others.

Apart from these sources of long-term capital, the small but growing firm may place particular reliance on finance by hire-purchase, trade credit and bank overdraft. Thus the Radcliffe Committee records that hire-purchase finance 'is also of much more importance to small and rapidly growing firms than to others' (para 204). On trade credit the Committee comments: 'Such information as we have obtained suggests that trade credit is more important in small firms than in large, and that small firms are on the whole more likely than large to be net receivers of credit. The same is true of young firms and of rapidly growing small firms' (para 306). On bank credit the Committee notes that: 'though the bank advance is conventionally a short term loan, the banks do in fact lend on a large scale to such customers (i.e. small concerns) to finance medium-term and long-term requirements' (para 941). The terms on which loans are made to small firms for these purposes were discussed in Chapter 2.

At a certain stage in its growth, a company may wish to make an issue of securities which carry a quotation (i.e. are dealt in) on a British Stock Exchange (often the London Stock Exchange). For this to be practicable, the company will need to offer prospects of return at least comparable with the average quoted company. It will also need to convert itself from a private to a public company, for the reasons explained in Section 2. Applications are considered by the Stock Exchange authorities only when they are satisfied that the market value of the Company's securities will total at least £250,000, while any one category of security should have a minimum expected market value of £100,000.

If the company has previously made a private placing of its securities, it will already be acquainted with the 'new issue' market, i.e. the network of arrangements by which companies (and public authorities) make an issue of their securities. More complex new-issue machinery is, however, utilized when a company plans an issue carrying a Stock Exchange quotation. For security issues up to £300,000, the company will usually seek a 'Stock Exchange placing'. Its broker (i.e. a member of the Stock Exchange acting on the company's behalf) will apply to the Stock Exchange Council for permission to have these securities dealt in on the Stock Exchange (Section 4). At the same time, the broker arranges with (mainly) a number of 'institutional investors', such as life insurance companies, pension funds and investment trusts, to take up the company's security issue. This differs from a private placing in that, since the securities in this case have a Stock Exchange quotation, they may easily be disposed of subsequently by the initial purchaser (Section 4).

For issues over £300,000, the company may invite subscriptions from the public at large, in which case it is required by the Companies Act, 1948, to publish a prospectus. This document sets out the background of the company, the purposes of the issue and so on, and since it is on the strength of this alone that many of the public will apply for securities, the Companies Act, 1948, specifies its contents in some detail, as well as closely defining various aspects of issue procedure. Even more rigorous requirements have to be met if the Stock Exchange Council is to grant (its essential) permission for the securities to be dealt in (Section 4). The business of handling a public issue will be undertaken for the company by an issuing house, which may be either a merchant bank or a firm specializing in new issue work. While a great deal of the administrative work is done by a commercial bank, acting as agent, it is only very occasionally that one or two of the clearing banks may undertake the whole range of new issue arrangements and sponsorship. One of the issuing house's most important tasks will be to arrange the underwriting of the issue, for example, by the institutional investors of the last paragraph. In return for a consideration of cash or fully paid up shares in the company, the underwriters agree in effect to take up that part of the issue not subscribed by the public. This is a very useful arrangement, since applications for securities in even attractive companies may be discouraged by a coincident economic or political crisis.

It is possible for a company to use the machinery of the new issue market without actually raising new funds. This happens when a company which has built itself up on its own resources decides to get its shares quoted on the Stock Exchange. Such a 'Stock Exchange introduction' is in the interests of its shareholders, since it greatly increases the marketability of the shares, as explained in Section 4. The company applies through a broker to the Council of the Stock Exchange, which has the application thoroughly vetted, as with a proposed placing arrangement. Further, an advertisement with the same contents as a prospectus must be published, in order to inform the public at large about the company. A similar publication is necessary for a Stock Exchange placing.

A large established company may also raise funds by inviting its existing shareholders to apply for a new issue proportionately to their current holdings. Such a 'rights' issue saves the company the expense of advertisements, of underwriting commission, and of new issue administration, as well as giving its own shareholders the opportunity to extend their investments. The popularity of this issue technique is shown by the fact that, in the last few years, rights issues accounted for, on average, about 37 per cent of new long-term funds raised by quoted companies in the new issue market. Placings, it may be noted, accounted on average for about 50 per cent, and public issues and similar techniques for the remaining 13 per cent.

While a 'rights' issue raises new funds for the company, a 'scrip' or 'bonus' issue simply represents the 'capitalization of reserves', and no fresh capital is introduced into the business. The elementary discussion of the balance sheet in Section 1 should make it clear that, in a company's balance sheet, the actual capital assets of the company are set out on the right-hand side while, on the left-hand side, are displayed the sources which (in total) financed their acquisition (Table 7.2). It follows that, when profits are retained in the business, the assets on the right-hand side of the balance sheet are increased by this amount, and some corresponding entry must be made among 'capital and liabilities' to explain these extra assets. One simple and appropriate entry would be 'Balance in Profit and Loss Account', or (less explicitly) 'General Reserve'. It is now a small step to issue fully paid up shares to the existing shareholders, in proportion to their current holdings, by the exact amount of the Reserve figure. The Reserve thus disappears from the balance sheet, to be replaced by an equivalent amount of share capital, which in its turn corresponds to the increase in the real assets of the company which is the result of profit retention.

Table 7.2 sets out a composite balance sheet of some 1,700 British

TABLE 7.2

Composite Balance Sheet of
1,692 quoted British companies end-1967

CAPITAL AND LIABILITIES	£ million	%	ASSETS	£ million
1. Shareholders' interest	14,184·8	53	*Fixed Assets*	
(a) Ordinary shares	5,610·3	21	9. Tangible fixed	
(b) Preference etc. shares	772·8	3	assets, net	10,970·5
(c) Capital and Revenue			10. Goodwill	765·4
Reserves	7,801·7	29	11. Trade investments	780·4
			12. Other assets	52·4
2. Long Term Loans	3,487·4	13		
3. Future Tax Reserves	712	3		
4. Minority interests	638·4	2		
Current Liabilities			*Current Assets*	
5. Bank overdrafts and			13. Stocks and Work in	
loans	1,710·1	6	Progress	6,482·2
6. Trade and other			14. Trade and other	
creditors, etc.	4,679·5	18	debtors, etc.	6,020·9
7. Dividends and interest			15. Tax Reserve	
due	547·6	2	Certificates	54·1
8. Current Taxation	685·2	3	16. Treasury Bills	1·0
			17. Quoted securities	313·5
			18. Unquoted securities	204·0
			19. Loans to local	
			authorities	13·4
			20. Cash	987·0
TOTAL LIABILITIES	26,645·0		TOTAL ASSETS	26,644·8

Note: (i) The figures relate to companies' accounting years ending between 6th April, 1967 and 5th April, 1968;
(ii) Column totals affected by rounding.

Source: Financial Statistics (H.M.S.O.)

companies whose shares are dealt in on a U.K. Stock Exchange. The companies all have assets of half a million pounds or more, or an annual income of £50,000 or more, and are mainly engaged in manufacturing, distribution, construction and transport. Before discussing the significance of the two principal sources of long-term capital (1 and 2), it is useful to note briefly the meaning of some of the other items.

It will be explained in Chapter 8 that a company may not actually have to pay certain taxes until some months after the close of its financial year, during which the tax liability was incurred. The company will of course make appropriate provisions (8), in the meantime either using the corresponding funds in its own business or buying Tax Reserve Certificates (15) (Chapter 8). Further, many companies will earmark a part of their current profits to meet *future* tax liabilities (3), meanwhile utilizing these retained profits in the business. A company will also have the use, for a short time, of dividends declared (7) but not yet handed over to shareholders. It is worth noting that Treasury bills (16), quoted securities (17) (of which some 13 per cent were British Government securities) and loans to local authorities (19) could be quickly turned into cash if necessary to finance the company.

Some of the companies whose assets are represented in Table 7.2 are subsidiaries of others among the 1,700. The parent company will hold a controlling but not necessarily an exclusive interest in its subsidiary. It is necessary therefore to show the minority interests of the other 'outside' shareholders in the various subsidiaries (4). The value (at cost) of shares held among the 1,700 in other 'associated' companies is given as 'trade investments' (11). The meaning of all the other items should be clear from the work of the chapter so far, except the distinction between Capital and Revenue Reserves (1c). In a nutshell, revenue reserves have been 'built up' from retained profits and so legally are available to finance dividend payments, though in practice they are more likely to be capitalized with a scrip issue. Capital reserves are not legally available to finance dividend payments: they arise from 'capital' transactions, for example, where a firm issues shares at a premium over their nominal value.[1]

It is interesting to observe the relative proportions in which these companies have financed themselves by ordinary shares on the one hand, and preference shares and long term loans (predominantly debentures) on the other. The ordinary share capital of a company, along with the retained profits which belong to the ordinary shareholders, is known as 'equity' capital. For any given company, the proportion of preference

[1] While reserves may still be described in this way, the distinction made by the Companies Act, 1967, is between 'statutory' and 'non-statutory' reserves. For most purposes 'statutory' can be taken as equivalent to 'capital' and 'non-statutory' to 'revenue'.

share (1b) and debt (2) capital to the total long-term capital is known as its 'gearing'. A first principle of company finance is that, the greater the riskiness of the enterprise upon which the firm is embarked, the lower should its gearing be. Thus if we consider the promotion of adventurous holidays, e.g. volcano visiting, as a risky business, it would be appropriate to finance it (almost) entirely with ordinary shares. The reason is that, should the business fail, which is very possible, the debenture and preference shareholders get no return at all, while if it succeeds they are limited to a fixed return, the fruits going to the equity investors. This difficulty may, however, be partly overcome by issuing a participating preference share, which entitles the holder to an extra dividend should the ordinary share dividend exceed a certain level.

For any given company, therefore, we may expect to find some correspondence between its gearing and the riskiness of its business. The position is, however, complicated by taxation rules, which may make debenture finance especially desirable in the interests of existing shareholders.

Finally, it is worth noting the outstanding contribution made by profit retention to the finance of the companies in Table 7.2, which may be regarded as typical. Even after allowance for the value of capital reserves, the figure (1c) probably understates this contribution, as reserves capitalized during the past would be represented in the balance sheet by ordinary shares. Some economic implications of profit retention are considered in Chapter 20, Section 6.

4. *The Stock Exchange*

The securities market denotes the network of arrangements by which company (and public authority) securities change hands. Most of these deals in the United Kingdom pass through a Stock Exchange, of which by far the biggest is the London Stock Exchange. In the U.S.A., by contrast, many more deals are made 'over the counter', i.e. simply by telephone arrangements among dealers.

The activities of the London Stock Exchange need to be understood in terms of its two categories of membership—stockbrokers and stockjobbers. To buy or sell securities on the Stock Exchange, a member of the public (i.e. any person or institution not a member of the Exchange) has to act through a broker. Brokers (who in early 1969 numbered 2,788, of whom 1,778 were operating in 195 partnerships)[1] carry out their clients' instructions to buy or sell the securities specified by dealing, in turn, with an appropriate jobber. Jobbers (590 in early

[1] Members have also, since July 1969, been able to form limited liability companies, in which outsiders can hold minority share interests. Directors

1969, of whom 288 operated in 33 partnerships)[1] specialize in one or more of a group of securities, for example, Government bonds, the securities of banking, insurance and shipping companies, the securities of brewing and distilling companies, and so on. The jobbers with the same specialist interests regularly occupy the same part of the Stock Exchange floor, and it is to this spot that any broker would go to effect a corresponding security transaction on his client's behalf.

A broker with a dealing commission will enquire a jobber's prices, e.g., 'How much are 3½ per cent War Loan?', and may be told '49¾-50'. This means that the jobber is prepared to buy this particular Government security, which has a nominal value of £100, for £49 15s., or sell it at £50. After ascertaining prices among other jobbers, the broker will want to do business with the jobber offering him the best price. Suppose that this broker has a buying commission from his client, and that '50' is in fact the lowest price at which 3½ per cent War Loan are available. He reveals to the jobber which way he wants to deal, asking to buy, say, £100,000 worth. For very small orders the jobber is bound by the rules of the Exchange to buy or sell as the broker requires. In other cases he is not so bound, but will usually accept the order either way provided the amount is not abnormal and the security is actively dealt in, as are Government bonds.

The details of this transaction are briefly noted by jobber and broker, the latter going on his way to buy or sell other sorts of security elsewhere on the floor of the Exchange, the jobber staying on his 'pitch' to undertake further business in Government securities. Such dealings by this and the other jobbers specializing in Government bonds make up the 'gilt-edged' market. In the case of Government (and local authority) securities, settlement is made the next day by the broker's and jobber's respective clerks. The gross profit for the broker lies in the commission he charges his client. The jobber derives his profit from any advantageous price movement after he has bought the securities and before selling them, or from the 'turn' between his buying (or 'bid') price and his selling (or 'offer') price.

Dealings in all other securities are 'for the account', unless arrangements are made to the contrary. The year is divided into twenty 14-day dealing periods, plus four 21-day periods around the great public holidays. Transactions in company securities which take place during a given dealing period have to be settled by the second Tuesday following the end of that dealing period. On this Settlement Day, all stock has to be delivered and paid for in cash.

---

must be Stock Exchange members, and retain personal liability for their company's debts. Such companies will not themselves be eligible for a quotation.   [1] Ibid.

Where securities are not actively dealt in, the jobber will merely record how the broker wants to trade, and will wait until he gets an inquiry for the same securities in the opposite direction before binding himself to the deal. For a security with a more active market, the price(s) any one jobber quotes will depend upon the relative weight of buying and selling orders that he anticipates. Thus suppose a certain company is likely to pay bigger dividends on its shares, because of a large and profitable contract it has acquired. Orders to buy off the jobbers would heavily outweigh selling orders, and the jobbers, realizing what was happening, would raise the prices at which they were prepared to do business. Their higher 'offer' price would discourage purchases, while their higher 'bid' price might encourage some holders to part with their securities. The quoted price(s) would rise until a new equilibrium was reached, reflecting the relatively greater popularity of this company's shares. In this sense, the prices of securities are determined by the forces of supply and demand.

In practice, of course, if the news of the company's good fortune were common knowledge, the jobbers would at once raise their prices to avoid the embarrassment of a large number of buying orders. In a similar way, any increase in Bank Rate may have been generally anticipated by a 'marking down' of Government security prices, so that the actual announcement of the increase has little or no effect on *current* security prices: in this case, the market is said to have 'discounted' the Bank Rate increase. Higher Bank Rate—other things being equal—depresses security prices (i.e. raises yields—Chapter 13) because it entails a rise in Treasury bill rate, and Treasury bills are a close substitute for very short Government bonds (Chapters 3 and 4). Further, a rise in Bank Rate makes bank finance by overdraft more expensive (Chapter 2), so that unless jobbers reduced prices they might have a preponderance of selling orders from firms seeking to liquidate their investments (compare item 17 in Table 7.2) in order to reduce their reliance on bank finance.

The jobber does not, however, react in a purely mechanical way to a preponderance of buying or selling orders, by automatically moving his prices up or down. If he feels that the increase in (e.g.) sales is a purely transient affair, and that there is no good reason why the security in question should be less popular, he may maintain his prices more or less unchanged, and adopt an 'unbalanced' position. This means that, in this example, he takes on his books a number of orders requiring him to buy from brokers without, for the time being, having as many orders to sell to brokers. By backing his own judgement in this way, the jobber is helping maintain price stability, damping down the fluctuations that purely temporary waves of buying and selling would otherwise induce. The adoption of an unbalanced position does, however, expose the jobber to a risk of loss, as he might have misread market feeling. Thus having bought a lot of shares in the belief that this was a temporary glut, he might have to bring prices down to get rid of them if their decline in popularity is more permanent than he had anticipated.

The willingness of the jobber to take this sort of risk is aided by the account system, his ability to borrow from the banks 'at short notice', and (for gilt-edged stocks) his ability actually to borrow securities through the agency of certain specialist brokers. However the two major contributors are, first, the size of the jobber's own fortune and, second, the pressure of competition from other jobbers, both of which have tended to decline in recent years. The inroads of taxation prevent jobbers today from building up the sizeable capital they need if they are to take risks on any but a small scale. (Access to outside capital, nonetheless, has recently been made easier by the Exchange: since 1966 members have been able to form partnerships with outsiders—who must be limited partners, while association in a limited company has been permitted since 1969—footnote, p. 145.) Second, the number of jobbers and jobbing firms has fallen in recent years, so that in some markets the jobber is not under strong competitive pressure in deciding his prices. This fall in the number of jobbers may be partly explained by the relative decline in the returns to jobbing, as an increased volume of business is transacted directly between brokers and institutional investors, with only nominal jobber participation.

The purchase of a company's securities on the Stock Exchange does not, of course, put any new funds at the disposal of the company. The company gets its funds when the share is first issued (and paid up), and any subsequent dealing merely represents a change of ownership to be recorded in the company's share register. The Stock Exchange is, nonetheless, an essential ally to the new issue market. When a company raises funds with a new issue, it applies the proceeds within its business to the finance of fixed and current assets. It would obviously be quite impracticable to give the shareholder his 'money back' any time he might want it, though some securities do carry a provision for their ultimate redemption. Thus companies do issue redeemable debentures and (much more rarely) redeemable preference shares. All ordinary shares and most preference shares, however, are irredeemable, while even with a redeemable debenture there may be a life of 20 years or more to maturity.

It follows that, without an organized market in which their securities may be sold, companies would find it much more expensive to raise funds from the public at large. Since the purchaser of a security would find it difficult to dispose of if his circumstances changed and he needed cash instead, the company would have to compensate him by offering the prospect of a substantially higher return. As it is, a security with a Stock Exchange quotation may always be disposed of on the market, so that people are much more willing to put funds at a company's disposal by taking up new issues.

The Stock Exchange, therefore, complements the new issue market by enabling investors to recover their cash, should they wish, with no disturbance to the business assets of the company. This does not mean, of course, that the investor is able at any time to make an immediate sale of his securities at the original purchase price. As previously noted, not all securities can be sold with equal readiness while, though the jobbing system may have some damping effect, security prices are likely to fluctuate. While the speculator may welcome this latter feature as his opportunity for capital gains, the investor who is interested only in investment income might prefer to surrender the prospect of capital gain to be relieved of the risk of capital loss. However, the only method of protecting the capital value of his investment is by buying a 'put option', which is limited (to 3 months) and expensive (at 5 to 10 per cent of the share value). Thus the holder of tobacco company shares standing at say 30s. in March may fear a rise in tobacco duty in the April budget, which would cause his shares to fall in value. He may buy from a specialist option dealer the right or option to sell him the shares at *today's* (March) price at any time during the next three months, whatever the market price should subsequently be.

A second function of the Stock Exchange lies in providing the new issue market with a guide to the terms on which new issues might successfully be made. Thus suppose the debentures of first-class industrial companies are changing hands in Stock Exchange dealings at prices which give the purchaser a return of 6 per cent per annum (Chapter 13). It is obvious that a new debenture issue will have to offer at least comparable terms if the issue is to be successful.

A third important function of the Stock Exchange lies in promoting various safeguards and advantages for the investing public. While companies formed under one of the various Companies' Acts of past years are subject to the Companies' Acts, 1948 and 1967, a company that wants a Stock Exchange quotation for any class of its securities will have to satisfy the Council's requirements, which can be more rigorous than the legal obligations. Thus the Act of 1948 requires any prospectus to reveal the company's profits over the last five years, while the Council's requirement is ten years. Again, where the directors know of any special trade factors or risks which could materially affect profits, the Stock Exchange requires their disclosure in the prospectus if it is unlikely that the general public would know of or anticipate them. Further, when 25 per cent or more of the voting share capital has not been issued, the company must undertake not to make an issue which could effectively alter control of the company without first obtaining the shareholders' approval in a general meeting.

F

These and many other provisions have given the public some guarantee of the business standards of the companies quoted on the Stock Exchange. The development of public confidence over the years has played a central part in creating a market for 'anonymous capital'. By security purchase people transform their personal capital into business capital, applied to projects of which in general they know nothing, under the guidance of directors over whom they generally exercise little influence.

5. *Investment Trusts and Unit Trusts*

An investment trust is a limited company formed to invest its shareholders' capital in the securities of other companies. The yields from its investments constitute its own gross profit, out of which in turn it will pay dividends to its shareholders. It may secure further funds for investment with a new share or debenture issue, by profit retention, and from any capital gain on the sale of its investments. The holder of shares in an investment trust who wanted to recover his cash would, of course, sell his securities on the Stock Exchange. The price he obtained would depend on the forces of supply and demand at work, and would be influenced but not determined by the underlying value of the trust's own investment assets.

Nearly 300 investment trusts submit returns to the Bank of England: on average in recent years, about 90 per cent of their total assets have consisted of ordinary shares—55 per cent in U.K. companies and 35 per cent in companies overseas. Before the war, the trusts held about half their assets in industrial debentures and preference shares, but the drawbacks of fixed interest securities in an inflationary period (Chapter 14) have prompted a revision of their portfolio distribution. Their appeal, accordingly, is to those who want an investment in ordinary shares, but have insufficient capital to take up the wide variety of shares desirable to reduce their risks. A wide investment spread is, however, the very feature which characterizes the trusts, which do not hold more than a small part of any one company's capital. Investment trust shares are also a useful outlet for some of the investment monies of the life insurance companies and pension funds.

In the capital market, the trusts are active as underwriters, and in Stock Exchange and private placings. Thus they play a part in the long-term finance of the smaller company, measured by their holdings of unquoted shares and debentures (3 to 4 per cent of total U.K. investments in recent years). Their substantial overseas assets provide a noteworthy contribution to the United Kingdom's investment income (Chapter 17).

The term 'investment trust' is misleading, since they are not trusts in the legal sense but limited companies. By contrast, the 'unit trust' is aptly named. The promoters of a unit trust arrange with, say, a bank or insurance company for it to act as trustee[1] for a pool of funds contributed by a number of subscribers. At the same time the promoters form a management company which, for a fee, undertakes the investment of these funds in suitable securities. The securities are held in the name of the trustee, for the benefit of the subscribers; as beneficiaries, they are paid a return out of the yields on the securities. All the details of administration are attended to by the management company.

At the inception of the fund each subscriber receives a number of 'units' proportionate to his contribution. The value of each unit is given by dividing the total number of units into the total value of the pool. As time passes, so the quoted prices of the securities in which the fund is invested will vary. Accordingly, a unit holder who wants to recover his cash is paid a price corresponding to the *current* value of the underlying securities. If necessary, the management company would sell an appropriate part of the trust's assets to finance the repayment. In practice, applications for new units provide a cash inflow, part or all of which may be used for this purpose. Occasionally, as a promotional device, management companies make a 'block offer' of a given number of units available during one week only at a fixed price. Units may, however, be bought at any time, at prices based on the most recent Stock Exchange quotations practicable. Unit trusts are, accordingly, described as 'open-ended': they expand and contract automatically, in consequence of net purchases or net sales by the public. By contrast investment trusts are 'closed-ended': they operate with a given (share) capital, which is increased only by the directors' decision.

Unit trusts have grown rapidly in recent years, both in numbers and volume of business, and in the sophistication of the investment facilities they offer. They have an especial appeal for the long-term equity investor who can save small but regular amounts. Because in the short run the general level of share prices may fall as well as rise, holdings of equities are not a good investment for a man who may want to sell them within a fairly short time of acquisition. However, the long term trend of equity prices is upwards, and (in the post-war period) an investor who can hold them for, say, three years or so can be reasonably confident of capital appreciation. The small saver can best obtain an equity investment by making regular purchases of trust units. By spending a constant sum in regular purchase the unit holder averages out his reduced purchases when the market is rising with increased purchases

[1] However, the Trustee Savings Banks and two or three of the clearing banks have themselves promoted unit trusts, setting up a subsidiary to act as management company with (say) an insurance company as trustee.

when the market is falling. Most trusts offer contractual savings schemes and, if these are linked with life assurance, the unit holder enjoys an income tax advantage.

Those trusts which have a widely spread portfolio also offer the small saver the advantage of a diversified investment. The managers will be alive to the profitability of 'switching' from one share to another, as prospects change for various companies or industries. The unit holder with confidence in his management company is perhaps less likely to sell in a panic than a small shareholder who relies on his own judgement. By interposing itself, therefore, between the small, uninformed investor and the Stock Exchange, the unit trust may make a contribution to the stability of the securities market.

6. *Insurance Companies and Pension Funds*

In its general or 'non-life' business, an insurance company undertakes, in return for an annual premium, to recoup the policy holder up to an agreed limit should a specified risk befall himself or his property. Such an agreement enables the insured to transform the possibility of a very large loss – say the theft of his property, or its destruction by fire, into the certainty of a very small 'loss', namely the sum paid annually to the company as a premium. In calculating the size of the premium for each category of business, the company aims at an annual income flow which will meet the claims of the relatively few unfortunates who actually suffer loss, while enabling them to cover expenses and provide a profit for their shareholders. In addition, companies will need to have accumulated from their income a reasonable working balance, and to have built up a financial 'reserve' of investments.

Should claims against a company exceed its income, it can meet the deficit initially by running down its working balances, and in turn 'liquidating' some of its investments. Subsequently, of course, it may need to raise its premiums for this type of business. It follows that, in their investment policy, the companies are keen to hold securities which always have a good market, for example, British Government securities rather than loans on mortgages. They are also attracted by high-yielding investments, as the returns form a valuable supplement to their premium income. Surprisingly, despite the relative certainty of their capital value, short bonds are not popular, as their yields are often relatively low and the capital necessarily requires frequent reinvestment.

Life insurance (sometimes called 'assurance') differs from general insurance in many significant respects. The policy holder pays premiums to the company usually over a number of years (perhaps 30 years or more), in return for an 'assured' benefit. If the policy holder has insured his own life in a 'whole-life' policy, his wife (or heirs) receives a capital sum upon his death. With an endowment policy, he receives a capital sum (or an entitlement to a pension) after a specified period, or his wife receives a capital sum should he die meanwhile. It follows that the policy holder (or his wife or heirs) is assured of a given capital sum (or its equivalent in annuity rights) at a future date, which the company has to meet by investing the premium income at interest. The investment funds which the life company manages are, therefore, at the very centre of its business. By contrast, the insurer against general risks has calculated (on past experience) that only a small number of policy holders will claim, and works out his premium rates correspondingly. His investment fund functions simply as an adjunct to the constant inflow and outflow of cash, serving to finance any unexpected excess of claims over premium (and investment) income.

Where the policy holder takes a whole-life or endowment policy upon his own life, the company cannot, of course, be certain of the amount of premium income it will receive from him, because of the risk of the policy holder's death. This uncertainty can, however, be allowed for in calculating premium rates when large numbers of people are insured, by working to the average life expectation for each age group as revealed by population statistics. A more difficult problem for the company is that, in quoting a premium, it has to try and estimate the interest which the investment of its premium income will yield over the years ahead, these yields in their turn being invested at interest. The bigger the (compound) rate of interest that can be safely assumed, the bigger the fund will have grown after a given period of time, so the lower the annual premium that need be asked of the policy holder in return for the assurance of a given capital sum. Companies are eager, accordingly, to invest a substantial part of their funds in assets which offer a virtually guaranteed income over a lengthy period, for example, long-dated bonds or debentures. The certainty of their returns enables the company to calculate with greater confidence the premium rates payable for any given scale of policy benefits.

Partly as a safeguard against the miscalculation of investment yields, companies offer a 'with-profits' endowment policy. The policy holder pays a rather higher premium for his assured capital sum, and this 'loading' provides the company with a margin should some investments prove less profitable than anticipated. The attraction of this sort of policy is that, should the company in fact enjoy a high profit level, the holder will receive substantial 'profit bonuses' on top of his minimum capital benefit. 'With-profit' policies have been especially popular in post-war years, because the promise of simply a fixed capital sum many years hence is less attractive in a period of rising prices (Chapter 14). Their popularity, in turn, has encouraged the life funds to hold more ordinary shares than before the war. Yields on equities are less certain than on debentures. However, they may offer better long-run prospects in a full-employment, inflationary economy (Chapter 14), and each company is aware of the competitive importance of a good 'bonus record'. The activities of the life companies in the new issue market have already been noted in Section 3.

Most general and life insurance business in this country is in the hands of British Insurance Association members, who number nearly three hundred. Over half their business, in turn, is conducted by the forty or so 'composite' companies which transact both general and life insurance. In 1959, equity investments became, for the first time, the largest single category in the life funds' portfolios. Since the late 1950s, however, gilt-edged securities and debentures have offered very high yields (Chapter 14), and this, coupled with their 'income certainty', soon restored gilt-edged to the lead. On average in recent years, Government bonds have represented about 24 per cent of total assets, ordinary shares 21 per cent, debentures 16 per cent, mortgages and loans 17 per cent, and property investments 10 per cent.

In offering a life pension on retirement in return for regular contributions during working life, the pension funds provide a service not unlike the life insurance companies. Indeed, about 30 per cent of premiums paid to the life companies are paid by smaller firms, for whose employees the companies have undertaken to organize a pension scheme. Self-administered pension schemes are run by larger firms, by nationalized industries and other public bodies, and by local authorities. All three groups have been particularly attracted by ordinary shares in recent years, as the buoyancy of company profits during an inflationary period should help the funds meet the demands for higher pensions that inflation also brings (Chapter 14). Some funds have, also, been 'making up lost ground', since until the Trustee Investments Act, 1961, their trust deeds prevented many funds from acquiring ordinary shares.

Over 1,000 self-administered funds are members of the National Association of Pension Funds. This body, like the British Insurance Association, has in recent years been asked by the Bank of England for its members' co-operation in restricting loans for certain purposes (Chapter 4) when the banks have been under comparable restraint.

Questions

1. What is a public limited liability company? What are the advantages and disadvantages of this form of organization?   U.L.

2. Explain and evaluate the role of ordinary shares in financing the activities of business firms.   U.L.

3. Compare ordinary shares, preference shares and debentures as a means of raising capital for private industry. U.L.

4. From what sources do firms raise money to finance their activities? What factors determine which sources a firm uses? U.L.

5. Outline the ways in which a firm can obtain capital in the various stages of its growth. S.U.J.B.

6. What considerations would the directors of a company have in mind in deciding the method by which they should attempt to raise additional capital for use in the business? I.M.T.A.

7. How can (a) a farmer and (b) an aircraft manufacturing company raise additional capital? U.L.

8. Describe and evaluate the functions of the Stock Exchange. U.L.

9. Discuss the role of the Stock Exchange in the finance of new firms. U.L.

10. Distinguish between the markets for new and existing capital, and explain the interaction between them. W.J.E.C.

11. Carefully explain the difference between the capital market and the money market. Describe the function of the latter in the British economy today. S.U.J.B.

12. Does the capital market meet adequately the financial needs of firms in the British industrial structure? J.M.B.

13. Is the capital market efficient? J.M.B.

8

Public Income and Expenditure

1. *The Public Sector*

Popular debate sometimes obscures the line between the affairs of the British Government and the activity of the British economy. Thus loans to the British Government by foreign governments (or international monetary institutions) are occasionally described, in a rather loose way, as loans to 'Britain'. This may be a vivid way of putting it, but if the same proposition is followed by the assertion that these loans are necessary because 'Britain' has failed to expand her exports, confusion may unwittingly result. People may also mix up the condition of the economy with the state of the Government's finances, and imagine that a Government policy designed to influence the former is in fact necessary to rescue the latter! To dispel any confusion of this sort, let us begin by making a few important distinctions.

First, for purposes of economic analysis or policy, the Government cannot be treated as identical with the British economy. The Central Government is one among the many institutions whose dealings, along with those of firms and households, local authorities and public corporations, make up the British economy. Unlike other institutions, of course, it has the power to finance its activities by taxing the other members of the economy (though some local authorities have the power to levy a type of local tax in the form of rates). Further, it is not limited in its spending by normal commercial criteria of, say, profitability. Because of the relatively large size of its activities, it is able to influence the remainder of the economic system by varying its taxation and expenditure levels, as well as by specific legislation. It also has available the instruments of monetary control described in earlier chapters.

Local authorities and public corporations are not in any sense 'part' of the Central Government, though they owe their life and powers to the various Acts of Parliament which brought them into being. They will, of course, have close financial and other relationships with the Government.

Central Government, local authorities and public corporations, and their affairs, may be classed together as the 'public sector' of the economy. The 'private sector' denotes the (economic) activities of households (the 'personal sector') and privately owned firms (though most firms of any size are public companies!—Chapter 7). 'Public finance' is the study of the finance of the public sector, both in the narrower sense of how its activities are financed, and in the broader sense of what effects all this may have on households and the firms in the private sector. Consideration of these broader aspects is postponed to Chapters 11 and 20.

The Central Government finances its activities mainly by raising taxes and borrowing. The taxes it raises may be labelled Government income, but never national income. The latter is a measure of the total output of goods and services for the economy as a whole, discussed in Chapter 9. On the other hand, the total debt the Government has accumulated over the centuries is known as the National Debt. It would be less confusing were it known as the Government Debt, as the uninformed may draw the false conclusion that it is 'what this country owes other countries', i.e. confuse Government and nation. However even this second description would be a little misleading in that, as explained in Section 4, some Government debt is held within the Government itself.

2. The Framework of Government Finance

A major principle of Government finance is the centralization of receipts into a common pool from which all Government payments are financed. For many years this pool took the form of just one fund, the Consolidated Fund, set up by the Customs and Excise Act, 1787, as a 'Fund into which shall flow every stream of public revenue and from which shall come the supply for every service'. However, in 1968 a second and parallel fund was established, to take over some of the payments and receipts handled until then through the Consolidated Fund. This National Loans Fund is operated as an official account at the Bank of England, as Chapter 4 noted. The Consolidated Fund is not itself an account, but has its balance held in the Exchequer account at the Bank; the two expressions are, therefore, often used interchangeably.

Exceptions have been admitted to the general principle of consolidation. Thus official dealings in the foreign exchange market, undertaken to influence the exchange value of the pound (Chapter 17), are conducted not through the Exchequer account but through the Exchange Equalization Account, established for the purpose in 1932. Again the National Insurance Fund was set up separately in 1947, to make it easier to relate contributions to benefits at least partly on an insurance basis. Clearly any comprehensive statement of Government finances must bring all the statutory funds into its reckoning.

Table 8.1 summarizes the contemporary system of Government finances operating through the Consolidated Fund and the National Loans Fund. It is easiest to outline the broad picture before proceeding

TABLE 8.1

Receipts (per year)	Units	Payments (per year)	Units
(I) Consolidated Fund			
1. Tax Revenue	100	3. Supply Services	82
2. Miscellaneous		4. Consolidated Fund	
Receipts	4	Standing Services including:	5
		4a. Interest Payment to N.L.F.	3
		5. Surplus on Consolidated Fund	17
(II) National Loans Fund			
6=5. Surplus on Consolidated Fund	17	11. National Debt: Interest and Expenses	9
7=4a. Interest received from Consolidated Fund	3	12. Loans to, notably, Nationalised Industries, Other Public Corporations and Local Authorities	15
8. Other Interest Receipts	6		
9. Repayments on Loans outstanding under (12)	4		
10. Net Borrowing Requirement	−6		

Note: The existence of the Exchange Equalization Account is ignored in entry 10. The E.E.A. is put in context in Table 8.4, and discussed in Chapter 18.

to examine the individual entries in this and the following sections. To give an impression of the proportions involved, imaginary units of value have been entered, based on data for the financial year 1969–70, with tax revenue taken as 100. The actual money values for this year will be found in Sections 3 and 4.

The proceeds of Government taxation (1) are paid into the Consolidated Fund, along with various miscellaneous receipts (2) (like T.V. licence fees). They thus provide the finance for the 'supply services'

(3), which is the name given to civil and defence expenditure by the Government which requires annual Parliamentary authorization (below). The revenue of the Consolidated Fund also finances certain standing charges on the Fund (4). Expenditure under 3 and 4 can be expected, in practice, to leave a surplus on the Fund (5), which is passed on to the National Loans Fund, to help finance N.L.F. payments.

One of the National Loans Fund's sources of income is interest received on past loans made by the Government under 12. It also receives the interest paid on the Government securities 'held' by the Issue Department of the Bank of England (Chapter 4), and the two together make up almost the whole of entry 8. This, in turn, is applied to meeting the interest due on Government debt, and the expenses incurred by the Bank of England in managing it (11). This will not be enough to meet the whole of the interest due and expenses (11), and a standing charge is imposed on the Consolidated Fund for the remainder (4a = 7). It follows that 7 plus 8 always equals 11.

Out of the National Loans Fund, the Government meets its lending to, notably, nationalized industries, other public corporations and local authorities (12). To meet these payments, it will have the capital repayments currently made on outstanding loans (9), along with the surplus on the Consolidated Fund (6 = 5). This, in Table 8.1, is more than sufficient to meet the whole of the Government's lending under 12, which means that the Government's net borrowing requirement—defined in entry 10—has for this year a negative value. This sum (10) is accordingly available to the Government to finance a net repayment of part of the National Debt.

We can now consider some of the administrative and Parliamentary background to the principal Consolidated Fund entries in Table 8.1, Supply Services (3) and Tax Revenue (1). Details of the various taxes and some Consolidated Fund payments follow in Section 3, while official borrowing arrangements—handled through the National Loans Fund—are reviewed in Section 4.

As an introduction to the Supply Services, it is useful to draw a rough distinction between revenue departments, spending departments and finance departments.

The first are the Departments of Inland Revenue and of Customs and Excise, which between them administer nearly the whole of the taxation system. Their tax receipts are paid into their own (subordinate) accounts at the Bank of England, and thence transferred to the Exchequer account. Any expenditure of their own is incurred solely in their work of raising tax revenue.

Second the spending departments are predominantly spenders of funds in providing the variety of Government services: Commonwealth and Foreign, Home and Justice, Industry Trade and Transport, Education and Science, the Armed Services, etc. Their activities may nonetheless yield a small revenue, e.g. the fines paid in the criminal courts.

Third are the finance departments foremost of which is the Treasury flanked by the Department of Exchequer and Audit, and the Pay Office. In the routine of financial administration, the Treasury is concerned, with the revenue departments, in constructing the taxation system; and, with the Audit Department, in superintending the expenditure of the spending departments. The Pay Office operates the Paymaster General's Account: this is a subordinate account at the Bank of England, fed from the Exchequer, on which the actual drawings of the spending departments are made.

Annually on 1st October, the departments will each receive a letter from the Treasury, asking for their expenditure estimates for the forthcoming financial year 1st April–31st March. In fact the Treasury will already have been acquainted with the major schemes of the spending departments over the past few years,[1] and informal co-operation will continue until the estimates are presented to the Treasury on 1st December. In the next two months the estimates receive further polishing and discussion, if necessary at Ministerial level. Final Cabinet approval is given early in February, and they are published and presented to the House of Commons.

Until recent years the estimates received formal consideration from the House of Commons sitting as a 'Committee of Supply' over a specified number of 'Supply Days'. These sittings were, in fact, used for debates on Government policy as reflected in its spending plans, and not for a systematic vetting of the estimates in financial terms. Since 1967 the Committee of Supply, as such, has been abolished, but the Supply Days (twenty-nine in total) have been retained. Material from the Estimates is still considered on these days, but the procedural change enables a wider range of other business to be undertaken as well. Supply Days may continue until early August, but the financial year begins on 1st April. Just before this date, therefore, the Government secures from Parliament a Consolidated Fund Act, authorizing expenditure by the departments for the time being.[2] Final approval is

---

[1] Since 1961 surveys of public spending over the next five years have been made annually, as an aid to forward planning. In April, 1969, the Government suggested (Cmd. 4017) that these surveys might be made more comprehensive, and published annually (instead of occasionally). Annual publication (probably in November) could become established in Parliamentary procedure as an occasion for debate of public spending trends.

[2] Cmd. 4017 suggests that this particular function of the C.F.A. be discharged instead by a clause in the preceding Appropriation Act, authorizing spending for the time being from the following 1st April.

obtained in the Appropriation Act, passed just before the end of the Parliamentary session.

By contrast with the Supply Services (i.e. departmental spending estimates considered on Supply Days), Consolidated Fund Standing Services do not require annual authorization in the Appropriation Act, since they are standing charges on the Consolidated Fund imposed by previous Acts of Parliament. The various categories of Supply Services and Standing Services are set out in Section 3.

House of Commons control over Government expenditure is exercised chiefly through two committees of the House. The Select Committee on Estimates (currently 33 members) picks out various items of Government spending for investigation, and publishes a Report on each inquiry which may be debated in the House of Commons. The Public Accounts Committee (15 members, chaired by a member of the Opposition) is entrusted by the House of Commons with the consideration of the Report and Appropriation Accounts submitted in November or December each year by the Comptroller and Auditor General. These are the audited accounts of each department for the financial year ended the previous 31st March, showing the sums voted each department (in the Appropriation Act) and the actual expenditure incurred under each head. The Committee publish a number of Reports, and those containing proposals for altering departmental financial practices will be taken up by the Treasury.

The Comptroller and Auditor General, though appointed by the Crown, is best thought of as a servant of the House of Commons; he is not a civil servant. He heads the Exchequer and Audit Department, which is primarily concerned with auditing the accounts of other Government departments. This is done by a continuous running audit, which builds up the material for the final Appropriation Accounts and the accompanying Report.

The Government's proposals for raising tax revenue for the year ahead are introduced into the House of Commons in Spring, usually in early April and generally on a Tuesday. Plans for changing current tax rates, modifying existing taxes or introducing new ones are set out in the Financial Statement. These form the basis of the Finance Bill, introduced at the same time to give effect to the Government's tax proposals. However, debate on the Finance Bill will generally continue until July before the Finance Act is passed. Accordingly the House will on the same day adopt by resolution the rates proposed for existing taxes, so that they take effect immediately without giving taxpayers an opportunity to forestall changes. Traditionally the close examination of the Finance Bill at the 'Committee stage' of its progress through the House of Commons has been undertaken by the whole House, sitting as a Committee of Ways and Means. This procedural form was, however, abolished in 1967, and in 1968 this stage was taken by a Finance Bill Committee of fifty members only. For 1969 it is proposed that part of the work at this stage be undertaken by such a committee and part by the whole House.

The proposals of the Financial Statement and Finance Bill are, of course, generally known as 'The Budget'. The Financial Statement, however, contains more than just the Government's tax plans. It also sets out in summary form transactions upon the Consolidated Fund and National Loans Fund, both those carried through in the year just ended and those planned for the year ahead. It thus provides an outline picture of tax yields, spending on Supply Services and standing charges on the Consolidated Fund, Government lending, and the net borrowing requirement for the year. Other information given by the Financial Statement is considered in Section 8.

Figures for Consolidated Fund and National Loans Fund transactions for the year just ended are necessarily provisional when published in the Financial Statement. A full and final account of payments into and out of the Funds is, however, prepared by the Treasury and sent to the Comptroller and Auditor General by the end of November in the same year. These accounts, after examination and certification by the Auditor General, are in turn laid with his report before each House of Parliament.

3. *Consolidated Fund Revenue and Expenditure*

We may now explore in greater detail the sources and destinations of the funds that flow into and out of the Consolidated Fund. The explanation in this (and the following) section is based on the Financial Statement (1969–70) presented to the House of Commons on 15th April, 1969.

Table 12 of the Financial Statement sets out the estimated tax revenue and miscellaneous receipts for the financial year 1969–70, both on the basis of the 1968–9 tax rates and after allowing for the changes proposed in the accompanying Finance Bill. The original 1968 Budget estimates are also given, with provisional figures for the 1968–9 outturn. This table (slightly modified and with footnotes omitted) is set out below as Table 8.2, though only the 1969–70 forecasts (allowing for Budget changes) are shown.

Of the taxes collected by the Department of Inland Revenue, the most fruitful is clearly the Income Tax. The outstanding feature of the income tax system is its progressive nature, which is easily understood by examining the way in which liability to income tax is assessed. Against his total annual income a person will often be able to set various tax

TABLE 8.2

Taxation and Miscellaneous Receipts

	1969–70 estimate £ million
TAXATION	
Inland Revenue	
Income Tax	4,881
Surtax	240
Corporation Tax	1,805
Capital Gains Tax	136
Death Duties	380
Stamp Duties	120
Special Charge	25
Other (i.e. Profits Tax)	3
Total Inland Revenue	7,590
Customs and Excise	
Tobacco	1,125
Purchase Tax	1,101
Oil	1,309
Spirits, Beer and Wine	844
Betting and Gaming	109
Other Revenue Duties	10
Protective Duties	220
Import Deposits	−175
Less: Export Rebates, etc.	−9
Total Customs and Excise	4,534
Motor Vehicle Duties	422
Less: Export Rebates, etc.	−2
	420
Selective Employment Tax (gross)[1]	1,920
TOTAL TAXATION	14,464
MISCELLANEOUS RECEIPTS	
Broadcast Receiving Licences	102
Interest and Dividends	87
Other	355
Total	15,008

[1] Revenue from the S.E.T. is stated gross, and the refunds, etc., entered as expenditure in the Supply Services (Table 8.3).

allowances. Thus allowances are made if the income is earned from a trade, a professional practice or from employment (as opposed to 'unearned' income received by way of interest, rents, dividends, etc.); if the taxpayer has a wife, children, dependent relatives, and so on. The total allowances are deducted from total income to give the balance liable to tax. On the first £260 of this balance tax is paid (1969–70 rates) at 6s. in the £. Thereafter tax is paid at the standard rate of 8s. 3d. in the £.

The basic rule is that all income (in money or kind) is liable to income tax, and this rule extends to a British resident's income from investments overseas, or a foreigner's income from investments in this country, even though he is resident overseas. From 1962, any capital gain arising from the disposal of land within three years or other assets within six months of acquisition became liable to income tax (and surtax—below). This liability was altered by the Finance Act of 1965, and now applies to capital gains from the disposal of land and other assets within twelve months of their acquisition. Capital gains on the disposal of assets after the twelve-month period are subject under the 1965 Act to a new Capital Gains Tax which, for individuals, is levied at a maximum of 30 per cent. This long-term tax should not be confused with the income tax liability on short-term capital gains, though both carry similar sorts[1] of exemption, e.g. the taxpayer's private house.

Companies, as well as private persons, were until recent years liable to income tax on their profits, paid at the standard rate since they had no allowances. They were also liable to a profits tax, which before 1958 was levied at a lower rate for undistributed than distributed profits. Shareholders, however, received their dividends without any further liability to income tax. Under the new system introduced by the Finance Act, 1965, *company* liability to income tax has been abolished, while the profits tax (then at 15 per cent) has been replaced by a corporation tax (currently at 45 per cent). Corporation tax is also applied to company capital gains.[1] Profits distributed as dividends, further, have become liable to income tax: at law this liability falls on the shareholder, though for administrative convenience the income tax is deducted by the company and paid on the shareholder's behalf. Profits retained by the company will have borne corporation tax, but are not liable to income tax.

After declaring its dividend, the company has between two and six weeks in which to remit the income tax to the Inland Revenue. Further, under the Pay-As-You-Earn scheme, companies and other employers are responsible for deducting the income tax from their employees' weekly wage or monthly salary. The proceeds are remitted to the

[1] Capital gains arising from the disposal of British government securities after the twelve-month period will not be taxed, under 1969 Budget proposals.

Inland Revenue at monthly intervals. By contrast, the corporation tax is paid at least nine months later than the end of the accounting period for which it was assessed. Most companies already trading when the 1965 Finance Act came into force will in fact continue to pay their tax on 1st January each year, which will often mean a significant delay between incurring the liability and paying the corporation tax. Thus a company in this category which had its books made up on 30th April, 1968, would not actually have to pay the tax until 1st January, 1970. The self employed, in professional practice or business, pay their income tax on a similar basis.

Surtax is an additional income tax payable on a sliding scale by people (not companies) with incomes in excess of £2,000 per annum. However, the effect of the surtax provisions of the 1961 Finance Act is to make earned income of £5,000 or less not liable to surtax.

Death duties are taxes on the estates (i.e. the property) of the deceased. Under the revised system proposed by the 1969 Budget, estates under £10,000 are exempt altogether: above this limit, each successive 'slice' of the estate will be subject to its own specified duty rate, on a progressive scale. The most lucrative stamp duties are those levied on the transfer of company securities and the conveyance of land. Others include the twopenny stamp duty on cheques.

The 'Special Charge' is an exceptional tax, operated on a sliding scale, which the 1968 Budget placed retrospectively on the investment income of individuals for the year 1967–8.

The taxes levied by the Department of Customs and Excise fall into three categories: customs duties, excise duties and purchase taxes. Customs duties are imposed on goods imported from overseas, and are traditionally classed as protective or revenue. Protective duties are designed to protect British firms from overseas competition in their home market, though many are in course of reduction in implementation of the 'Kennedy Round' (Chapter 19). Some concessions, moreover, may be given to imports from Commonwealth countries or members of the European Free Trade Area (Chapter 19). Thus the general tariff rate on imports of watches is $26\frac{1}{2}$ per cent, but imports from E.F.T.A. and the Irish Republic are admitted duty free, while imports from the Commonwealth pay $17\frac{1}{2}$ per cent. The current law on protective duties is contained in the Import Duties Act, 1958, which both consolidated previous legislation and defined the procedure for deciding the duties payable.

Customs duties may also be levied on imported goods simply to raise revenue. In this case home produced goods in the same class will be subject to an Excise duty at comparable rates. Thus spirits produced in this country (mainly whisky and gin) are subject to an Excise duty, while imported spirits (mainly rum and brandy) are subject to a Customs

166 ECONOMICS OF MONEY AND INCOME

duty. Imported tobacco is subject to a Customs duty, while an Excise duty would be payable on any tobacco grown commercially in this country. Excise duties may, further, be levied on certain commercial activities: an entertainments tax is payable on cinema performances, while a gaming licence is required to use premises for certain games of chance.[1] Customs and excise duties are charged on either an ad valorem or a specific basis, i.e. levied as a percentage or a fixed sum per unit.

Since 1940, customs and excise duties have been supplemented by purchase taxes on a wide variety of goods. These are ad valorem taxes, levied as a percentage of the statutory wholesale price, i.e. the price defined in the relevant Finance Act for the purpose of determining the tax. Purchase tax was first introduced partly to raise revenue and partly as an instrument for influencing the economy. Today, all Government income and expenditure must be considered from these two viewpoints, but implications for economic policy are held over to Chapters 11 and 20. Similarly, the economic background to tariffs (i.e. protective duties) is postponed for consideration in Chapter 19.

Firms which subsequently export goods on which a Customs duty was paid on import are entitled to a refund of the duty, known as a 'Customs drawback'. A similar return may be made of Customs or Excise duties paid on articles incorporated into goods which are finally exported. In October, 1964, the Government introduced a further scheme for making certain 'export rebates', the values of which are shown as offsets against tax revenue in Table 8.2. The scheme entitled exporters of goods wholly or largely produced in this country to a rebate of some of the indirect taxes that had entered into their costs of production, viz., certain items of *purchase tax* paid on goods used in manufacturing, duties on petrol and oil, and motor vehicle licence duties. The rebate scheme was introduced to encourage exports, in order to help reduce a U.K. balance of payments deficit (Chapter 18). It was abolished from April, 1968, but some rebates remained to be paid in the year 1969–70.

Along with its export rebate scheme, it may be noted, the Government also introduced in 1964 a temporary surcharge on imports. This tariff was intended neither to protect home industry nor to raise revenue, but to secure some quick relief for the problem of the U.K. external deficit (above), by discouraging imports. All imports except, in the main, books, foodstuffs and basic raw materials became subject to a surcharge fixed initially at 15 per cent, but reduced to 10 per cent in April, 1965.

[1] Section 13(5) of the Finance Act, 1966, lists them as: baccarat, big six, blackjack, boule, chemin de fer, chuck-a-luck, craps, crown and anchor, faro, faro bank, hazard, poker dice, pontoon, roulette, trente et quarante, vingt-et-un and wheel of fortune.

The surcharge was finally removed in November, 1966. In November, 1968, the Government introduced an import-deposit scheme, under which importers are (with certain exceptions) required to pay a deposit to the Customs and Excise—refundable 180 days subsequently—of 50 per cent of the value of the goods imported. The main exceptions relate to basic foodstuffs, fuel, raw materials, certain goods from the less developed countries, and goods intended for export.

Motor Vehicle Duties include driving licence fees, and the licence fees paid by all motor-vehicle operators known popularly as the 'road tax'. The duties are collected by County and County Borough Councils, and remitted to a 'Motor Tax Account' at the Bank of England, en route for the Exchequer account.

The Finance Act, 1966, introduced a Selective Employment Tax intended to fall upon the 'service' industries, e.g. distribution, banking, insurance, catering and laundries (but not transport). However, partly to simplify administration, *all* employers (not the self-employed) are required to pay the tax on each employee, and those employers on whom the tax is not intended to fall receive a refund. The tax is collected with the National Insurance contribution (Section 5), though intended for the Exchequer account like all other tax revenue. Since July, 1969, the rates of tax have been 48s. 0d. per man, 24s. 0d. per woman, 24s. 0d. per boy, 16s. 0d. per girl in employment. Under the original scheme, employers engaged in manufacturing received a refund larger than the tax paid, thus enjoying a small subsidy per employee (7s. 6d. for each man, less for others). This arrangement was discontinued from 1st April, 1968, except for manufacturers in Development Areas (Chapter 20). With this exception—which is also due to terminate in 1970—manufacturers today receive a plain refund as do transport firms, farmers, local authorities and, in general, public corporations. Some economic aspects of this and the other taxes previously described are considered in Chapter 20.

Loans by way of economic aid to less developed countries are not made from the National Loans Fund, but 'voted' out of the Consolidated Fund as part of the Supply Services. Interest on these and certain other loans similarly financed is still paid into the Consolidated Fund, along with dividends on the shares the Government owns in, e.g., British Petroleum, Ltd. However, the biggest item of miscellaneous revenue is the various receipts of the spending departments. The Government also derives a revenue from the sale (through the Post Office) of Broadcast Receiving Licences. These carry an excise duty of £1, distinct from the licence fee itself. Of the fee revenue, the bulk is made available from the Consolidated Fund for the finance of the B.B.C.

Table 8.3 is based upon Table 13 of the 1969 Financial Statement. Table 13 effectively summarizes the expenditure estimates of the depart-

TABLE 8.3

Supply Services and Consolidated Fund Standing Services

	1969–70 estimate £ million
SUPPLY SERVICES	
Defence Budget	
Defence (Central)	34
(Navy)	646
(Army)	600
(Air)	592
Ministry of Technology	209
Ministry of Public Building and Works	180
Atomic Energy Authority	5
Total Defence Budget	2,266
Other Supply	
(I) Government and Finance	200
(II) Commonwealth and Foreign	295
(III) Home and Justice	256
(IV) Communications, Trade and Industry	2,461
(V) Agriculture	413
(VI) Local Government, Housing and Social Services	4,876
(VII) Education and Science	449
(VIII) Museums, Galleries and the Arts	17
(IX) Public Buildings and Common Governmental Services	292
(X) Other Public Departments	17
(XI) Miscellaneous	29
Total Other Supply	9,305
Supplementary Provision[1]	229
TOTAL SUPPLY SERVICES	11,800
CONSOLIDATED FUND STANDING SERVICES	
Payment to the National Loans Fund in respect of service of the National Debt	478
Northern Ireland—share of reserved taxes, etc.	238
Other Services	35
Total	12,551

[1] An addition to the Supply Votes was necessary to take account of certain changes in (among other matters) the S.E.T. refund provisions and the cost of farming subsidies.

ments (published in detail in February, 1969), and also gives estimates for the standing charges on the Consolidated Fund. The Supply Services listed are self explanatory, though it should be recognized that the figures include spending by the departments on durable capital assets, such as hospitals. In other words, the Government is financing the growth of its stock of capital goods from its tax (and other current) revenue. It is also important to distinguish the grants to local authorities made by the Ministry of Housing and Local Government (included in item (VI)) from loans to authorities made by the Treasury (Table 8.4 below).

The Consolidated Fund Services, while much smaller in total, need more attention if they are to be understood. The first entry is identical with entry 4a in Table 8.1, explained in Section 2. The second entry reflects the financial arrangements made on the establishment of the Northern Ireland Government in 1921, when the United Kingdom Government reserved the right to collect certain taxes in Northern Ireland, notably income tax and customs and excise duties. The proceeds attributable to Northern Ireland are, however, remitted to that Government, less a contribution for the joint services enjoyed between the two countries, e.g. defence.

Among the other standing charges, a noteworthy entry is the 'post-war credit' repayments—or income tax refunds—the Government plans to make in the financial year ahead. During the 1939–45 war, the Government's anti-inflationary policy (Chapter 20) required high income tax rates (the standard rate was 10s. in the £), but at the same time it was necessary to avoid discouraging over-time work. The Government accordingly undertook to repay some taxation over the years after the end of the war. 'Other services' also include such items as the salaries and pensions of judges, Government incomes paid to the Sovereign and certain other members of the Royal Family, the salary of the Speaker of the House of Commons and the Leader of the Opposition, pensions to former Prime Ministers, etc.

4. *National Loans Fund Receipts and Payments*

Table 8.4 is based on Table 14 of the 1969 Financial Statement, with a little additional information from Table 15. It summarizes the receipts and payments estimated for the National Loans Fund in the financial year 1969–70, after allowing for 1969 budget changes (which would affect the size of the Consolidated Fund Surplus). Entries 1a, 1b, 2 and 5 have their counterpart in entries 8, 7, 6 and 11 respectively of Table 8.1, and no further comment is needed. Entry 6 breaks down the categories of National Loans Fund lending, but loans are stated net of repayments by the borrowers. Entry 6 is, accordingly, the equivalent of entry 12 minus entry 9 in Table 8.1.

If the possibility of changes in the sterling capital of the Exchange

TABLE 8.4

National Loans Fund
Summary of Receipts and Payments
1969–70 estimate

	£ million
I. RECEIPTS	
1. *Interest, etc.*	
(a) Interest on loans and profits of the Issue Department of the Bank of England	890
(b) Balance of interest met from the Consolidated Fund	478
Total	1,368
2. *Consolidated Fund Surplus*	2,457
3. *Exchange Equalization Account—* Changes in sterling capital	−826
4. *Net Borrowing*	
	2,999
II. PAYMENTS	
5. *National Debt* Interest and Expenses	1,368
6. *Loans (net of repayments)*	
(a) To nationalized industries	839
(b) To other public corporations	168
(c) To local and harbour authorities	540
(d) To private sector	4
(e) Within central government	80
	2,999

Note: A large part of 6e arises from official purchases of U.S. military aircraft.

Equalization Account is eliminated, then the figure for entries 3 and 4 gives the estimated net borrowing requirement of the Government for the year under review. That this is negative means that the Government will have the opportunity to make a net repayment of some of the outstanding N.L.F. debt over the course of the year. However, some of this

N.L.F. surplus could instead be applied to increasing the sterling capital of the Exchange Equalization Account; and vice versa. The relationship between the two funds is explored in Chapter 18.

Even abstracting from the E.E.A., we find various reasons why entry 4 will not necessarily measure the net decrease in National Loans Fund debt over the year. First, the figures given are estimates only, and tax yields and supply spending (especially) may differ somewhat from the values forecast, thus affecting the surplus forecast on the Consolidated Fund. Second, the Government may, anyway, introduce supplementary budgetary or spending proposals before the end of the financial year, raising tax revenue, or expenditure, correspondingly. Third, adjustments have to be made to the debt figure to allow for, e.g., the issue of securities at a discount. Fourth, the debt can, anyway, increase for reasons other than official borrowing: thus the Government might make an issue of securities to compensate shareholders on the nationalization of their enterprises. If, however, we could ignore all these qualifications, then the figure of £826 million would represent the decrease over the year 1969–70 in the size of the National Debt (as defined below).

Total sums borrowed and repaid over the course of the year would anyway be substantially greater than £826 million, as Treasury bill issues are made to finance expenditure ahead of tax receipts. Borrowing may also be necessary to finance some of each week's Treasury bill maturities and (unless a conversion issue is made) to redeem maturing bonds (Chapter 4).

At this point it is useful to summarize the sources of borrowing for the National Loans Fund, some of which have already been discussed in Chapter 4. First, the Treasury will seek to utilize the balances of statutory funds other than the National Loans Fund, and of official accounts with the Bank of England other than the Exchequer account. Thus current balances of the National Insurance Fund (Section 5) will be lent to the National Loans Fund as a Ways and Means Advance, or used to take up Treasury bills 'through the tap' (Chapter 4). A similar use is made of the sterling balances of the Exchange Equalization Account (Chapter 18) and of any funds standing to the credit of the departments in their subordinate accounts at the Bank of England (Chapter 4).

A second and closely related source of finance is the investment of certain statutory funds in Government securities. Thus the funds of the Trustee Savings Banks (Ordinary Departments) and of the Post Office (or National) Savings Bank ('ordinary accounts') are placed at the Government's disposal[1] through their investment in marketable bonds and certain non-negotiable securities (known as 'Terminable Annuities').

[1] Some Investment Department and 'investment account' funds are also invested in Government stocks (see Chapter 5).

Short-term Government debt apart, the National Insurance and National Insurance Reserve Funds (Section 5) are likewise invested in Government bonds (though the latter also holds some local authority securities).

The investment of these funds is undertaken by a small Government department, the National Debt Office, on behalf of the National Debt Commissioners. The Commissioners were first appointed in the eighteenth century, and charged with securing the reduction of the National Debt. An echo of this original obligation is found in the sale by the National Debt Office of life annuities, the capital sum payable being applied to security redemption. Its principal function today, however, is investment management. The only Commissioners ever consulted by the National Debt Office are the Governor and Deputy Governor of the Bank of England, and the Chancellor of the Exchequer. This provides an opportunity for the co-ordination of the Office's investment policy with the objectives of the Treasury and Bank of England in managing the National Debt.

A third source of finance is provided by the banking system, other financial intermediaries (including the Post Office giro) and the public at large, through their holdings of Treasury bills and marketable bonds (Chapters 2 and 5). There are currently over forty categories of marketable security in existence, dealings in which take place on the Stock Exchange. Approximately 20 per cent (by nominal value) are 'funded'; this means that while the Government may repay their nominal value at any time after the date (sometimes) mentioned in their title, it is under no obligation to do so. The holder's sole entitlement is to the annual interest. About half the total currently outstanding are $3\frac{1}{2}$ per cent War Loan, which became repayable in 1952 or after.

The remaining 80 per cent or so are 'unfunded', and will be redeemed at their nominal (or par) value some time between the dates mentioned in their titles. Thus $3\frac{1}{2}$ per cent Treasury Stock, 1979–81, will be redeemed at the Government's option at any time between these dates, and until redemption will carry annual interest at $3\frac{1}{2}$ per cent. The actual titles of these bonds—Exchequer stock, Conversion stock, etc.— have limited significance.

A fourth category of debt is made up of non-negotiable securities, comprising national savings securities and tax reserve certificates. The former are the savings certificates, national development bonds, premium bonds, etc., of interest to the small saver: their issue and management is conducted by the Post Office (after 1969, by the Department of National Savings). Tax reserve certificates may be purchased from the Bank of England (acting for the Treasury) by companies, professional men, etc., whose tax payments are particularly heavy at the start of the New Year (Section 3). The prudent firm will make provision for any future tax payments, and the sum set aside may be invested in a tax reserve certificate, which carries interest tax-free. The certificate may then be surrendered in payment of the tax when due, or (if necessary) surrendered for cash beforehand. When the certificate is first bought the purchase price is paid into the National Loans Fund, so that holdings may be regarded as short-term loans to the Government, financing part of its net borrowing needs.

Finally,[1] the Government may borrow from overseas Governments and international monetary institutions. While the National Loans Fund becomes indebted to these lenders, the loans *in themselves* do not place any new net balances at the National Loans Fund's disposal! The explanation of this paradox is to be found in the part played in these transactions by the Exchange Equalization Account, and is considered in Chapter 18.

Column 1 of Table 8.5 sets out the nominal value of the National Debt at 31st March, 1967 and 1968. Legally, this is defined as the total debt of the Government for which interest payments and any capital repayments have been charged by statute on the National Loans Fund, with recourse to the Consolidated Fund. Most of the Debt components have already been discussed in the preceding pages (except the Debt to the Bank of England, explained in Chapter 4). 'Other debt payable in sterling' represents mainly obligations to the International Monetary Fund (Chapters 18 and 19). 'Other debt payable in external currencies' represents obligations mainly to the United States and Canadian Governments. These two items should not be interpreted as defining either the form or the extent of the British Government's overseas debt liabilities, for reasons explained in Chapter 18.

Table 8.5 shows an increase of £2,208 million in the National Debt for 1967–8. It is not practicable to analyse this increase in terms of the financial categories defined in Section 2, as during this period the National Loans Fund had not been established, and all transactions were still routed through the Consolidated Fund. It is useful, nonetheless, to record that net loans by the Government, very largely of the sort defined in entry II (6) of Table 8.4, totalled £1,661 million, of which £330 million was met from a surplus of revenue over expenditure (similar to the Consolidated Fund Surplus (2) of Table 8.4). This left £1,331 million to be financed by borrowing. During the year the Government issued £508 million of securities by way of compensation to shareholders in the steel industry on its nationalization: this brings the figure for the Debt increase to £1,839 million. A further net increase in the Debt of £310 million is explained by certain transactions on the Exchange Equalization Account, other international transactions, and book-keeping adjustments made necessary by the sterling devaluation

---

[1] Government 'borrowing' through an increase in the fiduciary issue has already been considered in Chapter 4.

TABLE 8.5

	National Debt at:	
	(1)	(2)
	31st March	31st March
	1967	1968
	£ million	£ million
Funded Debt:		
(a) Marketable Securities	3,577	3,559
(b) Debt to the Bank of England	11	11
Life Annuities	5	5
Unfunded Debt:		
(a) Marketable Securities	16,276	16,530
(b) Terminable Annuities	640	558
(c) National Savings Securities	3,628	3,683
(d) Tax Reserve Certificates	289	308
(e) Floating Debt:		
(1) Treasury Bills	3,885	5,455
(2) Ways and Means Advances	273	278
(f) Other Debt Payable in Sterling	1,579	1,506
(g) Other Debt Payable in External		
Currencies	1,822	2,301
Total	31,985	34,193

Note: Column (2) does not add because of rounding.

Source: Annual Abstract of Statistics

of 1967. Finally, £59 million must be added in respect of certain technical adjustments, principally the issue of securities at a discount. The increase in the Debt over the year thus emerges as £2,208 million.

5. *The National Insurance Funds*

The present system of national insurance was established by the National Insurance Act, 1946, which set up three principal funds: the National Insurance Fund, the National Insurance (Reserve) Fund, and the Industrial Injuries Fund. The finances of all three are administered quite separately from the Consolidated Fund and National Loans Fund. The national insurance scheme divides the population aged between 15 and 65 into three categories: employed, self-employed and non-employed. Persons in each category make a regular weekly contribution to the National Insurance Fund, at rates for each group determined by the Government from time to time. Rates are rather lower for women than men, and lower still for boys and girls under 18 years of age. Employers are also required to make a weekly contribution in respect of each employee. Among the non-employed, married women and students are allowed to choose whether or not to make contributions. The major benefits provided under the scheme include retirement pensions for men at age 65 (for women at 60); regular weekly payments to people unemployed or away from work through sickness; various benefits for widows; payments in the event of industrial injury or death; an allowance for the guardians of orphan children; a lump-sum grant for women on maternity; and a grant on death (which would help meet funeral expenses). Details will be found in a popular guide published by the Department of Health and Social Security.

Important modifications to the scheme were made by the National Insurance Acts of 1959 and 1966. The 1959 Act introduced a graduated pensions scheme, which began operation in April, 1961. Employees participating in the scheme pay an extra contribution proportionate to their weekly earnings, and in return receive, on retirement, a bigger pension proportionate to the additional contributions they have made since 1961. The 1959 Act fixed the graduated contribution at 4¼ per cent of any weekly earnings between £6 and £15 (limits subsequently raised in 1963 to £9 and £18), and employers were required to make an equivalent contribution. The scheme is compulsory, except for employers who operate a private pension scheme with comparable minimum benefits, who are allowed to 'contract out' their employees. Male employees (over 18 years of age) who are 'contracted out' currently pay a flat-rate contribution of 19s. 1d.[1] per week; of itself, this entitles them to a retirement pension at the basic rate only. For male employees who are not 'contracted out' the current flat-rate contribution is 16s. 8d.[1] The corresponding flat-rate contributions for employers are 19s. 4d.[1] and 16s. 11d.[1] These contributions include relatively small sums for the Industrial Injuries Fund and the National Health Service, as well as—in the case of employers only—the Redundancy Fund (see below).

The 1966 Act provided for the payment of supplements to unemployment, sickness and widow's benefit, proportionate to the contributor's earnings. To finance these extra payments, all employees pay an additional ½ per cent on earnings between £9 and £30 a week.[1] For those employees contracted out of the main graduated pension scheme as such, these additional contributions will, nonetheless, also qualify them for a proportionate increase on their basic retirement pension. An identical contribution is made in each case by employers.[1]

[1] The National Insurance Bill, June, 1969, proposes an increase in each of these flat-rate contributions of 1s. per week, and an increase to 3¼ per cent of the ½ per cent payable on earnings from £18 to £30 per week.

The Government has, since 1947, made an annual contribution to the Fund, proportionate to the various rates currently in force. This 'Exchequer Contribution' is budgeted for annually in the Supply estimates and has, since 1962, been payable at a minimum of £170 million a year. The Fund also enjoys an income from the securities in which have been invested any surpluses of income over expenditure enjoyed in past years. Investments are controlled by the National Debt Office, which also handles the investments of the National Insurance (Reserve) Fund. This inherited, in 1947, the balances from previous Government insurance schemes. Interest on the Reserve Fund investments is paid as income to the National Insurance Fund. No capital may be transferred, however, without House of Commons approval.

Table 8.6 summarizes the receipts and payments of the National Insurance Fund for 1967–8. The biggest outgoing from the Fund, dwarfing all others, is the payment of retirement pensions. Since 1961, the finances of the Fund have been conducted on a 'pay-as-you-go' basis, which means simply that the Government aims at a rough balance of income and expenditure over the few years ahead (below). Given the ratio of retired people to working population in the community, the solvency of the Fund will thus largely depend on the level of benefit and contribution rates. Contributions have, in fact, been raised at intervals over the 1960s, and this has enabled some increase in the rates of benefit to be made. These, in turn, have gone some way to offset the effects of inflation (Chapter 14), but have been insufficient to secure for pensioners, and other beneficiaries, a corresponding share in rising community living standards (Chapter 15).

The difficulty of achieving regular pension increases on a largely flat-rate contributory basis partly explains why, in early 1969, the Government published proposals for a radically new national insurance scheme. The Government's plan, which is open to modification in the light of public discussion, provides for the establishment of two separate funds, the National Superannuation Fund, for pensions, widowhood benefits and death grants; and a Social Insurance Fund for the remaining benefits. In place of the flat-rate plus graduated contributions currently payable, all employees would pay a specified percentage on part or all of their earnings in each year (the self-employed, however, would continue to pay a flat rate). If their income was equal to, or less than, $1\frac{1}{2}$ times national average earnings, the percentage would apply to their whole income. If their income exceeded this figure, the percentage contribution would not fall on that part of their income above this figure. When the scheme started, the employee's contribution rate would be $6\frac{3}{4}$ per cent, of which $4\frac{3}{4}$ per cent would go to the National Superannuation Fund. Employees in occupational pension schemes could not be contracted out as under present arrangements, but could contribute

TABLE 8.6

National Insurance Fund
Receipts and Payments
1st April, 1967–31st March, 1968

		£ million
Receipts		
1. Balances at 1st April 1967		208
2. Contributions from insured persons and employers,		1,660
of which flat-rate contributions		1,242
3. Exchequer Contribution		300
4. Investment income (a) from National Insurance Fund		12
(b) from National Insurance (Reserve) Fund		50
5. Other		1
	Total	2,230
Payments		
6. *Benefits*:		
(a) Retirement pensions		1,385
(b) Sickness		323
(c) Widows		148
(d) Unemployment		122
(e) Maternity		37
(f) Death grant		9
(g) Guardian's allowance, etc.		1
7. Costs of administration		71
8. Other		19
9. Balances at 31st March 1968		116
	Total	2,230

Note: Totals do not add because of rounding.

Source: Accounts of the National Insurance Fund (House of Commons Paper 152, 1969). Most of this information is available, on a calendar-year basis, in the National Income and Expenditure Blue Book (H.M.S.O.)

a somewhat lower percentage in return for a reduced state retirement pension. Employers would contribute at the same rate, i.e. 6¾ per cent, which would be applied to their payroll without allowance for the earnings ceiling, though some concession would be made for occupational pension schemes. The Exchequer contribution would continue to run at around its current level, about 18 per cent of employers' and employees' contributions.

If the scheme is adopted, these contributions arrangements would be introduced in 1972, but the full pension benefits payable under the new scheme would not be available until 1992. People reaching pensionable age in the meantime will receive a pension calculated proportionately to their participation in each of the two schemes. Of itself, the new-scheme pension will be 'earnings-related': on retirement, a single person (for example) would be entitled to a pension equal to 60 per cent of his or her earnings up to half national average earnings, and 25 per cent of the remainder up to the scheme ceiling previously defined. 'Earnings' in this context are based on the average for the whole of the contributor's working life (taken to start at age 19), adjusted to reflect the levels of earnings current when he reaches pensionable age.

Like the current scheme, the new scheme will be run on the 'pay-as-you-go' principle. Unlike private pension funds, accordingly, the National Superannuation Fund will not be 'funded', i.e. the contributions of the participants are not invested in assets which, through the reinvestment of accumulating yields, ultimately finance the pension payments when due. Instead, the Government will meet current pension payments from the current contributions to the N.S.F. After 1972, accordingly, the Government will be able to finance old-scheme pension payments from the new-scheme contributions. With payments set as a given percentage of income, revenue will automatically rise as the community's money income grows. Even so, it will probably be necessary at some time in the late 1980s to increase the contribution rate, to allow for the growing proportion of retired persons getting the new-scheme pensions.

The Government proposes to review pensions payable under both schemes, along with other benefits, every two years. The buoyancy of the revenue should enable increases in old-scheme pension rates, as well as adjustments in new-scheme pensions to reflect the levels of earnings then current. In this way, pensioners might enjoy an almost automatic safeguard against inflation, along with participation in rising community living standards.

A further branch of the National Insurance scheme which must be mentioned is the Industrial Injuries Fund. This is a much smaller fund to which, currently, men over 18 years of age contribute 10d.[1] weekly, and their employers 11d.[1] Slightly lower rates apply to women and juveniles. A weekly injury or disablement benefit is paid to the victims of industrial accidents, apart from any damages recoverable through the courts for the employer's negligence. Benefit may also be paid to those who contract industrial diseases.

Though not strictly part of the National Insurance scheme, the

[1] The National Insurance Bill, June, 1969, proposes an increase of 1d. on these rates.

activities of the Redundancy Fund may usefully be reviewed at this point. Under the Redundancy Payments Act, 1965, employers are required to pay lump-sum compensation to redundant employees, related to their age, pay and length of service with employer. Employers making redundancy payments can claim a rebate of between two-thirds and three-quarters of the cost from the Redundancy Fund. This, in turn, is financed by contributions from all employers in respect of men and women employees. The current contribution for each man is 1s. 3d. per week, though this would be changed to ¼ per cent of his earnings when the new insurance scheme is introduced. Balances of the Fund are invested by the National Debt Office in the same range of securities as savings bank funds.

Finally, it may be noted that since 1957 each insured person has paid a few shillings weekly towards the finance of the National Health Service. The major part of expenditure by the Department of Health and Social Security on the Health Service, however, is met from the annual Supply estimates (Class (VI), Table 8.3). This Health Service contribution is collected with the flat-rate National Insurance and the Industrial Injuries contributions, and remitted by the employer to the Department of Health and Social Security, along with his own payments in respect of each employee. In addition to flat-rate insurance contributions, these are Redundancy Fund payments (for adult employees), payments of Selective Employment Tax (Section 3), and a very small sum payable per employee towards the National Health Service. On the other hand, graduated contributions from both employees and employer are paid by the latter through the P.A.Y.E. income tax system, the Inland Revenue remitting them in turn to the Department of Health and Social Security. Under the new insurance scheme these arrangements would be simplified by channelling all the payments through the P.A.Y.E. system.

6. *Local Authority Income and Expenditure* (*England and Wales*)

A number of social services—education, public health, housing, highways, fire service, police, etc.—are provided by local authorities. The inhabitants of large towns (generally 100,000 or more population) enjoying county borough status are served exclusively by their county borough council. In smaller towns and villages, some services, e.g. housing, are provided by the local municipal borough, urban or rural district council; and others, e.g. education, by the county council. A county council will thus have responsibilities in a number of municipal boroughs, or urban and rural districts, but not in a county borough.

Additionally, many authorities provide trading services—markets, harbours, cemeteries, bus services—which will not necessarily aim (except for transport) at covering costs from receipts. Since the social services may be provided free of charge (e.g. primary and secondary education) or at prices which do not fully cover the costs of provision (e.g. libraries), local authorities must clearly acquire funds to finance those activities, and to meet any deficit on trading services. Accordingly, having estimated their expenditure for the forthcoming year, authorities are obliged to budget for the means of financing it.

In their choice of methods, local authorities must observe a statutory restriction centring around the distinction between capital and revenue expenditure. In the main, capital expenditure results in the acquisition of a durable asset, e.g. a swimming pool. Revenue expenditure is incurred in running expenses and operating costs, e.g. the maintenance of the pool and the attendants' wages. Capital expenditure may be financed by borrowing; revenue expenditure (except temporarily) may not.

To meet some of their revenue expenditure, authorities will receive grants from the Consolidated Fund (Table 8.3). Under the completely revised arrangements introduced by the Local Government Act, 1966, local authorities submit estimates of the revenue expenditure (excluding trading activities) they propose to make over the following two years. The Government reviews these estimates in the light of its own policy, and then decides what overall grant total it will make available for each of the next two financial years. A part of this allocation will take the form of specific grants, intended to finance revenue expenditure on particular services; much the biggest grant here is for police expenditure. The remainder represents the sum available for distribution among the authorities as a 'rate support' grant.

The rate support grant is intended for the finance of local authority services in general. The grant is payable in three parts. First, county and county borough councils receive a 'needs' payment based upon, in the main, the size of their populations and the numbers under 15 years of age. Second, a compensating or 'resources' payment is made to any authority with rateable resources lower than the national average (in relation to population). Third, authorities responsible for levying rates (see below) receive a 'domestic' payment to enable them to reduce the rate levied on householders. The size of this reduction is decided on a national basis by the Minister of Housing and Local Government.

In accordance with these arrangements, local authorities submitted estimates in 1968 of their proposed revenue expenditure for 1969–70 and 1970–1. Their figures implied an increase in spending, expressed in 'real terms' (Chapter 9), of around 6 per cent per annum, which the Government considered too high in the light of current economic conditions (Chapter 20). It therefore decided that the 'relevant' revenue expenditure on which to base the overall grant would be a few per cent less than the authorities' own figures. This would allow for a 3 per cent 'real' increase in revenue expenditure in 1969–70 (relative to the 1968–9 level), and for a further 5 per cent real increase in 1970–1.

On this basis, the Rate Support Grant Order, 1968, fixed the aggregate of Exchequer revenue grants for 1969–70 at £1,666 million and for 1970–1 at £1,783 million. These represented respectively 56 and 57 per cent of the 'relevant' expenditure totals. Specific revenue grants for 1969–70 were to be £138 million, hence the value of the rate support grant for that year emerges as £1,528 million. For 1970–1, specific grants were put at £150 million, hence the rate support grant at £1,633 million.

The balance of local authority revenue expenditure is met from the general rate, which may also finance any deficit in the trading or housing revenue accounts. In principle, the general rate is levied on the occupiers of all property within the authority's area, but there are many exceptions to this rule. County councils, it may be noted, do not themselves levy rates, but notify their requirements to the municipal boroughs and urban and rural districts, which add the county 'precept' to their own rating needs.

Suppose, for a given rating authority, the sum to be raised from the general rate is £400,000. The total 'rateable value' of the property in the authority's area may be £480,000 (this is decided for each house, shop, factory, etc., by the Commissioners of Inland Revenue, on an estimate of its current annual rental value). Ignoring the complications presented by unoccupied property, etc., we calculate that a rate of one penny in the pound would raise 480,000 pence, or £2,000. To raise £400,000 a rate of 16s. 8d. (i.e. 200d.) in the pound must be levied. A householder, accordingly, with a house of rateable value £100 would this year pay a rate of 100 × 16s. 8d. Under the 'rate reduction' scheme (see above) this would be reduced by 1s. 3d. in the pound in the year 1969–70, or 1s. 8d. in the pound in the year 1970–1.

In the decade preceding the 1966 Act, the amount collected in rates increased by about 9 to 10 per cent per annum. This was much faster than the average growth of household income, and rate payments bore particularly hard upon the lowest income groups. To deal with the first problem, the Government aims to adjust the annual grant total in such a way that the average rate poundage need increase no faster than the growth in household incomes. The second problem the Government has sought to meet with the Rating Act, 1966, under which householders at low income levels may have their rate liability reduced.

For its capital expenditure an authority will, in the main, rely on borrowed funds, and borrowing for any given project (e.g. school building) must receive the sanction of the Ministry of Housing and Local Government, which in turn consults the appropriate Government

G

department (e.g. the Department of Education and Science). Capital expenditure in excess of the approved borrowing total may be met by levying a higher general rate. Further, capital expenditure on major highways is eligible for a capital grant from the Government, while expenditure on housing attracts various subsidies. The most recent (1967) of these is a grant which meets the interest cost on borrowing for house building in excess of 4 per cent per annum. Housing subsidies enable local authorities to charge their tenants rents lower than would otherwise be necessary if (e.g.) the full interest charges had to be met from rent revenue.

Funds may be borrowed 'on the market' or from the Government. Applications for loans from the Government are vetted (from a financial viewpoint) by the Public Works Loan Board and met, if approved, from the National Loans Fund (Section 4). Other things being equal, therefore, the more the local authorities borrow from the Government, the greater will be the Government's own net borrowing.

Between 1955 and 1964, the Government encouraged authorities to raise funds in the capital market, and severely restricted access to the P.W.L.B. Authorities were, however, reluctant to increase long-term borrowing during a period of generally high interest rates. There was, in consequence, a considerable rise in their 'temporary' borrowing, i.e. for a period of less than one year. The local authority temporary loan market was briefly described in Chapter 3, though it may be noted, additionally, that authorities are active in lending their temporarily surplus funds among themselves on a short-term basis.

Treasury disquiet with the growth of temporary borrowing led to the formulation, in 1963, of a general rule that each authority should limit its temporary debt to 20 per cent of its debt total for the current year. In return, for the financial year 1964–5 authorities were given access to the P.W.L.B. for up to 20 per cent of their long-term borrowing 'needs' (defined to include borrowing to pay off maturing debt). There was also the prospect of a rise in the 'quota' to 50 per cent over the next four years, but by 1967–8 it had progressed no further than 34 per cent, while for 1968–9 it fell back to 30 per cent. Moreover, for these years the quota was redefined as a proportion of actual net capital payments (i.e. excluding, in particular, borrowing to pay off maturing debt). The rate of interest charged on quota loans is based on the rate the Government pays for its own borrowing. Loans at the rates that local authorities would need themselves to pay are available for authorities demonstrably unable to meet the remainder of their needs by borrowing in the capital market.

Quite small loans (usually £500 upwards for between two and five years) may be accepted on the security of a mortgage of the authority's rates and revenues. These 'local authority mortgages' may have some appeal to local savers. A more up-to-date and simpler alternative is for the lender to be given a bond certificate. In essentials, this is the same as the 'yearling' bond discussed in Chapter 3, except that it is issued 'through the tap', i.e. over the counter of the town (or county) hall, instead of 'on block' by a placing.

Larger sums (from £20,000) may also be taken on mortgage for periods from one to seven years. Authorities and lenders are put in touch by specialist money brokers and some stockbrokers, most of whom are also active in the market for temporary loans. Restrictions on stock and bond issues (below) and on temporary borrowing have given this market an increased significance as a residual source of finance.

'Yearling' bonds apart, the bigger authorities may make issues[1] of their own (longer-dated) stock, carrying a Stock Exchange quotation. The Bank of England may act as the authority's agent, e.g. as with Swansea Corporation 6¾ per cent Stock, 1973–4, issued in June, 1965. Further, the Bank regulates the timing and terms of stock (and bond) issues, to ensure their co-ordination with the Bank's management of the market in Government stocks (for which to certain investors local authority securities are close substitutes).

7. The Nationalized Industries

A number of industries have, at various times (but especially between 1945 and 1951), been placed under public ownership: coal, gas, electricity, steel, railways, airways (very largely) and certain other transport undertakings. The technique in each case has been to establish by Act of Parliament a public corporation to take over the assets of the private firms in the industry, their shareholders being compensated with Government or Government-guaranteed securities. Each corporation is organized in accordance with its particular statute, which also requires it—in some broadly-worded formulation—to 'pay its way' over the years and to satisfy the demand for its product or service in 'the most efficient way'.

Disappointment with the financial performance of the nationalized industries prompted the Government, in 1961, to define more precisely their financial and economic obligations. The same obligations were also imposed upon the Post Office (whose transformation from Government department to public corporation was completed in 1969). In brief, they were expected to earn sufficient revenue from the sale of their product or service to cover their operating costs, to pay interest charges on outstanding capital obligations, to provide for the depreciation of

[1] Issues—subject to Treasury approval—on Continental capital markets seem (mid-1969) a likely development (compare page 185).

their fixed assets at replacement cost (Chapter 14), and to build up general reserves which would contribute to the finance of their investment projects (below). The differing circumstances of each industry were recognized, and the Government undertook to define an appropriate objective in each case. Typically, this was expressed as a rate of return on (i.e. profits as a percentage of) the capital of the business, to be achieved over a five-year period. Thus the target rate of return for the Post Office for 1963-4 to 1967-8 was put at 8 per cent, and for British European Airways for the same period, 6 per cent.

Most of the industries have, at some time or other, suffered losses, but the most persistent difficulties have been experienced by the rail and coal industries. By March, 1965, for example, the National Coal Board had accumulated a net operating deficit of £91 million, and it suffered a further deficit of £25 million in the year ending 26th March, 1966. The Coal Industries Act, 1965, provided for a capital reconstruction scheme under which both these losses and some unremunerative capital assets were written off. In short, the scheme involved reducing the Board's debt obligation to the Consolidated Fund by £415 million, an arrangement which also served to relieve it of interest payments worth, in 1966, £22 million. Assistance of a similar sort has, on occasion, been given to the rail industry. Both industries have been set targets requiring them to break even.

In 1967 the Government undertook a further review of the economic and financial objectives of the nationalized industries. This retained the principle of the target rate of return on total capital, but set alongside it two other principles intended to guide their pricing and their investment policies. In the first case, stress was laid on achieving a 'reasonable' relationship between prices and marginal costs of production, so that the cost to the consumer reflected the cost to the industry of providing him with that good or service. In the second case, all industries were expected to adopt the best financial methods for appraising new investment schemes, and the use of 'discounted cash flow' techniques (Chapter 13) was recommended. Projects which offered a rate of return below 8 per cent (a guide figure raised to 10 per cent in August, 1969) were to be rejected. The calculation of the rate of return offered by a new investment project (e.g. putting up a new electricity power station) should not be confused with the definition of a target rate of profit (or return) on total capital for the whole enterprise.

Through its statement of pricing and investment criteria the Government sought to encourage the nationalized industries towards greater efficiency in their use of the economy's resources, e.g. the avoidance of low-return investment projects. Alongside these commercial considerations, however, the industries would—it was recognized—need to take account of social and other factors, which could sometimes be reflected in the pricing or investment decisions taken. For example, the marginal cost pricing rule might require relatively high fares on an expensive-to-operate branch line, but these might be reduced in the interests of serving an isolated rural community.

Each industry's plans for investment over the next five years are reviewed annually by its 'sponsoring' Department (e.g. Ministry of Power for the electricity supply industry), the Treasury and the Department of Economic Affairs (Chapter 20). This enables the Government to agree capital expenditure for the forthcoming financial year, to give provisional approval for the following year's plans, and to review in outline the investment plans for the subsequent years. The bulk of capital expenditure proposed for the year ahead will be on projects already in hand, but some 'starts' on new projects will also come under consideration. Their ability to satisfy the minimum test discount rate (of 10 per cent) does not ensure their approval by the Government, which might choose to postpone some new schemes as a means of restraining the growth of public sector expenditure. The background to such decisions is considered in Chapter 20.

Of the industries' total annual capital requirements, about 55 per cent in recent years has been financed by borrowing from the National Loans Fund (before 1968, the Consolidated Fund), though this proportion does vary quite widely among the industries. The remainder has been met very largely if not exclusively from the industries' own internal resources. Loans are made for periods generally up to thirty years, at a fixed interest rate reflecting the Government's own borrowing rate when the loan is made. In one or two cases, however, this fixed-interest obligation has been converted to a requirement to pay a dividend out of any profits made. The most important internal resources are generally the reserves built up from the surplus of revenue over costs, though funds available (e.g.) through depreciation allowances are also utilized for this purpose (compare Chapter 7). Temporary loans are secured from the banks (on terms described in Chapter 2), and a net rise in overdrafts outstanding over the year may meet a tiny part of capital requirements. Up to 1956, the electricity, gas, transport and air undertakings issued their own securities (which carried a Government guarantee), instead of borrowing from the Consolidated Fund. This scheme was suspended because of the difficulties it created for the Bank of England in its execution of official monetary policy. In early 1969, however, the Gas Council was permitted by the Treasury to raise funds with an issue of (Government-guaranteed) bonds in Germany, and other nationalized industries may be expected to follow this precedent. Borrowing overseas in this way should be cheaper for the industry than borrowing from the Government. It also furthers the Government's objective of reducing the deficit on long-term capital account in the balance of payments, though at the cost of a greater interest-burden in later years—see Chapters 17 and 18.

8. *Statistics of the Public Sector*

Chapter 9 explains the construction of statistics of national income, output and expenditure for the economy as a whole. In Chapter 20 we shall see how this statistical information, coupled with the appropriate economic theory, forms a basis for Government economic policy. To build up the national income statistics, the Central Statistical Office relies, for the public sector, upon the figures presented in the accounts of the Consolidated Fund, the National Loans Fund, the other statutory funds, the local authorities and the nationalized industries. Clearly the accounts themselves were not designed originally for this purpose, but simply to facilitate financial administration. Accordingly, a great deal of their information, if it is to be used as a basis for economic policy and discussion, needs recasting in two ways.

First, a lot of consolidation can be undertaken. For example, the distinction between Consolidated Fund and National Insurance Fund need not be observed if the desired statistics are of total Government income and expenditure. It is also possible to consolidate information for the whole of the public sector, to give a measure of the combined weight of Central Government, local authority and nationalized industry transactions.

Second, the categories used in the accounts will not necessarily be appropriate for economic analysis, so that extensive reclassification needs to be made. Thus in the administration of the tax system, it is important to distinguish the agencies which collect the taxes: this explains the lay-out of Table 8.2. For economic analysis and policy, however, it is important instead to distinguish which taxes fall on income, which on capital and which on expenditure. This is not always a straightforward matter (for instance, the capital gains tax might possibly be regarded as a variety of income tax), but in principle it has nothing to do with which agency collects the tax for the Government. Taxes on expenditure, for example, are collected by (at least) three Government departments: Customs and Excise (purchase tax, etc.), Inland Revenue (stamp duties), and Department of Health and Social Security (selective employment tax). A similar sort of reclassification needs to be made for the various items of Government expenditure.

The Government has also sought in recent years to rationalize the structure and improve the presentation of its own published accounts. Thus before 1965 popular understanding of the Financial Statement was probably hindered by a highly technical distinction made between 'the

Budget above-the-line' and 'the Budget below-the-line'. This division in turn reflected the lay-out of the (now discontinued) Public Income and Expenditure Account, which followed the Sinking Fund Act, 1875, in distinguishing between 'expenditure' and 'payments' according to the

TABLE 8.7

Debt of the Public Sector

	31st March, 1968 £ million
Central government:	
National Debt (Table 8.5)	34,193
Accrued interest on national savings certificates	574
Balances in P.O.S.B. and T.S.B.s (Ordinary Departments)	2,740
Notes and coin in circulation (Chapter 4)	3,310
N. Ireland Government	244
Post-war credits	187
Local authorities:	
Gross loan debt (estimated)	12,950
Public corporations:	
Government guaranteed marketable securities (Section 7)	1,755
Loans from central government	10,381
Borrowing on bank overdraft	94
Finance from certain internal funds	279
1. Total outstanding debt	66,707
2. of which identified holdings within the public sector	23,915
3. Net debt of the public sector	42,792

Note: (i) Accrued interest on national savings certificates, since not charged on the National Loans Fund, is not included in the National Debt entry.
(ii) Notes and coin in circulation exclude those held by the Bank of England.

Source: Annual Abstract of Statistics, 1968

statutory authority governing their finance by borrowing. A new classification was introduced in 1965, which made a clearer distinction between revenue and expenditure on the one hand and, on the other, Government loans and the consequential estimated borrowing requirement. The establishment of the National Loans Fund in 1968 has enabled a further simplification of the Financial Statement, and the position of the Government as a net lender to the rest of the public sector emerges with particular clarity.

Improvements have likewise been made in the presentation of the Civil Estimates and the Defence Estimates. Thus in the former the Classes of expenditure (Table 8.2) were in 1962 reconstructed to bring together groups of Votes possessing a greater coherence. Each Vote, in turn, was designed to cover one important block of expenditure, while the Subhead classification was redesigned to follow as closely as possible the Departmental organization. These modifications were designed to make the economic implications of the accounts clearer, to facilitate Parliamentary, Treasury and departmental control, and to promote public understanding of the problems of Government finance.

Economic analysis of Government finances has also been facilitated by the addition to the Financial Statement and the Supply Estimates of tables which recast their information in the form used in the national income statistics. These supplementary tables will show, for example, what part of a given expenditure total represents current spending on goods and services, and what part fixed capital formation (see Table 9.2). An innovation of the 1968 Financial Statement, further, was the inclusion of a short assessment of the outlook for the economy up to mid-1969. The 1969 statement, re-styled 'Financial Statement and Budget Report', supplemented its forward assessment to mid-1970 with a review of the economy's progress over the past year. This assessment, along with the traditional Budget speech of the Chancellor, gives insight into the economic factors underlying the budgetary decisions, of the sort explained in Chapter 20.

Government debt represents another area in which official financial data may be presented in a different form to suit economic analysis. Thus in law the National Debt is the debt of the British Government charged upon the National Loans Fund, with recourse to the Consolidated Fund. We saw in Section 4, however, that a substantial part of this debt is in fact held by Government departments and other statutory funds like the National Insurance Fund. Further, public sector institutions like the nationalized industries and local authorities have substantial debt obligations to the private sector which are not charged upon the National Loans Fund, even though in the case of public corporation security issues they carry an official Government guarantee. The Radcliffe Committee (*op. cit.*) accordingly found it more helpful to use the term 'national debt' to denote the total net debt of the public sector. Table 8.7 sets out the national debt in this sense, as at 31st March, 1968. It is seen that national debt in the 'Radcliffe' sense means all the debt of government and public sector institutions less what they owe one another, i.e. the net debt of the public sector to the private sector (and to overseas debt holders).

Questions

1. Outline the main sources of income and the main lines of expenditure in the national budget presented each year by the Chancellor of the Exchequer to Parliament. A.E.B.

2. If government total expenditure exceeds revenue, from what sources can the British Exchequer obtain the necessary finance? I.B.

3. Set out the main sources of borrowing by the central government of the United Kingdom. I.B.

4. How does the House of Commons exercise control over public expenditure and taxation? I.M.T.A.

Note: Few questions on public finance call for descriptive material only; usually, some analysis or discussion is also required. Questions of this sort will be found after Chapter 20.

Part three

Part three

9

National Income, Output and Expenditure

1. *A Tale of a Shirt*

The purchaser of a 30s. shirt pays 30s. for it, so the value of his expenditure equals the value of the product. This is obvious, but what is less apparent is that the 30s. finds its way back as income to the people who made and sold the shirt. We may trace out this process in imagination with an artificial but nonetheless useful example.

The retailer (we assume) paid the wholesaler 22s. for it, and used 3s. from his net receipts of 8s. to finance the wages of his assistants, 1s. to help meet his rent and 2s. for current expenses such as heating, lighting, etc. His gross profit is 2s. of which 1s. is earmarked as a depreciation allowance (page 132). His net profit of 1s. represents a return of interest on the capital he has invested in the business, and a reward for his work in organizing the shop.

A similar breakdown may be made for the wholesaler's net receipts of (say) 7s. The manufacturer in turn received 15s. out of which he paid various suppliers (fuel, carriage costs, etc.), and remunerated himself, his employees, his landlord and any persons who had put up capital for his business. He passed on (say) 6s. to the textile manufacturer who in turn passed on 1s. to the planter who grew the cotton in the first place.

We are now able to see the value of the shirt from three different viewpoints. First, its value is equal to the customer's expenditure on the finished garment. Second, its value is equal to the sum of the incomes earned in its production, i.e. in making and selling it. Third, its final value is equal to the sum of the contributions made at each stage by the various industries and trades involved in its production. Thus the retailer contributed 5s. value (measured by 3s. wages and 2s. gross profit), the retailer's landlord contributed 1s. value (measured by his rent), and so on. These three approaches to the value of any product provide three avenues to the definition and calculation of the national output.

193

2. *Meaning of National Output*

The resources of an economy, used to produce goods and services of all sorts, comprise the labour power of its inhabitants, its natural resources and its physical capital (i.e. raw materials in course of production and capital goods—page 129). Labour power is, of course, provided by private people, who are rewarded for their contribution to production by wages and salaries. It is often convenient, for statistical purposes, to include one-man businesses, partnerships and farming companies in this broad category of 'labour'. A distinction is then drawn between those in employment, who receive wages and salaries, and those in self-employment, who enjoy fees and certain profit earnings.

The second contributor to the current output of goods and services is natural resources and physical capital. These resources will form the business capital (Chapter 7) of the firms in the economy or, alternatively, will be in the ownership of the Government and local authorities. The employment of business capital yields a profit for firms, while government sometimes derives an analogous return from the employment of some of its productive assets—e.g. local authority transport services (Section 3). The profits of unincorporated businesses and farming companies have already been accounted for in 'income from self-employment'. The profits of all other companies finance the payment of dividends and interest to share and debenture holders. These accordingly could be regarded as the ultimate 'owners' of the resources employed by these companies, if we ignore the strict letter of company law. While some firms derive (part of) their profits by leasing property, it is convenient for statistical purposes to distinguish between trading profits and rents from property lease.

As time passes, so the employment of these 'factors of production' by firms (and government) yields a flow of goods and services. This output flow is continuous, but we may take any two dates (say the start and end of a year, or of a quarter-year) and attempt to measure its value between them. In doing so, we must recognize that some goods and services will have become incorporated in yet other goods and services in the course of production. Thus the cloth in the example of Section 1 was incorporated in the shirt, and so was the transport service provided by the haulage contractor who, say, drove the cloth from the mill to the shirt factory! It follows that the value of the cloth and the value of the transport service will both already be included in the 'final' value of the shirt (Section 1).

If, therefore, we refrain from counting in the value of all these 'intermediate' goods and services a second time, we may define the value of the output yielded by the economy's resources during a given year as its domestic product for that year. Domestic product is said to comprise the economy's 'final' output of goods and services, in distinction to the intermediate goods and services which were also produced in the same period but became incorporated in the final output. The various categories of final output are considered in Section 4, but two important observations may be made in passing. First, while goods sold to households for their members' private 'consumption'—jam, shirts, furniture, etc.—are final goods, they represent in total just one category of domestic output, so that it is wrong to equate 'consumption' goods with final output. Second, the word 'final' is not equivalent to 'finished', so that—as explained in Section 4—final output does not consist only of final services plus goods sold in a technically finished condition.

With few exceptions, the domestic product is a measure of all those goods and services produced for sale 'in the market', even though—as with medical treatment under the National Health Service—the actual recipient may make little or no direct payment for what he receives. It follows that there are countless goods and services produced each year that do not enter into the domestic product. These are the things that people make and do for themselves and for one another on a non-monetary basis. Thus the shave a man gives himself, the spring-clean the housewife gives her house, or the cake she bakes, are all outside the domestic product. On the other hand, the purchase of a shave from a barber, of cleaning services from a charwoman, of a cake from the baker give rise to an identifiable economic transaction, yield an income to the barber, charwoman and baker, and are accordingly included in the domestic output.

The test for inclusion in domestic product is, accordingly, that the good or service is produced by factors who are rewarded for their contribution with a corresponding income. A few exceptions are admitted to this general principle, on the grounds that while no actual income payment is involved, the situations are so close to market transactions that to omit them would be misleading (see, however, Section 9). Thus domestic product calculations include an estimate of the annual value to house owners of their occupation of their own property, measured by the rents they would be paying were they instead renting their houses from a landlord. If this value were omitted, a rise in owner occupation would mean (other things being equal) a fall in domestic product, as the total rental value of actual tenancies would decline.

Domestic product is not quite the same thing as national product. British domestic output is derived from economic activity within the United Kingdom. However, some of the productive assets contributing to domestic output here are owned by foreign residents while, in turn, residents of this country own assets which are employed overseas. If, accordingly, we deduct from domestic output rent, dividends, interest and profits paid abroad, and add the corresponding income received by

British residents from their property overseas, we obtain the value of the U.K. national output. This is defined as the final output derived

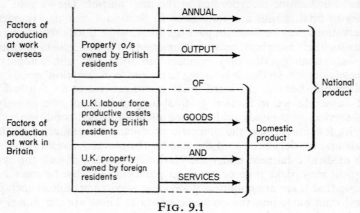

FIG. 9.1

from the U.K. labour force and U.K.-owned productive assets, whether the latter are employed in Britain or overseas. These relationships may be summarized in a simple diagram (Fig. 9.1).

3. Measurement of National Income

The national output must be expressed as a total money value and not as a total physical quantity, because it is impossible to add quantities expressed in different physical units—hogsheads of wine and kilowatts of electricity. We saw in Section 1 that the value of a 30s. shirt passes as 30s. of income to the factors responsible for its production. This suggests that, if we take all the incomes earned in a given year by labour and by other productive factors in the ownership of U.K. residents, we shall have a measure of national output for that year.

We may make a start, accordingly, by taking the total of personal incomes before tax received by residents of this country in 1968, amounting to £35,948 million (item 1 in Table 9.1). This figure includes their earnings received from property overseas, but of course excludes the earnings received by foreign residents from the assets they have in this country.

Personal income[1] in Table 9.1 includes wages, salaries, fees, dividends,

[1] The Blue Book figure of £36,093 million includes £121 million 'stock appreciation' for sole traders, partnerships and farming companies (see below), and £24 million taxes paid to overseas governments by private persons on property income from abroad.

interest, rent, unemployment and sickness benefits, etc. It also includes income in kind, such as the value of the farm produce consumed by the farmer's family, the value of the miner's coal allowance, of the serviceman's food and clothing, of the farm worker's 'free' cottage. By 'imputing' these incomes to the total of personal incomes, we ensure that the corresponding national output calculation takes account of the value

TABLE 9.1

United Kingdom National Output, 1968

	£ million
1. Total personal income before U.K. tax	35,948
2. *Less* National Insurance etc., benefits	3,687
3. *Less* Government debt interest	1,792
4. *Plus* Company undistributed profits	3,850
5. *Plus* Public Corporation undistributed profits	826
6. *Plus* Government trading etc., income	1,670
7. Residual error	−129
8. GROSS NATIONAL PRODUCT	36,686
9. *Less* Capital Consumption	3,375
10. NET NATIONAL INCOME AT FACTOR COST	33,311
11. *Less* Property income received from abroad	2,060
12. *Plus* Property income paid abroad	1,641
13. NET DOMESTIC PRODUCT AT FACTOR COST	32,892

Note: 7. *Residual Error*
The information in this and the other national income tables is derived by the Central Statistical Office from a variety of sources, notably government accounts, Inland Revenue tax assessments and the annual census of production. Any discrepancy is shown clearly as a residual error.

Source: National Income and Expenditure Blue Book, 1969

of the goods and services they represent. A further example of an imputed income is the annual rental value of owner occupied houses, discussed in the previous section.

However, personal income before tax would provide only a very rough measure of the national output, for two reasons. First, it includes a number of incomes not derived from any productive activity, so that there are no goods and services to correspond to them in the national output. Second, it omits a part of the incomes generated by production, a part which does not find its way as personal incomes into the pockets of private people. Let us explore these categories more fully.

The recipients of share dividends and debenture interest are, of course, making a contribution to production by the provision of capital. Part of the value of goods and services produced returns to them as income, so they are clearly not what is meant by the first category. On the other hand, a number of people will be in receipt of National Insurance benefits, such as pensions, unemployment and sickness benefits, in respect of which they are making no current contribution to productive activity. These incomes are known as transfer incomes, because financed by transferring current National Insurance payments ('transfer payments') to the beneficiaries (Chapter 8). Certain local authority grants such as university scholarships are also transfer incomes. This total of National Insurance etc., benefits (2) must be deducted from the total of personal incomes, to secure an income measure which is closer to the value of goods and services produced.

A less obvious example of a transfer income (3) is the debt interest paid by the Government and local authorities to the holders of Government securities, etc. The payment of Government debt interest is financed in the ways explained in Chapter 8. Interest on government debt is regarded as a transfer income because it does not readily correspond to part of the current production of goods and services. For example, of the capital sums borrowed by the Government in the past, the greater part has been spent in waging war, the benefits of which are intangible in their nature.

Merely to deduct these two transfer items will not give us a satisfactory income measure of national output. We also need to reckon with income yielded by production, but not received in private hands. There are three categories here. First, companies will not distribute all the profits they derive from production, as we saw in Chapter 7. These undistributed profits nonetheless represent a part of the value of the company's output, and must be added (4) to personal income before tax. Undistributed profits of public corporations (i.e. profits not paid as interest on Government finance) must be similarly treated (5). Both these profit totals are stated inclusive or gross of tax. Third, rental, trading and certain other incomes of government (6) must be added on to the total. Rental and trading incomes represent the net earnings of central and local government from activities so comparable with private enterprise that they may be regarded almost as 'government businesses'. Thus the Government enjoys the rents from the Crown Lands, runs a forestry business through the Forestry Commission, operates breweries and public houses in certain areas, and provides an export finance insurance service through the Export Credits Guarantee Department

(Chapter 2). Local authorities lease houses, operate bus services, rent markets and provide harbour facilities.

The calculation of personal income (before tax) *less* transfer incomes *plus* the undistributed profits of companies and public corporations *plus* the trading, etc., income of government provides one method of measuring the national output (8). The root principle behind the calculation is that, by totalling the income generated by production, we obtain a measure of the value of the product itself. Item 8 is described as 'gross' national product: what is the significance of the term 'gross'?

The profit totals of companies, public corporations and central and local government have all been stated inclusive of depreciation allowances (Chapter 7), while the depreciation allowances of partnerships, etc., were included in the personal income total (1). This means that the (gross) national product figure based upon this calculation includes both

(a) the incomes earned in producing replacement equipment, etc., to make good the partial consumption of the economy's stock of fixed assets; and

(b) that part of profits which firms, etc., earmark to make *financial* provision for deterioration and obsolescence (Chapter 7).

The concept of G.N.P. accordingly overstates national output by ignoring the deterioration of the economy's fixed assets caused by their use in production over the year. Unfortunately for our purposes, the sum a firm earmarks as its annual depreciation allowances does not accurately measure the extent to which its fixed assets are used up during that period. It is necessary, therefore, to estimate 'capital consumption' (9) by various sophisticated statistical methods. If we deduct this from G.N.P., we obtain a measure of net national income or product at factor cost (10). This is the value of national output calculated by summing the factor incomes generated in its production, after making good the capital consumption which the process of production has entailed.

As explained in Section 2, national output is not the same as the value of final goods and services produced in the year by the British economy, i.e. the domestic output. We may, however, calculate the value of net domestic product (13) by deducting from net national income the income received (11) by British residents from their productive assets employed overseas, and adding the income derived (12) by foreign residents from their property at work in the U.K.

4. *Composition of National Expenditure*

The example of Section 1 suggests that the value of the annual domestic product may also be calculated by adding all the final expenditure on goods and services in the course of the year. 'Final expenditure' is defined as all spending on currently produced goods and services *less* the intermediate spending which is, of course, represented already in the value of subsequent spending (Section 2). The addition of net income from abroad will then convert this domestic product total to a measure of the national output.

Let us define total domestic expenditure at market prices (5, Table 9.2) as all the final spending by the government, firms and households of the United Kingdom. Table 9.2 shows that this breaks down into four categories.

1. *Consumers' expenditure:* spending by private people (households) on consumer goods and services such as food, clothing, entertainment, etc. Expenditure on all durable consumer goods (e.g. cars and furniture) is included, except the purchase of (new) houses (see 3 below). 'Spending' here also includes various notional items of expenditure, such as the rents that owner occupiers of private houses may be imagined to pay themselves. Their inclusion is necessary to preserve consistency, since the corresponding notional incomes were counted in 1. Personal income in Table 9.1.

2. *Public authorities' current expenditure on goods and services.* Many goods and services are provided by government on a communal basis. Some of these services are enjoyed by everyone in general, for example, the collection of refuse, the provision of street lighting or the maintenance of law and order by the police. The armed services, too, may be considered to furnish a service of military defence for the general benefit. Other services are provided for particular individuals, wholly or largely free of direct charge to the actual recipients. This is true for people who receive medical treatment under the National Health Service, or for schoolchildren who 'consume' a final service, namely the teaching services of the school staff.

To provide these services, the central and local government will have to make expenditure on capital equipment of all sorts (see under 3 below), and will also need to meet current operating expenses. These are mainly the wages and salaries of the employees involved, such as policemen, nurses and teachers. Their salaries, of course, figure in 1. Personal income of Table 9.1, corresponding to an equivalent 'value of teaching services' etc., in the national output total. Expenditure on these operating expenses is described as 'public authorities' current expenditure on goods and services'.

3. *Gross fixed capital formation at home:* total spending on capital

goods such as plant, equipment, buildings which will in turn be used as factors of production. Capital expenditure is undertaken by companies (company capital formation); by public corporations, central and local government (public capital formation); and by unincorporated businesses, farming companies and professional men (personal capital formation). Personal capital formation also includes the purchase of

TABLE 9.2

United Kingdom National Expenditure, 1968

	£ million
1. Consumers' expenditure	27,065
2. Public authorities' current expenditure on goods and services	7,702
3. Gross fixed capital formation at home	7,798
4. Value of physical increase in stocks and work in progress	204
5. TOTAL DOMESTIC EXPENDITURE AT MARKET PRICES	42,769
6. *Less* Imports of goods and services	9,038
7. *Plus* Exports of goods and services	8,610
8. GROSS DOMESTIC PRODUCT AT MARKET PRICES	42,341
9. *Less* Property income paid abroad	1,641
10. *Plus* Property income received from abroad	2,060
11. GROSS NATIONAL EXPENDITURE AT MARKET PRICES	42,760
12. *Less* Capital Consumption	3,375
13. NET NATIONAL EXPENDITURE AT MARKET PRICES	39,385
14. *Less* Taxes on expenditure	6,960
15. *Plus* Subsidies	886
16. NET NATIONAL INCOME AT FACTOR COST	33,311

Source: National Income and Expenditure Blue Book, 1969

new houses by families; personal and company capital formation together may be described as private capital formation.

Part of this spending on capital goods can be regarded as providing 'replacement capital', necessary to make good the capital consumption entailed in the course of the year's production. Deduction of the appropriate estimate (12) from gross fixed capital formation gives net fixed capital formation at home. This represents the annual rate at which the economy is adding to its holding of fixed capital, in the hands of government, firms and households.

4. *Value of physical increase in stocks and work in progress.* In the course of the year, firms may have added to their stocks of raw materials, work in progress, and finished goods. These commodities have not yet come to the last stage in the production process with their sale as consumer or producer goods. Nonetheless, factors of production will have derived incomes from working on them in the course of the year, and for this reason they represent part of the final output for the year under review. Accordingly, we enter the value of the physical increase in stocks as a notional item of total domestic expenditure, even though the goods represented have not been bought by their ultimate purchasers as have goods and services in categories 1 to 3. In this way, account is taken of the incomes which the increase in stocks has brought about, and the product which it represents.

Not all of the total domestic expenditure will generate incomes for factors of production at work in this country. A part of it will go on imported goods and services, and so yields incomes in the foreign countries which supplied them. Conversely, foreign expenditure on British goods and services (i.e. our exports) will generate incomes for factors of production at work here, by absorbing part of our total product. Total domestic expenditure less imports (6) plus exports (7) is accordingly the spending total which absorbs the gross domestic product. The significance of its valuation 'at market prices' is explained below.

To obtain the value of national product, we recognize once again that some of the business assets at work here are owned by residents overseas, while U.K. residents in turn own assets which are employed overseas. We therefore deduct from G.D.P. (8) the income paid (9) to foreign residents who own property here, and add income received (10) by British residents from property overseas. The latter largely stems from spending by foreigners in their own countries on the contribution to foreign output of British owned factors of production at work there. The resultant (11) is the gross national expenditure at market prices. This may be defined as the total value of final output calculated in terms of the expenditure (actual and notional) made upon it, without allowance for the capital consumption entailed in its production. Deduction of the appropriate estimate (12) gives the net output figure (13).

To understand the significance of the market price valuation, consider once again our shirt example. In Section 1, the selling price of the shirt carried neither purchase tax nor subsidy. If there had been a purchase tax of (say) 5s., then 35s. spent on the shirt would have broken up into 30s. income to the factors and 5s. tax to the Government. On the other hand, a 5s. subsidy from the Government would have enabled its sale at 25s., though total factor income would have been 30s. It follows that the value of the net national output in terms of the market prices paid on sale (13) exceeds its value in terms of factor incomes (16) by the sum of taxes on expenditure (14) less subsidies (15). Taxes on expenditure include the revenue duties, etc., detailed in Chapter 8. They also include the rates paid to local authorities, as these represent a tax on the rent (actual or imputed) the occupier pays for the use of his property.

5. *National Product by Industry*

The example of Section 1 suggests a third approach to the calculation of the national output. The final value of the shirt may be imagined as comprising a series of productive contributions made by a number of industries and trades, the contributions of each being measured by the incomes its factors effectively derive from the sale of the shirt. Thus the shirt manufacturer paid the mill owner 6s. for cloth, and worked it up into a shirt which he sold the wholesaler for 15s. He and his employees 'added a value' of, say, 5s. to the original worth of the cloth, measured by the profit and wages respectively derived from its production. The other 4s. went on other raw materials, transport costs, fuel, etc., which represents the contributions made, in turn, by these industries at this particular stage in the shirt's career. The total 'value added' by, for example, the electricity industry would also include the supply of electricity at other stages in the shirt's manufacture and distribution.

Similarly, by taking the total of factor incomes generated in the various branches of economic activity, we obtain a measure of the contribution each branch makes to the domestic output; the sum of these contributions must then equal the domestic output. Table 9.3 contains estimates of the contributions to gross domestic product of the various industries, trades, etc., for 1968. Thus factors of production engaged in agriculture, forestry and fishing enjoyed a gross income of £1,127 million. This can be regarded as the contribution made by agriculture, etc., to the gross domestic output. The sum of these contributions gives gross domestic product, and gross national product is obtained by adding property income received from abroad, and deducting income paid abroad.

This is a gross national output measure, because the profit figures in the incomes total for each industry have been stated inclusive of depreciation allowances. If we wish to take account of capital consumption (Section 3), we may deduct an appropriate estimate (18) to obtain net national product at factor cost (19).

A few words are necessary on 'stock appreciation' (13). The calculation of a firm's profits must include as a cost of production the value of the raw materials it uses up. The usual method in this country is to value the raw materials consumed at the prices paid when the materials longest in stock were first acquired. This, however, overstates the book profit when prices in general are rising, as the firm will probably need to spend more than originally when it comes to replace the quantity of

TABLE 9.3

Gross National Product by Industry
United Kingdom 1968

	£ million
1. Agriculture, forestry and fishing	1,127
2. Mining and quarrying	687
3. Manufacturing	12,527
4. Construction	2,456
5. Gas, electricity and water	1,288
6. Transport and communication	3,065
7. Distributive trades	4,082
8. Insurance, banking and finance (incl. real estate)	1,206
9. Ownership of dwellings	1,801
10. Public administration and defence	2,258
11. Public health and educational services	1,818
12. Other services (e.g. domestic services to households)	4,731
13. *Less* Stock appreciation	650
14. Residual error (see Table 9.1)	− 129
15. GROSS DOMESTIC PRODUCT AT FACTOR COST	36,267
16. Net property income from abroad	419
17. GROSS NATIONAL PRODUCT AT FACTOR COST	36,686
18. *Less* Capital Consumption	3,375
19. NET NATIONAL INCOME AT FACTOR COST	33,311

Source: National Income and Expenditure Blue Book, 1969

materials consumed. In a period of rising prices, we may represent this 'overstatement of profits' by a sum labelled 'stock appreciation', and make allowance by deducting it from the total of values added by each industry, etc. 'Stock appreciation', it must be emphasized, is a quite different concept from that of 'increase in value of stocks' discussed in Section 4.

6. *Income and Expenditure Flows in the Economy*

Our analysis of national product, income and expenditure provides some insight into important relationships within the economic system. Fig. 9.2 is built up from the information in Tables 9.1–9.3, with additional information on the disposal of personal income from the Blue Book on National Income and Expenditure, 1969.

Starting in the top left-hand corner, we see that the factors of production at work in Britain in 1968 produced a gross output of £36,267 million. A part of the value of this output is attributable to foreign owned factors at work here, while an analogous contribution to foreign countries' domestic output was made by British owned factors at work overseas. Offsetting the one against the other gives a net income from abroad for British residents of £419 million. This balance is added to gross domestic product to show the value of the gross national product at factor cost. This is the value of the year's output from British (owned) productive factors, at work here and overseas, if we choose to overlook the capital consumption that this production entailed.

Gross national product yielded an equivalent gross national income, which appears in the top right hand corner of the figure. To calculate how much private people actually received as income (before paying tax), we first take account of the residual error in the statistics, explained in the footnote to Table 9.1. We recognize, second, that some people enjoyed a transfer or 'unearned' income to the value of £5,479 million; and third, that some of the income generated by production did not in fact find its way into private pockets. In the case of companies, it should be noted, this includes depreciation allowances as well as those retained profits which might have been distributed as dividends. Total personal income before tax emerges as £35,948.

How did the income recipients dispose of this sum? The answer is provided in the bottom right hand corner of the figure, which is largely self explanatory. Note, however, that the figure given for 'saving' includes the depreciation allowances of one man businesses, partnerships and farming companies. Consumers' spending reappears in the bottom left hand corner, as the first item of income-generating final expenditure. The addition of the other four items of final expenditure, already discussed in Section 4, gives a gross national expenditure at market prices of £42,760 million. Central and local government siphon off their taxes on expenditure (including rates) less subsidies, leaving a gross expenditure of £36,686 million to absorb a corresponding gross national product.

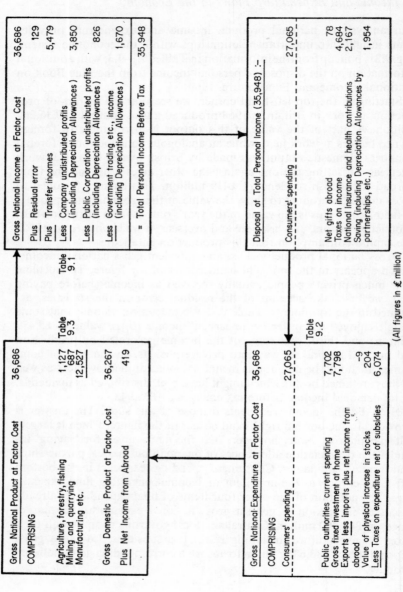

Gross National Product at Factor Cost	36,686
COMPRISING	
Agriculture, forestry, fishing	1,127
Mining and quarrying	687
Manufacturing etc.	12,527
	Table 9.3
Gross Domestic Product at Factor Cost	36,267
Plus Net Income from Abroad	419

Gross National Income at Factor Cost	36,686
Plus Residual error	129
Plus Transfer incomes	5,479
Less Company undistributed profits (including Depreciation Allowances)	3,850
Less Public Corporation undistributed profits (including Depreciation Allowances)	826
Less Government trading etc., income (including Depreciation Allowances)	1,670
	Table 9.1
= Total Personal Income Before Tax	35,948

Gross National Expenditure at Factor Cost	36,686
COMPRISING	
Consumers' spending	27,065
	Table 9.2
Public authorities current spending	7,702
Gross fixed investment at home	7,798
Exports less imports plus net income from abroad	−9
Value of physical increase in stocks	204
Less Taxes on expenditure net of subsidies	6,074

Disposal of Total Personal Income (35,948) :-	
Consumers' spending	27,065
Net gifts abroad	78
Taxes on income	4,684
National Insurance and health contributions	2,167
Saving (including Depreciation Allowances by partnerships, etc.)	1,954

(All figures in £ million)

FIG. 9.2

7. Changes in the General Level of Prices

Before investigating changes in the national income over a period of time, it is necessary to understand how changes in the general level of prices may be measured. The price of a commodity is the rate at which it exchanges for money, e.g. apples at 1s. 6d. per lb. The general level of prices is the level of prices ruling in the vast (but finite) number of transactions taking place in the economy at any given time. Some of these transactions are purely financial (notably, security dealings), while others involve dealing in goods and services (e.g. the purchase of a pound of apples, or a hair-cut). The expression 'the general price level' could accordingly refer to prices ruling in both financial and commodity transactions, or it may refer just to transactions involving goods and services. Clearly it is this second coverage which is appropriate in a context of income and output measurement.

While the general level of prices is an intelligible concept, it is not possible to measure it in absolute terms, i.e. it would not be possible to 'average out' all the prices ruling at a given time, even if the information were available. *Changes* in the general price level may, however, be estimated by devices known as index numbers. Thus a number of commodities may be discovered which, in the behaviour of their prices, are typical of a much wider range of goods and services. Their prices may be noted at a given date (the 'base date'), and at a subsequent date, and the later price for each commodity expressed as a percentage of its base date price. The average of these price percentages or 'price relatives' forms an index number showing the percentage change over the period of all the prices in the group. Since the commodities were selected as representative of a much wider range of goods and services, it is reasonable to infer that the prices of all the other goods and services in that range have changed (more or less) correspondingly. The calculation of index numbers in this way may be undertaken for various sectors of the economy, covering altogether retail prices, raw material and commodity prices, agricultural prices, etc. If all these index numbers show an increase, it is reasonable to conclude that the general level of prices has risen. None of these index numbers, of course, can on its own express the movement in the general price level; each is a guide only to the sector for which it is constructed.

References to the Annual Abstract of Statistics will show the variety of index numbers calculated by the Board of Trade. An especially important index number is, however, calculated monthly by the Department of Employment and Productivity. This is the Index of Retail Prices, which had its origin in an attempt during the 1914–18 war to measure changes in the cost of maintaining constant the standard of living enjoyed by the working classes before the war. It has since developed into a device for measuring changes in the prices of goods and services which figure in the budget of the average family. As such, it is an invaluable guide (of use, for example, in wage negotiations) to 'changes in the cost of living', if this expression is taken to mean changes in the prices of those goods and services on which households spend their incomes. It is no more than a guide, however, for it does not show variations in living costs between different parts of the country, nor are the commodities represented of equal importance to all families (but see below). Further, it is clear from the definition that the index

TABLE 9.4

Groups and group-weights used in Index of Retail Prices, 1968

Group		Weights
I	Food	263
II	Alcoholic drink	63
III	Tobacco	66
IV	Housing	121
V	Fuel and light	62
VI	Durable household goods	59
VII	Clothing and footwear	89
VIII	Transport and vehicles	120
IX	Miscellaneous goods	60
X	Services	56
XI	Meals bought and consumed outside the home	41
	Total weights	1,000

does not attempt to cover all family expenditure relevant to living standards (excluding, among other things, income tax payments).

The basic principle of its calculation follows the explanation already given. However, since some commodities are more important than others in the expenditure of the average family, the price relative of each commodity used in the index is multiplied by a given figure (a 'weight') to reflect its relative importance in family expenditure. Nearly 350 commodities are used for the index, divided into eleven groups and 93 sections. The eleven groups and the weights used in 1968 for each group are shown in Table 9.4. The Tobacco group, for example, is divided into two sections, Cigarettes and (Pipe) Tobacco, and their respective weights (in 1968) are 59 and 7. The percentage price changes for the cigarette and tobacco brands recorded are accordingly multiplied by 59 and 7 respectively, the products added and the total divided by 66 to obtain a price index for this group. The procedure is repeated for the other groups, and the resulting price indices multiplied by their group weights, totalled and divided by 1,000 to give the overall Index of Retail Prices in percentage form.

Information on prices is collected from a variety of sources to allow for differences between e.g. chain store and family business, city and country town. Any regional variations in prices are not, of course, shown up in the final index, though the use of supplementary index

TABLE 9.5

Index of Retail Prices
Base date: 16th January, 1962 = 100

	1965	1966	1967	1968	1969
Jan.	109·5	114·3	118·5	121·6	129·1
Feb.	109·5	114·4	118·6	122·2	129·8
Mar.	109·9	114·6	118·6	122·6	130·3
Apr.	112·0	116·0	119·5	124·8	131·7
May	112·4	116·8	119·4	124·9	
June	112·7	117·1	119·9	125·4	
July	112·7	116·6	119·2	125·5	
Aug.	112·9	117·3	118·9	125·7	
Sept.	113·0	117·1	118·8	125·8	
Oct.	113·1	117·4	119·7	126·4	
Nov.	113·6	118·1	120·4	126·7	
Dec.	114·1	118·3	121·2	128·4	

Sources: Annual Abstract of Statistics, Monthly Digest of Statistics

numbers for this purpose is being officially considered. Prices are recorded on the Tuesday nearest the 15th of each month, and the index number calculated on these prices is published by the end of the following month. Information for the weighting is provided by a continuous Family Expenditure Survey, which records spending details of a sample (10,400 in 1967, and a planned 17,000 by 1970) of private households of all types. Information about the spending habits of two less typical sorts of household is, however, excluded in calculating the weights. These are households with relatively high incomes (in 1967 where the family head earned £45 per week or more), and 'pensioner' households in which at least three-quarters of income comes from National Insurance retirement pensions and similar benefits. As a guide to the welfare of this second group, two supplementary index numbers have, since 1969, been constructed with weights based on the spending habits of, respectively, one- and two-member pensioner households. These are published not monthly but quarterly, as an average of the values for each of three months.

Since 1962 allowance has been made in the index for changing spending habits (as revealed in the Survey), by revising the weights at the start of each year and linking the modified series for the year back to 16th January, 1962, as base date. The same method is followed in the construction of the supplementary index numbers for pensioner households. Keeping the indexes in line with changing expenditure patterns helps make a comparison of index values over the years more meaningful. Difficulties do arise in such comparisons, however, from the development of new products and substantial changes in the quality of commodities. Table 9.5 sets out movements in the index since January, 1965.

8. *Comparisons of National Income over Time*

The first two columns of Table 9.6 show gross domestic and national expenditure (or product) at the market prices current in 1963 and 1968 respectively. It is seen that the totals and (with one exception) all their constituents are higher in the second year than in the first. This increase in the value of the national product was due partly to an increase in the quantity of goods and services produced, and partly to a rise in the general level of prices. Since a rise in the national output in real or quantity terms implies a rise in our living standards (Chapter 15), it is desirable to separate out the two factors at work and estimate the increase in the national output in real terms alone.

Such an estimate is made in column 3, which shows the 1968 national product and its constituents revalued in terms of the prices ruling in 1963. The increase recorded between the first and third columns is accordingly a real increase, showing how much greater was the value of the 1968 national output solely because more goods and services were being produced.

To obtain these column 3 estimates, two principal methods are followed. First, for some items, e.g. part of consumers' expenditure, the actual quantities bought by the public in 1963 and in 1968 can be ascertained. The 1968 quantities may be expressed as a ratio of the 1963 quantities, and this ratio multiplied by consumers' expenditure in 1963 to give the value of 1968 expenditure in terms of 1963 prices. Second, where actual quantities are not known, the alternative is to calculate a price index showing the (percentage) change in price of a given range of commodities between the two years. If the 1968 expenditure is divided by this index and multiplied by 100, an estimate is obtained of 1968 expenditure in terms of 1963 prices.

The problem of revaluing the national output in terms of another year's prices is also dealt with through the 'value added' calculation of

TABLE 9.6

United Kingdom National Output, 1963 and 1968

	1963 Output in 1963 Prices £ million (1)	1968 Output in 1968 Prices £ million (2)	1968 Output in 1963 Prices £ million (3)
1. Consumers' expenditure	20,125	27,065	22,562
2. Public authorities current expenditure on goods and services	5,184	7,702	5,851
3. Gross fixed capital formation at home	4,916	7,798	6,791
4. Value of physical increase in stocks and work in progress	219	204	160
5. Exports	5,815	8,610	7,321
6. TOTAL FINAL EXPENDITURE AT MARKET PRICES	36,259	51,379	46,685
7. *Less* Imports	5,946	9,038	7,609
8. GROSS DOMESTIC PRODUCT AT MARKET PRICES	30,313	42,341	35,076
9. Net property income from abroad	392	419	353
10. GROSS NATIONAL PRODUCT AT MARKET PRICES	30,705	42,760	35,429

Source: National Income and Expenditure Blue Book, 1969

national output. If the contribution of a given industry to the domestic product can be estimated in physical terms for, say, 1963 and 1968, then the ratio of the 1968 quantity to the 1963 quantity multiplied by the value of the 1963 net output will give the 1968 'value added' in terms of 1963 prices. Neither the expenditure nor the 'value added' approaches are statistically completely reliable, so a small discrepancy is found in the estimates of the domestic product by the two methods.

9. *National Income Calculations: Objectives and Difficulties*

Valuation of the economy's annual output of goods and services provides some measure of the living standards of its inhabitants, and this and similar questions have long been a centre of attention for economists. Thus Adam Smith, who is regarded as the founder of Anglo-Saxon economics, took as title for his principal work (1776), 'An Inquiry into the Nature and Causes of the Wealth of Nations'. In modern times, the construction of national income statistics was pioneered in this country in the inter-war years by such men as Sir Arthur Bowley, Lord Stamp, and Mr Colin Clark. Interest in national income measurement and analysis received a great stimulus in the late 1930s, with the publication in 1936 of J. M. (later Lord) Keynes' *General Theory of Employment, Interest and Money*. As the following chapters demonstrate, this provided a whole body of theory for explaining the level of national income and the interaction of the various components into which it may be analysed.

Keynes' ideas suggested ways in which the Government might influence the size of the national income and the general level of prices, for example through variations in tax rates (Chapter 20). However, if these instruments were to be used effectively, the Government would need its own national income calculations, with details of the various component items forming a system of 'national accounts'. The Government accordingly entered the field with, in 1941, a White Paper on the U.K.'s national income (which was not published till the end of the war, for security reasons). In post-war years, the national accounts (published in what has since become an annual Blue Book) have grown considerably in scope and refinement. Over the same period, further, much academic interest has been shown in the construction of a wider system of 'social accounts', intended to give a statistical picture of as much as possible of the whole network of economic relationships.

The official estimates of national income and its component parts (the 'national accounts') provide a statistical guide to many important aspects of the country's economic life. They enable comparisons to be made of the condition of the U.K. economy at different points of time, and between the U.K. economy and other economies. From such comparisons, it is possible to assess, for example, how much living standards have risen in this country over a given period, and how our living standards compare with those of other countries (Chapter 15). Forecasts of national income and its components are indispensable to the Government in formulating its economic policy. Larger firms, too, may take such forecasts into account in deciding their business policies. To understand why all this should be, it is necessary to work through the remaining chapters in Part III, before consulting Chapter 20.

Despite great improvements in their methods of construction national income statistics remain estimates, with varying degrees of reliability. The difficulties in compiling these estimates of the national accounts may be distinguished, in very broad terms, as *conceptual* and *statistical*. A prime conceptual difficulty exists in drawing the 'boundary' between what is output from economic activity and what is not. Thus the value of a housekeeper's services are included in the national output (page 195), but the same services performed by a housewife are excluded. The farm produce consumed by the farmer's family is included, but not the produce of the amateur gardener. The rental value of owner occupied houses is included, because owner occupation is analogous to letting a house one owns to oneself. The same argument could however be made for other durable goods owned by households, such as cars and T.V. sets, though no allowance is made in national income estimates for the annual value of the services they yield their owners.

The line has, of course, to be drawn somewhere, and the inclusion of certain items while similar items are excluded must reflect the availability of the statistics. It will be apparent, however, that the more goods and services are provided in economic transactions and the fewer on a non-monetary basis, the higher will money national income be. This in turn raises difficulties in comparisons of national income over a period of time, and between different countries, discussed in Chapter 15.

A second conceptual difficulty lies in the different basis of valuation for the goods and services provided by private enterprise, and those provided by government. The value of the first category is given by their prices, which are determined by the market forces of a free enterprise system. The value of the second category (containing, e.g., health and educational services) reflects the salaries of those engaged in their provision, which are not necessarily the same as the salaries they would command if their product were sold in the same way as, say, haircuts and entertainment. The national output, therefore, is a sum of values calculated on (at least) two different bases.

Of the many statistical problems in national income calculation, we need only note a common difficulty, that many of the figures used are devised originally for other purposes, and have to be adapted by the national income statisticians. In this connection, it is worth recalling the greater attention paid by the Government in recent years to presenting information in a form suitable for national income calculations (Section 8, Chapter 8). On the other hand, seemingly useful business information may in fact find no place in the national income statistics. Thus business depreciation allowances are calculated with reference to the original cost, not the current cost, of fixed assets, which makes them unsuitable for use in national income calculations which provide a

H

measure of output at current prices. Again, company accounts do not
distinguish between a rise in the value of stocks through a price increase
and through a quantity increase. Accordingly, as the 1969 Blue Book
notes (page 91): 'Considerable uncertainty (in the national income
statistics) attaches to the division of the change in value of stocks
between these two elements' (author's parenthesis).

Questions

1. From the following simplified set of figures (which can be regarded
   as annual estimates in £ millions), you are asked to calculate:

   (a) Gross national product at market prices.
   (b) Net national product at factor cost.

Wages and salaries	580
Profits before providing for depreciation	290
National insurance benefits	90
Direct income taxes	150
Consumers' expenditure on goods and services	630
Indirect taxes	160
Food and housing subsidies	30
Government expenditure on goods and services	170
Gross capital formation (private investment)	120
Depreciation	70
Sales and purchases of stocks and shares	220
Exports of goods and services	260
Imports of goods and services	180

   NOTE: You should use both the income and expenditure methods
   of calculation and you must show exactly how you arrive at your
   answers. All the relevant figures are given but not all the figures are
   relevant.

                                                    W. J. E. C.

2. (a) In 1960, the total domestic expenditure at market prices in the
       United Kingdom was £25,491 million. Exports and income re-
       ceived from abroad totalled £6,475 million, imports and income
       paid abroad was £6,734 million, taxes on spending amounted to
       £3,405 million and subsidies totalled £489 million.

       (i) What was the Gross National Expenditure at market prices?
           Show how you arrived at your figure.
       (ii) What was the Gross National Product at factor cost? Show
            how you arrived at your figure.

(iii) State what other information is required to enable the Net National Product at factor cost to be calculated.

(b) Discuss the principal reasons why the Government tries to evaluate the various aggregates of income in an economy.   J.M.B.

3. Would you include the following in a definition of the national income: (a) a wife's housekeeping money; (b) the earnings of a daily help; (c) family allowances; (d) an M.P.'s salary; (e) the prize-money on Premium Bonds? Give reasons for your answer in each case.   J.M.B.

4. (I) State precisely the difference between:
    (a) The *gross* and *net* national income;
    (b) The national income *at market prices* and *at factor cost*.
(II) Explain briefly how each of the following items are treated in calculating the size of the national income:
    (a) Pay of the armed forces;
    (b) Retained or undistributed company profits;
    (c) Social security benefits;
    (d) Football pool winnings.   W.J.E.C.

5. 'National income = national output = national expenditure.' Discuss.   U.L.

6. Describe how the national income can be calculated (a) by the income method and (b) by the expenditure method.   W.J.E.C.

7. Describe and explain the adjustments necessary to bring estimates of national expenditure into equality with estimates of total incomes.   W.J.E.C.

8. What is National Income? What problems are involved in estimating its magnitude? What are the purposes of such estimates?   J.M.B.

9. Explain what is meant by money national income. What difficulties arise in measuring it?   U.L.

10. Explain what is meant by:
    (a) money national income;
    (b) real national income?   U.L.

11. What is a price index number? How is one calculated?   U.L.

12. How would you measure the average level of retail prices? What difficulties are likely to arise in doing so?   U.L.

13. What is meant by the cost of living? Say how you might measure it, indicating the problems that will be encountered.   U.L.

10

Income Analysis (I)

1. *The Size of National Income*

The last chapter examined the measurement of national income, output and expenditure; in this and subsequent chapters we consider the economic forces that determine their size. The subject of national income determination is alternatively known as macro-economics, because of its concern with the aggregates and broad averages of the economic system (Greek *makros* means *large*). We have already met some of those concepts in the last chapter, e.g. the aggregate of all incomes (or national income), the total of consumption spending, the general level of prices, and so on. By contrast, micro-economics focuses attention on the small, individual units of the economy, i.e. the consumer, the firm and the industry. Macro-economics as a branch of economic science has made great progress in the last thirty or so years, under the influence pre-eminently of J. M. (later Lord) Keynes (1883–1946), whose seminal *General Theory of Employment, Interest and Money* was published in 1936.

The domestic product was defined in Chapter 9 as the flow of final output yielded by the resources at work within the economy. The value of this aggregate is expressed in money terms, which makes it important to distinguish (p. 210) between a change in its value caused by a change in the general price level, and a change which reflects an increase or decrease in the output of goods and services. Until Chapter 14, we shall assume that the general level of prices is perfectly stable, which enables us meanwhile to confine our attention to changes in output in real terms.

If all its resources are fully employed, the maximum size domestic product an economy can achieve is set by the size and abilities of its working population, the quantity and quality of its capital stock, and the efficiency with which the two work together. The size of national output will also reflect the value of income received from and paid abroad, but this is a quite minor complication without analytic significance in this context. As the years pass, the growth of the (total) population may lead to increases in working population, while net fixed capital formation will add to the economy's stock of capital goods. The quality of resources and the efficiency of work methods may also improve, all of which suggests a gradual rise in the maximum output the economy is capable of achieving.

Consideration of this prospect of income growth from year to year is, however, held over until Chapter 15. In this and the following two chapters we consider what determines whether resources get fully used or not at any given time, up to the limit set by the economy's current potential. It is convenient, accordingly, to take this potential as constant, which means assuming (until Chapter 15) that capital stock, labour force and work methods are unchanging. In this way questions about the rate at which resources grow are effectively separated out from the problem of how much use is currently being made of them. The key to this problem is to be found in the circular flow of income and expenditure, already touched upon in Chapter 9.

2. *The Flow of Income and Expenditure*

Fig. 9.2 on p. 206 showed national expenditure as a flow of spending on final goods and services, including net additions to stocks of raw materials and work in progress. This expenditure on final goods, etc., flowed as the national income to the factors of production. Most of it was spent, a part saved, and so on. This statistical picture of the whole economy is too complicated to serve as a starting point for our theory of income determination. We may start, therefore, by making three simplifying assumptions, the first two of which will be relaxed in Chapter 11 when the general picture is established.

First, we shall assume that there is no (central or local) government. This removes for the time being all consideration of government expenditure on the one hand, and on the other problems of taxes, rates and transfer incomes and payments.

Second, we may assume that there is no foreign trade or other economic relationships with overseas countries (i.e. we have a closed economy). In this way we can drop imports and exports out of the picture, while domestic product and national product necessarily become identical.

Third, we assume that all capital formation is in the hands of firms, which means that the only spending to be undertaken by individuals or households is consumption expenditure. In the national income statistics, as we have seen, house purchase is classified as personal capital formation.

Households get their living by selling services to firms. Most house-

holds sell labour services, i.e., one or more members of the family goes
to work in a factory, office, etc., in return for a weekly wage or monthly
salary. Some households, also, have parted with funds to firms, which
have been used to buy capital equipment and provide the circulating
capital. In this way these households make a contribution to production,
to be rewarded (if the firm is a company) with dividends on shares or
interest on debentures.

Fig. 10.1 shows our simplified economy in operation over a given

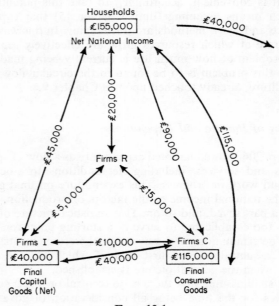

FIG. 10.1

period of time, say one month. The three arrows running in a straight
line from households represent their sales to firms of labour and other
factor services: £45,000 worth to Firms I; £20,000 to Firms R; and
£90,000 to Firms C. Coming back along these lines is a corresponding
flow, from firms to households, of remuneration in the form of wages,
salaries, dividends and interest. It is assumed that there is no profit
retention by companies. In our no-government, no-foreign-trade economy, the total value of this flow of income for the month is the net
national income. It is the total of incomes earned in the production of
goods and services.

The production of goods and services is carried on by the firms in the economy. A convenient simplification, which does not distort the real world too much, is to divide them into three categories.

Firms R produce the raw materials for other firms; they may do some processing, but do not sell their product direct to households.

Firms I buy their materials from Firms R, and use them to make capital goods. In reality these would be bought by both Firms R and Firms C, as well as by other Firms I. To simplify Fig. 10.1, however, it is assumed that sales of capital goods are made only to Firms C.

Firms C buy their raw materials from Firms R, and their capital goods from Firms I. Firms C final product comprises consumer goods and services, sold to households.

During the month, Firms R sell £5,000 worth of raw materials to Firms I, and £15,000 worth to Firms C. Firms I employ £45,000 worth of labour and other factor services to work their raw materials up into £50,000 worth of capital goods. To make their product of £115,000 worth of consumer goods and services, Firms C use up £15,000 of raw materials and £90,000 worth of factor services. In the process, their machinery and equipment deteriorates physically to the extent of £10,000, and they make good this deterioration by buying, during the same month, £10,000 worth of capital equipment from Firms I, to maintain their total capital intact.[1]

Firms C therefore 'add a value' of £90,000 to £15,000 worth of raw materials used up and £10,000 worth of fixed capital also used up. Firms I add a value to their raw material purchases of £45,000, while in working their land, quarries, etc., Firms R add a value of £20,000. The total of 'values added' by each category of firm is accordingly £20,000 + £45,000 + £90,000, which gives a net national product at factor cost of £155,000 (compare p. 203).

The final output of Firms C comprises £115,000 worth of consumer goods and services. This is shown in the box under Firms C in Fig. 10.1. The net final output of Firms I is £40,000 of capital goods. Firms I total output is £50,000 but of this £10,000 has been effectively 'incorporated' into Firms C final product, through the process of making good the depreciation which occurred in production. Likewise the raw materials of Firms R have been incorporated either into capital goods or into consumer goods.

The net national expenditure in the economy is the spending which takes place on these final goods and services. It comprises, first, the consumption spending of households, and a flow of £115,000 proceeds in Fig. 10.1 from households to Firms C. Back along this line comes a corresponding return of consumer goods and services. The second ingredient of net national expenditure is the purchase by Firms C of

[1] In contrast to the real world, therefore, depreciation allowances accurately measure capital consumption, and are immediately spent in making it good.

£40,000 worth of capital goods, to add to their productive capacity. This corresponds to the net fixed capital formation of p. 201. Gross fixed capital formation by Firms C is £50,000, i.e., it includes the £10,000 spent to make good depreciation. The value of this £10,000 has already been counted in the £115,000 total value of final consumer goods produced by Firms C. Note that in this example there are no additions to stocks of raw materials, work in progress, or finished goods. Net investment in stocks is zero.

Net national expenditure is not, of course, equivalent to total expenditure in the economy. Total expenditure includes, additionally, the intermediate spending among firms (p. 200). The £20,000 worth of raw material purchases is obviously intermediate expenditure, and we may similarly regard the £10,000 spent on making good capital depreciation.

Let us now consider how households dispose of their incomes when they receive them. A part—and for most people the greater part—is spent on consumer goods. In Fig. 10.1, households spend £115,000 on consumer goods out of a total income of £155,000. The balance of £40,000 is conveniently described as household savings, even though the households themselves would not necessarily regard the whole of this sum as 'nest eggs' set aside for the future. In this context, the word 'saving' is used simply as a shorthand expression for 'that part of income not spent on consumer goods'. The word does not carry the implication of 'purposefully setting aside', which perhaps it has in normal current usage.

A specialized meaning is also reserved in macro-economics for the word 'investment'. Investment describes the process of capital formation and stock accumulation already defined on pp. 201 f. 'Fixed investment' corresponds to 'fixed capital formation', and 'investment in stocks' to 'value of the physical increase in stocks'. Gross and net fixed investment, public and private fixed investment have exactly the same meaning as gross and net, public and private capital formation. In Fig. 10.1, the final net expenditure on £40,000 worth of capital goods is net fixed or capital investment. As previously noted, there is no stock investment in this example.

Households may dispose of the income they do not spend on consumer goods (their 'savings') in two ways: they may buy financial assets, or they may leave their money idle. Money left idle, in the form of notes, coins or clearing bank liabilities, may be said to be 'hoarded'. The purchase of financial assets may take the form of buying company securities or trust units. If we momentarily relax our simplifying assumptions (p. 217), government securities, savings certificates, shares in building societies, etc., may be added to the list. A person will often describe such purchases as an 'investment', but such a use of the word is best avoided in macro-economics. 'Investment' in macro-economics customarily denotes real investment, or the acquisition of capital goods or stocks, and not the acquisition of financial assets.

The company securities that some households buy may be new issues (Chapter 7), the proceeds of which could finance current investment. However, firms will not be restricted in their investment spending plans by the amount of funds that they can raise in this way, nor, on the other hand, will they necessarily want to spend in investment as much as they might finance by utilizing what households are prepared to save. Household savings, accordingly, do not of themselves generate an equivalent amount of investment spending by firms. They are, therefore, appropriately represented in Fig. 10.1 as a 'leakage' from the income flow among firms and households.

Let us now pull the threads together, and see what sort of pattern emerges. During the month, the factors of production produce a net output of £155,000 worth of goods and services, receive a corresponding income, and spend £115,000 on consumer goods and services, while the £40,000 balance leaks away into savings. Net national expenditure is nonetheless £155,000, as the consumption spending is augmented by £40,000 net investment spending, which may be regarded as offsetting the savings leakage. Net national expenditure, accordingly, 'absorbs' an equivalent value of net national output, thereby generating a corresponding net national income of £155,000.

Assume now that Firms C are planning to spend over each of the following months the sum of £40,000 as net investment, and that households are planning to save £40,000 from an anticipated income of £155,000. In these circumstances, the economy will continue in equilibrium, i.e. without any tendency for the values of income and expenditure to change. Each month, households spend their £115,000 and Firms C their £40,000. Net final expenditure is accordingly £155,000, which generates an exactly equal net national income. From their income of £155,000, people proceed to spend £115,000, and save £40,000. Just offsetting this leakage of savings from the expenditure flow comes an exactly equivalent sum of net investment spending, so that net national expenditure is maintained at £155,000.

So this economic model will continue to function, month after month, with no variation in income or output, *provided* that the planned net investment of firms remains equal to the planned savings of households. Investment plans, however, are made by firms: savings plans by households. There is no reason at all why they should coincide. What would happen, for instance, if firms decided to increase their investment spending, while households were planning to save the same amount as before? This suggests a disturbance to the economy, as if firms want to spend more, more may be produced, which implies bigger incomes, and more saving! Before we examine this question, however, we need first to look more closely at the relationship between household income and household consumption.

3. *The Consumption Function*

We need in this section to examine in some detail the relationship between the level of national income in the economy and the level of total consumption spending. The question we have accordingly to ask is: if the national income is low, or is high, what will be the desired level of consumption. We are not concerned, for the time being, with the reasons why national income should be high or low in the first place.

In the short run, it was explained in Section 1, an upper limit to the size of the national income is set by the full employment of the labour force. Failure to achieve this maximum, accordingly, implies a corresponding degree of unemployment among the working population. With this in mind, let us proceed to construct a graph to show the relationship between national income and household consumption. We may invent figures for an imaginary economy, and to give a touch of realism, work in units of £000 million and a time period of one year.

Fig. 10.2 measures the net national income of this imaginary economy along the horizontal axis, and consumption along the vertical axis. Savings may also be measured on the vertical axis, as they are defined (Section 2) simply as that part of household income not spent. It follows that income will always equal consumption plus savings. It is useful as a preliminary to draw the line OA at an angle of 45° with the horizontal axis. This serves a purpose as a guide line, because it shows at every level of national income what the equivalent total of savings and consumption must be.

Consider first a net national income of 20 (£000 million), as measured on the horizontal axis. If the economy is capable of producing a national income of 40 with full employment, then an income level of 20 implies widespread unemployment among the working population. It is not unreasonable to suppose that at so low a level of income and employment, the savings of people who are still at work would be offset by the dis-saving and borrowing of the large number of unemployed. Net savings for all households considered together would in this case be zero. Total consumption would actually equal net national income, and the value of consumption (at 20 units) is located on the 45° guide line.

Let us now take the other extreme, where the economy is enjoying full employment and the national income is at its maximum of 40 units. Clearly saving for households in the mass would be positive, as it is most unlikely that some households will be spending from past savings to such an extent as completely to offset the current savings of others. Suppose that, with national income 40, total household consumption is 35. This gives a second consumption value for a given national income total. Linking the first value (20) with the second (35) gives a graph CC.

This graph shows the relationship between household consumption

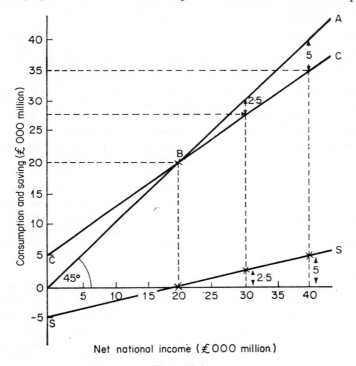

Fig. 10.2

spending and net national income for any given income level. Its construction for an actual economy would clearly be a very much more complicated affair, involving the highly skilled assessment of complex statistical material. However, the graph CC and its method of construction are quite adequate in a first approach to the subject. The relationship which the graph represents is known as the consumption function (sometimes also called the propensity to consume). The word 'function' is used here in the mathematical sense, to denote a relationship between two variables, which are net national income and total household consumption.

It is possible in the same fashion to construct a graph showing the relationship between household saving and net national income. In this example, at a national income of 20 units, net saving by households is zero, which gives one point on the savings graph. At a national income of 40, savings are 5, which gives the second point. The graph SS is known as the propensity to save. It will be apparent that, for any given value of income, say 30, the value of savings (2·5) will equal the distance between CC and the 45° guide line OA.

What significance may be attached to the extension of the graph CC to the left of the point B on the 45° guide line? This is something of a curiosity, which need not over-concern us. The graph here in effect states that, were income to fall below 20, consumption spending would exceed income. However, as income would (on circular flow principles) comprise this consumption spending,[1] income would immediately rise to 20. In other words, income in this economy cannot fall below the 'break-even point' B, where consumption equals national income.

The remainder of this section is devoted to considering some of the technical properties and implications of the graphs CC and SS. For this purpose, it is convenient to draw them again in Fig. 10.3.

First, the average propensity to consume may be defined as the ratio of consumption spending to national income at any given income level. Thus if national income is 20, consumption is 20, and the average propensity to consume (A.P.C.) is 1. At income level 30, however, total consumption spending is 27·5, and the A.P.C. is 27·5 ÷ 30, about 0·92. The A.P.C. therefore denotes the proportion of total income spent on consumption.

Similarly, the average propensity to save is the ratio of total savings to national income at any given income level. The A.P.S. accordingly denotes the proportion of total income saved. Thus at income 40, total savings are 5, so the proportion of total income saved (i.e. the A.P.S.) is 5 ÷ 40, or 0·125. Since the proportion of income saved plus the proportion spent must equal total income, it follows that A.P.C. + A.P.S. = 1. Thus at income 40, the A.P.C. is 35 ÷ 40, or 0·875, so that A.P.C. (0·875) plus A.P.S. (0·125) equal unity.

Marginal propensity to consume (M.P.C.) is defined as the ratio of the increase in consumption spending to a unit increase in national income. Marginal propensity to save (M.P.S.) is similarly defined as the ratio of the increase in saving to a unit increase in national income. It follows that M.P.C. + M.P.S. = 1, since a unit of extra income will be completely disposed of by spending a part and saving the remainder!

How big a 'unit of income' to take to calculate these ratios does not

[1] Provided firms make good their capital deterioration (compare p. 264), and provided that firms do not meet some consumer demand by running down stocks.

matter when the graph CC (and so SS) is a straight line. It is clear from
Fig. 10.3 that the ratio a/b where b is a small increase in income is the
same as the ratio 7·5/10, where 10 is a much larger increase in income.
Mathematically, the ratio a/b (or 7·5/10) represents the gradient of the
graph CC, which is constant since CC is a straight line. The value of
M.P.C. in Fig. 10.3 is accordingly calculable at 0·75. The value of
the M.P.S. (0·25) may be found either from the graph SS or, since
M.P.C. + M.P.S. = 1, by deducting M.P.C. from unity.

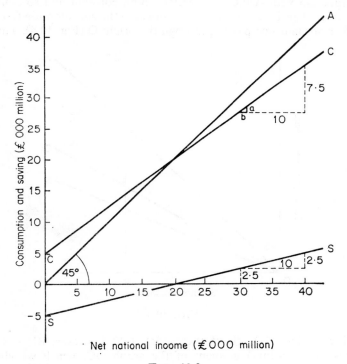

FIG. 10.3

The marginal and average propensities must be clearly distinguished
from each other. Thus the average propensity to consume is the proportion of a given total income devoted to consumption. The marginal
propensity to consume is the proportion of a unit *increase* in income
that will go the same way. If national income is 30, the A.P.C. is about
0·92: just over $\frac{9}{10}$ of income is devoted to consumption at this income
level. If now income rises by 10, the increase in consumption is 7·5, so
that only $\frac{3}{4}$ of the new income is devoted to consumption. This in turn

will mean that the A.P.C. will be lower at income 40 than at 30: it is in fact 0·875.

Where (as in Fig. 10.2) the consumption function CC intersects the 45° guide line, it is apparent that it will go on to cut the vertical axis at some point above the origin 0. This means that (when the consumption function is a straight line) the A.P.C. at any given income level will never have the same numerical value as the M.P.C. ($\frac{3}{4}$ in Fig. 10.2). For purposes of analysis, however, it may be convenient to use a consumption function with A.P.C. and M.P.C. both constant and so equal to each other. This is easily achieved by drawing the consumption function OC as a straight line passing through the origin O (Fig. 10.4). Thus at

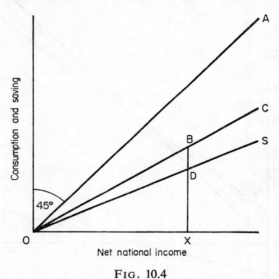

FIG. 10.4

any income level OX, the A.P.C. = BX/OX. However, BX/OX also defines the (constant) gradient of the graph OC, which we already know is equal to the value of the M.P.C. The graph OS is the savings function which corresponds to the consumption function OC. At any income OX, A.P.S. is given by the ratio DX/OX, which also defines the slope of OS, i.e. the value of the M.P.S.

Straight-line (or 'linear') consumption functions—whether passing through the origin or not—are, of course, based upon the assumption that M.P.C. is constant at all income levels. This is a reasonable simplification, made throughout the subsequent analysis. In the real world, however, M.P.C. may have a bigger value at low levels of income than at high levels of income, i.e., when income is low, a bigger proportion of a unit increase may be spent than when income is high. This means that the graph CC (and the corresponding savings function SS) will follow a curving path, shown in Fig. 10.5.

The size of the 'unit' income increase chosen to calculate M.P.C. now becomes very important, since the graph CC is not a straight line and its gradient accordingly changes as we move horizontally from O. When national income is OX, a unit increase in income (b) leads to a given rise in consumption (a), and the M.P.C. here is a/b. If we make b very

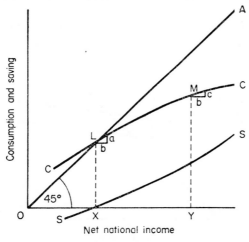

FIG. 10.5

small, then a/b represents the slope of the curve CC at point L. How-ever, when national income is OY, a similar rise in income (b) results in a now smaller rise in consumption (c). The M.P.C. at OY is therefore c/b, which likewise corresponds to the slope of CC at point M. The curve at this point is notably flatter than at point L: the slope, or M.P.C., is lower.

The community's consumption function portrayed in this section represents consumption spending as dependent on the current size of the national income. This relationship must rest upon the proposition that, for most people, the decision how much to spend in a given period (week, month or year) depends on the level of that period's earnings. There are, of course, other considerations. For example, the size of last week's income, and the expected size of next week's, may exercise some influence on this week's expenditure. Again, a person's ability to borrow, the price of borrowing (i.e. the rate of interest), the reward for saving (again the rate of interest), how much wealth he has already accumulated, how easily he could turn his wealth into cash to finance his spending, all these and other factors may be relevant to his spending decisions. Further, as we shall see in Chapter 11, the rates at which income tax is levied will influence households' consumption and saving plans. Additionally, dividend recipients will be affected by the rate of profits tax as well as their companies' policy on profit retention.

For the community as a whole, the distribution of income may also influence the position and slope of the consumption function. If the rich tend to spend a smaller proportion of their income than the poor,

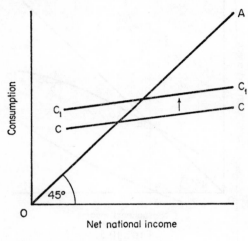

FIG. 10.6

then a community with marked inequality of incomes may be expected to have average and marginal propensities to consume with relatively low values.

To take into account all these features of the real world would, clearly, complicate the analysis very considerably. We may, accordingly, stress the primary importance of the relationship between current income and current consumption, and hold the other factors constant in the background. Even so, our diagram is capable of showing the implications of a change in any one other determinant of consumption spending. Thus suppose the expectation that the price level is going to rise takes root and spreads within the community. In consequence, people hasten to make their purchases now, and whatever the level of national income may be, households wish to spend rather more on consumer goods. This is represented diagrammatically by an upward shift of the consumption function (CC to C_1C_1 in Fig. 10.6). At any given level of income, consumption spending is represented as higher in the presence than in the absence of an expectation of price increases.

4. *Equilibrium Level of National Income*

With the aid of the consumption function, we are now able to represent afresh the determination of the equilibrium level of the national income. In Fig. 10.7, CC shows the total sum per year which all households will wish to spend at any given level of national income. Note that, from the slope of CC, the M.P.C. is calculable at 1/2. The sum which

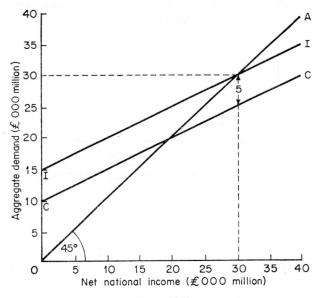

FIG. 10.7

firms plan to spend in net[1] investment each year is 5 (£000 million), and as a first step we may assume that they want to invest at this rate whatever the level of national income or consumption may be. The total final demand in the economy will accordingly proceed partly from households, partly from firms: this total is often known as aggregate demand. Net investment demand is shown diagrammatically with a line II, drawn parallel to the consumption function, at a constant distance of 5 (measured vertically) above it. This follows from the assump-

[1] As on p. 219, it is assumed that replacement capital spending is exactly met by that part of firms' revenue earmarked as depreciation allowances.

tion that, whatever the level of national income, investment demand is the same.

It is seen that II intersects the guide line OA at a net national income of 30. Aggregate demand, or net national expenditure, is also 30. This is the equilibrium level of national income. At this level, the consumption plans of households are such as leave a savings 'gap' or 'leakage' of 5 in the circular flow of income and expenditure. This leakage is exactly filled by the planned net investment spending of firms. The consumption plans of households and the investment plans of firms complement one another in such a way that, when net national income is 30, there is an equivalent aggregate demand to maintain it at that level.

The determination of the equilibrium level of national income may also be represented by using the propensity to save. In Fig. 10.8, II is

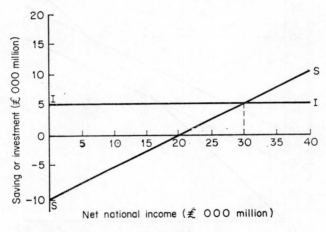

FIG. 10.8

drawn parallel to the horizontal axis, showing investment spending at 5 (£000 million) per annum independent of the level of national income. The propensity to save shows how much households wish to save at each income level. At an income level of 30, planned savings equal planned net investment, and the economy is in equilibrium.

The equilibrium level of national income need not represent full employment in the economy. Let us assume for simplicity (until Section 3, Chapter 12) that the general level of employment varies in direct proportion to the size of the national income. If with full employment the community would enjoy a national income of 40, then at 30 only 75 per cent of the working population are employed. The existence of so much unemployment would today undoubtedly prompt the government to seek to influence income and expenditure flows, to raise national income and with it the level of employment. But for the time being we are keeping the government out of the picture. The economy, in itself, is in equilibrium, and displays no tendency to change, despite the unemployment in its midst.

Suppose now that, in the under-employment equilibrium depicted in Figs. 10.7 and 10.8, firms decide (for one reason or another) to increase their annual net investment spending from 5 to 10 (£000 million). This means that they place on average twice as many orders as before for extra machinery and equipment, while the firms making capital goods place more orders (the 'intermediate' spending stage) for raw materials. The increase in net investment, of course, may also take the form of more orders for raw materials to add to stocks. Whatever form it takes, the increase in net investment spending will result in a direct increase in income, output and employment in the economy. If we follow the assumption just made, exactly $12\frac{1}{2}$ per cent more of the labour force will be newly employed in the capital goods and raw material industries.

However, an examination of Fig. 10.9 shows that moving the investment function up by 5 (from II to I_1I_1) has increased national income and expenditure not by 5, but by 10. We see too that total consumption, which formerly stood at 25, now stands at 30, and that total savings have increased from 5 to 10. Total employment must therefore have increased by yet a further $12\frac{1}{2}$ per cent, so that employment and national income have achieved their short run maximum.

The explanation of this agreeable result lies in the fact that, while the consumption function has remained unchanged, total consumption spending rose by 5 (£000 million) following the initial increase in net investment spending. Why should this occur? The rise in employment in the capital goods (and raw materials) industries will have increased household income by 5 (£000 million). This is of course an income they had not been expecting to receive, and is the consequence of the revised investment plans of the firms. From their new income they will have made purchases of consumer goods, thus occasioning a rise in demand for the products of the consumer goods industries. With greater sales, these firms have in this case reacted by taking on more men to increase output, leading to a further fall in unemployment. A part of the new income thus generated will, in turn, have been spent on consumer goods, thereby adding yet again to total consumption spending.

This process of expansion finally exhausts itself when, in this example, total consumption spending has risen by 5 (£000 million). The original increase in net investment spending of 5 has induced an increase in consumption spending of 5, so that the total increase in the national income and expenditure is 10. The ratio of the rise in national income to the rise in net investment is known as the multiplier. The value of the

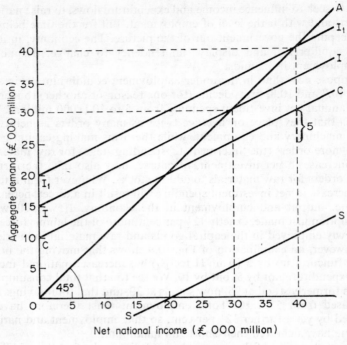

FIG. 10.9

multiplier in this example is 2. Every pound spent on extra investment
has led ultimately to a two pound increase in national income.

5. *The Multiplier*

The process by which economic activity expands if investment rises is
complicated, but some insight is offered by a simple (hence artificial)
example. We consider an economy suffering unemployment of labour
and other resources because aggregate demand is below the level necessary for full employment. Firms in the economy make either capital
goods or consumer goods, for which they procure raw materials themselves and do all their own processing, etc. Should firms for any reason
experience an increase in sales, they react immediately by taking on
more labour which is employed with plant, etc., previously standing
idle. At the end of each week, the full value of the sales increase is
paid out as wages to the men newly employed and as profit to the

business proprietors. The invariable reaction of these (and other) households to an increase in income is to spend three-quarters and save one-quarter (i.e. M.P.C. = $\frac{3}{4}$, M.P.S. = $\frac{1}{4}$).

Assume now that firms decide to increase their net investment spending on capital goods by £1 million per week. Orders are placed with capital goods firms, and at the start of the first week a given number of men are taken on their payrolls. At the end of the first week, the whole of the £1 million is paid out as wages and profits, and over the weekend a part of these earnings is spent on consumer goods. With an M.P.C. of $\frac{3}{4}$, consumption spending will rise by £750,000. Consumer goods firms react immediately to their increased sales by taking on more men at the start of the second week, and at the end the newly employed workers and the business proprietors will between them receive £750,000 as wages and profits. Over the second weekend, consumption spending rises by a further £562,500 (i.e. $\frac{3}{4} \times$ £750,000), and consumer goods firms react as before by taking on more men at the start of the third week. At the end of the third week, therefore, households receive an additional £562,500 as income, of which $\frac{3}{4}$ will be spent over the third weekend.

It is apparent that, by the end of the third week, the level of net national income has increased by:

$$£1 \text{ million} + £750,000 + £562,500$$

—remember that firms are keeping up the (original increase in) net investment spending at the rate of £1 million a week. This increase in net national income may also be written (£ million):

$$1 + \tfrac{3}{4}(1) + \tfrac{3}{4}[\tfrac{3}{4}(1)]$$

or

$$1 + \tfrac{3}{4} + (\tfrac{3}{4})^2.$$

This suggests that, at the end of the fourth week, the total increase (£ million) in net national income will be:

$$1 + \tfrac{3}{4} + (\tfrac{3}{4})^2 + (\tfrac{3}{4})^3$$

At the end of any given nth week, the rise in national income will be (£ million):

$$1 + \tfrac{3}{4} + (\tfrac{3}{4})^2 + (\tfrac{3}{4})^3 + \ldots + (\tfrac{3}{4})^{n-1}.$$

If the nth week is made sufficiently distant, the series forms a convergent geometric progression, with first term 1 and a common ratio of $3/4$. The formula[1] for the sum (S) is

$$S = \frac{a}{1 - r}, \text{ or } S = a \times \frac{1}{1 - r},$$

[1] Strictly, S gives the limiting value for the sum of the series as n is made larger, which implies that week n must be very far away indeed! This difficulty has arisen from the implicit assumption that each stage in the expansion occupies a calendar week, which makes the exposition easier but is unrealistic.

where a is the first term and r is the common ratio. Applying this formula to our series, we obtain

$$S = \pounds 1 \text{ million} \times \frac{1}{1 - \frac{3}{4}} = \pounds 4 \text{ million.}$$

The expression, $\frac{1}{1 - \frac{3}{4}}$, or $\frac{1}{1 - \text{M.P.C.}}$, accordingly represents a 'multiplier' (4) which, applied to the initial increase in the weekly rate of investment spending (£1 million), gives the value of the ultimate increase in net national income per week (£4 million). The multiplier may alternatively be expressed as $\frac{1}{\text{M.P.S.}}$, i.e. the reciprocal of the marginal propensity to save, since 1 − M.P.C. = M.P.S. (p. 224). Here the M.P.S. is 1/4, so its reciprocal is 4.

The value of the multiplier thus defines the ratio of the ultimate increase in national income to the initial increase in investment spending. Of the £4 million increase per week in household income, $\frac{3}{4}$ will be spent and $\frac{1}{4}$ saved: this savings leakage is exactly offset by the £1 million per week new investment spending. The same reasoning would, of course, apply had the investment increase taken the form of a rise in investment in stocks instead of an increase in fixed capital formation.

This example has been worked out in terms of an increase in the rate of net investment spending of £1 million per week. On the assumption that each stage in the expansion takes one week to operate, then by the nth week (when n is sufficiently distant) the total increase in national income per week will be £4 million. However, in the example of Fig. 10.9, we took the increase in investment spending as an increase *per year*. Net investment spending in this example was increased by 5 (£000 million) per annum, and net national income rose by 10 (£000 million), as the M.P.C. was 1/2, giving a multiplier of 2. Over what period of time is this process of expansion considered to operate?

The simplest solution to this problem is to ignore the rate at which the new £5,000 million of investment is spent *over* the year, and to assume that the whole expansionary process works itself out within the course of the year. In other words, an increase of £5,000 million investment spending per year (i.e. in this year, continuing at the same rate in following years) is treated as immediately leading to an increase in consumption spending (with M.P.C. = 1/2) of £5,000 million this year, which will continue at the same rate in following years.

An alternative is to take the view that, if the £5,000 million of investment is spent at the rate of just under £100 million a week, then each weekly 'injection' into the spending flow will have its expansionary influence on consumption. The increase in total investment spending for the year will then be the sum of the additional weekly expenditures, i.e. £5,000 million. The total consumption increase for the year will be the sum of the extra consumption spending induced in each successive week. This second method gives an answer approximately equal to the first, so the greater complexity of calculation it involves is hardly worthwhile.

The size of the multiplier, we have seen, varies inversely with the size of the M.P.S. If, for example, the M.P.S. is 1/5, the multiplier is 5; if the M.P.S. is 1/3, the multiplier is 3. This has important implications for the government's economic policy, should there be widespread un-employment because aggregate demand is too low. First, a rise in net investment spending raises national income (and thereby the level of

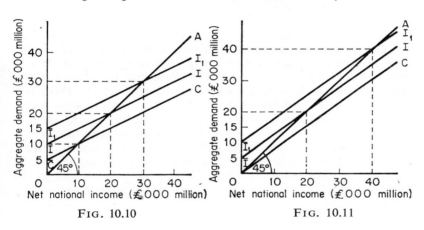

FIG. 10.10   FIG. 10.11

employment) more than proportionately. Second, the increase in national income will be the bigger, the larger is the marginal propensity to consume, i.e. the more of their new incomes people are prepared to spend.

This second proposition is illustrated by contrasting two economies in one of which (Fig. 10.10) M.P.C. = 1/2, while in the other (Fig. 10.11) M.P.C. = 3/4. It will be observed that the slope of the consumption function is steeper in Fig. 10.11 than in Fig. 10.10, though the fact that in Fig. 10.11 the consumption function passes through the origin 0 has no special significance. Both economies are initially at the same under-employment equilibrium income level of 20 (£000 million), with net investment running at the annual rate of 5 (£000 million). Suppose now that in both cases firms revise their investment plans, increasing net investment spending from 5 to 10 (£000 million). In the first economy (Fig. 10.10), an M.P.C. of 1/2 gives a multiplier of 2, and net national income rises from 20 to 30 per year. In the second (Fig. 10.11), an M.P.C. of 3/4 means a multiplier of 4: accordingly, the same size increase in net investment carries this economy on to an annual net national income level of 40 (£000 million).

It will be clear that the multiplier process will work in exactly the same manner in the reverse direction. Suppose, for example, that in Fig. 10.10 the level of investment spending fell from 10 (£000 million) to 5 (i.e. I_1I_1 shifts downwards to II). This entails a decline in consumption spending until a new equilibrium is reached with national income at 20, consumption at 15 and savings at 5.

6. *Changes in Consumption Plans*

It is well worth noting, in passing, that changes in consumption plans will also have a multiplier effect on income and employment, in the same way as changes in net investment spending. Suppose that, at each level of national income, households decide to spend a higher proportion of total income on consumer goods and services. This possibility has already been discussed in Section 3. In diagrammatic terms, the consumption function moves upwards, inducing a direct increase in employment and income, which in turn exercises a further expansionary influence on these two variables through the multiplier process. Fig. 10.9 will serve to illustrate the argument, if it is assumed that the consumption function moves from its original position CC to the position marked II, while net investment spending remains constant at 5 (£000 million) per year.

7. *Savings and Investment*

Our previous work tells us that a rise in net investment spending from an annual rate of 10 units to an annual rate of 16 units will, in the economy portrayed in Fig. 10.12, raise net national income from an annual value of 30 units to an annual value of 48 units. (A unit in this section denotes £1,000 million, though it will be apparent that the size of the unit is immaterial to the analysis.) It is useful, though difficult, to trace out the establishment of the new equilibrium in terms of savings and investment decisions.

Income is, initially, at the under-employment equilibrium level of 30 units per year. Firms wish to spend an annual 10 units in net investment, while households want (OS) to save $\frac{1}{3}$ of their current income. At an income level of 30 units, investment plans and savings plans are completely in harmony with one another, since the sum which households wish to extract from the income flow (30 units) as savings (10 units) is exactly offset by the sum which firms wish to inject into the income flow with net investment spending (10 units). The equality of 'planned savings' and 'planned investment' is thus seen as the condition of equilibrium for the income level.

Suppose now that, at the start of a new year, firms decide to spend an extra 6 units on net investment during the year. National income expands to 48 by a multiplier process $(6 + 4 + 2.66 + \ldots = 18)$, which we can take it works itself through within the year. To avoid various complications, we shall ignore the time sequence (as, for

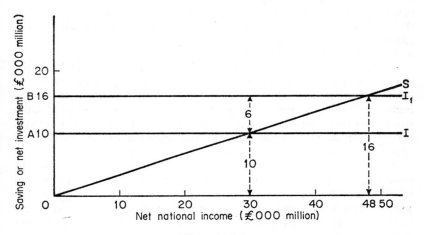

FIG. 10.12

example, in Section 5) by which this expansion occurs, and focus attention exclusively on the significance for savings and investment of each stage (6, 4, 2.66, etc.) in the expansion.

The first step (6 units) in the expansion brings national output from 30 to 36 units, with a rise in the output of capital goods and/or increase in stocks. Actual (and desired) investment spending is thus 16 units, and subtracting this value from national output of 36 units emphasizes that the output of consumer goods is, as yet, unchanged at 20 units. It follows that consumer spending is also 20 units, which puts the actual savings made by households at 16 units, since household income is of course 36 units. We may, however, regard 4 units of this as 'involuntary' saving since, with M.P.S. $= \frac{1}{3}$, households want to save only 2 units from their income increase of 6 units, and spend the other 4. Overall, therefore, households wish to extract 12 units as savings from the income flow, while firms wish to inject 16 units as net investment spending. Savings and investment plans are thus inconsistent with each other, which points to the next stage in the income expansion.

At the second stage, households increase their spending by 4 units, calling forth a corresponding increase in the output of consumer goods and services. Net national income accordingly rises from 36 to 40 units and, with consumption spending at 24, actual saving is necessarily 16 units. The increase in income of 4 units means that households raise the desired level of savings by M.P.S. ($\frac{1}{3}$) × 4 or 1·33 units, from 12 to 13·33 units. Alternatively, we may calculate the desired level of savings at income 40 units by applying the A.P.S. ($\frac{1}{3}$) to 40, to give 13·33 units. It follows that, at this stage, (16 − 13·33) or 2·66 units are being saved involuntarily, i.e. this is the sum which households want to spend from their income increase. Savings and investment plans still fail to synchronize, and income expands by the next step as households spend an additional 2·66 on consumer goods.

Analysis of each successive stage will show a progressively diminishing excess of planned investment over planned savings, until ultimately the two come into equality at an income level of 48 units. This accordingly represents the new equilibrium level, since with income 48 units the proportion that households want to save ($\frac{1}{3}$) occasions a savings leakage (16 units) exactly offset by the injection of net investment spending (16 units) which firms want to undertake.

While planned savings and planned investment are equal only in equilibrium, the actual savings made *at any given stage* equal actual investment, whether in equilibrium or not. Since actual savings is that part of national income not spent on consumer goods, it must necessarily be equal to that part of national output not sold as consumer goods, i.e. investment. Of course, at each income stage before equilibrium is achieved households found that their actual saving (16 units) was greater than their desired saving (12 units with income 36, 13·33 units with income 40, etc.) and, through raising their consumption spending, provided the mechanism that carried income up to 48 units.

Questions

1. Define the terms *investment*, *consumption* and *saving*. Explain the relationship between them.   J.M.B.

2. 'People who save and buy securities with the money are saving, but not investing, unless they buy a new issue.' Comment.   J.M.B.

3. What is the 'propensity to consume'? What variables other than income are likely to be important determinants of consumption?
                                                                                                    U.L.

4. Explain what is meant by the multiplier. How is it related to the marginal propensity to consume? U.L.

5. 'The vital factor in the determination of the level of the national income is the marginal propensity to consume.' Explain.   B.A. Gen.

6. 'An increase in the desire to save tends *other things being equal* to reduce output and employment.' Explain, paying particular attention to the meaning of *'other things being equal'* in this context.

S.U.J.B.

7. 'When savings and investment are equal the economy is said to be in equilibrium.' Explain. B.A. Gen.

8. 'In equilibrium, savings equal investment.' Elucidate this statement.

I.M.T.A.

9. 'Savings and investment are always equal.' 'Savings and investment are equal only in equilibrium.' Discuss these two statements.

S.U.J.B.

11

Income Analysis (II)

CHAPTER 10 showed how the level of aggregate demand was effective in determining the size of net national income, but limited the constituents of aggregate demand to two, i.e. household consumption and net investment by firms. This chapter broadens the analysis by introducing other sources of final expenditure, namely government spending and exports, and by showing how the level of demand is affected by imports, business saving and the rate of tax on household incomes.

1. *Introducing Government*

Chapter 8 presented a fairly complex picture of the finances of the British Government, but for the income analysis of this chapter a much simpler framework is required. We take it that a government spends money on goods and services only, financing its expenditure by a tax on household incomes and (if necessary) by borrowing.

To assess the implications of an income tax for consumer spending, it is useful to begin by considering just one individual. Suppose a man has a marginal propensity to consume (M.P.C.) of 0·75, which is constant at all levels of income. This means that if his income falls (rises) by £1 a week, he cuts (increases) consumption by 15s. and saving by 5s. a week. If now a tax of £1 a week is imposed upon his income, his personal disposable income falls by £1 weekly, though of course his pre-tax income is unchanged. His reaction to this cut in (received) income will be to reduce consumption spending by 15s. and savings by 5s. a week, given his M.P.C. of 0·75. Alternatively expressed, he pays his tax by cutting consumption 15s. and saving 5s.

Likewise for all households taken in the aggregate, the imposition of an income tax means that personal disposable income is correspondingly less than net national income. Households react by cutting consumption by M.P.C. × the value of the tax and savings by M.P.S. × the value of the tax. Diagrammatically, the consumption and savings functions shift downward correspondingly. Thus in Fig. 11.1 the pre-tax consumption function is CC, and pre-tax savings function SS. It is important to note that, from the slope of the graphs, M.P.C. is 0·66, M.P.S. is 0·33, and these values are constant at all income levels. Suppose now an income tax is imposed which requires the payment, at each national income level, of £3,000 million in taxation. Whatever the level of income may currently be, with an M.P.C. of 0·66 households react by cutting consumption spending in total by £2,000 million and savings

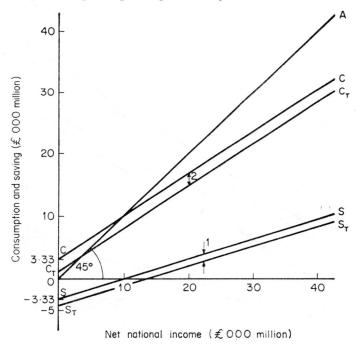

FIG. 11.1

by £1,000 million. This is shown by drawing a new consumption function, C_TC_T, £2,000 million—measured vertically—beneath the old; and a new savings function, S_TS_T, £1,000 million—measured vertically —beneath the old. The new graphs show that, at any given level of net national income, consumption spending is £2,000 million lower and savings £1,000 million lower than before the imposition of the tax.

It is easiest to analyse the effects of an income tax by assuming, as in this example, a lump sum tax. In practice, a government would operate a progressive income tax system, so that households paid more than proportionately bigger taxes at higher levels of income. C_TC_T

would in this case no longer run parallel to CC, but would diverge from it on a curving path as national income rose.

Fig. 11.2 shows the consequences of imposing the tax, though not the results of any government spending which it might finance (government spending is kept out of the picture for the time being). Before the tax is introduced, the net national income is running at an equilibrium level of £34,000 million a year; consumption spending is £26,000 million yearly, while private net investment spending proceeds at the

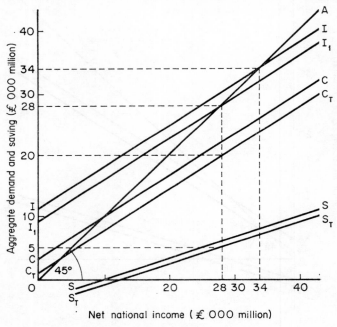

FIG. 11.2

rate of £8,000 million a year independently of the level of income. The initial fall in consumption of £2,000 million (M.P.C. × the tax) leads to a more than proportionate fall in national income through the multiplier process. With M.P.S. = $\frac{1}{3}$, the multiplier is 3 and hence the fall in national income £6,000 million.

The reduction in final demand is entirely a fall in consumption spending, initially £2,000 million which is multiplied to £6,000 million. Net investment demand is, of course, unchanged at £8,000 million a year, the investment demand function shifting down from II to I_1I_1 solely in consequence of the downward movement of the consumption function. At the new equilibrium income level of £28,000 million, consumption spending is £20,000 million, savings £5,000 million and tax payments £3,000 million. Together the 'leakages' of tax payments and planned savings are exactly offset by planned net investment spending.

At a technical level, this analysis has three features which are especially worthy of note. First, the downward shift of the consumption

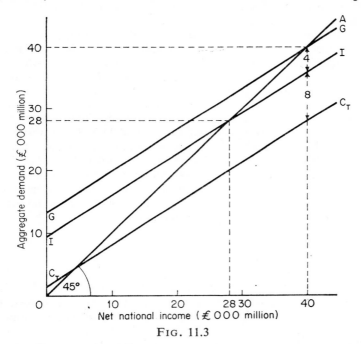

FIG. 11.3

function is given by the M.P.C. × the value of the (lump sum) income tax, i.e. $\frac{2}{3}$ × 3. Second, it is the change in the position of the consumption function, and not in the value of investment, which alters the equilibrium national income (p. 236). Third, since the initial change in consumption is negative, the multiplier carries through a contractionary process in the economy (p. 236).

An important reason (but certainly not the only one—Chapter 20) for levying income tax is to finance government expenditure. Government spending, like consumption or investment spending, is income generating. The fact that a pound is spent by the government, and not a firm or household, does not alter the fact that it is income for the recipient.

Suppose the government is planning to spend £4,000 million a year.

This is to be financed with an income tax yielding £3,000 million, the balance to be borrowed with an issue of government securities. The outcome is illustrated in Fig. 11.3. Suppose that, in the absence of taxation, the consumption function is the same as CC in Fig. 11.2. The imposition of a lump sum income tax yielding £3,000 million shifts it downwards by £2,000 million, measured vertically, to C_TC_T.

Private investment spending proceeds at a constant rate of £8,000 million a year, whatever the level of national income. As usual, this is shown by the graph II drawn parallel to the consumption function. Government spending is to be £4,000 million a year whatever the level of national income, so this can be shown in a similar fashion with a graph GG parallel to II. The vertical distance between GG and II measures the amount of government spending.

The consequence of this government intervention in the economy can be assessed by comparing the original equilibrium income (34) in Fig. 11.2 with the new equilibrium (40) in Fig. 11.3. The government's revenue raising and spending activities serve, on balance, to raise aggregate demand by an initial amount of £2,000 million. The fall in the consumption function of £2,000 million is more than offset in its effects by the government spending of £4,000 million. Assuming idle resources in the economy, and with a multiplier of 3, national income accordingly rises in total by £6,000 million.

2. *Introducing Foreign Trade*

A country engaged in foreign trade is importing some goods and services from various countries overseas and exporting others. For simplicity, we confine our attention to just two economies, and for convenience label the first 'Britain', and the second 'the rest of the world', or 'overseas': the inhabitants of 'overseas' are described as 'foreigners'. The analysis, however, continues at its abstract level, and the reader should not imagine that this section describes specific problems of the British economy in its external relationships. Analysis of some of those problems is undertaken in the course of Chapters 17–20.

To fit foreign trade into the analysis, it is important to keep in mind the basic proposition that expenditure upon a commodity generates income for its producers. It follows that British imports generate income for factors of production at work overseas; while British exports generate incomes for factors of production in this country. Allowance must accordingly be made for both imports and exports, in order to calculate the value of the aggregate demand which generates incomes within the British economy.

Consider first the total of final spending by British households, firms and government. Were there no foreign trade, this would constitute the final demand which generates income for British factors of production. However, some of this expenditure is in fact made on imported goods and services: this generates income for factors at work overseas. We need therefore to deduct imports from total final spending. At the same time, we add the value of exports, as this represents expenditure by foreigners on British goods, which will generate incomes for factors of production at work here. The value of total domestic expenditure *less* imports *plus* exports represents the expenditure aggregate which generates incomes for factors of production at work in Britain. It corresponds to the net domestic product or income, i.e. the net value of output from factors at work in Britain (compare Table 9.2).

To convert this to a net national income figure (p. 195), we need to add expenditure overseas which remunerates British owned property at work there, and subtract expenditure within Britain which remunerates foreign owned property at work here. This is too complicated to show in a diagram, so for simplicity we assume that British income from overseas always equals income paid abroad, from which it follows that national income equals domestic income. This problem has not risen before in this or the preceding chapter, since until this section we have assumed a closed economy, in which domestic and national income were necessarily identical.

Fig. 11.4 illustrates the contribution of exports from Britain to the generation of domestic income within Britain: for the moment, imports are kept out of the picture. The graph C + I + G represents the total final demand of British households, firms and government at the various levels of net national income. Note that, with M.P.C. at $1/2$, the multiplier is 2. It is seen that, in the absence of foreign demand for British goods and services, the equilibrium level of national income is 22 (£000 million). Suppose now that we allow for exports, which are to run at the rate of 3 (£C00 million) a year, irrespective of the level of the national income. The additional export demand can be shown by drawing EE parallel to C + I + G, the vertical distance between the two functions denoting the value of exports. The introduction of exports has a multiplier effect on the level of national income (assuming of course idle resources in the economy), and a new equilibrium is established at 28. A rise in exports (an upward shift of EE) would have exactly the same multiplier effect on national income as a rise in investment or government spending. The reader may check, for example, that a rise in exports of £2,000 million would lead to an income increase of £4,C00 million (assuming idle resources).

Expenditure on imports reduces income-generating demand within the economy. In Fig. 11.5, C + I + G represents final expenditure in a

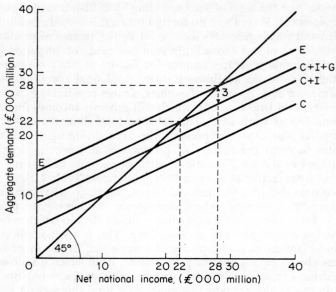

FIG. 11.4

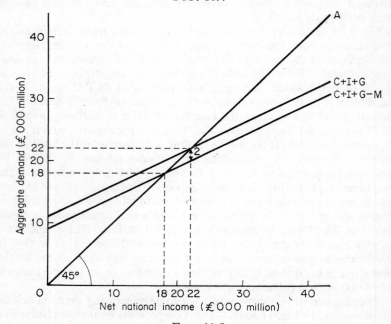

FIG. 11.5

closed economy. In an open economy (ignoring exports for the moment), we deduct imports (M) from final expenditure and are left with C + I + G − M to represent income-generating demand. The two graphs are drawn parallel, on the assumption that the level of imports is independent of the level of income. The value of imports in Fig. 11.5 is £2,000 million. The reader may check first, that the introduction of imports at £2,000 million reduces national income by £4,000 million; second, that a fall in imports (e.g. £1,000 million) has a positive multiplier effect on income (which rises to £20,000 million).

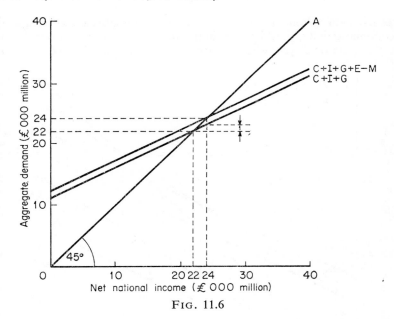

FIG. 11.6

To take account of both imports and exports, it is necessary merely to combine Figs. 11.4 and 11.5. The equilibrium level of net national income in the economy (Fig. 11.6) is £24,000 million, i.e. £2,000 million higher than the pre-foreign-trade equilibrium of £22,000 million. The corresponding increase in net national expenditure is made up of the £1,000 million surplus of exports over imports coupled with the consumption spending of £1,000 million thereby induced. The £1,000 million surplus of exports over imports may be described as this economy's net investment overseas (Chapter 16).

Broadening the analysis to take account of foreign trade or (in Section 1) taxation and government expenditure has not, so far, had any effect on the value of the multiplier. This is because imports, tax payments, exports and government spending were assumed to run at a constant level independent of the value of national income. A change in final demand, accordingly, was multiplied solely by those consumption changes which would operate anyway in the absence of taxation, etc. The next section considers how the multiplier is affected if tax payments and imports vary with the level of net national income.

3. *The Multiplier Further Considered*

Let us again assume a closed economy with, initially, no government economic activity, in which the equilibrium income level is currently 36 (£000 million) per year with net investment running at 12 (£000 million)

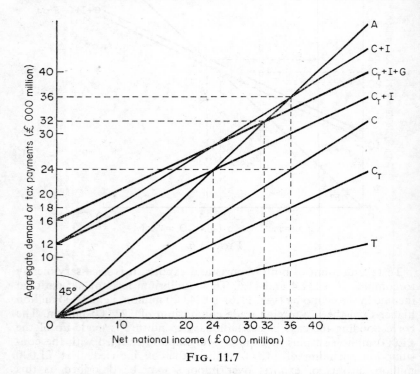

FIG. 11.7

per year (Fig. 11.7). For easier calculation, the consumption function is of the type drawn in Fig. 10.4, with A.P.C. = M.P.C. = $\frac{2}{3}$ (A.P.S. = M.P.S. = $\frac{1}{3}$).

Imagine next that the government imposes a tax at the rate of 25 per cent of income (shown by the graph OT). This means that, at any given income level, households are left with only 75 per cent of net national income as their *disposable income* after paying their income tax. This is split $\frac{1}{3}$ for savings, $\frac{2}{3}$ for consumption. It follows that their rate of saving now represents 25 per cent of net national income and their rate of consumption 50 per cent of net national income (OC_T). The slope of the consumption function accordingly flattens (Fig. 11.7) from $\frac{2}{3}$ (the old M.P.C.) to $\frac{1}{2}$ (the new M.P.C.).

To calculate the numerical value of the multiplier, we recognize that there are now two leakages from the flow of income-generating expenditure. The first is income tax at $\frac{1}{4}$ of net national income and the second is savings, also $\frac{1}{4}$ of net national income. Both leakages are represented if the multiplier is defined as $\dfrac{1}{\text{M.P.S.} + \text{M.R.T.}}$, where M.R.T. stands for the 'marginal rate of income tax' (i.e. 25 per cent). The value of the multiplier, accordingly, is $\dfrac{1}{\frac{1}{4} + \frac{1}{4}}$, i.e. 2.

It is important to realize that, in this illustration, households have not revised their desires about what proportion of their disposable incomes they save and what proportion they spend. They still wish to spend $\frac{2}{3}$ of what they receive, but now the income they receive is only $\frac{3}{4}$ of what they earn! Accordingly, as a ratio of net national income as opposed to disposable income, consumption is necessarily $\frac{2}{3} \times \frac{3}{4}$, i.e. $\frac{1}{2}$ of net national income. Similarly, savings are $\frac{1}{3} \times \frac{3}{4}$, i.e. $\frac{1}{4}$ of net national income, though of course $\frac{1}{3}$ of disposable income.

An income tax of 25 per cent when net national income is £36,000 million would reduce household disposable income by £9,000 million. Households react by cutting consumption by $\frac{2}{3}$ of the fall in disposable income, i.e. by £6,000 million. The introduction of the income tax thus means an initial fall in consumption spending from 24 to 18 units. This has a contractionary influence upon the level of income, given by

$$\frac{\text{Fall in aggregate}}{\text{demand (6 units)}} \times \text{Multiplier (2)},$$

i.e. net national income falls by 12 units to 24 (£000 million) per year. At this level, households pay an income tax of 25 per cent, i.e. 6 (£000 million), save $\frac{1}{3}$ of their disposable income ($= \frac{1}{4}$ of net national income), i.e. 6 units, and spend $\frac{2}{3}$ of their disposable income ($= \frac{1}{2}$ of net national income) i.e. 12 units. The economy is in equilibrium with total planned leakages (savings 6 units + tax payments 6 units) equal to planned investment (12 units).

If the government now decided to spend a *given sum* (say 4 units a year) on goods and services, then the level of national income will rise to $24 + (4 \times 2)$, i.e. 32 units per year. At this level, the government will be raising 8 units (i.e. $25/100 \times 32$) in tax, so that its 'budget surplus' would be 4 (£000 million) per year. Total planned leakages per year are now tax payments (8 units) + savings (8 units), which are equal to net investment by firms (12 units) + government spending (4 units). The consequences of introducing a 'balanced budget' in which government expenditure exactly equals tax revenue are considered in the next section.

An essentially similar analysis may be applied to the problem of

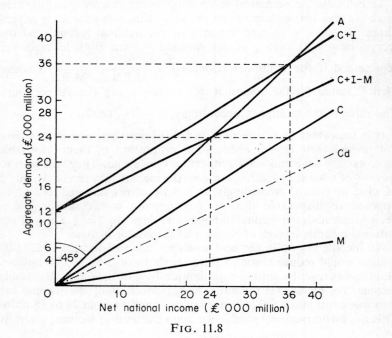

FIG. 11.8

income determination in an open economy. In Fig. 11.8, OC is the consumption function (with A.P.C. = M.P.C. = $\frac{2}{3}$) and, with net investment at 12 units per year, the equilibrium income level in the absence of foreign trade is 36 (£000 million) per year. To reduce complexity, government economic activity is ignored, while exports are kept out of the picture for the time being.

We define the average propensity to import (A.P.M.) as the ratio of imports to net national income at any given income level, and the marginal propensity to import (M.P.M.) as the ratio of the increase in imports to a unit increase in income. If now we allow for imports into this economy at an annual rate of 16·66 per cent of net national income (shown by the graph OM), then A.P.M. = M.P.M. = $\frac{1}{6}$. These imports may take the form of raw materials, capital goods, consumer goods (or services—Chapter 17) but, whatever their composition, 16·66 per cent of final demand in the economy is now deflected from its own products to the products of other economies. At any given income level, therefore, household savings represent one leakage from final demand of 33·33 per cent and imports represent a second leakage of 16·66 per cent.

The multiplier must, accordingly, be redefined as $\dfrac{1}{\text{M.P.S.} + \text{M.P.M.}}$, in this example $1/\frac{1}{3} + \frac{1}{6}$, i.e. 2.

The introduction of imports at an annual rate of $\frac{1}{6}$ of net national income means an initial fall in aggregate demand of $\frac{1}{6} \times 36$ i.e. 6 units. This exercises a contractionary influence upon the income level, given by

$$\text{Fall in aggregate demand (6 units)} \times \text{Multiplier (2)},$$

i.e. a fall in income from 36 to 24 (£000 million). At the new equilibrium income level, household consumption is $\frac{2}{3} \times 24$ or 16 units per year and, with net investment demand at 12 units a year, this puts total domestic expenditure at 28 units. Imports, however, are running at $\frac{1}{6} \times 24$ units, which means that 4 units from total domestic expenditure flow overseas on import purchases, leaving only 24 units income-generating demand within the economy. Planned savings by households are $\frac{1}{3} \times 24$ or 8 units a year and these, with planned imports of 4 units, equal planned net investment spending at 12 units.

Note that the fall in domestic income-generating demand is shown in Fig. 11.8 by rotating C + I to the position C + I − M. This is sufficient to define the new equilibrium income level, without raising the issue of the proportions in which investment demand and consumer demand are now being met by imports from other economies. Suppose, however, that all imports were of consumer goods and raw materials for direct processing as consumer goods. In this case, the consumption function could be rotated to OCd (dotted line in Fig. 11.8), to show spending on domestically produced consumer goods at each level of income.

Let us now allow for exports from this economy at the rate of 5 units per year. With a multiplier of 2, this should raise net national income to an annual level of 34 (£000 million). At this level, imports would run at an annual rate of $\frac{1}{6} \times 34$, i.e. 5·66 units, which is 1·66 units above the former import level. This country's imports, however, are the exports of other countries, so that the rise in imports (1·66 units) from them will have induced a more than proportionate increase in their national income levels, i.e. the expansion of their exports will have a multiplier effect on their national incomes. If, in turn, they have a positive marginal propensity to import, this country's exports to them will increase beyond the rate of 5 units per year. This small increase in its exports will, in turn, generate further income, leading to a slight rise in imports, and so on, until ultimately the effects of this interaction become so weak that they fade away.

It is apparent that, if we choose to allow for this feedback process, the value of the multiplier will be somewhat greater than $\frac{1}{\text{M.P.S.} + \text{M.P.M.}}$ and, in the example, the ultimate equilibrium income level will be higher than 34 units. The *foreign trade multiplier* may be defined as the value of the multiplier in an open economy, when allowance is made both for the leakage of the marginal propensity to import and for the 'feedback' effect on the economy's exports that the leakage engenders. It is not practicable to give its algebraic formulation here, though a more detailed discussion is undertaken in Chapter 16. Further, an analysis embodying both the 'import leakage' and the previously discussed 'taxation leakage' is attempted in the next section.

4. *Leakages and Injections Further Considered*

The discussion has so far proceeded with the aid of diagrams, but problems involving a number of terms are more easily analysed if expressed symbolically. To demonstrate the technique, we begin with a straightforward example involving a closed economy with no government economic activity. We know (Section 7, Chapter 10) that income will be at an equilibrium level if planned savings equal planned investment. Put another way, this condition means that in equilibrium the sum that households *want to* spend on consumer goods and services together with the amount that firms want to spend in net investment exactly absorbs the net national output. If, accordingly, we denote desired consumption by C and planned investment by I, we will know that net national income (Y) is at an equilibrium level if

$$Y = C + I \tag{1}$$

Suppose that, in this economy, households wish to spend $\frac{2}{3}$ of current income at any income level, i.e. A.P.C. = M.P.C. = $\frac{2}{3}$. We may denote this consumption function with the equation

$$C = \tfrac{2}{3}Y \tag{2}$$

It follows that, for any given value of planned net investment (I) per year, we may easily find the equilibrium income level (Y) by substituting equation (2) into equation (1), entering the value of I, and solving for Y. Thus if planned net investment is 12 (£C00 million) per year, equilibrium net national income is

$$Y = \tfrac{2}{3}Y + 12$$
$$\therefore \tfrac{1}{3}Y = 12$$
$$\therefore Y = 36 \ (\text{£000 m.}) \tag{3}$$

Alternatively, if I is 16 units, net national income is

$$Y = \tfrac{2}{3}Y + 16$$
$$\therefore \tfrac{1}{3}Y = 16$$
$$\therefore Y = 48 \ (\text{£000 m.}) \tag{4}$$

Note that, by using this method, we can calculate the effects of a change in investment (or in the consumption function) without first calculating the value of the multiplier. It is apparent, in fact, that the multiplier is 3, and multiplying the investment increase (4 units, i.e. from 12 to 16) correspondingly, shows the rise in net national income, i.e. 12 (£000 million).

As a next step, we may introduce government spending on goods and services (G) and taxation of household incomes (T). The condition for equilibrium now becomes the equality of the two leakages (planned savings and tax payments) with the two injections (planned net investment and government spending). Let us suppose that the government imposed taxation at the rate of 25 per cent of income per year, undertaking concurrent spending on goods and services at the rate of 4 (£000 million) (compare Section 3).

To discover how this would affect the equilibrium shown in equation (3), we first derive a new expression for the consumption function which recognizes that disposable income is less than net national income by the value of taxation (p. 249). Accordingly,

$$C = \tfrac{2}{3}(Y - T) \tag{5}$$

but

$$T = \tfrac{1}{4}Y$$
$$\therefore C = \tfrac{2}{3}(Y - \tfrac{1}{4}Y)$$
$$= \tfrac{2}{3}(\tfrac{3}{4}Y)$$
$$= \tfrac{1}{2}Y \tag{6}$$

We next reformulate the income equation to take account of government spending on goods and services (G),

$$Y = C + I + G \tag{7}$$

Substituting the new consumption function (6) and the appropriate values for I and G, we obtain

$$Y = \tfrac{1}{2}Y + 12 + 4$$
$$\therefore \tfrac{1}{2}Y = 16$$
$$\therefore Y = 32 \ (\text{£000 m.}) \tag{8}$$

The net effect, therefore, of government spending and tax raising is.

to reduce net national income from 36 to 32 (£000 million) per year (compare Fig. 11.7). At the new income level, savings (S) may be calculated from the savings function

$$
\begin{aligned}
S &= \tfrac{1}{3}(Y - T) \\
&= \tfrac{1}{3}(\tfrac{3}{4}Y) \\
&= \tfrac{1}{4}Y \\
&= \tfrac{1}{4}(32) \\
&= 8 \ (\text{£000 m.})
\end{aligned}
\tag{9}
$$

The tax revenue is similarly calculated from

$$
\begin{aligned}
T &= \tfrac{1}{4}Y \\
&= 8 \ (\text{£000 m.})
\end{aligned}
\tag{10}
$$

The government thus enjoys a 'budget surplus' of 4 (£000 million) per year.

We now take up a problem postponed from p. 250, and imagine that, in the situation given by equation (3), the government decides to spend the annual sum of 9 (£000 million) on goods and services, and to finance its expenditure by raising an exactly equal sum in income tax. The consumption function accordingly becomes

$$
\begin{aligned}
C &= \tfrac{2}{3}(Y - T) \\
&= \tfrac{2}{3}(Y - 9)
\end{aligned}
\tag{11}
$$

The income equation is

$$
\begin{aligned}
Y &= C + I + G \\
&= \tfrac{2}{3}(Y - 9) + 12 + 9 \\
&= \tfrac{2}{3}Y - 6 + 12 + 9 \\
&= 45 \ (\text{£000 m.})
\end{aligned}
\tag{12}
$$

The government's 'balanced budget' has thus raised income by its own value from 36 to 45 (£000 million) per year. Consumption (C) is $\tfrac{2}{3}$ (Y − T), or $\tfrac{2}{3}$ (36), i.e. 24. Savings (S) are $\tfrac{1}{3}$ (Y − T) or 12, and taxation (T) is, of course, 9.

When the tax is imposed households meet it partly by cutting consumption and partly by cutting savings. The tax is 9 units and, with M.P.C. = $\tfrac{2}{3}$, total consumption (and total income) would—if we momentarily ignore government spending—fall by

$$6 \ (\text{i.e. } \tfrac{2}{3} \times 9) + 4 + 2\cdot66 + \ldots = 18.$$

The government does, however, spend the whole of the tax proceeds concurrently, which has an expansionary influence on income given by

$$9 + 6 + 4 + 2\cdot66 + \ldots = 27.$$

Here the first term represents the government spending and the subsequent terms represent induced consumption spending. It is apparent, therefore, that consumption remains unchanged, while national income is greater by the value of government spending, i.e. 9 (£000 million).

To look at it another way, households meet part ($\frac{1}{3}$) of the tax by cutting savings, but the government spends the whole of the tax proceeds, so that the net effect is an initial *increase* in aggregate demand by the value of the sum that would have been saved, but is now paid as tax and spent by the government. In this example, therefore, there is an initial increase in final demand of M.P.S. ($\frac{1}{3}$) × 9, which leads to an income expansion by the multiplier process. The value of the multiplier is 1/M.P.S. or 1/$\frac{1}{3}$ (remember that in this example the tax is a lump sum), so that the value of the ultimate increase in national income is ($\frac{1}{3}$ × 9) × (1/$\frac{1}{3}$), i.e. 9. In more general terms, national income increases by (M.P.S. × Tax) × (1/M.P.S.), which simplifies to the value of the tax which, of course, is the same as the value of government spending.

The implications of 'business saving', i.e. profit retention by companies (Chapter 7), may be analysed in the same way as income tax, since both reduce personal disposable income below the level of net national income. We may allow for this in the consumption function—say equation (2)—by writing

$$C = \tfrac{2}{3}(Y - B) \qquad (13)$$

where B denotes business saving. If profits retained by companies represent in total $\frac{1}{10}$ of net national income, then B equals $\frac{1}{10}$ Y, and equation (13) becomes

$$\begin{aligned} C &= \tfrac{2}{3}(Y - \tfrac{1}{10}Y) \\ &= \tfrac{2}{3}(\tfrac{9}{10}Y) \\ &= \tfrac{3}{5}Y \end{aligned} \qquad (14)$$

If net investment is 12 (£000 million) per year, the equilibrium level of net national income is

$$\begin{aligned} Y &= \tfrac{3}{5}Y + 12 \\ \therefore \tfrac{2}{5}Y &= 12 \\ \therefore Y &= 30 \ (\text{£000 m.}) \end{aligned} \qquad (15)$$

Of this net national income, households receive only $\frac{9}{10}$ (i.e. £27,000 million), from which they spend $\frac{2}{3}$ × 27 (£000 million) and save $\frac{1}{3}$ × 27 (£000 million). Total planned savings comprise business saving (£3,000 million) and household saving (£9,000 million), equal to planned net investment at £12,000 million.

In these circumstances, accordingly, profit retention by companies has meant that net national income is 6 (£000 million) lower than it would otherwise be (equation 3). The explanation lies in the fall in aggregate demand which proceeds from the profit retention, readily apparent in the corresponding multiplier calculation. Initially the economy is in equilibrium with Y at 36, C at 24 and I at 12 (£000 million); A.P.C. = M.P.C. = $\frac{2}{3}$. Following the decision of companies to retain profits equal to $\frac{1}{10}$ of annual net national income, households' annual disposable income falls to $\frac{9}{10}$ of net national income. Of this they still wish to spend $\frac{2}{3}$ and save $\frac{1}{3}$, so that in relation to net national income A.P.C. and M.P.C. become $\frac{2}{3} \times \frac{9}{10}$, i.e. $\frac{6}{10}$, and A.P.S. and M.P.C. become $\frac{1}{3} \times \frac{9}{10}$, i.e. $\frac{3}{10}$. The remaining $\frac{1}{10}$ represents, of course, the average and marginal rates of business saving (R.B.S.). Business saving now constitutes a second leakage in the flow of income-generating expenditure, so that the multiplier becomes

$$\frac{1}{\text{M.P.S.} + \text{M.R.B.S.}} = 1/\frac{3}{10} + \frac{1}{10} = 1/\frac{4}{10} = 2 \cdot 5.$$

Profit retention by companies leads to a direct fall in disposable income of $\frac{1}{10} \times 36$ (£000 million), i.e. 3·6 (£000 million). Households react by cutting consumption by $\frac{2}{3}$ of the fall in disposable income, i.e. by 2·4 (£000 million). This cut in consumption expenditure forms, therefore, the initial fall in aggregate demand; its multiplication by 2·5 gives the full reduction in aggregate demand (entirely a fall in consumption spending), and hence in national income, of £6,000 million.

For a final exercise, we open the economy to international trade, and assess the implications of imports and exports for the income level given by equation (8). (This means, of course, that we pay no further attention to business saving.) Imports run at, say, an annual rate of $\frac{1}{5}$ of net national income, while exports are constant at 12 (£000 million) per year. The assumption that exports are constant means that we are ignoring the effect on export demand (p. 252) of variations in other economies' incomes caused by changes in this economy's imports (which vary with, since proportionate to, its national income).

Exports (X) represent an additional source of aggregate demand in the economy, while imports (M) form a leakage of aggregate demand onto the products of other economies (Section 3). The income equation accordingly becomes

$$Y = C + I + G + X - M \tag{16}$$

Imports (M) run at $\frac{1}{5}$ of national income, a relationship expressed in the equation

$$M = \tfrac{1}{5}Y \tag{17}$$

We already know that, in this particular example, $C = \frac{1}{2}Y$ (equation 6), so that substitution of equations (6) and (17) into equation (16) and the entry of the appropriate values for I, G and X gives

$$Y = \tfrac{1}{2}Y + 12 + 4 + 12 - \tfrac{1}{5}Y$$
$$\therefore \tfrac{7}{10}Y = 28$$
$$\therefore \ Y = 40 \ (\pounds 000 \ \text{m.}) \tag{18}$$

From equation (17) imports are calculable at 8 (£000 million) and with exports at 12 (£000 million), the economy has a surplus of exports over imports of 4 (£0C0 million). This is known as its 'balance of payments surplus on current account' (Chapter 16).

The introduction of imports and exports at these rates has thus had an expansionary influence on income, increasing it from 32 to 40 (£000 million). An alternative though more laborious method of calculating the income increase of 8 (£000 million) requires the calculation of the multiplier. The savings leakage (M.P.S. = $\frac{1}{4}$) and taxation leakage (M.R.T. = $\frac{1}{4}$) are now supplemented by an import leakage (M.P.M. = $\frac{1}{5}$). The multiplier accordingly becomes

$$\frac{1}{\text{M.P.S.} + \text{M.R.T.} + \text{M.P.M.}},$$

i.e. the reciprocal of the sum of the marginal rates of leakages. The formula gives a multiplier of $1/\frac{1}{4} + \frac{1}{4} + \frac{1}{5} = \frac{10}{7}$. The introduction of imports at $\frac{1}{5}Y$ would—of itself—occasion an initial fall in aggregate demand of $\frac{1}{5} \times 32$, i.e. 6·4 (£000 million). This exercises a contractionary influence upon income of $6·4 \times \frac{10}{7}$, or $9\frac{1}{7}$ (£000 million). More than offsetting this influence, however, are the expansionary consequences of exports at 12 (£0C0 million), i.e. $12 \times \frac{10}{7}$ or $17\frac{1}{7}$ (£0C0 million). Overall, therefore, income rises by $(17\frac{1}{7} - 9\frac{1}{7})$ i.e. 8 (£000 million).

To calculate the effects of a change in one or more constituents of final demand, it is necessary merely to enter the new value(s) in equation (16). Thus suppose planned net investment rose to 19 (£000 million) per year. We write

$$\begin{aligned} Y &= C + I + G + X - M \\ &= \tfrac{1}{2}Y + 19 + 4 + 12 - \tfrac{1}{5}Y \\ \therefore \ \tfrac{7}{10}Y &= 35 \\ \therefore \ Y &= 50 \ (\text{£0C0 m.}) \end{aligned} \tag{19}$$

The same result would also be obtained by applying the multiplier ($\frac{10}{7}$) to the investment increase (7), which gives $7 \times \frac{10}{7} = 10$ (£000 million). It is clear, however, that solving the equation for Y with different values of I, G or X (or with changes in the import or consumption equations) makes it unnecessary to calculate the value of the multiplier by formula, except as a check.

Questions

1. The following data describe the consumption function for a particular economy.

Income £m.	Consumption Expenditure £m.
2,000	750
2,500	1,125
3,000	1,500
3,500	1,875
4,000	2,250

(a) (i) Calculate the value of the average propensity to consume at £3,500 and the marginal propensity to consume at levels of income from £2,500 to £4,000.

(ii) If net investment increased by £40 million, by how much would you expect the level of the National Income to increase? Explain how you reach your result.

(b) Explain the assumptions involved in using the consumption function above and outline what additional factors are relevant in determining the effects of new investment on the level of income.

J.M.B.

2. Define 'investment'. To what extent does the value of the investment multiplier depend on the propensity to consume?   S.U.J.B.

3. What forces may alter the marginal propensity to consume, and what effects would a change in the marginal propensity to consume have on the national income?   B.A. Gen.

4. An imaginary economy is in equilibrium with no foreign trade or government activity. The *average propensity to consume* and the *marginal propensity to consume* are both $\frac{8}{10}$, the actual level of consumption expenditure being £16,000 in each year.

(a) Explain the italicized phrases.

(b) What is the level of investment expenditure each year?

(c) What is the value of the multiplier?

Suppose that with investment expenditure unchanged both average and marginal propensities to consume drop to $\frac{3}{4}$.

(d) What will be the new equilibrium level of national income?

(e) Explain *briefly* the effects, on the equilibrium of this simple system, of introducing foreign trade and government activity.

U.L.

5. (a) In a closed economy in equilibrium consumption expenditure is

at the rate of £80m. per year and investment expenditure at the rate of £20m. per year. There is no government taxation or expenditure. Assume that consumption is a constant proportion of disposable income at all levels of income. What is the level of national income in the economy, and what is the value of the expenditure 'multiplier'?
(b) Assume that government activity is incorporated into the example, taxation being one-quarter of all incomes, government spending £20m. per year (entirely on goods and services). Calculate the level of national income in the new situation, and the budget deficit or surplus.
(c) Suppose that in addition to government activity international trade is introduced into the model. Assume that the value of exports is constant at £20m. per year but imports comprise one-sixth of consumption expenditure in every year. What, now, will be the level of national income, and what is the size of the surplus or deficit on the balance of payments on current account?   U.L.

6. Explain briefly what is meant by the 'multiplier process'. What difference does the existence of a progressive tax on income make to the working of the process?   I.M.T.A.

7. In an open economy, does the multiplier have any effect on that country's international transactions?   S.U.J.B.

8. 'The operation of the multiplier is exactly the same in the field of foreign trade as in a closed economy.' Explain and discuss.
                                                       S.U.J.B.

12

Fluctuations in Output and Employment

THE INCOME analysis of the last two chapters shows that a change in any one of the constituents of final demand will induce a more than proportionate change in the national income through the multiplier process (if we assume idle resources in the economy, as appropriate). In the short run, however, the consumption function may be relatively stable while, until Section 3, we may abstract from government influence upon the level of economic activity achieved through its tax-raising and spending decisions.

This suggests a critical role for net investment, both domestic and overseas (Chapter 16), in determining the level of the economy's final output, up to the limit set in the short run by the full employment of its resources. Some of the determinants of the volume of imports and exports are considered in Chapters 16 and 18. This chapter shows how, on certain conditions, the investment decisions of firms could lead to a regular variation in the level of national output. Variations in national output imply variations in the level of employment: Section 3 examines this relationship, and discusses remedies proposed for the resultant unemployment. Other causes of unemployment are considered in Section 4, while Section 5 briefly considers the relevance of wage cutting as a remedy for unemployment.

1. *Investment and the Course of Sales*

As a first step, we need to consider how a firm's net investment would proceed if the management were determined to maintain a constant ratio between the firm's capital and its level of sales. We shall discuss this question first for fixed capital and then for stocks of raw materials, etc. To simplify the discussion, it is assumed that fixed capital consists only of machinery.

Suppose a firm has 10 machines of an identical type, with which it is producing an annual output worth £250,000. It seeks to maintain a constant ratio between its quantity of machinery and the annual value of sales, at 1 machine per £25,000 worth of sales. If we value each machine at its historic cost of £50,000, we can express this capital sales ratio as £500,000/£250,000, or 2. This figure is termed the coefficient of acceleration, or the accelerator, for this particular firm.

Each year 2 machines wear out and have to be replaced. The replacement cost of a machine is equal to its historic cost at £50,000. If sales are constant at £250,000 per annum, the firm will have no reason to buy any additional machines. The firm's gross investment is accordingly running at the rate of £100,000 a year, all of which is designed to make good capital consumption, i.e. the scrapping of 2 machines.

Assume next that, in a given year, sales rise to £500,000. If the firm follows quite rigidly the coefficient of acceleration we have defined for it, it will need a total capital stock of not 10 but 20 machines. Its order this year will accordingly be for 12 machines at £50,000 each, representing gross investment of £600,000. Of this, £100,000 (2 machines) is intended to make good the usual scrapping and £500,000 (10 machines) to increase the firm's fixed capital. Net investment by this firm is accordingly £500,000.

In the next and subsequent years, sales stabilize at £500,000 which means the firm is quite content with 20 machines. For the time being, its replacement investment continues at the rate of 2 machines per year. However, if the 12 machines which were bought in the same year all need to be scrapped at the same future date, then that year will show abnormally heavy replacement expenditure at £600,000. Even in that year, of course, gross investment will consist entirely of replacement spending, and net investment will be zero. This is because the firm, we have assumed, increases fixed capital only to meet extra turnover: it expands its capacity twofold for every unit increase in sales. Without a sales increase, therefore, there is no net investment.

This example assumed that the firm reacted immediately to a sales increase by increasing its capital stock in the given proportion. More realistically, however, we might imagine that the firm waits to see if the increase is maintained, meanwhile meeting its increased orders by, for example, running down stocks of the finished commodity, introducing overtime or shift working or patching up old machinery due for scrapping. If sales are maintained at this level (say in the second year), then it places its orders for new equipment. Even so, the time it took to get the new plant would depend on the current loading of the capital goods industries. If these were already working at full capacity, there would be a significant lag before they could deliver the new machines. A more sophisticated version of the accelerator, therefore, might take some account of these time lags by showing one year's net investment as dependent on a previous year's increase in sales.

The working of the accelerator might be modified in practice by changes in the rate of interest. Thus a firm which enjoys an increase in orders expected to be permanent may, nonetheless, postpone its investment project until the cost of raising necessary funds has fallen, in the meantime meeting orders as best possible by the ways indicated above. The connection between interest rates and investment decisions is, however, held over for consideration in Chapter 13; meanwhile we continue to abstract from reality by keeping interest rates out of the picture.

The example was worked through for a particular firm, but clearly for macro-economic analysis it is necessary to define a coefficient of acceleration for the economy as a whole. We might wish to limit our attention to the relationship between net investment and an increase in consumer sales. The accelerator may then be defined as the ratio of net investment to a given increase in total consumption. Alternatively, recognizing that all industries need to employ capital goods, we may define the accelerator as the ratio of net investment to a given increase in national expenditure. As our preceding discussion suggests, a more refined definition might express one year's net investment as dependent on a previous year's increase in national expenditure (or consumer sales).

The term 'accelerator' is normally reserved for the relationship between net fixed investment and growth of sales. A similar relationship, however, may exist between sales and stocks of raw materials (or finished goods). Thus if a firm's regular weekly sales are worth £10,000, it might like always to have a stock of £15,000 worth of the finished commodity, in case it should receive bigger orders. If its weekly sales jumped to £20,000 it would need a stock of £30,000 worth of goods to keep up its stock/sales ratio. This in turn implies an abnormally large raw materials order for just this week, to increase output both for sale and to add to stock. This will not be repeated if sales now settle at the £20,000 level.

Reasoning of this sort suggests that a firm's raw material orders will depend on both the current level of its sales and the size of any (recent) increase in its sales. Such a relationship may, as with the earlier accelerator concept, be usefully expressed in macro-economic terms.

2. The Trade Cycle

A tendency for national income (and employment) to fluctuate over a period of years has presented a grave problem for (in particular) advanced economies. However, the modern theory of income determination can prescribe policy measures for governments to dampen down, though not iron out, these fluctuations (Section 3). Wave-like variations in the real value of national income (i.e. its value after allowing for changes in the price level) are known as a 'business fluctuation' or 'trade cycle'. The concepts of accelerator and multiplier can be combined to provide a model of a trade cycle which, while artificial, will nonetheless give important insights.

To serve as a framework, we assume a closed economy with no government economic activity, and for the time being ignore changes in stocks of finished goods, etc. This means that the two components of final aggregate demand are consumption spending by households and net fixed investment spending by firms. For simplicity, firms are divided into the three categories of Section 2, Chapter 10, and it is assumed that only firms making consumer goods engage in either net or replacement investment spending.

We now make two assumptions about the relationship between consumption and net investment spending, which will enable us to produce a perfectly symmetrical fluctuation in the national income of this imaginary economy. Assume first that, should net investment rise in a given year, the multiplier effect by way of induced consumption spending will work itself through within the year; and that the value of the M.P.C. is $\frac{1}{2}$. Assume, second, that firms rigidly follow an accelerator coefficient of 1 in deciding this year's level of net investment with reference to last year's increase in consumer sales. This means, for example, that if this year's consumption is 5 units higher than last year, then net investment next year will be 5 units, i.e. firms want to increase their capital stock by the same value as this recent increase in consumer sales.

Table 12.1 shows the implications of these relationships for the behaviour of aggregate demand (and so of national output) over the years. The values in columns (2) to (6) may be £ thousand, £ million, etc., since the choice of unit is, as usual, immaterial to the argument. In Year 1, total consumption spending by households is 95, and net investment spending by firms is 5. Net national income and expenditure are accordingly 100, and household saving must be positive at 5. If we assume that, in Year 1, consumption spending is 5 higher than in Year 0, then (given the accelerator relationship previously defined) net investment in Year 2 will also be 5. There is, therefore, no change in consumption, investment or income in Year 2.

This must mean, however, that net investment in Year 3 will be zero, since the rise in consumer sales between Years 1 and 2 is zero. It follows that net investment in Year 3 is lower by 5 (column 5), and given an M.P.C. of $\frac{1}{2}$ and hence a multiplier of 2, this reduction means a fall in consumption of 5; net national income therefore falls overall by 10. In Year 3, total consumption spending generates an equal net national income, and *net* household saving is zero. This corresponds to the break-even income level with zero net investment represented in Fig. 10.2.

Total consumption falls by 5 between Year 2 and Year 3, so that in Year 4, there is 'negative net investment' of 5. Firms fail to make good 5 units worth of deterioration suffered by their fixed assets, a failure which has a contractionary multiplier effect on consumer

TABLE 12.1

(1)	(2)	(3)	(4)	(5)	(6)
	Total				Net National Income
Year	Consumption Spending	Change in Col. (2)	Net Fixed Investment	Change in Col. (4)	(Col. (2) + Col. (4))
1	95	+5	5	+5	100
2	95	0	5	0	100
3	90	−5	0	−5	90
4	85	−5	−5	−5	80
5	85	0	−5	0	80
6	90	+5	0	+5	90
7	95	+5	5	+5	100
8	95	0	5	0	100
9	90	−5	0	−5	90
10	85	−5	−5	−5	80
11	85	0	−5	0	80
12	90	+5	0	+5	90

spending. The equilibrium position for Year 4 is shown in Fig. 12.1, which is built up in the same way as Fig. 10.1. During Year 4, households receive a national income of 80, but spend 85 on consumer goods. Saving by households is, therefore, negative at 5, i.e. they are drawing down past savings. Firms C enjoy a revenue of 85, of which 50 is paid out as income to factors engaged in Firms C, 15 to Firms R and 15 to Firms I. Net national income is accordingly 80. Firms C are choosing to spend 15 instead of 20 on replacement capital goods; they want to run down their capital stock because of the previous fall in consumer sales. Their neglect of capital consumption is conveniently termed negative net investment; at −5 it is equal to household saving.

The fall in consumption of 5 between Years 3 and 4 is the same as the fall between Years 2 and 3, so that net investment in Year 5 remains constant at −5. There is, therefore, no change in income or consumption (though the value of the total capital stock falls by a further 5). In Year 6, accordingly, net investment is not negative but zero; this means that, in contrast to the two preceding years, firms make good all their capital consumption. Spending on capital goods therefore increases by 5, and this has a corresponding multiplier effect on consumption which rises by 5 to 90. This, of course, means positive net investment of 5 in

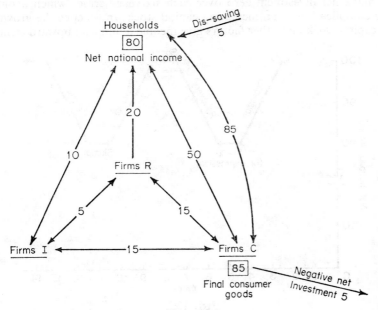

Fig. 12.1

Year 7, and a further consumption increase of 5 brings net national income to 100.

Given our assumed relationships between consumption and net investment spending, national income will continue to fluctuate indefinitely between the limits of 80 and 100. This in turn means some corresponding variation (Section 3) in the level of employment. For this reason, unemployment due to a deficiency of aggregate demand (as in Years 3–6) is sometimes known as cyclical unemployment. Fig. 12.2 plots column 6 of Table 12.1 against column 1: each national income value is put at the centre of its corresponding year.

In the boom period at the top of the cycle the economy obviously enjoys relatively high employment, though in the real world the boom may not be sufficiently strong to bring full employment. The recession

is characterized by rising unemployment, and perhaps by falling prices[1]
(p. 317). The recovery in turn will exhibit falling unemployment and a
more pronounced tendency to rising prices[1] (p. 316).

It need hardly be emphasized that, in the real world, the trade cycle
does not take so regular a form, nor is it merely the manifestation of the
very simple relationships initially assumed between consumption and
investment. Further, values for multiplier and accelerator were chosen
to make net investment zero over each six-year period, which avoids
the complication of an increasing capital stock. In practice the growth
of capital stock and other factors give income a long run upward trend,

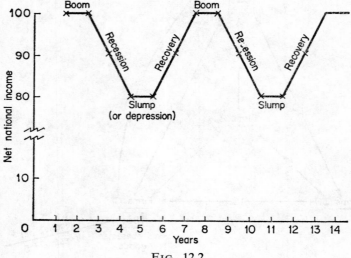

FIG. 12.2

so that the more realistic problem is that of instability in this trend.
This problem is taken up in Chapter 15 (Economic Growth).

In the model presented in Table 12.1, a fluctuation in national income
was induced by having fixed investment vary while maintaining the consumption function[2] constant. We could also produce a regular fluctuation in national output if we ignored fixed investment and assumed
an accelerator-type relationship between stocks of finished goods and
the level of sales (p. 262). A rise in sales in a given period then requires

[1] Remember, however, that to reduce complication we are until Chapter 14
assuming that the general level of prices is constant.
[2] The reader is recommended to plot the values of column 2 against
column 6 on graph paper. He will find that the consumption function is a
straight line with a slope of $\frac{1}{2}$, cutting the vertical axis at 45: its equation is
$C = 45 + \frac{1}{2}Y$.

a more than proportionate rise in orders next period, as firms need both to meet the extra current demand and to add to stocks. This in turn has an expansionary influence on consumption and income via the multiplier. The abnormal stocking orders are not, however, maintained at a constant rate, a failure which will have (via the multiplier) a contractionary influence on consumption and income. The ensuing cyclical variation in national output is sometimes described as a stock or inventory cycle.

In the real world, a business fluctuation dominated by a swing in fixed investment may take some seven to ten years to work through, while an inventory cycle may last two or three years from peak to peak. The working of the shorter cycle may thus be superimposed upon the longer, so that more than one cycle, of differing lengths, is operative at the same time.

3. *Aggregate Demand and the Level of Employment*

We have so far worked to the assumption that the level of employment in the economy varied in direct proportion with the value of net national income (p. 230). This proposition raises two problems, the first of which is quickly dealt with.

If the amount of capital 'consumed' in production varies from year to year, then orders for replacement capital goods will vary correspondingly, with clear implications for the employment level. Variations in replacement capital spending, however, show up most clearly in the concept of gross national expenditure, which suggests that the level of employment is more usefully related to gross, rather than net, final spending. We may, however, avoid this complication by assuming that capital consumption is a constant amount each year, and is regularly made good by spending the current depreciation allowances (compare Fig. 10.1). On these conditions, the employment level will depend on the value of net final expenditure only, as the possibility of swings in replacement capital demand also causing employment variations has, by assumption, been eliminated.

We turn now to the second problem, namely the relationship between the employment level and the value of net national income. The simplest assumption is that firms in the economy always experience 'constant returns' to labour, i.e. whatever the level of production, the employment of more men or less always changes output in the same proportion. Correspondingly, therefore, any change in (national) output always implies a uniformly proportionate change in the level of employment. It is more likely, however, that at relatively low employment levels when there is plenty of spare plant per man, many firms experience increasing returns to labour, i.e. if new men are taken on, they raise output more than proportionately. By contrast, as the full employment level is approached in the economy, many firms perhaps experience diminishing returns to labour. Extra labour makes a less than proportionate contribution to output, as greater demands are made upon a more or less limited productive capacity. In these circumstances, a rise

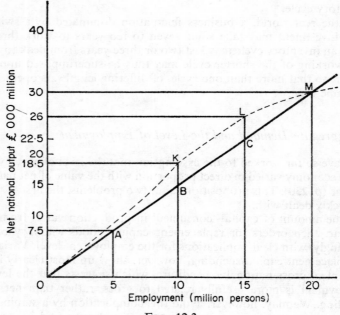

FIG. 12.3

in national output from a relatively low level entails a less than proportionate increase in employment. Thereafter, perhaps, constant returns are encountered, but as the economy approaches full employment, the weight of diminishing returns is felt. This will mean that output will rise less rapidly than employment.

These relationships between national output and the level of employment are shown in Fig. 12.3. If constant returns are assumed, then we have a straight-line relationship portrayed by, e.g., the continuous line OABCM. According to OABCM a rise in national output of £7,500 million always necessitates an increase in employment of 5 million men, irrespective of the level of national output. Alternatively, we may assume that constant returns (in these proportions) operate only between an employment level of 10 and 15 million persons (broken line KL). Below a figure of 10 million employed, increasing returns to labour mean that national output rises more than proportionately to an increase in employment (broken line OK). Above an employment figure of 15 million, diminishing returns imply less than proportionate increases in the national output (broken line LM).

If we take OKLM as the relationship between national output and employment, it is easy to read off the level of employment corresponding to a given level of aggregate demand. Thus a net national expenditure, of, say, £26,000 million generates an equal net national income, and results in the employment of 15 million persons. With national income and expenditure at £30,000 million, the corresponding level of employment is 20 million.

Let us suppose that, in the imaginary economy under review, 20 million persons are the maximum number who wish to offer their services in the labour market. Let us also for the time being ignore such difficulties a man may experience in seeking work as finding that there are vacancies only in occupations for which he is not qualified, or that the vacancies exist many miles away from his home town. In other words, we assume that labour is perfectly mobile—any man can and will do any job anywhere.

On these assumptions, we can say that there is full employment of the labour force if the whole of the 20 million working population is employed. Any lapse from full employment is the outcome of a deficiency of aggregate demand in the economy. In Fig. 12.3 a national output of £26,000 million requires the employment of 15 million persons. If aggregate demand rose from £26,000 million to £30,000 million, total employment would increase from 15 to 20 million persons. Total spending of £26,000 million is, therefore, inadequate to absorb the services of all those who offer them on the labour market.

This situation is illustrated in Fig. 12.4. The graph

$$(C + I + G + X - M)_1$$

denotes the usual relationship between the level of aggregate demand and net national income. The economy is currently in equilibrium with a net national income of £26,000 million per annum and a corresponding employment level of 15 million people. While this situation continues there is an annual waste of £4,000 million national product, which could have been produced by the 5 million people who would like a job but cannot get one.

This deficiency of aggregate demand may be a manifestation of the workings of the trade cycle, as discussed in the previous section. However, rather than wait for 'spontaneous' recovery—which may not, anyway, reach the full employment mark—the government would almost certainly choose by various means to stimulate aggregate and. For net national income to rise by £4,000 million and employment by 5 million people, it is necessary for aggregate demand to increase initially by only £2,000 million. This is because of the multiplier effect of the spending increase (the slope of $(C + I + G + X - M)_1$ is 1 in 2, giving a multiplier of 2). The distance marked ↑ at income £26,000 million is often known as the 'deflationary gap'. It is the amount by which aggregate demand falls short of full employment aggregate demand, when allowance is made for the multiplier effect.

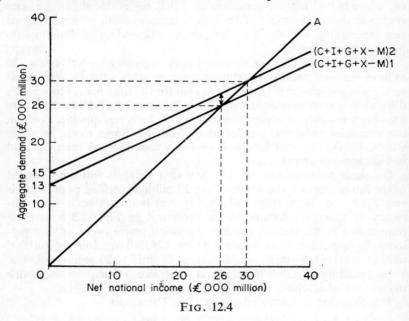

FIG. 12.4

The remedy for demand-deficiency unemployment is to push, somehow or other, $(C + I + G + X - M)_1$ into the position $(C + I + G X - M)_2$ i.e. increase aggregate demand. Reflection on the constituents of aggregate demand will reveal some of the possibilities here.

First, government policy may aim at encouraging firms to increase their net investment spending. The analysis of Chapter 13 gives grounds for thinking that, in its monetary policy, the government will seek to influence interest rates downwards, while in its tax (or fiscal) policy, the government could make taxation concessions in respect of investment spending (Chapter 20). However, the existence of a high level of unemployment would probably make businessmen pessimistic about the profitability of new capital schemes, and hence less responsive to a fall in interest rates or to fiscal inducements.

Second, the government itself might increase its expenditure on a variety of public works schemes (e.g. roads) or social services (e.g. school and hospital building). It might also encourage local authorities and public corporations to press ahead with capital schemes.

Third, an increase in exports would be income generating within the exporting country, even though the recipients of the exported goods are the customers overseas. It follows that, if there is danger within the economy of a deficiency of aggregate demand, one way of keeping it buoyant is for the government to give loans or grants to developing countries (Chapter 17). The spending of the recipients is then income generating in the donor country.

A fourth possibility is to try and deflect demand away from imports on to home produced goods, say by raising tariffs or introducing import quotas. However, a reduction in country A's imports from other countries (B) has a contractionary influence upon income in B, which may lead to a decline in B's imports from A. A might nonetheless benefit if the value of B's *marginal* propensity to import was low, e.g. at the extreme, B's imports might be constant at all income levels, so that A's exports were not affected by B's income contraction. On the other hand, the governments of the other countries (B) may retaliate by deliberately cutting imports from A.

Finally, the government could, through propaganda or tax cuts, encourage an upward shift in the consumption function. People are urged (or enabled) to spend more and save less. The result of any attempt by those in employment to save less will ultimately be, not that *total* household savings decline, but that the level of national income and employment rises. This proposition may be illustrated with a numerical example, using the same values as in Fig. 12.4. To avoid the complication of splitting 'income not spent' into saving and taxes, we shall ignore taxation in this example. Correspondingly, we may either ignore government spending, or assume that it is financed completely by borrowing.

With national income at 26 (£000 million), total consumption spending may be taken as 20, and (government spending plus) net private investment plus exports less imports total 6. It follows that savings also equal 6, since savings here equal income minus consumption. The multiplier is 2, which means that the M.P.C. is $\frac{1}{2}$ (we assume that imports have a constant value at all income levels, i.e. the marginal propensity to import is zero). Suppose now that, as a result of encouragement to spend more, households reduce their savings to 4, which means that consumption spending rises to 22. The economy is not in equilibrium, because the increased consumption spending will have a multiplier effect, and yet more people will be drawn into employment in the consumer goods industries. With a multiplier of 2, national income rises to 30, at which level total consumption spending is 24, and investment spending etc., 6. At the new equilibrium level, savings will also be 6. The reduction in savings (from 6 to 4) of those in employment when income was 26 has been offset by the savings of those who are newly employed in consequence (i.e., M.P.S. × the rise in income, or $\frac{1}{2} \times 4$).

The government's influence might also affect, to the good, the value of the marginal propensity to consume. If in this example the M.P.C. rose from $\frac{1}{2}$ to $\frac{3}{4}$, the multiplier would increase from 2 to 4. The deflationary gap would then be only £1,000 million instead of £2,000 million, and so twice as easy to fill by the various ways outlined.

It should not be imagined that a government faced with a problem of demand-deficiency unemployment would simply pull all these levers and hope for the best. Each course of conduct has various implications, and some methods of stimulating the economy may clash with others. For example, increasing government expenditure calls for more funds, but reducing tax rates yields less revenue. This in turn implies an increase in government borrowing, i.e. a rise in the national debt. A rise in the national debt means more interest to debt holders, and the necessity in future years to raise more tax revenue to pay that interest. Businessmen may interpret this as meaning higher tax rates in years ahead, and private investment may thereby be discouraged. The fall in private investment may more or less offset the increased government expenditure, so the economy is back at square one.

4. *Other Causes of Unemployment*

In the example of the previous section, an aggregate demand of £30,000 million a year was sufficient to maintain in employment the whole of the labour force of 20 million persons. A change in the pattern of demand for goods and services had no implications for the numbers in employment, since labour was assumed to be perfectly mobile: any man could and would do any job anywhere. Thus suppose the demand for some commodities declined, because of a change in the tastes of consumers, or because of the development of new products. If aggregate demand continues to run at an annual £30,000 million, this implies that some other commodities have proportionately increased in demand. With a perfectly mobile labour force, men simply leave the contracting industries (which have too much labour) and move into the expanding industries (which are short of labour). There is a change in the distribution of labour among occupations, but not in the overall level of employment.

In the real world, however, the labour force is less than perfectly mobile. This immobility may be occupational: men who leave one occupation do not have the training or perhaps the talent necessary to take up other jobs open to them. Or perhaps they underwent a long training period to qualify them for their previous work, and are reluctant to throw away the skills and standing thus acquired. Alternatively, their immobility may be geographical. Suitable employment exists in other towns or regions; but it may be difficult or more expensive to get housing in the new area, or people may be reluctant to sever the ties of a lifetime and move to a strange community.

Given imperfect labour mobility, it follows that unemployment may result from a change in the pattern of demand, even though the overall volume of demand remains sufficient to maintain everybody in work. Thus some industries may experience a decline in the demand for their products, while at the same time other industries experience an increase. Men become unemployed in the declining industries, but do not move to the industries which are seeking to expand, because of occupational or geographical immobility. The latter, accordingly, suffer a labour shortage. From one point of view, we may say that the unemployed are out of work because of the changing industrial structure, so their unemployment may be described as structural. From another viewpoint, the men are out of work because they do not move freely or without friction from one occupation to another, hence their unemployment may alternatively be labelled frictional.

The structure of industry will also undergo change—though of a different fashion—in consequence of changes in methods of production. Thus some industries may adopt techniques which require a lower ratio of labour to capital to secure the same output. This might come about through technical improvements, so that for the same expenditure it is possible for a firm to buy better machinery, which produces the same output with less labour. Unless there is an offsetting increase in demand, the introduction of this labour-saving machinery will result in some unemployment in the industries concerned. This may be called technical or technological unemployment. It might also be labelled structural unemployment, though here it is the result of a change, not in the pattern of output, but in the techniques of production. There may at the same time be other work available in the economy, if aggregate demand is appropriately high. If these men are unable to take up the jobs available through their immobility, their unemployment could also be classed as frictional.

The reasoning may be illustrated by considering, say, an individual master baker who has 10 ovens, each of which cost £2,000 and requires 2 men to operate. He may replace them by one oven, costing £20,000, which needs only 2 men to operate it. His method of production is now capital intensive (£20,000 equipment/2 men) instead of labour intensive (£20,000 equipment/20 men). Putting it another way, he has substituted capital for labour. With unchanged output he will dismiss 18 bakery operatives, who become technically unemployed.

If labour were perfectly mobile, then 'full employment' would mean literally that every single member of the population who wanted work was in a job. The only possible cause of unemployment (ignoring such factors as climatic conditions, etc.), would be a deficiency of aggregate demand. However, with imperfect labour mobility men may be unemployed because of changes in the structure of production, despite the fact that aggregate demand is sufficiently high to give them work. This in turn must mean that some industries are short of labour. Thus in early June, 1966, the Ministry of Labour recorded some 260,000 unemployed for Great Britain (excluding Northern Ireland), while in the same period there were about 450,000 unfilled vacancies. Despite the existence of a quarter of a million unemployed, this would be described as 'full employment': overall aggregate demand was sufficiently high to give everyone a job, even though for frictional reasons some vacancies were unfilled.

The expression 'over-full employment' is sometimes used to describe a situation in which the number of vacancies significantly exceeds the number unemployed (as in early June, 1966). This might be interpreted as evidence of 'excess demand' in the economy, considered in Chapter 14.

'Regional unemployment' denotes unemployment in a particular region or district which is above the national average. It is wrong to think that this is necessarily frictional. Suppose that the level of investment or export demand in the economy is abnormally low. The resultant unemployment is by definition due to inadequacy of aggregate demand. Yet the industries which make capital or export goods may happen to be concentrated in a few regions within the country. Unemployment is therefore concentrated in these regions. If all these unemployed became perfectly mobile overnight, they could not get work simply by moving elsewhere, as there are no job vacancies anywhere to be filled. By contrast, if in a generally buoyant economy with a high level of demand one particular industry, located in a given region, suffered a decline, its unemployed could procure work by moving elsewhere.

Just as aggregate demand deficiency unemployment may have regional manifestations, so e.g. technical unemployment may be spread fairly evenly throughout the country. Thus in the bakery example given earlier we might expect some unemployed bakery operatives in every town, in so far as there is a general tendency to introduce the capital intensive methods.

We may also note the influence on employment of essentially seasonal factors. The demand for some goods and services is seasonal, e.g. seaside hotel rooms, so that those who provide them in the high season must look for other employment in the remainder of the year. The weather, too, is a seasonal factor of great relevance in some industries, e.g. building.

Where regional unemployment is the consequence of changes in industrial structure, some relief may be afforded through official influence over the siting of new factories, coupled (where necessary) with encouragement to occupational mobility. In the U.K. today such measures merge into the broader policy of promoting 'balanced' regional development, explained in Chapter 20.

5. *Wage Cutting*

In reality it is very unlikely that trade union members or other wage earners would tolerate a reduction in their money wage rate, even if there were the prospect of partial compensation through a fall—to abandon temporarily an earlier assumption (p. 216)—in the price level. It is instructive, nonetheless, to consider what relevance wage cutting may have for unemployment, though the problem is much more complex than the following analysis might suggest.

We have seen that the price paid for (a unit of) any commodity finds its way as income to the factors which produced it. For easier illustration, imagine that the price paid per unit is distributed as income in the same proportions for every commodity: wages and salaries 75 per cent, rents 5 per cent and (interest and) profits 20 per cent. Suppose now that the economy is suffering widespread unemployment through a deficiency of aggregate demand and that—as a gesture of assistance—all wage and salary earners announce their willingness to accept a 10 per cent reduction in their rates of pay. How far will their sacrifice help create employment?

We explore this problem first in the context of a closed economy, with no government economic activity. Average and marginal propensities to consume are taken to be equal at $\frac{4}{5}$, and this ratio holds for households in each income group as well as in aggregate. It is useful to denote the value of national output before the wage reduction with the index number 100. The wage income derived from its production may accordingly be represented as 75 units, profits as 20 units and rents as 5 units. National output was absorbed by a national expenditure comprising consumption 80 units and investment 20 units. For the respective income groups, wage earners spent 60 units of their income and saved 15, while profit and rent recipients together spent 20 and saved 5 units.

Following the wage reduction, wage earners expect 10 per cent less money income, i.e. 67·5 units, though profit and rent recipients between them continue to expect 25 units. If these expectations are met, the general level of prices of currently produced goods and services must fall by 7·5 per cent. Accordingly, if national output is to remain at the same level in real terms as before the wage fall, national expenditure must now equal 92·5 units. If in fact it exceeds 92·5 units, then the extra demand will call forth an increase in output, which will necessarily raise the level of employment.

Assume that households make their spending plans with reference only to the size of their money incomes, taking no account of changes in the general level of prices. Such changes are also, we suppose, ignored by firms in reaching their investment decisions. It follows that, in the new situation, net investment spending would remain constant in money terms at 20 units, while consumption spending would fall by only 6 units (i.e. M.P.C. $\times$ fall in money wages of 7·5) from 80 to 74. The new value for aggregate demand (94 units) would thus exceed the new value of national output (92·5 units), and this excess could be expected to call forth an initial rise of 1·5 units in output, with some accompanying increase in employment. This rise would be multiplied, in turn, through the further spending of those newly employed.

This result was obtained only by assuming certain expenditures constant in money terms, so that (for the first effect) total final expenditure falls (6 per cent) less than money income (7·5 per cent). Suppose, however, that profit and rent recipients had kept expenditure constant in real terms, then with a fall in the price level of 7·5 per cent they would have reduced consumption to 18·5 units. If firms followed the same principle in their net investment spending, they also would have wished to spend only 18·5 units, so that aggregate demand would have totalled their 37 units spending plus 54 units (i.e. $\frac{4}{5} \times 67·5$) spending by wage earners, or 91 units altogether. This 'deficiency' of 1·5 units would have exercised a contractionary influence upon output and employment. Alternatively, wage earners might also keep spending constant in real terms (55·5 units), despite the fall in money income, so that aggregate demand remains constant in real terms at 92·5 units.

The outcome appears, therefore, to depend on the reaction of firms and profit and rent recipients to the fall in the price level. If they decide to increase expenditure in real terms, i.e. keep spending at least constant in money terms though the price level is lower, then this has an expansionary influence on output and employment. Wage earners cannot, it seems, automatically promote employment by accepting lower money wage rates. Their success depends on the appropriate reaction by other categories of spender to the accompanying fall in the price level. This weakness apart, wage-cutting involves some redistribution of income from the relatively poor to the relatively rich, which would almost certainly conflict with the community's social policy.

In an open economy, the fall in the price level might also affect employment through its implications for export demand. Suppose that the rate at which this country's currency (£'s) is exchanged for other currencies is 'fixed' at a given level (Chapter 17): in terms of dollars, say £1 = $4. With the exchange rate unchanged, the fall in the (sterling) price level makes this country's goods cheaper overseas. This would probably stimulate export demand and thus promote an increase in output and employment—though in the short run the additional orders could be met by running down stocks. Home produced goods would also become cheaper in relation to imports, which might serve to deflect some domestic demand to the products of the home economy.

Finally, we may briefly note that, by altering the relative prices of factors, a wage reduction might have some relevance to an unemployment problem in one specific industry. Suppose that an invention has raised the productivity of capital to labour in a given industry, and in consequence firms are switching to more capital intensive methods of production. If unions in this industry are prepared to accept a wage cut, the profitability of labour intensive methods is increased, and some technical unemployment may as a result be averted.

Questions

1. What is the consumption function? Discuss the part played by consumers' expenditure in the trade cycle.   J.M.B.

2. What is the 'multiplier'? Discuss the importance of the multiplier in the analysis of fluctuations in the general level of employment and output.   J.M.B.

3. Explain the connection between short-term changes in private investment and short-term changes in national income and employment.   U.L.

4. Explain how a change in investment could affect the level of employment in an economy.   J.M.B.

5. How may a government use fiscal policy to remove unemployment?   U.L.

6. How would you define the level of unemployment in a country? What factors cause unemployment?   U.L.

7. What do you understand by 'the mobility of labour'? To what extent do you think that unemployment is caused by low mobility of labour?   U.L.

8. Unemployment is usually divided into different types. Which type of unemployment is most likely to be cured by reductions in wages?
C.I.S.

9. 'Unemployment persists only because labour is immobile and trade unions refuse to accept cuts in money wages.' Discuss.   **U.L.**

10. 'The causes of regionalized unemployment must be kept quite separate from the causes of general unemployment.' Discuss.
B.A. Gen.

11. What are the causes and consequences of localized unemployment?
C.S.

13

Money, Interest and the Level of Income

A LEADING assumption underlying last chapter's trade cycle analysis was that the level of net fixed investment is determined by (recent) changes in consumer sales (alternatively, national expenditure). We now alter the emphasis, and consider how net investment may be influenced in any given year by the current level of interest rates (compare p. 262). First, however, it is necessary to discuss the determinants of the rate of interest: this will make it possible in the final section to trace a connection, via interest rates and investment decisions, between the level of income and the money supply.

1. *The Demand for Money Balances*

The theory of interest outlined in Section 2 rests upon an analysis of the motives people and firms have for holding money balances. Thus consider the behaviour of any person who, over the year, enjoys a flow of money income from his employment or from any assets he may own. He may receive this income per week, per month, per quarter, etc., but however frequently he receives it, he does not normally hasten to spend it all immediately. Instead, he holds a stock of money as a cash balance, gradually running it down over the interval till next pay day, to finance his various purchases and expenditures. This balance that he holds to finance his transactions may be labelled a 'transactions balance', and cash held for this motive is said to be held to satisfy the transactions motive.

If accordingly we listed the assets of a household on any given day, we would find a certain cash balance being held to finance transactions before the next pay day. The actual size of the balance would depend on the day chosen to compile the list, but it would be possible to calculate the average daily balance over the week, month, etc., whichever is the interval between pay days.

Thus suppose that each Friday at noon a man receives a wage of £21. If he spends the whole of this sum at a rate of £3 a day over the following seven days, then his average daily balance over the week will be £10·5. Had he spent all his pay by noon Monday at the rate of £7 a day, his average daily balance over the week would have been £4·5.

Now suppose the man is put on a salaried basis, but continues to be paid at the same rate. He receives £84 for a 28-day month, and if as before he continues to spend at a rate of £3 a day, his average daily balance will be £42, which is exactly 4 times his balance when he was paid on a weekly basis. If his pay were doubled to £168 a month, and he spent at the rate of £6 a day, his average balance per day would be £84; and if he reverted to a weekly wage system, at £42 a week, his average balance would be £21.

In these examples, the average size of cash balances held to finance forthcoming transactions depends upon the size of the income; how often it is received; and how often its recipient makes his transactions. It is conceivable that our salary earner, especially if he spent pretty regularly over the month, or bunched his spending up at the end of the month, might consider lending out his surplus balances over the first week or two, until he actually needed them. This is unlikely, because the trouble and cost involved would make the interest return hardly worthwhile. It is a useful first approximation, accordingly, to regard transactions balances as insensitive to any changes in interest rates.

It has been assumed in these examples that the income recipient spends the whole of his income on consumer goods. If he spends at a constant rate over, say, seven days, then with a weekly income of £21 his average daily transactions balance is £10·5. Suppose, however, he saved £3 a week. In this case his transactions balance at the start of the week can be taken as £18, and with a constant rate of spending averages £9 per day over seven days.

The £3 he saves may be used to buy some sort or other of financial asset. In the real world, there is a wide choice of assets open to the private saver, largely depending on the sum available: savings certificates, building society shares, company shares, government bonds, life insurance benefits, trust units, and so on. Alternatively, the saver may wish to add his current savings to a sum he has already accumulated and is holding in the form of cash. To hold wealth in the form of cash involves the holder in the loss of the interest he would have enjoyed had he instead used the funds to buy interest yielding financial assets. What rational motives may he have for behaving in this way? We have already, of course, distinguished the transactions motive: a household planning to spend a given sum over the week ahead will not find it worthwhile to lend it at interest in the interval. In this example, however, the income recipient has added £3 to a cash hoard he does not require for immediate consumption purposes. Why should he be holding it?

One possible motive is precautionary. A household may keep a precautionary balance, in the form of cash, to meet any emergency that may occur. Whether the precautionary balance is a few pounds, or a few hundred pounds, will depend largely upon the household's income, so that it is convenient to classify the precautionary demand as an extension of the transactions demand.

The transactions and precautionary motives are equally relevant to business enterprise. A firm will hold a 'working balance' to enable it to pay employees and suppliers before it is itself paid by its customers. Given the dates on which it makes payments and on which it receives payments, the size of this transactions balance will depend largely on its turnover. Further, the bigger its sales, the bigger its precautionary balance is likely to be. It is interesting to note that the transactions balances of firms and households, considered as two groups or 'sectors', will be inversely related to each other. Thus when wages are paid on a Friday, households' balances will be relatively high and firms' relatively low. As wages are spent during the week, the balances of households fall and of firms rise, until the cycle starts again on the following Friday.

The total size of the average cash balances held by all firms will clearly depend upon the number of firms there are. A reduction in the number of firms through the process of merger implies a reduction in the total of transactions balances held by firms, as previously independent units no longer need cash to finance their dealings with each other.

In the short run, over a year or so, it seems quite reasonable to assume constant the number of firms and the whole complex pattern of payments arrangements and customs among firms and between firms and households. On this assumption, it follows that the active determinant of the size of transactions and precautionary balances for households will be their incomes, and for firms their level of sales. Households' incomes and firms' sales in turn depend upon the level of national income, so we may express the total demand, in the economy, for transactions and precautionary balances as a function of (i.e. as dependent on) the size of the national income.

Will firms and households hold any cash over and above that required to satisfy the transactions and precautionary motives? For smaller firms and humble households, probably not. But for the rich, for larger firms, and for institutions like life insurance companies, there is a third possibility. This is that the household, etc., is taking a speculative view on share and bond prices, holding off the market for the time being in the hope of making a more advantageous purchase a little later on. In this case, it is holding a balance for a speculative motive.

For simplicity, let us ignore shares for the moment and assume that there is only one type of bond available, a Government security with no redemption date which was issued with a nominal value of £100 carrying 2½ per cent interest annually. Suppose further that since their issue the market value of these securities has declined greatly in Stock Exchange dealings, and their price now stands at £50. This means that a purchaser today at £50 will get £2 10s. 0d. yield a year, so the effective return to him as a percentage on his own investment of £50 is 5 per cent.

The name given in economics to the effective yield on undated or 'irredeemable' Government securities is the pure long-term rate of interest. 'Pure', in the sense that it contains no element of compensation to the investor for running the risk of default. There is really no possibility of the Government's defaulting on its obligation to pay interest, while even with the best companies there is always some risk of default (however slight) on their debentures. The pure long-term rate of interest (from now on in this and the following section referred to as 'the rate of interest') is inversely related to the level of bond prices. Thus the rate of interest on a 2½ per cent bond standing at £60 is 4⅙ per cent; standing at £70, 3⁴⁄₇ per cent, and so on.

A prospective purchaser may take a view forward. In so far as he holds off buying when the price is £50, he is losing 5 per cent interest on every £50 worth of 2½ per cent securities he could have bought. Thus a man holding in cash £100,000 which could be used for bond purchase is, while the price is £50, losing 2,000 × £2 10s. per year, or £5,000 interest annually, which is £416·6 per month. Suppose that he expects the price to fall to £40 (to take a very big change) in about a month's time. If he buys then he will get 2,500 securities for his money, and an annual return on his investment of £6,250. By waiting a month, he will have lost £416·6, but then enjoys a net gain of £1,250 a year as long as he has his securities. He will certainly hold on to his cash!

The sums that people 'hold back' for the time being from bond purchase, in anticipation of a fall in prices, are suitably labelled their 'speculative balances'. How much a person wishes to hold for this speculative motive is thus dependent on his expectations about the future level of security prices. Expectations vary from person to person, but it seems reasonable to suppose that, if prices are currently high by 'normal' standards, there will be more people who expect a fall in the near future than if prices are at present distinctly low. Further, when prices are high the interest sacrificed by holding cash is relatively small, which will reinforce people's willingness to back their judgement that prices are 'too high to last'.

We may, accordingly, define a relationship between the size of desired speculative balances and the *present* level of bond prices such that, the higher are bond prices, the more widely spread the desire among house-

holds, firms and financial institutions to hold speculative balances. The
level of bond prices varies inversely with the rate of interest, so the
relationship may be rephrased as: the lower the rate of interest, the
bigger the desired level of speculative balances. This relationship
between 'the speculative demand for money' and the rate of interest is
shown by the curve LL in Fig. 13.1, where the rate of interest is measured
on the vertical axis. For easier comparison, corresponding prices of 2½
per cent bonds have also been entered. The curve LL is a curve of

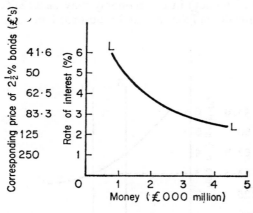

FIG. 13.1

liquidity preference, showing how much 'liquidity' people, etc., prefer
or desire for the speculative motive at any given interest rate. In this
context the 'liquidity' of an asset denotes the certainty of its value in
money terms. On this definition money possesses perfect liquidity, and
is contrasted with the undated bond, the value of which is liable to
fluctuate in money terms. In these circumstances, accordingly, 'preference for liquidity' means 'a desire to hold money balances in preference
to bonds'. In practice, speculative holdings would comprise bank
balances, since notes are more likely to be held under the transactions
and precautionary heads.

2. *The Liquidity Preference Theory of the Rate of Interest*

This analysis of the motives for holding money balances forms the basis
of a theory of the rate of interest, called accordingly the liquidity
preference theory. For the simplest version, we need to ignore the flow
of new savings and new security issues, and explain the interest rate

only in terms of a given liquidity preference, a given stock of money
and a given stock of bonds. Bonds are taken, initially, to be of the sort
discussed in the preceding section: company securities are brought
into the picture later in the section.

Suppose that the sum of money that people and firms want to hold
for transactions and precautionary reasons has, on average, a value
equal to $\frac{1}{3}$ of the annual net national income. If the latter were, say,
£30,000 million, then the demand for money balances for these two
motives would be £10,000 million. The total supply of money (i.e. the
total quantity of money) in the economy may be £12,000 million, in
which case £10,000 million would be absorbed in transactions and

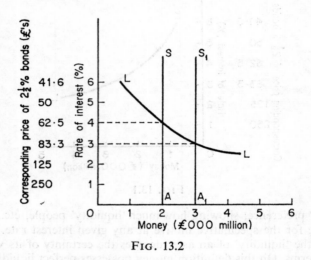

FIG. 13.2

precautionary balances, leaving a money supply of £2,000 million to be
held under the speculative head. The terms on which households and
others in the economy *want* to hold speculative balances of this size
can be read from the appropriate curve of liquidity preference, for
example LL of Fig. 13.1 which is reproduced in Fig. 13.2. This curve
shows that speculative balances of £2,000 million are wanted only when
the interest rate is 4 per cent per annum. 4 per cent must, accordingly,
be the equilibrium rate, since it is only at this level that firms, households and financial institutions are between them prepared to hold the
£2,000 million which is 'left over' after meeting transactions and precautionary requirements.

Equilibrium is represented in Fig. 13.2 by the intersection at interest
rate 4 per cent of the curve LL and the 'curve' AS, the latter showing
the supply or quantity of money actually available after meeting

transactions and precautionary requirements. It rises vertically because the amount *actually held* (here £2,000 million) is independent of the rate of interest. What is dependent on the rate of interest is the amount that people, etc., are *willing to hold* speculatively. When the price of $2\frac{1}{2}$ per cent bonds stands at £62·5, there are just sufficient people, etc., who are prepared, between them, to hold £2,000 million speculatively on the expectation that bond prices will fall fairly soon.

Expectations vary from person to person, and while some are holding balances (totalling between them £2,000 million) on the view that bond prices will shortly fall, there will be many others who do not share this expectation and so are quite happy to be holding bonds. Of course, a bond holder may change his mind and come to the view that prices will soon fall. In this case he will want to sell his bonds and hold cash for a short while, in anticipation of a price fall which will enable him to buy back a greater number of bonds. Correspondingly, some holders of speculative balances may also change their minds, and decide to buy bonds now as they no longer expect prices to fall in the near future. At any given time, therefore, members of this second category will want to buy bonds in the market, while members of the former category will want to sell them. Provided that the demand from the second 'group' to buy bonds is exactly matched by the offers from the first 'group' to sell them, transactions will go ahead at the current market price of £62·5, without disturbing it in any way.

This price of £62·5 will continue to rule in the market if two conditions are satisfied. The first is that the sum held under the speculative head remains unchanged overall at £2,000 million. Second, any changes in expectations among bondholders must be exactly matched by offsetting changes in expectations among holders of speculative balances.

Thus suppose that the size of the balances held under the speculative head increased from £2,000 million to £3,000 million (e.g. because of an increase in the money supply from £12,000 million to £13,000 million, with other factors remaining constant). We know from LL that there will not be enough people who are prepared, between them, to hold speculative balances of £3,000 million when the price of a bond is £62·5. Accordingly an excess demand will emerge for securities to the value of £1,000 million, coming from holders of the 'extra cash' who would prefer bonds instead. The excess demand will pull up the prices at which bonds change hands in current dealings, i.e. depress the interest rate, until a new equilibrium is reached. In Fig. 13.2, the increase in the quantity of money is shown by moving AS to A_1S_1, and the new equilibrium is given by the intersection of A_1S_1 with LL at 3 per cent. This means that, when the price of bonds has reached £83·3, there are sufficient people who—at this price—think the next price move will be downwards to absorb, between them, the £3,000 worth of

balances currently 'surplus' to transactions and precautionary requirements.

The new dealing price of £83·3 per bond will stand as long as those
who wish to sell on a revision of expectations are exactly matched by
those wishing to buy for the same reason. Suppose, however, that the
view that a price of £83·3 was 'too high to last' became much more
widespread in the community. The demand for speculative cash at the
current interest rate would rise beyond £3,000 million—shown in
Fig. 13.3 by moving LL to the right (L_1L_1). The preponderance of
sellers seeking to turn their bonds into cash would of itself depress the
price of bonds, and a lower price would establish itself as the new

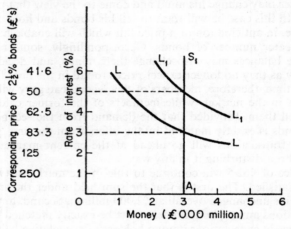

FIG. 13.3

equilibrium (£50 in Fig. 13.3). At this level the expectation that the
price of bonds will fall still further is less widely held than formerly,
and the £3,000 million surplus to transactions and precautionary
requirements is sufficient to satisfy the people who take this view.

The liquidity preference theory has been explained in terms of one
category of irredeemable Government bond. In fact, as we saw in
Chapter 8, of the £20,000 million or so Government bonds outstanding,
only about 20 per cent are irredeemable. The remainder have redemption dates, the nearness of which is relevant to the yield calculation.
Thus a 2½ per cent security redeemable in 20 years' time standing today
at £62·5 offers as its yield 4 per cent over 20 years *plus* a capital gain of
£37·5 payable in 20 years' time. In addition to Government bonds, there
is available a variety of fixed interest securities issued by local authorities,
foreign governments and public companies, as well as the issued share
capital of the latter (Chapters 7 and 8).

At any given time, there will be a definite pattern of investor preference as between these different types of security, which will find reflection in their relative prices and so in their relative yields. Thus in normal circumstances we might expect to find local authority securities slightly cheaper than comparable Government bonds, i.e. their yields fractionally higher, reflecting the greater marketability of the latter. Industrial debentures might be a shade cheaper still, in so far as the risk of default, though minimal with the bigger companies, is still greater than with government or local authority bonds. Traditionally in this country, ordinary shares have returned a significantly higher yield on average than government bonds, this 'yield gap' reflecting the relative uncertainty attaching to dividend prospects. Interestingly enough, this gap has (with few exceptions) been negative since 1959, which points to a change in investor attitudes discussed in Chapter 14.

We may accordingly visualize a great cluster of security prices, each with its particular position in the complex at any point of time. The relative position of each price depends on underlying investor preferences. As these change over time, so will the position of one security in relation to another (e.g. company A's shares rising and B's falling), and of one category of security in relation to another (e.g. bonds generally becoming cheaper and equities dearer). These relative changes apart, the general level of this complex of interest rates and dividend returns will depend upon the size of speculative balances and the terms on which the community is prepared to hold these balances.

3. *Fixed Investment and the Rate of Interest*

Consider an established company, the directors of which are contemplating an extension to the existing factory. They calculate that £1 million capital expenditure will be required to carry out the investment programme, and bring the new plant into operation. How are they to decide whether this project is profitable or not?

One relevant factor will be the estimated return on the new investment. For each year it is possible to estimate the output from the new extension, and the price at which it will probably sell. Multiplying the two gives the annual revenue yield. Against this, however, must be set the expenses involved in operating the new plant—the raw material purchases, the wages bill, the fuel used, and so on. Deducting each year's anticipated expenses from estimated revenue gives the net annual return from the investment.

It may be thought that, after a certain number of years, the new equipment will have worn out or become obsolete, and should be scrapped if efficiency is to be maintained in competition with other firms in the industry. The estimated scrap value will also have to be taken into account in setting out all the returns from the investment.

There are many problems involved in making these calculations, but just two may be mentioned here. First, the establishment of a new plant may yield some economies in the operation of the existing plant, which must clearly be taken into account in calculating the net return. Second, under current legislation, a company buying new plant may qualify for certain taxation and other benefits. Thus, under the initial allowance scheme, it will sometimes be able to defer tax payments to a future year, and in the meantime enjoy the use of the funds it would otherwise have paid as tax. It may, moreover, qualify for an outright gift of money from the Government, known as an investment grant. Both sorts of benefit are discussed more fully in Chapter 20: they should clearly be brought into any reckoning of the prospective returns from an investment programme.

The next step in appraising the project is to work out the cost to the firm of raising the initial £1 million capital sum. We have seen in Chapter 7 that to finance long-term investment a company may, typically, make a new share or debenture issue, or use its own undistributed profits. Again there are many problems in calculating the 'cost of capital', but we may content ourselves with a few straightforward observations. First, if a company raises funds with a debenture issue, the cost is the annual interest it has to pay on the debentures. Second, if it raises funds with an issue of equities, the 'cost' to the existing shareholders (who may be identified with the company) is the share in the company's total profits to which the new shareholders become entitled, which necessarily means that much less for the existing shareholders! Third, if the company uses its own funds, the 'cost' is the return it could have obtained had the funds been invested instead outside the company (e.g. in the shares of another company).

The firm now has its estimate of the returns from the investment project, and its calculation of the cost of raising the necessary finance. The next problem, at root, is to compare the two and discover whether any net profit remains for the company, after meeting the cost of capital. If the answer is yes, the investment is profitable and worth undertaking; if no, not worth undertaking. If the cost and return are the same, the firm would break even, with neither net profit nor net loss.

The comparison of the return on capital with the cost of raising it forms the basis of the firm's investment decision. While the principle is simple, the techniques are very much more complex. The bare bones of one such technique will be illustrated in the following example. Only enough detail is given to show the essentials of the calculation: it is quite impracticable to construct a fully life-like illustration.

Suppose that on an investment of £1,000 a firm anticipates one solitary return of £1,160 in a year's time. The rate of return (r) is 16 per cent, which may be understood as the rate at which the £1,000 (P) grows into £1,160 (V_1) by the end of one year. Arithmetically,

$$
\begin{aligned}
V_1 &= £1,000 + 0{\cdot}16\,(1,000) \\
&= £1,000\,(1 + 0{\cdot}16) \\
&= £1,160
\end{aligned}
$$

Symbolically,

$$V_1 = P\,(1 + r)$$

Another way of looking at this process is to see £1,000 as the present value of £1,160 receivable in one year's time. If this is the firm's current valuation of such a future benefit, it is said to be discounting the future return (£1,160) to a present value (£1,000) at 16 per cent rate of discount.

Arithmetically,

$$P = \frac{£1,160}{(1 + 0{\cdot}16)}$$

Symbolically,

$$P = \frac{V_1}{(1 + r)}$$

Suppose now that, instead of expecting £1,160 in one year's time, the firm expects £1,345·6 in two years' time. The rate of return is still 16 per cent, as this is the rate at which £1,000 (P) grows into £1,345·6 (V_2) by the end of two years.

Arithmetically,

$$
\begin{aligned}
V_2 &= £1,000\,(1 + 0{\cdot}16) + 0{\cdot}16\,(1,000\,(1 + 0{\cdot}16)) \\
&= £(1,000 + 0{\cdot}16\,(1,000))\,(1 + 0{\cdot}16) \\
&= £1,000\,(1 + 0{\cdot}16)\,(1 + 0{\cdot}16) \\
&= £1,000\,(1 + 0{\cdot}16)^2 \\
&= £1,345{\cdot}6
\end{aligned}
$$

Symbolically,

$$V_2 = P\,(1 + r)^2$$

The alternative way of looking at this process is once again to see £1,000 as the present value of £1,345·6 receivable in two years' time, when the firm discounts back the future value (£1,345·6) to a present value (£1,000) at a rate of discount of 16 per cent.

Arithmetically,

$$P = \frac{£1,345{\cdot}6}{(1 + 0{\cdot}16)^2}$$

Symbolically,

$$P = \frac{V_2}{(1 + r)^2}$$

Suppose now we are told that on an investment project of £1,000, a firm expects to earn a net return of £500 at the end of the first year, and £500 at the end of the second. The equipment then comes to the end of its useful working life, but may be sold as scrap for £160. The firm thus has three returns coming to it: one at the end of the first year (£500), and two at the end of the second year (£500 + £160). The reasoning of the previous paragraphs suggests that the present value (P_1) of the return after the first year is

$$P_1 = \frac{£500}{(1 + r)}$$

The present value (P_2) of the two returns obtainable after the second year is

$$P_2 = \frac{£500}{(1 + r)^2} + \frac{160}{(1 + r)^2}$$

It follows that the present value (P) of the return after the first year plus the two returns after the second year is

$$P = P_1 + P_2 = \frac{£500}{(1 + r)} + \frac{500}{(1 + r)^2} + \frac{160}{(1 + r)^2}$$

If the firm attaches a present value of £1,000 to this series of future returns, then this implies a certain rate of discount (r). Its value may be discovered by writing P = 1,000 in the foregoing equation, and solving for r.

$$1,000 = \frac{500}{(1 + r)} + \frac{500}{(1 + r)^2} + \frac{160}{(1 + r)^2}$$

Multiplying through by $(1 + r)^2$,

$$1,000 (1 + r)^2 = 500 (1 + r) + 500 + 160$$

from which,

$$r = 0 \cdot 10 = 10 \text{ per cent.}$$

This means that the rate of discount which equates two consecutive annual returns of £500 and a final lump sum of £160 to a present value of £1,000 is 10 per cent.

This method of calculating the return on an investment project is known in business as the 'discounted cash flow' technique. Essentially, one discounts back to a present value a series or flow of future cash benefits. In economics, the rate of discount is sometimes termed the 'marginal efficiency of capital': it is the yield on an additional or marginal capital project.

To ascertain now whether or not the investment project will show a net profit for the company, it is necessary to compare the rate of discount with the rate of interest at which the company can secure the initial funds (its 'cost of capital'). If the rate of discount exceeds the rate of interest, the project is profitable; if vice versa, unprofitable. If the rate of interest and the rate of discount are equal, the company will just 'break even' on the project.

To continue the last numerical example, suppose that the company can borrow £1,000 at 10 per cent, and suppose that it has the option of repaying the capital as and when it wishes. At the end of the first year, it will owe £1,000 capital plus £100 interest, or £1,100. It receives its first return of £500, and uses it to pay off £500 of this debt. It starts the second year owing £600 and by the end of the year, at 10 per cent

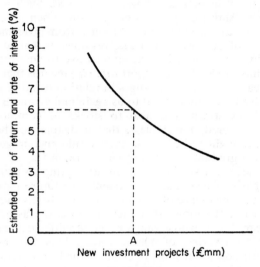

FIG. 13.4

interest, owes £660. This is exactly met by its end of year return of £500, plus the sale of the machinery for scrap at £160. It accordingly just breaks even.

The reader may entertain himself by calculating that, in this example, if the rate of interest on borrowed funds is 5 per cent, the company emerges from the two year period with a net profit of £82·5; while if the rate of interest were 12 per cent, it would suffer a net loss of £34·4.

Suppose that, at the start of a given period, it were possible to ascertain from businessmen the yields they had calculated on all the investment projects that might possibly be undertaken during the period ahead. Each project could be ranked in order of diminishing yield, giving a curve of the estimated rate of return for all contemplated new investment projects, shown in Fig. 13.4. If the pure long-term rate of interest is taken to represent the average cost of long-term finance and also measured on the vertical axis, the curve may be read as a 'demand curve' for new investment, showing how much will be undertaken at any given rate of interest.

Thus if the long term rate of interest is currently 6 per cent, net investment during the forthcoming period will be OA (£m.). A fall in the level of long-term interest rates (Section 2) would increase net investment, since it would make worthwhile some schemes formerly below the margin of profitability (to the right of OA). On the other hand, a shift of the curve to (say) the left would cause net investment to fall, even though the rate of interest was unchanged. Such a shift might reflect a more pessimistic attitude among businessmen, leading them to make lower estimates of the future net returns from investment projects.

The evidence of businessmen themselves suggests that, at least in the short term, investment decisions are insensitive to changes in the rate of interest. Thus the Radcliffe Report (*op. cit.*) records that (para. 451): 'The insignificance of interest changes in relation to other costs and to the risks involved was emphasized to us again and again, in relation not only to fixed investment but also to stocks of commodities.' The Committee considered, nonetheless, that a distinctive change in the level of rates, thought to be long lasting, would encourage/discourage fixed investment gradually over the years (para. 495).

There are various 'risks involved' in attempting to extend a firm's sales on the basis of new fixed investment: the future pattern of consumer tastes, the emergence of new products, the behaviour of business rivals, and so on. It follows that there is no easily ascertainable net return per year, but a whole range of possibilities depending on the weights given to a variety of market forces. This does not mean, of course, that firms do not trouble to evaluate the future return on investment projects. What it does mean is that in such calculations the range of possible outcomes is so wide that a change of 1 or 2 per cent in the rate of interest may have little significance for investment plans. It follows that the narrower the limits within which the rate of return can be calculated, the more relevance will interest changes have for investment decision. We might, for example, expect a company which constructs property for lease to pay more attention to interest rate changes than a manufacturing company: rents may be more accurately forecast than commodity prices. It does seem, at the very least, a useful first approximation to define the determinants of capital investment as the rate of interest and the rate of return.

4. *Investment in Stocks and the Rate of Interest*

A firm's 'stocks' consist of its raw material holdings, its semi-finished goods or 'work in progress', and its holdings of its own finished product. Carrying raw material stocks enables production to be carried on smoothly, despite temporary interruptions in supplies. Holding stocks of the finished product enables the firm to meet any unexpected increase in customers' orders. In both cases, some benefit is enjoyed should raw material prices subsequently rise. Against these benefits, however, must be set the cost of stock holding. There are expenses of warehousing, allowances for perishing, premiums for insurance against fire, etc.; there is the possibility that raw material prices may in future fall. Finally, there is the rate of interest payable on the funds used to finance the stock holdings.

If the firm has used a bank advance to finance raw material purchases, or to meet current costs of production and operation, then the rate of interest it pays will be geared to the Bank Rate (Chapter 2). Alternatively, it may have received its raw materials on credit terms from its suppliers (trade credit), in which case the relevant rate of interest is the discount it would have received had it paid the bill promptly (cash discount). The third possibility is that the firm is employing its own capital, in which case the interest cost to it is the foregone return on a short-term investment outside the firm (e.g. loans to local authorities for a large company, or deposits with a building society for a smaller concern).

It follows that a rise in short term interest rates (typically, following a rise in Bank Rate—Part I) will make stock holding more expensive to the firm. This in turn might be expected to prompt firms to reduce their stock levels, by placing smaller orders for raw materials. The raw material purchases of one firm, however, are the final product sales of another, so that some contraction in the level of output and employment would follow any general move to run down stocks.

In practice, it would seem that changes in interest rates are lost among the variety of other factors which are relevant to the size of the firm's stock holdings. In itself, a 1 or 2 per cent change in Bank Rate may be quite insignificant—see the quotation from the Radcliffe Report on p. 292. Further, Table 7.2 suggests that trade credit is a lot more important than bank advances in financing stock holdings, and the rate of interest on trade credit (i.e. cash discount) does not generally alter with other interest rates.

It would nonetheless be unwise to dismiss interest rates as unimportant in stock decisions for all types of business enterprise. Where the carrying of stocks is in the very nature of the business (in wholesaling and large scale retailing as contrasted with manufacturing), interest

costs may form a sizeable part of total costs, and exercise a proportionate influence. Some evidence for this view is found in para. 452 of
the Radcliffe Report. It appears, for example, that some wholesale
tobacconists and timber merchants have on occasions been directly
affected by a high level of overdraft rates (e.g. 7 or 8 per cent).

5. *Equilibrium of the Monetary and Income Systems*

We are now in a position to bring together the monetary theory of the
earlier sections with the income theory of the preceding chapters. For
this exercise we assume a closed economy with no government economic
activity, and invent appropriate values for the savings/income and
investment/interest relationships in Fig. 13.5; and for the supply of and
demand for money in Fig. 13.6.

The graph (i) in the lower right-hand quadrant of Fig. 13.5 shows the
annual value of net investment spending (I) that firms would want to
undertake at different levels of the pure long-term rate of interest (i),
which is chosen as representative of interest rates in general in the
economy. When the national income is at an equilibrium level, planned
investment (I) equals planned savings (S), shown by the graph in
quadrant (ii). The savings function (quadrant (iii)) in turn shows what
level of net national income (Y) corresponds to each given value of
planned savings (S).

Starting once more with graph (i), we see that at interest rate 5 per
cent firms would want to undertake annual net investment spending of
4 (£000 million). If the economy is to be in equilibrium this implies an
equivalent level of planned savings, shown by tracing a broken line to
quadrant (ii). Planned savings of 4 (£000 million) in turn suggest—
broken line to quadrant (iii)—an income level of 20 (£000 million) per
year. It follows that, with interest rate 5 per cent, only a net national
income of 20 (£000 million) is consistent with the equality of planned
savings and planned investment. The broken line is accordingly traced
down from quadrant (iii) and across from quadrant (i) to give, in
quadrant (iv), the one point where i = 5 per cent, Y = 20.

We return now to quadrant (i) and repeat the whole process, except
that this time we start with an interest rate of 4 per cent, at which
planned investment is 6 (£000 million). Planned savings would likewise
(graph (ii)) be 6 (£000 million) when the equilibrium income level
(graph (iii)) is 30 (£000 million). With the aid of a second broken line
a second point is entered on graph (iv) to show that, given the investment demand portrayed in graph (i) and the savings function of graph
(iii), an interest rate of 4 per cent is consistent with an annual net
national income of 30 (£000 million), and no other. Linking this and the

first point gives an 'IS' curve, which traces the equilibrium income level consistent with each interest rate. In brief, the curve IS shows—for each interest rate—the income level at which the savings planned equal the investment planned at that interest rate.

A similar technique may now be applied (Fig. 13.6) to the monetary sector of the economy, to show which pairs of interest rates and income

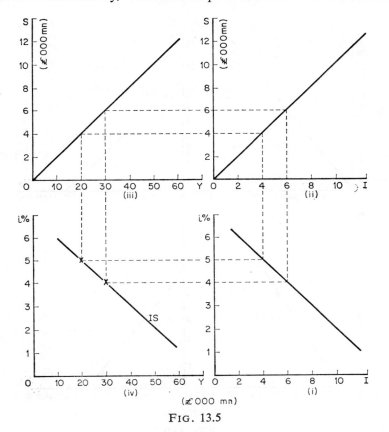

FIG. 13.5

levels are consistent with monetary equilibrium. Quadrant (i) gives the speculative demand for money, while from the graph in quadrant (ii) can be calculated how much money would be held under the transactions and precautionary heads (M_1), given the size of speculative holdings (M_2) and the value (M) of the total money supply (£12,000 million). Graph (iii) shows the transactions and precautionary demand for money balances as a function of net national income (Y). It is assumed that firms and households want to hold transactions and precautionary balances equal in value to one third of the net national income, at all levels.

If the rate of interest *is* 3 per cent, then (graph (i)) speculative balances

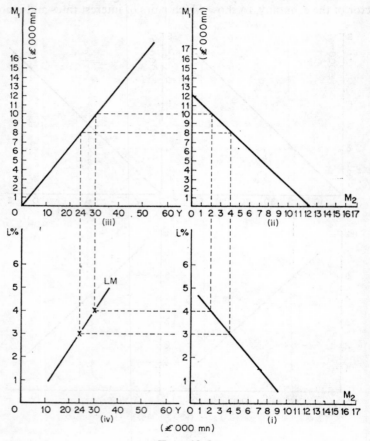

FIG. 13.6

will be 4 (£000 million). This is consistent (graph (ii)) only with transactions balances of 8 (£000 million), in turn consistent (graph (iii)) only with an income level of 24 (£000 million). It follows that the only income level consistent with an interest rate of 3 per cent is 24 (£000 million), if monetary equilibrium is to be achieved. For this pair of values, the total money supply is exactly absorbed by the transactions demand (given by the income level) and the speculative demand (given by the interest rate). With the aid of the broken line an appropriate entry is made in quadrant (iv), while similar reasoning will give a second point such that, when i = 4 per cent, Y = 30. Linking the two points establishes the position of the 'LM' curve, from which may be read what income level is consistent with each interest rate if the total demand for money balances is to equal the total money supply.

We now know (from the IS curve) which income levels are consistent with which interest rates if the income sector is to be in equilibrium, and

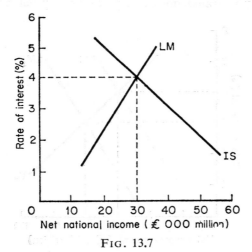

FIG. 13.7

(from the LM curve) the income level which corresponds to each interest rate if the monetary sector is in balance. Our remaining task is to discover the interest rate and income level consistent with general equilibrium, i.e. equilibrium in both sectors, and this is achieved by putting the two curves on the same axes in Fig. 13.7. Their intersection shows that the required pair is an interest rate of 4 per cent and an income level of 30 (£000 million). At these two values, planned savings equal planned investment, and the total demand for money balances is equal to the total money supply. At any other point on the IS curve, the second (i.e. monetary) condition is not satisfied; and at any other point on the LM curve, the first (i.e. income) condition is not satisfied.

This analysis is useful for assessing the full implications of a change in any of the system's determinants. Thus suppose that, in an economy with abundant unemployed resources, the quantity of money was increased by £5·33 thousand million. This would be represented diagrammatically by shifting the graph in quadrant (ii) of Fig. 13.6 to the right, parallel to its old position and distant from it by 5·33 (£000 million) on each axis. This would necessitate, in turn, drawing a new LM curve, which is in fact shown as LM_1 in Fig. 13.8. The intersection of LM_1 with IS gives the new general equilibrium values for the interest rate and the level of income.

It is apparent that, at the new interest rate of 3 per cent, planned investment will equal 8 (£000 million), while at the new income level of 40 (£000 million) planned savings will be 8 (£000 million). Further, the new income level requires 13·33 (£000 million) of the increased money supply in transactions and precautionary balances, while the

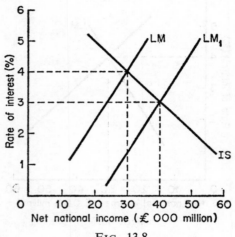

FIG. 13.8

remaining 4 (£000 million) is consistent with an interest rate of 3 per cent.

Fig. 13.8 gives the new equilibrium values for income and the rate of interest following the increase in the money supply, but provides no indication of the stages by which this equilibrium was reached. Let us suppose that the whole of the £5·33 thousand million increase in the money supply goes, at first, to swell speculative balances, so that income—hence transactions demand—are not immediately affected. The initial rise in speculative balances from 2 to 7·33 (£000 million) depresses the interest rate to 1·33 per cent, which provides (graph (i), Fig. 13.5) a strong stimulus to investment. National income, in turn, would begin to rise at a more rapid rate through the multiplier process, drawing some balances into transactions holdings away from speculative holdings. This would occasion some rise in the rate of interest, some retrenchment in investment plans, and a slackening in the rate of income expansion. In the outcome, accordingly, only 2 (£000 million) of the extra money supply has gone to swell speculative balances, establishing the rate of interest at 3 per cent. This fall in the rate of interest from the original level of 4 per cent has led to an investment increase from 6 to 8 (£000 million), and so a rise in income from 30 to 40 (£000 million). This in turn has necessitated an increased demand for transactions and precautionary balances, met by the other 3·33 (£000 million) of the increase in the money supply.

The figures taken in this example suggest that one remedy for demand-deficiency unemployment is an increase in the money supply. In practice however, the success of such an operation would depend on people's

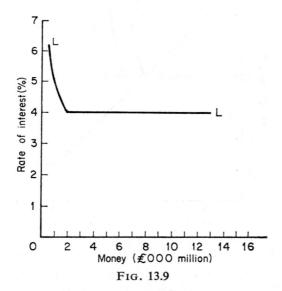

FIG. 13.9

expectations about the course of interest rates, as well as on the sensitivity of investment decisions to interest rate changes. Thus suppose that, at a time when 2½ per cent undated bonds stand at £62·5, there is a widespread view that the next price move will be downwards. This view may be sufficiently general for any increase in the money supply to be simply added to speculative balances, in anticipation of the fall in bond prices (Fig. 13.9). In these circumstances, a rise in the quantity of money occasions no net purchases of bonds, so there is no rise in their price and no fall in the interest rate (contrast p. 298). Unless, accordingly, they could influence expectations (i.e. cause the shape of LL to alter), the monetary authorities would be unable to depress the

rate of interest below 4 per cent: any extra liquidity is simply 'trapped'
in speculative balances.

If Fig. 13.9 is substituted for graph (i) in Fig. 13.6, then with a total
money supply of £12,000 million the corresponding LM curve will have

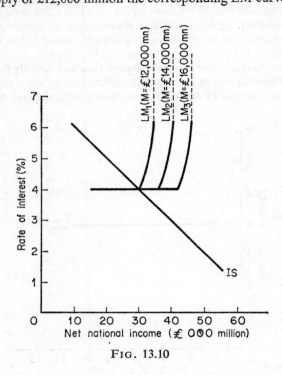

FIG. 13.10

the shape and position LM₁ shown in Fig. 13.10. The consequences of
two consecutive increases of £2,000 million in the money supply are
shown with LM₂ and LM₃. The introduction of the IS curve from
Fig. 13.7 demonstrates the impossibility, under these circumstances, of
stimulating investment through increasing the quantity of money.

Questions

1. What are the main reasons for the holding of money by households
   and firms?   U.L.

2. What do you understand by the demand for money? How does it
   differ from the demand for other commodities?   I.M.T.A.

3. Analyse the factors determining (a) the demand for and (b) the supply of money.   I.B.

4. What is meant by the statement that interest is the reward for surrendering liquidity?   J.M.B.

5. What is money? What is the connection between the volume of money and the rate of interest?   W.J.E.C.

6. To what extent is the rate of interest determined by liquidity preference?   S.U.J.B.

7. What factors determine the rate of interest?   B.A. Gen.

8. What factors determine the level of private investment in an economy?   U.L.

9. What are the main factors which influence a businessman's decision to buy a machine for his factory?   J.M.B.

10. Discuss the relationship between changes in interest rates and the investment decisions of business concerns.   I.M.T.A.

11. When a firm is deciding whether or not to buy a new machine, what considerations should it take into account?   C.I.S.

12. What determines the marginal efficiency of capital? What consequences may follow from a change in the marginal efficiency of capital?   B.A. Gen.

13. Define the 'marginal efficiency of capital' and consider the usefulness of this concept in economic analysis.   C.S.

14. How important is the rate of interest in determining the level of economic activity?   S.U.J.B.

15. What parts do (a) productivity and (b) thrift play in determining the rate of interest?   S.U.J.B.

16. Assuming the supply of money is constant, discuss the effects on the economy of an increase in the marginal efficiency of capital.
                                                              B.A. Gen.

17. What effect are changes in the rate of interest likely to have on the level of savings in an economy?   J.M.B.

14

The General Level
of Prices

THE INCOME analysis of the preceding four chapters has been governed
by the assumption (p. 216) that the general level of prices was quite
stable. Attention has accordingly been confined to changes in real
national income, i.e., changes in the value of national output which
reflect a change in the total quantity produced, and not a change in the
general price level. In this chapter we relax the earlier assumption, and
consider some of the influences operative upon the general price level.
These are considered in the context of three distinct theories, the first
centring around the quantity of money, the second concerned with
aggregate demand and the third with the upward pressure of production costs.

1. *The Equation of Exchange*

The ways in which the size of the total money supply may influence the
general price level are various, but one possible relationship may be
readily explored with the aid of the 'equation of exchange'. We begin
with the observation that, over a given period of time, say a year, sales
of all sorts of things will take place in the economy—sales of raw
materials, of finished goods, of services, and of financial assets such as
bills, bonds and shares. The total value of all these sales will obviously
exceed the quantity of money, as the units of the money supply will
change hands on much more than one occasion. If we could obtain an
estimate of the total value of sales, and divide it by the quantity of
money, the answer would give us the average number of times per
£ that the quantity of money was used in transactions. This may be
labelled the (transactions) velocity of circulation of money.

For example, suppose that the total value of all sales in an imaginary
economy in a given year is £100,000 million. The actual quantity of
money, we are further told, is £4,000 million. The average speed of

circulation per £ must accordingly be 25. It is useful to denote the quantity of money with the letter M, and the (transactions) velocity of circulation with the symbol V_T. It is then clear that the total value of all sales is given by the quantity of money (M) times its average speed of circulation (V_T).

We may, however, look at the total value of all sales from another viewpoint. It is the same as the number of sales (or transactions) that took place multiplied by the average value of each transaction. The number of sales and the average value of each cannot of course be calculated, but we may define them as abstract concepts. If we denote the number of transactions by T, and the average value of each by P, we conclude that the total value of sales may be re-written as P × T.

This accordingly gives us two ways of writing 'the total value of sales in the economy during a year': as M × V_T, or as P × T. Both expressions are always necessarily identically the same, because they are in fact different ways of expressing the same thing, i.e., the total value of sales. We write, therefore,

$$M \times V_T \equiv P \times T,$$

using the sign ≡ to show that mathematically this is an identity, i.e., both sides are always necessarily equal. The name given to this truism is the 'equation of exchange'.

This version of the equation of exchange is sometimes known as the 'Fisher equation' after its formulator, the American Professor Irving Fisher (1867–1947). The Fisher equation runs in terms of the total number of all transactions (T) and the average value of each (P). The total number of all transactions includes sales at every stage of production, both intermediate and final (p. 194), as well as all the purely financial transactions that take place (the sale of bills, bonds and shares, etc.). However, for purposes of economic policy we are more often concerned with the size and value of the national output, and not the all embracing total value of transactions. We may accordingly formulate a second version of the equation of exchange, which runs in terms of the quantity of national output and the average price of the 'final' goods and services which make it up. This alternative form is sometimes known as the 'Cambridge equation', because of its use in earlier work by Lord Keynes and other economists at Cambridge.

The national output is the total value of final goods and services produced in the course of the year, including additions to stocks. It was emphasized on p. 196 that it is impossible to calculate national output except as a money value, since clearly one cannot add commodities which are expressed in different physical units (tons, gallons, etc.). Nonetheless, we may conceive in the abstract of the great quantity of goods and services which make up the national output, even though we could never put any numerical value to it. Let us denote this quantity by the letter R. Now define the general level of prices as the average of the prices of the goods and services which make up the national output. This cannot be measured with an index number, as it will be recalled from p. 207 that the index number is only a device for measuring changes in the general level of prices, and not the absolute level. We may nonetheless conceive of the absolute level in abstraction, and denote it by the letter p (to distinguish it from the P of the Fisher equation). It follows that 'the value of the national output' may be re-written as p × R, i.e. the actual quantity of final goods and services times their average price.

The national expenditure was defined in Chapter 9 as the total value of expenditure on final goods and services (including 'notional' expenditure). If we divide this by the quantity of money, we have the average number of times per £ that the quantity of money was used in purchasing the national output. This may be termed the *income* velocity of circulation, and written V_Y. In 1968, net national expenditure at market prices for the U.K. economy was £39,385 million (Table 9.2), and the quantity of money (on an average over the year—Table 1.1) was £15,091 million. The income velocity of circulation was accordingly about 2·61 per £. It follows that the 'quantity of money (M) times the income velocity of circulation (V_Y)' is another way of writing 'national expenditure'.

We already know from Chapter 9 that national output and expenditure are necessarily always equal. We may accordingly write

$$M \times V_Y \equiv p \times R.$$

Like the Fisher version, this formulation of the equation of exchange is a truism, expressing the necessary equality of two different aspects of the same thing, i.e., national output or expenditure.

2. *The Quantity Theory of Money*

Either version of the equation of exchange may be used to formulate the quantity theory of money, which attempts to demonstrate the relevance of changes in the money supply to the general level of prices. On the Fisher equation, the theory states that in circumstances where V_T and T may reasonably be considered constant, a change in M will lead to a corresponding change in P. On the national income version, a change in M—given V_Y and R constant—leads to a corresponding change in p. It follows that the quantity theory is as much concerned with the behaviour of the velocity of circulation, etc., as with the quantity of money! It is necessary, accordingly, to look more closely at those other elements in the exchange equation, though discussion is limited to the national income version, because of its greater relevance to economic policy (Section 1).

The theory is, however, more easily understood if set out initially not in terms of income velocity of circulation, but with the aid of the 'twin' concept of the transactions demand for cash balances. It then becomes relatively straightforward to show how these concepts are related, and to re-express the theory in terms of income velocity. Chapter 13 distinguished three reasons why firms and households may hold money balances: a transactions, a precautionary and a speculative motive. For the time being, let us ignore the second and third by assuming that all cash balances are held under the transactions head. We assume, further, that the size of the (transactions) cash balances that firms and households wish to hold depends solely on the size of income, the frequency of receipts and payments and the number of firms in the economy (compare p. 281). Since the last two factors can reasonably be assumed constant in the short run, this suggests a stable short-run relationship between desired cash balances and the level of incomes (or national income). This relationship may be expressed with the equation

$$M = K(p \times R)$$

where K denotes what fraction of the value of national income (p $\times$ R) the desired level of money balances (M) represents. Thus if national income were £10,000 million a year, a value of $\frac{1}{5}$ for K would mean that people and firms found it convenient overall to hold cash balances of £2,000 million.

Suppose in this example that the quantity of money in existence is, in fact, £2,000 million. £10,000 million would then be—in this respect —the equilibrium value of national income, since £2,000 million is the sum that firms and households overall want to hold when national income is £10,000 million per annum. Assume next that the money supply is increased to £4,000 million. Firms and households would find that their actual cash balances were twice as high as their desired cash balances at the current income level. If people feel that they are holding more cash than they need, they may attempt to run down their balances by increased spending on goods and services. However, while some individuals may reduce their balances in this way, it is clearly impossible for the increased spending to reduce everyone's money balances, since spending by some entails receipts by others! Equilibrium can, therefore, be re-achieved only by a rise in national income (p $\times$ R), given that K is constant at $\frac{1}{5}$. If (p $\times$ R) rises to £20,000 million, then people overall will find that balances they previously thought were too big are now quite appropriate: they stand at $\frac{1}{5}$ (K) of the new income level.

Either p or R may have risen, but if we assume for the moment that R is constant, then the price level (p) must have doubled.

The argument is easily summed up by contrasting the *desired* cash balance/national income ratio (K) with the *actual* ratio, which may be distinguished as k. In the example, the value of income is initially in equilibrium with K ($\frac{1}{5}$) equal to $k\left(\frac{£2,000}{£10,000}\text{m.}\right)$. Disequilibrium results when a doubling of the money supply increases k to $\frac{2}{5}\left(\frac{£4,000}{£10,000}\text{m.}\right)$, but equilibrium is restored when a doubling of the price level brings k back to $\frac{1}{5}\left(\frac{£4,000}{£20,000}\text{m.}\right)$.

Where does income velocity of circulation (V_Y) fit into all this? If national income is £10,000 million for the year, and the money supply is constant at £2,000 million throughout the year, then V_Y is easily calculated as 5. This will be recognized as the inverse of the cash balance/national income ratio. The bigger the quantity of money in relation to national income, the more slowly it 'needs' to turn over. Had M been £5,000 million, the cash balance/national income ratio would have been $\frac{1}{2}$, and the income velocity of circulation only 2. A distinction may be drawn between the actual velocity of circulation (the inverse of k) and the 'desired' velocity (the inverse of K), in which case the condition of equilibrium is expressed as the equality of 'desired' velocity with actual velocity. The notion of a 'desired' velocity of circulation may, however, seem a little artificial, as while people desire certain size money balances, they have no desires about income velocity! The discussion is, accordingly, continued in terms of cash balances.

It is clear that an increase in M necessarily entails a rise in p if two conditions are satisfied. First, that the national output in quantitative terms, R, is constant. Second, that the desired cash balance/national income ratio, K, is constant (or that 'desired V_Y' is constant). Will these conditions in fact be satisfied?

R denotes, in material terms, the quantity of goods and services that make up the national output, an upper limit to which is set in the short run by the full employment of the economy's resources. It follows that, if the economy enjoys full employment, R may reasonably be treated as constant, in which case a rise in M (given K unchanged) must be associated with a rise in p. If on the other hand the economy's resources are not fully employed, then a rise in M (with K constant) might be offset by a rise in R leaving p—more or less—unaffected.

Whether or not the desired cash balance/national income ratio (K) can also be regarded as constant in the short run is a more critical question. If we recognize only the transactions motive for holding money balances, then K might reasonably be assumed constant given the short run stability of payments arrangements among firms and households (p. 281). However, even this conclusion is subject to a qualification not previously brought out in the discussion of Chapter 13. This is that firms and households expect the prices of goods and services to be reasonably stable in the period directly ahead. If in fact it were widely thought that prices were going to rise sharply, this would be a good reason for reducing cash balances by increasing current spending. In terms of the equation, K would fall and (with M and R constant) p would necessarily rise.

If people were simply aiming at a new but lower cash balance/ national income ratio, k would come into equality with K at a higher equilibrium price level. For example, if people decided on average to reduce their money balances from a level of $\frac{1}{5}$ of national income to a level of $\frac{1}{6}$, then with the money supply constant at £4,000 million, national income would rise from 20 to 24 (£000 million). With R unchanged, this means a rise in p of 20 per cent. On the other hand there might be a sustained 'flight from money', in the sense that people became increasingly reluctant to hold money balances at all! In this case, K would get smaller and smaller, the speed of circulation faster and faster, and prices higher and higher. The influence of expectations on people's willingness to hold cash balances thus plays an important role in hyper-inflation (Chapter 1).

Recognition of a second motive for holding money balances—the precautionary—does little if anything to upset the picture so far presented. Precautionary balances may reasonably be thought to represent a stable proportion of national income in the short run, provided that people feel that the level of prices—and employment—will continue much as before. The immediate prospect of sharp inflation would encourage a run down of precautionary balances (a reduction in K), just as the prospect of unemployment ahead might encourage a precautionary build-up (a rise in K).

The likelihood that K has a stable short-run value is, however, seriously weakened when it is recognized that, additionally, firms and households may hold money balances for a speculative motive. This will mean that the size of the total balances that firms and households wish to hold will depend not only upon the current level of income, but also upon the current level of interest rates (Chapter 13). It thus becomes impossible to conclude that, with R constant, a rise in M necessarily leads to a rise in p. More probably—in line with the general equilibrium theory of Chapter 13—the increase in the money supply will, at first, be held entirely under the speculative head, thus depressing the rate of interest.

This fall in the rate of interest does, however, provide an indirect link between changes in the money supply and the value of national output. It might encourage investment, and lead thereby to a more than proportionate increase in aggregate demand. If there are unemployed resources, output and employment will rise. If on the other hand there was already full employment, what would be the implications for the price level of the rise in aggregate demand? It is to an examination of this relationship that we turn in Section 3.

3. *Demand Inflation*

To deal with this question, we take as an example (Fig. 14.1) an economy in full employment equilibrium with an annual national income of £20,000 million and a stable price level. For simplicity, we

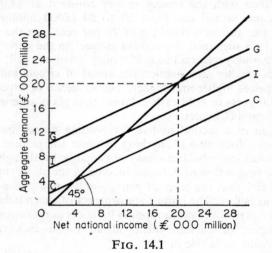

FIG. 14.1

shall consider only a closed economy (p. 217). The three sources of final demand are accordingly household consumption (at £12,000 million), net investment by firms (£4,000 million) and government spending on goods and services (£4,000 million).[1] Households are absorbing $\frac{3}{5}$ of the national output as consumer goods, and firms and government $\frac{1}{5}$ each.

Suppose now that either households or firms or government decide to increase their expenditure by £4,000 million per annum. We can show

[1] Government spending, we assume, is financed entirely by an income tax of the sort discussed in Chapter 11 (1). Its imposition has already shifted the consumption function into its position CC.

this in Fig. 14.2 by drawing $(C + I + G)_1$ £4,000 million higher (measured vertically) than GG in Fig. 14.1. If there were unemployed resources, this increased demand would of course draw them into employment and so increase the quantity of goods and services produced. However there is no unemployment, so the £4,000 million proposed spending constitutes an 'excess demand'. It has arisen because, at full employment level, one of the sources of final demand is seeking to increase its share of the national expenditure. Aggregate demand accordingly exceeds aggregate supply at the current level of prices, a

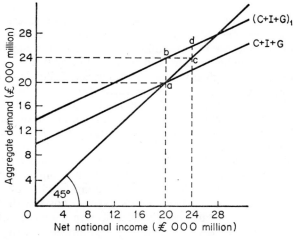

FIG. 14.2

situation known as 'demand inflation'. The excess demand ab may be conveniently labelled 'the inflationary gap'.

In the real world, it is true, there might be an increase in the economy's productive capacity over the year, for reasons explained in Chapter 15. This would enable some but not necessarily all of the increase in demand to be met in real terms (in the example, output would have to rise by 20 per cent to meet demand fully!). Allowance for this factor, therefore, will not necessarily 'close' the inflationary gap. It will simplify but not distort the analysis, accordingly, if we continue until Chapter 15 with the earlier assumption (p. 217) that, in the short run, output cannot be increased at all when resources are fully employed.

If markets in the economy are highly competitive, the consequences of the excess demand (ab) can be readily traced. In competitive markets, prices are determined by the interaction of the forces of supply and demand, and each firm in the market accepts the ruling price. With

L

supply constant in the short run, an increase in demand throughout the product markets can result only in a rise in prices. If a new short run equilibrium is to be achieved, prices must rise sufficiently to absorb the extra spending (ab) and 'choke off' the excess demand. Since households, firms and government want to spend an extra £4,000 million on final goods and services, prices in general will rise by 20 per cent. Households, etc., will now be spending £24,000 million on £24,000 million 'worth' of goods and services, but the value of the latter has increased (bc) only in consequence of a 20 per cent rise in the price level.

As final demand is bigger by £4,000 million, and prices in general are higher by 20 per cent, factors of production must be receiving £4,000 million more income. Money incomes, accordingly, have risen by £4,000 million, and we may surmise that some of the new income is going to firms as higher profits, and some as higher wages and salaries to employees. Why higher wages and salaries? Following the rise in price for its product, each firm will be eager to increase its labour force and expand production. The market demand for labour will accordingly rise but—with the supply fixed overall by the condition of full employment—this can result only in a rise in the price of labour, i.e. an increase in wage rates.

The consequences of the excess demand (ab) are, however, less certain if markets for products and labour are not highly competitive. Thus, more realistically, each firm may be considered to determine its own price, perhaps on the basis of its average costs with an eye as well on the policies of business rivals. Prices in a market where each individual firm fixes its own are said to be 'administered'. In the labour market wages are likely to be determined by collective bargaining between employers' representatives and one or more unions, so that employees of many different firms have their wage rates settled by the same bargain.

Administered prices are less likely to be directly responsive, in the short run, to an increase in demand. It is possible, nonetheless, that the excess demand for goods and final services may lead indirectly to a rise in their prices through its influence, first, upon the employer's wage bill. With order books full and delivery dates lengthening in consequence of the excess demand (ab), employers may accede the more readily to union requests for higher wage rates. They will probably be anxious to avoid industrial dispute when business is booming, perhaps hopeful of attracting additional labour, and anyway concerned not to lose men through failure to keep rates 'competitive' with other industries or occupations. They may also calculate that wage increases may easily be passed on as higher prices since markets are so buoyant. At the same time, unions may press claims more vigorously in the knowledge of the 'labour shortage' and the expectation that profits will be augmented by the rise in orders. They will be spurred on by any increase in (retail) prices that may already have taken place.

The outcome will probably be a rise in wage rates, which will raise average costs of production. Individually, too, firms may offer higher rates than the negotiated minimum, which will increase their average costs still further. All this provides a strong reason, accordingly, for firms to raise prices, especially since each knows that the others have experienced cost increases of roughly the same magnitude, to which they are likely to respond in the same way. We conclude that, even when markets are not highly competitive, a rise in demand (ab) may lead to higher prices via higher wage costs. In this case, however, the price response is not likely to be as immediate or as clear cut as under competitive market conditions. For easier analysis, therefore, we may assume that the latter prevail.

To return to Fig. 14.2, we see that national output has been brought into equality with aggregate demand by a rise (bc) in its value attributable only to a 20 per cent increase in the general price level. The economy, however, is not in equilibrium. It is apparent from $(C + I + G)_1$ that, with national income at £24,000 million, households, firms and government between them want to spend £26,000 million. There is still excess demand of £2,000 million (cd) in the economy. This suggests a further price rise of $8\frac{1}{2}$ per cent, and so on until equilibrium is apparently reached at a national income of £28,000 million, where $(C + I + G)_1$ cuts the 45° line.

To understand what this conclusion implies, let us assume that the original increase in aggregate demand came from business firms, which sought to increase their net investment from £4,000 million to £8,000 million. This is shown quite clearly in Fig. 14.3, which is built up from Figs. 14.1 and 14.2. In the initial equilibrium situation, households absorbed $\frac{3}{5}$ of the national output, firms $\frac{1}{5}$ and government $\frac{1}{5}$. Firms then sought to increase their share to $\frac{2}{5}$, in terms of the prices ruling at the time. In consequence of this excess demand, prices rose by 40 per cent, i.e. national income rose from £20,000 million to £28,000 million in money terms. At the new national income level, the relative shares of national expenditure have altered both in money and in real terms. Households are spending £16,000 million on consumer goods, government £4,000 million, and firms £8,000 million on net investment. However, the real worth of households' and government spending has fallen, while firms have not increased the real value of their expenditure by as much as they initially planned.

To compare the old position with the new, we make use of a technique explained on p. 210 for expressing the value of one period's output in terms of the prices ruling in another. If we take the pre-inflationary period (T_0) as the base date and express the then price level as 100, it is apparent that in the post-inflationary period (T_1) the price level has risen to 140. Accordingly, household expenditure of 16 (£000

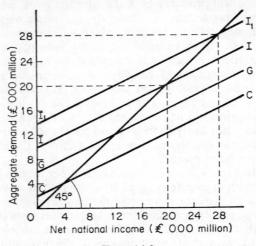

FIG. 14.3

million) in T_1 only buys as much goods and services as expenditure of $\dfrac{16 \times 100}{140}$ (£000 million) in T_0, i.e., $11\frac{3}{7}$ (£000 million). A similar calculation is made for firms' net investment and government spending, and the results set out in Table 14.1.

Table 14.1 shows quite clearly that the real worth of households' and government spending has fallen, in total, by $1\frac{5}{7}$ (£000 million), and the real value of firms' net investment spending has increased by $1\frac{5}{7}$ (£000 million). The process of inflation has accordingly entailed some redis-

TABLE 14.1

Sector	Money spending in T_0 (£000 million)	Money spending in T_1 (£000 million)	Value of T_1 spending allowing for 40% price increase (£000 million)
Households	12	16	$11\frac{3}{7}$
Government	4	4	$2\frac{6}{7}$
Firms	4	8	$5\frac{5}{7}$

tribution of resources from making goods for consumers and government to making investment goods for firms.

We obtain this conclusion by assuming that, as prices rise, households, firms and government do not alter their plans to take account of the rising level of prices. They are all victims of a 'money illusion': in a nutshell, they are concerned only with how much money they are spending, not how much goods and services they are buying. However, it is only if there is money illusion that, subject to the qualifications given below, equilibrium can be achieved. If firms are determined to have $\frac{2}{5}$ of national output, households $\frac{3}{5}$ and government $\frac{1}{5}$ at each consecutive level of prices, then there will always be excess demand to push prices up yet further.

The meaning of money illusion can be readily explained by examining how, in this example, households make their spending decisions. The consumption function CC in Fig. 14.3 shows a marginal propensity to consume constant at $\frac{1}{2}$ at all levels of incomes and prices. Up to a national income of £20,000 million (we assume) prices are stable, so that to increase consumption spending by $\frac{1}{2}$ when income rises by 1 unit represents a genuine, real increase in consumption. Beyond a national income of £20,000 million, however, prices rise proportionately with income. Accordingly, unless consumption spending is increased in proportion to the price rise, the value of consumption spending *falls* in real terms. Now, when income rises from 20 to 24 (£000 million), prices rise by 20 per cent. This means that the consumer goods and services which had cost 12 (£000 million) now cost 12 + ($\frac{1}{5}$ × 12) £000 million, or 14·4 (£000 million). To buy the same quantity of goods and services as before, therefore, households need to increase their consumption spending by 2·4 (£000 million), following their income increase of 4 (£000 million). However, in this example they react exactly as they would if prices were stable, and increase spending only by $\frac{1}{2}$ × 4 (£000 million). Their consumption therefore falls in real terms.

If, when prices are rising, households decide how much more to spend with an eye only on their bigger incomes and not on the higher prices, and if the government is content to maintain its spending constant at £4,000 million, then both sectors are losing out in real terms to firms. Even firms show money illusion in Fig. 14.3, since when prices rise they do not increase their spending plans proportionately in an attempt to double their real share of the national output. They end up accordingly with $\frac{2}{7}$ and not $\frac{2}{5}$ of national expenditure.

In Figs. 14.2 and 14.3, the achievement of ultimate stability of the price level (at 40 per cent higher than originally) depends on money illusion. In reality, it seems certain that government and households would increase money expenditure as prices rose, in an attempt to maintain the real worth of their spending. This does not mean, however, that in the real world price stability is necessarily impossible if aggregate demand rises at full employment level. Thus if the monetary authorities were to maintain the money supply unchanged, the increase in national income would draw money balances into transactions holdings away from speculative holdings, implying a rise in the rate of interest and so a curb on investment (Chapter 13).

Second we must recognize in reality that the government regularly intervenes in the economy, attempting by various methods (Chapter 20) to 'manage' aggregate demand in order to remedy any inflationary (or deflationary) gap.

Third, the analysis has been worked through on the assumption that, when resources are fully employed, output cannot be increased at all in the short run. In practice, an increase in aggregate demand may be (partly) met by the few per cent increase in the quantity of output that might sometimes be expected over a year (Chapter 15).

Finally, we have assumed for simplicity of analysis that all markets are highly competitive, with prices immediately responsive to increases in demand. In fact many prices will be administered, and relatively slower to change in response to a demand increase. A mild demand inflation may then manifest itself in a gradual upward movement of prices coupled with lengthened delivery dates and frustrated buyers. This second symptom assumes a greater importance if we relax an earlier assumption, and recognize the existence of foreign trade. Would-be buyers, disappointed at home, turn overseas for supplies; this movement will be reinforced by those who want to buy overseas because home prices have risen. At the same time, the thriving home market may weaken the incentive for firms to sell overseas, while their task will be made more difficult anyway in so far as the prices of goods are rising. In an open economy, therefore, an important symptom of demand inflation may be rising imports and constant if not declining exports.

4. Bottleneck Inflation

The picture so far constructed is of an economy in which rising aggregate demand exerts its pull upon output up to the full employment mark, and on the price level thereafter. The implication has been that the price level remains stable until all the economy's resources have been drawn into employment. In fact this can be true only if three extreme conditions are satisfied.

Assume, first, that all firms experience constant returns to labour (p. 267), as long as there is any unemployment in the economy. Assume, second, that all labour is perfectly mobile: in other words, any man can do any job anywhere (p. 269). Assume, third, that firms are prepared and able to turn their productive resources to the provision of any good or service whatsoever. Suppose now that, in these circumstances, there is a sufficient increase in aggregate demand to carry the economy up to full employment, but no further. The 'deflationary gap' is to be eliminated, but no 'inflationary gap' will emerge. Why will prices remain steady?

On these three assumptions, each firm will find that, as it increases output in response to the rising demand, the extra (or 'marginal') cost of each unit increase will remain constant. No firm, accordingly, has any reason for raising its own selling price, which means that the general level of prices must remain stable. First, every firm enjoys constant returns to labour, so that to increase production does not entail a more than proportionate increase in the labour force and a rise in the average wage cost. Second, since labour is perfectly mobile, any firm can get all the extra men it wants without bidding up wages, as long as there is any unemployment in the economy. Third, since firms are able to turn their resources to produce any commodity, no shortages of various final goods or raw materials can emerge as the economy expands, to act as a pull upon their prices.

A convenient way of consolidating these three assumptions is to say that, at the existing price level, resources are in perfectly elastic supply until full employment is achieved. An increase in aggregate demand then has no effect on the price level, but only on the supply of goods and services. In the previous section, we assumed (p. 309) that supply was perfectly inelastic once full employment was achieved. A rise in demand then did not raise output, only prices. The two situations are brought together in Fig. 14.4.

On the horizontal axis is represented national output in quantitative terms, while the general price level is represented on the vertical. They cannot, of course, be *measured* on their respective axes (Chapter 9), but it is clear enough that a movement up or down the vertical axis corresponds to a rise or fall in the price level, and a movement along the horizontal axis to an increase or decrease in the quantity of goods and services produced. When national output is below the full employment level OX, any change in aggregate demand has no effect on the price level, which remains constant at OP. At the full employment mark OX, any increase in aggregate demand has no effect on the total quantity produced, only on the price level. How far upwards the price level would rise along the path AB depends on the factors discussed in the last section.

Once we abandon the assumption of perfect elasticity of supply below the full employment level, we see that prices can in fact rise before full employment national output is achieved. Thus firms may experience diminishing returns to labour. As they increase output, they need to increase their labour force more than proportionately, so that average wage costs rise. Second, labour is not perfectly mobile. This means that, despite the persistence of unemployment, some firms will find it difficult to get the sort of labour they want, or get labour in the part of the country in which they are situated. Accordingly, wages in those occupations or industries will tend to rise. Third, not all firms can turn their resources to the production of any commodity. Some firms

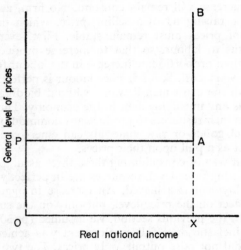

FIG. 14.4

therefore find their order books over full, while others are still looking for custom. Shortages develop, and some prices rise.

These three influences will all work to raise the level of prices before full employment is achieved, and explain why we might expect prices to rise in the recovery phase of the trade cycle (p. 266). This rise may be called 'bottleneck' inflation, as it is due to bottlenecks developing in the production of goods and services. There are 'shortages' of some sorts of labour and some sorts of goods, and their prices rise, thereby pulling up the general price level. 'Bottleneck inflation' is illustrated in Fig. 14.5, where the price level starts to rise at OW national output.

By the time OX national output is reached, the general level of prices has risen from XA (= OP) to XD. If we assume perfect inelasticity of supply, then a further increase in demand will draw prices up along the path DB. The demand may, however, be partly satisfied in real terms, if we recognize as significant the rise in the economy's productive

capacity that may take place in the short run (Chapter 15). In this
event, the response of output and the price level to rising aggregate
demand follows the path DEF.

We may briefly consider whether a fall in aggregate demand which
brought national output down from OX to OW would also bring the
price level back along the path DC (compare p. 266). The answer is
probably not. As demand contracts, prices may fall in some markets,
but there are at least two factors which make a fall to the former level
(OP) unlikely. First, unions may put up fierce opposition to a cut in

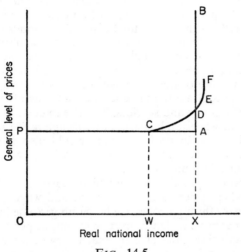

FIG. 14.5

money wages, and for most firms wage costs would be a big item in
total costs. Second, many prices are not determined by the forces of
supply and demand in a free market, but decided by firms themselves
after the fashion explained in Section 3. These 'administered prices' are
less likely to be marked down when sales are falling.

This 'downward inflexibility' of wages and administered prices may
in itself be an inflationary factor should the pattern of demand undergo
a rapid change. Prices and wages may rise in industries which are seeking to expand, without however declining in those industries faced with
contraction. On average, therefore, the general price level rises in
response, not to excess aggregate demand, but to 'demand shift'.

5. Cost Inflation

A third view of the inflationary process is provided by the 'cost-push' theory. In its simplest form, this theory holds that the upward pressure of costs is capable of causing a rise in the general level of prices, even if there is no excess demand in the economy. This proviso constitutes the essential distinction between the cost-push theory and the 'demand-pull' theory outlined in Section 3. We saw there that when prices are (largely) administered, and wages determined by collective bargaining, a rise in aggregate demand might operate indirectly to raise product prices through its influence first upon wage costs. The wage increases, accordingly, take place in the context of an excess demand for labour, which in turn reflects the excess final demand for goods and services. It is this excess demand which may be regarded as the ultimate 'cause' of the wage increase, even though superficially the increase may be attributed to union pressure, or employer competition for labour.

The unique feature of the cost-push theory is the proposition that a rise in costs may push up the price level even though there is no excess final demand for goods and services. The rise in costs may come about through a rise in wages and salaries, or through a rise in the prices of imports. An increase in profit margins would also exert an upward pressure on the price level, but this possibility is not considered here as an independent inflationary factor.

Consider first one possible way in which wage push might operate in an economy where prices are administered and wages determined industry by industry through collective bargaining. Some industries might be planning to achieve a significant rise in output per man in the year ahead, by introducing more efficient machinery or improving working methods. To obtain labour co-operation in the changes involved, they might be prepared to pay higher wage rates, which would be (more than) offset by the increased productivity, so that average labour costs and prices need not rise.

Workers in other industries may now react by making wage claims themselves on the grounds of 'fairness' or 'comparability', though no corresponding rise in productivity is anticipated. Their claims may, further, command public sympathy in so far as wages in these industries are generally thought to be 'low', i.e. provide a relatively low living standard. Employers may accordingly accede to their requests, and in turn raise prices to cover their increased labour costs. This must mean that the general price level rises, since prices in the first case have not fallen, and prices in the second case have risen. Firms need not be inhibited by the fear of losing sales at the higher prices, if they are confident that the government will actively 'manage' aggregate demand (Chapter 20) to ensure full employment.

A rise in the general level of prices may also be initiated by a rise in the prices of imports. If imported raw materials became more expensive, manufacturers might try and pass on their increased costs as higher prices. Despite the rise in prices, sales may be maintained if the government actively manages aggregate demand to ensure full employment. Households will, however, find that they have to spend more from a given income if they are to buy the same quantity of goods and services as before, since the 'cost of living' has risen. This in turn may encourage wage demands which, if successful, will increase average labour costs and lead to a further rise in prices. This second round of price increases may prompt a further round of wage demands, and wages and prices will follow each other upwards in a 'wage-price' spiral.

This reasoning may be illustrated with the aid of Fig. 14.6. It is less

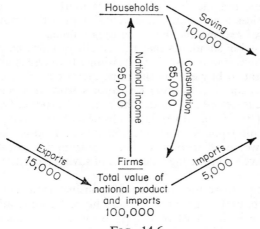

FIG. 14.6

complicated in this example to ignore the government's existence, and to assume that net investment at home is zero. The economy is initially in a full employment equilibrium: all figures are in units of, say, £ million.

Households are selling factor services valued at 95,000 units to firms who, with the addition of imports valued at 5,000, produce final goods and services to the total value of 100,000 units. Consumption spending absorbs 85,000 units of these, and export spending the remaining 15,000. This generates an income of 100,000 units, of which 95,000 pass as the national income to households and 5,000 remunerate the overseas suppliers of the imports. The national product is 95,000: this can be seen as the worth of what households add to imports with their productive services. It is equal to the value of (consumption) spending at home (85,000) plus exports (15,000) less imports (5,000). Saving in this economy is 10,000, which is equal to net investment overseas, i.e., the excess of exports over imports (compare Chapter 16).

Suppose now that the price of imports doubled. We ignore one possible consequence—a tendency among importers to turn to the products of the already fully employed domestic economy—and assume that exactly the same quantity as before is imported. With domestic costs (so far) unchanged, and the same physical import content now twice as expensive, we can see the next stage as an increase in final prices of 5 per cent, i.e., the quantity of goods and services formerly available to overseas and domestic buyers at 100,000 units is now offered at 105,000 units. The contribution made to this total by the economy's productive factors, i.e., the national income, is unchanged at 95,000 units, but the doubling in price of the import content has raised final prices 5 per cent. The purchasing power of money income, i.e. the value of real income, has accordingly fallen.

The fall in living standards that this entails can also be presented in terms of consumption and savings decisions. If overseas and domestic consumers want to buy exactly the same quantities as before, the first will need to spend 15,750 units on exports from this economy, and domestic consumers 89,250 units. The national product (95,000 units) plus imports (10,000 units) would be absorbed by consumption spending (89,250 units) plus exports (15,750 units). Households will thus be distinctly worse off in that, to keep consumption constant in real terms, they have had to reduce their rate of saving from 10,000 to 5,750 units.

In an attempt to restore real income, businessmen may raise their profit mark-up, and wage-earners secure higher remuneration because of the increase in the 'cost of living'. Both factors lead to a rise in production costs, which exerts an upward 'push' on the price level. It is apparent that households in aggregate cannot offset their loss by securing higher money incomes in this way (Section 6) but, while they try, a wage-price spiral is the consequence. No unemployment need result, provided sufficient spending is made from the higher incomes to take up the higher priced goods and services. In the example, this could be achieved by having overseas and domestic buyers decide to increase money spending in order to buy the same quantities as before. In reality (as already noted), the government would 'manage' aggregate demand in an attempt to ensure full employment.

6. *Consequences of a Changing Price Level*

The expression 'the value of money' has two quite distinct meanings, one of which we have already encountered in Chapter 1. First, it may mean the internal value of the money used within the country, e.g., in Britain, how much one can buy with £1. By contrast, the value of money in the external sense denotes the rate at which the money of one country exchanges for the money of another, e.g., how many American dollars one can buy with £1 sterling. These are two quite different concepts, though a change in the internal value of money may affect the rate of exchange, and vice versa. In this section we are concerned only with the direct consequences for the domestic economy of changes in the internal value of money. The implications of a change in the external value of money, and the relationship between internal and external values, are postponed for consideration in Chapters 16 and 18.

The value or purchasing power of money varies inversely with the general level of prices. Thus the lower the level of prices, the more one can buy with £1: the pound has appreciated in value. The higher the level of prices, the less one can buy with £1: the pound has depreciated in value. If we so choose, we may define inflation simply as a rise in the general level of prices, and deflation as a fall in the price level. The pound accordingly appreciates with deflation, and depreciates with inflation.

The term 'inflation', however, is not always used in this simple sense. Thus on p. 309, demand inflation was defined as an excess of aggregate demand over aggregate supply at full employment level. We saw that, if the prices of final goods and services are 'administered', then at least in the early stages the symptom of inflation is as likely to be frustrated buyers and rising imports as rising prices. This explains why the term 'disinflationary' is applied to a government policy which aims at curbing excess demand (Chapter 20). Its objective is to remove the inflationary gap, not actually to bring prices down to some former level. The word 'deflationary' may also be used in this way, or it may denote a policy designed particularly to bring prices down. 'Reflation' is a term sometimes used for the 'bottleneck inflation' of Section 4. However a 'reflationary' policy is designed, not to raise prices, but to encourage aggregate demand in an economy suffering unemployment because of demand deficiency.

In this section, we consider the effects of inflation and deflation using the terms only in the simple sense. The consequences of a changing price level may be traced out under three heads: first, the effect on the distribution of income; second, the effect on the ways in which people choose to hold their wealth; third, the effect on investment decisions. These consequences are easily grasped if we take note of an important fact about the behaviour of prices in the economy. During a period when most prices are rising, some will be rising faster than others, some will remain stationary, while others may even fall. Likewise when prices in general are falling, price behaviour will not be uniform. It follows that it is impossible to get one single, precise measure of a change in the value of money over a given period. If the majority of prices are rising, though at different rates, while a small minority are stationary or even falling, it seems reasonable to conclude that the *general* purchasing power of money is falling. By how much, however, would depend on the prices included in the particular index numbers chosen to calculate the change in the value of money (compare p. 207).

How are households' real living standards affected in a period of rising prices? A household's money income, of course, depends on the amount of services it sells to firms, other households (e.g., charwomen) or the government (e.g., civil servants), and the price at which it makes its sales. Its real income depends upon the size of its money income and the price level of the goods and services it buys. If the price the household gets for the sale of its services rises as fast as the 'average' of other prices, then it will just maintain its real income constant. But if its price stays constant, or rises less rapidly than others, then the purchasing power of the household's income will decline. For example, a landlord may have leased property at a ground rent fixed for 99 years. If other prices rise during the period, the purchasing power of his income will clearly decline. Income recipients in a similar category are people entitled under life insurance and pension schemes to benefits which are fixed in money terms when the agreement is first made, and the recipients of fixed interest on Government securities and company debentures.

The position of those who sell their services in the labour market will depend on how rapidly their own prices change when other prices are changing. The remuneration of public service employees is likely to be less responsive to changes in general economic circumstances than the incomes of industrial and commercial employees. Accordingly when prices in general are rising their own rates of pay tend to lag behind, so that for the time being their real incomes decline. This may impose a more general loss on the community if difficulties in recruiting teachers, nurses, policemen, etc., hold back the expansion of the corresponding services at the rate generally considered desirable.

Within industry and commerce itself, the remuneration of wage earners is likely to rise more rapidly than that of salary earners. If the rise in the price level is a manifestation of rising aggregate demand, we may expect a second sign to be an increased demand for labour in a number of industries. In a time of labour shortage, however, nationally negotiated wage rates may be augmented by locally agreed increases, bonus schemes and so on, which push actual earnings substantially above the level implied by the nationally agreed rate (Chapter 20).

A rising price level will prompt claims for higher wages and salaries generally throughout the economy. In so far as they are met, labour costs are increased, prices rise yet again, and the real value of the pay increase is reduced. This does not mean, however, that each union's efforts to increase or maintain real income are necessarily self-frustrating. Not all rates of pay will rise at the same speed, and those who push their increases furthest gain at the expense of those who lag behind. One union's decision not to make a wage claim would in itself do little (if anything) to moderate the inflation, so that its members' real income would be bound to fall.

Finally, we may consider the position of profit recipients in a period of rising prices. These range from the one man proprietors of small businesses to the equity shareholders of large public companies. A rising price level may be associated with a rising level of aggregate demand, which for most firms will mean rising orders hence buoyant profits. Specifically, firms may enjoy 'windfall' profits if rising demand enables them to increase their selling prices more rapidly than the rise in their wage costs. The share of profits in the national income would then increase relative to wages and salaries. This possibility does, however, seem stronger during hyper-inflation, or in competitive markets where price is immediately responsive to demand changes. It seems unlikely that profits would move far ahead of wages in an economy where most prices are administered and powerful unions keep a careful watch on the rate of profit growth.

Changes in the cost of keeping intact both fixed and circulating capital (Chapter 7) must be allowed for in assessing the value of any windfall profits a firm may enjoy. As an example, consider a firm which buys £100 of raw materials to manufacture into goods it plans to sell at £150, taking a profit for itself of £10. Assume for the illustration that the firm is selling in a competitive market, where it accepts the market price. Because of the upward pull of excess demand, the market price rises during the firm's manufacturing period, and it is able to sell its product at say £175, 16·6 per cent higher than originally expected. Superficially the firm enjoys a book profit of £35, but if raw material prices have risen in the same proportion (i.e. 16·6 per cent), it will need to pay £116·6 when it buys raw materials to replenish its stocks. If, accordingly, it is to maintain intact its circulating capital (p. 132), it must reckon its true windfall gain as £25 less £16·6, or £8·4.

Even this second figure may overstate the windfall profit if over the same period there is a rise in the replacement price of the fixed assets. Suppose, to take a fresh example, that a firm pays £100 for a machine which is estimated to have a life of 5 years, with no scrap value. If it uses the straight line method of depreciation (Chapter 7), it will make an annual depreciation charge against its revenue of £20. If in 5 years' time the price of an identical machine has risen, the £20 annual allowance (based on the historic cost) will have overstated the firm's profits, and understated the cost of keeping fixed capital intact. A prudent management will, in practice, earmark some profits to this end, though such profits are still liable to tax. The Government has not permitted firms to calculate their 'writing-down' allowances (i.e. the depreciation allowances approved for tax purposes) with reference to replacement cost, but this drawback has probably been more than offset by the investment allowance scheme and similar benefits introduced by the Government in post-war years (Chapter 20).

Correspondingly, at a time when prices in general are falling, the calculation of depreciation allowances with reference to historic cost will overstate the cost of keeping fixed capital intact. The book profits are accordingly lower than if depreciation was calculated on replacement cost. In consequence, companies may pay rather lower dividends which, through the restraint on consumption spending this implies, is hardly helpful if there is demand deficiency unemployment.

When the general level of prices is falling, the recipients of fixed money incomes will, of course, gain in real terms. Fees and salaries are unlikely to move downwards, so their recipients will also enjoy a real income gain. The position of the wage earner is more difficult to assess. In occupations where the labour force is strongly organized in trade unions, money wage *rates* are not likely to be reduced. Where the fall in the price level is a symptom of falling aggregate demand, earnings will fall in relation to the days of rising aggregate demand, when labour shortage typically results in payments above nationally negotiated rates. Business profits are likely to decline, not only because of windfall losses, but because of falling turnover where a fall in demand underlies the fall in prices.

We turn next to consider the implications of changes in the general level of prices for the ways in which people choose to hold their wealth. Clearly, if prices in general are rising, then the money value of one's own assets must increase at least in line with the average if a loss of real value is to be avoided. This explains why property, works of art and jewellery may be sought after as a personal investment during an inflation, as experience has shown that their prices are generally in the vanguard. Ironically, a price rise in consequence of their increased popularity may add to their attractiveness, if people interpret the rise as an augur of increases yet to come.

Equity shares are generally more popular[1] than bonds during in-

[1] Note, for example, the popularity in post-war Britain of trust units and 'with profits' life insurance policies (Chapter 7).

flation, as the first carry the prospect of rising dividend earnings while the second bear a return fixed in money terms. The shift in popularity causes a fall in bond prices and a rise in equity prices, so that the current return on a bond purchase may well be higher than on an equity purchase. The equity holder, however, is looking to the future when he expects both an increase in share prices and a rise in business profits. It would be unwise to take our initial proposition as a day-by-day guide to stock market behaviour. Thus a sharp bout of inflation might depress share prices somewhat if investors anticipated a vigorous disinflationary policy from the Government, which might reduce business profits over the next year or so.

A feature of the securities market in Britain since 1959 (with few exceptions) has been the lower dividend yield on leading ordinary shares compared with the rate of return on government bonds. As noted on p. 287, this constitutes a reversal of the traditional 'yield gap' or 'risk premium', whereby equities normally yielded a higher return than bonds in reflection of their greater riskiness. It would, however, be wrong to attribute the reversal of the yield gap entirely to the implications of inflation. The greater popularity of equities is also in part a consequence of the government's post-war success in maintaining full employment, and its emphasis on economic growth (Chapter 20), both of which foster the expectation of buoyant company profits and minimal company failures.

Finally, a changing price level may influence the rate and the composition of investment. This in turn will affect both the current level of economic activity and its subsequent rate of growth. Thus rapid inflation would encourage firms to build up stocks of commodities rather than engage in fixed investment. A slackening in the growth of fixed capital, however, may slow down the rate of growth of national output (Chapter 15). On the other hand, investment generally may be encouraged in so far as the process of inflation redistributes income in favour of profits (but see above), which may be ploughed back into the business.

A rise in the price level implies a decline in the real burden of business debt (e.g., debenture obligations), which is fixed in money terms. Thus to embark on a capital scheme a company might need to borrow long term at interest rates which make the whole venture seem—at the current prices for its products—only modestly attractive. However, it may be estimated that a gradual rise in prices over the years may increase the margin of return for the company, since of course the interest charge will be fixed in money terms. Capital investment may thus be encouraged by the expectation that the current upward 'creep' of prices will continue. This will prove a stimulant to the current level of employment (Chapter 12) and the future growth of output (Chapter 15).

Correspondingly, a falling price level which induces expectations of a continuing decline is likely to discourage capital investment, by increasing the anticipated debt burden. Thus through its influence on investment decision a falling price level may aggravate a slump, and a rising price level accelerate a boom (Chapter 12).

Questions

1. How far is the quantity theory of money likely to be accurate? What use can be made of this theory?   A.E.B.

2. Is an increase in the supply of money invariably inflationary?
                                                                   B.A. Gen.

3. Under what circumstances would you expect a 10 per cent increase in the supply of money to have no effect on the general level of prices? Give reasons for your answer.   J.M.B.

4. 'Inflation is impossible without an increase in the quantity of money.' Discuss.   U.L.

5. It has been said that 'with inflation the Quantity Theory comes into its own'. Discuss this statement.   I.B.

6. Show how, if the conditions of the supply of money are given, it will be the public's liquidity preference that determines its value. I.B.

7. What is the effect of an increase in the quantity of money on (a) the rate of interest, (b) national output, (c) the general price level?
                                                                   B.A. Gen.

8. 'The price level is determined by the level of effective demand.' Explain and discuss.   U.L.

9. How may incomes and prices be affected by (a) an export drive, and (b) a successful national savings campaign?   W.J.E.C.

10. 'Saving may be a private virtue but it is also a public vice.' Do you agree?   S.U.J.B.

11. Analyse the effects on the price level and aggregate employment of an increase in households' propensity to consume. Distinguish in your answer between conditions of full employment and unemployment.   U.L.

12. Since savings and investment are by definition always equal, why is it necessary to stimulate investment in a depression or encourage savings in an inflation?   S.U.J.B.

13. 'An increase in investment leads to an increase in employment *via* the multiplier.' Explain carefully what is meant by this statement, making clear the assumptions necessary for it to be true.   U.L.

14. What is inflationary pressure and how does it arise?   B.A. Gen.

15. 'The multiplier only operates at conditions of less than full employment.' Comment.   B.A. Gen.

16. Explain the distinction which is often made between 'cost-push' inflation and 'demand-pull' inflation, and discuss the usefulness of the distinction.   I.M.T.A.

17. What determines the value of money? How can changes in its value be measured?   J.M.B.

18. What is meant by the term 'the value of money'? If the stock of money is held constant, what factors determine changes in its value?   I.B.

19. Examine the probable economic consequences of a significant *appreciation* in the value of money.   I.B.

20. Consider the economic effects of a prolonged fall in the value of money.   I.B.

21. A clever, but dishonest, Englishman went to Sweden for a holiday. He decided to buy some souvenirs for his friends and paid for them with forged kroners. The forgeries were never discovered. What were the effects of his behaviour and who paid for the souvenirs?   J.M.B.

15

Economic Growth

1. *Capital Accumulation and Population Increase*

Chapters 10 to 12 discussed the role of net investment in generating income, but not the significance of the additions to the economy's capital stock which it also represents. Changes in the size of the labour force and the efficiency of work methods were similarly ignored. By taking the size of the economy's resources as constant (p. 217) in this way, attention was more easily focused on aggregate demand as the determinant of the current income level.

Analysis of income in terms of the use currently made of some given amount of resources is described as 'short-period'. Analysis of the implications for the income level of the growth of resources over time is known as 'long-period'. On this definition, analysis would be long-period even if concerned with the influence on the income level of only a few months' growth of resources. On the other hand, once the size of capital stock, etc., has been 'frozen' by appropriate assumption, short-period analysis is conveniently conducted in income and spending values expressed as rates per year, perhaps extending over a period of years. Such analysis nonetheless remains short-period, since it ignores the implications for the income level of the growth of resources (and of course, any improvements in efficiency). In this sense, the trade cycle example of Chapter 12 is short-period: it simply shows how, on certain conditions, interaction of multiplier and accelerator could generate a regular fluctuation in aggregate demand. It leaves out of the picture the possibilities of population change, or improvements in production methods, while the net investment pattern is such that capital stock remains constant over the cycle.

The analysis of this chapter is long-period: it takes into account the growth of population and the capital stock, and improvements in work methods, and considers their implications for the growth of income from year to year. However, the only form of capital growth considered is an increase in the economy's stock of capital goods (due to net fixed capital formation). This means leaving out the other type of net

328

domestic investment, namely increases in holdings of raw materials, semi-finished and finished goods. It also means leaving out overseas investment, i.e. a net increase in a community's claim upon foreign residents reflecting an excess of exports over imports (Chapter 16). Overseas investment augments national income of future years by the interest etc., yielded by the claims acquired on foreign residents.

To form a first assessment of the influence on national income growth of the rate of fixed capital formation, we consider a closed economy, with no government economic activity. Final spending is made up accordingly of consumption and net domestic investment, taken to consist exclusively of fixed capital investment. The working population is assumed to increase at exactly the same rate as the capital stock, and neither it, the capital stock nor methods of production ever improve or deteriorate in efficiency. Aggregate demand is assumed to be always sufficient just to maintain full employment.

TABLE 15.1

Year	Working Population (million)	Net National Income (£000 million)	Savings (£000 million)	Consumption (£000 million)	Net Investment (£000 million)
1	20	100	25	75	25
2	21	105	26·25	78·75	26·25
3	22·05	110·25	27·56	82·69	27·56

At the start of each year, the new equipment produced over the previous year comes into commission, and the output it produces during the year represents the increase in national income in relation to the previous year. Thus in Year 1 of Table 15.1 net investment is £25,000 million, so that firms start Year 2 with this much extra equipment. This enables them to produce, say, £5,000 million more goods and services than in Year 1 so that—assuming all resources in a full employment equilibrium—net national income rises to £105,000 million. The ratio of the increase in capital (£25,000) to the increase in output (£5,000 million) is known as the marginal capital output ratio: here 5/1. Its inverse is known as the marginal coefficient of capital (0·2). It is also possible to define an average capital output ratio. Thus if at the start of Year 1 the total capital stock had been valued at £500,000 million, the average capital output ratio would also have been 5/1: its inverse is the average coefficient of capital.

Let us now assume that the marginal capital output ratio is constant at 5/1, and that M.P.C. (= A.P.C.) is constant at 3/4. This second assumption means that consumption during Year 2 will be 78·75 units so that—on the previous full employment assumption—net investment must be 26·25 units. The economy accordingly starts Year 3 with extra capital worth 26·25 units, and is capable of producing an extra 5·25 units national income. National income accordingly rises to 110·25 units, of which ¾ is consumption (82·69) and 27·56 net investment.

It is clear that net national income is growing at the rate of 5 per cent a year. The analysis suggests that this rate of growth reflects two factors, namely the value of the marginal capital output ratio (5/1), and the proportion of income devoted to net investment (1/4). With the economy each year in full employment equilibrium (above), realized investment will equal planned savings, so that the proportion of income devoted to net investment will (with the sort of savings function shown in Fig. 10.4) equal the marginal propensity to save. The relationship may accordingly be expressed in the formula

$$G = S/Y \div K/Y,$$

where G is the rate of growth of income, S/Y is the marginal propensity to save, and K/Y the marginal capital output ratio. In this example S/Y is 1/4, K/Y is 5/1, so that the growth rate (G) is $\frac{1}{20}$, or 5 per cent per annum.

Working population is also growing at 5 per cent per annum, and so is total capital stock (which can be taken as £500,000 million at the start of Year 1). Income, population and the stock of capital thus advance together in 'balanced growth'. Income per head, however, remains constant at £5,000 a year. The possibilities and implications of raising it are discussed in Section 2.

2. *Achieving Faster Growth*

The formula just defined suggests that the rate of income growth may be increased by raising the 'savings ratio' (S/Y) or by reducing the marginal capital output ratio (K/Y). Thus—to take up the first possibility—suppose that the savings ratio rises to 2/5 so that (with full employment assumed) net investment becomes 40 units in Year 1 (Table 15.2). If for the time being the marginal capital output ratio is taken as constant at 5/1, income will rise at the rate (G) of 2/5 ÷ 5/1, or 8 per cent per annum. Working population is still increasing at the yearly rate of 5 per cent, so that income per head grows at a little under 3 per cent a year.

Consumption now forms a smaller proportion (⅗ instead of ¾) of an income growing more rapidly, and itself now grows at the annual rate of 8 per cent instead of 5 per cent. After a certain number of years, accordingly, consumption will catch up with the level it would have reached had the original consumption cut not been made, while thereafter the consumption level is higher. On this basis, the sacrifice of current consumption enables the economy to achieve higher consumption subsequently than would otherwise have been attainable, because of the fruitfulness of the intensified capital investment.

Table 15.2 makes it clear that capital per head is increasing since the capital stock (at 8 per cent) is growing more rapidly than the labour force (at 5 per cent). This process is known as 'capital deepening'. Table 15.1, by contrast, represents a process of 'capital widening', if the capital stock at the start of Year 1 is taken as £500 thousand million.

TABLE 15.2

Year	Working Population (million)	Net National Income (£000 million)	Con- sumption (£000 million)	Net Invest- ment (£000 million)	Capital Stock (£000 million)	Income per Head (£000)	Capital per Head (£000)
1	20	100	60	40	500	5	25
2	21	108	64·8	43·2	540	5·14	25·7
3	22·05	116·64	69·98	46·66	583·2	5·29	26·45

Capital stock and labour force increase at the same rate (5 per cent), so that capital per man remains constant.

Unless certain conditions are satisfied, the increase in the amount of capital per man (Table 15.2) must, however, lead to a fall in the productivity of the additional units of capital. As each man had more and more capital placed at his disposal, so the usefulness of the extra capital would diminish, and the marginal capital output ratio would increase. This means a slow-down in the rate of income growth and so a slow-down in the rate of growth of the capital stock. In the limit, the rate of income and of capital growth would revert to 5 per cent, i.e. the rate set by the growth of working population. In this event, with the savings ratio at 2/5, the marginal capital output ratio would have risen to 8/1: income per head would now be constant, but at a higher level than before the rise in the savings ratio took place.

However, a fall in the productivity of the additional capital may be avoided if certain other influences come into operation. One is an improvement in the quality of the labour force, the second a rise in the efficiency of work methods, and the third an improvement in the design and efficiency of the capital goods themselves. All three factors are generally operative over the years, and enable a given number of men to use successively more equipment without a fall-off in the productivity of the additional units.

It appears, therefore, that an increase in the savings ratio would need to be supplemented by other influences if the prospective increase in the rate of growth is to be achieved. Otherwise, it is argued, the marginal capital output ratio would rise as the expansion of capital relative to labour depressed—at the margin—the productivity of capital. These 'other influences'—three examples of which were noted above—are conveniently designated by the term 'technical progress'.

Technical progress may also operate as a growth factor independent (at least conceptually) of the savings ratio, since progress along one or more of the lines indicated would reduce the marginal capital output ratio. Table 15.3 shows the implications, with a savings ratio of 1/4, of a fall in the marginal capital output ratio from 5/1 to 2·5/1 (the fall can be considered to date from Year 2).

TABLE 15.3

Year	Working Population (million)	Net National Income (£000 million)	Con- sumption (£000 million)	Net Invest- ment (£000 million)	Capital Stock (£000 million)	Income per Head (£000)	Capital per Head (£000)
1	20	100	75	25	500	5	25
2	21	110	82·5	27·5	525	5·24	25
3	22·05	121	90·75	30·25	552·5	5·49	25·06

The growth rate (G) of net national income becomes

$$G = 1/4 \times 1/2\cdot5 = 10 \text{ per cent.}$$

Net investment now rises more rapidly than in Table 15.1 (10 per cent a year instead of 5 per cent), since while it represents the same proportion of net national income ($\frac{1}{4}$), income itself is increasing at the rate of 10 per cent instead of 5 per cent per annum. Both income and capital per head are rising, which suggests a need to maintain technical progress in the economy if diminishing returns to capital are to be avoided.

Technical progress may be 'embodied' in improvements in equipment design and efficiency, or it may take other forms, e.g. improvements in the educational standards of the labour force. In the first case, the improved versions will be bought not only to add to capital stock (net investment) but also to make good capital depreciation (replacement investment). 'Embodied' technical progress thus works to reduce the marginal capital output ratio by increasing the productivity not only of additional fixed capital but also of replacement fixed capital. Further, a rapid rate of progress in plant design may lead to increased replacement investment spending, as firms feel the need to scrap their quickly obsolescent plant to maintain efficiency relative to competitors. The average productivity of the capital stock thus increases more rapidly but —faced with an increased replacement 'burden'—firms may modify their net investment spending.

3. *Instability in the Rate of Growth*

The role of aggregate demand in the process of income growth has, so far, been kept quite neutral by the assumption that each year's final expenditure was just sufficient to maintain full employment of the economy's resources. This section relaxes that assumption and considers, first, some consequences and, second, some possible causes of variations in the rate of growth of aggregate demand.

In the economy depicted in Table 15.1, the capital stock and labour force are both 5 per cent higher in Year 2 than in Year 1. With a marginal capital output ratio of 5/1, the economy is now capable of producing in Year 2 an income which is bigger by 5 per cent than Year 1. However, for this potential growth to be achieved, aggregate demand is required to rise by 5 per cent. On the assumption that the economy enjoyed full employment in Year 1, this increase will maintain resources in full employment in Year 2. Since consumption is a stable proportion of income ($C = \frac{3}{4}Y$), it is net investment which will need to rise by 5 per cent (1·25 units), since this will induce a corresponding percentage increase in aggregate demand (of 5 units) by way of the induced rise in consumption spending (3·75 units). However, the net investment of Year 2 adds to the capital stock with which the economy starts Year 3. Accordingly, with the same percentage rise in the labour force and the marginal capital output ratio unchanged, net investment is required to rise by a further 5 per cent (i.e. a bigger absolute amount than in Year 2), if full employment is to be maintained and the potential growth achieved.

Suppose now that, in Year 2, aggregate demand failed to grow by 5 per cent. The consequence would be some unemployment among the working population and some idle capital resources. To firms the latter would appear as 'excess capacity', and its emergence would probably discourage investment spending in Year 3, with effects for aggregate demand multiplied by the induced fall in consumption spending.

Suppose, on the other hand, that aggregate demand grew by more than 5 per cent in Year 2. The consequence would be excess aggregate demand (Chapter 14), hence a shortage both of labour and of capital equipment. The latter shortage would probably encourage firms to increase investment spending (by more than 5 per cent) in Year 3, with a more than proportionate increase in aggregate demand through the induced consumption spending.

It appears, therefore, that there is just one critical growth rate for aggregate demand if the economy of Table 15.1 is to avoid large-scale unemployment on the one hand or demand inflation on the other. With consumption a stable proportion of income, net investment is required to rise by a constant percentage (hence an increasing absolute amount) each year, to maintain full employment without inflation. This rigorous requirement must, however, be modified when allowance is made for the possible instability of the consumption function, or the existence of other sources of aggregate demand. Thus suppose that net (private domestic) investment spending did not rise by 1·25 units in Year 2. Full employment can still be maintained if there is an offsetting rise in consumption spending, or if there were government spending or net investment overseas. Further, the failure of net fixed capital formation to increase by 5 per cent in Year 2 means that the economy starts Year 3 with a capital stock which has increased by less than the customary 5 per cent. Real output could[1] not therefore rise by as much as 5 per cent in Year 3, which means that the required growth rate for aggregate demand is correspondingly reduced.

It is instructive, nonetheless, to continue with the highly abstract example of Table 15.1, and suppose that net investment will rise at 5 per cent a year in the absence of technical progress, and as long as the labour force increases at an annual 5 per cent. This will provide a framework in which to consider the implications for aggregate demand of a change in the rate of population growth, and of technical progress.

If capital stock and labour force are increasing at an identical rate then, in the absence of technical progress and economies of scale, there is no reason for the general level of unit production costs to rise or fall from year to year. With a rate of interest assumed constant, the critical determinant of the level of net investment spending thus becomes the prospective growth of sales. Suppose that firms estimate the likely growth of next year's sales with reference to last year's experience. Thus if sales grew by 5 per cent last year, they may reckon that sales will grow by 5 per cent next year; accordingly, they place appropriate in-

---

[1] The marginal capital output ratio would, however, be likely to fall in Year 3, since the labour force is now growing more rapidly than the capital stock. Despite the more rapid growth of the labour force, the economy could still enjoy full employment if production methods changed appropriately.

vestment orders this year for equipment they want by the start of next year. If 'appropriate' is taken to mean 5 units worth of equipment for each anticipated unit increase in sales, then we have a construction which exactly fits the situation depicted in Table 15.1.

For example, a rise in final sales (i.e. net national expenditure) of 5 per cent in Year 2 prompts firms to expect a corresponding percentage increase (on Year 3's level) in Year 4. In absolute terms, this will be a rise of $5/100 \times 110 \cdot 25$, i.e. $5 \cdot 5125$ units, so that during Year 3 firms place orders for $5 \times 5 \cdot 5125$, or $27 \cdot 56(25)$ units worth of extra equipment. They want this for the start of Year 4, to meet the anticipated extra demand. It is apparent on these conditions that, once the economy has achieved 5 per cent growth in two consecutive years, it is set on this path in perpetuity. Each year the expectation of a rate of growth next year which is proportionate to last year's entails a level of net investment spending just sufficient to ensure full employment of this year's additional resources. Thus in Year 3 aggregate demand rises by 5 per cent just because firms are getting ready, by way of increased investment, to meet the 5 per cent extra demand they expect in Year 4.

Disturbance to this economy's smooth rate of growth may, however, come about through a change in the rate of population growth, or through the achievement of some technical progress. Thus suppose that the rate of population growth fell below 5 per cent in a given year, and persisted at its new level. One immediate consequence is that real output could not rise by 5 per cent in this year. Second, in the assumed absence of technical progress and economies of scale, the productivity of this year's capital will fall, in so far as labour and capital are not perfect substitutes for each other. Firms are thus faced with a fall in the rate of expansion and a rise in the level of operating costs, both of which will serve to reduce the marginal efficiency of capital. With the rate of interest unchanged, this suggests a fall in the net investment level, and a more than proportionate decline in aggregate demand.

The outlook for this economy is not one of alternation between full- and under-employment, but rather one of 'long-run slump', more usually called 'secular stagnation'. Government monetary policy might be aimed at a fall in the rate of interest (following Chapter 13, through an increase in the money supply), in order to induce some revival in net investment (see, however, the difficulties mentioned on p. 299). In the fiscal field, a case might be argued for (increased) public expenditure to offset the inadequacy of private investment: the former need not be restricted by the prospect of a low (zero, negative) rate of return.

Policy measures apart, the stagnation might be relieved by the 'natural' factors of population increase or technical progress. Thus by raising the productivity of capital more rapid population growth would provide a boost to the rate of return and so to the rate of net investment spending. This, in turn, suggests the possibility that, at least over the generations, the alternation of periods of fast and slow population growth may find some reflection in upswings and downswings in economic activity.

The introduction of technical progress into the economy of Table 15.1 may also make for instability in growth, via its implications for net investment spending. Thus the development of more efficient capital goods implies a period of high yields on investment projects, and hence a strong stimulus to net investment. The same holds for the development of new sorts of consumer goods. A slackening in the rate of innovation might, correspondingly, depress net investment. Such a variation might be echoed long afterwards in the pattern of gross final expenditure, and so in the employment level (p. 267). As the equipment bought so widely in the boom comes to the end of its working life, its replacement *en masse* may stimulate another burst of economic activity.

Section 2 took the level of aggregate demand as given, and discussed the implications for the growth rate should capital stock be increasing more rapidly than the labour force, or should the economy achieve some technical progress. In this section the assumption that aggregate demand is neutral has been relaxed: the concluding discussion has shown how, by their influence on investment decisions, these two factors may introduce some instability into the rate of income growth through the effects on aggregate demand.

4. *Growth and Welfare*

Consider a community in which, out of a total population of 50 million, 20 million people working on average a 40-hour week for 50 weeks produce, in a given year, a national output valued at £100 thousand million. Suppose for the illustration that, because of (miraculous!) technical progress, the productivity of this same work force is 25 per cent greater in the subsequent year. The community may enjoy its increased powers of production in three ways. First, it may have a higher real national income per head; second, it could have more leisure—either a shorter working week or longer holidays per year; third, it could have a smaller proportion of its total population at work.

In the first event, the economy would yield a national output of £125 thousand million: average annual income per head of total population would rise from £2,000 to £2,500, and per head of working population from £5,000 to £6,250. Alternatively, with productivity 25 per cent higher and national income and numbers in employment unchanged, the working week could fall to an average length of 32 hours.[1] In this event, average income per head of total population and working population would be unaffected (respectively £2,000 and £5,0C0 a year), but the total number of man hours devoted to producing this income would fall from 40 × 20 × 50 million hours to 32 × 20 × 50 million hours per year. It follows that national income per hour worked would rise from £2·5 to £3·125. The opportunity for greater leisure might also be taken in the form of longer holidays in the year: if the length of the working week remained unchanged at 40 hours, the labour force need work only a 40 week year.[1]

The third possible outcome is that, with national income, the working week and holidays unchanged, the benefit of the increased productivity is enjoyed through a reduction in the numbers of the working population. This could mean fewer married women in paid employment, a longer period of compulsory education, more young people in college, and an earlier retirement age. Since in our example productivity has increased by 25 per cent, a working population of 16 million[1] working 40 hours a week for 50 weeks could produce a national income of £100 thousand million over the year. National output per head of total population would be unaffected, but annual income per head of working population would rise from £5,000 to £6,250. The total number of hours worked per year would fall from 40 × 20 × 50 million to 40 × 16 × 50 million, so that national output per hour worked would rise from £2·5 to £3·125.

The way(s) in which the community uses its increased powers of production may affect its future rate of income growth. For example, if the working population (or working week) falls with the expansion of educational facilities for young people, the capabilities of the future labour force will be greater and so—it may be supposed—will its productivity. In the short run, however, the more 'progress' is made in one direction (e.g. higher real income per head), then the less room there is for progress in the others (e.g. more leisure). There is no simple mechanism by which a community may choose in what proportions to have the greater leisure, the smaller labour force or the more goods that increased powers of production make possible. Historically, we find that all three benefits characterize the rise in living standards that stems from capital investment and technical progress. Thus in England today, people have a higher real income per head, a shorter working week and longer holidays per year, and a longer period in school than was the average experience fifty years ago.

The achievement of a faster rate of economic growth has become a major policy goal of governments in both advanced and 'developing'

[1] It is assumed for simplicity that output varies in direct proportion to man hours worked.

countries (Section 6). Military and prestige reasons apart, the reason for this emphasis lies in the benefits of rising living standards that economic growth confers upon the inhabitants of the economy. It is clear, however, that in assessing how far living standards have improved it is necessary to take into account not only the percentage increase in G.N.P. over a given period, but also changes in the average working week and in the numbers and age distribution of the working and total population.

Even if real income per hour worked has risen, it is still not possible to establish that the standard of living (or 'economic welfare') has unambiguously increased. First, the distribution of the real national income may alter with the process of growth. Thus where growth is accompanied by inflation, the distribution of real income may change (for example, the relative share of some public service employees may diminish), while those on fixed incomes actually become worse off in absolute terms than they were originally (Chapter 14). It is then difficult to establish that the greater well-being of the majority more than offsets the reduced well-being of the minority.

Second, the living standards of a community may find more accurate reflection in the level of consumption than in the level of national income. Thus if a greater proportion of national expenditure is devoted to net domestic investment, income per head should rise immediately but, for the time being, consumption per head will fall (compare Tables 15.1 and 15.2). In this case the community sacrifices some current consumption for the sake of higher living standards at some time in the future.

However, whether or not people *feel* worse off when they reduce current consumption will depend, at least partly, on their freedom of choice. An economy could be imagined in which the government engineered lower consumption spending (say) by raising tax rates, so that people feel worse off because their take-home pay is smaller. On the other hand, people might develop a greater thriftiness (i.e. the propensity to save increases), so that investment can expand without creating excess demand. People may accordingly consider themselves better off as they are doing what they now prefer, i.e. consuming less and saving for the future.

Third, living standards in an open economy will depend on the volume and prices of imports and exports, as well as net national income per head. Thus if imports and national product are unchanged an increase in exports entails less goods for home consumption (or home capital formation). On the other hand, a rise in imports (with exports and national product unchanged) provides more goods for domestic consumption (or home capital formation), though at the expense of increased liabilities towards (or reduced claims upon) the foreign suppliers (Chapter 17). Excess aggregate demand in an open economy may lead to an excess of imports over exports (p. 314), so that overall its inhabitants are 'absorbing' more than they produce by a net intake of supplies from the rest of the world. Living standards may also be affected by a change not in the quantity of imports, but in their prices—as the example of Chapter 14 (Section 5) demonstrates.

Fourth, improvements in the quality of consumer goods will contribute to higher living standards, even though real income per head is constant. On the other hand, some commodities can never become widely available however much average income rises, because of the natural factors which operate to limit supply. It is not possible, for instance, for everyone to have a house in its own grounds fairly near the town centre, though the relatively rich can afford this. In the same vein, more extensive car ownership as income rises does not confer the same benefits as when ownership was more restricted, since increased road congestion reduces the pleasures of motoring.

Further reservations are necessary when we turn to the relationship between economic growth and community welfare in the broad sense. Thus, at least in mature economies where human beings have been relieved of much of the drudgery of physical labour, it is by no means obvious that a reduction in the working week or an earlier retirement is an unqualified gain in welfare. Work provides personal satisfactions other than the wages received, and a reduction in working hours may bring a 'problem of leisure'.

Second, the growth of national output and the extension of economic activity may occasion 'social costs', so called because they inflict no monetary loss on the individuals responsible but are nonetheless detrimental to the members of the community. Some of these are social costs of production—for example, river and air pollution and the destruction of natural beauty by industrial processes. Some are social costs of consumption—for example, the noise, smell and danger introduced to city streets by motor traffic.

Third, it is clear that it is a man's feelings about the size of his income, rather than the size of the income in itself, which are relevant to his well-being. It follows that a rise in his income, which introduces him to the prospect of a better life while taking him no further than the threshold, may sharpen his recognition of his own relative poverty and increase his discontent.

Finally, the achievement of a more rapid growth rate may entail deep social changes as, for example, industrialization brings people from the countryside to the town. This may entail the sacrifice of ways of life which some people would prefer to more rapid growth and may, anyway, carry its own problems (for instance, of increased delinquency).

5. *International Comparisons of Income*

Comparison of each country's national income statistics (Chapter 9) seems a useful method of establishing how big and how fast-growing each country's output is in relation to others. Thus the size of gross domestic product per head, valued at factor cost, may be used to compare productivity, and an income measure at market prices used for a comparison of living standards. Such information may serve as a guide to the distribution of the economic aid given by richer to poorer countries (Section 6). It may also be used to decide the relative shares of the costs of international organizations (such as U.N.O.) to be borne by the member countries. In addition to its immediate practical significance, information of this sort may inspire, and be used to test, theories about the nature and characteristics of economic development. Thus it may be thought that the higher the national income per head, the greater the proportion of the working population engaged in manufacturing ('secondary') and service ('tertiary') activities, as opposed to the 'primary' activities of agriculture, fishing and mining. To discuss such a theory, it is important to be able to say whether national income per head is higher in one country than another, and to compare the occupational distribution of their respective labour forces.

Unfortunately, the comparison of national (or domestic) income per head possesses many difficulties, which cannot be fully resolved by even the most refined economic and statistical techniques. These difficulties may be grouped into three broad categories. First, countries show a wide variation in the adequacy and reliability of their social statistics. Second, countries vary considerably in their economic and social structure, and their physical environment. Accordingly, it is necessary but very difficult to ensure that the same sorts of economic benefit are uniformly included in the concept and measurement of 'income' in differing economies. Third, each country has its own structure of relative prices of goods and services, and its own currency in which these prices are expressed. There is, accordingly, a valuation problem in expressing the income 'bundle' of goods and services for each country in one appropriate common monetary measure.

The difficulty of obtaining adequate and reliable social statistics is at a minimum in mature economies like the U.K. or U.S.A. Even for this country, however, it is necessary to emphasize the highly tentative nature of some part of the national income calculations—for example, the valuation of the physical increase in stocks or of capital consumption (p. 214). In developing countries, by contrast, even information on basic material such as output and prices may be difficult to obtain, or very unreliable. Population statistics, too, may be unreliable, so that on this score alone there may be a wide margin of error in the calculation of income per head. For example, a census of the Nigerian population conducted in 1952 put the total population at 31,500,000, while the United Nations Monthly Bulletin of Statistics for December, 1961, gives a figure for mid-1961 of some 35,700,000. A census of May, 1962, estimated the population at 53,200,000, but these results were annulled by the Nigerian Federal Government in February, 1963, because they were considered unreliable. A second census was taken in November, 1963, which put the total population at 55,600,000. This result was accepted by the Federal Government though criticized in turn by, among others, the Premier of the Eastern Region.

The second difficulty in making income comparisons lies in ensuring that goods and services which satisfy comparable wants in both countries are included in the national incomes of both countries. This means that the boundary between economic and non-economic activity has to be drawn in as uniform a manner as possible for economies which are sometimes very different in structure and set in contrasting social contexts. In a highly developed market economy, many goods and services will be provided through the economic system which, in a developing country, will be provided within the family or the village community, without giving rise to a money income. It follows that the value, for example, of foodstuffs consumed by the peasant farmer's family, or of the recreational activities of the village community, need to be 'imputed' (p. 197) in the national income of the developing country.

The bigger the area of imputation, the more acute the statistical problem of deciding the prices at which to value the imputed goods and services. It is necessary, for example, to decide whether the peasant farmer's home produce should be valued at the price he could sell it wholesale, or the price he would have to pay for it retail. The choice of solution could make a significant difference to the value of national output if imputed consumption of home grown produce formed a substantial part of national expenditure.

A further example of an imputation problem is the treatment of 'free goods'. In tropical climates, for instance, the need for fuel and warm clothing is much smaller than in countries of the temperate zone. If national income comparisons are used as a measure of relative living standards, allowance should be made for the goods and services produced in some countries to alleviate discomforts which in other countries do not arise.

The third difficulty stems from the fact that countries have different price structures, and use different currencies in which to express these prices. In 1966, for example, the G.D.P. at factor cost per head of population in the U.K. was £587, while in the U.S.A. the same income measure was $3,504 (U.N. Yearbook of National Accounts Statistics, 1967). One way of comparing the two is to convert the U.K.

M

figure into $'s at the (then) official rate of exchange of £1 = $2·8: this
puts U.K. income per head at $1,644. This is the sort of calculation
used in the construction of Table 15.4. The regional domestic product
totals in Column 1 have been calculated by taking the G.D.P. for each

TABLE 15.4

*Gross Domestic Product (at
market prices) by Major Regions*

Region	(1) G.D.P. 1960 ($000 million)	(2) G.D.P. per head 1960 ($)	(3) Average annual compound rate of growth (%) (1955–60)
All market economies	1089·9	558	1·4
1. Developed market economies	920·1	1410	2·0
(a) North America	539·8	2718	0·5
(b) Western Europe:	314·3	946	3·3
E.E.C. (Chapter 19)	180·6	1068	4·1
E.F.T.A. (Chapter 19)	110·0	1229	2·0
Other W.E. (incl. Turkey)	23·7	322	2·6
(c) Japan	39·0	418	8·5
(d) Oceania and S. Africa	27·0	948	1·7
2. Developing market economies	169·8	130	1·8
(a) Latin American republics	61·4	300	1·6
(b) Africa (excl. S. Africa)	27·0	113	1·6
(c) Far East (excl. Japan)	68·3	85	1·8
(d) West Asia (excl. Turkey)	10·9	214	2·4
(e) Others (mainly Carribean countries)	2·2	472	4·6

Source: U.N. World Economic Survey, 1963

country in the region, applying the rate of exchange between its currency and U.S. dollars, and summing the results which are expressed in
U.S. dollars. Column 2 is obtained by dividing by the appropriate
population estimate. Column 3 shows that average annual compound
rate of growth which would result in the increase in G.D.P. per head
between 1955 and 1960 which was in fact achieved.

The weakness of this method is that £1 spent in the U.K. does not
have the same purchasing power as $2·8 in the U.S.A., so that a G.D.P.

per head of £587 in the U.K. in 1966 does not represent $1,644 worth of goods and services in the U.S.A. This difficulty has prompted the development of other techniques for comparing national incomes. Thus suppose that two countries produced identical goods in different quantities, and that in both economies the pattern of relative prices of the various goods was the same. On these two conditions the comparison of national income would be straightforward, provided all the statistics were available. The physical quantities of each good (or appropriate units of each service) could be multiplied by the price ruling either in the one country or in the other. The values obtained in the one currency could then be totalled for each country, to give two national income totals expressed in one currency unit.

In the real world, of course, countries do not produce the same commodities, though this difficulty may be partly overcome by working in terms of categories of commodity, e.g. 'fruit', 'meat', 'clothing' and so on. Further, relative prices are not the same, so different estimates are obtained depending on the price 'weights' chosen. Thus suppose country A produces 100 lb. of fruit a year selling at 2s. a lb., and 50 lb. of meat a year selling at 4s. a lb. (small figures are chosen to simplify the arithmetic). Country B produces 80 lb. of fruit at $1 a lb., and 60 lb. of meat at $3 a lb. If we use A's prices, then its 'national output' of fruit and meat is (200 + 200)s., i.e. 400s., and B's 'national output' is (160 + 240)s., also 400s. However, if we use B's prices, A's 'national output' is $(100 + 150) i.e. $250, and B's 'national output' is $(80 + 180), i.e. $260. Consideration of this problem belongs to the science of statistics.

6. Growth in the Developing Countries

Whatever the difficulties in measuring differences in living standards and productivity, there is no doubt that, in both respects, some countries are substantially worse off than others. These are the countries often described as 'underdeveloped' or 'developing', though the use of these labels does not carry the implication that more 'mature' or 'advanced' economies, like the U.K. or U.S.A., have exhausted their potential for further growth. The United Nations Organization defines them as Africa (excluding South Africa), North and South America (excluding U.S.A. and Canada), Asia (including Cyprus but excluding Japan, China (mainland), North Korea, North Vietnam, Mongolia and Turkey), and Oceania (except Australia and New Zealand). The Organization for Economic Co-operation and Development has the same coverage in its definition, save for the inclusion of Greece, Spain, Yugoslavia and Turkey.

For each of these countries, the acceleration of the rate of growth of national output per head is today a major goal of economic policy. Their growth problems are also of concern to the more mature economies, which provide economic aid both bilaterally (i.e. from one country direct to another) and through various international agencies (Chapter 19). However, the countries listed above differ widely among themselves in the stability and maturity of their political institutions, in their level of economic development, in their social structure, and in their past achievements. It follows that it is both difficult and dangerous to treat their growth problems in general terms. Nonetheless, by confining our attention to the countries in the U.N. coverage, we may attempt an exploration of some difficulties which are common, in greater or lesser degree, to a large number of countries.

In comparison with the more mature economies, all these countries are characterized by a low ratio of fixed capital per head of working population. This suggests that the growth of output per head might be accelerated by additions to the *per capita* stock of social capital. If we do not at this point inquire too closely into the economic structure of the countries concerned, we might conclude that this calls for an increase in the rate of saving, which might free domestic resources for employment in capital production. Further, given that equipment must often be imported from abroad, an increase in saving might free resources for an expansion of exports. This in turn may increase export earnings, which would finance the purchase of equipment overseas. As a supplement to this self help, the import of capital goods might be financed by economic aid from other countries. Unless this took the form of a grant, such aid would necessitate an increase in export earnings in subsequent years, in order to finance the repayment of the loans (along with any interest they might carry).

These suggestions are, however, subject to some very important qualifications about the structure and functioning of these economies, and the particular path along which it is desired that a given economy should develop. Growth of income and the capital stock must not be confused with industrialization. It is clearly possible for a country to expand her output per head by specializing in the production of primary commodities, i.e. foodstuffs, raw materials and fuels. International trade will then enable it to procure a wide range of manufactured goods.

At the present time, in fact, the production of primary goods for domestic consumption and for export is the predominant activity of most of the underdeveloped countries. This suggests that the application of new capital resources to primary production would pay an immediate dividend, by increasing the volume available for export. Second, the development of existing agricultural and mining activities would carry with it the minimum economic and social dislocation, in contrast to a programme of industrialization. There are, however, major drawbacks to primary specialization.

First, the growing of crops or the working of mines may have, in some countries, overtones of 'colonial exploitation'. This would make them unattractive in comparison with industrialization, to which considerable prestige may be attached. Second, the world demand for primary commodities tends to be insensitive to price changes ('inelastic'), in which case an increase in output will depress actual export earnings. Further, demand or supply conditions may be subject to short run variations, leading to substantial fluctuations in export earnings. Third, it is impossible to forecast the long run trend of world demand for a given primary (or any other) commodity. In consequence, a change in tastes or the development of synthetic substitutes may, in years ahead, significantly reduce the demand for a commodity to the production of which a country has heavily committed her capital resources.

Many of the countries with a low income per head have only a rudimentary exchange economy. This presents a second group of difficulties for any proposal to accelerate growth by increasing savings, or by imports of capital financed by overseas assistance. Countries like Nigeria or Uganda, for example, have within their economies a large subsistence sector. This means that much of economic activity takes place within peasant communities, which very largely provide themselves for their own wants. The overall degree of specialization in these economies is accordingly low, with a correspondingly small volume (by mature standards) of domestic trade.

In these circumstances, any scheme for 'increasing savings' must be given its appropriate interpretation. Thus in some of the West African countries, the government has used the marketing boards as an instrument for achieving forced community 'savings'. These boards were established to market the export crop of peasant farmers, and to stabilize their incomes from year to year in the face of fluctuations in world commodity prices. However, by running a surplus over the years, the boards can 'save' on the farmers' behalf, placing the funds at the Government's disposal for the finance of capital projects.

In this latter case, the problem of harnessing the farmers' 'savings' to the finance of real investment does not arise. Otherwise, the undeveloped condition of capital markets may make this a considerable problem. Further, the employment of an increasing volume of labour on capital schemes—for example, road building, dam construction, railway building—calls for a progression from a subsistence economy to a market economy. The workers who are employed in those activities must be fed and clothed, which means that peasant farmers must produce at least part of their crop for a domestic market. They will, however, only have an incentive to do this if there are (durable?) consumer goods for them to buy with their newly acquired money incomes. It follows that the import of consumer goods may have a part to play in the fostering of the exchange economy, by helping provide economic incentives. The growth of an exchange economy, in turn, is necessary for the support of labour specializing in capital schemes.

A corollary of the increased use of capital equipment per head is, of course, the reorganization of methods of production and the achievement by the working population of appropriate technical and educational standards. This in turn requires the diversion of resources to the provision of education, either domestically or through the use of overseas earnings (or aid) to finance education abroad. Expenditure on education, therefore, may be regarded as a variety of capital investment, necessary if fixed capital is to be fully exploited.

A third sort of problem arises if, for a large sector of the population, national income per head is so low that an increase in savings could not be achieved without an impossible sacrifice. Suppose, however, that such a country received substantial economic aid from overseas, and assume that this did in fact enable an initial increase in income per head. This may prompt an increase in the rate of population growth, which will tend to bring income per head back to its former level. If any increase in output entails (sooner or later) a corresponding population increase, a *permanent* increase in income per head can never be achieved, which precludes the possibility of a permanent increase in saving. We are presented, accordingly, with a 'vicious circle', in which living standards are held down to a bare minimum[1] by the tendency for resultant population growth to offset any initial income increase.

It may be, however, that population growth will never rise above a certain percentage rate, however big the increase in income. Assume for the illustration that this maximum rate is 3 per cent per year. It follows that if, through overseas assistance, national income could be increased at a minimum rate of, say, 4 per cent over a number of years, then in each year output per head would rise. The annual increase in output per head would enable increasing positive savings, and a point would sooner or later be reached where the domestic investment corresponding to these savings was sufficient in itself to achieve a growth of output in excess of 3 per cent a year. The economy would then be launched on the path of self sustaining growth, and overseas economic aid could be withdrawn.

[1] Its usual description as a 'subsistence level' uses the word 'subsistence' to denote 'minimum living standards'. This is quite different from the earlier use of the word in the phrase 'subsistence sector'. The latter denotes a part of the economy in which peasant communities cater for their own needs, at what may indeed be a fairly high level of achievement.

Questions

1. Explain what is meant by the proposition that growth of real national product depends on the accumulation of capital.   U.L.

2. 'Wealth creates income. Income creates wealth.' Discuss.   J.M.B.

3. What is the National Capital? What factors determine the rate at which capital is accumulated in countries like Britain or America? J.M.B.

4. If the marginal product of capital is positive, does it follow that all investment, unless it is embarked upon in error, must increase the national income?   C.I.S.

5. 'It is more sensible to use all unemployed labour before trying to make the men and machines actually at work produce more.' Explain this statement.   C.I.S.

6. 'In a fully-employed economy a rise in investment requires a fall in consumption.' 'In an under-employed economy a rise in investment causes a rise in consumption.' Explain these statements and show whether they conflict with each other.   B.A. Gen.

7. What is meant by the statement that investment demands abstinence?   J.M.B.

8. 'The introduction of new machinery, while it may lead to higher national income, could also displace labour and cause unemployment.' Discuss.   U.L.

9. 'The quality of a country's labour force is much more important than its size in determining real income per head.' Discuss.   U.L.

10. Examine the effects of technical advance on the economic development of nations.   U.L.

11. Analyse the relationship between population growth and economic development.   W.J.E.C.

12. How is money national income calculated? Does money national income correspond exactly to the level of national welfare?   U.L.

13. Does an increase in real per capita income necessarily lead to an increase in welfare?   B.A. Gen.

14. Can a country have a high national income with a low standard of living?   A.E.B.

15. Define the national income. Since the United States has a national

income roughly eight times that of Britain, is there an equivalent difference in the two countries' national welfare?   S.U.J.B.

16. To what extent is the size of a country's national income a good indication of its economic prosperity?   S.U.J.B.

17. Define national income and explain fully its relationship to the standard of living of a country.   S.U.J.B.

18. What are the problems which arise in comparing the national incomes of two countries?   A.E.B.

19. Why do standards of living differ between economies?   J.M.B.

20. What are the main obstacles to economic development in the poorer countries of the world at the present time?   W.J.E.C.

21. 'The economic development of backward countries depends chiefly on their rate of industrialization.' Explain and discuss.   U.L.

22. How far is industrialization a necessary part of economic growth? Give examples.   U.L.

23. What are the main classes of information about which you would try to obtain knowledge before preparing an outline investment plan for a country in an early stage of economic development?   B.A. Gen.

Part four

Part four

16

Principles of International
Economic Relationships

ECONOMIC RELATIONSHIPS between the residents of different
countries form a complex pattern, and to identify some important
elements it is best to begin by exploring a few simple situations unclut-
tered by the detail and variety which characterize real-world economic
life. Significant relationships and concepts can then be discerned more
clearly, and subsequently used in the analysis of more realistic problems
of international economic affairs. This chapter proceeds, accordingly, by
inventing two economies (generally referred to as country A and country
B), each of which produces only two commodities, most easily described
as X and Y, which are the same in both countries. Initially the inhabitants of the two countries live in complete economic isolation, but
subsequently they start trading with each other, and it is with the
resultant interaction of the two economies that this chapter is concerned.
The picture that is built up in this way cannot, it is clear, be taken as a
literal representation of the real world, but it does contain much which
(to repeat) is helpful in getting to understand real-world situations and
problems.

1. *The Principle of Comparative Costs*

Consider, then, a world containing just two countries, A and B, both
of which produce just two commodities, X and Y, but nonetheless live
in complete economic isolation. In both countries, economic resources
(i.e. land, labour and capital) can be freely moved between X and Y
production, though such a shift carries different consequences in A
from B, for reasons considered later. If Y production is cut back by 1
unit per week in A, the resources freed can produce 2 more units of X.
In B, by contrast, the resources freed by reducing Y output by 1 unit are
capable of an extra 5 units of X. Conversely, reducing X production
by 1 unit raises Y output by $\frac{1}{2}$ unit in A, but only by $\frac{1}{5}$ unit in B. 'Units'

may be understood in terms of millions of tons, bushels, gallons, etc., according to the nature of commodities X and Y.

If all resources are fully employed, the production of 2 more X per week in A means giving up the opportunity to have 1Y: we may accordingly say that the 'opportunity cost' of 2X is 1Y, or of 1X is $\frac{1}{2}$Y. The opportunity cost of 1Y must, therefore, be 2X. In B, the opportunity cost of 1Y is 5X, and of 1X, $\frac{1}{5}$Y. The A's have a comparative advantage in Y production, in the sense that to get 1Y more they sacrifice only 2X while the B's need to sacrifice 5X. Put another way, the B's have a comparative advantage in X production, since they can get 5X more by giving up 1Y, while the A's get only 2X more if they give up 1Y.

A's biggest possible weekly output of X may be, say, 60 units, while devoting all her resources instead to Y production would yield 30 weekly units of Y. The corresponding limits for B are 100X and 20Y. Within these respective limits A and B can produce any intermediate combination of X and Y in accordance with the opportunity cost ratio in each country, i.e. for each unit reduction in Y output, A can produce 2 more X and B 5 more X. Some of the possible X and Y output combinations for each country are set out in Table 16.1.

TABLE 16.1

Production Possibilities in A and B
(units per week)

Country A	X	60	50	40	30	20	10	0
	Y	0	5	10	15	20	25	30
Country B	X	100	80	60	40	20	0	
	Y	0	4	8	12	16	20	

To understand how output and price may be determined in each country, it is necessary to make some assumption about market structure. Let us assume that in fact markets are highly competitive. This means, first, that production is carried on by a large number of small firms, so that no one firm can exercise a significant influence on prices; second, that firms are free to switch between X and Y production, as they choose; third, that all parts of the market are in perfect communication, so that in all transactions X and Y change hands on the same terms. Under these conditions, the quantities of X and Y produced in each country will depend on their relative popularity, while the equilibrium price at which they change hands will be governed by their opportunity costs. This price may, however, be temporarily disturbed by a change in relative popularity, in which case the reactions of firms to this disturbance will alter the ratio of X and Y output and lead to the restoration of the equilibrium price.

Thus suppose for the illustration that firms in A are currently producing 40 X and 10 Y per week, and that the price of Y in terms of X is in fact 1Y = 2X. Assume next that a rise in the popularity of Y relative to X raises the price at which Y changes hands in the market to 1Y = 3X. Firms in the X business now find it profitable to produce 1Y in place of every 2X they are capable of producing, since 1Y will exchange in the market for 3X. Y production therefore increases and X production declines, until the growing abundance of Y and the diminishing availability of X bring the terms of exchange in the market back to 1Y = 2X. This exchange ratio is reached, say, when X output has fallen to 30X and Y output increased to 15Y. With the exchange ratio once again at 1Y = 2X, no firm has any reason to switch between X and Y production. This price, accordingly, continues to hold in all exchanges until temporarily disturbed by any subsequent change in the pattern of demand.

As long, then, as A and B are living in economic isolation, X and Y change hands in A at the rate of 1Y = 2X (or 1X = $\frac{1}{2}$Y), and in B at the rate of 1Y = 5X (or 1X = $\frac{1}{5}$Y). Imagine now that the inhabitants of A and B abandon their policy of economic self-sufficiency, and open up their economies to the sale of each other's goods. In this case, countries A and B together will form one big market and, if transport costs are ignored, the same price for X and Y in terms of one another will rule throughout this market. This price will be determined by the relative popularity of X and Y in the joint A + B market, but cannot settle outside the limits given by each country's opportunity cost ratio.

Thus assume that the first price to establish itself in the joint market happens to be 1Y = 3X. At this rate, A firms will specialize exclusively in Y production, since for each unit of Y they could themselves produce only 2 units of X. B firms, on the other hand, would specialize exclusively in X production, as for each 3 units of X they could produce only $\frac{3}{5}$ unit of Y. Joint output by the two countries will therefore consist of all the Y that A is capable of producing (30Y per week) and all the X that B is capable of producing (100X per week).

Suppose next that X became rather more popular relative to Y. Previous reasoning suggests that the price of X would rise, say to 1Y = 2·5X. At this rate, B firms would continue to specialize exclusively in X production, while A firms are still better advised to produce Y rather than X. It follows that the pattern of total output would be unchanged at 30Y (from A) and 100X (from B). Suppose, however, that X became so popular relative to Y that the price of Y fell to 1Y = 1·5X. All B firms would continue to specialize in X, and A firms would also start switching from Y to X production! Their movement into X production would continue until the increased supply of X and reduced supply of Y had brought the price of Y up to $1Y = 2X$. In the outcome, B is completely specialized in X, but A is also producing some X—such is the popularity of X relative to Y.

To sum up, the equilibrium price of Y cannot be lower than $1Y = 2X$, in which case B will be specializing exclusively in X production but A will be producing both X and Y. Nor can it be higher than $1Y = 5X$, in which event A will be exclusively specialist in Y production while B produces both X and Y. If the price lies between these limits, A will be engaged solely in Y production, and B in X production. Whether the inhabitants of both A and B derive a gain from inter-nation trade depends upon this outcome. It can be shown that more X and Y becomes available in both countries if the price lies between the opportunity cost ratios, so that each country specializes exclusively in the commodity in which it has a relative advantage. However, if the pattern of demand (and so the equilibrium price) is such that only one country specializes, then the gain is limited to that country.

Before trade between the two countries begins, the inhabitants of A can have 2 more X only if they sacrifice 1Y, and the B's can have 1 more Y only at the sacrifice of 5X. Suppose that, on the establishment of trading relationships, the equilibrium price in the two-nation market settles at $1Y = 3X$. Then a movement of A's firms into Y production enables A inhabitants to secure 3X for each Y sold in the inter-nation market, which clearly represents a gain on the 2X sacrificed in domestic production for each unit expansion in Y output. Alternatively expressed, for each 2 units by which X production is contracted, Y production can be expanded by 1 unit, $\frac{2}{3}$ of which will purchase 2X in the inter-nation market. The inhabitants of B also benefit, since each unit contraction of their Y industry enables B firms produce 5 more X, 3 of which command 1Y in the two-nation market. Clearly, the nearer the equilibrium price is to the opportunity cost ratio in B, the smaller is the gain to the B's, and the bigger the gain to the A's. In the limit, had the equilibrium price settled at $1Y = 5X$, the inhabitants of B would have been no better off, while the A's would have derived the maximum benefit. Vice versa, if the price had settled at $1Y = 2X$.

This reasoning may be illustrated by picking two pre-trade output combinations for A and B from Table 16.1, and working out the consequences of complete or one-sided specialization. Suppose that, before trade begins, A is producing 40X and 10Y, B 40X and 12Y per week; and that, after trade, the price in the joint market is $1Y = 3X$. A firms are accordingly completely specialized in Y production with an output of 30Y and B firms completely specialized in X production with 100X. Since Y and X change hands at the rate of $1Y = 3X$, the inhabitants of A might between them export 15Y and import 45X in return from B. This means that the domestic availability of X and Y is now 45X and 15Y per week in A, and 55X and 15Y in B. Each country has clearly benefited. Alternatively, perhaps A exports 20Y for 60X, so that she enjoys 60X and 10Y domestically, while B enjoys 40X and 20Y: this also represents a mutual gain.

For a second example suppose that, before trade between the two countries, A is producing a weekly 50X and 5Y, while B is producing 60X and 8Y. When a joint market is established, the first price to emerge is, say, 1Y = 2·5X. All B firms accordingly start to switch to X production, and A firms to Y production. However, when Y output has reached 15 units in A (and so X output dropped to 30 units), the price of Y falls to 1Y = 2X. A firms accordingly have no incentive to expand Y output further, while the new price has no effect on the B firms' move to exclusive specialization. If A now exports 10 of her Y for 20X from B (i.e. 1Y for 2X), she is in exactly the same position as before trade, with 5Y and 50X (30X home produced and 20X imported). B, on the other hand, is 20X and 2Y to the good!

These ideas are conveniently summed up in the principle of comparative advantage or comparative costs. Where two countries (A and B) are both producing two commodities (X and Y) at differing opportunity costs, it is always possible to increase the joint output of the two commodities if each country moves resources into the field in which it has the relative advantage. Further, both economies enjoy a gain in the resultant trading relationship if each specializes exclusively, an outcome which depends upon the establishment in the joint market of a price intermediate between the respective opportunity cost ratios.

The law of comparative costs is a principle of quite general application. Thus suppose two neighbours, with differing capabilities as handymen, both want to put up an outhouse. For each 50 bricks laid, A could instead put up 2 feet and B 4 feet of shelving. There is a joint gain if they pool their efforts and B works on the shelves, A on the brick-laying. For example, A might lay 50 bricks for himself, then 50 for B, while B does 3 feet of shelving for A, then 5 feet for himself. Each enjoys a net gain of 1 foot of shelf!

2. Why Comparative Costs Differ

The significance for international trade of differences in opportunity cost makes it desirable to look at some of the reasons why these differences should arise. Consider, first, two countries, C and D, each of which has identical factor endowments of 100 units of labour and 100 units of capital, which are used to produce just two commodities, X and Y. The method of X production is the same in both countries, 1 unit of capital and 1 unit of labour producing 1 unit of output per week. The method of Y production in C has exactly the same requirements as X production, but to produce Y in D a less efficient method is used which takes up 2 units of capital and 2 units of labour for each weekly unit of output. Since capital and labour are always used in the same (here, equal) proportions to produce both commodities, it is legitimate to work in terms of a 'unit of resources' comprising one unit of each.

It is apparent that if C devotes her 100 units of resources exclusively to Y production she will have 100Y, or if exclusively to X production, 100X. If C cuts back Y production from 100 units to 80 units per week, she frees 20 units of resources which can produce 20X, and so on. The opportunity cost of 1X is therefore 1Y, and this ratio is the same at all levels of X and Y production. D's resources, on the other hand, will yield either 100X or 50Y. Moving 20 units of resources out of X into Y production reduces X output by 20 units and increases Y output by 10 units; opportunity cost is constant at 1Y for 2X.

In Y production, C enjoys an absolute advantage over D in that she can produce twice as much Y per unit of resources: in X production, both countries are equally efficient. Nonetheless, the difference in opportunity cost enables an increase in joint output if C moves resources from X into Y production and D from Y into X production. As C reduces her X output by 1 unit she can increase Y output by 1 unit, while D at the same time cutting back Y production by 1 unit achieves 2 more units of X. Before specialization, for example, C may produce 40X, 60Y, and D, 50X, 25Y; considered together 90X, 85Y. If demand conditions are such that both countries specialize completely, C will produce 100Y and D, 100X; considered together, 100X and 100Y—joint gain, 10X, 15Y. To sum up, both countries have identical endowments of the factors of production, and the difference in opportunity costs arises from a difference in the method of producing one commodity (Y). If D adopted the more efficient C method, the difference in comparative advantage—and the prospective gain from specialization—would disappear.

Consider, second, two countries, E and F, with different endowments of the factors of production. E has 100 units of capital, 50 units of labour, while F has 50 units of capital and 100 units of labour. Both countries use the same methods to produce X and Y, but X production calls for 1 unit of labour and 2 units of capital (per unit per week), while a weekly unit of Y output requires 2 units of labour and 1 unit of capital. This difference in the required factor proportions for the two goods now makes it impossible to work in terms of 'units of resources'.

On this information, it is apparent that E could produce either 50X (thereby using her 100 units of capital and 50 units of labour) or 25Y (using 50 units of labour but leaving 75 units of capital unemployed).

Reducing X output by 10 units from e.g. 50 to 40 units would free 10 units of labour and 20 units of capital, enabling an extra 5 units of Y to be produced. The opportunity cost of 1Y is thus 2X, and this is constant at all production levels. Similar reasoning will show that F can produce either 25X or 50Y, with a constant opportunity cost at 1Y for ½X. Joint output will be increased as E moves resources from Y into X and F from X into Y.

E can produce more X than F, and F more Y than E. Given the production methods used, this reflects the fact that E has more capital than F, and F has more labour than E. Accordingly, joint output is increased if E specializes in X, which is relatively 'capital intensive' in its production method (2 units of capital/1 unit of labour), while F specializes in Y, which is relatively 'labour intensive' (1 unit of capital/2 units of labour). This basis for specialization could be removed by the

TABLE 16.2

Country	Capital Stock Endowment	Labour Force Endowment	Maximum Possible Weekly Output X or Y	Opportunity Cost of 1X
G	120 units	40 units	40 units or 40 units	1Y
H	60 units	30 units	20 units or 30 units	1·5Y

growth of population, the accumulation of capital, or the adoption of different production methods.

Consider, finally, a situation in which one country, G, has both more labour and more capital than its neighbour, H. If the same methods of X and Y production are used in both countries, G will be able to produce both more X and more Y than H. Suppose now that the method of X production is more capital intensive than the method of Y production, and that, in relation to H, G has a bigger capital than labour endowment. G's relative advantage will then be greater in X production or, alternatively expressed, H's disadvantage will be smaller in Y production. This difference in comparative advantage may be exploited to increase joint output if G moves resources from Y into X production and H from X into Y production.

For example, 1 unit of X (per week) may require 3 units of capital and 1 unit of labour, and a weekly unit of Y 2 units of capital and 1 unit of labour. The method of producing X is more capital intensive than Y, and the method of producing Y is more labour intensive than X. The factor endowments of the two countries and their maximum potential outputs of X and Y are shown in Table 16.2.

G has twice as much capital as H, but only 1·33 times as much labour. This gives her a bigger lead in X production, which calls for relatively more capital to labour than Y. If in fact both countries are producing some X and some Y, joint output will increase as G moves resources into X and H into Y production. For the illustration, G may be producing 5 units of X and 35 units of Y, and H 4 units of X and 24 units of Y. If H gives up producing her 4X, she can produce 6Y instead, while at the same time G may increase X output to 10 units and cut back Y to 30 units. Joint gain, 1 unit X, 1 unit Y.

The reader may use the data in Table 16.2 to calculate the various combinations of X and Y that G and H are capable of producing on their own: switching resources, as indicated, will then always increase output. The figures for factor endowments, however, have been carefully chosen for maximum simplicity. Experiment with them will complicate the analysis, but will not upset the conclusions established.

3. *Exchange Rates under Competitive Conditions*

The economic systems discussed in Section 1 operated on simple barter principles, one commodity exchanging directly for another without the use of money as an intermediary to facilitate exchange. More realistically, however, each economy, A and B, may be supposed to have its own separate money supply, so that goods are sold for and prices expressed in (say) $'s in A and £'s in B. The results obtained in Section 1 still hold good, though the currency difference does introduce a complication into dealings between the nationals of A and B.

It is not possible to say just how much X and Y would cost in terms of £'s in B, or $'s in A, but it is possible to define their *relative* prices, both before and after trade between the two countries. Thus assume for the illustration that, at a time when the two countries are isolated, the price of a unit[1] of X is $5 in A and £1 in B. Since in A a firm can as readily produce 1Y as 2X, it follows that the price of 1Y in A must be $10 if the division of production between X and Y is currently in equilibrium. Similarly, the price of 1Y in B must be £5.

The difference in currencies, and the absence of any conversion rate between them, make it impossible to determine whether Y at $10 per unit in A is cheaper or dearer than Y at £5 per unit in B. It is apparent, nonetheless, that Y is five times dearer than X in B, but only twice as expensive in A; or, to look at it the other way, X is five times cheaper than Y in B, but only twice as cheap in A. This difference in the price relationships suggests that, on the commencement of trade between the

[1] A 'unit' in this and subsequent sections can be taken to represent one millionth part of the 'unit' defined on page 352.

two countries, A firms will seek to sell Y in B, and B firms will attempt to sell X in A. The situation will, however, be complicated by the need of any A firms which achieve sales in B to sell for $'s the £'s in which they are paid, while B firms will want correspondingly to sell their $ earnings for £'s. They have an obvious opportunity. Their dealings in the currencies of their two countries constitute a foreign exchange market, and the rate at which £'s and $'s change hands 'in' the market is the rate of exchange.

The rate of exchange may be expressed either as the price of $1 in terms of pounds or as the price of £1 in terms of dollars. If transport and exchange dealing costs are ignored, the £ price in B of any Y imported from A will depend upon its $ price in A (given at $10 a unit) and the rate of exchange. Likewise, the $ price in A of any X imported from B depends upon its £ price in B (given at £1 a unit) and the rate of

TABLE 16.3

Rate of exchange (i) or (ii)	Price of X in B	Price of B-produced X sold in A	Price of Y in A	Price of A-produced Y sold in B
$1 = 10s. or £1 = $2	£1	$2	$10	£5
$1 = 8s. or £1 = $2·5	£1	$2·5	$10	£4
$1 = 6s. 8d. or £1 = $3	£1	$3	$10	£3·33
$1 = 6s. or £1 = $3·33	£1	$3·33	$10	£3
$1 = 5s. or £1 = $4	£1	$4	$10	£2·5
$1 = 4s. or £1 = $5	£1	$5	$10	£2

exchange. Some possible exchange rates and corresponding X and Y prices are given in Table 16.3.

If the rate of exchange were £1 = $2, then X imported from B into A would sell there at $2 a unit, compared with the $5 a unit for domestically produced X. This would clearly prompt A firms to switch exclusively to Y production, given that a unit of Y can be produced in place of every 2 units of X, and can be sold at $10, or its sterling equivalent of £5. In B, on the other hand, imported Y would sell at the same price as the domestically produced commodity, i.e. £5 a unit, so that B firms, lacking an incentive to specialize in X, may be expected to continue with some Y production. An exchange rate of £1 = $2 accordingly implies specialization by A, but not by B. Similar reasoning suggests that, at a rate of £1 = $5, specialization will be achieved by B (in X), but not by A.

Specialization by one only of the two countries reflects the outstanding popularity of one commodity relative to the other, already discussed in non-monetary terms in Section 1. It may easily be deduced that, if the exchange rate lies between £1 = $2 and £1 = $5, the resultant pattern of prices in A and B will promote specialization by both countries. For example, at a rate of $1 = 6s. 8d. any A firm will find it more profitable to produce 1Y (selling price $10 or £3·33) rather than 2X, since 1X produced by a B firm will sell at $3 in A. Likewise, a B firm is better off selling 5X at £1 ($3) apiece, than 1Y at £3·33.

The rate of exchange which actually establishes itself will be an equilibrium rate, balancing the forces of supply of and demand for the two currencies in the foreign exchange market. These forces, in turn, are the expression of the demand in each country for imports from the other at the price which corresponds to the equilibrium exchange rate. Accordingly, by setting out the quantities each country would want to

TABLE 16.4

(1) Rate of Exchange	(2) Price of X imported from B	(3) Quantity of X Demanded (million units)	(4) $'s Offered (millions) (2) × (3)	(5) £'s Demanded (millions) £1 × (3)
£1 = $4	$4	50	200	50
£1 = $3·33	$3·33	54	180	54
£1 = $3	$3	56	168	56
£1 = $2·5	$2·5	60	150	60

import at various rates, it becomes possible to identify the equilibrium rate as that which equates the demand for and supply of each country's currency.

Table 16.4 (column 3) shows the amount of X that the inhabitants of A would want to buy at four different prices, each of which corresponds to a given rate of exchange applied to a constant sterling price of £1 per unit in B. The figures have been chosen on the assumption that, with money incomes and the domestic price of Y ($10) unchanged, the inhabitants of A would want to buy more X at lower prices. If the inhabitants of A themselves made their purchases in B, they would need to offer dollars for sale in the foreign exchange market, to acquire the sterling to pay the B sellers. If the B firms take the initiative in selling to A inhabitants, and accept dollars in payment, then they will sell dollars in the foreign exchange market to acquire their own currency. Either way, the consequence of A's importing X is that a supply of $'s seeking exchange into £'s comes onto the foreign exchange market.

TABLE 16.5

(1)	(2)	(3)	(4)	(5)
	Price of Y	Quantity of Y	£'s Offered	$'s Demanded
Rate of	imported	Demanded	(millions)	(millions)
Exchange	from A	(million units)	(2) × (3)	$10 × (3)
£1 = $4	£2·5	24	60	240
£1 = $3·33	£3	18	54	180
£1 = $3	£3·33	15	50	150
£1 = $2·5	£4	10	40	100

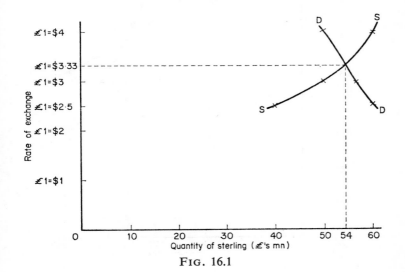

FIG. 16.1

A similar table may be constructed for country B (Table 16.5). Column 3 shows the demand in B for imports of Y, on the assumption that money incomes and the domestic price of X (£1) are constant. In B, of course, purchasers of Y who buy on their own initiative from A will offer sterling in the foreign exchange market to acquire dollars to pay their A suppliers, or A firms which export to B will want to repatriate their earnings by buying dollars in return for pounds.

A comparison of columns 4 and 5 in the two tables shows that the supply of pounds (or the demand for dollars) is brought into equality with the demand for pounds (or supply of dollars) at an exchange rate of £1 = $3·33. Were the rate higher, say £1 = $4, the excess of sterling offered (£60 million) over sterling demanded (£50 million) would push

the dollar price of sterling downwards. Were the rate lower, say
£1 = $2·5, the net excess of demand over supply (£20 million) would
push the exchange rate upwards. Only at £1 = $3·33 is the exchange
market in equilibrium. The argument may easily be illustrated diagrammatically.

In Fig. 16.1, the rate of exchange of £1 in terms of dollars is measured
on the vertical axis, while sterling is measured on the horizontal axis.

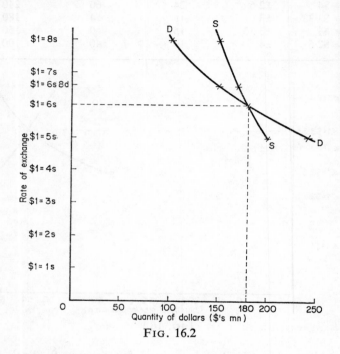

FIG. 16.2

The quantity of sterling offered at each exchange rate is plotted as a
supply curve of sterling, and the quantity of sterling demanded at each
rate is plotted as a demand curve for sterling. The intersection of the
two curves gives the equilibrium rate.

In Fig. 16.2, alternatively, the rate of exchange of $1 in terms of
pounds is measured on the vertical axis, and dollars are measured on the
horizontal axis. With the aid of column 1, Table 16.3, the quantity of
dollars offered at each exchange rate is plotted as a supply curve of
dollars, and a demand curve for dollars is similarly constructed. The
equilibrium rate is again given by the intersection of the two curves.

The position and slope of the supply and demand curves for currency reflect the underlying relationship between price and demand for the imported commodity. In country B, each fall in the price of Y (column 2, Table 16.5) results in a more than proportionate increase in demand (column 3): in this case, demand is considered sensitive to price changes, and is said to be 'elastic'. The consequence is that sterling expenditure on Y increases (column 4) with each price reduction, i.e. the supply of sterling increases with a rise in the value of the pound in terms of the dollar (column 1). The supply curve of sterling (Fig. 16.1) accordingly slopes upwards from left to right. In country A, by contrast, the demand for X is insensitive to price changes, or 'inelastic'. As the price falls (column 2, Table 16.4), so the quantity demanded increases, but less than proportionately. The dollar expenditure on X accordingly decreases as the dollar grows in value in relation to the pound (column 1), so that the supply curve of dollars (Fig. 16.2) slopes upwards from right to left.

The equilibrium rate of exchange not only balances the forces of supply and demand in the foreign exchange market; it also brings into equality the ratio of the prices of the two products in the two countries. The prices of X and Y both before and after trade are set out in Table 16.6.

TABLE 16.6

	Before inter-nation trade		After inter-nation trade	
	A	B	A	B
Price of X (per unit)	$5	£1	$3·33	£1
Price of Y (per unit)	$10	£5	$10	£3

With trade, A and B form one joint market for the sale of X and Y. When the market is in equilibrium, A firms will sell Y in B at their home price ($10) converted into £'s (£3) at the exchange rate (£1 = $3·33), and B firms sell X in A at their home price (£1) converted into $'s ($3·33) at the same exchange rate. It follows that the ratio of the price of Y to the price of X (here, 3 to 1) must necessarily be the same in both countries.

It also follows that the equilibrium exchange rate equalizes the price of X in A and B, and equalizes the price of Y in A and B. This means that £1 in B will buy 1 unit of X in B, or $3·33 on the foreign exchange market, which in turn would buy 1 unit of X in A. $1 in A will buy one-tenth of a unit of Y in A, or 6s. on the foreign exchange market, which would buy one-tenth of a unit of Y in B. The domestic purchasing power of the pound and the dollar are thus brought into parity, or equality, at the equilibrium exchange rate.

A change in the domestic purchasing power of one currency (i.e. a change in the general level of prices—Chapter 14) will take its effect upon the exchange rate, and not upon the price level in the other country. Thus if the general level of prices doubles in A, the value of the dollar will fall correspondingly in the exchange market: it will take twice as many dollars as before to buy £1. If the general price level fell by a half in A, the external value of the dollar would double.

Tables 16.7 and 16.8 illustrate the consequences for the external value of the dollar of an inflation in A which leads to a doubling of the domestic price level. The demand table for Y in B at certain sterling prices is already known (Table 16.5). Since the price of Y has doubled in

TABLE 16.7

(1)	(2)	(3)	(4)	(5)	(6)
			Quantity of		
		£ Price of Y	Y Demanded	£'s Offered	$'s Demanded
Rate of	Price of	imported	in B	(millions)	(millions)
Exchange	Y in A	from A	(million units)	(3) × (4)	(2) × (4)
£1 = $2·5	$20	£8	—	—	—
£1 = $3	$20	£6·66	—	—	—
£1 = $3·33	$20	£6	—	—	—
£1 = $4	$20	£5	—	—	—
£1 = $5	$20	£4	10	40	200
£1 = $6	$20	£3·33	15	50	300
£1 = $6·66	$20	£3	18	54	360
£1 = $8	$20	£2·5	24	60	480

A, it becomes necessary to calculate what exchange rates, applied to the new price of $20, would give these sterling prices for Y in B (Table 16.7).

The price of imported X has also, by definition, doubled in A. This means that, whereas before the inflation the inhabitants of A would pay $2·5 a unit for 60 million units of X (Table 16.4), they are now prepared to pay $5 a unit for the same quantity. Likewise, they are now willing to pay $6 a unit for 56 million units of X, and so on. The consequences are set out in Table 16.8.

A comparison of columns 5 and 6 in the two tables shows that equality in the demand for and supply of sterling (and dollars) is now achieved at an exchange rate of £1 = $6·66. The external value of the dollar has fallen by half, in that £1 will now buy twice as many dollars as before. The counterpart of this external depreciation of the dollar is thus an external appreciation of the pound. The price of X in B is (of course) unchanged at £1 a unit, while the price of Y, though $20 a unit in A, is unchanged in B since £1 now buys $6·66 on the foreign exchange market. The value of sterling offered and demanded is unchanged at £54 million, since sterling prices are unchanged. The value of dollars demanded and offered, however, has increased twofold from $180 million to $360 million. The results for the foreign exchange market may also be shown diagrammatically. In Fig. 16.3, DD and SS represent the demand and supply curves of Fig. 16.1, while the new supply and demand relationships are plotted as S_1S_1 and D_1D_1.

TABLE 16.8

(1)	(2)	(3)	(4)	(5)	(6)
			Quantity of		
		$ Price of	X Demanded	£'s Demanded	$'s Offered
Rate of	Price of	X imported	in A	(millions)	(millions)
Exchange	X in B	from B	(million units)	(2) × (4)	(3) × (4)
£1 = $2·5	£1	$2·5	—	—	—
£1 = $3	£1	$3	—	—	—
£1 = $3·33	£1	$3·33	—	—	—
£1 = $4	£1	$4	—	—	—
£1 = $5	£1	$5	60	60	300
£1 = $6	£1	$6	56	56	336
£1 = $6·66	£1	$6·66	54	54	360
£1 = $8	£1	$8	50	50	400

A change in the rate of exchange could also come about through a change in tastes in A and/or B, in which case relative prices will also undergo a change in both countries. Thus suppose Y became more popular relative to X in country B. For any given price of Y, accordingly, the inhabitants of B would want to buy more of it than previously, which would also mean that, with a given total expenditure, they would have to buy less of X. Since the demand for X and Y is unchanged in A, the net effect is that Y has become more popular and X less popular in the joint A + B market, which suggests that Y will rise in price relative to X.

The consequences in the foreign exchange market can be worked through with the aid of Table 16.9. At each price (column 2) the inhabitants of B would now like to buy more Y (3) than previously (Table 16.5), which means that at each corresponding exchange rate (1) they would offer more sterling (4) (or wish to buy more dollars (5)) in the foreign exchange market. However, at each given exchange rate the demand for sterling (or supply of dollars) is unchanged in A (Table 16.4). Accordingly, at a rate of £1 = $3·33, the supply of sterling (£72

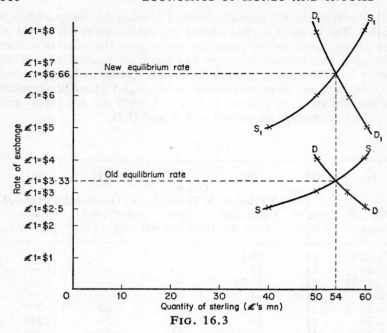

FIG. 16.3

million) exceeds the demand (£54 million), and the excess supply (£18 million) depresses the value of the £ in terms of the $. As the $ appreciates in value, so the price of X falls in A: quantity demanded increases (Table 16.4), and with it the amount of sterling demanded. A new equilibrium is achieved at £1 = \$2·5, at which rate the supply of and demand for sterling are equated at £60 million. This result is also shown diagrammatically in Fig. 16.4, where DD and SS have the same meaning as in Fig. 16.1, and S_1S_1 is derived from Table 16.9.

TABLE 16.9

(1) Rate of Exchange	(2) Price of Y imported from A	(3) Quantity of Y Demanded (million units)	(4) £'s Offered (millions) (2) × (3)	(5) \$'s Demanded (millions) \$10 × (3)
£1 = \$4	£2·5	30	75	300
£1 = \$3·33	£3	24	72	240
£1 = \$3	£3·33	21	70	210
£1 = \$2·5	£4	15	60	150

In the new equilibrium position, the price of X has fallen to $2·5 a unit in A while the price of Y has risen to £4 a unit in B. At the new prices, the inhabitants of B are in fact able to import less Y (15 million units) than previously (18 million units), while X consumption has increased in A from 54 to 60 million units.

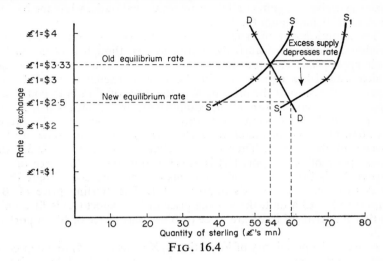

FIG. 16.4

4. The Terms of Trade in Competitive Conditions

The relationship between a country's export prices and her import prices is conveniently designated her 'terms of trade'. The relationship is easiest to demonstrate for a simple barter economy (such as A in Section 1), which trades only one commodity (Y) for a second commodity (X) produced by a second simple barter economy (B). The two countries together form a joint market for X and Y, and the rate at which Y exchanges for X throughout this market is determined by the relative popularity of X and Y (Section 1). It follows that, if the equilibrium price of 1Y is 3X, then this ratio also defines A's terms of trade with B, since A residents who export Y to B residents in return for imports of X will necessarily be doing so on these terms. The price of B's export (X) in terms of her import Y is $1X = \frac{1}{3}Y$, so that B's terms of trade are, of course, the inverse of A's.

Given the opportunity cost ratio for each country defined in Section 1, both countries enjoy a gain at these terms of trade (p. 354). If, however, Y became more popular relative to X, the price of Y would rise relative to X, e.g. to $1Y = 4X$, and A's terms of trade would 'improve' or become 'more favourable', while B's terms of trade 'deteriorate' or become 'less favourable'. An improvement in A's terms of trade in this situation means that A derives a greater gain from trade, while B's gain is correspondingly reduced. In the limit, if B's terms of trade deteriorate to her opportunity cost ratio of $1X = \frac{1}{5}Y$, then she derives no gain at all from international trade, while the benefit to A is at its maximum (p. 354).

The adoption of a monetary system by the two economies (compare Section 3) does not disturb these conclusions, though it does call for their appropriate re-expression in money terms. The rate of exchange which establishes equilibrium in the foreign exchange market also equalizes the ratio of the price of X to the price of Y in both countries. This is a necessary feature of the equilibrium, since it means that X and Y are traded on the same terms throughout the joint A + B market (p. 363). Once again, therefore, each country's terms of trade are the inverse of the other's. Thus if the exchange rate is £1 = $3·33, the dollar price of A's import (X) is $3·33 a unit, the dollar price of her export (Y) is $10 a unit, and A's terms of trade are accordingly Price of A's export/Price of A's import = 3/1. The sterling price of B's import (Y) is £3 a unit, the sterling price of her export (X) is £1 a unit, so that B's terms of trade are Price of B's export/Price of B's import = 1/3.

A rise in the popularity of Y relative to X leads (p. 365) to a depreciation of sterling (say to £1 = $2·5), and so a fall in the dollar price of A's import ($2·5 a unit) and a rise in the sterling price of B's import (£4 a unit). The decline in A's import price improves her terms of trade from 3/1 to 4/1 or, if the original terms of trade are represented by the index number 100, from 100 to 133·33. The rise in B's import price spells a deterioration in her terms of trade from 1/3 to 1/4 or, expressed as index numbers, from 100 to 75. The change in import prices leads A to increase and B to reduce quantities imported (p. 367), so that the improvement in her terms of trade confers a real gain on A and the matching deterioration imposes a real loss on B.

A change in the terms of trade may come about through a change in tastes, but not through a change in the absolute level of prices. Clearly, if prices (say) doubled in both countries, the price *ratios* of imports and exports would remain exactly the same. If the price level rose in one country only, e.g. doubling in A, this would be matched in a free exchange market by a corresponding depreciation of its currency (p. 364). Thus while their respective dollar prices would be doubled, the sterling prices of B's export and import would be unchanged.

5. The Balance of Payments and the Rate of Exchange

The export of goods by B residents to A residents for cash payment means that the former give up one sort of asset—the goods—in return for another of equivalent value—the dollars in which they are paid. Correspondingly, the import of goods by B residents means that they acquire one sort of asset (the goods imported) but lose another, the sterling they part with in payment. Each type of transaction has thus a twofold aspect, and this is clearly brought out by using the book-keeping technique of double-entry to record them in tabular form. Conventionally, the sale (export) of goods is shown as a 'credit' in the left-hand column of the account, while in the right-hand column the corresponding increase in money assets is entered as a 'debit'. Since a sale is recorded as a credit, it is necessary to enter a purchase (import) of goods as a debit in the right-hand column. This means, in turn, putting the matching 'decrease in money assets' as a credit in the left-hand column.

TABLE 16.10

International transactions planned by residents of B,
week beginning 19th February, 1968

Credit	£ million	Debit	£ million
Export of X to A	54	Increase in $ assets	54
Decrease in £ assets	54	Import of Y from A	54

Table 16.10 uses this double-entry method to present the international transactions which, at the start of a given week, the residents of B are proposing to undertake in the course of that week. Before assessing how their trading plans will work out, it is useful to re-arrange the information in Table 16.10 to form not one, but two accounts. The entries for exports and imports represent trading items, while the entries showing changes in money assets may be distinguished as monetary items. In Table 16.11, the trading items are separated into a current (or trading) account, and the monetary items into a monetary (sometimes called, capital) account. These two accounts form the planned 'balance of payments' of B residents with A residents at the start of a given week.

During the previous week's business (we may take it) the rate of exchange in the foreign exchange market was stable at £1 = $3·33, and B residents are assuming that this 'current' rate will rule in the week ahead. The dollar price of Y is $10 a unit and, at the corresponding sterling price of £3, B residents between them want (Table 16.5) to buy 18 million units of Y from A firms (1b). This means that they will need to part with £54 million to A exporters (2a). The sterling price of X is £1 a unit and, at the corresponding dollar price of $3·33, B firms anticipate (Table 16.4) selling 54 million units of X in A (1a). Their anticipated earnings are accordingly $180 million—worth £54 million (2b) at the current exchange rate.

B's planned balance of payments is clearly in balance in the sense that the total of credit entries in the left-hand column equals the total of debit entries in the right-hand column. This is an automatic balance, reflecting the construction of the account on a double-entry principle:

TABLE 16.11

B's Planned Balance of Payments with A,
week beginning 19th February, 1968

Credit	£ million	Debit	£ million
1. *Current Account*			
(a) Export of X	54	(b) Import of Y	54
Balance on current account : 0			
2. *Monetary Account*			
(a) Decrease in £ assets	54	(b) Increase in $ assets	54
Net change in money assets : 0			

each credit entry made is matched by an equal debit entry, and vice versa. More interesting, B's planned balance of payments is in balance in the sense that it is entirely consistent with the current equilibrium of the foreign exchange market. As these proposed transactions are put into effect during the course of the week, so B exporters acquire (overall) $180 million which are sold for the £54 million earnings of the A exporters at a rate of £1 = $3·33. This, however, is exactly the rate which must rule in the market if B residents are fully to carry through their import and export plans. B's *actual* balance of payments, recording the transactions which have taken place in the week ending 24th February, will thus be a replica of Table 16.11.

B's planned balance of payments may, however, be in disequilibrium in the sense that the planned level of imports and of exports is not consistent with the current equilibrium of the foreign exchange market. In this case, the attempt by B residents to put their plans into execution will cause a change in the exchange rate, and so in relative prices. The change in relative prices will lead them to modify their plans, and the import and export levels actually achieved will be such as to equate the supply of and demand for the two currencies at the new exchange rate. The actual balance of payments will thus diverge from the planned, and will reflect the new equilibrium in the exchange market.

For example, in consequence of a rise in the popularity of Y relative to X B residents might plan, at the start of a given week, to increase their imports of Y to 24 million units, at a total sterling value of £72 million (Table 16.9). B firms have no reason to alter their estimates of forthcoming X sales in A, so that the planned balance of payments will show a deficit of £18 million on current account (Table 16.12). This deficit represents, in the foreign exchange market, a potential excess supply of sterling at the current exchange rate of £1 = $3·33 (compare

TABLE 16.12

*B's Planned Balance of Payments with A,
week beginning 26th February, 1968*

Credit	£ million	Debit	£ million
1. *Current Account*			
(a) Export of X	54	(b) Import of Y	72
Balance on current account:	−18		
2. *Monetary Account*			
(a) Decrease in £ assets	72	(b) Increase in $ assets	54
Net change in money assets:	−18		

Fig. 16.4). The £ accordingly depreciates, relative prices alter, and B residents change their plans. Changed trading plans, in turn, mean changed currency requirements, and a new equilibrium rate is established which equates the supply of and demand for sterling. Following Fig. 16.4, this rate is £1 = $2·5, at which the sterling value of B's imports and exports are equal at £60 million (Table 16.13).

To sum up, as long as economic relationships between A and B are limited to trading relationships conducted in competitive conditions, the actual value of imports for any given period must always equal the actual value of exports. This equality is a simple expression of the fact that, at the equilibrium exchange rate, the quantity of sterling offered must necessarily have equalled the quantity demanded. Planned imports and exports may, of course, diverge in value, in which case it is a movement in the exchange rate which effects reconciliation via the change in relative prices and the consequential adjustment of trading plans.

In the real world, however, economic relationships are not confined to simple trading activities, in which goods are sold for cash payment and the foreign currency proceeds immediately converted into domestic currency. Thus exporters may be paid in cash but find it convenient to hold some balances in account with the banks in the country in which they do business, or perhaps invest short-term in securities there. Or they may sell their exports on credit terms, so that they acquire not cash but a claim upon the foreign importer. Further, residents of one country may wish to buy securities or other interest-yielding assets in countries overseas, for example, because of a higher level of interest rates or greater political stability than at home. All these 'capital movements' can be written up in a country's balance of payments, and illus-

TABLE 16.13

B's Actual Balance of Payments with A, week ending 2nd March, 1968

Credit	£ million	Debit	£ million
1. Current Account			
(a) Export of X	60	(b) Import of Y	60
Balance on current account:	0		
2. Monetary Account			
(a) Decrease in £ assets	60	(b) Increase in $ assets	60
Net change in money assets:	0		

trations of the necessary credit and debit entries will be found in the following pages and in the next chapter.

A capital movement may serve to counter-balance a disequilibrium in a country's planned balance of payments on current account, which will mean that import and export plans otherwise inconsistent at the current exchange rate will in fact be carried through. If, however, equilibrium is to be preserved in this way, there will need to be an equivalent increase in domestic saving in the country proposing to make the overseas 'investment'.

Thus suppose that, at the start of a given week, some A residents are planning to buy £18 million worth of securities in B during the week ahead, and hold them beyond the end of that week. Assume, second, that A residents in general are planning to reduce purchases of Y by 6 million units during the forthcoming week. This means cutting their domestic expenditure—or increasing their saving—by $60 million. Assume, third, that with the exchange rate currently at £1 = $3·33, B residents are simultaneously planning to import £72 million worth of Y from A, and export £54 million worth of X (compare Table 16.12). Table 16.14 sets out B's planned balance of payments for the week.

A capital account is introduced in Table 16.14, and the purchase of bonds by A residents (2a) is enterered as a *credit*. This is because the sale of the bonds by B residents (2a) is analogous to the export of goods (1a) in its exchange market consequences: both result in a dollar demand for sterling. If the B residents are paid in dollars, their dollar assets increase correspondingly (3c), and during the week they will sell $60 million and B exporters $180 million on the foreign exchange market. If on the other hand the B sellers of securities are paid in sterling, then it is the A purchasers who sell $60 million, which comes to the same thing. In this second case, however, the counter-entry to 2a would be, not 3c, but a deduction of £18 million from 3a.

TABLE 16.14

B's Planned Balance of Payments with A, week beginning 26th February, 1968

Credit	£ million	Debit	£ million
1. *Current Account*			
(a) Export of X	54	(b) Import of Y	72
Deficit on current account:	18		
2. *Capital Account*			
(a) Purchase of bonds by A			
residents	18		
Surplus on capital account:	18		
3. *Monetary Account*			
(a) Decrease in £ assets (1b)	72	(b) Increase in $ assets	
		(1a)	54
		(c) Increase in $ assets	
		(2a)	18
Balance on monetary account:	0		

It is clear that B's planned balance of payments is quite consistent with the current equilibrium exchange rate of £1 = $3·33, in that $240 million will change hands for £72 million. B's actual balance of payments for the week ending 2nd March will accordingly be a replica of Table 16.14. B may be said to enjoy an 'inflow of capital' (2a), so that her deficit on current account is 'financed' by her surplus on capital account. Item 2a might also be described as 'Private investment (by A) in B', though the term 'investment' is also used to denote the surplus of A's exports over her imports (Section 6).

It is, of course, quite incidental that A's investment in B took the form of a bond purchase. Thus having sold £72 million worth of Y in B, A exporters might decide for the time being to hold £18 million of their sterling earnings in account with banks in B. Accordingly, in the

N

week under review, they sell only £54 million on the foreign exchange market, which exchanges for $180 million (B's export earnings) at £1 = $3·33. Conventionally, the acquisition of bank balances in this way is regarded as a short-term investment, and the transaction is entered up in the monetary account. With the capital account deleted, the monetary account for the week ending 2nd March would read:

Credit	£ million	Debit	£ million
2. *Monetary Account*			
(a) Decrease in £ assets (1b)	72	(b) Increase in $ assets (1a)	54
Increase in £ liabilities due externally: 18			

The entry 'increase in sterling liabilities due externally' represents the fact that A residents are now the holders of £18 million worth of bank balances in B.

In this example, the movement of capital from A to B coincided with a reduction in A residents' own domestic expenditure on Y. This second decision made it possible for B to expand her imports without creating any excess demand for Y, while the first decision served to match up the supply of and demand for the two currencies in the foreign exchange market. Both the foreign exchange market and the markets for X and Y were accordingly in equilibrium. A decision to invest overseas, however, may not be paralleled either by a domestic decision to increase savings or by a decision overseas to increase imports. In these circumstances, the new position of apparent equilibrium for the exchange rate will in fact be inconsistent with equilibrium in the trading markets.

Thus suppose that, at the start of the week, B's planned imports and exports are given by Table 16.11. In addition, B residents are planning to use previously idle sterling balances to buy (say) £6 million worth of securities in A. It is apparent that, during the course of the week, the supply of sterling will exceed the demand at the current exchange rate (£1 = $3·33), and sterling will depreciate. When it has reached £1 = $3, the quantity of Y which B residents want to import will have fallen to 15 million units at £3·33 each (Table 16.5): they accordingly offer on the exchange market a total of £56 million, i.e. £50 million to buy Y plus £6 million to buy securities. Correspondingly, the amount of X that A residents want to import (Table 16.4) will have increased to 56 million units, and they offer $168 million to buy £56 million on the foreign exchange market.

It was explained in Section 3 that the ratio of the price of Y to the price of X reflects the relative demand for the two commodities in the joint A + B market. When this market was initially in equilibrium, Y was three times the price of X, as given by the exchange rate of £1 = $3·33. The relative popularity of X and Y in the joint market has not changed, and yet the price ratio given by the new 'equilibrium' exchange rate puts Y at 3·33 times the price of X. Two conclusions follow. The first is that the joint market for X and Y will not be in equilibrium at the new set of prices, which suggests a change in import and export levels and thus a further change in the exchange rate. Second and more generally, unless the conditions previously defined are satisfied, international capital movements mean that the balance of payments on current account is not automatically kept in balance through variations in the rate of exchange.

6. *The Balance of Payments and the Level of Economic Activity*

The interaction and adjustment of two economies has, so far, been explained purely as a process of achieving equilibrium in the markets for commodities and in the foreign exchange market. Disturbance to this equilibrium has been caused (Section 3) either by a change in the price level in one country, or by a fall in demand for one commodity matched by an increase in demand for the other. A new equilibrium has been reached by a change in the relative value of the two currencies in the foreign exchange market, accompanied in the second case by a change in relative prices within each country. There has been a tacit assumption that aggregate demand in each economy kept at a stable level, which (by implication) was sufficient to maintain full employment of its resources. The possibility that this might not be the case was, however, foreshadowed towards the end of Section 5.

This micro-economic (p. 216) approach thus serves to focus attention on only one set of problems in the process of inter-nation adjustment. Other problems arise from variations in the level of aggregate demand and its constituents, and their analysis requires the use of the macro-economic theory developed in Part III. The significance of exports and imports in the flow of income-generating expenditure has in fact already been outlined in Chapter 11, and this section will simply apply those conclusions more explicitly to the problem of inter-nation adjustment.

Table 16.15 sets out a given week's final expenditure in economies A and B, broken down into the categories appropriate for income analysis (compare Table 9.2). It is assumed that, in the week under review, the equilibrium rate of exchange was £1 = $3·33, and that A exported 18 million units of Y to B at a dollar price of $10 a unit, while B exported 54 million units of X to A at a sterling price of £1 a unit.

Both economies enjoyed full employment, which means that A produced a further 12 million units of Y for domestic sale, and B likewise a further 46 million units of X (see Table 16.1 and footnote, p. 358). For simplicity, domestic investment in each economy is limited to the purchase by firms of part of the output of the home-produced good, so that households' consumption expenditure absorbs the remainder of home production and all the imported commodity. For convenience,

TABLE 16.15

A's National Expenditure
Week I

	$mn.
1. Consumers' expenditure (8mn. Y, $10; 54mn. X, $3·33)	260
2. Domestic net investment (4mn. Y, $10)	40
3. Total domestic expenditure	300
4. *Less* Imports (54mn. X, $3·33)	180
5. *Plus* Exports (18mn. Y, $10)	180
6. Net National Income	300

B's National Expenditure
Week I

	£mn.
1. Consumers' expenditure (26mn. X, £1; 18mn. Y, £3)	80
2. Domestic net investment (20 mn. X, £1)	20
3. Total domestic expenditure	100
4. *Less* Imports (18mn. Y, £3)	54
5. *Plus* Exports (54mn. X, £1)	54
6. Net National Income	100

actual quantities bought and prices paid in each category are shown in brackets.

As a first exercise, the problem presented on p. 372 may be reconsidered explicitly in income terms. Suppose that, at the start of Week II, households in A decide to reduce their consumption spending to $200 million. This they plan to achieve entirely by cutting down their consumption of Y to $20 million. At the same time, households in B are planning to increase their consumption of the imported good Y from £54 million to £72 million. Table 16.16 shows that, at the end of the week, national income remains unchanged in both countries. In A the decline in domestic consumption spending has been offset by the increased value of her exports to B. In B the increased consumption spending has been directed exclusively at imports from A, which means that national expenditure (comprising domestic consumption spending, domestic investment and exports) is unchanged.

The excess of A's exports over imports represents, of course, a surplus

TABLE 16.16

A's National Expenditure
Week II

	$mn.
1. Consumers' expenditure (2mn. Y, $10; 54mn. X, $3·33)	200
2. Domestic net investment (4mn. Y, $10)	40
3. Total domestic expenditure	240
4. *Less* Imports (54mn. X, $3·33)	180
5. *Plus* Exports (24mn. Y, $10)	240
6. Net National Income	300

B's National Expenditure Week II

	£mn.
1. Consumers' expenditure (26mn. X, £1; 24mn. Y, £3)	98
2. Domestic net investment (20mn. X, £1)	20
3. Total domestic expenditure	118
4. *Less* Imports (24mn. Y, £3)	72
5. *Plus* (Exports (54mn. X, £1)	54
6. Net National Income	100

on her current account with B (Table 16.17). This excess may be termed 'net investment by A in B' (though the same expression may be applied to the corresponding financial transaction, say a bond purchase, which has preserved the rate of exchange in equilibrium at £1 = $3·33). It is apparent that this overseas investment by A is able to generate income within A in the same way as domestic investment by A firms (compare p. 247). A's overseas investment has also made it possible for B's consumption and domestic investment expenditure together to absorb £18 million worth of goods more than the value of her national product.

This excess represents the sum by which B's exports fall short of her imports, and might be described as B's 'external disinvestment'.

Table 16.15 will also serve as a starting-point from which to investigate the repercussions of an initial fall in income in one of the two countries. To keep this problem within manageable limits, two important assumptions must be made. First, any prospective imbalance in the current account is always exactly offset by counter capital movements: the rate of exchange thus remains stable at £1 = \$3·33. Second, any change in income has no effect on relative prices or the general

TABLE 16.17

A's Balance of Payments with B
Week II

Credit	\$ million	Debit	\$ million
1. *Current Account*			
(a) Export of Y	240	(b) Import of X	180
Surplus on current account:	60		
2. *Capital Account*			
		(a) Purchase of bonds from B residents	60
Deficit on capital account:	60		
3. *Monetary Account*			
(a) Decrease in \$ assets (1b)	180	(c) Increase in £ assets (1a)	240
(b) Decrease in \$ assets (2a)	60		
Balance on monetary account:	0		

level of prices in either country. Suppose now that, in each country, the average and the marginal propensity to consume have an identical value, which is the same at all levels of income (compare p. 226) and therefore calculable from the data in the table. These properties are likewise assumed for the marginal and the average propensity to import (Chapter 11). In A, therefore, A.P.C. = M.P.C. = 13/15, and A.P.M. = M.P.M. = 3/5; in B, A.P.C. = M.P.C. = 4/5, and A.P.M. = M.P.M. = 27/50. Each country's national income (Y) is equal to the sum of final income-generating expenditure. In the notation of Chapter 11,

$$Y = C + I + X - M.$$

Accordingly, in the week recorded in Table 16.15,

$$Y_A = 260 + 40 + 180 - 180 = 300 \text{ (\$mn.)}$$
$$Y_B = 80 + 20 + 54 - 54 = 100 \text{ (£mn.)}$$

Assume now that, at the start of some subsequent week, firms in B decide to reduce their domestic investment expenditure to £10 million per week. If B's exports could be assumed constant, the ultimate fall in B's income may be calculated by the multiplier formula

$$\frac{1}{\text{M.P.S.} + \text{M.P.M.}}$$

(p. 251). This is $\frac{1}{1/5 + 27/50}$, or $100/74 = 1.35$. B's national income thus falls by (1.35×10) £ million, from £100 million to £86.5 million. Imports are maintained at $27/50$ the level of current national income, which means accordingly a decline (£7.3 million) from £54 million to $\frac{27}{50} \times 86.5 = £46.7$ million.

B's imports are, of course, A's exports so that, in dollar terms, A's exports will have fallen from $180 million to ($46.7 \times 3.33$) $ million, or $155.5 million. This fall of $24.5 million in income-generating expenditure in A will, through the multiplier process, induce a more than proportionate fall in A's national income. A's imports will thus decline to $\frac{3}{5}$ of the new, and lower, income level. A's imports are, however, B's exports, so that the earlier assumption that B's exports remain unchanged is, in fact, not warrantable. The decline in B's exports will induce a more than proportionate decline in B's national income, which will once again affect A's national income through the associated decline in B's imports (i.e. A's exports). This 'feedback' effect from one economy to the other will get smaller and smaller since, at each stage, the decline in imports is a constant proportion of a fall in income which is itself smaller than the income decline at the previous stage. Ultimately both economies reach a new equilibrium level of income, which is lower than that suggested by the multiplier formula $\frac{1}{\text{M.P.S.} + \text{M.P.M.}}$, in consequence of the induced fall in export demand (compare p. 252).

We may now attempt to assess the significance of these income changes for each country's balance of payments. Since the two economies have in each case different values for the marginal propensity to save and the marginal propensity to import, there is no reason to suppose that income has declined in each country by the same percentage. Thus in A income may have fallen by 28 per cent to $217 million per week; in B, income may have fallen by 34 per cent, to £66 million per week. If each country's imports bear a constant ratio to national income, it follows that, in this example, A's imports will stand at $\frac{3}{5} \times 217 = $130 million per week, while B's imports are $\frac{27}{50} \times 66$ or £36 million per week. Valued at an exchange rate of £1 = $3.33, B's exports are thus worth £39 million, and A's exports $120 million.

In the original equilibrium situation, each country's current account was exactly in balance at an exchange rate of £1 = $3·33 (Table 16.15). The change in income (initiated by a fall in B's domestic investment) has led to a surplus on B's current account and a corresponding deficit on A's current account. If, therefore, the exchange market is to remain in equilibrium, inhabitants of B must be willing to accumulate claims in A at the rate of £3 million ($10 million) per week.

7. *Limitations on a Free Market Analysis*

The analysis of the first five sections suggests that, if they develop free trading relationships with each other, countries will specialize according to comparative advantage (Section 1), trading their products internationally at prices which, within defined limits, are determined mutually with the rate of exchange by underlying demand conditions (Sections 3 and 5). A comparison of price ratios with what they were (more realistically, might be) in the absence of international trade then provides a measure of each country's gain from foreign trade (Section 4). While this analysis affords important insights, its results need modification or may be upset when capital movements are brought into the picture (Section 5). Further, the level of imports, exports and the rate of exchange are also influenced by economic forces more appropriately analysed in terms of income flows (Section 6) than the establishment of price/output equilibrium in product markets. These matters have already been considered, and it is necessary finally to specify three further limitations on the use of the price analysis developed in the earlier sections.

First, the assumption that in both countries (A and B) opportunity cost is constant at all production levels represents the simplest but least realistic way of dealing with the problem of costs. Within the limits set by each country's opportunity cost ratio, a change in demand in the joint market effects a change in relative prices without the complication of any reaction from the supply side, as each country's resources remain completely specialized. To bring the theory closer to the real world means recognizing that the opportunity cost may vary continuously as output of one good increases and the other diminishes. In this event a change in demand will react back upon supply through the change in price, and the new equilibrium will reflect both the changed demand and the changed cost conditions. Supply conditions, accordingly, can be expected in reality to play a more active part in determining the equilibrium values of price and output than that assigned by a theory in which opportunity costs are assumed constant.

Second, markets in the real world will seldom satisfy the rigorous conditions of perfect competition defined on p. 352, which makes it very unlikely that conclusions obtained within a perfectly competitive framework will emerge in the real world with the same starkness and simplicity. It is, indeed, conceivable that the pattern of prices established under imperfectly competitive conditions may lead to a flow of trade in the reverse direction from that suggested by the principle of comparative advantage. By way of example, suppose that in country B the production possibilities are those defined in Section 1, and that markets are perfectly competitive. While they are living in economic isolation, B inhabitants buy 19 million units of Y per week at a price of £5 each, and 5 million units of X per week at £1 each—an output pattern which accurately reflects the relative popularity of X and Y. In A, on the other hand, the production possibilities defined in Section 1 would be available if resources were able to move freely between X and Y production. In fact, the supply of Y is exclusively in the hands of the firms already established in the Y industry, and firms in the X industry are prevented from switching resources into Y production whatever its relative profitability. The maximum output of which the Y industry is capable may be taken at 10 million units a week which sell—since Y is particularly popular—at a price of $18 each. Firms in X production manufacture 40 million units per week, selling at a unit price of $3.

It is apparent that Y is six times the price of X in A, and only five times in B. When accordingly trading ventures are essayed between the two, it should, for example, be profitable (ignore transport costs) for B firms to sell Y in A and finance purchase of X for home sale with the proceeds, i.e. we might expect a flow of X from A to B and of Y from B to A. For brevity, we proceed to what appears to be the only possible equilibrium in this example, which depends on certain assumptions about demand conditions in A and B. Suppose that the inhabitants of A would be quite prepared to buy 1 million more units of Y at $18 each, if they become available. Suppose, too, that at a price of £5/6 a unit, B inhabitants would wish to purchase 6 million units of X. We may now envisage that B firms specialize exclusively in Y, producing a weekly 19 million units for home consumption and 1 million units for export to A, where they will sell at $18 each. A inhabitants reduce their expenditure on X by $18 million per week, i.e. from $120 million ($3 × 40 million) to $102 million ($3 × 34 million), which prompts A firms engaged in X production to sell their 'surplus' 6 million X in B at a price (by assumption) of £5/6 a unit.

A firms thus earn £5 million per week, which they sell on the foreign exchange market for the $18 million the B exporters have for disposal. This puts the exchange rate at £1 = $3·6, which equalizes the price ratio between the two countries, and appears to restrict the gain from trade to B. It must be recognized, however, that A inhabitants may feel themselves better off since they now absorb 11 million units per week of the popular Y commodity (of which 10 million units are still home-produced), compared with the previous level of 10 million units which the monopolization of the home industry set at a maximum. Of course, had the Y industry been competitive, the price of Y would have been only twice that of X; the country could have specialized exclusively in Y production; and much more striking gains would have been available.

Finally, it must be recognized that the price (and income) analysis of this chapter has paid no regard to government economic policy. In reality, of course, governments may exercise a direct influence upon the volume and prices of imports and exports; the flow of capital into and out of the country; currency dealings between its own and overseas residents; and the rate of exchange ruling in the foreign exchange market. Its policy in these fields may be partly shaped by its membership of international organizations and its subscription to international agreements. It is to an examination of these issues that we turn in the following three chapters.

Questions

1. Under what conditions would two persons:
    (a) exchange possessions if they have exactly the same quantities of the same range of goods?
    (b) specialize in the production of two commodities X and Y when both of them can produce both commodities?   I.M.T.A.

2. 'The reasons for specialization between individuals are essentially the same as the reasons for international trade.' Discuss.   U.L.

3. What are the gains to be had from trade between economies producing the same range of products and how do they arise?
                                                                        J.M.B.

4. 'If one country is more efficient than another in all fields of production, no trade between them is possible.' Discuss.   J.M.B.

5. 'International trade takes place because each country is differently endowed with resources.' 'International trade takes place because comparative costs of production differ amongst countries.' Are these explanations contradictory? Explain your answer.   U.L.

6. In Malanesia a unit of resources will produce either 100 yards of cloth or 20 units of steel. In Indolaysia a unit of resources will produce 90 yards of cloth or 15 units of steel. Explain the effects of international trade on production of each of the commodities in each country.   U.L.

7. The following data refer to the labour costs of production (measured in man days) of certain commodities in two countries.

	Commodities						
Country	Wheat	Oats	Beef	Mutton	Wool	Iron	Steel
A	25	30	40	40	50	150	110
B	15	15	35	30	40	100	50

(a) Explain whether trade is possible between country A and country B? If so, state which three commodities country A is most likely to export to B.

(b) Discuss the factors other than labour costs which are likely to affect the possibility of trade between these two countries. J.M.B.

8. 'International trade takes place because of differences in comparative costs.' 'International trade takes place because of differences in prices.' Reconcile these statements. U.L.

9. Show how differences in comparative costs between two countries may make it profitable for importers and exporters in each country to buy from and sell to the other country. U.L.

10. Explain the relationship, in a free market for foreign exchange, between exchange rates and domestic and foreign price levels.
S.U.J.B.

11. How far is it true to say that, in a situation of free exchange-rates, if the cost of living in a country rises the exchange rate of its currency will fall? B.Sc.(Econ.)

12. Discuss the inter-connections between the level of domestic employment and the balance of payments. W.J.E.C.

13. Discuss the proposition that the economic effects of a rise in exports are equivalent to those of a similar rise in investment.
B.Sc.(Econ.)

14. Would you expect an expansion of exports to relieve or increase inflationary pressure within the exporting country? C.I.S.

17

The British Balance of Payments: (I) Structure and Content

1. *A Fixed Exchange Rate*

At any given time firms, private persons and Government departments in the U.K. will be planning to buy or sell (or give away!) goods or services abroad, or engage in capital transactions with overseas residents. In some cases, alternatively, the initiative will rest with overseas residents who are planning trade and capital deals with U.K. residents. Either way, some (but not all—Section 2) of these transactions will give rise to a sterling demand for foreign currencies in the foreign exchange market, and a demand for sterling among the holders of foreign currencies. Accordingly, if the Government did not intervene in the market, the rate of exchange would be determined from day to day solely by the interaction of currency supply and demand on business account, as explained in Chapter 16.

That chapter also showed, however, that in certain circumstances (p. 375) a freely floating or 'flexible' exchange rate might be rendered less stable by short-term capital movements. Instability of the exchange rate could, in turn, discourage international trade and (long-term) investment, as the parties to the various transactions would be less sure of the home currency values of their prospective payments or receipts. Historically, this particular sort of difficulty had not confronted the U.K. monetary authorities (i.e. Bank of England and Treasury) in the years before 1931 as, except for a period of war-time emergency (1914–1925), the country had participated in the international 'gold standard' system, which provided a mechanism for narrowly restricting exchange rate fluctuations (Chapter 19). U.K. abandonment of that system in September, 1931, prompted the authorities in the following year to adopt a new technique for stabilizing the rate of exchange.

A stabilization fund was established, in the form of an account held by the Government at the Bank of England, under the control of the Treasury but operated on its behalf by the Bank itself. This account, named the Exchange Equalization Account, was equipped at first with sterling assets only, from which sales of sterling could be made in the foreign exchange market whenever a temporary shortage of sterling relative to foreign currencies threatened an undue appreciation of sterling. Sales of sterling, of course, meant purchases of foreign currencies, and in this way the Account built up foreign currency holdings which it could subsequently use to buy sterling whenever a temporary glut of sterling relative to foreign currencies threatened an undue depreciation of sterling. The foreign currency assets of the Account were strengthened, in September, 1939, by the transfer from the Issue Department to the Account of nearly all the gold the Bank had, until then, been holding as part of the backing for the note issue (Chapter 4): gold is, of course, readily saleable for national currencies throughout the (non-communist) world.

The establishment of the International Monetary Fund (Chapter 19) in 1945 placed upon the U.K., as a member, the obligation to maintain the value of sterling within narrow limits either side of the parity agreed with the Fund (Chapter 19). In terms of U.S. dollars the parity first chosen valued sterling at £1 = \$4·03, but subsequently the parity was twice reduced, first to £1 = \$2·8 in September, 1949, and second to £1 = \$2·4 in November, 1967. The machinery by which the U.K. Government could meet this obligation to stabilize the external value of sterling lay, of course, to hand in the Exchange Equalization Account.

Let us take the currently agreed rate (£1 = \$2·4) for illustration. If an excess of sterling supply over demand in exchange dealings pushes the value of the pound down towards the lower limit[1] of £1 = \$2·38, the Bank will sell foreign currency from the Account to absorb the excess sterling or, alternatively viewed, make more foreign currency available in the market. It can do this, of course, only while the Account has stocks of—or access to—foreign currencies and gold, but this problem is taken up in Chapters 18 and 19. Alternatively, if an excess demand for sterling is drawing the exchange value of the pound towards the upper limit[1] of £1 = \$2·42, the Bank will sell sterling from the Account to absorb the excess supply of foreign currency, i.e. make more sterling available in the market.

The analysis of Chapter 16 was developed in a context of freely competitive markets, in which (Section 5) the rate of exchange was determined solely by the interaction of currency supply and demand on business account. The fact that the rate is stabilized around a fixed level must call, therefore, for some modification of the conclusions derived from a free-market analysis. In particular, it will be necessary to reconsider the conditions of balance of payments 'equilibrium', and the

[1] These are the limits to which, in practice, the authorities work under an agreement made with other European monetary authorities.

international implications of changes in one country's price level. These problems are, however, best held over until Chapter 18, to follow this chapter's review of the U.K. balance of payments structure and contents.

2. Composition of the Balance of Payments

Table 17.1 sets out the general balance of payments of the United Kingdom for 1968, i.e. it forms a record of all transactions between United Kingdom and overseas residents which took place in that year, expressed in sterling values. The information for the table is derived from a variety of sources, notably Customs returns for commodity imports and exports, banking statistics for monetary movements, official statistics, and inquiries undertaken by, especially, the Board of

TABLE 17.1

General Balance of Payments of the United Kingdom, 1968

			£ million
1. CURRENT ACCOUNT			
(a) Imports (f.o.b.)			6,910
(b) Exports and re-exports (f.o.b.)			6,233
		Visible balance	−677
Invisibles			
(c) Shipping	Debits		895
	Credits		956
(d) Civil aviation	Debits		213
	Credits		233
(e) Travel	Debits		271
	Credits		282
(f) Other services	Debits		421
	Credits		862
(g) Interest, profits, dividends	Debits		754
	Credits		1,173
(h) Government	Debits		506
	Credits		44
(i) Private transfers	Debits		225
	Credits		147
Total invisibles	Debits		3,285
	Credits		3,697
		Invisible balance	+412
CURRENT BALANCE			−265

2. LONG-TERM CAPITAL ACCOUNT

(a) Loans made by the U.K. government (less repayments)	−60
(b) Loans made to the U.K. government (less repayments)	+54
(c) Other U.K. official long-term capital (net)	+27
(d) Private investment abroad (net)	−736
(e) Private investment in the U.K. (net)	+573
BALANCE OF LONG-TERM CAPITAL	−142
BALANCE OF CURRENT AND LONG-TERM CAPITAL TRANSACTIONS	−407
BALANCING ITEM	−130

3. MONETARY MOVEMENTS

(a) Net change in external liabilities in sterling	+166
(b) Net change in liabilities in other currencies:	
(i) overseas sterling area currencies	−46
(ii) non-sterling currencies	+53
(c) Net miscellaneous capital	−24
(d) Change in account with I.M.F.	+525
(e) Gold and convertible currency reserves	+114
(f) E.E.A. loss on forwards	−251
BALANCE OF MONETARY MOVEMENTS	+537

Note: + denotes a credit entry, and − a debit entry. In the long-term capital and monetary accounts, a − sign denotes an *increase* in U.K. assets (or decrease in liabilities), and a + sign denotes a *decrease* in U.K. assets (or increase in liabilities). See text.

Source: United Kingdom Balance of Payments, 1969

Trade. This diversity means that, while the table is based on the double-entry principle, it is not for the most part possible to build it up step by step with a succession of entries and counter-entries (as was done in Section 5, Chapter 16). Instead, most pieces of information are entered separately in the double-entry framework, and the underlying pattern of relationships must then be deduced by the standard rules of the double-entry system.

Except where necessary to explain the significance of certain entries, discussion of these underlying relationships is held over until Sections 3 and 4. This section is, therefore, largely concerned with the meaning of each item, and its particular status as a debit or credit entry. From the use of the system in Chapter 16, it will be apparent that a sale of goods by a British to an overseas resident (i.e. an export) is entered as a credit, while the purchase of goods from foreign residents by British residents (i.e. imports) is entered as a debit. Instead of goods, the British resident might have sold the foreigner his IOU, and this sale would also have been entered as a credit. The IOU would give the foreign purchaser interest and captial redemption rights against the British resident, so that U.K. liabilities due externally have risen (equivalent to a *net* decrease in U.K. assets overseas). By extension, therefore, the acquisition by foreign residents of capital rights of any sort against British residents is entered as a credit (compare p. 373). This requires, in turn, a debit entry for the acquisition by British residents of capital rights on foreign residents, signifying an increase in U.K. assets overseas (or a *net* decrease in liabilities).

One important consequence of the method used to construct Table 17.1 is that, since the statistics are neither complete or (in some cases) fully reliable, the accounts will not (except accidentally) achieve that automatic balance which follows when each entry (debit or credit) has been individually matched with its own counter-entry (p. 370). Only if the statistical coverage and reliability were complete would the total of credit entries in the table necessarily equal the total of debit entries. An adjustment is accordingly made for the statistical inaccuracy by entering a 'balancing item' of appropriate value and sign. Thus if total debits exceeded total credits, the difference would give the value of the balancing item, which would be entered as a credit $(+)$; and vice versa. Since 1962 the balancing item has been positive in three years, and negative in four. While its value has varied quite widely from year to year, its annual average value (1962–68) was only— £4 million.

The first part of the current account gives a record of the U.K.'s 'visible trade', so called because it comprises imports, exports and re-exports of physical (hence visible!) commodities. The difference between them is termed the 'visible balance' or the 'balance of (visible) trade'. The valuation of the goods excludes the freight charges incurred in getting them from their port or airfield of origin, and the cost of insurance while in transit. In commercial terms, the goods are said to be valued 'free on board', i.e. the seller's price includes the cost of getting the goods (say) on board ship in the harbour of origin, but freight and insurance charges from that point on are met by the buyer. If the seller's price included a quotation for this freight and insurance, it would be described as c.i.f., i.e. cost (of the goods), insurance and freight.

It is, of course, possible to make an export by selling a foreign resident not a commodity but a service. Thus a British shipping firm may lease a vessel to an American who wants to transport goods from Zanzibar to Panama. In this event the British firm has exported (i.e. provided an overseas resident with) a service, by placing the vessel at his disposal for a given period in return for payment. In the same fashion, a British airline which carries foreign residents on its flights is exporting a service, while British residents who travel on foreign airlines are importing a service. The use of British ships to carry British exports overseas represents, in itself, an invisible export. While the British exporter may charter the vessel, the freight is effectively paid by his foreign customer who (in this case) is charged a c.i.f. price. These freight charges are not, of course, included in 1b, since exports are valued f.o.b. in the table. On the other hand, a British importer who charters a U.K. vessel to import his goods is neither importing nor exporting a shipping service, since he is dealing with another British resident and would, of course, have paid his foreign supplier an f.o.b. price.

The first two items in the second part of the current account thus represent imports (debits) and exports (credits) of shipping and aviation services—which are, of course, invisible! Holiday and business trips overseas by British residents entail purchases of services, etc., from foreign residents, which are accordingly entered as debits under 'Travel'. Vice versa, holidays, etc., spent in Britain by overseas residents represent invisible exports, and are entered as a credit. 'Other services' gives the value of a variety of miscellaneous transactions, such as the international sale or rental of film and television rights, the grant of licences under foreign patents, the underwriting of insurance risks in other countries, and so on. The provision of these services by British to foreign residents corresponds to the preceding 'invisible exports', and is accordingly entered as a credit. Vice versa, the provision of these services to British residents by foreigners resembles an import, and is entered as a debit.

British residents who own assets in other countries (company shares, foreign government securities, etc.) are, in a sense, providing overseas residents with a service by having placed their capital at the latter's disposal. The provision of this service is analogous to an export, and its annual value—as measured by the overseas residents' dividend and similar obligations—is therefore entered as a credit (1g). On the same principles, the interest and similar obligations of British to foreign residents is entered as a debit, since it represents the worth of the service provided for British residents by overseas residents through the latter's employment of their capital here.

Government transactions under 1h fall into two categories, though the two are not shown separately in the statistics in Table 17.1. The first comprises trading transactions, in which the Government buys goods and services from or sells them to overseas residents. Thus the Government purchases supplies overseas for the upkeep of embassies, foreign-based armies, and so on. These purchases are a form of import, and are entered as debits. Corresponding to exports, on the other hand, and hence a credit entry, is the Government's sale of services and other supplies to, for instance, American forces based in the U.K.

The nature of the second sort of entry under 1h is best explained with an example. Suppose the Government gives a grant in sterling to the government of a developing country, with the condition that it must be spent on British goods. The goods subsequently bought and exported appear as a credit under 1b, but there will be no corresponding debit entry in the capital or monetary account. It is necessary, therefore, to enter the value of the grant as a debit under 1h, to provide an offset for the previous credit entry in accordance with the double-entry principle. This sort of debit entry under 1h is known as a transfer payment, since the Government is transferring (giving) purchasing power to the developing country without any *quid pro quo*. The biggest item among the Government's transfer payments is, in fact, grants by way of aid to developing countries.

The same principle underlies 1i, Private transfers, which cover a variety of transactions between private residents in the U.K. and overseas residents undertaken without a *quid pro quo*. Thus a British resident may make a gift of, say, a valuable painting to a friend overseas. This will appear initially as a credit under exports (1b) and is subsequently offset as a debit under 1i. A gift of goods by an overseas to a British resident would appear first as a debit under imports (1a), and then be offset as a credit under 1i. A cash payment to a British resident from an overseas source, such as a legacy or a pension, first figures (in principle) as a debit under (3) Monetary Movements (Section 4), and an offsetting credit entry is made under 1i.

The invisible balance is struck as the difference between total invisible debits and total invisible credits. Its addition to the visible balance gives the overall balance on current account.

Loans by the U.K. government (2a) are long-term and almost all by way of economic aid to developing countries. They are entered as a debit, since they represent the acquisition of claims by the British government on overseas governments. It should go without saying that loans differ from grants (above) in that loans are repayable (generally with interest) whereas grants are not. The loan figure (2a) is stated net of capital repayments on former loans. Loans to the British government under 2b consist entirely of £98 million lent (in dollars) by the American authorities to buy certain U.S. military equipment, repayable by instalments over seven years. It is entered as a credit item (since here a foreign government is acquiring a claim on the British government), but is in some part offset by £44 million worth of U.K. repayments on previous loans from overseas governments (including earlier loans for U.S. military purchases).

'Other official long-term capital (net)' is typically a debit entry, largely representing capital contributions to international agencies like the International Development Association (Chapter 19), which lend to developing countries, and loans by the Government's own Commonwealth Development Corporation. The credit entry under 2c for 1968 is exceptional, and reflects a small loan and a loan repayment to the Government. Subscriptions to bodies like the United Nations, it may be noted, are not capital contributions but transfer payments designed to meet running expenses, and accordingly figure in the current account under 1h.

'Private investment abroad' (2d) falls into two main categories: portfolio and direct. The first denotes the (net) purchase by U.K. residents of the securities of overseas governments, corporations and companies. Direct investment denotes the acquisition of claims by U.K. companies against associated companies, subsidiaries or branches overseas. By either method the acquisition by British residents of claims on foreign residents makes this a debit entry.

U.K. companies may invest directly overseas by taking up more shares or debentures in the associated or subsidiary company, or through an increase in the associate's (etc.) net indebtedness to the parent company in the inter-company accounts. Thus the associate may purchase equipment in the U.K. (a credit entry under 1b), which is paid for by the parent, to which the overseas associate accordingly becomes indebted (a debit entry under 2d). Profit retention by associates or subsidiaries also gives rise to overseas investment by U.K. parent companies, since each parent's 'claim' upon the overseas company is increased by the value of its share of the retained profits. The credit entry under 1g already includes the value of these unremitted profits, thus forming the counterpart to this element within 'Private investment abroad'.

'Private investment in the U.K.' (2e) takes exactly the same forms as 2d, though here—since overseas residents acquire claims on British residents—the appropriate entry is a credit.

The third account records the acquisition of short-term financial assets, and the movements of funds to finance current or long-term capital transactions. Entered under 3a is the acquisition of claims, payable in sterling,[1] on British residents by overseas residents in two principal ways. First, commercial banks and other firms resident overseas may increase the working balances they hold with London banks, or increase their short-term lending to British finance companies and local authorities. Second, overseas central banks may take up more U.K. Treasury bills or (short-dated) Government stock, either to increase their working and other balances held in sterling or to provide short-term financial assistance to the U.K. Government (Chapter 18). On the other hand, British banks acquire sterling claims on overseas residents when, for example, a London bank gives an overseas resident an advance in sterling, or accepts a bill of exchange in sterling on behalf of an overseas resident.

[1] See, however, p. 428.

In 1968, the total sterling claims (of the sorts indicated) held by overseas residents on British residents rose by £452 million or, alternatively expressed, U.K. residents' liabilities due overseas or 'externally' increased by this amount. At the same time, the claims of British banks on foreign residents rose by £286 million so that, on balance, U.K. external liabilities in sterling went up by £166 million. This net acquisition of claims worth £166 million on British residents by foreign residents is, of course, entered as a credit.

Some claims against and liabilities due to overseas residents are expressed in currencies other than sterling, and net changes in their value are given in 3b. A distinction is drawn between liabilities and claims (i) expressed in the currencies of the overseas sterling area, and those (ii) expressed in the currencies of other countries (conveniently designated 'non-sterling currencies'). The overseas sterling area denotes a group of countries—many of which are Commonwealth members—with close financial associations with the U.K. Its significance and precise coverage is considered in Chapter 19. The first entry under 3b shows the net change in British banks' liabilities which are due to overseas residents in overseas sterling area currencies. Thus British banks may build up their working balances with banks in Australia (a sterling area member), thereby increasing U.K. claims on overseas residents due in an overseas sterling area currency. On the other hand, overseas residents may make deposits with U.K. banks denominated in overseas sterling area currencies, which will increase the latter's liabilities due overseas under this head. In 1968, liabilities of U.K. banks in these currencies fell by £20 million while their claims rose by £26 million. This net increase in U.K. banks' assets held overseas is accordingly entered as a debit, since it represents an increase in the claims of U.K. residents on overseas residents.

Liabilities and claims in non-sterling currencies fall into two categories. The first comprises official liabilities to overseas central banks for foreign currency deposits placed at the disposal of the British monetary authorities, explained in Chapter 18. The second denotes the liabilities and claims of British banks on overseas residents outside the sterling area. This covers, for instance, the working balances British banks hold in dollars, deutschemark, etc., in account with banks in New York, West Germany, etc. More significant, however, are the sums deposited with them in non-sterling currencies (very largely U.S. dollars) by overseas residents, which the banks mostly 'on-lend' to the residents of other countries in need of dollar finance. The U.K. banks mainly active in this 'Euro-currency' market (Section 4) are the merchant banks and London offices of overseas banks (Chapter 2).

Foreign currency deposits placed with U.K. banks represent an increase in their liabilities due overseas, while loans they give (or balances they acquire) overseas mean an increase in their claims against overseas residents. In 1968 the banks' liabilities increased more than their claims by £35 million, which ranks as a credit entry. The figure given in 3b (ii) is, however, £53 million, which means that in the same year the U.K. authorities increased their liabilities to overseas central banks by fresh borrowing under this head to' the value of £18 million.

The entries so far considered in this account reflect the dealings of the U.K. banking system (including the Bank of England) with overseas residents, though for convenience changes in the sterling liabilities of U.K. finance houses and local authorities are also included in 3a. It is apparent, however, that business firms in the U.K. may have financial dealings directly with banks and other firms overseas without involving a U.K. bank, and the net outcome of these transactions is included under 3c, Net miscellaneous capital.

Thus firms in the U.K. may reduce or increase balances in account with overseas banks as, for example, they buy or sell goods overseas. Further, U.K. exporters may extend short-term credit to overseas customers, and importers here may enjoy credit terms from their foreign suppliers. The outcome of these and similar transactions over the year is summed up under 3c. If U.K. firms grant more trade credit overall than they receive and/or increase their overseas balances, this means a net increase in their claims against (or a net decrease in their liabilities to) overseas residents—hence a debit entry. If, on the other hand, they are net recipients of trade credit, etc., liabilities due overseas increase, which requires a credit entry. The figure under 3c excludes changes in credit between parent and subsidiary company (or branch) and associated companies here and overseas. It would not be practicable to disentangle this information from the long-term changes in inter-company indebtedness with which it is included in 2d and 2e. Further, changes in certain official balances held in non-sterling currencies are also included under 3c, to avoid confusing them with 3e.

Item 3d mainly records foreign currency drawings by the British Government from the International Monetary Fund, or repayment to the Fund of previous drawings. Fresh drawings from the I.M.F. increase the Government's liabilities to an overseas institution, and accordingly rank as a credit entry. Repayment to the Fund reduces the Government's liabilities due overseas, hence a debit entry. The role of the I.M.F. and the significance of the Government's dealings with it are considered in Chapter 19.

The 'reserves' of 3e are the official reserves of gold and foreign currencies—notably U.S. dollars—which can be freely[1] sold (hence 'convertible') for other currencies in the foreign exchange markets of

[1] Further explained in Chapter 19.

the world. These holdings of gold, foreign currencies and foreign currency securities form part of the assets of the Exchange Equalization Account, the remainder comprising sterling and sterling securities. It will be recalled from Section 1 that, to keep the exchange value of sterling centred on the I.M.F.-approved parity, the Bank of England will sell foreign currency from the Account to prevent an undue sterling depreciation, and buy foreign currency for the Account to prevent an undue sterling appreciation. The sale of foreign currency (or gold) from the Account represents a fall in U.K. claims on foreign residents, hence a credit entry; the purchase of gold or foreign currency adds to U.K. claims on foreign residents, hence a debit entry.

Until quite recently the official reserves were supplemented by a portfolio of U.S. securities held by the Treasury since, in 1940, it had used war-time emergency powers to buy a substantial part of the U.S. securities in private hands in the U.K. A part of the portfolio was sold off in February, 1966, and the remainder in November, 1967, the foreign currency proceeds being incorporated in the official reserves.

The final entry (3f) is exceptional, and reflects the loss suffered by the Exchange Equalization Account on its 'forward exchange' commitments in consequence of the sterling devaluation of November, 1967 (Section 1). As explained in Chapter 18, Section 5, the Bank of England may at times use the resources of the Account to make sales of foreign currency for delivery at a future date, but at an exchange rate agreed when the contract is initially made. A devaluation of the pound before these forward contracts have been discharged then means that the Account sells the foreign currency to the people concerned on more favourable terms than they would have got by dealing at the new official parity. This implies a loss for the E.E.A., which has been included with all the other operations of the Account to give the overall figure for the year which emerges in 3e. Item 3f forms the corresponding counter-entry to this loss; it may be defined as the reduction in the E.E.A.'s foreign currency liabilities following the Bank's discharge of its forward exchange obligations.

3. *Analysis (I): the Finance of Trade*

The next task is to explore the relationships which underlie the debit and credit entries of Table 17.1, and to link them, where appropriate, with the workings of the foreign exchange market. The network of relationships is highly complex, and the task is made easier by building up a simplified representation of Table 17.1 in two distinct stages, using the formal double-entry method employed in Chapter 16, with imaginary figures to give a complete coverage.

Table 17.2 provides the first stage in the exercise, focusing attention exclusively on U.K. trade with the rest of the world in goods and services

TABLE 17.2

Credit	£ million	Debit	£ million
1. CURRENT ACCOUNT			
(a) Exports and re-exports		(e) Imports (f.o.b.)	51
(f.o.b.)	50	(f) Transport	2
(b) Transport	5	(g) Travel	2
(c) Travel	1	(h) Private gifts	1
(d) Private gifts	2	(i) Government purchases	4
		(j) Government grants	1
CURRENT BALANCE —3			
2. LONG-TERM CAPITAL ACCOUNT			
(a) Loans to U.K.		(c) Loans by U.K.	
Government	1	Government	3
(b) Investment in U.K.		(d) Investment in overseas	
subsidiaries, etc.	2	subsidiaries, etc.	1
BALANCE ON LONG-TERM CAPITAL ACCOUNT —1			
3. MONETARY MOVEMENTS			
(a) Increase in trade credit		(e) Increase in trade credit	
extended to U.K. firms	2	extended by U.K. firms	3
(b) Net decrease in foreign			
currency balances	1		
(c) Net increase in sterling			
liabilities	2		
(d) Decrease in official			
reserves	2		
BALANCE ON MONETARY MOVEMENTS +4			

(for the illustration—shipping, civil aviation, travel), and the ways in which this trade is financed. It accordingly provides a hypothetical and partial balance of payments for the U.K. for a given year. Since the problem of statistical coverage and reliability does not arise, there is, of course, no 'balancing item'. Small values have been chosen, partly for simplicity and partly to emphasize that the figures are quite imaginary.

During the year, the economy exported goods worth £50 million (1a), and provided foreign residents with transport and tourist services to the value of £6 million (1b + 1c). Of these goods and services, customers in developing countries bought £1 million with the aid of Government grants (1j), and £3 million by drawing on Government loans restricted to purchases in the U.K. (2c). A further £1 million worth of goods was taken by the overseas associates, subsidiaries and branches of U.K. companies. The latter paid for the goods, and their increased claim on their foreign associates etc., is entered under 2d. £1 million worth of goods was also sent abroad as private gifts (1h). Over the year, trade credit extended by British firms to their overseas customers increased by £3 million (3e), which means that receipts over the year were £3 million less than the value of the year's exports (1a + 1b + 1c) simply because overseas customers were given time to pay. The total of debit entries so far listed is £9 million, which leaves the finance of £47 million worth of exports (goods and services) to be explained.

The economy's imports of goods on private account (1e) totalled £51 million, and purchases of services a further £4 million (1f + 1g). The Government also bought goods and services worth £4 million from overseas residents, so that total imports of goods and services came to £59 million. Of these, £2 million worth came as gifts to British from foreign residents (1d), while the Government was able to buy £1 million worth with a loan from a foreign government (2a). The British-based subsidiaries, etc., of foreign companies bought £2 million worth of goods abroad, which were paid for by their foreign parents, leading to an increase in U.K. (private sector) indebtedness overseas of £2 million (2b). Trade credit extended by foreign suppliers to U.K. firms rose by £2 million (3a), which means that payments over the year were £2 million less than the value of the year's imports (1e + 1f + 1g + 1i) simply because U.K. importers were given time to pay by overseas suppliers. Total credits so far amount to £7 million, which leaves the finance of £52 million worth of imports (goods and services) to be explained.

At this stage, we consider how, in principle, U.K. firms may make payment to and receive payment from their customers overseas. For simplicity, it is easiest to ignore methods involving recourse to bank credit (as, in general, would the bill of exchange). A U.K. exporter may be paid by his overseas customer in three different ways. First, the latter may pay in his own (or another foreign) currency, thereby increasing the foreign currency balances held by the U.K. exporter, or by the U.K. exporter's bank (to whom he may have sold his foreign currency earnings in return for a sterling balance at home). Second, if the overseas customer holds a working balance in account with a London bank, he may instruct the bank to make payment from his account. Third, his own bank overseas may arrange payment on his behalf, out of the balance the foreign bank itself keeps in account with a London bank. In either case, there is a reduction in the sterling liabilities of U.K. banks to overseas residents.

British importers pay for their purchases overseas in an analogous fashion. They may pay in sterling, thereby increasing the sterling balances held in account with British banks by the overseas suppliers (or by the latter's own banks overseas). Alternatively, if the British importer holds a working balance in account with a bank located overseas, he may instruct the bank to make payment from his account. Finally, his own bank in this country may arrange payment on his behalf, out of the balance it keeps in account with a bank located overseas.

It will be recalled that we have still to explain the finance of £47 million worth of exports and £52 million worth of imports. These are the goods and services which were paid for during the year in foreign currency or in sterling, in the ways just described. In many cases, of course, banks (and sometimes firms) will be able to match up their payments with receipts, and thereby maintain overseas balances at an appropriate and roughly even level. Thus a London bank may acquire a foreign currency balance when one of its U.K. customers is paid for an export, and use these funds shortly afterwards to finance an import payment on behalf of another U.K. customer. Or an overseas firm may increase its balance in account with a London bank when it is paid by a U.K. importer, and may subsequently draw on these funds to finance its own purchases in the U.K.

However, in order to give the illustration precise numerical values, we shall ignore these arrangements and assume that all sterling and foreign currency requirements are satisfied through the foreign exchange market. This means that overseas firms and banks which deplete their sterling balances (having paid in sterling for U.K. exports) will, after a few transactions, usually want to build them up again to their customary level. This they can do by selling their own (or another) currency for sterling in the foreign exchange market. They are joined by U.K. exporters and banks who have received payments in foreign currencies, and now want to convert them into sterling. Since £47 million worth of U.K. exports have been paid for in these two ways, the resultant foreign currency demand for sterling will be £47 million, provided that firms and banks in aggregate maintain their working balances at a constant level.

In the same way, British banks (and firms) which deplete their foreign currency balances (having paid in foreign currencies for U.K. imports) will, after a few transactions, usually want to bring them back up to their normal level. To do this they need to sell sterling for the appropriate foreign currencies in the foreign exchange market. They are joined by overseas firms and banks who have been paid in sterling, and now want to convert it into foreign currencies. Since £52 million worth of U.K. imports were paid for in these two ways, the resultant sterling demand for foreign currencies will be £52 million, provided that banks and firms in aggregate maintain their working balances at a constant level.

Table 17.2, however, shows that these important provisos are not satisfied. Entry 3b records a net decrease of £1 million in the foreign currency balances of U.K. banks and firms. This means that British banks and firms decided, in aggregate, that their working balances held in foreign currencies were inappropriately high, and accordingly—on balance over the year—repatriated £1 million worth by, say, selling the equivalent sum for sterling. On the other hand, entry 3c indicates a net increase in sterling liabilities of £2 million, which represents the size of the increase in working balances held in sterling by foreign residents. Overseas firms and banks must, therefore, have decided in aggregate that their sterling holdings were inappropriately low, and—on balance over the year—increased the level by, say, not repatriating £2 million worth of their sterling earnings.

To present the *net* outcome in the foreign exchange market for the year, it is appropriate to calculate the foreign currency demand for sterling as £48 million (£47 m. + £1 m.), and the sterling demand for foreign currency as £50 million (£52 m. − £2 m.). These figures are, however, limited to the demand for and supply of sterling on private or business account (including the commercial needs of the U.K. Government under 1i). For the complete picture, accordingly, it is necessary to summarize the year's operations of the Exchange Equalization Account. Table 17.2 shows a decrease in the official reserves of gold and foreign currencies of £2 million. This means that, over the year, the Exchange Equalization Account was a net seller of £2 million worth of foreign currency on the foreign exchange market, thereby bringing the foreign currency demand for sterling to £50 million.

Retrospectively, therefore, it may be said that of £52 million worth of imports, £47 million were financed by export earnings, £1 million by running down the foreign currency balances of U.K. banks and firms, £2 million by increased sterling (bank account) liabilities to foreign residents, and £2 million by a fall in the official gold and foreign currency reserves.

While the Exchange Equalization Account emerges over the whole year as a net seller of foreign currencies, it is clearly not possible from the balance of payments table to chart its operations day by day during the course of the year. Thus there may have been occasions when the Account was a net buyer of foreign currencies, say at times when payments to British exporters were particularly heavy, or payments for imports were lagging. Again, while on balance over the year foreign residents increased their sterling holdings by £2 million, there may well have been times during the year when working balances were hastily run down (Chapter 18). In this case the Account would have sold considerably more than the £2 million worth of foreign currency recorded in Table 17.2, only to recoup its sales later on when these balances were rebuilt. Any fluctuations of this sort in either sterling or foreign currency balances would have brought total turnover in the foreign exchange market above £50 million. The previous figures for sterling demand (£48 million) and supply (£50 million) on business account are, therefore, meaningful only in calculating the *net* requirement imposed on the E.E.A. for the whole year.

4. *Analysis (II): the Finance of Capital Movements*

Table 17.2 dealt exclusively with trading relationships between U.K. and overseas residents, and the transactions they undertook in order to pay for the goods and services traded. Other capital and monetary transactions are, however, made which are not motivated by a need to finance U.K. imports or exports (though clearly any resultant exchange market transactions will, in the real world, merge indistinguishably with trading settlements). This second category of transactions is covered in Table 17.3, which represents the second stage in our construction of a hypothetical U.K. balance of payments record.

Of the £3 million entered under IA, only £2 million represents interest, profit and dividend earnings actually remitted to U.K. residents as a return on the employment of their capital overseas. The remaining £1 million comprises the share of U.K. companies in the profits retained by their subsidiaries and associates overseas. This is regarded as direct investment overseas by the U.K. companies, and figures accordingly as part of IIE (Section 2). Similarly, the overseas (parent) companies' share in profits retained by their U.K. subsidiaries and associates, amounting to £1 million, has been included under IIA, with a counter-entry of the same value as part of IC.

In neither of these two cases is there, of course, any actual movement of funds. They thus contrast with all the other entries in the first two accounts, which entail payments of the corresponding sums between U.K. and overseas residents. These payments may take place in the ways described in the previous section, but it is easiest to ignore the intermediate adjustment of working balances and deal directly with the resulting demands of one currency for another.

The remittance of interest, etc., by overseas to U.K. residents will over the year have occasioned a foreign currency demand for sterling of £2 million. To this must be added the requirements (£1 million, IB) for private transfers from overseas to U.K. residents by way of legacies, money gifts, pensions, and so on. Third, overseas companies furnished their associates, subsidiaries and branches in the U.K. with £1 million in sterling as capital funds for expansion (bringing the entry under IIA to £2 million), which necessitated an equivalent sale of foreign currencies on the foreign exchange market. Finally, £3 million sterling was required to finance the (net) purchase of U.K. securities by overseas residents

TABLE 17.3

Credit	£ million	Debit	£ million
I. CURRENT ACCOUNT			
(A) Interest, profits, dividends	3	(C) Interest, profits, dividends	2
(B) Private transfers	1	(D) Private transfers	1
CURRENT BALANCE +1			
(II) LONG-TERM CAPITAL ACCOUNT			
(A) Investment in U.K. subsidiaries, etc.	2	(C) Loans by U.K. Govt.	2
(B) Portfolio investment in U.K. (net)	3	(D) Repayments by U.K. Govt.	2
		(E) Investment in overseas subsidiaries, etc.	2
		(F) Portfolio investment overseas (net)	1
BALANCE ON LONG-TERM CAPITAL ACCOUNT −2			
(III) MONETARY MOVEMENTS			
(A) Increase in foreign currency liabilities	50	(C) Increase in foreign currency assets	45
(B) Increase in £ liabilities	10	(D) Account with I.M.F.	8
		(E) Increase in official reserves	6
BALANCE OF MONETARY MOVEMENTS +1			

(IIB). This brings the total foreign currency demand for sterling arising from the first two accounts (entries IA to IIB) to £7 million.

The calculation of the sterling demand for foreign currencies under heads IC to IIF follows the same pattern. Interest, profits and dividends (IC) actually remitted overseas by U.K. residents came to £1 million (above), and a second million pounds worth of foreign currencies was required for legacies, money gifts, missionary payments, etc., made overseas (ID). Third, the U.K. government made sterling loans to developing countries of £2 million (IIC), without 'tying' them to the purchase of U.K. products. The recipients chose, we assume, to spend the entire loan overseas (say in the U.S.A.), resulting in a further sterling sale for foreign currency, of £2 million. Fourth, the Government paid, in dollars, £2 million mixed interest and capital (IID) on the long-term debt outstanding to U.S.A. and Canada from early post-war years.

Of the £2 million entered under IIE, £1 million represents U.K. investment through profit retention by overseas subsidiaries, etc. (above), and £1 million the direct provision of capital to overseas subsidiaries and associates through the sale of sterling on the foreign exchange market. To this must be added the £1 million of foreign currencies required by U.K. residents to finance (net) security purchases overseas (IIF). This brings to £8 million the total sterling demand for foreign currencies under heads IC to IIF.

Entry IIIA records an increase in foreign currency liabilities of £50 million. For our purposes in this section, the whole of this figure can be taken in conjunction with IIIC as reflecting the participation of London banks in the 'Euro-currency' market. To assess the implications this activity may have for the foreign exchange market, it is necessary briefly to review how the Euro-currency market works.

The leading currency involved in the market is the U.S. dollar (hence, alternatively, 'Euro-dollar' market), and the leading operators are U.K. banks, especially merchant banks and the London offices of overseas banks. They accept deposits in U.S. dollars from overseas residents and 'on-lend' them at a margin to other overseas residents in need of dollar finance. Most of the depositors and borrowers are themselves banks, though large companies also participate. The depositors may be resident in the U.S.A., but more often are residents of other countries, especially Western Europe, who want to hold on for the time being to dollar balances acquired in the U.S.A., but are reluctant to leave them on time deposit with U.S. banks because of the interest restrictions imposed under 'Regulation Q' (Chapter 6). They may seek, accordingly, to place them outside the U.S.A., and the London (or other) banks which take them place them in their turn at the disposal of banks and firms in various countries (including the U.S.A.) currently in need of dollar finance.

An example may be helpful. Following a sale in the U.S.A. by one of its own customers, a French bank may acquire a dollar balance in account with a New York bank, which it may decide to hand over (in effect) to a London merchant bank in return for a deposit with the latter denominated in dollars. In turn, the London bank may place the balance it now has in account with New York at the disposal of a German bank, which draws on it to make certain payments in the U.S.A. on behalf of one of its customers in Germany. In a few weeks, say, the German bank acquires a balance in account with New York following an export to the U.S.A. by one of its customers, which it may use to repay the London bank. The latter may use these dollar funds to repay the French bank, whose deposit claim against it is thereby extinguished.

The objective of the London bank in all this is to derive a profit from the margin between its lending rate (to the German bank) and its borrowing rate (from the French bank). However, if short-term rates rose sufficiently in the U.K., the London bank would consider selling fresh dollar balances it acquired for sterling, which it could lend short-term to (say) U.K. local authorities and finance companies. The danger here, however, is that of capital loss to the London bank when it comes to sell sterling back for dollars, should sterling have been devalued in the interval. To guard against this risk, accordingly, the London bank would invariably make appropriate 'forward exchange' arrangements, which would subsequently provide it with dollars on terms only a little inferior to the current rate in the exchange market (see Chapter 18). It follows that the London bank would find the initial 'switch' from dollars into sterling profitable only if the lending rates in the U.K. exceeded lending rates in the Euro-currency market by more than the cost of forward exchange cover.

Acceptance by London banks of foreign currency deposits does not entail dealing in the foreign exchange market, unless the deposits (instead of being on-lent abroad) are switched into sterling for employment in the U.K. Table 17.3 shows that over the year foreign currency liabilities rose by £50 million while foreign currency assets rose by only £45 million, which must mean *net* switching from foreign currencies into sterling of £5 million. Entries IIIA and IIIC simply show how much bigger were assets and liabilities at the end of this year than they were at the end of the previous year, and so provide no guide to changes in their values in the course of the year. It follows that the total sum switched into sterling during the year may have been notably greater than £5 million.

Since Table 17.2 covered the working balances held by overseas residents for the day-to-day finance of trade, entry IIIB can be taken to refer exclusively to sums attracted into short-term sterling investments at times when U.K. interest rates are high relative to the rest of the world. Table 17.3 records a £10 million increase over the year in sterling liabilities, which means that at the end of the year foreign residents held £10 million more than at the beginning in deposits and loans with finance companies, local authorities, accepting houses, the London offices of overseas banks, and so on. These deposits and loans were, of course, made in sterling and to procure it the overseas residents, we may assume, made *net* sales over the year of £10 million worth of foreign currencies. Once again, however, total transactions occasioned in the foreign exchange market would probably have been much bigger than this figure, as overseas residents moved into and out of short-term sterling investments in response to changes in the international pattern of interest rates and re-assessments of the likelihood of sterling devaluation (Chapter 18).

The net outcome of the year's operations by the Exchange Equalization Account can now be estimated by calculating the difference between foreign currency supply and sterling supply over the entire year. Entries in the current and long-term capital accounts gave rise to an £8 million sterling demand for foreign currencies and a £7 million foreign currency demand for sterling. A further net foreign currency demand for sterling of £5 million proceeded from the 'switching' operations of U.K. banks, and of £10 million from the net acquisition by overseas residents of short-term sterling investments. Movements into and out of sterling during the year mean, of course, that total sterling supply on private account would have been higher than £8 million, and total foreign currency supply greater than £22 million. Nonetheless, the difference between the two gives the value of the *net* sterling sales made by the Account during the year. Of its corresponding foreign currency purchases, however, only £6 million remained in the Account (IIIE), as £8 million was used to pay off part of a debt outstanding to the International Monetary Fund (IIID).

5. *Interpretation of the Balance of Payments*

The partial balance of payments of the two preceding sections are brought together in Table 17.4, which is recognizably closer to Table 17.1 though, of course, it remains at the same level of simplification as its two constituents. In particular, no account has been taken of the use of sterling as a 'vehicle' or 'reserve' currency; of the restrictions on currency dealing (i.e. exchange control) imposed by the U.K. Government; or of the support given to the official reserves by overseas central banks and international monetary institutions. These matters are, however, taken up in the course of the next two chapters.

The use of imaginary figures to construct Tables 17.2 and 17.3 made it possible to illustrate the relationships which underlie the three balance of payments accounts. In particular, we saw that the finance of some current and long-term capital transactions is explained within these two accounts, while the finance of the remainder is reflected—along with various short-term capital transactions—among the monetary movements. In the real world, of course, much of this background information is not available or, where it is available, could not be conveyed in just one table. For this reason it is important to develop another (in a sense more superficial) technique of interpretation.

Totalling the debits and credits of the current account shows an excess of debits of £2 million, described as the deficit on the current account. A similar calculation shows a deficit of £3 million on the long-term capital account, hence a combined deficit of £5 million on the two accounts. The difference between total credits and debits on these two

TABLE 17.4

£ million

1. CURRENT ACCOUNT

(a) Imports [1e]		51
(b) Exports [1a]		50
	Visible balance	−1
Invisibles		
(c) Transport	Debits [1f]	2
	Credits [1b]	5
(d) Travel	Debits [1g]	2
	Credits [1c]	1
(e) Interests, profits, dividends	Debits [1C]	2
	Credits [IA]	3
(f) Government	Debits [1i + 1j]	5
	Credits	0
(g) Private transfers	Debits [1h + ID]	2
	Credits [1d + IB]	3
Total invisibles	Debits	13
	Credits	12
	Invisible balance	−1
CURRENT BALANCE		−2

2. LONG-TERM CAPITAL ACCOUNT

(a) Loans made by U.K. Government [2c + IIC]	−5
(b) Loans made to U.K. Government (less repayments) [2a − IID]	−1
(c) Private investment abroad (net) [2d + IIE + IIF]	−4
(d) Private investment in the U.K. (net) [2b + IIA + IIB]	+7
BALANCE OF LONG-TERM CAPITAL	−3
BALANCE OF CURRENT AND LONG-TERM CAPITAL TRANSACTIONS	−5

3. MONETARY MOVEMENTS

(a) Net miscellaneous capital [3a − 3e]	−1
(b) Net change in external liabilities in sterling [3c + IIIB]	+12
(c) Net change in liabilities in other currencies [3b + IIIA − IIIC]	+6
(d) Change in account with I.M.F. [IIID]	−8
(e) Gold and convertible currency reserves [3d − IIIE]	−4
BALANCE OF MONETARY MOVEMENTS	+5

Notes: 1. + denotes a credit entry, − a debit entry. In the long-term capital and monetary accounts, − denotes an increase in assets or decrease in liabilities, + denotes a decrease in assets or increase in liabilities.
2. Entries 3a, 3b, 3c are brought into line with the definitions in Section 2 by assuming that no U.K. firms hold bank accounts overseas, i.e. all their transactions are routed through their U.K. banks' overseas balances.

Source: Derived from Tables 17.2 and 17.3

accounts is often referred to as the 'basic-balance'—here negative to the value of £5 million. The third account can now be interpreted as showing both the net outcome of short-term capital movements and how the negative basic balance was financed.

Miscellaneous capital movements (3a) show a net deficit of £1 million, which increases the deficit so far accumulated to £6 million. Had there been no other monetary movements on business account, this would have meant a net drain on the official reserves of £6 million. However, entry 3b reveals a £12 million increase in sterling liabilities, while foreign currency liabilities rose by £6 million (3c). These credits, totalling £18 million, offset the £6 million deficit by £12 million and—in terms of exchange market transactions—enabled the E.E.A. to make a net acquisition of £12 million worth of foreign currencies. Of this sum, however, the Government used £8 million to repay part of an outstanding debt to the I.M.F., so that the reserves for the year show an increase of only £4 million. It may be said, therefore, that an 'inflow of short-term capital' (3b + 3c) financed the deficit on the current and long-term capital accounts, and enabled the authorities both to increase their foreign currency reserves and repay part of an old debt to the I.M.F.

The acquisition by a U.K. resident of a capital claim on a foreign resident is, of course, entered as a debit, either in the long-term capital or monetary account, while the converse is entered as a credit. It is clear, accordingly, that the deficit on long-term capital account represents a net increase in U.K. long-term claims on overseas residents, i.e. over the year the U.K. made net long-term investment overseas worth £3 million. The fact that this coincided with a deficit on current account may seem, at first sight, to contradict the reasoning built around Table 16.14, in which a country's deficit on current account was financed by her external long-term disinvestment (i.e. by another country's long-term investment *in her*). To resolve the paradox, it is necessary to recognize that net U.K. liabilities on short-term capital account rose by £5 million over the year, which might be described as short-term disinvestment by the U.K. In the full picture, therefore, the £5 million increase in U.K. residents' short-term liabilities enabled them finance both a current account deficit of £2 million and the net acquisition of long-term assets of £3 million.

Questions

See questions after Chapter 18.

o

18

The British Balance of Payments: (II) Features of Disequilibrium

1. *The Meaning of Equilibrium*

Balance of payments equilibrium was defined in Section 5, Chapter 16, in terms of the equilibrium of the foreign exchange market. Thus, within that section's theoretical framework, a community's planned balance of payments was in equilibrium if the resultant supply and demand for currency would be equal at the ruling exchange rate. If not, the planned balance of payments was in disequilibrium, which meant that the exchange rate would alter under the influence of excess supply/demand, entailing a revision of trading plans. A new exchange rate would emerge at which currency supply and demand were equal and—provided this brought equilibrium in the commodity markets (p. 375)—the exchange market would be in equilibrium. The revised version of the planned balance of payments would necessarily be in equilibrium, since merely a list of the proposed trading (and capital) transactions which would give rise to the now harmonious currency requirements.

In the contemporary world, by contrast, the U.K. authorities operate a stabilization fund (i.e. the Exchange Equalization Account) precisely to prevent the sterling exchange rate moving outside certain narrow limits, when currency supply and demand diverge at the ruling level. Accordingly, if trading and capital plans result in currency requirements inconsistent with the officially approved parity, there is no (significant) alteration in the rate, and so no stimulus (on this score) to revise trading plans. Instead, the disequilibrium in the exchange market, i.e. the net excess supply of or demand for sterling (on private or business account, including the commercial and military needs of Government) is offset by the E.E.A.'s purchase or sale of foreign currency.

Suppose that, over a given year, the E.E.A. has made a net purchase or a net sale of foreign currency. This must mean that the U.K. balance of payments for that year was in disequilibrium, in the sense that transactions gave rise to a currency supply and demand inconsistent (in the absence of E.E.A. intervention) with the official parity for the rate of exchange. The balance of payments record will accordingly show—if we ignore the compensatory activities of the E.E.A.—either a surplus of credits over debits, or a deficit of credits against debits. The first may be described as a 'surplus disequilibrium', and has entailed a net purchase of foreign currency by the E.E.A. The second may be described as a 'deficit disequilibrium', and has entailed a net sale of foreign currency by the E.E.A. If over the year the E.E.A.'s day-to-day purchases are exactly offset by its day-to-day sales, then its net sales or purchases are zero, and the balance of payments for the year will have been in equilibrium.

When selling foreign currency, the authorities may be able to avoid over-depleting the reserves by borrowing some of the foreign currency they sell from the I.M.F. or from overseas central banks. In turn, their purchases of foreign currency may be used to pay off outstanding loans which originated in that way. The operation of a stabilization fund with the support, should need arise, of overseas institutions is conveniently designated 'compensatory financing'. In effect, the authorities *compensate* for the disparity in currency supply and demand on business account by *financing* the deficit or surplus.

It follows that, in assessing the scale of the E.E.A.'s net sales or net purchases during the year, it is necessary to consider both the net change in the reserves and the net change in official indebtedness to overseas monetary institutions. It may happen, for example, that the extent of official borrowing during the year is more than sufficient to meet the E.E.A.'s net sales of foreign currency, so that at the end of the year the Account records an increase in its foreign currency holdings. On the other hand where net purchases of foreign currency have enabled the repayment of some outstanding debt, the authorities may have gone further and actually depleted the reserves for this purpose. For this reason, the movement of the reserves alone is not an accurate indicator of deficit or surplus disequilibrium.

If the Government expected the balance of payments to show a deficit disequilibrium, it might well aim to limit the scale of its compensatory finance by stimulating the supply of foreign currency on private or business account. In particular, the authorities might engineer a rise in short-term interest rates, so that deposits with merchant banks, finance companies, local authorities, etc., become more attractive to overseas residents. The resultant sale of foreign currency for sterling will thus offset part or all of the deficit the authorities would otherwise have had to finance. In the second case, the E.E.A.'s net sales of foreign currency over the year are zero, and on the earlier definition the balance of payments will have been in equilibrium. It is, however, a precarious equilibrium in that (other things being equal) deficit disequilibrium is avoided only by maintaining an appropriate margin between short-term interest rates in the U.K. and overseas.

Apart from influencing short-term capital flows, the Government might turn its attention to transactions in the current and long-term capital accounts. Thus, to anticipate a deficit disequilibrium, the Government might bring in measures aimed at reducing import demand (a current account debit) and long-term investment overseas (a long-term capital account debit). It might, for instance, introduce regulations limiting quantities imported, make import finance more difficult, raise tariffs, restrict foreign currency purchases, or hope to discourage import demand by depressing the level of economic activity at home. Overseas investment might be restrained by controls on the purchase of foreign exchange, unfavourable tax rules governing the returns from overseas investment, or direct requests to firms to limit their investment voluntarily. In these ways the Government might succeed in so restricting the demand for foreign currency that deficit disequilibrium is avoided. In the absence, however, of these constraints a deficit disequilibrium would emerge, so that the balance of payments could be said to exhibit 'suppressed disequilibrium'.

The term 'surplus on the balance of payments' is sometimes applied to a 'surplus disequilibrium', as a way of emphasizing that the statistics record a surplus of credits over debits offset by E.E.A. net purchases of foreign currency. Similarly, a 'deficit disequilibrium' may be described as a 'deficit on the balance of payments', since here the record shows a deficit of credits against debits offset by E.E.A. net sales of foreign currency. However, in assessing the policy implications of disequilibrium the overall result of 'surplus' or 'deficit' is less important than the outcome on each of the three accounts.

The situation which appears to present the more urgent problem is that of deficit disequilibrium, since the ability of the authorities to maintain their sales of foreign currency is limited by the size of the reserves and the goodwill of monetary institutions overseas. It may be, however, that a country in deficit disequilibrium has a substantial surplus on current account, which is more than offset by her deficit on long-term capital account. The latter represents, of course, net long-term investment overseas, hence an increase in residents' net ownership of capital assets in other countries. On the other hand, a country in surplus disequilibrium may have a substantial deficit on both current and long-term capital accounts, more than offset by a short-term capital inflow in response to abnormally high interest rates.

A balance of payments which is in equilibrium may also present problems for economic policy. Thus the equilibrium may cover up a suppressed disequilibrium, and be maintained only by tolerating e.g. an abnormal level of unemployment. Again, the equilibrium may possess features inimical to welfare in the long run. Thus suppose a country achieves equilibrium with a deficit on current account offset by a surplus on long-term capital account, i.e. a net inflow of long-term capital. This will probably be welcome where the current account deficit reflects the import of capital goods, which may contribute to the more rapid growth of domestic production and perhaps a subsequent export expansion. If, however, consumer good imports are disproportionately large, then the country effectively enjoys its current living standards[1] only through the (net) transfer of capital assets into foreign ownership.

This short discussion suggests that the concepts of equilibrium and disequilibrium (as defined in this section) are not in themselves adequate for evaluating a country's balance of payments and determining appropriate economic policy. Rather, information is required about the balance on current account and on capital account(s), and the ways in which economic policy is being used to influence the country's external economic relationships. On the first score, the U.K. balance of payments has since 1964 been characterized (except for a small current account surplus in 1966) by a deficit on both current and long-term capital account, financed by depletion of the official foreign currency reserves and borrowing from overseas monetary institutions. The pressure on the reserves has at times increased with a net outflow of short-term capital, and at others fallen with a net inflow.

While this is a picture of deficit disequilibrium, it is insufficient to define the objective of official policy simply as the 'removal of the deficit in the balance of payments'. More explicitly, the immediate goal of official policy is to convert a current account deficit into a surplus, though without prejudice to full employment at home, continuing development aid and military expenditure overseas, and conformity to international agreements on the use of tariffs and other import restrictions. If the current account surplus is allied with a reduction in U.K. net investment overseas (again without prejudice to development aid), a positive 'basic balance' (p. 405) may be achieved. In the absence of a net outflow of short-term capital, this could enable the authorities repay some of the loans outstanding and (perhaps) add to the official reserves. It is these specific targets, then, which provide the criteria[2] against which to assess U.K. balance of payments performance.

[1] This ignores the possibility that the high level of consumer good imports has enabled a cut in domestic production for consumption, thereby freeing resources for increased domestic investment (compare p. 449).

[2] In a Letter (May, 1969) to the I.M.F., the Chancellor of the Exchequer specified an objective of at least £300 million surplus on current and long-term capital accounts for the financial year ending March, 1970.

2. *The Current Account Balance*

The work of Chapter 17 has served to emphasize the distinction between the balance on (visible) trading account and the overall balance on current account. As well as the balance of visible trade the latter reflects, of course, the net provision or receipt of transport, travel, insurance and other services, Government net purchases of goods and services overseas, Government grants and the net value of private transfers, and the net inflow or outflow of interest payments.

From the diversity of the current account entries it is clear that a variety of influences will operate to shape its outcome. Thus imports and exports of commodities (visible trade) and of services like transport and travel will depend, in particular, upon the level of economic activity and the behaviour of prices here and overseas. On the other hand it is for the Government to decide, within its political and economic policy, the scale of its net expenditure overseas on goods and services (largely military), and the level of grants for overseas governments (largely economic aid). Finally (private transfers are ignored), the flow of interest payments will mainly reflect the value of the short- and long-term capital held overseas by U.K. residents and held in the U.K. by overseas residents.

In analysing changes in the value of imports and exports of goods (and services), it is essential to distinguish between changes in the quantities traded and changes in prices. Thus an increase in the sterling value of total U.K. exports could mean that more goods were being exported at the same sterling prices, or conceivably that rather less goods were being exported at substantially higher sterling prices. A fall in the sterling value of total U.K. imports might mean, for example, that less goods were being imported at the same sterling prices, or that the same quantity (or, indeed, a greater quantity) of goods was being imported at (much) lower sterling prices; and so on.

From the analysis of earlier chapters it is clear that the value of U.K. imports and exports will be influenced by quantity changes occurring in response to changes in aggregate demand, both here and overseas. Thus excess demand in the U.K. is likely—apart from price effects—to draw in increased imports and discourage exports (Chapter 14), while a fall in economic activity would probably dampen U.K. import demand. Similarly, a decline in activity in other economies is likely to depress U.K. exports, and expansion overseas to encourage them (Chapter 16). In practice, of course, policy measures aimed at promoting full employment would serve to limit the multiplier interaction described in Chapter 16.

Changes in import and export values will also reflect the movement of import and export price levels, and these price changes may, in turn, be associated with changes in quantities traded. If international economic relations were limited to competitive trade with freely floating exchange rates, then a rise in one country's price level would be matched by an external depreciation of its currency (and vice versa), with no consequences either for the volume of international trade or for other countries' price levels (Chapter 16). The maintenance of a fixed exchange rate by the U.K. and many other countries makes these conclusions much less relevant to the contemporary world, and requires a re-assessment of the foreign trade implications of changes in the domestic price level.

With the official exchange parity unchanged, a rise in the general level of prices in the U.K. entails a roughly equivalent increase in the foreign currency prices as well as the sterling prices of U.K. exports. The consequences for the volume—and hence the value—of exports will depend, other things being equal, on the elasticity (p. 363) of demand in overseas countries for imports from the U.K. Thus if demand is sensitive to price changes, the rise in U.K. export prices will prompt a significant switch among overseas customers to other sources of supply, i.e. to home suppliers or to export rivals of the U.K. Provided the latter can meet the new orders, this will entail a more than proportionate fall in quantity demanded and so a decline in the value of U.K. exports. It is unlikely, however, that the U.K. will be alone in experiencing a rising price level, which suggests that 'other things', notably other countries' price levels, cannot be taken as constant. It follows that rising prices in the U.K. may nonetheless be associated with an expanding volume of exports if prices in other (relevant) countries are rising even more rapidly, i.e. the prices of U.K. exports are showing a *relative* decline.

A general price rise in other countries which carries (some) U.K. import prices up with it must mean, with fixed exchange rate, an increase in the sterling prices as well as the foreign currency prices of U.K. imports. Consequences for the value of imports will, accordingly, depend on the response in the U.K. to this increase in prices. If demand is elastic and if U.K. firms are able to meet the orders which are switched to them, then the volume of imports will contract more than proportionately, and the value of imports decline. If these two conditions are not satisfied, the value of imports will rise. Any assessment must, of course, be related to the behaviour of the domestic price level. Clearly, imports may become *relatively* cheaper despite inflation overseas if U.K. inflation is more rapid.

It is clear that, with fixed exchange rates, changes in the terms of trade (i.e. the ratio of export to import prices) come about by a different path from that described in Chapter 16. The implications such changes have for living standards must also be reconsidered, while it is important to set the associated movements in import and export values against the targets of balance-of-payments policy (Section 1).

For a first exercise, assume that a rising price level in the U.K. has carried export prices up with it, while U.K. import prices are unchanged (or, at least, have risen less than proportionately). Conventionally, this is described as an improvement in the terms of trade. If overseas demand is elastic then (on the conditions previously mentioned) the price rise will lead to a more than proportionate decline in quantity exported, and a fall in the level of total export earnings. The implied decline in the U.K. employment level could, however, be averted by appropriate management of the domestic level of aggregate demand (Chapter 12). With full employment maintained but imports cheaper in relation to home produced goods, it is likely that the volume of imports will rise. In the outcome, therefore, it appears that the value of imports will have risen, while the value of exports will have declined.

This result, of course, runs counter to the targets of official policy, though there is an immediate gain to U.K. residents, who are now parting with less exports for a bigger quantity of imports, i.e. U.K. residents are 'better off' in the sense that the economy is absorbing a bigger total quantity of goods and services than before. This gain is achieved, however, only through a decline in the surplus or increase in the deficit on current account, which must mean in turn a reduced deficit or increased surplus on capital account, i.e. a reduced rate of asset accumulation overseas or an increased rate of U.K. indebtedness overseas. Thus U.K. residents have become 'better off' only in the sense of currently absorbing more goods and services while slowing down the accumulation of— or actually depleting—their (net) capital overseas.

For a second exercise, we assume a rise in import prices in a context of full employment at home, so that importers are unable to turn readily to domestic sources of supply. There is, accordingly, no reduction in the quantity imported, which means an increase in the value of total imports. Following the illustration of Chapter 14 (Section 5), the rise in import prices will exert an upward pressure on the general price level in the U.K., so that U.K. exports become more expensive. At least initially (p. 320), the rise in the general (and export) price level is smaller than the rise in the import price level, so that the terms of trade are said to deteriorate. Of itself, the price increase would serve to discourage exports, though this effect could be offset by inflation and buoyant income levels overseas, associated with the original rise in U.K. import prices (i.e. overseas suppliers' export prices).

Should foreign customers buy the same quantity as before, then the total value of exports increases, but less than the increase in the value of imports (since the relevant prices have changed by different amounts). Superficially, it might seem that U.K. residents are no worse off, since they exchange the same quantity of exports for imports as before. They are able to do so, however, only by running a smaller surplus or bigger deficit on current account, which means reducing the rate of asset accumulation or increasing the rate of U.K. indebtedness overseas, on capital account. In the example of Chapter 14, households could maintain consumption constant only by cutting their savings, which certainly appears as a fall in living standards. The counterpart to their savings reduction was the fall in investment overseas, i.e. the reduced surplus on current account.

3. Rectifying a Current Account Deficit

The discussion of Section 2 suggests that a deficit on current account may be reduced or perhaps eliminated by appropriate changes in U.K. relative prices or in U.K. aggregate demand. Such movements will affect not only the visible trading balance, but also the values of such invisibles as transport, travel and other services. The outcome for the overall balance on current account, however, must also reflect the behaviour of the other invisibles, notably interest payments and receipts and net current expenditure overseas by the Government.

If overseas demand for U.K. exports is elastic then, with exchange rate unchanged and other factors constant, a fall in the general price level in the U.K. will result in a more than proportionate increase in the quantity of U.K. exports demanded. Provided, therefore, that domestic resources are available to satisfy this increase in demand, the value of U.K. exports will rise. In practice, it is highly unlikely that the U.K. authorities would want or be able to engineer an absolute fall in the price level, since an attempt to do so by depressing aggregate demand would entail considerable unemployment and an attempt by cutting wage rates would provoke labour disputes. The same result may, however, be achieved if the U.K. Government is more successful than others in slowing down the rate of domestic price increase, so that U.K. exports become cheaper relative to the commodities of overseas competitors. In this case, the tendency to lose sales through the rise in U.K. prices may be more than offset by the shift of new orders to U.K. suppliers in the changed circumstances of the market.

A reduction in the foreign currency prices of U.K. goods may also be achieved by a devaluation of sterling, i.e. by reducing the official parity at which the U.K. Government undertakes to maintain its external value. Thus a devaluation of the pound from (in terms of the U.S. dollar) £1 = $2·8 to £1 = $2·4 means that a U.K. exporter who sells his product in the U.S.A. at $2·8 a unit could reduce his price to $2·4, i.e. by 14·3 per cent, and still enjoy an identical sterling return of £1.

Provided, therefore, that U.K. firms charge the same prices in their foreign markets (excluding transport costs) as in their home market, the foreign currency prices of U.K. exports will fall proportionately to the devaluation (here, 14·3 per cent).

If demand for U.K. exports is relatively elastic, then (other things being equal) quantity demanded will rise more than proportionately to the fall in price. Providing, therefore, that U.K. firms have the resources available to meet the new orders, the sterling value and the foreign currency value of U.K. exports is increased. If, on the other hand, overseas demand is relatively inelastic, the increase in sales is insufficient to offset the fall in the foreign currency price, and foreign currency export earnings are reduced. The *sterling* value of exports would, nonetheless, record an increase, since the sterling price is unchanged while— unless demand is completely insensitive to price changes—there is at least some increase in the quantity of goods sold overseas.

The consequences for U.K. imports can be assessed in a similar way. If foreign exporters charge the same prices in the U.K. as in other markets, a devaluation of the pound will raise the sterling price of imports proportionately to the appreciation of other currencies. Following the devaluation of the earlier example, an American firm selling a $2·8 product for £1 in the U.K. would need to raise its price to £1⅙, i.e. by 16·66 per cent, in order to maintain its return of $2·8. Unless U.K. demand for imports is completely inelastic, the *foreign currency* value of imports is bound to decline, since less goods are imported at prices unchanged in foreign currencies. However, if U.K. demand is inelastic, then the *sterling* value of imports will rise, since quantities imported fall less than proportionately to the sterling price increase; in this case, the decline in the foreign currency value of imports is relatively small. If on the other hand U.K. demand is elastic, the *sterling* value of imports will fall, since quantities imported fall more than proportionately to the sterling price rise; in this case the foreign currency saving is relatively large.

Since U.K. imports are, of course, the exports of other countries, any fall in their value entails some decline in aggregate demand—and so in income—among our foreign suppliers. Especially where these suppliers are also U.K. export customers, this fall in income could have a depressing effect on overseas demand for U.K. exports, perhaps offsetting the encouragement afforded by the relative fall in export prices. However, advanced economies which export manufactured goods to the U.K. would probably so manage aggregate demand anyway as to offset this income fall. Further, U.K. demand for the exports of primary producing countries is likely to be inelastic, at least in the short run, in which case the fall in U.K. primary import quantities—hence the supplying countries' incomes—would be small.

It is clear that devaluation may bring some benefit to the visible trading balance even where both overseas demand for U.K. goods and U.K. demand for imports are inelastic, provided that the (fairly small) foreign currency saving in import payments is nonetheless bigger than the decline in foreign currency earnings from export markets. The prospective benefit is, however, at its greatest when both overseas demand and U.K. demand are elastic, though this prospective gain can be achieved only if incomes remain reasonably stable abroad (see above), and only if certain supply conditions are satisfied in the U.K. Since to meet an increase in export orders U.K. firms must—to ignore stocks— have the resources available, it follows that devaluation would be a doubly appropriate policy were the economy suffering both an adverse trade balance and demand-deficiency unemployment (Chapter 12). Where, however, the economy enjoys full employment, the Government must necessarily restrict domestic spending in an attempt to free resources to meet the (anticipated) increase in export orders. Full employment at home may also put difficulties in the way of import substitution, if lengthy delivery dates for home produced goods deter U.K. purchasers from the switch.

If firms charge the same prices (adjusted for transport costs) in overseas as well as home markets, then a sterling devaluation will necessarily worsen the U.K. terms of trade. Expressed in sterling, U.K. import prices rise while export prices (at least initially) are unchanged; expressed in foreign currencies, U.K. import prices are unchanged while export prices (at least initially) decline. It is, however, unlikely that this initial reduction in (foreign currency) export prices will be maintained. First, the rise in (sterling) import prices will work its way through to the price level of final goods and services, as firms which use or sell imported goods experience a cost increase. Given uniform prices in home and overseas markets, export prices (expressed in sterling or in foreign currency) must accordingly rise. Second, the increase in final prices entails a fall in living standards for U.K. households, since while money incomes are unchanged the price level has risen. In an attempt to restore real income, wage-earners may seek higher wages, and business-men bigger profit mark-ups. If they secure bigger money incomes and if productivity is unchanged the result will be a second round of price increases, and a cost inflation may be set under way (compare Section 5, Chapter 14).

So far, two policies have been considered for improving the visible trading balance, i.e. the restraint of domestic price increases and devaluation. Both of these, in short, operate through an alteration in relative prices, here and overseas. However, price changes apart, the volume of imports will also respond to variations in U.K. aggregate demand (compare Chapter 16), which suggests the possibility of reducing the value of imports by putting curbs on domestic spending. Where the economy is suffering excess demand, such a policy would also serve to restrain the rate of price increase. Otherwise the curb on domestic spending would entail (other things being equal) a deficiency of aggregate demand and a lapse from full employment. However, raising the unemployment level as a means of reducing import demand represents an attempt to 'suppress' rather than 'rectify' a current account deficit—a distinction explained in Section 4. Meanwhile, it is important to distinguish such a policy from one of restricting domestic spending to free resources for an export expansion. In this second case, estimated aggregate demand (including, of course, export spending) is sufficient to give full employment, though there may be some short-term frictional unemployment before the reallocation of resources is achieved.

Changes in relative prices or the level of domestic spending which affect the visible trading balance may also affect net receipts from the services which figure in the 'invisibles' section of the current account. Thus a sterling devaluation will make U.K. shipping and aviation rates cheaper to overseas residents, and vacations in the U.K. cheaper to the foreign tourist. At the same time, the corresponding services overseas become more expensive to U.K. residents. The responsiveness of demand to these changes and (in some cases) the availability of resources will—as for visible trade—shape the outcome for net U.K. receipts under these heads.

A devaluation will also reduce the foreign currency required to make U.K. interest and profit payments overseas (unless an obligation is expressed in foreign currency terms). Assume the pound is devalued from (in terms of the U.S. dollar) £1 = \$2·8 to £1 = \$2·4. Then for each £100 profit that an American subsidiary in the U.K. remits to its parent in the U.S.A., its foreign currency requirement is reduced from \$280 to \$240. On the same principle, it is clear that the foreign currency value of U.K. interest and profit receipts is unaffected by devaluation (except for a reduction where obligations are expressed in sterling). In sterling terms, however, the value of these earnings is increased proportionately to the appreciation of other currencies. Thus a \$280 remittance from U.S.A. to U.K. is recorded at a value of £100 before the devaluation (above), and at £116·66 afterwards. Devaluation thus increases net foreign currency earnings under the heading of interest and profits, not through a rise in gross earnings (since the foreign currency value does not rise) but through a fall in gross payments (since the foreign currency value falls).

4. *Suppressing a Deficit Disequilibrium*

In its economic policy, the Government is not, of course, exclusively concerned with the balance of payments targets specified in Section 1, but pursues simultaneously a variety of other objectives. At home, these include the maintenance of full employment and the promotion of domestic product growth, goals which are further considered in Chapter 20. Externally, it seeks to meet the requirements and further the objectives of the international organizations to which it belongs, and the international agreements to which it is a party (Chapter 19). These relate, among other things, to tariff levels, to economic aid for developing countries, and to the operation of controls on sterling/foreign currency transactions.

Faced with a deficit in the balance of payments, the Government could conceivably attempt to eliminate it by compromising one or more of these policy objectives, both domestic and external. For example, to reduce a deficit on current account, it might raise tariff levels or depress the employment level, hoping thereby to dampen import demand. Measures of this sort will not necessarily be successful (below), but— if they are—the disequilibrium is 'suppressed' rather than 'rectified'. While its original cause (e.g. disparity between U.K. and foreign price levels) remains uncorrected, the disequilibrium can be expected to open up again once the Government makes a fresh move towards the objective(s) which were sacrificed in getting rid of the deficit. Thus if imports fall with a rise in tariff levels or an increase in unemployment, they must (other things remaining equal) rise again with a reduction in tariff levels or any attempt to stimulate economic activity.

Measures which suppress a disequilibrium may, accordingly, be contrasted with those considered in Section 3 for rectifying a current account deficit, i.e. the restraint of domestic price increases, devaluation, and the elimination of excess demand. In broad terms, the latter are all consistent with the variety of policy objectives earlier defined. The distinction is, however, analytical, and a group of policy measures may include some designed to rectify a disequilibrium and others which will work to suppress it. Thus a negative basic balance might be met with devaluation, restraints on domestic price increases, restrictions on import finance, and a reduction in overseas economic aid.

A rise in tariff rates, the introduction of import quotas or an increase in the unemployment level all carry unfavourable implications for U.K. export demand, considered abstractly in Chapters 12 (p. 271) and 16 (Section 6). The outcome for the current account balance would, accordingly, be difficult to predict. Uncertainty also attaches to the use of two other sorts of 'suppressive' measure, considered in this section.

These are reductions in overseas economic aid, and the extension of exchange restrictions on capital transactions.

Suppose that the U.K. has a deficit on both current account and long-term capital account, which the Government hopes to reduce by cutting the grants and loans it makes as aid to developing countries. The reduction in grant expenditure is recorded as a fall in debits in the current account, and the reduction in loans appears as a fall in debits in the long-term capital account (Chapter 17). The net outcome for the balance of payments must, therefore, depend on the consequences for the relevant credit entries, both in these two accounts and under the 'monetary movements' head.

Part of their current aid receipts may be applied by developing countries to the payment of interest or the repayment of capital on existing loans, or to finance pension and similar obligations to retired colonial officials. A reduction in aid would add to the difficulties some experience in maintaining these payments, and so increase the possibility of default. Default on current interest obligations should, of course, be distinguished from the long-run interest yield sacrificed by the U.K. when the Government reduces the current level of loans (not grants).

The consequences of a cut in aid for U.K. exports are more complex and best considered—along with the implications for monetary movements—with the help of a numerical example. However, distinguish first between aid which is 'tied' or restricted to expenditure in the U.K., and 'untied aid' which can be spent in any country of the recipient's choice. Consider now the case of a developing country which annually sells goods worth £8 million in the U.K., using £3 million of its export earnings to finance interest and capital payments and £5 million to finance imports from the U.K. Apart from its export earnings, this country receives £10 million a year aid from the U.K. Government, three quarters of which is tied to U.K. purchases, while the remainder it converts into U.S. dollars in the foreign exchange market to pay for some of its imports from the U.S.A. This entails an annual 'direct cost' to the official reserves of £2·5 million worth of foreign currency, since over the year the E.E.A. either pays out £2·5 million more dollars than it would otherwise have done, or it fails to accumulate £2·5 million of dollars it would otherwise have got.

Suppose now that, as part of a general retrenchment in its aid programme, the Government decides to cut its aid to this country to £5 million a year, all of which henceforth has to be spent in the U.K. This appears to eliminate completely the direct cost to the reserves, since the developing country is no longer allowed to sell any of its aid receipts for U.S. dollars. In fact, this particular gain is illusory if the developing country chooses to switch £2·5 million of its £8 million *export earnings* from U.K. purchases to purchases in the U.S.A.

Assume that such a switch is made, and that the developing country cuts imports from the U.K. by £5 million a year. With other factors constant the basic balance is unaffected by the aid reduction, since credits (the exports) will have fallen by the same amount as debits (the aid). Other factors, however, may well undergo a change: two possibilities are considered, the first detrimental and the second beneficial to the basic balance. First, other donor countries may cut their aid programmes if the U.K. cuts hers, leading to a further export loss in so far as the recipients of other countries' aid had been spending part of it in the U.K. Second, U.K. export industries may be able to secure other orders to replace those lost with the U.K. aid reduction, because they are now able to offer shorter delivery dates. Such a result would, however, imply that U.K. export industries were faced with excessive demand in relation to their productive capacity, in which case the Government might have promoted export sales by heavier restraints on domestic spending.

Restrictions on capital transactions between U.K. and overseas residents operate very largely within the context of official exchange control. 'Exchange control' denotes the system of regulating financial transactions between U.K. residents and non-residents, originally introduced in 1939 to conserve U.K. foreign currency resources in the interests of the war effort. The system has been retained since the war, as by dampening the sterling demand for foreign currencies (below) it serves ultimately to protect the official reserves. It has, however, undergone many modifications, of which probably the most outstanding was the de-control, in 1959, of current transactions, i.e. payments for the goods and services featured in the current account.[1] The administration of the control is in the hands of the Bank of England, though final responsibility rests with the Treasury.

To outline the operation of the control on capital transactions, and assess its implications, it is necessary to distinguish between portfolio investment and direct investment overseas (Chapter 17). Foreign residents are allowed to buy U.K. securities quite freely, to sell their holdings of U.K. securities, and to exchange the sterling proceeds for other currencies without any penalty. On the other hand, if U.K. residents wish to purchase the securities of countries outside the sterling area (Chapter 19), they are obliged to buy the necessary foreign currency in the 'investment dollar market', i.e. from other U.K. residents who have acquired it by selling their own foreign securities to overseas residents. The exchange rate at which the deal takes place varies with supply and demand, but foreign currency bought in this way is usually more expensive than foreign currency bought in the 'official market'.

[1] A restriction on overseas travel expenditure outside the sterling area was, however, reintroduced in July, 1966.

This system gives U.K. residents the opportunity to buy foreign securities if they wish, though at an artificially increased price, while giving complete protection to the official reserves. Relaxation of the rule would probably cause an immediate loss to the reserves, in so far as U.K. residents have a positive net demand for foreign securities, i.e. if the market were freed purchases overseas would outstrip sales overseas. In 1965, however, the authorities tightened the control by requiring the seller of a foreign security to dispose of 25 per cent of the foreign currency proceeds in the official market. This means an equivalent saving to the official reserves (e.g. with this inflow coming onto the market the E.E.A. need sell less foreign currency itself when supporting sterling). On the other hand—until the rule is relaxed—it spells the gradual shrinkage of the U.K. investment portfolio overseas, with an accompanying decline in the interest and dividend return.

Except for a programme of voluntary restraint covering four developed countries,[1] direct investment in the overseas sterling area (Chapter 19) is uncontrolled. Investment outside the sterling area is, by contrast, subject to quite severe limitations, though these do vary with the character of the investment undertaken. Investment through profit retention by subsidiaries is permissible, provided that the rate of profit repatriation does not fall much below the record of previous years. This increases U.K. assets overseas and hence their prospective profit yield, at the immediate 'expense' to the official reserves only of the foreign currency the E.E.A. would have acquired had the profits actually been remitted.

On the other hand, the purchase of foreign currencies outside the sterling area to provide overseas associates with capital (compare p. 401) has not been permissible *at all* since July, 1965. U.K. firms are, however, able to make security issues overseas to finance their activities there or—where there is the prospect of a quick, significant and continuing foreign currency return—to buy foreign currency in the investment dollar market. Investment so financed imposes no burden on the official reserves, which should in fact subsequently benefit under several heads. First, there is a prospective profit return to the U.K. parent company. Second, part of the foreign currency raised abroad or in the investment dollar market might be spent in buying U.K. capital goods (say, to equip a new factory). Third, the U.K. subsidiary may in future years look to the U.K. for further supplies, for which it will pay in its own national currency.

Were U.K. firms allowed to finance direct investment by foreign currency purchases in the official market, these various benefits would, sooner or later, outweigh the initial loss to the official reserves. How long this would take cannot be readily calculated because measurement

[1] Australia, New Zealand, South Africa and Eire.

of the benefits is so uncertain, and in the meantime the authorities would be open to embarrassment from a depleted stabilization fund.

5. *Pressure on the Official Reserves*

Suppose that, at the end of a given year, U.K. balance of payments statistics record a deficit on both current and long-term capital account, financed by attracting short-term capital, by official borrowing overseas and by depleting the official reserves of foreign currencies. This end-year picture gives little guide to the course or sequence of events during the year. In particular, it does not show up monetary movements which might at times have caused much bigger losses to the reserves than that finally recorded. These may stem from temporary changes in payments habits among traders, or represent outflows of short-term capital more than offset by inflows at other times during the year.

Some possible combinations of debits and credits are illustrated in Table 18.1, which is not however meant in any way to indicate realistic magnitudes or ratios. 'Private short-term capital' represents the sum of monetary movements on private account,[1] and all the other entries and the signs used in the table can be understood from Chapter 17. The results for each quarter are shown separately in Columns 1 to 4, and their addition in Column 5 gives the outcome for the year as a whole.

It is seen that this end-year picture exactly fits the description of the preceding paragraph. However, while the end-year statistics record a small inflow of short-term capital, figures for the first two quarters show a relatively large outflow. This outflow, combined with the negative basic balance, had by end-June led to a loss from the official reserve of foreign currency worth £110 million. While the basic balance remained negative in subsequent months, a reversal of the short-term capital flow coupled with official borrowing from overseas enabled the authorities add to the reserves in the second half of the year. In the outcome, therefore, the loss to the reserves is less than half the loss accumulated by end-June.

The outflow of short-term capital shown in the first half of the year could have originated in any of three ways. First, the level of interest rates might have risen in other world financial centres, e.g. New York, Paris, Tokyo, etc., or perhaps fallen in London. With other factors constant, this would have made short-term sterling investments less attractive to overseas residents than corresponding investments in other parts of the world. The consequence, therefore, could well be an outflow

[1] Including sterling balances held as reserves by overseas sterling area countries (Chapter 19).

of short-term capital as overseas residents realize their investments here and sell the sterling proceeds for foreign currencies to invest elsewhere.

Second, it will be explained in Chapter 19 that the foreign currency reserves of the Exchange Equalization Account may also be drawn on by members of the overseas sterling area, enabling them finance deficits in their payments with non-sterling countries. It may be that in the first three or six months of the year, a number of them were in deficit with non-sterling countries (U.S.A., Japan, Germany, etc.). Their sale of sterling for foreign currency would then have reduced U.K. net liabilities (as does any capital outflow) at the cost of depleting U.K. reserves.

TABLE 18.1

(*All values in £ million*)

	(1) End-March	(2) End-June	(3) End-Sept.	(4) End-Dec.	(5) Total End-Year
Current A/c Balance	−20	−20	−20	−20	−80
L-t Capital A/c Balance	−10	−10	−10	−10	−40
Basic Balance	−30	−30	−30	−30	−120
Foreign currency reserves	+50	+60	−30	−35	+45
Private s-t capital	−20	−30	+30	+25	+5
Official borrowing	0	0	+30	+40	+70

Note: See note (1) to Table 17.4

Had the U.K. itself been in current account surplus with non-sterling countries at that time, it might have more or less offset the overseas sterling area deficit, leaving the reserves (on this score) broadly unchanged.

Third, the deficit on current account—perhaps a continuation from the previous year—may itself have set off the short-term capital outflow in the first six months, if it became widely thought that the Government might devalue sterling as a remedy (see below). In this case, the figures suggest that, about mid-summer, the Government was able to restore confidence in the continuation of the official parity, i.e. that sterling would not be devalued. This it might have done by announcing a loan from overseas central banks to 'support' sterling (Section 6), the evidence of which figures in the statistics for the next two quarters. Further, the Government might have introduced disinflationary measures at home (compare p. 472), including a rise in Bank Rate. The resultant rise in other interest rates would also have made the U.K. relatively more attractive for short-term investment funds (above).

A devaluation imposes a loss upon the overseas holders of assets in the U.K., since of course the foreign currency value of their assets declines in proportion. For example, a devaluation of sterling from (in terms of the U.S. dollar) £1 = $2·8 to £1 = $2·4 reduces the dollar value of a £1 million holding in the U.K. from $2,800,000 to $2,400,000. Where the asset is held on a long-term basis, say a British company as a subsidiary by an American, this consideration seems to have little relevance. In other cases, however, holdings will be short-term, in the form of balances with U.K. banks, Treasury bills, deposits with finance companies and local authorities, and so on. Where these short-term investments have not been covered in the forward exchange market (below), the prospect of devaluation gives a strong incentive to realize them and sell the sterling proceeds for a 'safer' currency.

A protective 'hedge' against devaluation may be secured by the overseas resident through an appropriate contract in the forward exchange market. In this case, he would arrange with a foreign exchange dealer to sell the latter sterling in return for (e.g.) U.S. dollars, in (say) three months' time, at a rate of exchange agreed between them at the time the contract is made. Thus having bought sterling at the 'spot' rate (i.e. for immediate delivery) of £1 = $2·80, an American may make a contract enabling him to sell sterling three months hence at (say) £1 = $2·77 whatever the spot rate should happen to be on that particular date. If it should still be £1 = $2·80, the arrangement will have cost him 3 cents per £1, since had he not made the arrangement he would have got 3 cents more per £1 at the spot rate. If, however, sterling has been devalued to £1 = $2·40, he will have avoided losing 37 cents per £1 (i.e. $2·77 − $2·40). The American thus avoids a big loss if sterling is devalued, at the expense (in this example) of a small loss if it is not. The latter, however, he would have taken into account in first assessing the profitability of investing short-term in the U.K.

While the spot rate is stabilized within narrow limits on either side of the official parity, the authorities are under no corresponding obligation in respect of the forward rate. Suppose, however, that the fear of devaluation led to heavier forward sales of sterling and so a widening of the 'discount' on the forward rate relative to the spot rate—in the example, a fall in the forward rate from £1 = $2·77 to, say, £1 = $2·75. In this event, the authorities may intervene in the market by themselves selling foreign currencies forward, in order to absorb the supply of forward sterling and prevent the forward rate diverging too far from the normal. This could help reduce the immediate loss to the reserves in at least two ways. First, by keeping down the cost of forward cover the authorities give practical encouragement to overseas residents who were contemplating selling their sterling assets to hedge them instead with a forward contract. Second, by masking the full impact on the forward rate of heavy sterling sales forward, the authorities may help limit the spread of a lack of confidence in the continuation of the official parity.

Apart from inducing an outflow of short-term capital, the prospect of devaluation may add to existing pressure on the official reserves by giving traders an incentive to alter the timing of their import and export payments. Clearly, if he anticipates a devaluation of sterling it is in the interests of the U.K. importer to pay as quickly as possible for as many orders as he can. Similarly, the interests of U.K. exporters are best served by delaying conversion of their foreign currency receipts into sterling, since a devaluation increases the sterling value of their earnings. Export customers who pay in sterling have a similar incentive to delay the sale of their own currencies for sterling.

It follows that the immediate loss to the reserves occasioned by a current account deficit is aggravated by any tendency for importers to *lead* with import payments or for exporters to *lag* in the repatriation of foreign currency receipts. The reserves will, of course, subsequently benefit when goods are imported which have been previously paid for, and export earnings are repatriated in a flood. In the meantime, however, the increased losses to the reserves occasioned by the 'leads and lags' in trade payments may of themselves serve to weaken confidence in the continuation of the official parity, thereby encouraging a precautionary outflow of short-term capital. In practice, opportunities for accelerating and delaying payments are limited by the exchange controls operated by the Bank of England (Section 4). Thus U.K. banks and trading companies are restricted in the size of the balances[1] they can hold on account overseas, which represents some constraint on their ability to delay repatriation. Further, payments for imports are not in general permitted until the goods have been despatched (though before 1965 payment was permissible once the contract had been made).

6. *Official Compensatory Finance*

The assets of the Exchange Equalization Account are held in two primary forms, on the one hand sterling and on the other gold and foreign currencies. The principal sterling asset consists of short-term Government debt since, apart from a small working balance, any sterling the E.E.A. buys in the course of its operations it lends to the National Loans Fund either as Ways and Means Advances or in return for Treasury bills issued 'through the tap' (Chapter 4). The foreign currency

[1] Building up these balances would be a form of short-term investment overseas.

assets of the E.E.A. comprise foreign securities and balances held in account with banks overseas. A purchase of foreign currency by the E.E.A. leads to the crediting of these balances, and a sale results in their debit. For convenience, the E.E.A. also holds some of its gold stocks overseas, an arrangement which makes it particularly easy for the E.E.A. to restore its foreign currency balances following a sale. For example, having sold dollars from its account with the American Federal Reserve, the E.E.A. might then acquire more dollar balances by selling some of its gold held 'on earmark' with the U.S. Treasury to the Federal Reserve (which buys as agent for the U.S. Treasury—Chapter 6). The remainder of the E.E.A.'s gold is physically located in the Bank of England, but must not be confused with the very small gold stock 'belonging to' the Issue Department (Chapter 4). The value of the E.E.A.'s assets is not entered in the weekly Bank Return, the form of which was established in 1844, but separate figures for the gold and foreign currency holdings are published monthly.

To understand some of the banking implications of the E.E.A.'s operations, it is useful to construct a simplified illustration. Suppose that an American firm decides to repatriate part of a (sterling) balance it holds in account with a London clearing bank. Having received the appropriate instruction, the London bank—in its role as foreign exchange dealer—offers the sum for sale in the foreign exchange market, i.e. among other foreign exchange dealers. It happens that, at the time, sterling sales are relatively heavy and, to prevent an undue depreciation of sterling, the Bank of England is 'operating in the market', i.e. using the E.E.A. to buy some of the sterling offered. If the Bank takes up this particular offer, it credits the E.E.A. correspondingly and debits the account of the bank which made the sale. The latter of course debits the account of its American customer, so that its liabilities on account and its cash reserve fall by the same amount.

The American firm now receives a cheque drawn on the E.E.A.'s account at the Federal Reserve, which it pays into its account with an American commercial bank. The latter pays the cheque into its account with a Federal Reserve bank, enjoying an increase in its cash reserves while at the same time it increases its liabilities by crediting the firm's account (Chapter 6). The total assets of the E.E.A., meanwhile, are unchanged, since the fall in its dollar balances (in account with the Federal Reserve) are exactly matched by the rise in its sterling holdings.

Though net purchases of sterling by the E.E.A. deplete the cash reserves of the clearing banks, the transfer of these balances from the E.E.A. to the National Loans Fund (above) gives the authorities a ready opportunity to offset the resultant cash shortage. Thus assume that the clearing banks are exactly on their 8 per cent cash ratio when the E.E.A. buys 100 units of sterling off them in the fashion described.

Since the banks' liabilities to customers also fall by 100 units, they will now be short of 92 units cash if they are to maintain their 8 per cent cash ratio. To take one possibility, the banks may now sell Treasury bills (value 92 units) to the Bank (at the back door), and thereby have their cash reserves restored. To buy the bills, the Bank uses the new balances in the National Loans Fund, to which the E.E.A. acquisitions have been transferred in return for tap Treasury bills. In this way, the Bank utilizes (here, most of) the otherwise surplus balance in the National Loans Fund to minimize the interest cost of Government debt (compare p. 72, and Chapter 4 generally). However, the clearing banks have maintained their cash ratio only at the expense—following their bill sale—of their liquidity ratio, which represents some constraint upon the level of bond holdings and/or advances.

In this example, the Bank effectively returned (92 per cent of) the cash the clearing banks had lost by immediately buying bills off them 'at the back door'. Where, however, a continuing balance of payments deficit entails a succession of net sterling purchases by the E.E.A., it is clear that the Bank will be able to reduce the number of Treasury bills on offer at the weekly market tender. Since a part of the National Loans Fund's needs are met by selling tap bills to the E.E.A., which is regularly buying sterling in the foreign exchange market, it will not be necessary to raise as much as otherwise through the sale of bills to the market. Again, therefore, the liquid assets base of the clearing banks comes under some pressure, though now of longer duration, through a continuing shortage of Treasury bills.[1]

The banking consequences of E.E.A. net sales of sterling can be analysed in a similar way. To prevent an undue appreciation of the pound in exchange market dealings, the authorities will increase the supply of sterling by buying foreign currency. Since the E.E.A. holds only a small working balance, it will find it necessary to recall some of its Ways and Means Advances to the National Loans Fund, or perhaps sell back some of its tap Treasury bills, in return for the funds to finance its foreign currency purchases. The E.E.A.'s sterling assets thus decline, but its purchases of foreign currency mean a corresponding increase in balances held on account overseas.

The E.E.A.'s sale of sterling means a corresponding increase in the cash reserves of the clearing (and other) banks, while their deposit liabilities rise (or have risen) equivalently. At the same time, the National Loans Fund is in need of additional finance to meet the cash payment it has made to the E.E.A. Accordingly, by offering fresh

[1] The implied constraint on bank credit (Chapter 4) is disinflationary, which could help correct a current account deficit. Correspondingly, the reflationary implications of E.E.A. net sterling sales (subsequently described) could serve to limit a current account surplus.

Treasury bills in the market, the Bank can absorb the surplus cash of the clearing banks, and thereby largely make good the initial cash outflow from the National Loans Fund. This does, however, entail an increase in market Treasury bills which, via the liquidity ratio, represents an expansionary influence upon the level of bank credit.

If the E.E.A. is continually making net purchases of foreign currency, it will eventually run short of sterling assets. In itself this shortage represents a simple problem of domestic finance for the Government, which solves it by making a fresh issue from the National Loans Fund, held until needed in the form of tap Treasury bills. A much more serious problem arises when the E.E.A. is continually making net sales of foreign currency, since this entails the eventual exhaustion of the foreign currency reserves. The drain on the reserves can be stopped by eliminating the underlying balance of payments deficit but—while appropriate policies (Sections 3 and 4) are introduced and work themselves through—the Government may arrest the decline by borrowing overseas.

The principal sources from which the Government can borrow foreign currencies are the International Monetary Fund and the central banks (or sometimes the Governments) of other countries. The general conditions governing this assistance are considered in Chapter 19; meanwhile, it is useful to outline the mechanics of this sort of international finance, particularly its implications for the National Loans Fund and the E.E.A.

Assume that the I.M.F. is willing to provide the U.K. Government with foreign currencies up to a certain value. Technically, the Treasury does not *borrow* the foreign currency from the I.M.F., but *buys* it in return for sterling. This foreign currency it gives to the E.E.A., which surrenders a corresponding value of tap Treasury bills. The sterling received by the I.M.F. is immediately *lent* back to the U.K. Government, in return for a special sort of Government security, interest-free notes. There is, accordingly, no net cash outflow from the National Loans Fund. In the outcome, the I.M.F. holds more U.K. Government securities and less 'foreign' currencies, the E.E.A. holds less Treasury bills and more foreign currencies, and the National Loans Fund owes more (on interest-free notes) to the I.M.F. and less (on bills) to the E.E.A.

The *debt* of the Government to the I.M.F. is now in sterling, but the true burden of its obligation lies in accumulating enough foreign currency through the E.E.A. to sell back to the I.M.F. by the repayment date. When it makes repayment, the Treasury will secure the foreign currency from the E.E.A. in return for tap Treasury bills, redeem its interest-free notes held by the I.M.F. with sterling, and then (the essential step) buy the sterling back off the I.M.F. with the foreign currency. The I.M.F. has thus replaced its sterling assets with other currencies, the E.E.A. some of its foreign currency assets with tap Treasury bills, and the National Loans Fund its sterling debt (in interest-free notes) to the I.M.F. with a debt (in Treasury bills) to the E.E.A.

The same sort of interaction between National Loans Fund and E.E.A. takes place when the Government borrows from overseas governments or from overseas central banks. Thus in the first case the Treasury secures (say) U.S. dollars from the U.S. Government in return for an appropriate undertaking to repay the dollars, with interest, according to the conditions of the loan (compare p. 173). The dollars it passes to the E.E.A., against the latter's surrender of the corresponding worth of tap Treasury bills. The National Loans Fund's external obligations (to the U.S. Government) increase, and its domestic obligations (to the E.E.A.) diminish.

In the second case, the Treasury might secure foreign currency from an overseas central bank on a 'swap' for sterling, which is, however, invested on the latter's behalf by the Bank of England in Treasury bills. The National Loans Fund's liabilities due externally thus increase, while there is a corresponding reduction in its liabilities to the E.E.A., since the latter surrenders tap Treasury bills in return for the foreign currency. Alternatively, the overseas central bank might just lend the foreign currency to the Treasury, which passes it to the E.E.A. against tap Treasury bills. Either way, the E.E.A. secures foreign currency balances in account with an overseas central bank, and either way the E.E.A. must part with foreign currency when repayment is made. Statistically, however, 'swaps' are treated as an increase in sterling liabilities (to be included in entry 3a in Table 17.1), and 'foreign currency deposits' as an increase in liabilities in non-sterling currencies (to be included in entry 3b (ii) in Table 17.1).

Questions

1. The following figures in random order include all the items of a Balance of Payments Statement. The 'monetary movements' section has been simplified by consolidating into one figure the various changes in short term assets and liabilities except for the change in the gold and convertible currency reserves. The long-term capital account has been simplified by merging all official long-term capital movements.
   (All figures are in £m.)
   Balancing item +35.
   Transport (net) 2.
   Private investment abroad (net) 228.
   Exports and re-exports (f.o.b.) 4471.

Change in short term borrowing 599.
Government current expenditure abroad (net) 439.
Government long term lending abroad (net) 116.
Travel (net deficit) 71.
Imports (f.o.b.) 5005.
Interest, profits, and dividends (net) 405.
'Other services' (net) 248.
Fall in gold and convertible currency reserves 122.
Private transfers (net deficit) 23.

(a) Construct a Balance of Payments Statement distinguishing:
    (i) Current account (visible trade and invisibles)
    (ii) Long term capital account
    (iii) Balancing item
    (iv) Monetary movements.

(b) What broad differences would you have expected in the figures for the following year if sterling were devalued?   U.L.

2. Define (a) The Balance of Payments on Current Account; (b) The Balance of Payments on Capital Account. What is the connection between the two?   U.L.

3. Outline (a) the different forms that international long-term capital investment can take and (b) the implications of such investment for the balance of payments of an investing country.   I.B.

4. 'The important question for any country is not *whether* its accounts with the rest of the world balance, but *how* they are balanced.' Discuss this statement.   I.B.

5. 'The balance of payments always balances.' Explain and discuss.   U.L.

6. Show how a balance one way or the other in a country's current external accounts is reflected in a change in its assets or liabilities. Illustrate your answer by reference to British experience.   I.B.

7. What is meant by disequilibrium in the balance of payments? How may it come about?   U.L.

8. What is the Exchange Equalization Account? What are its functions?   I.M.T.A.

9. 'The rate of exchange is a price, and like any other price is determined by supply and demand.' Discuss.   B.A. Gen.

10. What is meant by the expression 'an equilibrium rate of exchange'? How would you decide whether the rate of exchange for any particular currency was in equilibrium or not?   I.B.

11. 'A major objection to inflation is that it leads inevitably to an adverse balance of payments.' Explain and discuss.   U.L.

12. What is meant by a worsening of the terms of trade? Is this the same thing as devaluation of a country's currency? Give a reasoned answer.   U.L.

13. Show how an 'unfavourable' movement of the *terms of trade* might produce an 'improvement' in the *balance of trade*.   U.L.

14. Distinguish carefully between:
   (a) the balance of trade;
   (b) the balance of payments; and
   (c) the terms of trade,
   and explain how they are related to each other.   B.Sc.(Econ.)

15. To what extent are deflation and devaluation alternatives as methods of correcting a balance of payments deficit?   I.M.T.A.

16. Assess the relative merits of devaluation and tariff imposition as instruments for correcting an adverse current balance.   J.M.B.

17. Why did the United Kingdom government find it necessary both to devalue the pound and introduce deflationary measures?
                                                                                    B.A. Gen.

18. State and assess the main arguments for and against devaluation as a means of solving a country's external payments problem.
                                                                                    W.J.E.C.

19. Comment on the following statement: 'Devaluation leads to a deterioration in the terms of trade and, therefore, to a fall in the standard of living.'   J.M.B.

20. 'Devaluation always worsens the terms of trade of the devaluing country.' Discuss, showing whether this is always a decisive argument against devaluation.   B.A. Gen.

21. How is a balance of payments deficit financed?   C.S.

22. 'To increase exports we must first reduce demand at home.' Do you agree?   S.U.J.B.

23. In what ways can a deficit on a country's current balance of payments be (a) financed and (b) reduced? Illustrate your answer by reference to recent experience.   I.B.

24. State and discuss the remedial measures which a country can take when faced with a deficit in its balance of payments.   W.J.E.C.

25. Discuss the case for and against restricting British investment overseas.   S.U.J.B.

19

International Economic
Policy and Institutions

THREE IMPORTANT areas of international economic policy are singled
out for consideration in this chapter. Sections 1–3 explore the workings
of the international payments system; Section 4 briefly considers the
work of leading international organizations in development finance;
and Sections 5 and 6 outline the working of tariff and other related
schemes. Survey of these fields gives an opportunity of examining the
major international institutions (like I.M.F.) and agreements (like
G.A.T.T.). It also serves to uncover further problems of the U.K.
economy in its external relationships.

1. The International Gold Standard

Imagine that the central bank in each of a number of countries is prepared to deal in gold in unrestricted quantities, with all comers, at a
price fixed in terms of its own national currency. Thus the central bank
of country A may buy or sell gold at $16 per oz; of country B at
£4 per oz; of country C at 32 francs per oz, and so on. These prices
establish the 'gold value' of each country's currency (sometimes referred
to in technical writing as its 'mint par'). Suppose now that the cost of
transporting gold between any two central banks is invariably 5 per cent
of the dealing price per unit of gold transported. Thus to send gold from
A to B would cost 80 cents (i.e. 5 per cent of $16) per ounce of gold
in the shipment. In these circumstances, no country's currency can
appreciate in the foreign exchange market by more than 5 per cent of
the ratio between the gold value of other currencies and its own gold
value. The ratio between the gold value of the dollar and the gold value
of sterling is (on these figures) £1 = $4, and vice versa $1 = 5s. On this
prediction, accordingly, sterling cannot appreciate beyond £1 = $4·2
(i.e. 5 per cent above the gold value ratio), and the dollar likewise could
not appreciate above $1 = 5s. 3d.

To illustrate the reason, suppose that at a given time the sterling-dollar rate in the foreign exchange market just happens to coincide exactly with the gold value ratio of the two currencies, at £1 = $4. Suppose next that, with other factors unchanged, the dollar demand for sterling increases because, say, A residents wish to increase imports from B. The excess demand for sterling which emerges at the ruling rate will draw the price of sterling upwards (compare Chapter 16), until it reaches a level of £1 = $4·2. At this rate, however, it is equally as cheap for A residents to buy gold from their central bank at $16 per oz., send it to B at a cost of 80 cents per oz., and sell it to the central bank in B for £4 per oz. For each $16·8 he parts with in A, the A resident thus secures £4 in B, equivalent to an exchange rate of £1 = $4·2. It follows that, while he can get sterling on these terms through by-passing the foreign exchange market, no dollar holder would pay more than $4·2 for £1 on the foreign exchange market. In the outcome, therefore, some of the dollar demand for sterling is met in the foreign exchange market at a rate of £1 = $4·2, while the remainder is satisfied through shipments of gold from A to B which procure sterling for dollars on identical terms, though outside the exchange market.

In the contrary situation, an excess sterling demand for dollars at the original parity of $1 = 5s. (equivalent to £1 = $4) would lead to an appreciation of the dollar until it stood at $1 = 5s. 3d. The dollar-sterling rate could rise no higher in the foreign exchange market, since at this level it would be equally profitable for a B resident to buy gold from the B central bank at £4 per oz., ship it to A for 4s. (i.e. 5 per cent of £4) per oz., and sell it there to the A central bank at $16 per oz. In this way he would secure $16 in return for £4 4s., equivalent to an exchange rate of $1 = 5s. 3d. Quoted in sterling, this represents a rate of £1 = $3·81 (approx.).

These calculations have served to define the lower and upper limits outside which the sterling-dollar rate cannot move in exchange market dealings. Expressed in terms of sterling, the upper limit of £1 = $4·2 is known as B's gold 'import' point, since it is at this level that gold will start to move into B. Correspondingly, the lower limit of £1 = $3·81 represents B's gold 'export' point, at which gold starts to leave B. (Vice versa, £1 = $3·81 is A's gold import point, and £1 = $4·2 her gold export point.)

If an increase in B's imports from A depresses the sterling-dollar rate to £1 = $3·81, with an accompanying outflow of gold, then B's 'export' of gold effectively finances her increased imports of goods and services. This represents a form of external disinvestment by B, since she is reducing her stock of an asset—gold—which is as readily accept-able overseas as the appropriate foreign currencies. If an increase in B's exports to A (i.e. A's imports from B) pushes up the sterling-dollar rate to £1 = $4·2, with an accompanying inflow of gold, then B's 'import' of gold represents the return for her increased supply of goods and services to overseas residents. This forms a variety of external investment by B, as she is adding to her stocks of an asset—gold—which constitutes a claim upon overseas residents in the same way as holdings of foreign currency balances.

Faced with a gold outflow of abnormal size or duration, a central bank would need to take corrective measures to protect her gold reserves. By drawing other interest rates upwards a rise in the central bank rediscount rate might serve to attract short-term capital from overseas, and the consequent increase in foreign currency demand for the home currency could pull the latter off its gold export point, at least for the time being. More radically, a country losing gold might adopt a deflationary policy designed, by discouraging imports and encouraging exports, to improve its current balance, though its need to adjust price and income levels would be reduced if the countries enjoying the gold inflow simultaneously pursued a reflationary policy.

This picture of international monetary relationships, though presented at an abstract level, nonetheless comes close to the essentials of the international 'gold standard' system which operated among leading nations in the thirty or forty years preceding the First World War. The Bank of England had dealt freely between gold and sterling as far back as 1821,[1] but not until the last decades of the nineteenth century had most other major powers established free convertibility at fixed prices between their currencies and gold. The system thus adopted served not only to stabilize exchange rates (around their gold-value ratios) but provided a means (through gold movement) of financial offset among surplus and deficit countries. Chronic surplus or deficit, however, implied a need[2] for reflation or deflation, which would work on the current balance and so prevent an abnormal gold accumulation or drainage.

As mentioned in Chapter 1 the 'full-gold' or 'gold-coin' standard operative in the U.K. up to 1914 was—after the war-time suspension— replaced in 1925 by a 'gold-bullion' standard under which the Bank of England was obliged to sell gold only in minimum units of 400 fine

[1] And indeed in the eighteenth century before the suspension of convertibility in the Napoleonic Wars.

[2] The gold backing system introduced in England and Wales by the Bank Charter Act of 1844 was intended—following the Quantity Theory of Money —to ensure automatic deflation by causing the note issue to contract in line with a gold outflow. In practice contraction on this pattern did not occur as, among other reasons, the Bank moved to protect its gold reserve with a rise in Bank Rate. However, such a rise coupled with credit restraint would also represent a deflationary monetary policy.

ounces. This economized the Bank's stock of gold while nonetheless enabling participation in the international gold standard system which was gradually restored in the mid-1920s. America had re-adopted a full-gold standard in 1919 but most other leading countries adopted either a gold-bullion standard, like the U.K., or a gold-exchange standard. The latter meant that a central bank held most of its reserves, not in gold, but in the securities or currency (i.e. bank balances) of a country on either a full-gold or gold-bullion standard. By this arrangement a central bank could earn interest on its foreign currency/security reserves, while (in principle) gold was always available to it from the foreign central banks.

The restored gold standard of the 1920s was, from the beginning, subject to various strains. First, some countries (including the U.K.) adopted mint par values which 'overvalued' their currencies, so that their exports appeared unduly expensive to foreign buyers while foreign goods appeared abnormally cheap to importers at home. In the U.K.'s case, this prevented her from achieving a current account surplus sufficient to finance all her long-term investment overseas, and the difference was financed by an inflow of precariously-held short-term capital. Second, countries which had overvalued their currencies found deflation at home difficult or impossible,[1] while their problem of adjustment was made no easier by the general unwillingness of countries receiving a gold inflow to follow a domestic policy of economic expansion. Third, the gold holdings of gold-bullion and full-gold standard countries were exposed to abnormal drains and associated crises of confidence as and when gold-exchange countries chose to switch reserves from currency into gold.

These weaknesses in the international monetary system, coupled with serious depression in world production and trading levels, led to the progressive collapse of the international gold standard system from 1929 onwards. The U.K. left the gold standard in September, 1931, to be followed by the U.S.A. in April, 1933. Unlike the U.K., however, the U.S.A. returned in 1934 with the adoption of a system—described as a 'limited gold-bullion standard'—which survives to this day. Under these arrangements (Chapter 6), sale of gold by the U.S. Treasury is (mainly) limited to overseas central banks and international monetary institutions at the fixed price of $35 per oz., though the Treasury will buy at this price from any source. A few European countries (notably France) also persevered with the gold standard through into the second half of the decade but—as a system for stabilizing the exchange rates and adjusting the economic relationships of the world's leading coun-

---

[1] In the U.K. opposition to wage cuts in the coal industry (which had suffered a sizeable contraction in post-war export markets) culminated in 1926 in a General Strike by trade union members.

tries—the international gold standard system may be regarded as finished in 1931.

2. *The International Monetary Fund*

It was with the hope of achieving more satisfactory regulation and development of the post-war international monetary system that forty-four nations, meeting at Bretton Woods, U.S.A., in 1944, drew up and signed the Articles of Agreement of the International Monetary Fund. The Fund itself came into existence in 1945 and began operations from its Washington headquarters in 1947. Today it has over a hundred members, including almost every non-communist country except Switzerland[1] but excluding every communist country except Yugoslavia. While the Fund is technically a specialized agency of the United Nations, control of the Fund is in the hands not of the U.N. but of its own member governments. Each appoints one representative (thus the Chancellor of the Exchequer represents the U.K.) to serve on the Fund's Board of Governors; the Board, which meets annually in September, attends to such basic issues as the admission of new members, proposed changes in the Fund Agreement, or revision of 'quotas' (i.e. member countries' financial subscriptions to the Fund—below). Otherwise, administration of the Fund is left to the twenty directors who make up the full-time Executive Board (five are the individual representatives of the five countries with the largest quotas, while each of the remaining fifteen represents a group of countries). The U.K. qualifies for its own nominee under these arrangements, and representation on the Executive Board is shared between a Treasury and a Bank of England official. On both boards, voting powers broadly reflect the quota size of the country (or countries) represented.

The objectives and activities of the Fund fall into three broad categories. First, the regulation of monetary relationships among member countries, in accordance with the 'code of good conduct' set out in the Fund Agreement. Second, the provision of finance to members in balance of payments deficit, again in line with the principles set out in the Agreement and developed by the Fund. Third, the promotion of consultation among member countries on international monetary problems, with an advisory service for individual members from its technical staff.

A corner-stone of the international monetary system envisaged in the Fund Agreement is stability of members' exchange rates. Under the 'par value' system adopted by the Fund, each member is required to define the value of its currency in terms of weight of gold, thereby

[1] Which is reported (mid-1969) to be considering joining.

establishing a scale from which the external value of one currency in terms of any other can readily be calculated. Strictly, members are required by the Articles to prevent the exchange values of their currencies moving more than 1 per cent either side of the parities thus defined, in all transactions within their territories. The United States meets this obligation by its willingness to sell gold for dollars to (or buy gold with dollars from) the monetary authorities of other countries at the fixed price, per ounce, of \$35 plus (or minus) $\frac{1}{4}$ per cent handling charge. Thus if the dollar were depreciating all round against Western European currencies, the monetary authorities of U.K., Germany, France, etc., would all sell their respective national currencies for dollars, which would serve to support the dollar rate in the exchange market. The dollar balances so acquired they could turn into gold at the Federal Reserve Bank of New York any time they chose (Section 3).

Other member countries are not prepared to sell gold freely like the U.S.A., and accordingly need to adopt different techniques for stabilizing their currency values. Britain and other Western European countries follow the same system of each 'pegging' its own currency on the dollar. This means that the monetary authority in each country buys its own currency to prevent it falling unduly against the dollar and sells it to prevent an undue appreciation (compare Chapter 17 and Section 3). Their choice of margins—about[1] 0·75 per cent either side of parity— might appear to raise difficulties on 'cross-rates'. Thus the official sterling-dollar parity is £1 = \$2·4, and the official dollar-deutschemark parity \$1 = D.M.3·66, which implies a sterling-deutschemark (cross) rate of £1 = D.M.8·78. Suppose now that sterling appreciates 0·75 per cent above the official parity on the dollar, while the deutschemark depreciates on the dollar by 0·75 per cent. This entails a sterling-deutschemark rate 1·5 per cent above £1 = D.M. 8·78, which is a half per cent more than strictly permitted by the Fund Agreement! This arrangement has, nonetheless, been sanctioned by the Fund, which also permits a margin of 1 per cent either side between any currency (say sterling) and the second currency on which it is pegged (the dollar).

Stabilization of exchange values around their approved parities protects them from the gross disturbances which short-term capital movements might otherwise create, and thus helps make a stable foundation for international trade and investment. However, in the changing pattern of world trade and capital flows, a parity may come to lose the suitability it once possessed, so that some adjustment appears desirable. In this event any member has the right to alter its currency's par value by up to 10 per cent of the original parity chosen. A bigger alteration

[1] The statistics of p. 385 show that, for the U.K., the percentage is currently 0·83.

or a further alteration, while still necessarily proposed by the member, must be approved by the Fund.

The Fund will give its approval only if the applicant's balance of payments is in a condition of 'fundamental disequilibrium'. This term has not been defined by the Fund, and it might be thought unduly self-restrictive for it to attempt to do so. While the rule covers proposals for revaluation[1] as well as for devaluation, its practical importance lies in restricting the use of the latter as a remedy for deficit disequilibrium (Chapter 18). Thus the Fund would be unlikely to approve a devaluation where the deficit reflected essentially temporary problems, such as a crop-exporting country's bad harvest, or the interruption of trade through a short-lived and local war. Deficits originating in this way could be financed from the country's reserves, or by borrowing from the Fund (below). On the other hand, devaluation would probably be approved for a country which was persistently troubled by a negative trade balance, where reserves were low, and the deficit was largely financed by short-term capital inflow.

The Fund's par value system is thus designed to give its members stability of exchange rates without rigidity. Each rate is stabilized around a given parity, but the parity itself can be adjusted in appropriate circumstances. Where a member does devalue, the Fund can make a further contribution to rate stability by restraining other members, over-fearful of increased competition in export markets, from following suit. On the other hand, devaluation by a leading country like the U.K. could be expected to bring similar moves by other countries which align their exchange rates on sterling.

The 'code of good behaviour' for members defined by the Fund Agreement also prescribes the removal of current transactions from exchange control. In effect, Article VIII requires each member to allow free dealing in its currency for trading and similar purposes between resident and non-resident alike, at a uniform exchange rate centred on the official parity. The currency of a country satisfying these conditions is described as 'convertible' (compare p. 393). Many leading members were unable to accept this obligation for some years after the war, because of the help exchange restrictions gave them in suppressing deficit disequilibrium in their balance of payments (compare p. 408). Today, however, all the principal industrial countries—though relatively few primary producers—have adopted Article VIII. A very slight retreat from full convertibility was made by the U.K. in 1966 when (with Fund consent) a restriction on residents' overseas travel expenditure was reintroduced.

The second category of Fund activities consists in providing finance

[1] Thus Germany and Holland raised the par values of their currencies by 5 per cent in 1961, and Germany by 9·29 per cent in October, 1969.

P

for members in balance of payments deficit, out of the pool of resources built up from members' contributions. The conditions for drawing on this pool were defined originally in the Fund Agreement, but have undergone considerable elaboration through the subsequent decisions and operations of the Fund. Further, under a recent amendment to the Fund Agreement, the Fund has been enabled to supplement these arrangements with a new scheme by which members could enjoy additional finance through 'Special Drawing Rights'. This system is held over for consideration in Section 3.

The value of each member's contribution to the Fund is represented by its 'quota', the size of which it agrees with the Fund. Quotas are reviewed periodically when, as in 1959 and 1965, the Fund may decide on a general rise, though any member is free to opt out of the increase. Contributions are (normally) payable in the proportion 25 per cent gold and 75 per cent the member's own national currency. The currency contribution is in practice lent back to the member until needed (if ever) by the Fund to meet calls upon its resources. This resembles the procedure followed when a member uses its own currency to 'draw' (i.e. buy) other currency from the Fund—a technique explained in Chapter 18.

That drawings on the Fund are intended to cover 'temporary' disequilibria only is apparent from the Articles of Agreement and from the Fund's requirement that they be repaid within three to five years. The drawing country is, accordingly, expected within that period to convert its deficit into a surplus, in order to finance the repayment of the drawing to the Fund. If it failed to do so, it might secure another drawing from the Fund to finance the repayment, though this would certainly entail increased Fund surveillance over its domestic policy (below). Such circumstances would, however, suggest that the disequilibrium was 'fundamental', and Fund and member might consider devaluation as a means of bringing the latter's price level closer in line with world conditions. The Fund Agreement does not permit it to lend on a long-term basis to finance imports of capital goods, as part of a development programme: this activity is left to its sister institution, the World Bank (Section 4).

Given these conditions, a member's access to the resources of the Fund will depend primarily on the size of its quota, the amount of assistance sought and the amount (if any) already outstanding. To explain the system followed, it is useful to construct a simple illustration. Suppose that, valued in U.S. dollars, a member's quota is 100 ($ million) which has been paid 75 units in national currency and 25 units in gold. The Fund has made no use of this member's currency in meeting other members' drawings, so its holding of the currency is at present 75 units. The member now has a fully automatic right to draw up to 25 units in appropriate currencies from the Fund, should it need assistance in meeting a balance of payments deficit. This is the difference between the member's quota (100 units) and the Fund's holding of its currency (75 units), usually referred to as the gold 'tranche' (which means 'slice') because of its general equivalence to the member's gold subscription. If the member exercises this facility up to the limit of its gold tranche, the Fund's holding of its currency will rise to 100 units, i.e. 75 units original subscription and 25 units paid for the currencies now purchased.

Further or bigger assistance by the Fund would take the member into its first 'credit' tranche, where the Fund's holding of its currency lies between 100 and 125 per cent of quota. The Fund's attitude to an application in this range is liberal, provided that the member undertakes to make reasonable efforts to reduce its balance of payments deficit. Movement into the second (126 to 150 per cent) and subsequent tranches requires a progressively stronger justification by the member, and meets stiffening conditions by the Fund, until the limit is reached at 200 per cent of the applicant's quota.

A member may, however, apply for a 'compensatory drawing' of up to 25[1] per cent of quota, even if this brings Fund holdings of its currency beyond the normal limit of 200 per cent of quota. This facility, introduced in 1963 largely for the benefit of primary producing countries, is available to a member whose export receipts fall short of the normal for reasons largely outside its control (e.g. a decline in world prices), provided the member will co-operate with the Fund in working (where appropriate) for the solution of its balance of payments problem.

More generally, the conditions imposed on members seeking to draw within their credit tranches may relate both to the Fund Agreement and to the domestic economic policies pursued by the applicants. In the first case, the Fund can clearly use its financial powers to help keep members' external policies in line with the Fund Agreement. Thus it could make assistance conditional upon the applicant's attempting, at the same time, some progress towards the convertibility defined in Article VIII. In the second case, the Fund is likely to emphasize the importance of restraining domestic inflation in overcoming a balance of payments deficit. To this end it might expect the applicant to give clearly specified undertakings on, for instance, Government spending, tax policy and the level of bank credit.

Drawings on the Fund which take the member beyond its gold tranche carry a once-and-for-all service charge of about $\frac{1}{2}$ per cent and an annual interest charge which varies with the size of the drawing and the

---

[1] 50 per cent since 1966. A complementary scheme introduced in 1969 permits drawings up to 50 per cent to finance buffer stocks (*re* international commodity agreements). Drawings under the two schemes must not together exceed 75 per cent.

time it is outstanding. The currency or currencies drawn would most often be fully 'convertible' and, other things being equal, the Fund would prefer to use the currency of countries in overall balance of payments surplus. Repayment must be in gold or a convertible currency, in the second case not necessarily the currency originally drawn. As explained in Chapter 18, a member makes 'repayment' by buying its own currency back from the Fund—bringing the Fund's holding of its currency down to its original subscription level, i.e. 75 per cent of quota.

In addition to the drawing facilities so far described, the Fund offers members the benefits of two other schemes, the first introduced in the early 1950s and the second in the early 1960s. A member who anticipates a need for assistance may, under the 'Stand-By Arrangements', apply to the Fund for advance authorization of a drawing, which it may or may not take up in the following twelve months, depending on its balance of payments outcome. In considering a request for a 'stand-by credit' the Fund applies the same criteria, according to tranche, as it would to a request for an immediate drawing. While the stand-by facility carries a very low interest charge, its arrangement may of itself be immediately beneficial to the member's balance of payments. Thus it could represent evidence of the Fund's willingness to co-operate with the member to avoid a devaluation of its currency, which would serve —in association with other measures—to reduce any risk of a 'flight' from the member's currency (compare p. 422).

In contrast to other Fund facilities, assistance under the 'General Arrangements to Borrow' is limited to the ten members who are parties to them. The arrangements were made in 1962 between the Fund and ten leading industrial nations[1] ('The Group of Ten'), subsequently joined in 1963 by Switzerland (not a Fund member). The scheme envisages a situation in which one of the ten seeks a very large drawing from the Fund, to meet an outflow of short-term capital so serious as to threaten the stability of the international monetary system (Section 3). In order to satisfy such a request without excessive strain the Fund can call upon the other nine for a supplementary contribution, additional to their standard quotas. These contributions are made in the respective national currencies, but only if the members of the Group, after consultation, approve the Fund's request. Switzerland will also provide assistance. Repayment by the drawing member is made to the Fund, within three to five years or sooner if practicable, and the Fund in turn reimburses the donors. By these arrangements, then, the Fund is able in appropriate circumstances to get hold of additional 'strategic' currencies on a very large scale, while avoiding any general increase in quotas.

[1] Belgium, Canada, France, West Germany, Italy, Japan, Netherlands, Sweden, United Kingdom, United States.

3. *The International Payments System Today*

Two outstanding features of the contemporary system of international payments are the use of the U.K. pound sterling and the U.S. dollar as 'vehicle' currencies and as 'reserve' currencies. To explain the meaning of, first, a 'vehicle' currency, it is useful to construct a simple illustration involving the use of sterling in this role.

Suppose that a New Zealand firm with a balance in account with a London bank draws on it to finance an import from Germany. The sterling balance acquired in this way by the German exporter is soon sold on the foreign exchange market for deutschemarks, supplied by another German firm which uses sterling to finance its import business with, say, West Africa. A subsequent German import from Nigeria is accordingly paid for by the transfer of the balance to a Nigerian bank, which may, in turn, use it to settle payment on a Nigerian import from Australia.

Ownership of a U.K. banking liability has thus passed among the residents of a variety of countries, serving on each occasion to finance an international movement of goods. In this way sterling has acted as a 'vehicle' for the finance of international trade, though none of the trade had any connection with the U.K. Throughout the example, the sole effect on Britain's external position was a successive change in the direction of her external liabilities, from New Zealand through Germany and Nigeria to Australia. To round the illustration off, it might be the case that this particular bank balance is used by the Australian to finance an import from the U.K., thus terminating (at least for the time being) its career in international finance. At the same time, of course, another U.K. firm may be paying its Australian supplier in sterling . . . , and so on.

Suppose that the international use of sterling as a vehicle currency began to increase. This would mean that more banks and merchanting houses outside the U.K. wanted to hold sterling balances and other short-term assets in the U.K., to use in financing trade with countries other than the U.K. Their acquisition of sterling would show up in the U.K. balance of payments as an inflow of short-term capital, i.e. an increase in U.K. short-term liabilities. If on the other hand sterling became less popular as a vehicle for financing international trade, the consequential run-down of sterling balances would show up as a decrease in U.K. short-term liabilities.

Since the 1950s sterling has lost to the U.S. dollar its position as the world's leading vehicle (or 'trading') currency. Sterling is similarly overshadowed by the dollar in its role of 'reserve' currency, and arrangements exist (below) which will limit its role even further in years ahead. A reserve currency is the principal foreign currency held as an external reserve by a nation's monetary authority. Its holdings are used, along with other international reserve assets (notably gold), to stabilize the external value of the currency at the I.M.F.-approved parity and finance a balance of payments deficit should one arise. For members of the Overseas Sterling Area the function of reserve currency is performed by sterling, though official holdings of U.S. dollars are significant and can be expected to increase. For most other countries (including Britain) outside the communist blocs, the reserve currency is the U.S. dollar.

The Overseas Sterling Area comprises the U.K. colonies; the Commonwealth except Canada; Iceland, Eire, South Africa and certain Arab countries. Membership, cohesion and function have all variously changed since, amidst the disintegration of the international gold standard in the early 1930s, the O.S.A. first assumed an identity as a group of countries which aligned their exchange rates on sterling. Its importance for the international payments system today reflects the dominant role of sterling in the finance of O.S.A. members' overseas trade. Privately, the use of sterling as a vehicle currency is more widespread among O.S.A. members than in the rest of the world. At an official level, all the members (except S. Africa, which chiefly holds gold) hold their external reserves mainly as short-term sterling assets—namely balances in account with London banks, Treasury bills and short-dated Government bonds.

To see how sterling functions as a reserve currency, it is convenient initially to ignore the outside, non-sterling world, and begin by supposing that one O.S.A. member (X) is in overall deficit with the rest of the O.S.A. In outcome the deficit will be financed by a switch of sterling balances from the ownership of X to the ownership of the surplus countries. Of itself this change in the ownership of the U.K.'s external liabilities would have no effect on their level, or on the U.K. balance of payments. Assume next that X is in deficit with the U.K., reflecting (say) an excess of imports over exports. This would entail a run-down of X's sterling balances, as some of her bill and bond holdings were sold and bank balances drawn on to pay off U.K. creditors. From the U.K.'s viewpoint, her excess of exports to X has enabled (or financed) a reduction in sterling liabilities to X. On the other hand if the U.K. were in deficit with X, the immediate consequence would be a rise in X's sterling balances, representing from X's viewpoint an increase in her external reserves. Finally, if X's surplus with the U.K. coincided with an exactly equivalent deficit by X with the rest of the O.S.A., then X's sterling balances would, in the outcome, remain unchanged.

To sum up, within the Sterling Area (i.e. O.S.A. plus Britain) O.S.A. official holdings of U.K. short-term liabilities provide a reserve currency for the finance of deficits and surplus among Sterling Area members. An overall deficit of the U.K. with the O.S.A. would (to ignore temporarily the outside, non-sterling world) increase the external reserves held by the latter, and vice versa. If the U.K. were exactly in balance overall with the O.S.A. then (on the same proviso) the stock of external reserves among O.S.A. members would remain constant.

For most non-communist countries outside the O.S.A., the function of reserve currency is carried out, after a similar fashion, by the U.S. dollar. Thus an overall deficit by Germany with the rest of the world would entail—if we ignore momentarily official German gold holdings —a corresponding fall in the German authorities' holdings of dollar balances. In terms of exchange market operations, the German monetary authorities would have been net sellers of dollars (below) for D.M.s over the period, in order to support the latter's exchange value. Vice versa, a German surplus overall would have entailed an accumulation of dollar reserve holdings. A deficit by the U.S.A. with the rest of the world entails (at least initially) a rise in U.S. short-term liabilities, hence an increase in other countries' international reserves; vice versa, a U.S. surplus implies a contraction in other countries' official dollar holdings.

Relationships between the O.S.A. and the non-sterling world centre mainly around the reserve holdings of the United Kingdom. Thus an O.S.A. member in overall deficit with the non-sterling world would procure the appropriate foreign currency by running down its official sterling balances in London, which would impose a corresponding burden on the Exchange Equalization Account. Other things being equal, U.K. short-term liabilities to an O.S.A. member would fall, but U.K. external reserves would fall by a similar amount. If the same country happened concurrently to have an equivalent overall surplus with the rest of the O.S.A., her sterling assets would in the outcome remain unchanged. Should the O.S.A. in total have an overall surplus with the rest of the world then (other things being equal) E.E.A. external assets would rise and sterling liabilities would rise. This would reflect O.S.A. members' sale of their 'excess' foreign currency acquisitions for sterling on the foreign exchange market (but see below). If at the same time, however, the O.S.A. had an exactly equivalent deficit with the U.K., the level of U.K. sterling liabilities would remain unchanged though E.E.A. external assets would rise as before.

A country's external reserves do not, of course, consist exclusively of one reserve currency. Thus Western European countries hold their reserves part in U.S. dollars and part in gold, in proportions varying from country to country. A monetary authority can at its discretion switch between dollars and gold by dealing with the U.S. authorities at their fixed gold price (Section 2). Western European countries may also have relatively small official holdings of other convertible currencies, which would be counted as part of their external reserves. For most of these countries, however, the regular currency for exchange market intervention is the dollar, so that (for example) the U.K. authorities would not usually seek to stabilize the sterling exchange rate by operating in D.M.s or francs, nor would the Germans try and stabilize the D.M. with sterling sales or purchases. If sterling were depreciating against the dollar, the D.M., and so on, it would normally be sufficient for the Bank of England to sell dollars in appropriate quantities: any sterling holder who wanted D.M.s would then profitably move from sterling into dollars and thence into D.M.s, thereby relieving the pressure on the sterling-D.M. rate.

Members of the O.S.A. hold their reserves 'mainly' in sterling, which means that they will in some cases also have significant holdings of gold and U.S. dollars, as well as working balances in other currencies. The practice of 'diversifying' reserves in this way has gained ground among O.S.A. members in the past decade. Clearly, growth in O.S.A. holdings of gold and dollars limits the reserve function of sterling, and is achieved at the expense of E.E.A. external assets. An O.S.A. overall surplus with the non-sterling world increases E.E.A. gold and currency holdings only in so far as O.S.A. members do not hold on to their 'excess' foreign currency acquisitions as a reserve, but sell them off for sterling to hold in their place.

To sum up, the contemporary international payments system may be characterized as a 'gold-exchange' standard. Gold represents the 'final' international monetary asset: it could always be used to buy any (non-communist) country's currency, and hence will always serve to finance the holder's balance of payments deficit. Unlike bills and bonds, however, gold does not yield interest. This is one reason why countries generally hold a reserve currency in addition to gold, though the proportions vary widely from country to country. Many countries favour the U.S. dollar as a reserve currency, since it can readily be turned into gold (by sale to the U.S. monetary authorities) and because it is the currency of so rich and powerful a country. However, one important group of countries—the Overseas Sterling Area—largely (but by no means exclusively) holds sterling in place of both gold and dollars. This they do partly because O.S.A. members have easier access to British capital sources under U.K. exchange control regulations (Chapter 18), partly from strength of tradition, partly because of sterling's importance to them as a trading currency, and partly because sterling is, anyway, convertible into dollars and so into gold.

Foreign holders of dollar or sterling balances would, of course, suffer a capital loss if the U.S. dollar or the pound were devalued. This means, first, that the American or the British authorities might hesitate to propose devaluation of their currencies to the I.M.F., even though they thought it otherwise appropriate as a way of correcting an external payments deficit. It also means, nonetheless, that American and British official reserves can be exposed to heavy pressure by the withdrawal of foreign funds, if balance of payments disequilibrium raises the prospect of a dollar or a sterling devaluation (Chapter 18).

During the persistent American and British payments deficits of the 1960s, official dollar and sterling holdings (i.e. balances held by the monetary authorities of other countries) have in general been more stable than commercial holdings (notably dollar and sterling balances held for trading purposes). It might be thought that this would have afforded U.S. gold reserves some protection, since a switch by commercial holders from the dollar into other currencies simply means that monetary authorities accumulate dollars in their official reserves, as they sell their own currencies to support the dollar on the exchange market (Section 2). However, since a dollar devaluation means that the U.S. authorities raise their official gold price from $35 per ounce, the holder of dollar balances (or indeed other currencies) might prefer[1] to speculate on the devaluation by buying gold on the free London market. Until 1968, relatively heavy purchases on the London market entailed a gold loss for the U.S. authorities, since they played the leading role in a consortium of central banks which had, from 1961 onwards, operated in the market in an attempt to stabilize the price of gold. The abandonment of the arrangement in March, 1968, means that the U.S. authorities are no longer exposed to a gold drain along this particular channel, though (of course) they may still suffer a gold loss if other monetary authorities choose to alter their reserve composition by switching from dollars into gold.

A very large outflow of short-term capital from the U.S.A. or the U.K., inspired by a fear of devaluation, could conceivably compel the U.S. or U.K. authorities to devalue simply to halt the speculation and bring the reserve loss to an end. A devaluation of—in particular—the U.S. dollar would prompt other countries to reconsider—and in many cases readjust—their own par values, and the consequence might be a period of marked instability in the international monetary system. It was principally to ensure its ability to assist the U.S. authorities in the event of a speculative 'run' on the dollar that the I.M.F. negotiated the General Arrangements to Borrow in 1962, though of course assistance is available to any of the participants on the terms described in Section 2. This scheme apart, both the U.S. and the U.K. authorities began in the

[1] Residents of the U.K. and U.S.A. are not allowed to hold gold, except for approved purposes, e.g. industrial use. In many countries, however, private gold holding is quite legal, and demand can be met through the London and various other world markets. Supply comes from private hoards, current mining production and, occasionally, the Soviet Union and China.

early 1960s to develop arrangements with leading central banks for special, short-term assistance in the event of an outflow of short-term capital.

In the U.K.'s case such arrangements were first made in 1961 at Basle with the central banks of Belgium, France, West Germany, Italy, the Netherlands, Sweden and Switzerland: similar plans were later agreed with the U.S.A. The Basle agreement of 1961 enabled the U.K. authorities to borrow short-term (by the techniques described in Chapter 18) to offset some of the reserve losses occasioned by an outflow of private capital. The arrangements were periodically renewed and, in 1966, significantly broadened with a provision for assistance in meeting sterling sales by official overseas holders (this was negotiated with, additionally, Austria, Canada and Japan, while France gave a separate facility).

A fresh and more radical agreement was reached at Basle in 1968, when the parties to the 1966 scheme were joined by Denmark, Norway and the U.S.A. The 1968 agreement gave the U.K. a very large 'stand-by' credit, initially available for three years, against the run-down of official (and private) sterling balances by members of the O.S.A. Any U.K. borrowings under the scheme would be repayable within ten years. The U.K. thus enjoys a medium-term protection against loss to E.E.A. reserves through 'diversification' by O.S.A. members (a trend which had accelerated after the 1967 sterling devaluation). At the same time, O.S.A. members have undertaken to limit the rate at which they switch official sterling balances into dollars while maintaining minimum sterling holdings, and to control their own residents' private conversions. In return for this restraint, the value of official O.S.A. sterling balances has been (largely) guaranteed against any future devaluation of the pound (relative to the dollar). The likely outcome, accordingly, is the decline of sterling's reserve role in the finance of payments (via the E.E.A.) between the O.S.A. and the non-sterling world, though it should continue to function as a reserve currency in the finance of intra-Sterling-Area payments.

The problems of the reserve currencies also form part of wider issues centring on the appropriate level and forms for 'international liquidity'. In this sense a country's 'liquidity' is measured by the size of its external reserves plus its borrowing powers under I.M.F. and central bank arrangements, i.e. the total resources it can draw on to finance a balance of payments deficit. 'World liquidity', accordingly, denotes the total value of external reserves (in gold and currency) held by non-communist countries, along with the borrowing facilities available under I.M.F. and central bank schemes. In brief, an 'excess' of world liquidity implies that, even though their disequilibrium is 'fundamental', deficit countries may be over-slow to adjust their external payments by way of disinflation and/or devaluation, since finance for the deficit is so readily to hand. By contrast, a 'shortage' of world liquidity suggests that countries may be embarrassed by even quite temporary external deficits, and be obliged to resort to disinflation or trade, capital and exchange controls. Excess liquidity thus carries the danger of inflation, while inadequate liquidity threatens restraint on the growth of domestic product and international trade.

It would be very difficult to put a numerical value on the growth of total world liquidity (as defined) in the post-war period. However one constituent, reserve holdings of gold and currency, showed by end-1968 a 47 per cent increase on the 1951 level of $48 thousand million. Of this increase a little under one-quarter represented bigger official gold holdings, while the remainder very largely reflected an increase in official dollar balances. This second source of world liquidity cannot be expected to grow significantly in future years. While persistent U.S. deficits originally furnished other countries' monetary authorities with their dollar holdings, their continuation would heighten the anxiety already experienced and thus precipitate dangerously heavy switching from dollars into gold.

Alternative methods of securing an adequate level of international liquidity have been widely discussed. On one approach emphasis is laid not on expanding the supply of liquidity but on reducing the requirement, through more rapid adjustment to balance of payments (notably, current account) disequilibrium. Thus a measure of automatic adjustment might be achieved through greater exchange rate flexibility, say by permitting rates to vary a few per cent either side of the official parity. If sterling, for example, were allowed to vary between margins of £1 = $2·5 and £1 = $2·3, deficit disequilibrium would imply not only a loss to the U.K. reserves but a market rate which was bumping along the lower level. In sterling terms U.K. imports would become perceptibly more expensive, while U.K. exports would become slightly cheaper in foreign currency prices. With appropriate elasticities (Chapter 18, Section 3) these price movements would improve the balance on U.K. current account, so that (other things being equal) the need to run down the reserves or borrow overseas is reduced. In fact, of course, 'other things'—notably short-term capital movements— would be affected by the modest sterling depreciation, but in what ways and with what consequences cannot be considered here.

Other proposals centre on ways of raising the level of world liquidity. One possible way of increasing the value of world reserves is through a rise in the official U.S. price of gold, accompanied by a corresponding reduction in the gold values (Section 2) of other I.M.F. members' currencies. Exchange rates would thus be unchanged in terms of each other, but gold would be worth more in terms of each currency. Gold revaluation is not, however, a means of maintaining liquidity expansion but a way of overcoming an existing shortage, since, if countries are to remain willing to hold currencies after such a revaluation, it would need to be interpreted as a once-and-for-all increase. A gold revaluation would, of course, give an especial benefit to South Africa as the leading gold producer in the non-communist world, to countries holding a high proportion of gold in their reserves, and to private gold hoarders. A further weakness in the scheme is the risk of instability in the period immediately preceding the change, since rumours of the proposal would almost certainly prompt a scramble from dollars (and, where possible, sterling) into gold. Finally, by increasing the importance of gold and gold mining in international monetary affairs, the revaluation would run counter to the long-run trend (both domestic and international) towards a 'managed' money supply in which 'book-keeping entries' are dominant.

Strongly representative of this trend is the Special Drawing Rights scheme which was written into the I.M.F. Articles of Agreement in July, 1969, and is due to be activated in January, 1970, for an initial period of three years. Under these arrangements the Fund would set up a new account, quite separate from the existing pool of subscriptions, in which all members who wished to participate would be credited each year with Special Drawing Rights proportionate to their standard quotas. These credits would *not* require any contribution from the members concerned. A participant (X) who ran into a payments deficit would then be able to draw on its 'holding' of S.D.R.s and present them to another participant (Y) who would give in return an equivalent value in convertible currencies, which the recipient (X) could (of course) use in financing its deficit.

Participants would be required to maintain a minimum average S.D.R. holding of 30 per cent over the first five-year period, so that a participant (e.g. X) who ran down its S.D.R. holdings heavily in (say) the first two years would need to make net purchases of S.D.R.s from other participants in the three subsequent years, to achieve the prescribed five-year average. The Fund would be able to designate participants to receive S.D.R.s from their fellow participants, and would in general select members who needed to 'reconstitute' their S.D.R. holdings (above), or were 'surplus' countries with strong reserve positions. However, no participant would be obliged to accept S.D.R.s if this would increase its holdings beyond three times its allotment. Members accumulating S.D.R.s would receive interest, financed by charges levied on participants whose holdings had fallen below their allotment level.

Despite their name S.D.R.s are better regarded not as a borrowing facility but as an international monetary asset, which can be turned automatically (subject to the five-year average requirement) into convertible currencies for the finance of payments deficits. In the U.K. the authorities would treat S.D.R.s, like gold and convertible currencies, as part of the official reserves, and include them among the assets of the E.E.A. By providing for the creation of a new form of 'international money', the scheme thus represents a deeply significant innovation in international monetary affairs. Through progressive increases in participants' S.D.R. allocations, the I.M.F. could achieve an expansion in the world level of reserves in line with the growth of international trade and investment, and thus minimize the dangers of a world liquidity shortage. The need for external adjustment by countries in 'fundamental' payments disequilibrium would, however, remain.

4. The World Bank

The provision of finance by mature economies can help promote the economic growth of developing countries (Chapter 15) in two principal ways. First, by providing professional assistance, developing labour skills and raising educational standards, 'technical assistance' in the context of official aid programmes can increase the efficiency of an economy's labour force. Second, the growth of the economy's capital stock can be accelerated by drawing on external funds, both private and official. To clarify the role of external finance under this second head, it is useful to construct a simple and quite abstract example.

Suppose that at the moment a developing country is operating with its current account exactly in balance, and is engaged in no capital transactions with the rest of the world. To achieve a more rapid growth in its capital stock, it may follow one—or both—of two paths. First, it could attempt an increase in the rate of domestic saving, in order to free resources for the desired increase in the level of net investment. Second, it could increase the value of its imports, and finance the deficit on current account by long-term borrowing overseas (i.e. a surplus on capital account). If these extra imports took the form of capital goods, their addition to the economy's capital stock would bring about a corresponding rise in its rate of growth. Conceivably, however, this same result could be achieved if all the extra imports took the form of consumer goods, provided domestic production of consumer goods was cut back correspondingly, and the resources thus freed switched to investment activity. This latter path would not be appropriate if the economy's productive resources could not be easily switched in this way, or perhaps were at a comparative disadvantage in producing capital goods.

Some of the sources of external finance available to developing countries were indicated, in passing, in Chapters 17 and 18. Privately, these were direct investment and—less important in value terms—the sale of securities in world capital markets; at an official level, loans and grants by way of economic aid. Much the greater part of governmental aid is given bilaterally (i.e. directly by donor to recipient), though some is channelled through international economic agencies (below). Where aid is given bilaterally, arrangements often exist for co-ordination of aid programmes. These arrangements may involve donors only, or both donors and recipients. Illustrative of the first variety is the Development Assistance Committee of the Organization for Economic Co-operation and Development, which has eleven European nations—including the U.K.—and Australia, Japan, U.S.A. and Canada as its members. Illustrative of the second is the Colombo Plan for Co-operative Economic Development in South and South East Asia, which has eighteen participants within the region and six (including the U.K.) outside.

The organizations which provide development finance on a fully international basis are the International Bank for Reconstruction and Development (the 'World Bank'), and its two associates, the International Finance Corporation and the International Development Association. The World Bank was conceived towards the end of the Second World War as a sister institution to the I.M.F., designed to specialize in the finance of reconstruction and development which, it was envisaged, would present urgent problems after the war. The Bank's Articles were drawn up at Bretton Woods in 1944 jointly with the Fund Agreement, and the Bank came into operation from its Washington headquarters in 1946. Organization of the Bank largely parallels that of the Fund, with defined policy areas reserved to the Board of Governors but administration otherwise in the hands of twenty Executive Directors. All Fund members were, in early 1969, members of the Bank, though membership—while limited to Fund members—is not binding upon them.

While the Bank's first efforts were devoted to assisting European countries in their post-war reconstruction, it has since the late 1940s been concerned exclusively with development finance. To qualify for assistance, an applicant must be a member of the Bank, and would most often be a developing country with relatively low income per head of population. Assistance may, however, be given—though, since 1965, on less advantageous terms—with development projects in mature economies. Financial assistance by the Bank almost invariably takes the form of loans, either to governments or (in practice, much less often) to government-guaranteed private organizations. Loans are given only for specific investment projects, and normally only the foreign currency costs of the project are covered. This means that the Bank lends to finance the import of necessary goods, the employment of foreign technicians, and so on, but not (save exceptionally) for the finance of local labour and similar costs. Loans are made at near-commercial interest rates (below), and for less developed countries the maximum loan period is thirty-five years, beginning after a grace period of, at the maximum, ten years.

The Bank lends only for 'sound', high priority projects which will make a significant contribution to the borrowing country's economic development. The scale of the loan must, however, be reasonable in relation to the borrower's prospective foreign exchange earnings, so that repayment prospects do not appear prejudiced. So far electrical and transportation schemes, respectively, have each absorbed about one-third of the Bank's total lending, though more recently agricultural and educational programmes have received increased attention from the Bank. Applicants for assistance must submit detailed proposals, which are prepared with the help of technical advisers provided by the Bank. In practice the latter generally assume the broader function of helping the applicant review the range of development possibilities open to it, and select the most suitable for immediate execution with Bank finance. They may also advise on the economic and financial policies desirable if the growth rate is to be raised and the benefit from the Bank's assistance maximized. This support does not cease with the grant of the loan, as the Bank maintains close supervision over the project and the use of the loan funds. The 'technical assistance' provided in this way represents an important supplement to the Bank's primary financial activity.

The Bank's loan resources are derived from its own share capital, the sale of bonds, the sale of its investments, its interest receipts, and capital repayments. Each member has a capital share in the Bank, based on its I.M.F. quota, and 10 per cent of the share capital has been called up by the Bank to provide loan finance. A more important source of funds is the bonds that the Bank periodically issues, either by offer to the public at large (the U.S.A. has taken the biggest proportion of this sort of issue) or by a direct placing with financial institutions, especially central banks. Interest rates offered on these bonds need to be in line with general market levels, which explains why the Bank's own interest charges are on a conventional pattern. The other source of funds to require explanation is the Bank's sale of its own investments, i.e. in return for a capital sum the Bank may transfer to a private investor its rights in an outstanding loan. Since 1967 this technique has, in practice, been limited to inviting private investors to participate with the Bank in putting up funds when a new loan contract is signed.

The 90 per cent uncalled capital of the Bank serves to guarantee bonds issued or investments sold, and cannot be called up to replenish the Bank's lending resources. The guarantee means that, if countries which had borrowed from the Bank were to default, the Bank could meet its obligations to the bond or investment holders by calling on member governments for appropriate contributions up to the limit of their share capital. It follows that a general increase in the share capital, as in 1959, is primarily designed to safeguard the attractiveness of Bank bonds, by maintaining a substantial margin between the capital total and the level of commitments guaranteed by the Bank.

This financial structure explains why the Bank sees itself principally as a 'bridge' between the private investor and countries in need of development finance. By guaranteeing their funds with the resources of its member governments and by vetting the uses to which the funds are put, the Bank encourages private citizens and financial institutions to put up development finance in circumstances which, without these features, would often be relatively unattractive. In principle the Bank may also guarantee private bonds issued to raise development finance, though in practice this power has been very little used. However, to encourage the direct flow of private capital to developing countries the Bank in 1966 sponsored the establishment of the International Centre for the Settlement of Investment Disputes, which provides machinery for settling disputes between private investors and the governments of the countries where their investment is located. At a purely national level, further, the Bank seeks to increase the effectiveness of bilateral aid programmes by undertaking to organize co-ordinating machinery for the countries concerned.

While World Bank assistance is limited to governments and to private concerns which offer a government guarantee of repayment, the International Finance Corporation exists specifically to help finance private enterprises which do not satisfy this guarantee condition. I.F.C. was established in 1956 as an associate (in effect, subsidiary) of the World Bank, and all the latter's members are eligible for membership. The I.F.C. operates only within its members' territories, providing finance for productive enterprises both on a loan basis (conventional interest rates are charged) and by taking up equity capital. I.F.C. is also active in encouraging local development finance companies, and in promoting the growth of local capital markets, typically by underwriting (Chapter 7) security issues. Since 1965, I.F.C. has been able to supplement the resources provided by its own share capital with funds borrowed from the World Bank. I.F.C. economizes on resources, further, by arranging where possible for other institutions to participate in its finance of an enterprise, while it is always eager to sell off its existing investments (in each case giving first offer to the original entrepreneurs behind the venture).

The third member of the 'World Bank group' is the International Development Association, set up as a Bank associate in 1960 to help developing countries on terms more flexible than those offered by the

Bank itself. I.D.A. has two categories of membership, the first comprising more mature economies whose share subscriptions are payable in gold or convertible currency, the second consisting of less developed countries whose subscriptions are paid very largely in their own national currencies. These resources, which may be augmented by supplementary subscriptions from its first category members and by grants from the World Bank, enable I.D.A. to lend to its second category members to cover the foreign currency costs (and, exceptionally, the local currency costs) of priority development schemes. Loans are made to governments and private concerns (in the latter case, sometimes without guarantee), on 'soft' terms which have typically provided a ten year grace period, a fifty year repayment period, and no charges except a 0·75 per cent service charge. In contrast to World Bank loans repayments may be made in the borrower's own national currency, thereby avoiding a drain on the borrower's foreign currency earnings.

5. *General Agreement on Tariffs and Trade*

If plans laid in early post-war years had come to fruition, the two leading international economic agencies, I.M.F. and I.B.R.D., would have been joined in the late 1940s by a sister institution, the International Trade Organization. Just as the I.M.F. Agreement was constructed in the light of pre-war monetary difficulties, so the proposals for an I.T.O. reflected the trading problems of the 1930s, when widespread resort to import restrictions (in an attempt to safeguard domestic employment levels) had aggravated the contraction of world trade. The I.T.O. was planned, accordingly, as an institution which would facilitate its expansion in the post-war era, by supervising the gradual dismantling of tariffs and other barriers to the free international movement of goods. The difficulties of reconciling national interests led, in fact, to the abandonment of the I.T.O. project in 1950, but meanwhile in 1947 a number of countries had taken the opportunity, concurrently with I.T.O. negotiations, to agree tariff concessions among themselves on a reciprocal basis. These arrangements were codified in the General Agreement on Tariffs and Trade, which survives in place of the more ambitious I.T.O. scheme.

At end-1968 seventy-eight countries (including, from the communist bloc, Czechoslovakia and Poland) had acceded to the General Agreement, while its provisions were also applied in practice by a further twelve countries. Between them, these nations are responsible for about four-fifths of the total volume of world trade. The general objectives to which the contracting parties to the G.A.T.T. subscribe may be summarized as the promotion of world trade and income growth. The specific paths to this goal prescribed by the General Agreement are the elimination of discrimination in trade, the reduction of tariff[1] and other barriers to trade, and the encouragement of consultation where trading interests appear to conflict. Progress in these directions is achieved, in particular, through periodic conferences of the contracting parties, at which the participants negotiate trading concessions for a given number of years ahead. Six major conferences have been held since 1948, the most recent at Geneva from 1964 to 1967.

The elimination of trade discrimination among the contracting parties is sought through the application of what is termed the 'most-favoured-nation' principle. This requires any concession (say a tariff cut) made by one contracting party to another to be extended equally to all the other parties. Exceptions are, however, admitted to this rule. Thus the special trading relationship between a former mother country and her ex-colonies is recognized, so that Britain may legitimately maintain preferential duty rates for Commonwealth members. A more difficult problem is presented by customs unions or areas (see Section 6), though the principle here is that contracting parties outside the union (or area) should at least be no worse off as a result of its formation.

Before the Geneva Conference of 1964–7, tariff reductions under G.A.T.T. auspices had made only modest progress, probably because of the cumbersome negotiating procedure adopted. This involved bargaining between pairs of countries on a product-by-product basis, with generalization of any concessions thus secured to the other conference participants under the most-favoured-nation clause. At the 1964–7 Geneva Conference, the eleven leading industrial nations among the forty-nine participants adopted a more thorough-going multilateral approach, holding joint discussions aimed at a uniform percentage reduction in all their tariffs with minimal exceptions. In the outcome the Kennedy Round (as it was called) achieved tariff reductions by the leading industrial participants averaging nearly 40 per cent,[2] and covering over two-thirds of their dutiable imports (certain agricultural produce excepted). These reductions are to be introduced by stages up to 1972.

The General Agreement also stands opposed to other forms of interference with free international trade, notably quantitative restrictions on imports (i.e. import quotas) and the grant of subsidies on exports (designed for example to boost a nation's foreign currency earnings, but see also p. 458). Import quotas may, however, be tolerated as a means of suppressing deficit disequilibrium in the balance of payments, more

[1] I.e. protective duties, not revenue duties where a corresponding tax is imposed on similar domestic products (p. 165).
[2] For example, a 40 per cent reduction on a 10 per cent tariff would bring it down to 6 per cent.

especially in the case of developing countries. However, quotas to limit certain agricultural imports are also operated in practice by some contracting parties. Subsidies for exports of manufactured goods were proscribed in 1960, but subsidies for primary exports are still permitted though not encouraged.

Nearly two-thirds of the contracting parties to the Agreement are developing countries, and in 1965 their special problems received explicit recognition with the adoption of supplementary provisions aimed specifically at accelerating their income and trade expansion. The more mature nations undertook, except where prevented by compelling reasons, to reduce tariff and other barriers to imports from the less developed countries, without expecting concessions in return. They also agreed to try and reduce any revenue duties (compare p. 165) or other taxes which had the effect of discouraging the consumption of goods from the developing countries.[1]

Some of the problems involved in tariff reductions under this head may be usefully considered in the light of the comparative costs discussion of Chapter 16. Their characteristically high ratio of labour to capital suggests that—relative to more mature economies—the developing countries enjoy a comparative advantage in manufactures produced by labour-intensive methods (certain sorts of textile provide an example). Accordingly tariff protection of the domestic production of these goods by more mature economies blocks the path to an expansion of manufacturing exports by the less developed, while the reduction or removal of the tariffs would give them the opportunity to found or develop their labour-intensive industries on an export basis. This, in turn, offers the prospect of benefits both in increased foreign currency earnings and in the stimulus given the rest of the economy by the industrial development. Likewise in the case of certain agricultural products, developing countries may be prevented from exploiting to the full any climatic or other advantage they possess, through the imposition of revenue duties on their produce, or through tariff or quota restrictions designed to protect domestic agricultural interests.

Tariff reduction by more mature economies does not, however, automatically entail an export expansion for the developing countries. The

---

[1] These provisions notwithstanding, the concessions of the Kennedy Round barely touched upon the products of export interest to the developing countries. Their more likely path to tariff concessions appears accordingly to be through the United Nations Committee on Trade and Development. Following its last full meeting in 1968, a special U.N.C.T.A.D. committee was established to draw up a plan which would, without reciprocal concessions, give all the less developed countries free or preferential access to all the developed countries for their manufactures, semi-manufactures and processed primary products.

industries thus exposed to competition may respond with a search for greater efficiency, notably by adopting more capital-intensive methods. Success will enable them to free labour resources for alternative employment, thereby raising the economy's productive potential. On this outcome, the benefit from the tariff reduction is secured by the mature economy itself, through the stimulus it affords to previously stagnating industry and the implications this has for the rate of income growth.

If on the other hand exposure to foreign competition entails the contraction of the relevant domestic industries, consumers in the mature economy will nonetheless gain through their enjoyment of the lower-priced import(s). Resources will, likewise, be freed for alternative employment and, with appropriate factor mobility, this will enable an increase in the output of other goods and services. Against any increase in output, however, there must now be set the currency earnings of the developing country, which represent an 'entitlement' to a corresponding increase in exports from the mature economy. Further if through lack of appropriate mobility labour resources freed by the contraction became unemployed, the potential increase in the output of other goods and services will not be achieved. As long as they remain unemployed, the consequent loss of income (or production) must be weighed against the gain to consumers and the benefit to the developing country.

While the developing countries are eager to secure tariff reductions from the more advanced, they are themselves reluctant to grant tariff concessions in return. This reluctance may be attributable to one or more of three factors. First, the ease of collection of taxes on imports (at ports and airfields) may be an important consideration to a government whose system of public administration is relatively weak. Second, any tendency to inflation caused by an ambitious development programme will probably be reflected in a tendency towards current account deficit. A government would, in these circumstances, be reluctant to increase the stimulus to import demand by reducing tariffs. Third, the developing country may be eager to protect an industry which, while relatively inefficient at present, is subject to decreasing cost (a case not considered in Chapter 16). In this event the expansion of the industry behind its tariff barrier will bring a fall in unit costs, through the achievement of economies of scale. The fall in costs would allow the withdrawal of the protection and, perhaps, the former infant might emerge as a competitor itself in international markets.

6. *European Economic Community and European Free Trade Area*

The 1957 Treaty of Rome defined the common objective of the signatories, France, Germany, Italy, Belgium, Netherlands, Luxembourg as the achievement of economic integration among their six countries. Specifically, this meant bringing their economies closer together by the progressive introduction of a customs union, the removal of restraints on factor movements, the adoption of common economic policies in some directions and their gradual harmonization in others, and the creation of new institutions to serve the economic community thus brought into being. The executive body designed to implement these proposals was a nine-member Commission, which submits its recommendations to ministerial representatives of the six governments meeting as the Council of Ministers.

The adoption of a customs union was planned in three stages, extending over a total period of twelve years. These arrangements secured the step-by-step abolition of any quotas originally operated by members against each other's trade, and the progressive removal by members of tariffs on imports of one another's goods. At the same time, progress was made in establishing a system of common external tariffs, in general calculated from the average of duties hitherto levied by each member. The common external tariff must be applied uniformly by each member against imports from countries outside the Community, with some exceptions in favour of dependencies, former colonies and two countries —Greece and Turkey—which have reached a special agreement with the Community. By 1st July, 1968, all duties on trade within the Community had been abolished, and a common external tariff barrier adopted for industrial goods. This incorporated the concessions made by the Community in the 'Kennedy Round' (above), in which the Six had negotiated as a unit.

While its popular description 'The Common Market' ignores some important features of the Community, the title nonetheless draws attention to the ambition of the Six to create one market not only in commodity trade but also for the productive factors of capital and labour. In this second respect official policy is largely restricted to removing obstacles to migration within the Six, since personal considerations may continue to limit the flow of labour over national frontiers. Progress has already been made by giving workers from each member country equal access to employment opportunities throughout the Community. The establishment of a common capital market is likely to take many years longer, and presents problems at two levels of difficulty. First, the reconciliation of the highly complex national rules governing security dealings and financial transactions presents a formidable task, while special arrangements might also be needed should capital movements within the Community lead to balance of payments dislocation. More fundamental, however, is the problem of developing national financial machinery sufficiently to match the continental scale on which much of European industry may operate within the customs union.

In general the degree of economic integration envisaged by the Six entails the alignment of members' economic and social policies rather than the adoption of one common policy by all alike. Three exceptions to this rule will, however, be provided by external trade, transport and agriculture. Of these the formulation of the common agricultural policy proved the most controversial and, in outcome, contrasts sharply with the U.K. system. In broad terms, the Six attempt to ensure 'satisfactory' incomes for the farming sector by maintaining prices at an appropriately high level in the markets for farm produce. Several techniques are employed, but the widest in application is a system of levies which requires the agricultural exporter to the Community to pay whatever the difference might be, should his price at the importer's frontier be lower than the Community's target price. Proceeds of this sliding tariff may be used to finance subsidies on the export of 'surplus' produce from the Community, and have also been applied to the Community's farm modernization programme. Support for the agricultural sector within the E.E.C. thus falls directly on the consumer; the U.K. system, on the other hand, puts the burden on the taxpayer (Chapter 20).

Areas in which the Six have made progress towards policy alignment include regional problems, short-run stabilization of employment and prices, social measures, and the system of taxation. In the latter field interest has focused especially on the harmonization of indirect taxes, as differences here might restrict the freedom of intra-community trade. Members are, accordingly, committed to the adoption (by 1970) of a standard 'tax on value added' (T.V.A.) to be levied, for the time being, up to the wholesaling stage in production.[1] Equalization of the tax rate may come later, though this is controversial.

Institutions created to serve the needs of the Community are the European Social Fund and the European Investment Bank. The first was seen as a means of meeting some of the 'social cost' of the creation of the E.E.C., notably by providing finance for re-training and re-settling workers in a period of rapid structural change. The second is designed to finance modernization programmes, schemes of joint interest to several members, and the development of regions (and of associated countries overseas) with special growth problems.

It is apparent, first, that E.E.C. membership entails more than participation in a customs union and, second, that the relative plasticity of the Community at the present time still gives new members an opportunity to influence the direction in which it evolves. The implications of joining the E.E.C., therefore, cannot be fully assessed against existing

[1] T.V.A. is a tax paid at each stage in the productive-distributive process proportionate to the value added (compare the shirt example of Chapter 9) at that stage.

E.E.C. practices, since some of them might be modified to accommodate a new member who would, in turn, be able to influence their subsequent operation and development.

Analysed in the light of the comparative costs discussion of Chapter 16, a customs union could enable each member to specialize in activities in which it enjoys an advantage relative to other members. This is not always as beneficial as it may look, however, since yet more efficient producers in the world outside will be restricted in their access to the market by the common external tariff. Membership may, therefore, be detrimental to any country which is relatively efficient by world standards in its specialisms, in so far as it gets its imports at prices intended to suit its—by world standards—relatively inefficient partners in the union. However, to calculate benefits on these lines before entry is difficult, since participation in the union can itself bring reductions in cost levels. These may arise from increased investment (as firms anticipate increased competition) and economies of scale (as some firms expand output).

The proposed establishment of a customs union among the six signatories to the Treaty of Rome led seven other European countries to suggest a further arrangement for incorporating the Six with themselves in a free trade area. Their scheme was to remove restrictions on movements of industrial goods within the area (i.e. among the thirteen members), while reserving the right of each member to impose its own tariff scale on goods from outside the area. This second feature—the absence of a common external tariff—distinguished their proposal from a customs union, though of course the arrangement would have permitted the Six to operate their common tariff against goods from countries outside the area. The proposal did not receive the support of the E.E.C., but was nonetheless adopted by the other seven countries concerned, in the Stockholm Convention of 1959. This brought into being, in 1960, the European Free Trade Area among Britain, Sweden, Switzerland, Norway, Denmark, Austria and Portugal. Finland became an associated member in 1961.

Within six or seven years the formation of E.F.T.A. had led to the removal by the eight participants of quotas and (with few exceptions) tariffs on industrial goods in trade among themselves. Following the free-trade-area principle, however, each member operates its own tariff scales against goods from outside the area. Non-members are not allowed to exploit this arrangement by sending their goods first to a low-tariff member and thence re-exporting them to a high-tariff member. The multilateral abolition of tariffs and quotas is restricted to industrial goods but, in recognition of the special interests of Denmark, Norway and Portugal, the Convention requires members to attempt to expand intra-Area trade in fish and agricultural products. To this end, concessions made under bilateral agreements would be extended to other E.F.T.A. members.

Despite these achievements in liberalizing trade among themselves, a prime objective of E.F.T.A. remains the establishment of a single European market. The seven full members of the Area have accordingly made various attempts to achieve either association with, or membership of, the E.E.C.

Questions

1. How far does the present international monetary system resemble that existing under the gold standard? I.B.

2. To what extent does gold have any significant functions in the present-day international monetary system? I.B.

3. How true is it that the world economy has returned to the gold standard in recent years? S.U.J.B.

4. 'The international monetary system today depends to a considerable extent on the dollar and sterling acting as reserve or key currencies.' Explain what is meant by this statement and consider any advantages and disadvantages of such a system. I.B.

5. 'For the international payments system to function properly, it is essential that creditor countries as well as debtor countries fulfil their obligations.' Comment on this statement. I.B.

6. Discuss the advantages of the sterling area system at the present time from the point of view of Great Britain. B.Sc.(Econ.)

7. Describe the main characteristics of the sterling area today. I.B.

8. Explain what you understand by the problem of 'international liquidity'. B.A. Gen.

9. Explain briefly, and critically, any *one* of the current schemes for increasing international liquidity. I.M.T.A.

10. What is meant by 'international liquidity'? Why have suggestions been made for increasing it? J.M.B.

11. What is the problem of international liquidity? Discuss alternative methods of dealing with it. U.L.

12. Describe and evaluate the functions of the International Monetary Fund. U.L.

13. Describe the purpose and operations of the International Bank for Reconstruction and Development.   I.B.

14. Why do countries sometimes borrow from abroad? In your answer distinguish short-term borrowing from long-term borrowing.   U.L.

15. What is G.A.T.T.? Discuss its relevance to current problems of world trade.   U.L.

16. What are the hindrances to international trade? How far can international agencies limit or remove them?   A.E.B.

17. 'The main justification of tariffs is to protect the industries of advanced nations from the unfair competition of backward ones.' Discuss.   U.L.

18. 'The Common Market is a beginning, not an end.' Consider the implications of this statement.   C.I.S.

Part five

20

The Management of
the Economy

---

1. *Objectives of Economic Policy*

Several important objectives of Government economic policy are concerned with the 'stabilization' of the economy in the period immediately ahead, say the next twelve months or so. These goals of short-run stabilization policy include trying to achieve the growth in output which expanding productive capacity makes possible, a high level of employment, stability of the general level of prices, and satisfactory (p. 409) external economic relationships.

As the work of Part III would suggest, the economic magnitude of especial relevance to these four objectives is the level of aggregate demand. To influence or 'manage' this level and its constituent parts, the Government relies on both fiscal and monetary instruments of policy. These are operated in accordance with the principles of modern macro-economic theory, though with due regard for other considerations of economic and social policy (below). The development of these principles since the 1930s (p. 216) has, accordingly, exercised a radical influence on the nature and scope of economic policy in these fields. Historically, the first major policy instrument to bear the full imprint of the new thinking was the Budget of 1941 (for the date, compare p. 212). The leading role in its construction was, in fact, played by J. M. (later Lord) Keynes, who had become an adviser to the Treasury in 1940. This gave him an opportunity to implement his ideas on the management of aggregate demand by fiscal methods. The Budget, accordingly, set out to relieve the pressure on the price level that Keynes anticipated would be generated by the many demands upon the economy's resources during war.

These ideas have continued to dominate fiscal and monetary policy in the post-war era. They thus represent the theoretical background against which most of contemporary policy (Sections 2–4) must be understood. Demand management by fiscal and monetary instruments has not, however, prevented a slow upward creep in the general level of prices. In recent years, therefore, considerable interest has been expressed in a policy designed to supplement their influence, viz. an incomes policy, or latterly a prices and incomes policy. Through this policy, considered in Section 5, the Government attempts to introduce appropriate criteria of its own into the process of determining prices, wages, salaries and dividends. While the immediate concern is greater stability of the price level, this in turn has considerable relevance to the achievement of a surplus on the balance of payments current account.

The four goals of short-run stabilization policy are not, of course, the sole objectives of official economic policy. Other objectives—the provision of economic aid and the satisfaction of international obligations—have already been encountered in Chapters 18 and 19. Domestically, two further important tasks are the achievement of greater equality in the distribution of the national income, and the promotion of a faster rate of economic growth in the long term. Relevant to this first objective are the characteristics of the taxation system the Government chooses to operate, and the scale and nature of its social services programme. Thus the progressive structure of the income tax system implies a less unequal distribution of income after tax than before. Second, the operation of some social services entails a supply of goods and services at (as with education and medical treatment) little or no direct cost to the recipient. Some of the ways in which income redistribution is achieved through the public finances are considered in Section 6.

The achievement of faster real income growth is served by two sorts of policy measure, the first carrying a stress on the more efficient use of existing resources, and the second a stress on the expansion and improvement of resources. Representative of the first, for example, is the Government's monopoly and restrictive practices policy (an attempt to achieve more efficient market structures), its decisions on public corporation pricing policy, and its regional policy. Representative of the second is the Government's use of the public finances to promote activities, such as fixed investment or education (especially higher education), which seem particularly relevant to faster growth. Some of the fiscal techniques adopted are explained in Section 6.

Finally, the Government has in the 1960s made several attempts to work out the implications and requirements for the economy of a given 'target' rate of growth, and has incorporated its findings in comprehensive medium-term development plans. These attempts are briefly considered in Section 7.

2. Short-run Demand Management

Chapter 12 explained the relevance to the full employment objective of avoiding a 'deflationary gap', while the importance to price stability— and to equilibrium in the balance of payments current account—of avoiding an 'inflationary gap' was shown in Chapter 14. Eliminating a deficiency or excess of aggregate demand does not, it is true, remove all problems of unemployment, inflation or current account deficit. It will, however, remove the threat to the employment level implied by demand deficiency, and the danger to price stability and the current account balance presented by excess demand.

The use of policy measures to secure the appropriate management or 'adjustment' of aggregate demand may appear to be a continuous process. It is useful, nonetheless, to distinguish two phases in official demand management. First, in its annual Budget, the Government takes the opportunity to vary tax rates and effect marginal adjustments in public sector expenditure plans, to achieve a balance between aggregate demand and productive capacity forecast for the year ahead. This matching of aggregate demand to supply potential may, accordingly, be defined as the principal short-run task of Budgetary policy today. Second, in the interval between Budgets, the Government will often need variously to modify and to reinforce the measures originally introduced, and this it may achieve through both fiscal and monetary instruments of policy. Intervention of this sort is frequently (but not invariably) necessary, when the actual course of events—especially in external economic relationships—has differed from that anticipated.

It is clear that Budgetary decisions about tax rates and public sector spending levels must rest on a forecast of developments in the economy over the year ahead, based initially on the assumption that fiscal and monetary policy remain unchanged. This should show up the likely emergence of demand deficiency, or of inflationary pressure and adverse movements in the balance of payments, and enable appropriate counter-influences to be introduced through the medium of the Budget. The forecasts will, accordingly, need to specify the probable growth of productive capacity, the course of aggregate demand and the likely outcome on balance of payments current and long-term capital accounts.

The Treasury's forecast of the growth of productive capacity is based upon the current estimate of gross domestic product, with an allowance for such factors as the recent value of fixed capital investment, changes in the working population and any changes in the length of the working week. The forecast of aggregate demand is based partly upon direct information, for example on investment plans as ascertained by survey, and partly upon relationships established statistically as relevant and informative. Examples of the latter are the accelerator-type relationship between the level of income in one year and the level of fixed investment in the subsequent year, and the relationship between changes in the level of consumption and the level of stocks. Allowance would also be made for the multiplier effects of any increase forecast in (say) investment spending. The forecast of final expenditure will already contain figures for anticipated import and export values, and these can be combined with estimates of certain long-term capital movements to provide a partial balance of payments forecast. The forecasts are all drawn up on a quarterly basis, as this gives a clearer impression of the course of events than would a year-end forecast.

Suppose, first, that the forecast for the year ahead indicates a probable deficiency of aggregate demand in relation to productive capacity. This will require a reflationary Budget, designed to give appropriate stimulus to final expenditure. On the other hand, a forecast that aggregate demand is likely to outstrip the growth of the economy's real output potential will require a disinflationary Budget, aimed at preventing the emergence of the excess demand. A constraint will also be put on the Budgetary decision by any targets set for the balance of payments on current account. Thus a big increase in export demand may be anticipated on the basis of a sterling devaluation. In this event some restraint on domestic expenditure might be necessary, to accommodate the enlarged export spending without exceeding the 'maximum permissible' level of aggregate demand, defined in relation to output potential.

Superficially it might seem that the Budget could attempt to adjust all or any of the domestic constituents of aggregate demand. There are, however, major difficulties in the way of manipulating investment and government spending in the interests of short-run stabilization. In practice, therefore, the main burden of adjustment has fallen on household consumption, though this (as explained in Section 4) is not without its drawbacks. Some attempt was made in the 1950s to encourage or retard private fixed investment for these purposes, by modifying from time to time the benefits available to firms under the system of initial and investment allowances (Section 6). A disadvantage here, however, is that any discouragement (in a disinflationary Budget) to fixed capital accumulation has unfavourable implications for the rate of income growth. Further, since plans for forthcoming fixed investment will in most cases have been laid some time ago, quick expansion would not generally be practicable nor quick contraction free from costs. Manipulation of the level of stock investment is free from these disadvantages, but fiscal[1] instruments for this task do not, in fact, lie to hand.

The relative inflexibility of spending programmes in the short term also makes it impracticable to attempt any but marginal adjustments in

---

[1] Changes in interest rates and credit restrictions may, however, have some influence (Section 3).

the level of public sector expenditure, both on current and capital account. Further, the Government has since the early 1960s been committed to the comprehensive planning of public expenditure on a long term basis, within the scope offered by the expected growth of the economy's productive capacity. Any need for disinflation, accordingly, will typically be reflected in the public sector as a cut-back in the planned rate of expansion (compare Chapter 8), and not an absolute contraction.

The spending plans of households are, by contrast, relatively flexible, so that policy measures aimed at influencing consumer demand can be expected to take a quick effect. Further, instruments for this purpose lie readily to hand, especially variations in the rates of expenditure taxes and (in principle) of income tax.[1] It is, accordingly, upon the level of consumer demand that the Budget seeks primarily to operate, whenever it is necessary either to stimulate or dampen aggregate demand in the period ahead.

The implications for consumer spending of changes in tax rates will be broadly apparent from the work of Part III. A rise in income tax rate(s) reduces disposable income after tax (Chapter 11), which will (though this in fact depends on the nature of the consumption function) entail a fall in both consumption spending and saving. Vice versa for a fall in income tax rate(s). To assess the implications of a rise in expenditure tax rates, we may reasonably assume that (for the most part— Section 4) the taxes fall on commodities the demand for which is relatively but not completely insensitive to price changes. On this assumption any rise in tax rates will lead to a relatively small reduction in the quantities that households want to buy, but an increase in total money expenditure on the commodities concerned. An increased proportion of this expenditure will, of course, now be taken by the Government as tax revenue. The increase in money expenditure on some commodities means that households will also have less to spend (from their current income) on other goods and services, so that on both scores the quantity of goods and services that households will be able to buy will tend to fall. Vice versa for a reduction in expenditure tax rates.

In the use of tax rate variations to influence consumer spending, emphasis—more especially in recent years—has been on changes in

---

[1] The 1969 Budget also attempted a less direct influence over consumption spending with tax measures designed to promote the habit of regular saving. Under the Save-As-You-Earn scheme operated by the Department of National Savings, a person saving (say) £1 a month for five years would be repaid his £60 with a bonus, tax-free, of £12, which would be doubled if the £60 were not withdrawn for two further years. Similar contractual savings schemes (all limited to a maximum savings rate of £10 a month) are to be operated by the T.S.B.s and building societies.

expenditure tax rates rather than income tax rates. The progressive nature of the income tax system does, however, suggest that it has stabilizing properties 'built into' its structure. Thus of two equal and consecutive increases in pre-tax pay, the second will give a lower rise in disposable income after tax than the first, in so far as the second increase carries a liability to higher income tax rates. If consumption rose by a given fraction of the increase in disposable income, the second increase in pre-tax pay would have led to a smaller rise in consumption than the first increase. Vice versa, of two consecutive and equal decreases in pre-tax income, the first (on the same condition) is associated with a smaller consumption decline than the second.

The progressive nature of the income tax will, on this basis, impose some restraint on the development of either inflation or recession, even though the rates of income tax remain unchanged. In an inflation, however, households may increase their spending when incomes rise with reference, as well, to the rise in the price level (compare p. 313). Suppose that households decide to keep their consumption constant in real terms, at a time when prices are rising at the same rate as pre-tax incomes. In this case they will need to *raise* the proportion of the increase in disposable income which they spend on consumer goods, cutting savings to meet the rise in tax payments. Money expenditure on consumer goods will, accordingly, now rise in line with the increase in pre-tax income.

While the principal short-run objective of the Budget is to match aggregate demand with supply potential over the year ahead, it may nonetheless be necessary for the Chancellor to modify his Budgetary measures before the year has run its course. In principle, this might be because—contrary to the forecast results for his policy—either a deflationary or an inflationary gap has emerged. In practice, the reason is more likely to be the emergence of a balance of payments 'crisis', typically a worsening of the deficit on current account coupled with a precautionary outflow of short-term capital (compare Chapter 18, Section 5).

Such an outcome on current account may indeed reflect a build-up of inflationary pressure in the economy, in which case the Chancellor will need to introduce immediate disinflationary measures. It could be, however, that the growth in aggregate demand has kept step with the expansion of productive capacity. Even so, it may be thought desirable to slow down the rate of demand growth, in order to effect some restraint on (the growth of) import demand, given the positive relationship between the two. In this event, following the definition of Chapter 18, the authorities would be 'suppressing' rather than 'rectifying' the disequilibrium. In the interests of external balance, a second policy goal is compromised, since some potential output growth is sacrificed. The resultant benefits to the balance of payments are noted in Section 3, and the broader problem thus revealed—of conflict among policy objectives—is considered in Section 4.

The disinflationary measures introduced by the Chancellor in either set of circumstances will usually be a 'package deal' of fiscal and monetary restraints. The latter, which would often include a rise in Bank Rate and generally a tightening of credit restrictions, are held over for consideration in Section 3. The fiscal restraints might be expected to comprise some marginal reductions in the investment programmes of the public corporations, local authorities and central government, and an increase in the rates of some of the taxes particularly relevant to consumption spending. To alter income tax rates in mid-year is not really practicable, but expenditure tax rates are more easily adjustable. Further, since 1961 it has no longer been necessary to introduce a special supplementary Budget for this purpose, as in that year the Government took the power, subsequently renewed and broadened, to vary the principal expenditure taxes by up to 10 per cent during any fiscal year. These 'regulator' powers—which have given fiscal policy a needed measure of flexibility—have since been used on three occasions. The use of the regulator and/or the introduction of other measures (both fiscal and monetary) is conveniently (though unofficially) described as a 'mini-budget', which should not be confused with a supplementary 'full-scale' Budget.

The management of aggregate demand through the Budget, or through a mini-budget, achieves an indirect influence on the balance of payments current account. Restrictions on domestic spending may be used to discourage import demand or to free resources to satisfy an expansion in export demand (above). Budgetary measures may also be used, however, to operate directly on the current account. Thus the supplementary Budget of October, 1964, introduced both an export-rebate scheme and a surcharge on imports (Chapter 8). This tariff (which, it may be noted, contravened U.K. obligations to her E.F.T.A. partners) was intended to operate as an immediate though temporary check on the growth of imports.

3. *The Role of Monetary Policy*

As already suggested, some monetary instruments are used to achieve a quick effect on the level of domestic demand, when balance of payments considerations make this imperative. Thus the Government may wish quickly to dampen the level of domestic expenditure to ensure the availability of resources to meet an anticipated export expansion, as at the time of the 1967 sterling devaluation. Again, quick effects are necessary when a marked deterioration (say a sharp rise in the deficit) on trading account, associated with buoyant domestic demand, prompts a precautionary outflow of short-term capital.

In this second case, the use of monetary (and fiscal) instruments of disinflation can be expected to have the more rapid effect on the short-term capital account. A measure of domestic disinflation makes it less likely that sterling will be devalued as a remedy for the trading account weakness. Accordingly, if foreign holders of sterling balances are reassured, the introduction of such a policy—coupled, perhaps, with support of the forward exchange rate (Chapter 18)—will have an immediate effect in stemming the outflow of short-term capital. The desired effect on foreign 'confidence' and the restraint on domestic demand are thus achieved, without conflict, by the same set of policy instruments.

On the monetary side these instruments will, typically, include an increase in credit restrictions and, often, a rise in Bank Rate. Any tightening of hire purchase deposit and repayment requirements will be intended to act upon the level of consumer demand. Quantitative and qualitative restraints on loans by banks and other financial institutions are designed to bear especially upon consumption spending, on investment in stocks (of raw materials, etc.) and on import demand. They may also achieve an indirect effect on aggregate demand in so far as businesses, anticipating difficulties in raising loans should they want them, resolve to hold bigger precautionary cash balances. Their attempt (e.g. by cutting down stock levels) will be disinflationary, even though —with money supply and other factors constant—they cannot all succeed. However, since the gradual extension of 'requests' in the 1960s suggests that firms are able to develop ways around credit restrictions, the efficacy of whatever measures are currently in force will—on past experience—tend to be suspect.

The import-deposit scheme introduced in the mini-budget of November, 1968, will also operate in part through its influence on the availability of short-term funds. The scheme is intended primarily to serve as a quick (though temporary) check on the growth of imports, though unlike the import surcharge of October, 1964, it is (probably) not technically in breach of E.F.T.A. undertakings. Additionally, in so far as importers are unable to get extra credit from their banks or from overseas suppliers, their need to tie up funds in this way may prompt the restriction of their spending plans (other than on imports).

In the circumstances under review, a rise in Bank Rate is, perhaps, intended primarily to 'catch the eye' of overseas holders of sterling balances, as an earnest of the Government's intention to disinflate. Domestically it might, for the same sort of reason, lead firms to take a more cautious view of the immediate future, and perhaps postpone some spending plans. This is thought more likely if the rise in Bank Rate carries it from a level considered 'normal' (perhaps 4 or 5 per cent) to a level considered 'high' (perhaps 6 or 7 per cent). The associated rise in the cost of bank finance is unlikely (p. 293) to have a big impact on stock levels, but what marginal effect it does have is not unimportant, since the overall demand adjustment required is relatively small. A further disinflationary consequence of a Bank Rate increase—unlikely to be welcomed by the Government—could well be a slackening in private house construction. This would reflect a temporary fall in available funds from the building societies, which are slow to increase their own interest rates when others are rising (Chapter 5).

As Chapter 18 (Section 5) explained, an outflow of short-term capital might also reflect, not a devaluation scare, but a rise in interest rates in other world financial centres. In this event, a likely means of protecting the official reserves would again be a rise in Bank Rate, to maintain the relative attractiveness of short-term investment in the U.K. Where the economy is also showing signs of inflationary pressure, such a rise would be doubly appropriate. If, however, the current domestic problem were one of mild recession, the authorities would be placed in conflict, in so far as a rise in Bank Rate, through its effects on most other leading interest rates, would tend to aggravate the recession at home.

It was with this sort of problem in mind that, in January, 1963, the Bank of England announced that in future it reserved the right to help the discount houses at Bank Rate plus a premium of up to 1 per cent (Chapter 4). Assistance on these terms would prompt a rise in Treasury bill rate, while leaving undisturbed (for example) the cost to business of finance by bank advance. The 'primary' London money market would thus become more attractive to short-term foreign funds and—more important—some effect might also show on interest rates in the 'secondary' money markets (below).

The use of the quick-acting measures so far described represents only one level of official monetary policy. At a more fundamental level, the conduct of monetary policy is a continuous activity of the authorities, as they engage in the management of the National Debt—conveniently defined in this context as the 'net debt of the public sector' (Chapter 8). As Chapter 4 demonstrated, some of the principal categories of this debt —Treasury bills, bonds and currency—lie at the centre of the monetary system. Accordingly the day-to-day management of the debt gives the authorities the opportunity to influence this system, in line with various policy goals. Their exercise of this opportunity nonetheless remains subordinate to their primary objective, of ensuring that the borrowing needs of the Government can always be met.

As Chapter 4 explained, by their pursuit of a 'funding policy' the authorities avoid the embarrassment to monetary restraint that large-scale reliance on bill finance would present. Moderation in the issue of Treasury bills is not in itself, however, sufficient to bring firm pressure on the growth of clearing bank assets (hence liabilities), for reasons set out in Chapter 4. Further, official requests for restriction (as described in Chapter 4) relate to the level (and composition) of advances (and latterly of bill finance), and not to the overall level of assets and liabilities. Total liabilities (the greater part of the money supply) may thus expand significantly even during a credit squeeze, if the clearing banks have a sufficiently large liquid asset 'base' and expand by taking up Government bonds (the less-liquid asset 'alternative' to advances). Expansion in the banks' bond holdings may in turn reflect the positive net borrowing requirement of the Government (explained in Chapter 8, and summarized below), and the reluctance of institutions and people outside the banking sector to meet it fully by themselves lending all that the Government needs to borrow.

This suggests that restraint on the growth of the money supply may be difficult so long as the Government is a net borrower. (In this context it is interesting to recall from Chapter 4 that an increase in the note issue—much the smaller part of the money supply—also represents a form of Government 'borrowing'!) Accordingly, the Government's recent achievement of a 'negative' net borrowing requirement (Chapter 8 and below) implies that, in this respect, a curb on the growth of the money stock may be more readily secured.[1] Whether or not such restraint is important represents, of course, a different issue. Thus according to the theory of Chapter 13, the money supply has only an indirect influence on the level of aggregate demand, via the rate of interest on the level of investment. By contrast, an explanation of inflation in terms of the quantity theory of money (expressed in terms of a demand for money balances) would assign a critical part to the control of the money supply.

The Bank of England's daily operations in the discount market give it a dominant influence over the short-term rates ruling in the market from day to day, and over the Treasury bill rate (Chapters 3 and 4). It uses this influence partly to eliminate erratic fluctuations, which might be communicated to the bond market (Chapter 4), and partly to main-

---

[1] In 1969 the Government has expressed a keener interest in restraining the growth of the money supply and associated variables, as an instrument of anti-inflationary policy. Interest centres particularly on the rate of 'domestic credit expansion', defined as the increase in the money supply plus overseas lending to the public sector (including any reduction in E.E.A. foreign currency reserves). Since net official selling of foreign currency reduces the Government's reliance on borrowing from the banking sector (Chapter 18), the concept of D.C.E. helps 'correct' for the retarding influence such sales will have on the growth of the money supply in a period of balance of payments deficit.

tain the relative attractiveness of the U.K. for the investment of short-term foreign capital. Though the secondary markets are today the principal outlet for private short-term funds from overseas, rates of interest here will to some extent reflect those ruling in the London discount market.

In the bond market, as Chapter 4 noted, the frequency of the Bank's dealings, and the size of its resources, give it an opportunity to influence the prices at which bonds change hands. Thus the Bank will seek to prevent quite fortuitous disparities in supply and demand causing erratic movements in prices. These it may counter by making purchases or sales of its own, as appropriate. More fundamentally, the Bank's concern is to maintain at all times the 'marketability' of Government securities. This means that it attempts to ensure that prospective buyers or sellers are always able to carry through their business in the market, and that the resources of the jobbers are never overwhelmed by the pressure of net purchases or net sales. To this end, the Bank 'stands behind' the jobbers in the gilt-edged market (Chapter 7), buying or selling securities as necessary to 'maintain the market' in Government bonds.

If it is able to utilize underlying market trends, the Bank will seek to encourage bond prices (hence long-term interest rates) in the direction which best suits the immediate requirements of Government policy. Suppose, for example, that the current policy emphasis was on disinflation, which implies a need for some rise in long-term interest rates if fixed investment is to be checked at the margin (but see below). It may happen that at the time prospective sellers of securities outnumber would-be buyers. In these circumstances, while operating in the market to prevent a violent price fall,[1] the Bank would probably reduce gradually its own buying price. Prices would thus move gently downwards, until they reached a level the Bank judged appropriate to market feeling, at which prices could be expected to stabilize.

On the other hand, while the Bank might wish to see bond prices fall, it may happen that the broad equality of buying and selling orders is serving to keep the level stable. In these circumstances, it seems very unlikely that the Bank would try and push the price level downwards

---

[1] Of course, if the Government had raised Bank Rate as part of a 'disinflationary package', a sharp fall in bond prices (unless previously discounted) would occur (Chapter 7) which the Bank would not attempt to moderate. On occasions, further, in late 1968 and early 1969, the Bank judged it appropriate, as an accompaniment to domestic disinflationary measures, to allow fairly sharp price falls (i.e. rises in yields) to result from the pressure of net sales. It might be thought that the Bank considered there to be little danger, on these occasions, that the falls would destabilize the market by exciting yet further selling.

with a significant increase in its own sales. Such intervention by the Bank would probably be resented by security holders, who might conclude that their capital values (i.e. the prices of their bonds) were being artifically depressed by the Bank for the sake of official interest rate policy.

The motive underlying the Bank's policy is its desire to extend as far as it can the demand or 'appetite' for Government debt outside the banking sector,[1] while minimizing its reliance on the latter for bill finance. An important reason why banks, discount houses, insurance companies, etc., and large industrial and commercial companies hold the bonds is that they possess a high degree of marketability. These holders probably take it for granted that, such is the volume of turnover, they will not in normal circumstances have any difficulty in putting their orders through. If this assumption proved false, government bonds would lose an important attraction for the big holders mentioned. Hence the Bank's customary willingness to act as a 'jobbers' jobber' (above). Hence also its reluctance to give the appearance of 'juggling' with bond prices, lest the arbitrary movements thus imparted to prices make bonds less attractive to the big institutional holders.

The Bank's desire to maximize the demand for Government debt outside the banking sector is partly explained by the implications this has for the growth of the money supply. Second, as Table 8.5 demonstrates, about four-fifths of the outstanding bond issue is redeemable, which means that the authorities must be concerned with maintaining the attractiveness of bonds as investments, to facilitate re-finance through further issues. This apart, the authorities have generally[2] needed to increase each year the amount of Government debt outstanding, to assist in the capital finance of public corporations and local authorities (Chapter 8).

The Government's need to provide some of the capital finance for these institutions largely explains the continued growth of the National Debt (as legally defined), from £21,366 million at end-March, 1945, to £34,193 million at end-March, 1968. Its own spending needs—on capital as well as revenue account—are in fact more than covered by tax

---

[1] This provides one reason why the authorities are keen to attract small savings through the National Savings Movement. A second is that the sale of savings certificates, etc., is broadly disinflationary, in so far as official propaganda persuades households to substitute an act of saving for an act of spending.

[2] A substantial Consolidated Fund surplus gave the Government a negative net borrowing requirement over 1968–9, and the National Debt fell to £33,963 million at end-March, 1969. A negative net borrowing requirement is forecast also for 1969–70 (Chapter 8).

revenue and other current receipts, leaving a margin to spare for local authority and public corporation capital finance. The former will to some extent borrow on the capital market, while some of the latter will be able to contribute to their own capital finance by charging prices which earn them a net revenue. The excess of their capital expenditure over the funds they themselves put up is met by the Government. For this the Government relies in part on its own surplus, and in part on fresh borrowing.[1] Other things being equal, therefore, the bigger the surplus the smaller the Government's borrowing requirement. This relationship establishes an obvious bridge between fiscal and monetary policy.

Whether or not the growth of the National Debt will impose a burden on future generations is a complex question. Two relatively simple observations are, however, relevant. First, its growth means a rise in the total interest payable to the holders of the debt, which entails a bigger transfer of income from the general body of the tax-payers to the smaller group of debt holders. In itself this would tend to accentuate any existing inequalities in income distribution. Second, the expansion of the public debt might impose some constraint on the rate of private sector fixed capital formation, in so far (say) as it increased the cost or reduced the amount of long-term finance available for the private sector. Future generations would then be worse off in that the (private sector) capital stock they inherited would be smaller, and the goods and services yielded by this stock correspondingly diminished.

It must be recognized, on the other hand, that the peace-time expansion of the National Debt will have been matched by an increase in public sector assets. Future generations will, accordingly, benefit from the flow of goods and services these will provide. Further, it might be thought that a more fundamental constraint on private net fixed investment—given full employment of resources—was the proportion of domestic product absorbed by the other sectors of the economy, notably households, Government and exports (less imports). Third, the growth of real national income may well ensure that interest payments on the debt do not rise as a proportion of national income. Finally, as Section 2 demonstrated, the level of taxation is decided with reference to the desired impact the Government wishes to make on aggregate demand, though it is conceivable that the Government's ability to borrow could also be taken into account. Changes in tax rates, therefore, are very much more likely to reflect the needs of demand management, than any need to cover the debt interest (essential though this is).

Although the prospect of thereby burdening future generations seems small, the expansion of the public debt may conceivably impose some disability on the present generation. This may follow from the

[1] Ibid.

restrictions placed on monetary policy by the authorities' need to ensure that the Government's borrowing requirements can always be met. In consequence, monetary policy may be less efficient than if the debt were growing less rapidly, or, indeed, stood at a lower absolute size. For example, if the authorities were less pressed in their need to make fresh bond issues and ensure the re-finance of existing issues, they might feel able to adopt a more flexible policy on the long-term rate of interest.

By way of illustration, assume that the Government desires some measure of disinflation. If through sales of their own they were actively to bring about a fall in bond prices, the authorities might serve this purpose in several different ways. First, other security prices (e.g. debentures) would tend to fall in sympathy, making external finance by security issue more expensive for companies. Second, firms which held bonds as a financial reserve might be less likely to part with them if this entailed selling at a loss, so that, meanwhile, some of their funds would be 'locked in'. Third, for the same sort of reason, the clearing banks would be less likely to run down their bond holdings, to make room for an expansion of advances.

Against these arguments, however, it must be recognized, first, that in the interests of long-term growth the Government is unlikely to want to impose any direct discouragement on fixed investment, even though hindrances do unfortunately result as a by-product of other policies (Section 4). Second, as the theory presented in Chapter 13 would suggest, expectations about future price movements have a dominant influence on current bond prices. Any attempt by the Bank of England to push prices to some target level could then be frustrated by the way the market reacted to the Bank's manœuvre, with unpredictable consequences.

4. Difficulties of Stabilization Policy

The Government's management of the economy in the interests of short-run stabilization policy is likely to encounter difficulties of various sorts. First, as Section 2 illustrated, some of its short-run policy objectives may be in conflict with one another, so that progress towards one objective may entail the compromise of a second. Similarly, some of the longer-term goals of economic policy may carry implications unfavourable for the immediate problems of stabilization. Second, the policy instruments the Government uses in pursuit of any one objective may have undesirable side effects, which tend at least in part to frustrate other policy goals. Third, since official (or other) forecasting is necessarily imperfect, and since delayed repercussions of official measures may appear as disturbances in a later year, it is conceivable that attempts at demand management may at times have a destabilizing influence upon the economy.

Two outstanding features of the post-war economy have been, first, the maintenance of—by historical standards—a very high level of employment; and, second, a persistent tendency for the general level of prices to creep upwards. Thus the level of unemployment has tended generally to stand between 1·5 and 2·5 per cent of the working population in any given year, while the annual rate of increase for the index of retail prices has a value, typically, between 2 and 4 per cent. Moreover, periods when the unemployment rate falls (e.g. from 2 to 1·5 per cent) tend to be those which show the more rapid rate of price increase. These (and other, more refined) observations point to a conflict between the enjoyment of high employment levels and the achievement of price stability. This is taken up in Section 5.

A conflict between policy goals may also arise should the Government decide to disinflate in order to achieve a quick improvement on the balance of payments current and short-term capital accounts. In this event, as Section 2 noted, the economy will sacrifice some of the output growth it might otherwise have achieved: unemployment also, after some time lag, will tend to increase. In this set of circumstances, alternation in official emphasis between minimizing unemployment and averting external crisis could result in a 'stop-go' sequence of restraint and relaxation in demand management. Thus having through disinflation achieved some improvement in the balance of payments, the Government might subsequently attempt to reduce the unemployment level by relaxing restrictions on (notably) consumer demand. In consequence import demand may once again surge forward, precipitating another balance of payments crisis and leading to the reimposition of restraint.

This mechanism has probably played an important part in the 'stop-go' sequence which has characterized demand management in the 1950s and 1960s. This, in turn, may have had a discouraging influence on the level of fixed investment, through the periodic setbacks to business plans and the atmosphere of uncertainty thus created. Alternation in emphasis on short-run policy objectives may thus be prejudicial to long-run growth prospects.

In so far as it contributes to price stability, growth of real national output per head over the years may give indirect help in achieving external balance. Output growth might contribute to price stability in two ways. First, it enables a rising aggregate demand to be (partly) met in real terms. Second, the corresponding rise in productivity per man could enable wages to rise without an increase in average wage costs (Section 5). Greater stability of the domestic price level would, in turn, increase export competitiveness, and help home-produced goods in their price competition with imports. Against these benefits, however must be set the tendency for imports to rise with the income level—first as more commodities are absorbed anyway and, second, as with rising living standards consumers develop their tastes for foreign clothes, furniture, holidays, etc. The net implications of growth for external balance will, therefore, reflect the weights attached to these opposing forces.

Discussion so far has focused on conflict among policy goals. However, a similar difficulty may be presented by the use of policy measures to serve one specific objective, if these measures have side effects which partly frustrate the achievement of other objectives. Some disinflationary measures, for example, carry unfavourable implications for economic growth. Thus, conceivably, a tightening of the credit supply may indirectly create difficulties for some firms in the finance of their capital projects, even though the banks are encouraged to lend for such purposes. Hire-purchase restrictions, too, may entail a small set-back to fixed investment in so far as some capital goods are bought on hire-purchase terms. A credit squeeze carries the danger, moreover, that newly established and expanding businesses may experience the relatively more acute difficulty in their short-term finance. Finally, the frequent use of Bank Rate as part of a disinflationary package, or to attract short-term funds from overseas, will be one factor operating to depress bond prices (Chapter 7), hence raising the cost (Chapter 13) of long-term finance to the company.

Fiscal instruments of policy may likewise work to slow the growth rate. Thus a rise in income tax rates (particularly the standard rate) may serve to discourage the 'supply of effort', both from entrepreneurs and from the labour force, since the net financial reward for extra work is (in most cases) thereby reduced. Further, while expenditure taxes fall largely on consumer goods and services, there is nonetheless some burden (though small) on capital goods. A sharp rise in rates may, therefore, effect some marginal discouragement to private fixed capital formation. The same holds for exports, which explains why—from 1964 to 1968—many exports carried a rebate entitlement.[1]

The use of disinflationary measures also carries the danger of dislocation, if not unemployment, in industries making durable consumer goods. Thus within the range of consumer goods and services, expenditure taxes fall with particular weight on a relatively narrow range of commodities (tobacco, alcohol, cars, motoring, other durable goods).[2]

---

[1] The scheme was discontinued when the 1967 sterling devaluation gave U.K. exporters a significant price advantage.

[2] Another important consumer 'commodity' subject to expenditure tax is house occupation, on which rates are levied by the local authority. Rates are not, of course, varied in line with central government demand management.

Further, hire-purchase facilities are used by households very largely for the acquisition of cars and other durables, like refrigerators, T.V. sets, furniture, etc. Demand for cars and other durables may well be sensitive to price changes, while demand is anyway likely to fall if credit terms become more onerous. Motor manufacturers may be able to expand export sales if their home market is depressed, representing a diversion of resources from domestic to export production in line with official policy. Manufacturers of durables with less market flexibility will have production plans upset and may need to reduce output.

Use of the same measures to achieve disinflation also seems to be at odds with a second policy objective of greater equality in income distribution. Thus an increase in expenditure tax rates to check consumer demand appears to impose an unfair burden on the poorer sections of the community (Section 6). Similarly, the use of hire-purchase restrictions is likely to be particularly burdensome for low-income groups with very limited funds of their own. On the other hand, policy measures which particularly benefit low-income groups may have inflationary implications. Thus the U.K. system of supporting farmers' incomes (Section 6) results in notably lower prices for foodstuffs than the E.E.C. method (Chapter 19). Accordingly, households are left with more to spend on other commodities than they would have if food imports were (say) subject to a sliding tariff on the E.E.C. model. Similarly, occupants of subsidized council housing pay less than an 'economic' rent for housing and so have more to spend on other goods and services. Against this, however, it must be recognized that the imposition of a tariff on food imports, or the abolition of subsidies on local authority housing rents, would enable the Government to relax taxation in other directions.

A final drawback to increasing expenditure tax rates to check demand lies in the impetus it may give to cost inflation. Where the commodities taxed are inelastic in demand, price is likely to rise by most or all of the tax increase. While this serves (other things being equal) to reduce demand for other commodities, it is unlikely that—with many prices administered—their prices will fall. The level of retail prices is, accordingly, likely to rise. With money incomes (so far) unchanged, this represents a fall in real living standards, to which unions may react by seeking a wage increase.

It remains to consider briefly the possibility that official attempts at demand management could have a destabilizing influence upon the economy. One obvious way in which this might happen is through error in the official forecast, which leads the Government to apply its influence in the wrong direction. For example, suppose that the economy currently has an unemployment level of (say) 2·5 per cent of the working population, which the Government is anxious to reduce. Its forecast may predict that, without a change in policy measures, there will be an insufficient increase in aggregate demand to realize this objective. The Government may therefore decide on a reflationary policy of, say, cuts in expenditure tax rates and a relaxation of credit restrictions. Clearly, if the original forecast were wrong, and an upsurge in aggregate demand was in fact just imminent, the authorities' measures will reinforce the boom and create excess demand in the economy.

Forecasting errors apart, any influence that the Government currently exerts on aggregate demand may well have delayed repercussions, which contribute to (though they do not entirely create) the need for further official intervention at a later date. For example, a restriction on consumer spending this year may contain the seeds of a recession next year, through an accelerator-type relationship with stock- or fixed-investment. The prospective emergence of this recession may be correctly diagnosed, and the authorities respond with an appropriate stimulus to aggregate demand. This, however, may after a time lag have repercussions in yet a later year, which require a curb on domestic spending; and so on. It appears, therefore, that the management of aggregate demand may in part contribute to an instability in the level of economic activity which it is intended to correct.

5. *Prices and Incomes Policy*

Section 1 defined prices and incomes policy as an attempt by the Government to introduce appropriate criteria of its own into the determination of money incomes and prices. Such attempts were first made between 1948 and 1950 but, after intermittent experiment in the 1950s, it was not until 1962 that the policy became firmly established as an instrument for the management of the economy. The title then adopted, 'incomes policy', reflected the emphasis initially placed on the regulation of wage, salary and (though perhaps to a lesser extent) dividend increases. Since 1965, however, prices have been specifically included within the policy's scope.

The operation of a prices and incomes policy requires a Government decision both on the nature of the criteria to be applied and on the methods of applying or implementing them. This second decision may, in turn, entail the establishment of new governmental machinery. The criteria and—to some extent—the ways they are implemented will be shaped by the specific objectives the policy is designed to serve. Three principal objectives may be distinguished. First, the policy may play a part in dealing with a sharp deterioration on current account, especially where this is associated with a speculative outflow of short-term capital. It may, second, contribute to price stability in an economy with a high employment level, thereby helping to minimize the conflict between these two objectives noted in Section 4. Third, it may contribute to increased economic efficiency and more rapid real income growth.

A switch in emphasis between the first (short-run) objective and the other two (long-run) objectives provides one reason why policy criteria may vary from time to time. Thus in response to a balance of payments crisis, the Government might introduce a 'freeze' or 'standstill' on money incomes and (with minimum exceptions) on prices. Such a freeze will apply for a limited period only, say six months or a year, and is aimed specifically at the immediate balance of payments problem. This may enjoy some relief both from any rise in export competitiveness and from any stemming of the precautionary capital outflow, should the freeze be interpreted by foreign opinion as an earnest of the Government's intention to 'hold prices' rather than devalue. The criteria here are simple, since in each case the Government expects a 'nil increase' except where—for prices—rises in import costs or seasonal factors make this inevitable. In the period following the freeze, further, money incomes should not be increased to compensate for the preceding standstill.

Construction of appropriate criteria for the two long-term objectives represents a much more complex problem. From 1962 to 1965 emphasis lay on trying to keep the average annual growth of wages and salaries within the annual growth rate of real national output per head. This 'guiding light' for wage and salary increases was, at first, decided on recent productivity experience, but from 1963 it was based on the output increase forecast for the period ahead. The definition of a 'norm' was not, of course, intended to imply that all wages and salaries should increase by exactly this amount. Indeed, in its 1962 policy statement the Government considered that only in three situations would there be any clear justification for pay increases. First, where workers themselves made a contribution to increasing productivity, for example, by giving up restrictive labour practices. Second, where a manpower shortage in a given industry threatened that industry with a decline, or was likely to frustrate its expansion. Third—though this was expected to carry less weight than in the past, where wages or salaries had risen in other comparable employment.

A policy restatement of 1965 reaffirmed the use of the guiding light (or norm) to provide a criterion for defining the average rate of increase of money income per head, based on anticipated real product growth. Increases beyond the norm might, however, be justified in any of four special cases. One of these was identical with the productivity criterion defined in 1962, while two others were similar to the manpower-shortage and comparability criteria. The fourth covered circumstances where wages and salaries were generally recognized as too low to provide a 'reasonable' standard of living. Increases beyond the norm were, nonetheless, to be regarded as exceptional since, if the average were to be maintained, they would mean that some other increases would necessarily fall short of the norm.

The scope of the policy was, further, broadened in 1965 by the definition for the first time of criteria directly relating to prices. Firms were not expected to raise their prices, except in certain specified circumstances. Broadly stated, these covered the award of exceptional pay increases (above), unavoidable increases in costs which could not be offset in other directions, and a need to raise capital from the firm's own resources. Where unit costs fell, or where anyway profits rested on excessive market power, firms were expected to reduce prices.

After a period of 'freeze' followed by a 'severe restraint' (necessitated from mid-1966 to mid-1967 by balance of payments difficulties), further attempts were made to construct an appropriate long-term formula for income increases (criteria for price increases reverted to the 1965 pattern). The most important modification has been the abandonment of the attempt to define, in terms of a norm, the permissible average rate of increase of money incomes per head. This attempt had, it is considered, suffered at least two drawbacks. First, the figure chosen as norm might prove an inaccurate guide, since it rested on a forecast of real output growth that might not, in fact, be achieved. Second, its publication served to foster expectations of a pay increase based on the norm as a minimum, when of course the norm was intended to define the average of all money income increases.

The central position of the norm in incomes policy has been taken over by the four criteria originally defined in 1965 as providing grounds for an increase beyond the norm. Accordingly, since mid-1967, proposed increases in wages and salaries have required justification under any one of these four heads. A notable exclusion under this rule is thus the pay claim based solely on a rise in the cost of living. Having satisfied the first test, a proposed increase has, since 1968, been subject to a 'ceiling' defined—for 1968 and 1969—at $3\frac{1}{2}$ per cent per year. This limit is also intended to govern proposed increases in dividends on ordinary shares. The sole exception to the ceiling relates to pay claims based on the productivity criterion. The nature of this exception illustrates one of the ways in which the policy may be used to encourage more rapid real income growth.

The definition of appropriate criteria to govern money income increases and changes in prices represents, of course, only one part of prices and incomes policy. The second part consists of putting the criteria into effect. In this task, the primary objective of the Government is to stimulate and to enlist the voluntary co-operation of both trade unions and business enterprises. In recent years, nonetheless, the Government has taken far-reaching statutory powers, intended mainly as a deterrent in cases where voluntary allegiance appears in danger of breaking down.

The principal executive agency for the policy is the National Board for Prices and Incomes, set up in 1965 as successor to the National Incomes Commission (itself established only in 1962). The task of the Board (which includes representatives of business and trade unions) is to consider cases, within the broad field of the policy, referred to it by the Government, and to publish a report (with recommendations) on each of its investigations. The cases referred by the Government will often (but by no means invariably) relate to proposed pay or price increases notified to it under the 'early warning' system. This scheme was voluntarily introduced in late 1965, though statutory authority to this end was subsequently taken in the following year. By these arrangements, manufacturers of various 'key products' are expected to notify the Government of any rise in prices they propose to make, while trade union and employer organizations have undertaken to give notice of proposed pay claims or increases (except, in general, where one hundred or less workers are involved). Similar arrangements exist for unions and employers not members of an organization, and for the public sector itself.

A proposal to make a pay claim or raise a price will not necessarily be referred to the N.B.P.I. The increase may clearly conform with the criteria of official policy, or the Government may wish (in the case of a pay claim) to see how negotiations proceed. Where a reference is made, the party or parties are expected (and may, by statute, be required) to suspend further action until the Board has published its report. The report itself is likely to contain a variety of suggestions for improving efficiency in the industry concerned, as well as specific recommendations on the proposed pay or price increase. If the Board does not recommend the increase, the Government has statutory authority[1] to compel a delay before the increase is put into effect. Under the Prices and Incomes Act, 1968, the maximum delay is for twelve months, dating from the initial notification to the Government. This Act also authorized[1] the Government, where it had asked the Board on a price reference whether the price in question could be reduced, to compel any reduction—recommended by the Board—for a period up to twelve months.

The early warning system introduced in late 1965 did not cover proposed increases in dividends on ordinary shares, though statutory power to require notification was taken by the Government in 1966. A request

---

[1] This authority expires at end-1969 and—according to Government policy statements—will not be renewed.

for voluntary notification and restraint was made in 1968, while the 1968 Act (above) subsequently prohibited[1] companies from increasing their ordinary share dividends above the rate for the preceding financial year without first obtaining Treasury consent.

To assess the contribution the policy might make to the restraint of inflation at high employment levels, it is necessary to consider the implications it has for some of the inflationary forces that may be at work in the economy.

Chapter 14 drew attention to the inflationary significance of 'bottle-necks' in an economy for which—on the definition of Chapter 12—full employment might be claimed. Changes in the pattern of demand (or, indeed, in production methods) coupled with less than perfect mobility of labour and capital can entail labour shortages in some industries or regions, while unemployment persists elsewhere in the economy. In the absence of any official restraint the labour shortages imply a rise in wage costs, as employers raise remuneration to try and attract more labour, or under pressure from unions which are themselves, perhaps, responding to employers' buoyant profit levels (compare Chapter 14).

A possible remedy for the inflation thus generated lies in the use of orthodox fiscal and monetary instruments to reduce the level of aggregate demand. This will ease the pressure on resources in especially short supply, and help remove the 'tightness' in labour and product markets which is at the centre of this inflationary mechanism. However, a fall in aggregate demand implies a rise in the level of unemployment and, while at some level or other price stability may in the end be achieved, it would be very difficult to estimate just what this unemployment level would be. Further, the incidence of unemployment varies regionally, so that a U.K. average of 2 per cent may include a level of, say, 3 per cent in Scotland and 6 per cent in Northern Ireland. A fall in aggregate demand would almost certainly aggravate these regional unemployment problems. Finally, a reduction in the employment level does entail some output sacrifice, and hence (in itself) is prejudicial to the rate of real income growth.

Unwillingness to accept a higher level of unemployment points, accordingly, to the need for policy instruments other than those of demand management for the restraint of 'bottleneck' or 'demand-shift' inflation. One such instrument is a prices and incomes policy, designed simply to dampen the rate of inflation at any given level of (relatively low) unemployment. Other measures could include the encouragement of labour mobility, and a policy of attracting capital (Section 6) to those regions with an unemployment problem.

An alternative approach to the problem of inflation stresses the

[1] This authority expires at end-1969 and—according to Government policy statements—will not be renewed.

importance of cost-push factors, operating independently of the level of aggregate demand. In such circumstances prices and incomes policy may contribute significantly to price stability, by inhibiting the inflationary mechanisms at work.

Thus suppose that wage increases based on a rise in productivity in one group of industries prompt wage claims in a second group which are based on the comparability principle (Chapter 14). If these claims are successful then, given unchanged productivity in this sector, prices of their manufactures will rise. However, the stress in contemporary prices and incomes policy on the productivity criterion, coupled with a tendency to play down the comparability criterion, might alternatively encourage a search for ways of raising productivity, to enhance the prospects of succeeding with the pay claim. In this event, the cause both of price stability and of economic growth would have benefited from the policy. Further, in so far as the rise in productivity in the first (or, indeed, second) sector—since not completely matched by wage increases—led to a fall in unit costs, there would be a case under the policy for a reduction in prices. This would give the whole community the chance to benefit from the productivity increase.

A second inflationary mechanism directly attacked by the policy is the wage-price spiral. By current criteria, increases in the cost of living are excluded as a basis for wage or salary claims. The policy thus attempts to prevent a rise in import prices (or expenditure tax rates—Section 4) from reacting back on the price level via increases in wage costs.

These benefits will, however, remain hypothetical unless the criteria defined for the policy meet with compliance. Difficulties in the way of successful implementation are considerable. One problem stems from the practice of supplementing national wage agreements with further bargains made at plant or local level, to take account of plant or local conditions. In such cases an 'earnings gap' may be expected between the centrally negotiated wage rate (per hour) on the one hand and actual earnings (per hour) on the other. A tendency for this gap to drift upwards in value over time ('wage drift') may thus reflect continuing 'tightness' in the labour markets (above). Whatever the interpretation of this (complex) phenomenon, incomes policy is clearly made ineffectual if national agreements for wage-rate increases are in line with policy criteria, while the actual increases in earnings are not. This explains why, in its 1968 policy restatement, the Government expects the $3\frac{1}{2}$ per cent ceiling to govern the overall increase, where wage negotiations take place at more than one level.

A second difficulty in implementing the policy is that, in itself, it may serve to redistribute income in favour of shareholders, which would put workers' voluntary allegiance under strain. Such a redistribution would follow from any tendency for undistributed profits to rise in consequence of the $3\frac{1}{2}$ per cent limitation on wage and dividend payment increases. This consideration probably played a part in prompting an increase in Corporation Tax from 40 to $42\frac{1}{2}$ per cent in the 1968 Budget. A rise in Capital Gains Tax would also be relevant, in so far as swelling assets from profit retention boost the market value of a company's shares.

This points to a more fundamental obstacle to the long-run voluntary acceptance of the policy. Compliance with the criteria defined for income increases and price changes will result in a pattern of income distribution different from that which would otherwise obtain. This has implications both for the allocation of resources among industries (e.g. how many workers want to follow a given occupation) and for the living standards of different economic groups (e.g. members of various trade unions). To consider this second feature: implementation of the policy requires a sacrifice from those trade unions and firms which could, in the alternative, have done better for themselves than the policy criteria in fact allow. For example, members of unions who do not qualify for a pay increase under one of the four criteria will suffer a fall in real incomes as import prices or expenditure tax rates rise. Without the restraint of the policy, their bargaining power may have been sufficient to keep their wage rates up with the price increases. Voluntary allegiance to the policy is thus in constant danger of failure through the re-assertion of self-interest. A statutory system, on the other hand, would be even more fully destructive of freedom of operation in labour and product markets.

6. *Public Finance, Growth and Income Distribution*

Previous sections have shown how, through variations in tax rates, the Government can influence the level of aggregate demand in the interests of short-run stabilization policy. This section shows how longer-term objectives of policy may be served through appropriate design both of the taxation system and of the system of public expenditure. The goals considered are the promotion of, first, greater equality in income distribution and, second, the more rapid growth of real income.

Redistribution of income is achieved through the agency both of taxation and of public expenditure. Thus on the taxation side the progressive nature of the income tax (which accounts for about one-third of total tax revenue) entails a more than proportionate tax payment from higher income groups, and thus secures greater equality in the distribution of post-tax income. Further, income from capital—relatively more important for higher income groups—is subject to special taxation burdens. First, dividend income from company shares is subject to income tax, though the profits from which the dividends are paid have already borne a corporation tax. Second, dividend and similar income received by private persons does not qualify for the 'earned income' allowance. Third, capital gains accruing on the disposal of assets are in general subject to tax, either an income tax or a specific capital gains tax. Finally, the operation of death duties tends to restrict the perpetuation of income inequalities arising from capital inheritance. All the taxes mentioned have been described in Chapter 8.

Against these redistributive features of the tax system, however, must be set the less favourable implications of the expenditure taxes, which bring in about one-third of total tax revenue. These taxes are levied on either a specific or a percentage basis (p. 166) in relation to the good or service taxed, and are not in any way adjusted to take account of the incomes of the persons paying the tax. It follows that two consumers who buy the same quantities of identical goods and services will pay equal taxes, but the total tax paid by the poorer of the two will form a bigger proportion of income than the tax paid by the richer. In this sense expenditure taxes may be considered 'regressive'. On the other hand, where commodities are taxed on a percentage basis, and where expensive varieties are likely to be bought by the rich, the tax payment becomes more nearly proportionate to income. Thus a man with an annual income of £10,000 may buy a £6,000 car carrying a tax of £2,000, while a man with an income per year of £1,000 buys a car costing £600 carrying a tax of £200. For each the tax paid represents one-fifth of annual income.

The taxes raised by the Government finance the public provision of a wide variety (Chapter 8) of goods and services. Some of these—like the 'service' of defending the country—are enjoyed 'collectively', while in other cases goods and services are provided on an individual basis: leading examples are the state education system, and the National Health Service (financed chiefly from tax revenue). Goods and services supplied wholly or largely free of (direct) charge represent a part of their recipients' real income, i.e. an addition to the goods and services they can buy with their own money incomes. It follows that a family which pays less taxes than the value of the direct benefits it enjoys, effectively receives a net income (in kind) from the Government. In this way, the goal of income redistribution is served through the expenditure as well as the taxation side of the public finances.

Services like the defence of the modern state are invariably both financed through and provided by the Government, and separation of the finance from the provision of the service would appear impracticable. In other cases, however, where goods and services are supplied by the Government largely to ensure that poorer people get them, such a separation might be achieved. For example, primary and secondary education might conceivably be re-established on a private-enterprise basis, perhaps with minimum standards secured by Government inspection. To meet the fees charged, poorer families would be given subsidies by the Government out of its tax revenue, specifically for this purpose. Richer families would themselves pay for their children's education, but would benefit from any cut in tax rates reflecting the (net) reduction in Government spending. A similar scheme might be outlined to replace the National Health Service. A feature of both schemes is the increased freedom given to, or responsibility placed on, 'consumers' of educational and medical services. However, whatever the merits or demerits, the example clearly shows that Government concern with the redistribution of income in favour of poorer families need not involve it in the actual provision of goods and services.

A reassessment may also be made of any subsidy schemes which serve to reduce the cost of living. Thus under the present arrangements for supporting farmers' incomes, agricultural produce enters the country largely at world prices and, where these are below officially 'guaranteed' prices, the Government makes up the deficiency to the U.K. farmer. The U.K. consumer thus gets the benefit of low world prices, while the burden of support for the agricultural sector falls on the taxpayer. This system is clearly more beneficial to poorer families than the alternative use of, say, a sliding tariff after the E.E.C. fashion, which can push prices of farm produce above the world level. However, should the E.E.C. system be adopted, poorer families could be protected against a fall in real income by the payment of an appropriate personal cash subsidy. Higher income groups would lose by the rise in food prices, but gain from any associated fall in taxation.

The Government's payment of housing subsidies to local authorities also reduces the cost of living for local authority tenants, since their house rents are in consequence lower than they would otherwise be. If it were desired to restrict this benefit to poorer tenants, they might be paid personal rent subsidies, and an 'economic' rent (i.e. covering full cost) then charged to all. The real income of poorer tenants would thus be unchanged, while that of other tenants would be reduced. The rest of the community would, however, benefit from any associated fall in tax rates.

The objective of income redistribution has found reflection in the design of the public finances from, at least, around the turn of this century. By contrast, only since the end of the Second World War has the promotion of real income growth become an explicit objective of fiscal policy. Of course, the pattern of the public finances has always had (complex) implications for the growth of the economy: for example, as Section 4 noted, the structure of the tax system can influence the 'supply of effort' from the labour force and from entrepreneurs. Nonetheless, it is only in the past decade or so that fiscal policy has been expressly used to modify and exploit this relationship, in the interests of more rapid growth. In the field of taxation, attention has centred particularly on promoting fixed investment, stimulating economic activity in relatively 'sluggish' regions, and encouraging the expansion of the manufacturing sector of the economy.

Expansion of manufacturing industry relative to the service industries may result in faster growth of the gross domestic product. This could be achieved through the economies of scale that expanding manufacture is likely to enjoy, accruing to the firm both from its own expansion and from that of the industry of which it forms part. It was to serve this long-term objective—as well as an immediate disinflationary purpose—that the Selective Employment Tax was introduced in 1966 (Chapter 8). First, the tax helped remove the current bias in the indirect tax system against manufactured goods, since services (as such) were not liable to excise duty or purchase tax. Second, any resultant rise in the price of services would tend to reduce output, thereby freeing labour (and other resources) for manufacturing employment.[1] In some cases, further, consumers might substitute manufactures for services, e.g. washing machines for laundry services. Third, the incentive to greater economy in the use of labour would also tend to release manpower from the service industries. The need for active encouragement of the labour supply towards manufacturing employment is, however, questionable, since it is uncertain whether in fact U.K. manufacturing growth has been impeded by labour shortage.

The promotion of fixed investment has been attempted through tax benefits on depreciation allowances, cash grants on equipment purchase (both considered below), and modifications to the system of company taxation. Of these modifications, the most fundamental was the introduction in 1965 of the Corporation Tax (Chapter 8).

The new system may encourage fixed investment by increasing the attractiveness to the company of profit retention (Chapter 7). Thus under the (directly) preceding rules, a company's £100 of profits bore profits tax at 15 per cent and income tax at the standard rate of (say) 41·25 per cent (i.e. 8s. 3d. in the £), leaving £43·75 after tax. The distribution of any part of this residue brought no further liability to income tax. Under the current system, the company is left with £55 profit after paying corporation tax at 45 per cent on £100 profits. In general, this residue will not be liable to further taxation if retained within the company. Any part which is distributed, however, becomes

---

[1] The S.E.T. scheme as first introduced gave manufacturers a small subsidy per employee (Chapter 8). In principle this might have encouraged the demand for manufactures, in so far as it led to lower prices or increased sales promotion.

liable to income tax at the standard rate. This suggests that companies with a relatively low ratio of dividend payments to total profits pay less tax (overall) than they would under the old system. Accordingly, companies with a tradition of high distribution have a tax incentive to move towards bigger retentions.

While of itself a rise in company saving may encourage fixed investment, the system nonetheless posseses drawbacks. Thus a company with more internal funds to spend on investment projects will not necessarily have expansion opportunities which offer a high rate of return. If all the same it persists with its project it will add to the pressure of demand on resources while the work is in progress, only to create a 'white elephant' capable in its turn of a quite limited contribution to future production. A rise in company saving, further, implies a reduced supply of funds in the new issue market, in so far as with lower dividends shareholders have smaller incomes from which to finance new share purchases. Companies with projects offering a better rate of return might thus experience greater difficulty in raising funds in the market, while the existing imperfections of the capital market are thereby augmented.

One advantage of the new system which may be noted in passing is the separation it achieves between company and personal taxation. This enables the Government to secure greater refinement in its fiscal policy. Thus under the old arrangements any attempt to restrict private consumption with a rise in the standard rate of income tax would (with profits tax unchanged) necessarily have entailed a *pro rata* reduction in post-tax company profits, thereby reducing the internal funds available (assuming dividends unchanged) to finance expansion. A second important feature is the associated reconstruction of the rules governing the liability to U.K. tax of income derived from overseas investment. The opportunity was taken to make these rules distinctly less favourable than before, in the expectation that a fall in the rate of return after tax would discourage the outflow of long-term capital in the years ahead (compare Chapter 18).

For most of the post-war period, an attempt was made to influence the rate of private fixed investment through the use of initial allowances (introduced in 1945) and investment allowances (1954), which gave firms tax benefits on their depreciation allowances for specified fixed assets. The system can best be explained with a simple example.

Suppose a firm buys a machine costing £1,000, and—for purposes of tax assessment—depreciates it on the reducing balance method (Chapter 7) by 20 per cent a year over ten years. Its allowance in the first year is accordingly £200, and this the firm will be able to set against its tax liability on its profits. If the firm received an initial allowance of 20 per cent, it could claim tax relief on a second £200 in the first year, i.e. £400 altogether, though tax relief in subsequent years would be correspondingly reduced. Accordingly, provided that tax rates remained unchanged, the firm would benefit by paying rather less tax than otherwise in the first year, even though it paid rather more in subsequent years. This would give it an interest-free 'loan' of that tax revenue the payment of which it had postponed from the first to later years.

With an initial allowance the firm (given tax rates unchanged) paid the same tax overall, but altered the timing of the payment to its benefit. An investment allowance, by contrast, brought an actual reduction in the total tax payable. Thus an investment allowance of 20 per cent would have increased the firm's tax relief by £200 in the first year, without reducing it in the subsequent years. Provided, therefore, the firm made enough profit fully to utilize its investment allowance, it would enjoy an indirect subsidy on the purchase of the machine equal to the value of the allowance (here £200) times the rate of tax per £ of profits.

The initial allowance was introduced as an incentive to capital reconstruction in the immediate post-war period. During the 1950s both it and the investment allowance served as instruments of demand management, as the Government sought through changes in rates and coverage to adjust fixed investment in the interests of short-run stability. Subsequently, the system (fundamentally modified) has been developed as a means of encouraging investment selectively, in certain sectors and in certain geographical regions of the economy.

Sectors where fixed investment receives especial encouragement are the manufacturing, extractive, constructional and ship-repairing industries. In 1966, the Government made purchases of plant or machinery within these industries eligible for a new investment grant at a standard rate of 20 per cent. A factory buying a new £1,000 machine may thus claim a £200 subsidy (from the Board of Trade). At the same time, investment allowances were abolished for *all* sectors of the economy, though initial allowances were retained (at increased rates) for new industrial buildings, and for machinery purchases in those sectors (e.g. commerce, catering) which did not qualify for investment grants. Advantages claimed for the grant over the allowance are that the grant benefits the firm more promptly; that it is more certain, since independent of tax rates or business profitability; and that it is more likely to be included in the estimate of a project's rate of return.

Through the offer of more generous rates, the system is also used to promote capital development in areas troubled by a relatively slow rate of economic progress and a relatively high rate of unemployment. Thus firms in specified Development Areas obtain a 40 per cent investment grant for eligible assets, instead of the standard 20 per cent, and a 25–35 per cent grant on new buildings which is not available elsewhere in the country (but see below). Under the Industrial Development Act, 1966, the Development Areas comprise most of Wales, Scotland and England north of York; Merseyside; Cornwall; and North Devon.

Initial allowances might be expected to encourage fixed investment through their 'liquidity' effect i.e. they increase the internal funds at the disposal of the business. In addition to a liquidity effect, investment grants (and the former allowances) will also have a subsidy effect: the grant (or tax saving) gives the firm a higher return on its investment than it would otherwise enjoy. Both factors may be helpful in promoting growth in the Development Areas. First, the boost to the rate of return will at least in part offset any drawbacks a firm might experience if it moved to, or expanded activities in, one of these Areas. Second, firms which are eager to expand but are hindered by a shortage of funds might be attracted by the prospect of increased liquidity. On the other hand a localized unemployment problem, while assisted by any rise in regional economic activity, would be aggravated should the grants encourage the substitution of capital for labour.

Any such tendency will, however, be partly countered by the system of Regional Employment Premiums introduced in late 1967. Under this scheme, manufacturers in the Development Areas are able to claim a premium[1] of 30s. per week for each man in full-time employment (less for women, juveniles and part-timers). The objective here is to bring down the unit costs of manufacturers operating in these Areas, in order to increase their competitiveness in national markets. This may enable them win orders at the expense of firms in (say) the Midlands and South East, thereby relieving some of the pressure on areas so often characterized by labour shortage. By utilizing otherwise idle resources in the Development Areas the scheme can thus contribute to economic growth, while by relieving pressure of demand elsewhere in the economy, it may at the same time contribute to price stability. The minimum life for the scheme is to be seven years, after which premium payments may be progressively tapered off.

7. *Planning for Growth*

It remains to consider the attempts made in the 1960s to bring about more rapid income growth through the construction and execution of comprehensive, medium-term development plans. The first plan

[1] From 1st April, 1970, however, their 7s. 6d. S.E.T. refund subsidy will be discontinued, the Government applying its saving to finance assistance to specified 'grey areas'—intermediate between Development Areas proper and the rest of the country. This assistance is likely to include 25 per cent grants towards industrial building costs.

appeared in 1963, and covered the period 1961–6, while a second followed in 1965, covering the years 1964–70. The agency responsible for the 1963 plan was the National Economic Development Council[1] which, with its secretariat the National Economic Development Office, had been established primarily for this purpose in 1962. By contrast, the 1965 plan was drawn up by the Department of Economic Affairs, though after consultation with industry and with the N.E.D.C. The D.E.A. was established in 1964 specifically to assume the central responsibility for the Government's growth programme, i.e. to formulate a development plan and co-ordinate the relevant official policy.

Both the 1963 and the 1965 plans were set out on broadly similar principles. Each defined a rate of real income growth which, it was hoped, would represent a reasonable target for the U.K. economy over the period of the plan. The annual average compound rate of growth of gross domestic product set in the first plan was 4 per cent, and in the second 3·8 per cent. The requirements for, and implications of, this growth rate were then assessed.

Thus the expansion postulated by the 1965 plan was judged to require a significant rise both in output per man and in the level of employment in the Development Areas, if the target growth rate was to escape frustration through manpower shortage. Again, within the overall increase of G.D.P., fixed capital formation was required to rise more rapidly than private consumption, in order to furnish an appropriate increase in the community's capital stock. Further, to achieve the necessary expansion of aggregate demand, balance of payments crises and their associated need for disinflationary measures would necessarily have to be avoided. The 1965 plan accordingly set a more rapid rate of growth for exports than imports, to improve the current account, while detailing a change, over the six-year period, from a net outflow to a net inflow on long-term capital account.

For the pursuit of these goals the Government needed to rely on the customary workings of private enterprise as well as on the public sector within the economy. Influence on the decisions of firms in the private sector was sought partly through publication of the plan itself, partly through the N.E.D.O. and associated machinery, and partly through the fiscal system.

Section 6 has already noted the fiscal devices introduced, between 1965 and 1967, to encourage domestic fixed investment, to restrain long-term investment overseas, and to promote the growth of the Develop-

[1] Its original membership of twenty has since been increased to twenty-four, and currently comprises the Prime Minister, five other Ministers, fourteen representatives of industry (both employers and unions), two 'independents', the Director-General of N.E.D.O., and the Chairman of the National Board for Prices and Incomes.

ment Areas and of the manufacturing sector (where, it was hoped, economies of scale would help achieve the desired rise in output per man). In addition, by creating an expectation of faster growth in the years ahead, the publication of the plan in itself was thought likely (both in 1963 and in 1965) to stimulate fixed investment. Thus, on an accelerator-type principle, the prospect of a more rapid increase in demand might encourage firms to increase capacity at a faster rate. In this way, the plan's publication might serve to counter the discouragement to fixed investment occasioned by the 'stop-go' sequence of aggregate demand management (Section 4). Finally, opportunities for an exchange of views between Government and industry on specific growth problems were provided by the meetings of N.E.D.C. and its associated 'little Neddies'. The latter are the Economic Development Councils set up for many of the large industries from late-1963 onwards, to encourage intra-industry co-operation in expanding exports, raising productivity, planning investment, and related growth matters.

Both these attempts at planning for growth thus consisted of looking forward over the next five years or so; indicating the various objectives that must be met for a given growth rate to be achieved; and applying appropriate policy measures. The co-operation of the private sector was sought both in the construction and the execution of the plan, though for the latter fiscal influences have also been brought to bear. Clearly, 'indicative' planning of this sort differs both in scope and in methods from planning in an economy (like the U.S.S.R.) where material resources are collectively owned and where the disposal of resources and the pattern of output are largely determined, firm by firm, by the central planning authorities.

Within a year or so of publication it became apparent, in the case of both plans, that the postulated rate of growth of G.D.P. would not be achieved. The immediate reason lay in deterioration, during 1964 and afterwards, of the balance of payments on both current and long-term capital accounts, which led to a series of foreign exchange crises. The disequilibrium on external account was judged to require a policy of domestic disinflation, to slow down import expansion, help increase export competitiveness, and reassure overseas holders of sterling balances. In consequence production failed to rise sufficiently to reach (or, in the case of the 1965 plan, to make it possible to reach) the plan specification.

Despite this failure to achieve the target rate of expansion, both attempts at planning for faster growth may have had some valuable results. First, the construction of a development plan helps maintain a balance in official policy between the objective of long-term growth on the one hand and, on the other, immediate problems of employment, prices and external equilibrium. This has found reflection in recent years in the use of fiscal measures to help promote growth as well as to balance aggregate demand and supply. It has also served to emphasize the capital-creating role, in addition to the income-generating role, of fixed investment spending (both private and public), and thereby discouraged the use of variations in the fixed investment level for the short-run management of aggregate demand.

Second, the attempts at planning have led to the creation of agencies specifically concerned with the difficulties of increasing the growth rate and with possible solutions to them. Investigation of these problems is undertaken by the N.E.D.C., which, of course, lost its direct responsibility for plan construction on the formation of the D.E.A. in 1964. The twenty-one 'little Neddies' are likewise active in their specific fields, though against any benefits that may result from their work (e.g. the more rapid spread of new production methods within an industry) must be set the risk that closer collaboration among firms in the interests of faster growth might also serve to discourage competition.

Third, the D.E.A. continues to work on problems of medium- and long-term planning, and in early 1969 published a fresh assessment of the prospects for the U.K. economy up to 1972. Unlike the two earlier and more ambitious 'plans', this 'planning document' did not attempt a close definition of expansion targets for the economy. Rather, it sought to indicate the problems the economy would face in the few years ahead (in expanding exports, raising productive potential, improving labour mobility, deciding appropriate consumption and investment levels, and so on), and the broad directions of official policy. Its publication was intended to serve as a basis for consultation between Government and both sides of industry (i.e. management and unions) on how performance might be improved, leading in turn to appropriate action by the parties concerned.

Finally, the interest in national development planning has been associated with, and has in part stimulated, a fresh approach to regional problems. Concern with the relief of regional unemployment has, in the 196Cs, been absorbed in a broader policy of promoting 'balanced' regional development, in the interests both of the regions and of the economy as a whole. Thus parts of the country (notably the Development Areas specified in Section 6) with a tendency to unemployment rates above the national average have come to be re-assessed as 'reservoirs' of untapped resources, the utilization of which would accelerate U.K. income growth. At the same time the efficient use of resources in prosperous regions like the Midlands and South East may, it is recognized, be prejudiced by congestion within these areas, where levels of economic activity might be thought 'excessive'. On this interpretation, more rapid national income growth could be achieved through balanced regional development, whereby growth is stimulated in the sluggish

R

areas and regulated in others. This objective prompted the establishment, in 1965, of eleven Regional Economic Planning Councils, covering the whole of the U.K. The task of each is to advise the Government on the appropriate development of its own region, the necessary co-ordination being undertaken (except for Northern Ireland) by the D.E.A.

Changes in the Machinery of Government

Governmental changes made in October, 1969, included the dissolution of the Department of Economic Affairs. Its responsibility for medium- and long-term economic assessment (p. 497) passed to the Treasury, while the newly-created Department of Local Government and Regional Planning acquired the job of co-ordinating Regional Economic Planning Council affairs. Administration of the investment grant system (p. 493) was transferred from the Board of Trade to the Ministry of Tecnnology.

Questions

1. What are the principal objectives of economic policy in Britain today? How consistent are these objectives with one another?
S.U.J.B.

2. Set out the various economic and financial factors which a British government takes into consideration when framing a modern budget. I.B.

3. 'What is prudence in the conduct of every private family, can scarce be folly in that of a great kingdom' (Adam Smith). Does this dictum provide an acceptable basis for budgetary policy today?
C.I.S.

4. 'British experience has shown that full employment can be maintained only at the expense of other objectives of national economic policy.' Discuss. I.M.T.A.

5. Discuss the various objectives at which a government may aim when framing a present-day budget. I.B.

6. How may a government use fiscal policy to remove unemployment?
U.L.

7. What measures can a government take to deal with inflation?
J.M.B.

8. Should Chancellors of the Exchequer aim at a balanced economy rather than a balanced budget? J.M.B.

9. 'Subsidies are deflationary because they lower the prices of products.' Discuss. U.L.

10. 'If levels of voluntary saving were higher then taxes in the United Kingdom could be lowered.' Comment.   B.A. (Gen.)

11. How can the budget be used to influence the balance of payments?   S.U.J.B.

12. 'Taxation today is unfair, too high and a disincentive.' Comment on this view.   W.J.E.C.

13. What limits are there to fiscal policy as an instrument of stabilization?   J.M.B.

14. 'The sole object of the purchase tax is to raise revenue.' Discuss.   S.U.J.B.

15. If the Chancellor of the Exchequer decides to increase revenue from taxation, what general principles should he follow in levying such taxation?   I.B.

16. What are the main weapons of monetary policy? Give examples of circumstances in which they may be used.   U.L.

17. 'Monetary measures today do not represent a policy in themselves but are part of general economic policy.' Discuss this statement.   I.B.

18. Is the Bank Rate an effective weapon as a short-period stabilizer of demand?   J.M.B.

19. The national debt in Britain today is more than three times its pre-war level. To what extent does this represent an increase in the 'burden' on the British economy?   I.B.

20. Show clearly the nature and composition of the National Debt. In what sense, if any, is it a burden?   J.M.B.

21. What are the objectives of an 'incomes policy'? What practical problems may arise when governments implement such a policy?   C.I.S.

22. How might taxes and subsidies be used to influence the distribution of income in a country?   U.L.

23. Describe and assess the tax system as a means of redistributing income.   U.L.

24. Describe briefly the tax structure of the United Kingdom, giving some indication of the objects and principles involved.   S.U.J.B.

25. Describe the main taxes levied in the U.K. (or your own country) and account for their relative significance.   U.L.

26. Compare and contrast direct and indirect taxes as sources of government revenue.   U.L.

27. The Selective Employment Tax discriminates against employment in service trades. Consider the justification for this on grounds of national economic needs.   I.M.T.A.

28. Discuss the use of planning as a means of raising a country's rate of growth. Illustrate your answer by the experience of the United Kingdom (or that of your own country).   U.L.

Appendices

Appendix A

1. *The Decimal Currency System*

On Monday, 15th February, 1971 ('Decimal Day'), the £ s. d. currency system changes to a decimal system, based on the pound sterling (£), which is retained, and the new penny (p), which is one-hundredth part in value of the £. The six decimal coins to be issued are set out in column 2 of the table, with the £ s. d. values alongside.

Decimal Coins

(1) Metal	(2) Denomination	(3) £ s. d. value
Bronze	$\frac{1}{2}$p	1·2d.
Bronze	1p	2·4d.
Bronze	2p	4·8d.
Cupro-Nickel	5p	1 shilling
Cupro-Nickel	10p	2 shillings
Cupro-Nickel	50p	10 shillings

The halfpenny ($\frac{1}{2}$d.) of the present system loses its status as legal tender (be 'demonetized') from 1st August, 1969, and the half-crown from 1st January, 1970. 5p, 10p, and the new 50p coins are already in circulation.

On and after Decimal Day, the banks will be working exclusively in terms of the new currency, and during the subsequent 'change-over' period all other organizations will convert to this basis. It is not expected that this change-over period will extend beyond August, 1972, and a shorter period might be practicable. At the conclusion of the change-over period, the (by then) 'old' penny (1d.), threepenny piece (3d.) and sixpence (6d.) will be demonetized. Outstanding shilling and two shilling pieces will remain in circulation as coins of value 5p and 10p respectively.

From Decimal Day, legal tender limits for bronze coins will be raised from 1 shilling to 20 new pence (equivalent to four shillings); and for cupro-nickel coins, from £2 to £5.

Further information can be found in the publications of the Decimal Currency Board (published by H.M.S.O.); and in 'Decimal Currency in the United Kingdom', Cmd. 3164 1966, and 'Decimal Currency: The Change-Over', Cmd. 3889 1969.

2. *A Specimen Cheque* (*by courtesy of Lloyds Bank Ltd*)

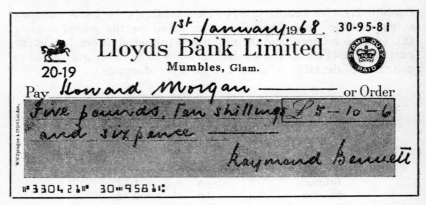

1. Raymond Bennett is the drawer of the cheque, Lloyds Bank the drawee, and Howard Morgan the payee.
2. Morgan might:
   (a) present the cheque for payment at the counter of Lloyds Bank, Mumbles;
   (b) pay it into his own bank account; or
   (c) give it to a third party (say) in settlement of his own debt.
3. Had the cheque been crossed with two parallel lines //, alternative 2a would be eliminated. Lloyds would pay only to another banker (who would be collecting on the cheque after Morgan, say, had paid it into his account). If the name of a banker, say Midland Bank, is written across the face of the cheque, Lloyds would pay only to the Midland Bank. Had the words 'Account Payee' been written between the parallel lines, alternative 2c would also, in practice, be eliminated.
4. If, as in 2c, Morgan wants to give the cheque to a third party (say to Geoffrey Cottle for some boating equipment) he will need to indorse it. He might write on the back of the cheque 'Pay Geoffrey Cottle' and add his (Morgan's) signature, or put his signature only.

5. If Morgan puts his signature only, the cheque may now undergo further transfer without further indorsement by the person(s) transferring it. Suppose the cheque (so indorsed) were stolen from Cottle and used to buy some goods off Gerald Griffiths, who accepted it in good faith. Griffiths would get a good title to it. However, had the cheque been crossed with two parallel lines and the words 'Not Negotiable', Griffiths would not have a good title, even though he accepted it in good faith.

6. In this context, therefore, 'Not Negotiable' (with the crossing) means that the taker of the cheque acquires no better title to it than the giver enjoys. It does not restrict its transferability, and Griffiths might pass it to Frank Wardle, Wardle to Bill Bailey, and so on.

7. In practice, the great majority of cheques are not passed around in this way.

3. *A Negotiable Sterling Certificate of Deposit* (*by courtesy of Morgan Grenfell and Co. Ltd*)

4. *A Specimen Bill of Exchange* (*from* The Bill on London, *Gillett Brothers Discount Co. Ltd, Chapman and Hall. Reproduced by permission*)

5. *A Treasury Bill* (*reproduced with the permission of the Bank of England and the Controller of Her Majesty's Stationery Office*)

6. *Notice of Tenders for Treasury Bills* (*by permission of the Controller of Her Majesty's Stationery Office*)

TENDERS FOR TREASURY BILLS.

1. THE Lords Commissioners of Her Majesty's Treasury hereby give notice that Tenders will be received at the Chief Cashier's Office, at the Bank of England, on Friday, the 25th November, 1966, at 1 p.m. for Treasury Bills to be issued under the Treasury Bills Act, 1877, the National Debt Act, 1889, and the National Loans Act, 1939, to the amount of £150,000,000.

2. The Bills will be in amounts of £5,000, £10,000, £25,000, £50,000 or £100,000. They will be dated at the option of the Tenderer on any business day from Monday, the 28th November, 1966, to Saturday, the 3rd December, 1966, inclusive, and will be due 91 days after date.

3. The Bills will be issued and paid at the Bank of England.

4. Each Tender must be for an amount not less than £50,000 and must specify the date on which the Bills required are to be dated, and the net amount per Cent. (being an even multiple of one penny) which will be given for the amount applied for. Separate Tenders must be lodged for Bills of different dates.

5. Tenders must be made through a London Banker, Discount House or Broker.

6. Notification will be sent by post, on the same day as Tenders are received, to the persons whose Tenders are accepted in whole or in part and payment in full of the amounts due in respect of such accepted Tenders must be made to the Bank of England by means of **Cash or by Draft or Cheque drawn on the Bank of England** not later than 1.30 p.m. (Saturday, 11.00 a.m.) on the day on which the relative Bills are to be dated.

7. Members of the House of Commons are not precluded from tendering for these Bills.

8. Tenders must be made on the printed forms which may be obtained from the Chief Cashier's Office, Bank of England.

9. The Lords Commissioners of Her Majesty's Treasury reserve the right of rejecting any Tenders.

TREASURY CHAMBERS,
18th November, 1966.   **(1745)**

7. *A Form of Tender for Treasury Bills (by permission of the Controller of Her Majesty's Stationery Office)*

No._____

London,_____ 19

To the Lords Commissioners
of Her Majesty's Treasury.

My Lords,

In accordance with the terms of the notice in the London Gazette of

the_____

we hereby beg to tender for the undermentioned Treasury Bills, for which, or

for any less amount that may be allotted to us,

we agree to give the sum of * £_____ : :

say,_____

_____ per cent.

PARTICULARS OF BILLS.

			PLEASE LEAVE THESE COLUMNS BLANK		
_____ of £5,000 each = £		,000			
_____ of £10,000 each =		,000			
_____ of £25,000 each =		,000			
_____ of £50,000 each =		,000			
_____ of £100,000 each =		,000			
TOTAL † £		,000			

‡ To be dated the_____day of_____ 19___

To be due 91 days after date.

We have the honour to be,

My Lords,

Your Lordships' most obedient Servants,

Signature_____

Address_____

* The price per cent. offered must be an even multiple of one penny and must be written in
  words at length, as well as in figures.
† Each Tender must be for not less than £50,000.
‡ Separate Tenders must be lodged for Bills of different dates.

(27)

Appendix B

References and Further Reading

DEVELOPMENT OF THE MONETARY SYSTEM

FEAVEARYEAR, Sir Albert, *The Pound Sterling* (revised edition E. V. MORGAN), Oxford University Press 1963
The standard work on the development of the monetary system in England.

MORGAN, E. V., *A History of Money*, Penguin Books 1965
A wide-ranging survey of the origins and development of monetary institutions and the evolution of monetary theory and policy up to the present.

UNITED KINGDOM FINANCIAL INSTITUTIONS

SAYERS, R. S., *Modern Banking*, Oxford University Press, 7th ed. 1967
Contains an authoritative and detailed exposition of the workings of the financial system and of various issues in monetary economics.

GASKIN, M., *Scottish Banks*, Allen and Unwin 1965

REPORT OF THE COMMITTEE ON THE WORKING OF THE MONETARY SYSTEM (*The 'Radcliffe Report'*) Cmd. 827 1959 H.M.S.O.
A major source of information on the financial system and on monetary policy, though some of its material is now dated.

The Bill on London published for GILLETT BROTHERS DISCOUNT CO. LTD by Chapman and Hall, 3rd ed. 1964
A fascinating and practical exposition of the use of the bill of exchange.

SCAMMELL, W. M., *The London Discount Market*, Elek Books 1968
A major reference work on the market's functions and history.

NATIONAL BOARD FOR PRICES AND INCOMES, Report No. 34, *Bank Charges* 1967, H.M.S.O.
A wider-ranging survey than the title might imply.

MONOPOLIES COMMISSION, *A Report on the Proposed Merger of Barclays, Lloyds and Martins Banks* 1968, H.M.S.O.
Contains much valuable material on the banking system.

CENTRAL OFFICE OF INFORMATION, *Reference Pamphlet No. 65 The British Banking System*, H.M.S.O.

CLAYTON, G. and OSBORN, W. T., *Insurance Company Investment*, Allen and Unwin 1965.

MORGAN, E. V. and THOMAS, W. A., *The Stock Exchange: Its History and Functions*, Elek Books 1962

CLEARY, E. J., *The Building Society Movement*, Elek Books 1965

NATIONAL BOARD FOR PRICES AND INCOMES, Report No. 22, *Rate of Interest on Building Society Mortgages* 1966, H.M.S.O.
Contains a very useful and succinct account of building society operation.

CENTRAL OFFICE OF INFORMATION, *Reference Pamphlet No. 24 British Financial Institutions*, H.M.S.O.

STUTCHBURY, O., *The Management of Unit Trusts*, Skinner 1965

FERRIS, P., *The City*, Penguin Books 1965
An informative and entertaining introduction to financial institutions.

BUSINESS FINANCE

PAISH, F. W., *Business Finance*, Pitman, 3rd ed. 1965
Contains an authoritative exposition of the principles of business finance and the provision of finance.

WOOD, F., *Business Accounting*, *Books I and II*, Longmans 1968
A simply-written introduction to accounting.

BANKING AND MONETARY POLICY IN THE U.S.A.

CHANDLER, L. V., *The Economics of Money and Banking*, Harper, Row and John Weatherhill, 4th ed. 1965
Contains an authoritative and detailed account of the American banking system, and of monetary policy in the U.S.A. May also be consulted for monetary theory and international monetary relations.

BANKING IN NIGERIA

BROWN, C. V., *The Nigerian Banking System*, Allen and Unwin 1966

FINANCES OF THE PUBLIC SECTOR

PREST, A. R., *Public Finance*, Weidenfeld and Nicolson, 3rd ed. 1967
Deals authoritatively with theoretical and policy issues in public finance, and also describes institutional arrangements.

BRITTAIN, Sir Herbert, *The British Budgetary System*, Allen and Unwin 1959
A major reference work.

CENTRAL OFFICE OF INFORMATION, *Reference Pamphlet No. 10 The British System of Taxation*, H.M.S.O.
A concise but relatively thorough exposition.

DRUMMOND, J. M., *Finance of Local Government*, Allen and Unwin, 2nd ed. 1962

National Superannuation and Social Insurance, Cmd. 3883 1969, H.M.S.O.
The Government's proposals for reconstructing the National Insurance scheme. Further official publications can be expected.

Nationalised Industries: A Review of Economic and Financial Objectives, Cmd. 3437 1967, H.M.S.O.
The most recent Government statement of policy.

NATIONAL INCOME STATISTICS

STONE, R. and G., *National Income and Expenditure*, Bowes and Bowes, 8th ed. 1966
An authoritative, lucid and concise exposition of national income statistics.

MAURICE, R. (ed.), *National Accounts Statistics: Sources and Methods*, H.M.S.O. 1968
The official and detailed explanation of the construction of the official national income statistics.

INCOME THEORY

DERNBURG, T. F. and McDOUGALL, D. M., *Macro-Economics*, McGraw-Hill, 3rd ed. 1968
A very clear presentation of macro-economic theory, which considers in greater depth the material contained in Part III.

LESS DEVELOPED COUNTRIES

MYINT, H., *The Economics of the Developing Countries*, Hutchinson University Library 1967
A very clear and readable account.

INTERNATIONAL ECONOMICS

KINDLEBERGER, C. P., *International Economics*, Irwin, 4th ed. 1968
Relatively advanced, but authoritative and very clear.

YEAGER, L. B., *International Monetary Relations*, Harper, Row and John Weatherhill 1966
As before.

HIRSCH, F., *Money International*, Penguin Press 1967
An exciting and detailed account of international monetary relationships and affairs, with material as well on domestic economic policy.

ECONOMIC POLICY

PREST, A. R. (ed.), *The U.K. Economy: A Manual of Applied Economics*, Weidenfeld and Nicolson, 2nd ed. 1968
An analysis of contemporary features and problems of the British economy especially written for students: very informative, penetrating and wide-ranging.

DOW, J. C. R., *The Management of the British Economy 1945–60*, Cambridge University Press 1964
Relatively advanced, but searching and very clear.

HACKETT, J. and A.-M., *The British Economy: Problems and Prospects*, Allen and Unwin 1967
An introduction to U.K. economic policy: both an account and an appraisal of recent economic developments and policies.

CAVES, R. E. and Associates, *Britain's Economic Prospects*, Allen and Unwin 1968
An assessment of the U.K. economy in its various aspects by a group of distinguished American economists: relatively advanced, but highly rewarding to study.

FRIEDMAN, M., *Dollars and Deficits*, Prentice-Hall 1968
Analysis of problems of inflation, monetary policy and the balance of payments by a distinguished American economist and leading exponent of the quantity theory of money.

DEPARTMENT OF ECONOMIC AFFAIRS, *The Task Ahead: Economic Assessment to 1972*, H.M.S.O.
The Government's 'planning document' published in January, 1969: further publications can be expected.

Productivity, Prices and Incomes Policy in 1968 and 1969, Cmd. 3590 1968, H.M.S.O.
The latest official statement of the Government's prices and incomes policy. Further publications can be expected.

STATISTICAL SOURCES

Financial Statistics is published monthly, the National Income and Expenditure Blue Book and the Balance of Payments Red (or Orange) Book annually.

The 'Notes and Definitions' published separately as an accompaniment to Financial Statistics contain much useful information on the financial system. Useful statistical information may also be found in the weekly Board of Trade journal (e.g. on hire purchase finance, the investment of insurance funds); and the monthly Employment and Productivity Gazette (e.g. on the index of retail prices). *Economic Trends*, published monthly for the Central Statistical Office by H.M.S.O., provides statistics and background articles on trends within the economy.

PERIODICALS AND OCCASIONAL PUBLICATIONS

The Bank of England's Quarterly Bulletin is a rich source of information on monetary developments, policy and institutions. For the U.S.A., the Federal Reserve Bulletin, published monthly, plays a similar role. Articles on various aspects of the economy and of economic policy are to be found in the reviews published quarterly by Lloyds, Barclays, National Westminster, The 'Three Banks' (the National and Commercial Banking Group, Ltd) and Midland. The latter's review concerns itself particularly with monetary affairs. Papers on various aspects of economic policy are regularly published by the Institute of Economic Affairs.

Index

Accelerator, 260–2, 467–8, 482
  and multiplier interaction, 263–7, 328
Accepting houses, *see* Banks, Merchant
'Administered' prices, 310, 314, 317, 321, 323
Aggregate demand,
  management (U.K.), 465–82, 486, 497
  meaning, 229, 240
Agricultural incomes,
  in Common Market, 458, 481, 490
  U.K. method of support, 458, 481, 490
Agricultural Mortgage Corporation Ltd, 140

Balance of payments,
  achievement of balance in competitive conditions, 369–75, 406
  automatic balance, 370, 388
  and economic growth, 344–5, 409, 449
  implications of capital movements for equilibrium, 372–5, 375–80
  principles of construction, 369–375
  see also Exports; Imports
Balance of payments (U.K.),
  basic balance—meaning, 403–5
  contents defined, 388–94
  and economic growth, 470, 479–480
  and inflation, 410–13 *passim*, 415, 470, 472
  interpretation, 403–5
  leads and lags, 424
  and level of economic activity, 408, 410, 413–17 *passim*, 470, 471–2

meaning of 'equilibrium' under fixed exchange rates, 406–9
  principles of construction, 386–8
  simple version constructed from first principles, 394–405
  statistics for 1968, 386–7
Balance sheet, structure explained, 129–31
Balanced budget, effect on income level, 254–5
Balanced growth, meaning, 330
Bank Charter Act, 1844, 13, 15, 63, 433n.
Bank of England,
  balances of other banks with, 26, 29, 30, 40–2, 63, 65, 68–81 *passim*, 425–7
  Bank Return, 63–6, 425
  cash deposit scheme, 48, 49, 88
  central-bank role defined, 62, 63
  channels of influence over commercial banks summarized, 85–88
  commercial banking business, 62, 65
  control over clearing banks' cash and liquid assets, 76–81, 81–3
  Exchequer account and National Loans Fund management, 62, 65, 68–71, 71–5, 103, 119
  functions summarized, 62–6
  funding policy, 80–1, 86, 473–4
  history, 12–16, 62, 83, 107, 122, 433
  money market operations, 71–5, 425–7, 474
  organization, 63, 65, 83–4
  relations with discount houses, 50, 52, 53, 54, 55–6, 63, 65, 69–70, 70–5, 76–80, 85–6, 88, 473

514

522

International Monetary Fund,
dealings with U.K. authorities,
63, 173, 393, 403, 405, 407,
409n., 427–8
establishment and organization,
435
functions summarized, 435
methods of providing finance,
427–8, 439–40, 448
policy on provision of finance,
438–40, 449
quotas, 435, 438, 440, 448, 451
'sister' institutions to, 450, 453
stability of members' exchange
rates, 122–3, 385, 423, 435–7,
442
International payments, example involving British and American
banking systems, 425
leads and lags, 424
methods of making, 396–8
working of contemporary system,
441–9
International reserves, 441–6
see also Exchange Equalization
Account; International
liquidity
International specialization,
explained with reference to
opportunity cost, 351–5
explained with reference to relative prices, 358–63, 380–2
International Trade Organization,
453
'Intervention' currency, 444
Inventory cycle, 267
Investment,
appraisal techniques, 184, 287–92,
325–6
and demand management (U.K.),
468, 472, 473, 475, 478, 479,
480, 496, 497
determinants of, 260–2, 270, 272,
276, 287–94, 325–6, 333, 336,
477, 492–4
'equality' with savings, 221, 230,
236–8, 253, 264, 320
meaning in income theory, 220–1

negative net, explained, 264–5
and real income growth, 325, 328–
336, 344–6 *passim*, 468, 477, 479,
480, 491–4
Investment allowances, 139, 324,
468, 492–3, 494
Investment dollar market, 419–20
Investment, Fixed, measurement, 201
Investment goods, defined, 129
Investment grants, 139, 288, 493–4,
498
Investment, Overseas, *see* Overseas
investment
Investment, Stock,
and income flow, 224n.
measurement, 202, 203–4, 214,
323, 340
Investment trusts, 140, 141, 150–1
Issuing houses, 108, 141–2

'Kennedy Round', 165, 454, 455n.,
457
Keynes, Lord, 212, 216, 303, 465

Labour-intensive   production
methods, 273–4, 277, 357–8,
455
Labour mobility, 269, 272–4, 315,
316, 456, 457, 458, 486
Land, a productive factor, 129
Limited companies,
balance sheet of 1,692 quoted
British companies, end-1967,
143–5, 293
as a business form, 133–8, 139,
194
Limited Partnerships Act, 1907, 134
Liquidity preference, meaning, 283
Liquidity trap, 299–300
Local authorities,
activities, 96, 179–80
borrowing and debt instruments,
59, 60, 73, 97, 99, 100, 101, 103,
105, 144, 159, 169, 170, 182–3,
188, 198, 293, 391, 393, 402,
407, 423, 476, 477; *see also*
Securities
grants to, 169, 180–1, 182